Professor Torbjörn N … **zerland** – *"Having adopted the first edition, I am* … *ern, easy-to-read and well-structured text has bee*… *e interesting and accessible cases, bringing to the fore themes such as technology and sustainability. Highly recommended!"*

Professor Zoe Radnor, Cass Business School, UK – *"As we have seen during the recent COVID-19 pandemic, operations management really matters to ensure that society continues to function. This book is a leader in the field being both clear and practical, as well as rigorous. It is a lively account, full of interesting new examples and at the same time anchored in the important business and management issues of the day."*

Professor Giovanni Perrone, University of Palermo, Italy – *"It is a pleasure to present the second edition of Operations Management by Steve Paton, Ben Clegg, Juliana Hsuan and Alan Pilkington. The new edition is clear, easy to read and has a special focus on issues of particular relevance to operations management today, such as technology and sustainability. This textbook is a perfect guide for students and a helpful support for instructors."*

Professor Amrik Sohal, Monash Business School, Australia – *"The first edition of the book was part of a highly relevant and valuable online and offline package for teaching and learning about operations. The authors brought together their many years of teaching, research and industry experience. The new edition has been improved very significantly in all aspects, incorporating the feedback the authors have received from users and other academics and industry experts. The new edition takes a decidedly international and contemporary perspective, including major changes made to chapters covering people and performance, sustainability and emerging technologies."*

Professor Jose A.D. Machuca, University of Seville and International University of Andalucía, Spain – *"The second edition of this book is again an excellent contribution to the field of operations management (OM). The content is well designed and, in addition to traditional topics, covers new contemporary issues faced by OM managers such as digitalization, service operations, sustainability and managing people. Furthermore, the online materials provide extra support for students and instructors, which will be highly appreciated in this current period of increasing online learning due to the COVID-19 pandemic. I am happy to recommend this book!"*

OPERATIONS MANAGEMENT

OPERATIONS MANAGEMENT

Steve Paton, Ben Clegg,
Juliana Hsuan and Alan Pilkington

Mc Graw Hill

London Boston Burr Ridge, IL Dubuque, IA Madison, WI New York San Francisco
St. Louis Bangkok Bogotá Caracas Kuala Lumpur Lisbon Madrid Mexico City Milan
Montreal New Delhi Santiago Seoul Singapore Sydney Taipei Toronto

Operations Management, Second Edition
Steve Paton, Ben Clegg, Juliana Hsuan and Alan Pilkington
ISBN-13 9781526848222
ISBN-10 1526848228

Published by McGraw Hill
338 Euston Road, 8th Floor
London
NW1 3BH
Telephone: +44 (0) 203 429 3400
Website: www.mheducation.co.uk

British Library Cataloguing in Publication Data
A catalogue record for this book is available from the British Library

Library of Congress Cataloging in Publication Data
The Library of Congress data for this book has been applied for from the Library of Congress

Portfolio Manager: Rosie Churchill and Isabel Berwick
Content Developer: Nina O'Reilly and Georgia Martin
Content Production Manager: Adam Hughes
Marketing Manager: Melanie Sutcliffe

Text design by Kamae Design
Cover design by Adam Renvoize

ISBN-13 9781526848222
ISBN-10 1526848228

Dedication

"To Mandy, Karli and Ethan" – SP

"Thanks to my wife Anna and my children,
Harry and Ella for their support and encouragement" – BC

"To my dear family in Europe, Americas and Asia
for their love" – JH

"To my family in all the places I call home" – AP

Brief Table of Contents

Detailed Table of Contents

Guide to Case Studies

Guide to Case Studies

Chapter	Case type	Company	Sector	Region	Page
8: Supply Chain and Supply Relationship Management	Opening	Barilla	Manufacturing	Europe	249
	Short	FitMe	Services	Europe	269
	Short	Pampers	Manufacturing	USA	273
	Short	Carvana	Services	USA	276
	Short	LEGO	Manufacturing	Europe	281
	Short	Lauritzen Bulkers	Services	Europe	278
9: Inventory Management	Opening	Amazon	Services	Global	289
	Short	Cathay Pacific	Combined	Asia	301
	Short	Nike	Manufacturing	USA	310
10: Lean Operations	Opening	Subway	Services	USA	324
	Short	Primark	Services	UK	330
	Short	Apple iPhone	Manufacturing	USA	337
	Short	National Health Service	Services	UK	339
11: Project Management	Opening	Crossrail	Services	UK	347
	Short	Airbus 380	Manufacturing	Europe	350
	Short	Human Genome Project	Services	USA	359
	Short	Bolshoi Ballet renovation	Services	Europe	369
	Short	Qatar World Cup	Manufacturing	Asia	378
12: Performance and People Management	Opening	W.L. Gore & Associates	Manufacturing	UK	391
	Short	NHS hospitals	Services	UK	395
	Short	Severn Trent Water	Services	UK	403
	Short	Four Seasons Health Care	Services	UK	408
	Short	Higgs & Sons Solicitors	Services	UK	416
	Short	GE	Services	Global	422
13: Quality Management	Opening	Dasani water (Coca-Cola)	Manufacturing	USA	429
	Short	Harley-Davidson	Manufacturing	USA	432
	Short	7-Eleven (retailing)	Services	Asia	435
	Short	Carlsberg	Manufacturing	Europe	441
14: Future Directions in Operations Management	Opening	Beth's Chocolate Ambitions	Manufacturing	USA	479
	Short	Foxconn	Combined	Global	484
	Short	Walmart	Services	USA	490
	Short	Fashion Industry	Manufacturing	Global	492
	Short	Royal Houthandel G. Wijma & Zonen BV	Manufacturing	Europe	495
	Short	The Apprentice	Combined		497

Preface

There are numerous operations management textbooks in publication, and producing something new and different is a daunting task. Before writing this book we felt it was important to understand both what its purpose would be and where it would fit into the already crowded market. It is always best to practise what you preach and, luckily for us, writing a textbook is itself an exercise in operations management. So like all good operations managers, at the outset we created an operations strategy to guide the book.

One of the key strategic activities when designing something is to understand the trade-offs. Designing a product is fundamentally about compromise as no product can be everything to everyone. We discovered there are several trade-offs in designing an operations management textbook. That between the need for a concise text and the need for comprehensive coverage of material. That between the inclusion of older, well-established and still relevant material and newer, less well-known but more current material. That between theoretical rigour and ease of practical application. And finally, that between depth of detail for the specialist versus scope of coverage for the generalist.

The decisions taken to balance these trade-offs are made more difficult by the way the field of operations management is currently evolving. It is shifting from a subject that is somewhat narrow in scope and manufacturing-focused, towards a broader subject that encompasses pretty much all the activity of modern business.

We believe that by considering these trade-offs and the evolving nature of the subject we have made the correct decisions for this textbook.

For this second edition we have added some new content that is becoming increasingly important to the field of operations management. First, we recognise the larger strategic context and specifically the increasing importance of operations strategy and its linkage with corporate strategy. Second, we emphasize the importance that design activity plays in creating fit-for-purpose products and services, reliable processes and robust supply chains, and how it affects the value created for customers. Third, we infuse the 'traditional' operations management material with fresh subjects such as innovation, agile thinking and the use of technological solutions for operational control. And fourth, we provide context for the reader by describing the careers of several operations managers and examining how the insights gained from these inform us about the occupation of operations management as a whole.

This book is therefore intended to be accessible to the student with no prior knowledge of operations but still useful to the experienced operations manager. It is contemporary in its approach but respectful of the classics. And finally it is theoretically rigorous but still useful to practitioners.

The key aims of the text are to:

- Explore fundamental operations management principles that are applicable to both manufacturing and service situations
- Offer a contemporary and novel treatment of the subject areas that comprise operations management
- Reflect on recent developments in operations management theory and practice
- Provide a balanced approach to qualitative vs quantitative coverage
- Integrate theory and practice using examples and case studies
- Encourage students to read and engage with the material in an interactive way

- Highlight key developments and practices by exploring how operations management has evolved in recent years.
- Emphasize the themes of Globalization, Business Integration and Corporate Social Responsibility (CSR).

Our intention has been to provide well-chosen content that maps easily and directly onto a typical course in operations management, thereby conveying a sense of value and relevance to students and lecturers alike. This text is targeted at both undergraduate and postgraduate audiences and offers a comprehensive treatment of operations management. It is designed to be used in specialized operations management courses and as a part of a broader degree in business and management.

This book therefore seeks to overcome the main challenges lecturers and instructors face in delivering an operations management module. Challenges such as deciding what subjects to include, what level to teach them to and how to make them relevant and interesting.

Overview of the Book

This book is organized in four parts – 'Directing', 'Designing', 'Managing' and 'Improving' – to reflect the current nature of operations managers' roles.

Part 1 Directing

This section introduces the principles, theory and concepts used to guide organizations in building an operational capability. Broadly speaking, it deals with the strategic issues which senior operations managers must consider in their decision-making. In addition to the core material that deals with making operations strategy it also contains a comprehensive treatment of adjacent subjects such as making corporate strategy and managing innovation without which operations strategy would be somewhat unmoored from the wider strategic context. This book takes the view that operations is the 'engine' that drives the business and to do this effectively operations must be fully aligned with the broader strategic direction of the business.

Chapter 1 introduces the strategic environment that operations exists within and provides an understanding of the decision-making that creates the corporate strategy that operations managers must support. Only by understanding the techniques used at corporate level to create strategy can operations managers shape activity at the operational level to fit coherently with it.

Chapter 2, while still strategic in nature, focuses more closely on operations management itself, looking at the concepts that will help managers to formulate useful operations strategy and take the correct decisions that will in turn support and enable the overall corporate strategy.

Chapter 3 deals with the topic of innovation, both what it is and how it is managed. As the pace of change in business increases, managing innovative activity effectively and efficiently is becoming a strategic consideration. Therefore a strong understanding of how to manage innovation is crucial to formulating strategy at both at the operational and corporate levels.

Part 2 Designing

All operational systems, simple or complex, must be consciously designed. This section outlines the methods which help operations managers both design and produce the products and services that organizations sell.

Chapter 4 takes a closer look at how products and services can be designed in order for companies to stay competitive. It covers strategies and techniques that companies use to develop innovative product and service solutions and also looks at more contemporary approaches, such as modularity and service architecture. Only by understanding the new product and service development processes can organizations ensure that the correct solutions can be introduced to the market. Capability in design is a key advantage in the struggle to stay ahead of the competition.

Chapter 5 introduces the importance of process design in operations management. It describes the theoretical background to processes and how they impact upon order processing, operations layout and operational practices. Techniques for modelling, designing and improving business processes are given and the role of technology is explained.

Chapter 6 introduces supply networks and how they are designed and also considers the management of enterprises. First, it presents the differences between supply chains, networks and multi-organization enterprises. Then the theoretical background is discussed and practical techniques introduced that aid decision-making, both strategically and tactically. Trends such as outsourcing and supplier rationalization are also included.

Part 3 Managing

This section explains the tools and techniques which ensure an operation, once up and running, will continue to operate smoothly and efficiently on an ongoing basis.

Chapter 7 discusses the concepts of capacity and how an organization deals with constraints that limit what it can deliver. It discusses the nature of capacity and how it can be matched with varying or unpredictable demand. Methods of forecasting are considered and the chapter evaluates strategies for services and queuing techniques.

Chapter 8 focuses on issues that operations managers need to consider when managing supply chains and supply relationships, and looks at various strategies to balance agility and efficiency in supply relationships and supply chain management of services and products. As the goal of all companies is to ensure that their customers are satisfied, it is important that the flow of goods and services take place as smoothly as possible throughout the supply network.

Chapter 9 examines how to manage the flow of materials within the operation. Today this is largely achieved using computerized and integrated systems under the heading Enterprise Resource Planning (ERP).

Chapter 10 examines how lean techniques can be used to the improve operational processes. Lean is a methodology that helps operations managers to design extremely efficient processes that produce products and services in the desired quantities, exactly when they are needed with the minimum if waste. This chapter also discusses the limitations of the lean approach enabling managers to make a practical assessment of how to deploy lean methods in the real world.

Chapter 11 introduces project management and deals with a unique set of problems facing those organizations that do not carry out the same set of 'routine' activities for a long period of time, but find themselves undertaking just one set of activities before moving onto something completely different. In order to manage projects effectively, project managers rely on administrative skills to ensure the time, cost and performance criteria of the project are met. This chapter includes the mechanistic elements of project management such as the tools/frameworks and the organic elements such as leadership.

Part 4 Improving

No operation can succeed by standing still. A key feature of operations management is the need to continually adapt to changing market conditions while improving performance and enhancing the competitiveness of the firm – this section tackles the issues that arise due to these requirements.

Chapter 12 introduces performance management as an organizational system that allows managers to take an integrated and coherent approach in ensuring the achievement of strategic objectives. It introduces the basic components of performance management systems and describes the most useful models for implementing performance management. It then goes on to describe how people fit within this system.

Chapter 13 introduces some key concepts of quality management and explains why quality is an important issue for all organizations. It illustrates why quality is becoming more challenging to manage as the demands of customers and the environment become more complex. The philosophy of quality management is discussed and the most useful tools for managing product and process quality are described.

Chapter 14 is a summary chapter that brings together the important themes in the book – which are corporate social responsibility (CSR), business integration and globalization. This chapter investigates these themes comprehensively before discussing their future impact on careers and the profession of operations management.

About the Authors

Dr Steve Paton, University of Strathclyde

Steve is a senior lecturer in Operations Management at Strathclyde University. He holds an MBA from Glasgow University and a PhD from Strathclyde University. Prior to entering academia, he spent 20 years in industry within the Aircraft and Defence sectors. Steve initially trained as an electrical engineer and then held a number of positions in operations and project management, gaining experience of all aspects of these disciplines. His research interests include the management of operations and projects in high value complex, engineering environments. His aim is always to generate useful knowledge which is academically rigorous but can be transferred to business practice.

Steve has published extensively in journals such the *International Journal of Operations and Production Management, British Journal of Management, Production Planning and Control and New Technology, Work and Employment.*

Contact: steve.paton@strath.ac.uk

Professor Ben Clegg, Aston Business School

Ben has over 20 years' experience in operations management. He holds a BSc (Hons.) in Management Science from Loughborough University, a PhD in Systems Engineering from De Montfort University and is a Chartered Engineer. He is a Fellow of the Institute of Engineering and Technology (FIET), a Fellow of the Higher Education Academy (HEA), an active participant in the European Operations Management Association (EurOMA) and the Production and Operations Management Society (POMS). Ben joined Aston Business School in 2003 and has also taught at the University of Central England, EM Lyon Business School in France and was a visiting scholar at Stanford University's Centre for Integrated Facilities Engineering, USA. Prior to entering academia Ben undertook a university sponsorship and graduate apprenticeship with GEC in operations and project management, worked as a practising manager in both the private and public sector and worked for a university start-up company. As well as teaching, Ben regularly consults and trains others in operations management and has won awards for his teaching and research.

Ben has contributed towards many books and has published in leading journals such as the *International Journal of Operations and Production Management, International Journal of Production Research, International Journal of Production Economics, IEEE Systems, Management and Cybernetics, and Supply Chain Management: an International Journal.* He also reviews for journals such as the *International Journal of Productivity and Performance Measurement,* and the *Journal of Manufacturing Technology Management.* Ben's senior academic roles include EurOMA Board member, and Associate Dean for Business and Community Engagement and Head of the Operations and Information Management Department at Aston Business School. His interests include process improvement, strategic thinking for operations management and systems thinking improvement methodologies.

Contact: b.t.clegg@aston.co.uk

Professor Juliana Hsuan, Copenhagen Business School

Juliana Hsuan is Professor of Operations Management & Supply Chain Management at Copenhagen Business School, Denmark. She serves as the Concentration Coordinator of CBS Master of Science in Supply Chain Management. She is also an Affiliated Professor at the Division of Service Management and Logistics, Chalmers University of Technology, Sweden. Juliana was an automotive electrical design engineer and executive trainee with Motorola in the USA before joining academia. She served in the board of leading academic associations including EurOMA (European Operations Management Association) and INFORMS (Institute for Operations Research and the Management Sciences) TIMES (Technology, Innovation Management and Entrepreneurship).

Her research has been published in leading academic journals such as *International Journal of Operations & Production Management, Decision Sciences, Journal of Product Innovation Management, IEEE Transactions on Engineering Management, Production Planning & Control, Technovation, R&D Management, Supply Chain Management: An International Journal,* among others. She is the co-author of *Managing the Global Supply Chain,* 4th edition, published by Copenhagen Business School Press. Her teaching and research interests include (service) operations management, (reverse) supply chain management, servitization, innovation management, modularization strategies, mass customization, and portfolio management of R&D projects.

Contact: jh.om@cbs.dk

Professor Alan Pilkington, University of Westminster

Alan Pilkington is Professor of Technology Management at Westminster Business School in London. He holds a B.Eng. (Hons.) degree in Engineering from Leicester Polytechnic University and a PhD in Manufacturing Strategy from Aston University. Prior to his time in academia, he was a manager for a UK automobile producer working on introducing new manufacturing systems and on joint venture projects with Japanese car makers.

Alan is a Chartered Engineer, past Chair of the IEEE Technology Management Society, a Senior Member of the IEEE, and member of the IET, and European Operations Management Association. He has published many articles in the *Journal of Operations Management, California Management Review; Technovation;* and *International Journal of Operations and Production Management.* His current research involves work on outsourcing design and manufacturing, bibliometric analysis and the adoption of 3D printing technology.

Contact: a.pilkington@westminster.ac.uk

Acknowledgements

We hope you enjoy this book, and are inspired to go on to become the great strategic and operations managers of the future. There are a number of individuals we must acknowledge who contributed at various stages in one way or another to this textbook.

First we should mention those who helped us from the initial planning stages right through to the development and final publication of the book: Rosie Churchill, Adam Hughes, Georgia Martin, and all others working behind the scenes at McGraw-Hill. Also, a special thank you to Rebekah Taylor at Just Content.

Other people who have also helped shape the book include: William Ho, Prasanta Dey and Tim Baines (Aston Business School); Harry Sminia (Strathclyde Business School); and Peter Ball (Cranfield University).

The authors and publisher would like to pay special thanks to all those who participated at various stages in the text development, be it by reviewing chapters, attending our focus group, or participating in our interview series; each has made a positive contribution to the final product:

Robert Allan, JWF
Amr Arisha, Dublin Institute of Technology
Viktor Avlonitis, Copenhagen Business School
Ozlem Bak, University of Greenwich
James Baldwin, University of Sheffield
Steven Barsanti, GC Aesthetics
Anu Bask, Aalto University
Jens Bengtsson, Norwegian School of Economics and Business Administration
John Bicheno, Cardiff Business School
Heidi Bjorstad, Bergen University College
Thorsten Blecker, Hamburg University of Technology
Jürgen Bode, International School of Management
Lennart Bogg, Malardalen University
Tommy Bood, Karlstad University
Owen Brady, Institute of Technology, Carlow
Louis Brennan, Trinity College Dublin
Naomi Brookes, Aston University
Martin Butler, University of Stellenbosch
Peter Byrne, Dublin City University
Declan Carew, Dublin City University
Luc Chalmet, Ghent University
Stephen Disney, Cardiff University
Alexander Douglas, Liverpool John Moores University
Veronica Earle, University of Hertfordshire
Roy Edwards, Staffordshire University
Thomas Frandsen, Copenhagen Business School
Helgi Gestsson, University of Akureyri
Stein Erik Grønland, Norwegian School of Management
Allan Gowans, Walker Precision Engineering
Ida Gremyr, Chalmers University of Technology
Árni Halldórsson, Chalmers University of Technology
Graham Heaslip, Institute of Technology, Carlow
Behzad Hezarkhani, Brunel University London
Alex Hiller, Nottingham Trent University
Ian Hipkin, University of Exeter
William Ho, Aston University
Julie Hodges, Durham University
Ian Holden, University of Lincoln
Jeffery Holden, University of Westminster
Bill Hollins, University of Westminster
Juanling Huang, Birmingham City University
Donal Hughes, University College Dublin
Ola Hultkrantz, Chalmers University of Technology
Stanley Hutchinson, Saxion University
Alessio Ishizaka, University of Portsmouth

Christer Karlsson, Copenhagen Business School
Bruce Kibler, Cologne Business School
Yearnmin Kim, University of Ulsan, Korea
Katri Karjalainen, Manchester Business School
Gyöngyi Kovács, Hanken School of Economics
Björn Lantz, University of Gothenburg
Benn Lawson, Queen's University Belfast
Reda Lebcir, University of Hertfordshire
Moren Levesque, York University
Kevin Maher, Institute of Technology Tralee
Morag Malins, University of Warwick
Thomas McNamara, Rennes School of Business
Eðvald Möller, University of Iceland
Jan Mouritesen, Copenhagen Business School
Michael Nelson, University College Dublin
Michael O'Mahony, Cork Institute of Technology
Leonard O'Sullivan, Limerick University
Garry Priddis, University of Brighton
Vijayender Reddy, Nyenrode Business University
Gwenny Ruël, University of Groningen
Anders Segerstedt, Luleå University of Technology
Chris Seow, University of East London
Angela Short, Dundalk Institute of Technology
Karin Smidt-Destombes, Vrije Universiteit A'Dam
James Smith, Coventry University
Sean Stevenson, imv-imaging
Jan Stentoft Arlbjørn, University of Southern Denmark
Trevor Stocker, Nottingham Express Transit (NET)
Roy Stratton, NTU
Mikko Tarkkala, Helsinki School of Economics
Rudd Teunter, Lancaster University
Markku Tinnilä, Alto University
Sandra Transchel, University of Mannheim
Norbet Trautmann, University of Bern
Joris Van de Klundert, Maastricht University
Whitey van der Linde, University of Johannesburg
Karl Van der Merwe, Nelson Mandela Metropolitian University
N. Van der Zee, NHL University
Allard Van Riel, Radboud University Nijmegen
V. Venugopal, Nyenrode Business University
Chris Voss, London Business School
Stephen Wagner, Otto Beisheim School of Management
Ying Yang, University of Aberystwyth
Linda Zhang, University of Groningen

We would also like to thank the following contributors for the material that they have provided for this textbook and its accompanying resources:

Angela Short, Dundalk Institute of Technology
Bang Gun Je, STX
Carl Wegeberg, J. Lauritzen
Choi Yeon Woo, Hyndai Heavy Industries Co., Ltd
Curt Corneliussen, J. Lauritzen
Dave Piper, Lightning Source UK Ltd
Garry Copeland, British Airways
Gary Craine, Barlcays Bank
Glyn Morris, Higgs and Sons Ltd.
Graham Jones, Farnborough International Ltd
Ian Briggs, MCT Aspire Engineering
James Rowell, University of Buckingham
Jan Sjulstok, J. Lauritzen
Jose Artuto Garza-Reyes, University of Derby
Judy Scully, Aston University
Kim Young Jum, Hyndai Heavy Industries Co., Ltd
Martijn De Lange, TNT Post UK
Olga Matthias, University of Bradford
Priyanka Roy, University of Hertfordshire
Sebastian Kitching, University of Swansea
Soroosh Saghiri, Kingston University
Steffen Ring, Motorola
Tommy Hjordt, Motorola
Y.S. Kim, Hyndai Heavy industries Co., Ltd

Guided Tour

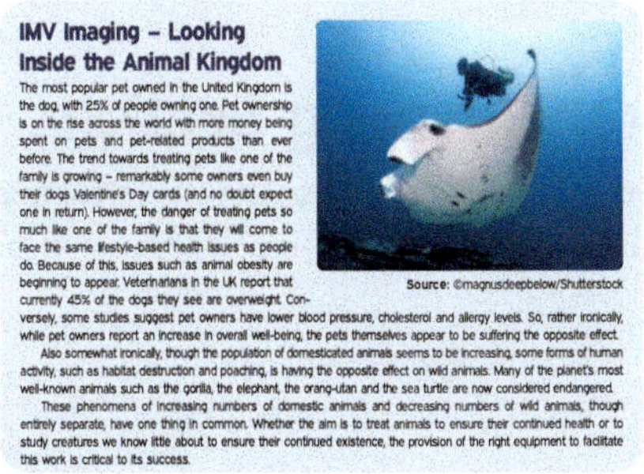

IMV Imaging – Looking Inside the Animal Kingdom

The most popular pet owned in the United Kingdom is the dog, with 25% of people owning one. Pet ownership is on the rise across the world with more money being spent on pets and pet-related products than ever before. The trend towards treating pets like one of the family is growing – remarkably some owners even buy their dogs Valentine's Day cards (and no doubt expect one in return). However, the danger of treating pets so much like one of the family is that they will come to face the same lifestyle-based health issues as people do. Because of this, issues such as animal obesity are beginning to appear. Veterinarians in the UK report that currently 45% of the dogs they see are overweight. Conversely, some studies suggest pet owners have lower blood pressure, cholesterol and allergy levels. So, rather ironically, while pet owners report an increase in overall well-being, the pets themselves appear to be suffering the opposite effect.

Also somewhat ironically, though the population of domesticated animals seems to be increasing, some forms of human activity, such as habitat destruction and poaching, is having the opposite effect on wild animals. Many of the planet's most well-known animals such as the gorilla, the elephant, the orang-utan and the sea turtle are now considered endangered.

These phenomena of increasing numbers of domestic animals and decreasing numbers of wild animals, though entirely separate, have one thing in common. Whether the aim is to treat animals to ensure their continued health or to study creatures we know little about to ensure their continued existence, the provision of the right equipment to facilitate this work is critical to its success.

Source: ©magnusdeepbelow/Shutterstock

Chapter Opening Case Studies

Each chapter begins with an opening case study introducing the key topics that follow in an engaging way for students. In many instances, real company examples will be discussed and highlighted in these sections.

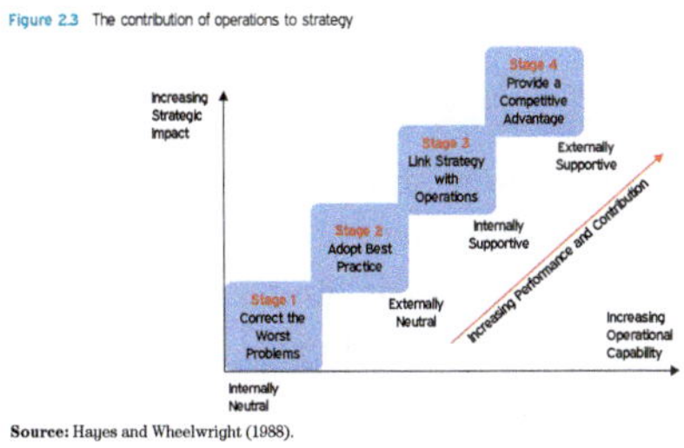

Figures and Tables

This text makes extensive use of data, and presents them in various figures and tables. Explanations in the narrative, worked examples and end-of-chapter problems will refer to many of these exhibits.

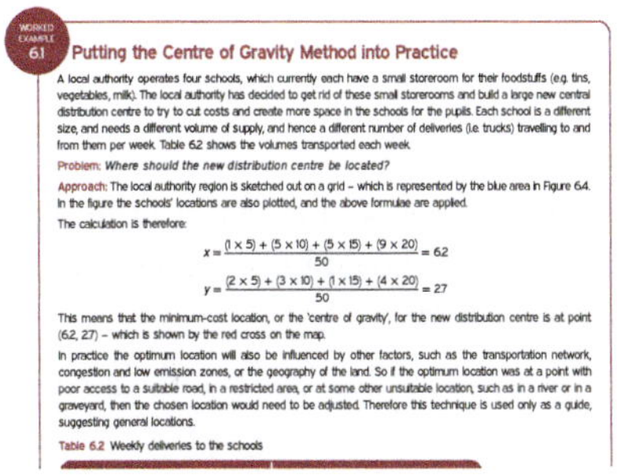

WORKED EXAMPLE 6.1 Putting the Centre of Gravity Method into Practice

A local authority operates four schools, which currently each have a small storeroom for their foodstuffs (e.g. tins, vegetables, milk). The local authority has decided to get rid of these small storerooms and build a large new central distribution centre to try to cut costs and create more space in the schools for the pupils. Each school is a different size, and needs a different volume of supply, and hence a different number of deliveries (i.e. trucks) travelling to and from them per week. Table 6.2 shows the volumes transported each week.

Problem: *Where should the new distribution centre be located?*

Approach: The local authority region is sketched out on a grid – which is represented by the blue area in Figure 6.4. In the figure the schools' locations are also plotted, and the above formulae are applied.

The calculation is therefore:

$$x = \frac{(1 \times 5) + (5 \times 10) + (5 \times 15) + (9 \times 20)}{50} = 6.2$$

$$y = \frac{(2 \times 5) + (3 \times 10) + (1 \times 15) + (4 \times 20)}{50} = 2.7$$

This means that the minimum-cost location, or the 'centre of gravity', for the new distribution centre is at point (6.2, 2.7) – which is shown by the red cross on the map.

In practice the optimum location will also be influenced by other factors, such as the transportation network, congestion and low emission zones, or the geography of the land. So if the optimum location was at a point with poor access to a suitable road, in a restricted area, or at some other unsuitable location, such as in a river or in a graveyard, then the chosen location would need to be adjusted. Therefore this technique is used only as a guide, suggesting general locations.

Table 6.2 Weekly deliveries to the schools

Worked Examples

Separate worked examples are integrated throughout the chapters. Each worked example illustrates an intuitive way to solve either qualitative or quantitative problems in a step-by-step format.

SHORT CASE 2.2 Teekay Corporation: The Marine Midstream Company

When you turn on a control on your cooker, gas will flow and ignite on the ring. When you insert the nozzle of a petrol pump into the filler of your car and pull the trigger, petrol flows into the tank. The journeys taken by these fuels from deep underground to kitchens and garage forecourts are generally invisible to us unless an ecological disaster and the resulting news story forces it onto our TV screens. Without energy, though, society would be unable to function. Energy powers industries, fuels transportation systems, and generally improves the quality of our lives. But first, that energy must be moved from where it is produced to where it is consumed. You will probably not have heard of the Teekay Corporation, but it is an essential link in the global energy supply chain. Teekay was founded in 1973 by Torben Karlshoej, whose initials provided the Teekay name. Teekay helps its customers link their upstream energy production seamlessly to their downstream processing operations. Teekay's vision is 'to bring energy to the world'.

Teekay's reputation for safety, quality and innovation has earned it a position as the world's leading marine service company; the strength and flexibility of its fleet create a significant competitive advantage for the corporation, and for its customers. At the heart of operations, multi-functional ship teams are fully responsible for the day-to-day operations of the fleet, with each team focused on a dedicated group of vessels. Every team is equipped to efficiently deliver the entire service process of vessel operations. Supporting these teams are dedicated competence and performance management systems, including centres of excellence with expertise focused on ensuring

Source: ©G-Valeriy/Shutterstock

Short Case Studies

Located throughout the chapters are short case examples strategically placed to demonstrate how the key theories and issues discussed relate to the real world.

CRITICAL PERSPECTIVE

How Does Current Operational Activity Influence Operations Strategy Making?

In both Chapter 1 and this chapter we present strategy-making as a purposeful process of planning based on a set of rational decisions. This school of strategizing can broadly be labelled as 'strategy by design' and is associated with the rationalist approach. Where operations strategy is concerned, this approach to strategy-making seems a rather uncomfortable fit. Often capabilities cannot be planned, it is very difficult to 'force' the development of a new competence. There is another approach termed 'strategy as process' and this approach is useful when thinking about operations strategy. Strategy as process is best thought of as a process of emergence. This tends to be associated with incrementalism, setting an initial direction and continually adjusting, often by trial and error, until some idea emerges. With this approach there is some planning involved but this is subordinate to, and is expected to be changed by, the learning that emerges along the way. Lately a school of thought termed 'wayfinding' (Chia, 2017) has been proposed, which pushed this idea of emergence a step further. Wayfinding represents the view that 'strategic coherence can emerge inadvertently from local coping actions and decisions taken on the hoof' (Bounty *et al.*, 2019: 1). Here there is no initial direction set; insights emerge from the ongoing operational work of the organization. This is a useful way to think about operations strategy making from the 'bottom up'. In reality this type of emergence has been characterized before in the 'continuous improvement' philosophy as operations improves and adapts organically.

The key point is ...

that this thought-provoking view seeks to characterize the way strategy emerges unplanned from other forms of organizational activity. It suggests that the interweaving of seemingly unrelated actions may produce a useful outcome: a phenomenon that organizations would do well to take note of and exploit.

Critical Perspective Boxes

These separate sections are distributed throughout the text to demonstrate an alternative theoretical perspective, to encourage and promote critical thinking.

Contemporary Thinking: Servitization

The concept of operations strategy, or manufacturing strategy as it was known initially, was born out of work done by Skinner (1966, 1969, 1971, 1974) as he attempted to understand what was wrong with US manufacturing firms as they struggled to compete in the international market. Broadly, Skinner concluded that production performance in the US was sub-optimized in two ways. First, it was fixated on Taylorist methods which, although useful, were becoming outdated and somewhat inflexible, and second, it rarely tied in neatly with the overall strategy of the firm.

As time moved on and the tools and techniques that are associated with operations management became increasingly common in arenas other than manufacturing, the terminology changed in favour of the label operations strategy: a phrase more easily applicable to all industry sectors.

Though still traditionally associated with the manufacture of tangible products, the tools and techniques of operations management are now recognized as equally applicable to the delivery of intangible services. Furthermore, we now recognize that products and services are not discrete, they lie on a continuum with tangible products occupying one end and intangible services the other. This 'product-service continuum' shown in Figure 2.5 has forced manufacturing firms to rethink how they structure and compose their value propositions.

Most companies exist somewhere in the middle of the continuum between pure product and pure service. Pure service companies do exist, for example professional practices such as legal and accounting firms. Most companies these days are a combination of product and service provider. A restaurant is considered as a service, but it is supported by the manufacture of food products; and the entertainment experience provided by a cinema would not be possible without the production of a film. Most consumer goods are products that are wrapped in a service package. Ironically, pure product companies are the most difficult to define, because most products need some form of service and support.

Contemporary Thinking Sections

These sections of text introduce and explain the latest academic thinking on a particular topic.

Stage 4: Externally Supportive

This stage resonates most clearly with the resource-based view. Here operatior
state from that achieved in Stage 3 is a subtle but significant one. The level of p
made it best in class, achieving a competitive advantage, but now at Stage 4 o
driving forward towards future markets by creating products and services tha
tion. Here senior management is so confident of operations that it can base
operations is truly in the driving seat.

Stop and Think

Corporate strategy should never be developed without taking operations management into statement. Do you agree with it?

Operations Contribution and Competencies

From a resource-based perspective it is critical that the maturity of operations i
be impossible to build a strategy around the creation of operational competen

Stop and Think Questions

Using these reflective questions students are invited at regular intervals to 'stop and think' about a particular concept or issue, encouraging them to apply their own ideas and analysis, thus reinforcing concepts and promoting critical thinking.

Organizations facing high levels of uncertainty in their markets and the exte
develop their own internal resources, and look for low-risk projects and organ
often have their own back-up power plants to ensure that they always ha
However, such risk aversion usually means more expense, and slower rates of

The key point is ...

that all the above assumptions affect transaction costs. If other factors are favourable, then v
transaction costs with external organizations are higher than its internal transaction costs, it
cheaper and easier to do activities in house. Conversely, if internal transaction costs are high
organization can benefit from downsizing or outsourcing noncompetitive parts of its operatio
get another organization to perform these activities.

TCE is often criticized for:

- Failing to explain clearly situations when suppliers should collaborate a relationships
- Focusing too much on cost minimization rather than on value maximi

The Key Point is. . .

These short summary statements highlight and reinforce the key aspects that students should have understood, following a particular text section.

BUSINESS INTEGRATION

GLOBALIZATION

Key suppliers were included throughout the design and manufacturing process. For instance, I
Group was one of only two engine suppliers. Rolls-Royce built the new Trent 900 engines – one c
engines ever built. The other engine (the GP2700) was built by the American Engine Alliance
companies are General Electric and Pratt & Whitney. Rolls-Royce and AEA are the main partne
investing time, money and knowledge right from the beginning.

Rolls-Royce joined up with its key suppliers in risk- and revenue-sharing arrangements, wher
the development of the new engine in exchange for a percentage of their sales revenue. Seven
as risk- and revenue-sharing partners (from Spain, the USA, Italy, Sweden and Japan). Three
included as programme associates (from South Korea and Japan). These companies had an input into
but did not share in the overall risk-and-revenue partnership. In addition, hundreds more supp
conventional, openly competitive arrangements.

Much responsibility rested with the supplier management team at Rolls-Royce. They manage
global suppliers to try to ensure that parts and services were delivered on time, every time
This involved recruiting new suppliers, developing new processes, planning and scheduling, material
facturing, assembly, and final delivery to the customer. In short, the supplier team provided the lin
chain together. As a result, Rolls-Royce is now a major player in Singapore's aerospace industry, a
of the country's aerospace output via joint ventures with local industry. Eight out of the first 11 airli
chose the Trent 900 engine.

However, at around US$26,000 per hour or US$50 per seat-hour, the A380 has proven
Comparing this to a new Boeing 777 which costs just US$44 per seat-hour the A380 may be c
new economically viable variant cannot be conceived. The A380 will remain in service unt

Key Theme Icons

Located throughout the text in the margins', these icons highlight the important trends and themes in operations. *Business Integration* icons highlight the cross-functional areas of business operations. *Globalization* icons indicate passages that relate to the nature of international/global operations, or where globalization is affecting business. *Corporate Social Responsibility (CSR)* icons highlight key sections that relate operations management to this increasingly important topic.

Review Questions

1. Explain what each of the five generic performance objectives represents.
2. Explain the difference between order winners and order qualifiers.
3. In relation to the product life-cycle describe some characteristics of the operational system used to produce a product in its mature phase.
4. Explain how flexibility of service and speed of service might require a trade-off decision.
5. Briefly describe the four stages in the Hayes and Wheelwright model of operations contribution.

Discussion Questions

1. Reflect on the value disciplines – do they seem relevant to the companies that you are familiar with?
2. In relation to a company that you are familiar with define how each of the five generic performance objectives might be used.
3. Consider Hayes and Wheelwright's four-stage model – how could this be used to shape a performance improvement plan for your operation?
4. Consider the concept of trade-offs. What trade-offs might a police force have to think about when planning its operational activity?
5. Discuss the product life-cycle model – do you think it is as relevant today as it was when it was first conceived in the 1960s?

Further Reading

Hayes, R., Pisano, G., Upton, D. and Wheelwright, S.C. (2005) *Operations Strategy and Technology: Pursuing the Competitive*

modular solutions. *International Journal of Operations & Production Management*, 39(5), 630-657.

End of Chapter Questions

These are separated into three assessment sections: Review Questions, Discussion Questions and Problems. Each section enables either independent and/or group learning with plentiful opportunities to practise concepts and ensure understanding of key topics; and, where relevant, reinforce qualitative or quantitative material and methods.

Operations Strategy

tions Strategy?

is about decision-making. Like decisions made in relation to corporate made in relation to operations strategy must focus on the achievement of nd the 'signposts' that inform the decision-making process may be formal- h as a vision or a mission. Unlike decisions made in relation to corporate made in relation to operations strategy tend to be short term and tactical, he initiation and directing of action at the lower levels of the organization.

es that operations strategy can be defined as:

bout, and management of: core competencies, capabilities and processes, urces and key tactical activities necessary in the function or chain of te and deliver product and service combinations and the value demanded

Operations strategy: the set of major decisions about core competencies, capabilities and processes, technologies, resources and key tactical activities necessary in the function or chain of functions that create and deliver product and service combinations.

captures the various elements that operations may call upon to support corporate strategy; it l level of operations; and it emphasizes the integration of activity into a single entity that nd effective way to meet the goals of the organization.

ons Strategy Made?

Key Terms

These are highlighted in boldface throughout the chapters, and are defined in the margin notes for easy reference.

Introduction

Unlike Warner Bros described in Chapter 1, IMV do not rely fully on corporate strategy and methods such as diversification into new product markets to find success. IMV has tended to stay within one arena, basing its strategy on its core competence in the design, production and support of imaging equipment.

Chapter 1, p23

Therefore it could be argued that IMV prioritizes operational strategies over corporate ones, embracing a resource-based approach that emphasizes the building and strengthening of core competencies. But this is not the whole story. More recently, this internal focus has been supported by a market awareness that informs its deployment of these products into many different niches. Indeed, IMV's market awareness extends beyond simply expansion into new geographical regions and increasingly diverse applications. IMV recognized that selling a service is seen by much of the market as far more valuable than selling the physical product alone. They are therefore developing an operational strategy based on a **servitization** model. Servitization (described later in the chapter) is an operational strategy that draws on both market- and resource-based thinking. This case serves to illustrate that there needs to be a balance found between different views of how strategy is made.

Servitization: the addition of services to complement the sale of a manufactured product

The purpose of this chapter is to pick up where the previous chapter ended and investigate how the operational systems and processes are conceived that will support the company in reaching its strategic goals. The treatment of operations strategy in this chapter will set the context for your study of the more detailed processes and systems that are the concern of the remainder of this book, as without an understanding of operations strategy to guide you, it may be difficult to piece together each aspect of operations management theory and method into a coherent whole.

This chapter will begin by detailing how operations strategy is generated and how it can contribute to and support the overall corporate strategy. It will continue by discussing how operations strategy is related to the overall performance of the organization. It will then look at more generic operations strategies that can be adopted to simplify the decision-making done when generating operations strategy.

Chapter links

Highlight topic connections in the book. Chapter and page number are provided in the margin for quick cross-referencing.

However, for servitization to succeed as an operations strategy for manufacturing firms, changes must be made to how they work. Operationally, a firm's service activity must change from simply making sure the customer uses their tangible product properly, to making sure the product-service bundle fulfils the customer's needs. Commercially, the relationship must move from a product-orientated, often short-term, transactional arrangement to a solutions-oriented, longer-term, strategic arrangement.

Studies have classified three different types of servitization strategy (Cusumano *et al.*, 2015). The addition of 'Smoothing' services helps to regularize and control sales. The addition of 'Adapting' services expands the functionality of the product or assists customers in using the product in new ways. And finally the addition of 'Substituting' services makes the outright purchase of the product unnecessary.

Manufacturers are motivated to servitize for a number of reasons. These include competitive pressures that stem from the need to differentiate a mature product by adding services; demand-based forces driven by customers who may want to outsource some non-core activities; and economic factors such as the need to find a new source of revenue by accessing the often more profitable service market. Martinez *et al.* (2017), when studying how servitization as a strategy is generated, found that it was an emergent process with both market and resource-based considerations contributing to the eventual shape of the solution.

Servitization therefore both highlights another step in the evolution of operations management and illustrates the importance of a robust process for generating operations strategy.

Summary

In this chapter we have built on the content of Chapter 1 by relating strategic thinking to the operations management of organizations. We have defined what operations strategy is and presented a model that can be used to make sense of the activity required to generate an operations strategy.

We have proposed that one of the main purposes of generating an operations strategy is to define the required performance of the operation and we have introduced five generic performance objectives, quality, time,

Summary

This section briefly reviews and reinforces the main topics covered in each chapter, to ensure students have acquired a solid understanding of the key topics.

Key Theories

The key theories discussed in this chapter were:

- **The five generic performance objectives** – those aspects that customers value most and therefore must be delivered by the operation. These include quality, speed, cost, dependability and flexibility.
- **Order-winning and order-qualifying criteria** – those features that customers see as the key reasons to buy or not to buy a product or service.
- **Performance profiling and prioritizing** – the process of measuring the performance of the operation against that of the competition to identify what improvements must be carried out to create an advantage.
- **Operational trade-offs** – the prioritizing of important performance objectives over those that are less important.
- **The product life cycle** – the five stages that a product will pass through from the point of introduction to the point of withdrawal. These are birth, growth, maturity, decline, and withdrawal. Each stage requires a change of emphasis in operations strategy.
- **Value propositions** – those generic operations strategies that help focus the process of strategy-making to create competence in specific areas. The six propositions introduced are innovators, brand managers, price minimizers, simplifiers, technological integrators and socializers.

Suggested Answers to Stop and Think Questions

1. **World-leading operations:** Most markets are occupied by numerous companies, all attempting to gain the greatest share. The pace of technological change creates a challenge, because it is making it increasingly difficult to gain a leadership position and, more importantly, maintain it because a new process or device may soon be invented that will displace the previous best, either by direct replacement or by substitution. Communication and information availability creates a challenge as it

Key Theories and Equations

These sections briefly recap and summarize the key theories and equations covered in the chapter, to aid revision and student learning.

Connect® for Management

We have a wide selection of resources on hand to help students gain valuable practice during their course. By applying what they have learned to real world scenarios and consistently testing their knowledge of the subject matter, these tools help prepare them for the real world of management.

Application-Based Activities (ABAs)

Provide students with valuable practice, using problem-solving skills to apply their knowledge to realistic scenarios. Students advance through understanding basic concepts, to using their knowledge to analyse complex scenarios and solve problems. Along the way, students see the implications of their decisions and are provided with feedback on how management theory should be informing their actions.

Each activity has been created to align with higher order thinking skills and are also categorized by difficulty to cater to each students' abilities.

Assignable Videos

By studying the selection of topic relevant videos provided, students will develop robust critical analysis skills, whilst relating this to relevant companies and situations. Each video is accompanied by questions to test understanding and application of theory and concepts understood from the video.

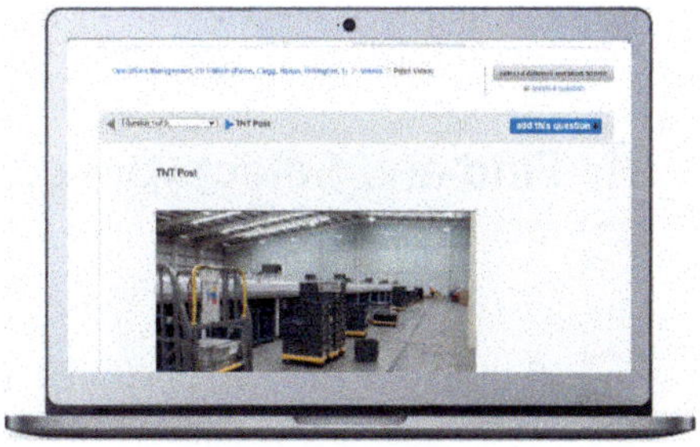

Assignable within Connect, these videos keep the subject matter contemporary and allow students to relate key theories with real-world concepts.

Test Bank

Build your own question banks relating to end-of-chapter material, featuring video case content to both test student knowledge and ability, and ensure engagement with existing real world cases.

Introduction

Learning Outcomes

After reading this chapter you should be able to:

- Define the term 'operations management'
- Describe the conversion process model of operations management
- Use the conversion process to analyse the operations of organizations
- Discuss the role of the operations manager
- Use the 4Vs model to analyse operations systems
- Reflect on the practice of operations management

Breathing Life into Operations Management

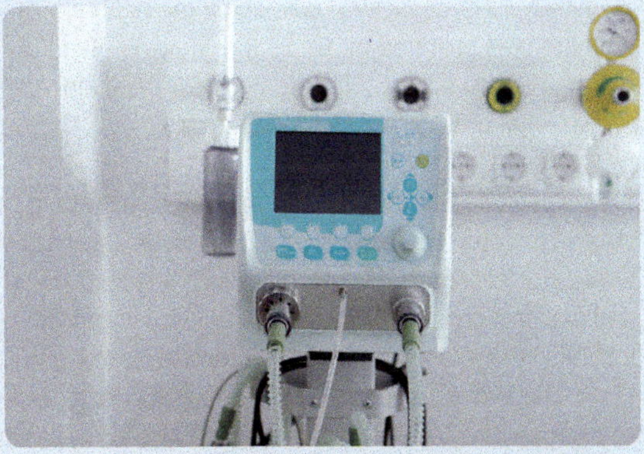

Source: ©Nenov Brothers Images/Shutterstock

On 31 December 2019, health authorities in Wuhan, China, confirmed that they were treating dozens of people affected by a new virus. On 11 January 2020, the Chinese media reported the first known death from this virus. Then, on 23 January, Chinese authorities closed down Wuhan. By 30 January, amid thousands of new cases, the World Health Organization had declared a 'public health emergency of international concern'. By the end of February the virus had globalized. The end of March saw many countries implement some form of lockdown on public activity. Shockingly, by the end of April reports stated that approximately 3.3 million people worldwide had been infected with around 234,000 deaths recorded.

Little has done more to place operations management front and centre than the Covid-19 crisis. Though medical professionals received the majority of attention, it was operations managers who were tasked with providing the resources required to support the work of the medical services. While operations management could be found in many strands of the unfolding Covid-19 narrative, initially one story dominated.

The Ventilator Story

Galen, the noted 2nd-century Greek physician, studied respiration and concluded that breathing was required to maintain circulation, that is, the act of breathing caused the heart to beat. Though this conclusion was not entirely correct, it might represent the first attempt to understand how the cardiovascular system works. For the next 1,500 years this view seems to have persisted. Then, in 1543, Andreas Vesalius published his seven-volume treatise on anatomy entitled

De Humani Corporis Fabrica (*On the Fabric of the Human Body*) which contained, in its description of a tracheotomy, the first reference to respiratory ventilation.

For air to enter the lungs via ventilation a pressure gradient must exist between the airway and the alveoli (air sacs) within the lungs. This gradient can be accomplished by either raising pressure in the airway or lowering the pressure at the alveoli. So, simply speaking, ventilation can be done in two ways: by applying positive pressure or by applying negative pressure.

Negative-pressure machines were first described in 1838 by Scottish physician John Dalziel. This 'tank' ventilator was essentially an airtight box into which the patient, excluding the head, was inserted. This type of ventilator predominated for over a century, reaching its pinnacle during the Poliomyelitis epidemics of the mid-20th century when it became popularly known as the 'Iron Lung'.

By the 1960s, there was a movement away from negative pressure machines in favour of positive pressure machines. Despite the early adoption of the negative pressure system, positive pressure ventilators incorporating a bellows and mask arrangement may actually have been first to appear, introduced in the late 18th century by French anatomist Francois Chaussier. Interestingly, the method of mouth-to-mouth resuscitation, another positive pressure method, appeared at around the same time but was discarded as it was assumed, wrongly as it (rather fortunately) turned out, that expired air lacked the necessary oxygen content as it had already been processed by another's lungs.

To complicate matters somewhat, positive pressure ventilators come in two types: the previously described non-invasive which creates increased pressure at the patient's airway, most often using some form of mask; and the invasive which, in effect, introduces an artificial airway (intubates) the patient. By the 1970s positive pressure ventilation had become the preferred method for most conditions.

Ventilators of all types have undergone substantial technologically enabled change over the last 60 years becoming smaller, lighter, more capable, and much more reliable. The development of ventilators is itself a testament to technological innovation.

The Ventilator Challenge

In March 2019 in response to growing fears that the Covid-19 outbreak might overwhelm the National Health Service (NHS), the UK government announced that measures were to be taken to increase its operational capacity. One critical piece of equipment that emerged as an apparent capacity constraint was the ventilator.

Initially, NHS capacity – defined by the numbers of ventilators it had access to – was unclear. The most specific estimate was provided by Sir Simon Stevens, Head of NHS England, who informed the House of Commons that the NHS had 6,699 adult ventilators and 750 paediatric ventilators. The NHS then managed to secure a further 35 from the Ministry of Defence and 1,200 from private hospitals. This meant that there were around 8,684 ventilators in the system.

It was stated at that time by the government that, based on modelling done in China, 30,000 ventilators might be required to cope with the peak of the outbreak. This peak was predicted to arrive in mid-April, at that time around 3 weeks away. So, meeting this total would require a production rate of approximately 7,000 per week. To put this into some sort of operational context, the combined production capacity at that time of two of the established ventilator suppliers Smiths and Penlon was, according to some reports, as low as 60 machines per week.

To bridge this gap in production volume, the rather ambitious assertion was made that other groups of manufacturers – for example, the VentilatorChallengeUK Consortium that included BAE Systems, Meggit and a host of other engineering firms – would 'pull together' and with their 'scale and resources' supplement this manufacturing capability. At the same time, and in an even more bullish move, it was widely reported that Dyson had accepted an order (though placement of this order was later disputed), from the government to supply 10,000 machines. Oddly, Dyson had no approved design for a ventilator and no track record in supplying this product. The understandable panic that gripped the nation at this time and the frenzied activity accompanying it, led to what seemed to be a widespread disregard for the operational actualities of the situation.

In reality, there were many issues associated with the announcements being made.

First, even assuming a fully designed and certified product is available, increasing production capacity by several orders of magnitude is no easy task. Operational systems are designed to work efficiently at a relatively narrow range of volumes. Reconfiguring a low-volume production system to become a high-volume production system takes a large investment in machinery and labour and often requires fundamental changes to the processes. In other words, low volume is rarely upgraded to high volume by simply doing the same things more times and more quickly. Adding other companies, regardless of their size and success in producing for other markets, is quite simply not a quick and easy a solution. This is because the vast majority of production lines are not capable of producing a wide variety of products; they are specialized to a specific product range. Put more simply, a system that produces a car on Monday cannot be reconfigured to produce a ventilator on Tuesday.

In addition, the production of parts for the medical industry, like many industries that produce safety-critical products, is tightly governed. Not only does the product have to be certified by specific governing bodies to meet certain standards, but the companies in the supply chain and their processes also need to be certified as fit to produce. The Medicines and Healthcare Products Regulatory Agency (MHRA) is the UK body that oversees the approval of medical equipment.

While much of the rhetoric was bullish, some better informed sources were more cautious. Ventilator manufacturer Penlon's Product Chief was quoted as stating that 'asking non-specialist manufacturers to make a ventilator was unrealistic'. Other sources suggested that it could take months for non-medical manufacturing companies to ensure their production facilities were suitable for making ventilators.

While scaling-up to produce higher volumes of existing products presents problems, Dyson's position was even more challenging as it needed to design and certify an entirely new product before putting it into production could even be considered. A ventilator is a sophisticated piece of equipment and it must be designed to meet a huge number of requirements in relation to functionality, safety, usability, reliability, maintainability and testability. Below are listed a very small subset of requirements and they state, for example, that ventilators must:

- be reliable and able to keep working 100% of the time for at least 14 days
- sense when a patient stops breathing
- be fitted with an alarm that alerts medical staff in case of a fault or some other interruption
- support a range of 10 to 30 breaths per minute, rising in increments of two, with the settings adjustable
- be intuitive to use, requiring no more than 30 minutes of training for an experienced medical professional.

Even after the design of a product is complete, certifying a product such as this takes time, some reports suggested up to 2 years. More alarmingly, one report indicated that standards may be relaxed to allow a quicker certification process.

After design is complete, certification is gained and production has begun, a new ventilator must be integrated into its operational environment, in this case a complex socio-technical system that includes patients and medics and a host of other equipment. Finally, a system for service and support must be set up to ensure its ongoing viability.

The Ventilator Outcome

Fortunately, as events unfolded, the initial requirements of 30,000 ventilators were revised downwards to 18,000 and ultimately even this number proved to be an over-estimate. The peak of the UK outbreak passed in April 2020 and the NHS coped with little more than its initial number of ventilators.

Despite this fortunate escape, much work had been done to meet the objectives set. Most notably Penlon and the VentilatorChallengeUK Consortium did manage to certify a modified design creating the Prima EOS 2 ventilator. This was done in a very short timescale and represents a great achievement, and, at the time of writing, work involving many companies is still ongoing to upscale production capacity.

Providing a sensible and informed summary Peter Elsy, Head of the VentilatorChallengeUK Consortium (quoted in the Engineering and Technology News) summarized the issues facing industry by describing the fundamental operational trade-off at the root of this challenge by noting that 'it is vital that we balance the twin imperatives of speed of delivery and the absolute adherence to regulatory standards that is needed to ensure patient safety'.

Sources: www.nytimes.com/article/coronavirus-timeline.html; www.statista.com/statistics/1105235/coronavirus-2019 ncov-cases-recoveries-deaths-most-affected-countries-worldwide; www.wired.co.uk/article/uk-coronavirus-ventilators; www.med-technews.com/news/government-orders-15-000-penlon-ventilators; www.emedecine.medscape.com; www.eandt.theiet.org; Corrado, A. and Gorinin, M, (2002) 'Negative pressure ventilation: Is there still a role', ***European Respiratory Journal,*** **20,** 187–197.

Introduction

Providing medical care effectively and safely involves the management of one of the most complex operational systems on the planet. It is a service that is supported by sophisticated technology, utilizes complex supply chains and relies on complicated processes. It employs skilled workers who carry out intricate tasks often at the boundary of what is known by science. Providing healthcare is challenging, relentless and stressful work, it is required 24 hours a day, 365 days a year. Delivering medical services successfully requires the most effective operations management.

The early stages of the Covid-19 crisis very clearly highlight how important good operations management is in keeping the public safe and society functioning. The development and certification of new tests, vaccines and equipment, their production, distribution and deployment brought operations management very quickly into the spotlight. In the longer term, operations management will be required to reconfigure how society works, to redesign and re-engineer the systems and processes such as transport and security that facilitate human activity.

Operations management was once the poor relation in managerial work, it existed in relative obscurity, used mainly in factories, camouflaged behind esoteric practices and bewildering jargon. It lived in the shadow of other, more glamorous and highly paid activities such as marketing, sales and strategic management. In recent years though, operations management has begun to emerge from the shadows. This is happening for two reasons: first, it is gradually finding application outside its traditional production environment; and second, it is starting to receive greater exposure in the mainstream media with its terminology and models being increasingly used to explain economic and industrial phenomena, such as Brexit with its focus on 'frictionless' supply chains, and the Covid crisis that brought the need to reconfigure how many industries work.

It has been some time in coming, but these days there is now some prestige associated with being an operations manager. As the case study shows, good operations management is not only crucial to success in business but critical to our survival.

The purpose of this chapter is threefold. First, to introduce the basic concepts and language that underpin operations management, and so create an understanding that will enable you, as a student of management, to think like an operations manager. Second, to create the foundation for effective study of the material contained in the chapters to come. And lastly, and possibly most importantly, to stimulate your interest in what, we would argue, is the most important skill-set within contemporary management.

What Is Operations Management?

Today's Management Challenges

> *The Matrix is a system, Neo. That system is our enemy. But when you're inside, you look around, what do you see? Businessmen, teachers, lawyers, carpenters – the very minds of the people we are trying to save . . . Many of them are so inured, so hopelessly dependent on the system, that they will fight to protect it.*
>
> Morpheus to Neo, *The Matrix* (1999)

In making the statement above, Morpheus is attempting to open the mind of his student Neo to the true nature of life in *The Matrix,* and the shocking revelation that reality is a fabrication, a virtual world created to enslave the human race. The challenge Morpheus faces is that Neo, like the rest of humanity, is so embedded in his perception of reality that he cannot imagine another state of being.

Those living in the first-world societies of the 21st century exist in very much the same way. The degree of organization applied in our everyday lives is so pervasive that it is difficult for most to conceive of a different form of existence. Lives are lived in a state of systematization, every waking moment in some way supported by an operational process. When we leave our beds, we engage in personal processes for cleaning, dressing and feeding. When we leave our homes, we step into processes for transport and security. When we arrive at our places of work, we seamlessly fold into processes for producing products or delivering services. We are never free of process. Our lives are continually 'managed' within the system that is our society.

Whereas the fictional Matrix is a system for exploiting and enslaving the human race, the processes and systems in our everyday lives exist, we tell ourselves, for the opposite purpose. They are there to make our lives easier and safer. They exist to enable us to be more productive. Transport systems get us to where we want to be reliably and predictably, health care systems keep us fit and well, security systems keep us safe from harm, and manufacturing systems produce goods that are reliable and affordable and meet our needs.

Therefore, it could be argued that, for all society's bewildering complexity, the overall challenge faced by humanity is simply to create better systems. This challenge lies squarely within the remit of operations management.

The Operations Challenge

Let's investigate this overall challenge in a bit more detail. Operations management can be defined as *the activity of managing the resources of the organization that deliver goods and services.*

The way to perform this activity well is to implement systems and processes that are:

- *repeatable* – can be done over and over again
- *consistent* – produce the same result every time
- *reliable* – do not break down randomly.

The achievement of these three conditions has been the goal of operations managers since the first factories were established. These days, the standard of performance required of operational systems is governed by a number of factors such as:

- Globalization where more companies operating in each market push the boundaries of operational performance
- Advances such as automation and information technology inventing new ways of doing things more cost effectively
- Technology-push creating more sophisticated products
- Market-pull creating demand for more differentiated products
- Growing legal constraints such as employment law
- Tighter environmental restrictions on pollution
- Increased focus on ethical issues, such as exploitation of labour.

So it is not enough to have processes that are repeatable, consistent and reliable, they must also perform more efficiently than those of the competition while being compliant with the regulation within the wider environment. In simple terms this means that they must produce the greatest output for the least input, while not breaking any moral or legal codes.

SHORT CASE

Slicing Up the Profits

One of the original skills developed by early humans was hunting animals for food. In tandem with this came the skill of cutting up the catch into edible chunks. Part of the trick here was in producing as much food as possible from a single carcass, to sustain the tribe for as long as possible. Today, much the same logic applies, but now the key driver towards an efficient process is not survival, but profit. As you read this case study, consider how little waste there is in modern food production processes.

Source: ©Tatjana Baibakova/Shutterstock

The Sharp End of the Food Industry

In the meat industry, like every other, efficiency is measured by how much output is gained from a given input. In this case the output is the price that can be commanded for selling the cuts of meat, and the input costs are the cost of material, the carcass, the cost of the butcher's labour, and the overheads of running the facility. The main factors influencing this process are the speed of work, the skill of the worker, and the effectiveness of materials utilization.

The need for speed is obvious, as the quicker the activity is carried out, the higher the throughput will be, and the greater the number of units that are processed.

The skill of the butcher is critical: a highly skilled butcher will be more precise in his activity, resulting in less waste and a larger proportion of high-quality meat, which can be turned into more desirable cuts that can be sold for a premium price.

High materials utilization in this context means reducing to a minimum the parts of the carcass that cannot be sold. In the meat industry the process produces very little waste. What cannot be sold as steak will be sold as minced beef, what cannot be sold as minced beef will be sold as sausages, and what cannot be sold for human consumption will be sold as animal food.

The process for butchering animals has evolved over many centuries, with techniques, skills and tools being upgraded as technology and facilities have changed. Repeatability, consistency and reliability are key factors in the success of this industry. The process must be repeatable, as it must happen numerous times, over and over again; it must be consistent, in that it must result in the same quality of output each time an animal is processed; and it must be reliable, in that it must not break down. Failure to meet any of these objectives will result in reduced efficiency and therefore loss of profit.

What, once upon a time, were groups of hunters huddled around a fire, with flint axes and crude knives, has turned into a multi-million pound industry that is crucial to society, with a supply chain stretching from farm to high street, in a process that utilizes the latest technology, automation and management principles in the search for the most efficient and profitable process for converting meat to money.

Question

1. The process of producing fresh meat is a long one, beginning essentially with the birth of the animal. Think of the number of opportunities within this journey for the process to break down, by becoming inefficient or inconsistent.

The Conversion Process

The first step in designing an operational system is to conceptualize all work activity as a *conversion process* – so called because it represents the conversion of a specific set of input resources into the specific output (or set of outputs) that is the product. Some texts call this the transformation process, the terminology is interchangeable.

Figure 0.1 represents a model of the concept of the conversion process. In its most basic form, a set of input resources – raw materials, people, information and money – enter a 'black box' representing the processes of the organization. Here the organization converts these inputs to an output that is the product or service to be sold. The resources can be sorted into two categories: **transforming resources** are the resources that carry out the conversion process but are not themselves altered, and **transformed resources** are the resources that are converted by the process and therefore become the product.

> **Transforming resources:** facilities such as buildings, equipment and tools and process technology; all the staff involved in the conversion process; and the capital that is needed to buy materials, and pay for the facilities and staff.
>
> **Transformed resources:** materials to be converted into products for sale, and information.

Resources

Transforming resources are:

- *Facilities:* the buildings, equipment and tools.
- *Staff:* the people working to complete conversion activities, operate machinery or maintain the equipment.
- *Capital:* the money to buy materials and pay for the facilities and staff.

Transformed resources are:

- *Materials,* such as metal, wood and plastic, which become parts such as nuts and bolts, structures, or printed circuit boards, which are built into products such as cars, buildings or computers. As the input materials move through the conversion process, their physical form will be changed in some way to form the eventual product.
- *Information,* such as market requirements, assembly instructions, engineering formulae, scientific concepts or business intelligence. Information is useful in two ways in the conversion process: first,

Figure 0.1 The conversion process

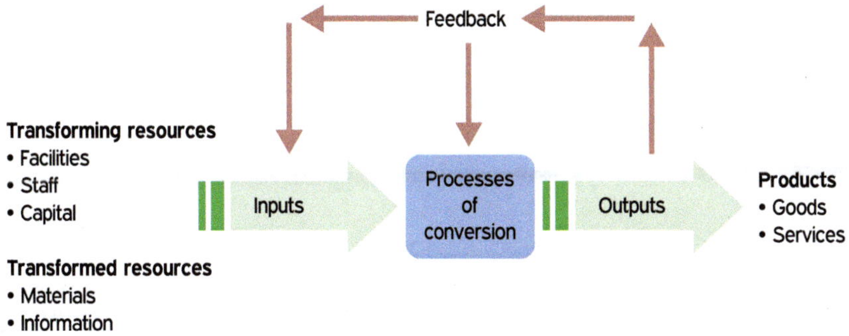

where it informs the process of conversion, for example in design specifications and diagrams, without which the product could not be built; and, second, where it is itself part of the product, and is sorted, recombined or repackaged to form different information. Accountants do this with financial information, which is converted from its raw form into published accounts, and journalists do this when news is reconfigured and packed into a story for a newspaper or television report.

Figure 0.1 also shows a feedback system. This monitors the conversion process, and captures any deviations from process norms that may occur. Feedback is needed to ensure that the process performs the way it should, repeatably, reliably and consistently. As nothing is perfect, and processes do change over time, they must be constantly monitored and measured to ensure they do not deviate from their required norm.

Feedback

Feedback broadly falls into two categories:

- Feedback that is *internal* to the conversion process. This ensures that the process remains stable and produces exactly the same product, over and over again. This feedback is usually quantitative. For example, the dimensions of the product, such as the weight of a chocolate bar – too high, and product is being given away; too low, and the customer is being short-changed; or oven temperature in a cooking process – too high and the food products may be burned as they pass through this part of the process, too low and it may be under-cooked.
- Feedback that is *external* to the conversion process. This can be either qualitative, such as how the customer perceived the product, or quantitative, such as what percentage of the market buys the product. This feedback can inform the design of the product: a poorly selling product, or one that attracts a lot of complaints, will need to be modified to ensure it more closely meets the customer's needs.

Figure 0.2 illustrates the conversion process in terms of the manufacture of a motor car.

Most complex operations involve a number of conversion processes. Figure 0.3 shows how the operation is actually made up of linked chains of conversion processes.

Figure 0.2 A simple conversion process

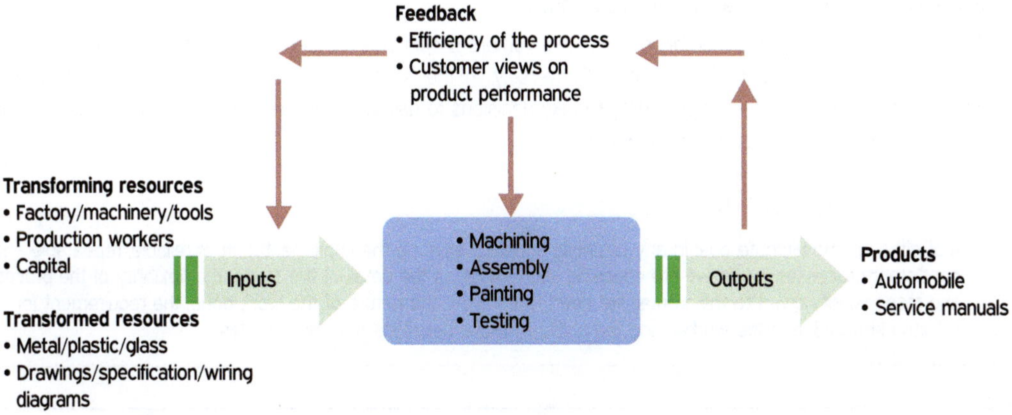

Figure 0.3 The conversion process expanded

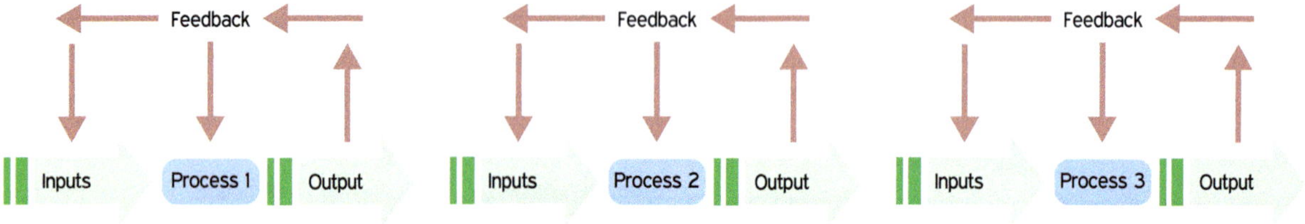

We can view the entire conversion process as a series of sub-processes, with the output of one process becoming the input of the next, all working to produce the product to be sold to the end-user. Of course, in most industries the overall process will comprise many parallel process chains, all converging to create the final product. With this conceptualization of an operations system, it is critical to see the next stage of the process as 'the customer' regardless of whether it is carried out within your organization or by another organization. Remember, the output from one stage becomes the input to the next, and it must be correct or the next stage cannot be performed properly.

CRITICAL PERSPECTIVE

When Is a Process Not a Process?

In simple terms, operations management argues that the utilization of reliable, repeatable and consistent processes will create the most efficient operation. This argument has been proved time and time again, as evidenced by many systems such as the production lines of car companies, for example Toyota, and the service systems in fast-food outlets, for example McDonald's.

As managers analyse their operations, and attempt to implement greater systematization, the question that emerges is therefore: how much process is too much process? Or put another way, which activities, if any, cannot be systematized?

There is no easy or universal answer to this, but fundamentally the answer must be based on the amount of randomness that will remain within the work process, despite our best attempts to remove it.

For example, in building a car, it should be possible to create a process that is totally non-random. If the design is robust, if all the processes of manufacture are well thought out, if the facilities are well constructed and immune to external influence, if the feedback loops are correct and the workforce well disciplined, then every unit of output should come together in exactly the same way, with no surprises.

Any breakdown in the process will be due to external, unanticipated events such as labour strikes, or to extreme environmental conditions, such as earthquakes, that impinge on the closed environment of the factory.

But now consider, for example, the process of carrying out common surgical procedures, such as cataract operations or appendectomies. These processes are repeatable, and – some might argue – no more complex than building a car, but they are subject to more randomness. Variations in the physical features and underlying health conditions of the input resource – the patient – may necessitate decisions during the process of surgery that lead to its being changed, or even abandoned.

This means that in the car assembly process the workers should be expected simply to follow the process, as any decision taken by them would disrupt it. Conversely, in the surgical process the surgeon must possess the knowledge and be given the responsibility to take decisions to deviate from the process, if issues arise, in order to ensure the ultimate success of the operation.

The key point is ...

that although the ultimate goal in any business should always be the implementation of reliable, repeatable and consistent processes, when we are choosing such things as the detail of the steps, the flexibility of the process and responsibility given to the worker, we need to consider the nature of the work done, the requirement for retained knowledge in the worker, and the ability to make decisions that this enables.

Stop and Think

Surgery is performed by a skilled surgeon, supported by a team of people, who complete the entire operation. What prevents routine surgery being performed on a production line basis, with each worker trained in only a small part of the procedure?

The Nature of Products

It is common to associate the term 'product' purely with something tangible – a physical artefact that can be seen, held, and used. Until very recently, this association was correct; very little of what was bought and sold did not have some sort of physical or tangible presence. These days, though, with the growth of the service sector, the word 'product' is increasingly applied to intangibles, such as financial services, package holidays, health care or legal advice. A mortgage is no less a product than a car or a watch. It is designed for a purpose, sold, paid for, and used. It is important that, as operations managers, we see the 'production' process of these intangible products in the same way that we see the production process of tangible products. In other words there are still inputs, outputs, processes and feedback loops.

The product that is sold in restaurants is the experience of the meal. Although eating out is considered a service, it is a combination of the tangible product that is the meal and the intangible service that is provided by the attentiveness of the staff and the ambience of the surroundings.

Nowadays, it is becoming increasingly difficult to draw a distinction between a tangible product and an intangible service as very few physical products are sold without some form of service package attached. This 'blurring' of distinctions between the tangible and intangible and how it affects the management of operations systems is becoming very important and will be explored more fully throughout the remainder of this book. At this point, however, the fact that needs to be emphasized is that the conversion process model is as applicable to services delivery systems such as those that exist in restaurants, banks, schools and hospitals as it is to the production systems that exist in factories.

Figure 0.4 shows a conversion process for a typical service: the service of education provision. Although the operational logic of the conversion process applies to both production and service delivery, there are nevertheless some differences between them. The main one is that in service delivery the customer is present in the conversion process at all times, though it may seem somewhat odd, the customer can be considered as one of the 'raw materials' that is 'converted'.

This conversion might be from being a non-graduate to a graduate; or from a customer with long, untidy hair to one with styled hair; or from a patient who is ill to one who is well.

Within service work the customer's presence in the conversion process is, admittedly, rather inconvenient and it has consequences for operations managers. In the manufacture of tangible products such as chairs, cars or clothes, most of the work is done in a factory and, if the operations managers have set this up correctly, this will be a closed system: closed, that is, to the customer and the risk of their interfering.

Figure 0.4 The conversion process of education

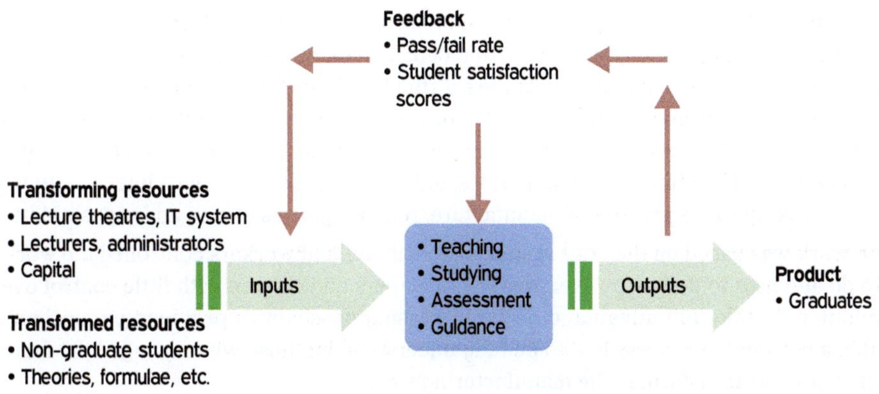

But in the provision of services such as hairdressing, education or policing, the customer is an integral part of the operational process and, unfortunately, customers have the potential to behave unpredictably and disrupt the reliability, repeatability and consistency of the process. So the service system needs to be able to handle the randomness that this brings. The way to deal with this tends to be to build-in more flexibility, generally in the form of staff who are knowledgeable and empowered enough to manage the random events before they get out of hand.

There are knock-on effects too. A customer's presence will cause inconsistencies in the delivery of a service that may affect other customers and this means that each customer may have a slightly different experience. This is easy to recognize where a dining experience may be made better or worse depending on the atmosphere created by the presence or absence of other customers.

There are other differences between production and service delivery that also cause problems. For example, the intangible nature of the service experience makes it more difficult to ensure that a quality service is being produced and maintained. It is more difficult to measure the service experience than it is to measure the utility of a physical product and therefore it is more difficult to judge if it is of the correct quality.

Also, services tend to be difficult to store. If a hotel room is left vacant for a night, then this represents a loss of revenue as the next night is a different revenue-generating opportunity. Similarly, the experience of going to a theatre show or a rock concert cannot be wrapped and mass-produced. The closest thing might be the product equivalent that is the DVD of the show or the CD of the rock concert, but these proxies are always a poor imitation of the real thing.

These issues affect several aspects of operations management, and we shall explore them in more detail, later in the book.

Stop and Think

Have you ever sought legal advice for any reason? Perhaps buying a house, claiming compensation, or even defending a criminal charge? From a lawyer's perspective, how can consistency, reliability and repeatability be guaranteed in the process of delivering legal services?

How Is Operations Management Practised?

The Importance of Process

When we walk into McDonald's, first we may enter a process for queuing, we are then served by someone who is not a trained waiter, we purchase a meal that is cooked by someone who is not a skilled chef, and we eat in an environment that can only by quite a stretch of the imagination be called a restaurant. Moreover, the meal we buy has been designed to specific standards of quality, is the product of a process of manufacture, and will be produced in exactly the same way, regardless of where or when it is bought. McDonald's is the ultimate in service systematization.

Organizational processes evolved in different places and at different rates, but the father of process design is usually recognized as Fredrick Winslow Taylor (1911). In the late 19th and early 20th centuries the United States experienced rapid industrialization. Driven by new technologies, more complex forms of organization emerged, and many of the world's best-known companies were founded, including Esso, General Motors and Ford. Skilled workers were scarce, and even basic language skills were difficult to find. Taylor, and his system of *scientific management* solved this problem by making the attributes of the worker mostly irrelevant. Taylor and his supporters believed in *rationalism* – the view that if you understand something, you should be able to state it explicitly, and write a rule or law for it. The effect of applying rules and procedures is to replace uncertainty with predictability. By applying this thinking to the process of manufacture, reliability, consistency and repeatability will result.

Before Taylor, work was based on the craft system, where individual workers controlled the work process, as they knew what to do and how to do it. However, this left managers and owners with little control over the production process. In addition, to take full advantage of the increasing possibilities provided by mechanization, all of the activities within a conversion process had to be fully understood by those who managed the factory. Taylor advocated five principles that transformed the manufacturing world.

1. A clear division of task and responsibility between worker and manager – the manager planned and organized; the worker carried out the tasks.
2. The use of scientific methods to determine the best way of doing the job – the separation of *conception* (the planning of the work) and *execution* (the doing of the work). In effect this meant that the craft knowledge possessed by the worker was taken by the management, formalized, improved, and assimilated into the process of production.
3. Scientific selection of the person for the newly designed job – simply speaking, choosing the right person for the job.
4. The training of the worker to do a job in a specific way – implementation of the division of labour to the point where each worker was specialized in an extremely limited piece of work and was trained specifically to do it.
5. Surveillance of workers – the implementation of rudimentary performance management systems.

Taylor's five principles were based on experiments he carried out almost exclusively in the steel industry in 19th-century America, but his ideas endured and spread becoming the basis of operations management in all industries today. In the early 20th century Taylor's ideas were developed by Henry Ford into the production line system that came to dominate manufacturing work, and more recently have been applied in the service sector, as evidenced in the aforementioned McDonald's and similar global fast-food outlets.

Stop and Think

Look around at the organizations that you come into contact with in your daily life. Try to identify the processes that they use. Can you find any that are not underpinned in some way by Taylor's principles?

Characteristics of Operations Management

Operations management models and frameworks are useful because they are generalizable, that is, they apply to a number of different types of operation. The conversion process model is a good example of this. All operations systems transform input resources into output products. All operational activity, regardless of what it is or where it takes place can therefore be characterized by this model. However, while all operations are similar in this respect they also differ in several ways.

The four most fundamental characteristics that lead to differences in how operations systems are designed are called the 4Vs of operations management. The 4Vs are the *Volume of Output*, the *Variety of Offering*, the *Variation in Demand* (for the output), *Degree of Visibility* (of the conversion process). These Vs are often called 'dimensions', as each represents a continuum ranging from high to low.

The Volume of Output

Volume refers to how many units of a given type of product are produced or how many times a particular type of service is delivered. Before explaining this further it is important to point out that there is no absolute scale against which to measure volume. In other words there is no specific volume at which an operations system changes state from a high-volume system to a low-volume system or vice versa. For example, ballpoint pens are often cited as an example of one of the most-produced goods: some estimates propose that there is a worldwide demand for 14 million pens per day, this equates to over 5 billion per year. In contrast, the global demand for cars in 2019 was a relatively modest 75 million. Despite this disparity the operational systems used for manufacturing these products would both be considered high volume.

When considering the volume dimension the absolute volume of each product or service is not really the key consideration at all. The volume dimension is relevant because the form of the production system tends to alter as companies search for the best efficiency as volumes change. What is important here is the concept of economies of scale. This concept states that as production volumes increase the cost of each individual unit should fall. This is because as volumes increase more revenue should be generated and therefore more money should be available to invest in the production process. This investment will buy more efficient and specialist machinery, machinery which would ultimately remove the less efficient worker from the process of production.

Figure 0.5 The Volume/Variety dimension

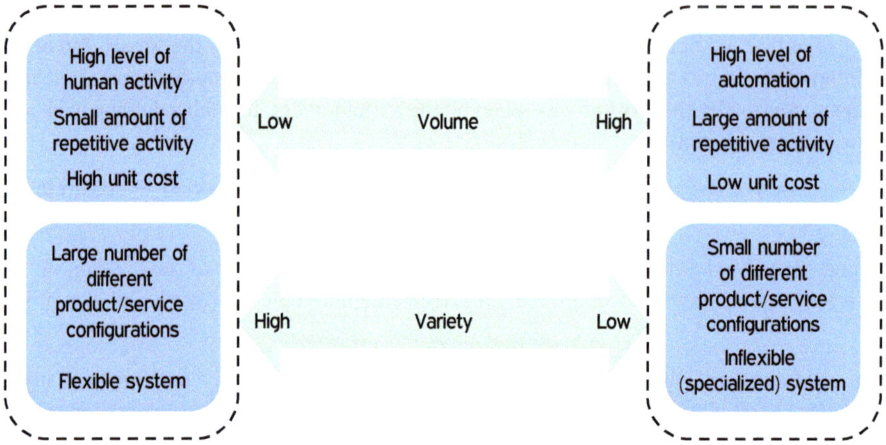

The foundational logic supporting this argument dates back to the first industrial revolution. It dictates that workers are flexible (they can do a lot of different things) but inefficient (it costs a lot to have them do these things). Conversely machines tend to be inflexible, they can do only one thing but they do it very efficiently. Although technology has changed hugely in the last two centuries, one of the effects of which has been to increase the flexibility of automation, the superiority of machines for carrying out repetitive tasks in volume is still one of the most basic pieces of logic that continues to shape industry.

These days the provision of fast-food is possibly the most quoted and most visible example of this phenomenon as McDonald's and similar companies provide testament to. In these service systems some form of specialist automation has been implemented wherever possible and where humans are still used, as much as possible has been done to ensure they behave like the machines that they have yet to be replaced by.

Figure 0.5 illustrates the characteristics displayed by an operations system that exists at each extreme of the Volume dimension.

The Variety of the Offering

Variety refers to how many types of product are manufactured by the same facility. If a standard product such as a mass-produced car is to be built numerous times, the process used can become very specialized both in equipment and worker skills. However, if the factory was required to produce many types of custom car, then more general hand-tools and more widely skilled staff would be needed to provide the necessary manufacturing flexibility.

In reality, manufacturing systems are generally not required to swap at the drop of a hat between entirely different products. For example, a production system would not regularly be asked to switch back and forth between producing a family saloon and producing a sports car. More commonly, the production system would be designed to produce one type of car but with the flexibility to accommodate different configurations of that type.

Variety in service delivery is similar. A train service tends to be very inflexible. It delivers the same journey repetitively, in shorter journeys often many times a day. However, a taxi service may deliver many different journeys over the course of a day, never repeating the same one. Figure 0.5 illustrates the characteristics displayed by an operations system that exists at each extreme of the Variety dimension.

CRITICAL PERSPECTIVE

The (not so) Simple Relationship between Volume and Variety

Understanding the detail when you are considering Volume and Variety is fundamental to the design of operations systems. As shown in Figure 0.5, Volume and Variety tend to be related in what mathematicians might describe as an inversely proportional relationship. To put this more simply, high-volume/low-variety operational systems will tend to have one set of characteristics and low-volume/high-variety operational systems another.

This relationship is rarely questioned, it forms part of the bedrock of operations dogma. However, while it is often correct, it is not always correct. Let's explore this contention by examining a common example.

One of the usual ways educators explain the Volume/Variety relationship is by quoting service-system examples such as restaurants or hotels. For example, a top-notch, Michelin-starred restaurant might commonly be described as low-volume/high-variety and a fast-food, city-centre diner might be described as high-volume/low-variety.

In relation to the Volume dimension this relationship is easy to defend. A branch of, for example, TGI Fridays will serve many more meals in a day than an eatery like, for example, The Fat Duck (for non-gastronomists, this is Heston Blumenthal's restaurant which boasts 3 Michelin stars).

However, the Variety dimension is a bit more troublesome and the main issue is found in how we characterize Variety. Let's assume Variety refers to the range of options, or put another way, the number of different meals that the restaurant can produce. The greater the range of options, then the greater the Variety. Applying the standard Volume/Variety dogma would indicate that the fast-food diner should have a less extensive menu and the Michelin-starred restaurant a more extensive menu. Clearly, this is not always the case. Often the fast-food diner boasts a much larger choice.

But what about another tenet of this relationship which states that the higher-volume system will have less flexibility than the lower-volume system? Let's assume that flexibility is defined as the ability to change the output of the operational system at short notice, this ability to change in effect creates greater Variety of output. Again, our standard Volume/Variety thinking would assert that the fast-food diner would be much less flexible. But again, this isn't always the case in reality. For example, often city-centre diners will accommodate any reasonable customer request, for example, removing a particular component, such as a sauce, or replacing one component, such as potatoes, with another such as fries. Conversely, the Michelin-starred restaurant might baulk at a change request, shocked by the audacity of the customer who might want to 'mess around' with the composition of the award-winning meal that has been so lovingly crafted by the highly skilled chef.

Indeed, rather bizarrely, this lack of flexibility may be one of the main selling points of the Michelin-starred restaurant!

The key point is ...

that the underlying characteristics of each dimension and the context within which it is deployed must be understood in detail before applying the Volume/Variety logic.

Variation in Demand

Variation in demand refers to how the required number of products may differ over a period of time, for example, from day-to-day, or week-to-week. This can be most easily seen in holiday resorts, where the facilities have to cope with huge differences in throughput across the year. A ski resort, for example, may be working at full capacity throughout the winter, but may have no business at all during the summer.

Variation in demand and volume of output are linked. Operations systems are designed to deliver a particular volume of output and will therefore be at their most efficient when producing this volume. If the rate of production of output and the rate of demand for this output are steady and matched then there is no issue. However, if the demand varies – for example, falls – then the production output must vary to match it and absorb the attendant reduction in efficiency or the output must be maintained with the unsold product stored until (hopefully) the demand rises. Both of these options incur cost. In addition, in service work storage is often not an option as consumption and production must be done simultaneously. Figure 0.6 illustrates the characteristics displayed by an operations system that exists at each extreme of the Variation dimension.

Degree of Visibility

Degree of *visibility* refers to how much of the operational system is visible to the customer. While at first glance this seems a relatively simple dimension to conceptualize, there are different degrees of visibility. Degree of

Figure 0.6 The Variation dimension

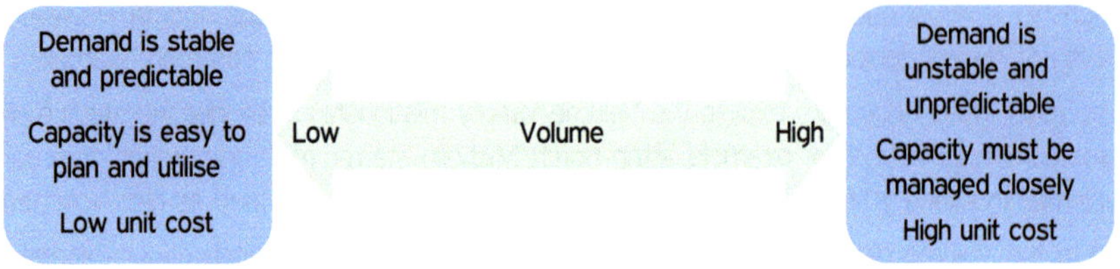

Figure 0.7 The Visibility dimension

visibility tends to be closely related to the level of customer participation in the system. Unfortunately, though more accurate, calling this dimension 'participation' does not lend the same alliterative elegance to the model.

While processes can be visible in both manufacturing operations and service operations, this dimension applies mainly to services because the customer's presence as a transformed resource is necessary to the execution of the service process.

Production systems are generally low visibility, locked behind factory doors and closed to the eyes of the public. This means that the customer is normally only aware of the finished product. This is not always the case though – some companies are now opening their factories to the public. At the most rudimentary level the degree of visibility afforded by this policy may be limited to customer observation of certain activities. For example, the opening up of limited sections of a whisky-making operation for the interested customer to view. Here, this level of increased visibility is not a necessity but an operational choice (possibly) based on the strategic imperative to increase revenue through tourism. Some companies, such as high-profile, drinks-manufacturer Guinness, are taking this further and making their factories into a sort of theme-park experience, where customers can tour, view, taste and buy. In cases like this, the process of manufacture has become more visible but customers are restricted to the periphery and there is little impact on the process sequencing and little increased risk of intervention.

Even in service delivery, some aspects of the process are out of sight or only partially visible to the customer. Airport terminals are a good example of this. After check-in, baggage disappears until it hopefully emerges at the destination. The customer does not see the majority of the process that delivers it.

In service delivery though, many processes must not only be designed to consider customer observation, they must also be designed for customer participation. In airports while the operational processes for moving baggage may be out of sight, the operational processes for moving customers such as security, check-in and boarding are impossible to hide.

While the need to make a process visible may only require minor alterations to ensure it is visually appealing, there are many, much more impactful, issues that arise when customers participate in processes. Figure 0.7 illustrates the characteristics displayed by an operations system that exists at each extreme of the Visibility dimension.

Who Is the Operations Manager?

The Role of the Operations Manager

Much has changed since the time of Taylor and Ford. Back then, operations managers were inward-facing, concerned only with the minutiae of process implementation, and the single-minded drive for efficiency. Those in operations roles in the early 20th century, if transported forwards in time to the early 21st, might experience a mix of emotions when confronted with what their role has become.

Would their overwhelming feeling be one of pride? Operations management, previously a member of the minor nobility in the hierarchy of management disciplines, has now risen in status to management royalty. Operations managers command large numbers of employees and operations systems are seen as the engines that power industry. Once imprisoned in the production line, operations models and techniques have now broken out and travelled extensively, emigrating to all parts of the organization and all types of industries.

Accompanying pride might be a feeling of satisfaction that the philosophy of system and process has been proven, it has become the new management religion, with disciples in all management specialisms attempting to implement routinized systems wherever possible.

But pride and satisfaction might be tempered by feelings of unease as they consider the daunting size of the current role. These days, it could be argued, the operations role is much more challenging, both in content and in scope. The nature of the operations manager's role will depend on the type of organization and the characteristics of the industry, but in addition to the traditional tasks such as process design and capacity planning, many of the following responsibilities will be found:

- *Strategizing:* aiding in the development of corporate strategy, and devising and implementing operations strategies to support it
- *Performance management:* devising methods to increase the performance of the entire organization
- *Change management:* engaging in initiatives to continually update and improve the organization and re-engineer processes to meet ever-increasing competitive pressures
- *Design of products and services:* where once the scope of operations was limited to the manufacture of products to an existing design, these days it is increasingly absorbing the design work due to the realization that the design of the product and the design of the process of manufacture are inextricably linked.

CRITICAL PERSPECTIVE

No Place for the Operations Function!

The drive towards system and process began in earnest during the Industrial Revolution, where new technology in the form of steam-driven machinery enabled products to be manufactured faster, and more consistently. This new system supplanted the previous craft-based system; large factories were built, where people and machines worked together in the process of manufacture. Early management systems, based on the division of labour and scientific management (Taylor, 1911), were quickly established to shape the labour force around the needs of the machine, and of the process.

These factories became characterized by the process of the production system. The term 'operations management' did not come into use until the mid-20th century, and was coined in association with the manufacture of products. Manufacturing at this time dominated the industrial landscape, and companies were structured in discrete functions such as production, marketing, finance and sales. This structure, combined with the historical legacy, associated the operations function with production activity. This situation still persists today within some companies, and indeed some textbooks, still use this terminology. But as industrial activity in the service sector has grown, there has been a consequent association of the term 'operations' with a far wider variety of industries. Operations management has been adopted by many companies that do not produce any physical product. It is now associated more with techniques such as process thinking and problem solving, which can be applied to any organization in any industry.

Nowadays banks label call centres as operations hubs, and retailers associate operations with the movement and sale of merchandise.

The key point is ...

that operations management is no longer confined to one organizational 'function', but can be applied as process and method across the entire organization.

Operations Management Skills

With the role of the operations manager growing, it is difficult to distil a specific set of skills needed to be an effective operations manager from the seemingly endless set of general management skills within the toolkit of the 21st century manager. As the scope of operations widens, merging and overlapping with other areas of the organization, operations managers are increasingly seen as mini-general managers. Planning and organizing, influencing and communicating, leading and motivating, implementing change and shaping culture, making decisions and problem solving, all fall under the remit of the operations manager. It is not easy to make sense of this bewildering assortment of skills, but it is possible to tidy things up somewhat and gain a better sense of what is required to be a success in the operations management role.

If we assume the basic activity of management is decision-making, then we can set the foundation of the operations role as deciding:

- *What* resources will be needed: material, infrastructure, people, information and capital
- *When* each resource will be needed: scheduling and sequencing of tasks
- *Where* the work will be done: in company or externally
- *How* the work will be done: system, process and activity
- *Who* will do the work: types of worker.

To build on this, though, it is not enough to merely list what an operations manager does. The following *bundles of skill* should provide a clearer picture of what the operations manager needs to be good at.

- *Managing process:* This is still the keystone of the operations manager's role. It requires skills in process planning and systems thinking, coupled with an understanding of technology and the ability to utilize it effectively, it also requires the ability to manage the people who inhabit the process.
- *Managing complexity:* With the size and diversity of today's operations, the challenge is not in the individual tasks or decisions that are taken, but in how they interact as a whole, and the complex relationships that result.
- *Linking conception and execution:* For Taylor, process designers and process workers were different sets of people. These days, in many organizations, both conception and execution are controlled by operations managers. The management of these different sets of people will require different approaches.
- *Balancing today and tomorrow:* The short-term is key, as it is the efficiency of the current conversion process that provides the profit and keeps the organization afloat, but the longer term must not be neglected. A balance must be struck between doing what is important today, and planning for what may be important tomorrow.

Therefore, operations managers must be able to process large amounts of varied and complex information, coordinate large numbers of tasks, prioritize effectively, solve complex problems and, most crucially, remain calm while under the pressure created by doing all of the above.

The Evolving Nature of Operations

GLOBALIZATION

While we have argued that operations management has undergone many changes since the days of Taylor and Ford, its evolution is not yet complete. When the external environment changes, ultimately the organization will look to operations management to deal with it. There are, broadly, three external forces that serve to alter the way operations management is practised.

Globalization

Globalization: the increasing integration of internationally dispersed economic activity, and the extension of an organization's operational activity to cover the whole world.

There has been international commerce since the earliest times when merchants traded spices and cloth across the ever-expanding known world. More recently this tendency to operate internationally has grown much more quickly. A much greater proportion of business than ever before is done across national boundaries, and many more companies see their markets on a global scale. Indeed, for many companies, such as travel and logistics firms, their sole purpose is to operate internationally.

Several factors are driving this rise in global business. Market-based factors, such as increasingly homogeneous customer requirements and more efficient and comprehensive international distribution networks; economic factors, such as international economies of scale and resource cost differentials; regulatory factors, such as the reduction in trade barriers increasing coherence in product standards; and technological factors, such as increasing sophistication in communications channels.

Operations management has been at the forefront of this trend, where (mainly) lower labour costs in the developing nations have caused a large-scale shift of low-skill manufacturing activities, such as mass production, and service activities, such as call centre work, from Europe and the USA to developing nations such as China, India and South America.

Globalization, therefore, results in a larger-scale canvas on which to practise operations management and a greater need for an external perspective.

Business Integration

BUSINESS INTEGRATION

While globalization is serving to expand the geographical boundaries that businesses operate within, there is a complementary effect whereby organizations are integrating more effectively with other organizations through supply chain relationships, to better capture the expanding opportunities provided by these global markets.

External integration is seen mainly in the creation of longer, larger and more complex supply chains, with companies specializing and then partnering with other companies to produce the final product or service. The necessity for closer relationships means companies must find new ways to communicate and interface with one another.

Similarly, as globalization increases efficiency and shortens product life-cycles, companies need to work more effectively at breaking down internal barriers between functions, departments and culturally diverse groups. Companies can no longer afford to allow internal politics and culturally abrasive relationships to impact on performance. Closer team-working is required to remove conflict and build consensus.

Corporate Responsibility

Milton Friedman, the economist, believed:

> *In a free economy there is one and only one social responsibility of business – to use its resources and engage in activities designed to increase its profits so long as it stays within the rules of the game.*
>
> Friedman (1962: 133)

CSR

This cosily simplistic notion advises companies to obey the rules of free competition, 'rules' that refer mainly to the avoidance of the crimes of deception and fraud. This was a view based on the notion that a free economy, with all parties acting on self-interest, will ultimately enhance the greater good. As has been most clearly evidenced in the 'credit crunch' of 2008, this thinking contains some flaws. These days, responsibility extends to more than just economic and legal imperatives. Carroll (1999) adds *ethical responsibility,* which encourages companies to do the right thing in relation to the wider social interest, such as supporting the environment or a disadvantaged group; and *discretionary responsibility* to contribute to the community in any way possible.

Corporate responsibility therefore encourages companies to strike an even balance between public good and private gain.

Corporate responsibility: the awareness, acceptance, and management of the wider implications of management decisions.

As you read through this book, each theme will be signalled as it appears in the text. This will allow you to consider the ways in which these forces are shaping the theories, tools and techniques of operations management.

Key Theories

The key theories discussed in this chapter were:

- **Conversion process** – the system of operational activity that takes a specific set of inputs and turns them into a specific output (or set of outputs) that is the product
- **The 4Vs of operations management** – volume of output, variety of offering, variation in demand for the product or service, and visibility to customers of the production or service delivery process

- **Scientific management** – a management system developed by Fredrick Winslow Taylor that encouraged the use of rational methods to plan operational processes in great detail.

Suggested Answers to Stop and Think Questions

1. **Process of surgery:** In simple terms it should be possible to design a process of surgery for routine operations that could be done by staff that are not trained to the same level as a fully qualified surgeon, much as a car is built by semi-skilled staff rather than by a fully qualified mechanic. In practice, though, there are reasons why this approach maybe difficult to implement. The main one is that the input, that is, the patients, are not all the same in terms of underlying health and severity of condition to be operated on. Therefore decisions will have to be taken during the process of the operation, and these require a skilled surgeon. Also, if something untoward occurs during the procedure, the staff might need to be skilled in techniques beyond those required for the operation in order to deal with it. In reality there is also another, less practical, reason in that the profession of surgery is highly enclosed, with a governing body that would not look kindly on the profession being diluted by the introduction of operations management methods to this degree.
2. **Legal services:** A legal service must be based on a defined process, but it differs from the production of goods or the delivery of more standardized services such as transport or fast food, in that the key element is not how well the process is defined; it is the knowledge possessed by the professional delivering the service.

   Specialization is important. Much as the medical profession is built upon areas of specialist knowledge, so is the legal profession.

   Process is not the only factor, but it still has a part to play. Those elements of the service that can be systematized and managed, such as the process of interaction with the customer (the meetings, communications and so on), should be standardized. Likewise, maintaining the same lawyer throughout a particular case will result in a more consistent approach for the client.

   People skills are important in the delivery of this service too. They will provide a degree of empathy between the involved parties and make for a more supportive and comfortable experience for the client.
3. **Taylor's principles:** It is difficult to find an organization that does not employ some measure of scientific management. The important thing to consider is the degree of systematization. A large company engaged in high volumes of repetitive, low-skill activities within production lines or call centres will embrace process management as much as possible. Conversely, a smaller organization with activity that requires a high level of decision-making, such as R&D or legal services, will be less process based.

connect

Further Reading

Ackroyd, S. and Thompson, P. (1999) *Organisational Misbehaviour,* Sage, London.

Blowfield, M. and Murray, A. (2008) *Corporate Responsibility: A Critical Introduction,* Oxford University Press, Oxford.

Ritzer, G. and Dean, P. (2019) *Globalization: The Essentials,* Wiley, Oxford.

Sprague, L.G. (2007) 'Evolution of the field of operations management', *Journal of Operations Management,* **25**(2), 219–238.

References

Carroll, A.B. (1999) 'Corporate social responsibility', *Business and Society*, **38**(3), 268–295.

Friedman, M. (1962) *Capitalism and Freedom*, University of Chicago Press, Chicago.

Taylor, F.W. (1911) *Scientific Management*, Harper & Row, New York.

PART 1 Directing

Contents

JOBS

We are looking for an operations director to play a central role in running the critical processes and systems to support the achievement of our global mission.

This position has primary responsibility for planning and implementing our operational routines, including: making decisions about the location and capacity of our facilities; working with our partner firms to procure and manage the flow of parts and services; and developing our systems to world-class levels through implementing lean principles.

The right candidate will be a self-starter and team player with relevant experience and proven success in operational and strategic management.

What does it take to become an Operations Manager?

We talk to Sean Stevenson at IMV Imaging about what it takes to manage operations in high-tech, global company.

How did you get into Operations Management?
I had a variety of roles prior to entering service operations management, my background is in IT software and hardware and for as long as I can remember I have always had a passion for understanding how things work. As I worked through various roles within IT, I stopped asking 'how does this work?' And started to ask 'what can I do to make this better?' I then started to apply the same thinking to business and to how processes come together to allow the business to operate efficiently day-to-day. This led me to operations management.

What was the most useful skill or experience that prepared you for your current role?
I would say my technical background has provided me with a good stepping-stone. In my early career, I would often implement new IT processes that affected how a user would operate their computer and now I am changing processes within our business to improve how we deliver our services.

What role does operations management play in the company's strategy-making process?
As a company grows, small issues may become bigger issues and big issues can not only waste a lot of time and money, but can also damage the company reputation. How we run our operations day-to-day has a massive impact on the future strategy of our business. Selling product is one thing but we also need to think about how we support these products in the field to ensure optimum 'up-time' for our clients. Looking internally at our processes and efficiency plays an important part in how we achieve on-time delivery to our clients. We also need to think about smarter ways to do things and this might be updating existing processes or looking at ways in which technology can help us improve customer focus.

What decisions do you typically take when thinking about operations strategy?
There are various elements to take into consideration here. Development of our workforce is something I have a deep passion for and something that we review regularly within our business. As we work with technology that is changing fast, we need to ensure our teams are up to date with the latest techniques. I also like to look at the equipment we use to do our business and how we can utilize it better. A recent example would be the implementation of 3D printing to print common parts used within our equipment. Using this means that rather than having to hold stock or wait on a shipment from our supplier we are able to print small, commonly used, parts in around 15 minutes. This represents a saving to our business and it also provides a quicker reaction time for our customers.

You are currently implementing a 'servitization' strategy – can you briefly describe what this consists of?
Traditionally, service has been a reactive part of our business. However, over the last five years, we have been growing our service business and investing into our service infrastructure. We are now at a stage where we need to adopt a much more proactive approach. We also need to look at how we deliver our services in an efficient way globally. We are currently adopting 'Lean' principles in pursuit of this.

What changes do you see happening in your industry and how might this affect how you do your job in future?
Globalization has already affected our industry significantly and created a very turbulent market place. Due to greater investment in our industry, competition is becoming much more intense and this is only going to get worse.

What do you consider to be essential skills for your role?
The ability to take time out of the day-to-day management and take a step back to look at the bigger picture. To look outside our businesses and industry even and see what other companies are doing and how can this be made useful to us. Also being able to listen to our clients and understand their needs.

1 Business Strategy and Customer Orientation

Learning Outcomes

After reading this chapter you should be able to:

- Define what is meant by strategy and strategic management
- Effectively use key strategic terms
- Describe the difference between market-based and resource-based approaches to strategy
- Discuss the nature of organizational competencies and capabilities
- Explain the nature of competitive advantage

BUSINESS INTEGRATION

Warner Bros: From Humphrey Bogart to Harry Potter

Source: ©Oscity/Shutterstock

It is over a century since four Polish immigrant brothers opened their first film studio on Sunset Boulevard in Hollywood. Now, Warner Bros stands at the forefront of every aspect of the entertainment industry, including film and TV, gaming, consumer products, comic books and cinemas.

From Exhibition to Production

Film production was not the brothers' first business. They began by buying a movie projector with which they showed films in the mining towns of Pennsylvania and Ohio. With the proceeds, they opened a theatre, and within a few years, they were distributing movies across a four-state area. However, they recognized that their power to sell tickets for movie viewings was limited by the films available to them. In order to grow their business further, they needed more control over what films they distributed, and so they made their first strategic move by diversifying into film production. Then, in 1918, they opened their studio on Sunset Boulevard, Hollywood. In 1923 they formally incorporated as Warner Brothers Pictures Incorporated, and the first major stars to work with the studio included John Barrymore, Douglas Fairbanks Jr, and rather excitingly, a dog called Rin Tin Tin. This trend continued with Bette Davis, James Cagney, Humphrey Bogart, and even the future American president, Ronald Reagan.

Strategic Directions

By the end of 1924, Warner Bros was arguably the most successful independent studio in Hollywood. As the studio prospered, it grew initially through strategic acquisition, with the purchase of the Vitagraph Company, which had a nation-wide distribution system, and further diversification, with the establishment of a successful radio station, KFWB, in Los Angeles.

Determined to embrace new technology – a strategy that continues to this day – Warner Bros signed a contract with the sound company Western Electric, established the Vitaphone sound process, and began making films with music and effects. These included ***The Jazz Singer***, starring Al Jolson, which signalled the end of the silent era and the birth of 'the talkies'. All this was done despite the misgivings of Harry Warner, who famously wondered, '***Who the hell wants to hear actors talk?***'

Further acquisitions followed, with additional theatre chains, a string of music publishers (which later formed Warner Bros Music), and several radio companies. Then began a period of success in films that saw Warner Bros follow market trends, beginning with the production of musicals before shifting into swashbucklers, then gangster movies, war epics and westerns. This period also saw possibly their most significant strategic acquisition so far with the purchase of Schlesinger's cartoon unit, and the introduction of Bugs Bunny and Daffy Duck, characters that quickly came to define the company's image.

Although by the late 1960s movie audiences were shrinking, Warner Bros continued to believe in the public's affinity for stars, signing deals with big names such as Paul Newman, Robert Redford, Barbra Streisand and Clint Eastwood, a policy that carried the studio successfully through the 1970s and 1980s. This period also saw the relabelled Warner Communications engage in joint ventures for distribution with Columbia Pictures and Walt Disney Pictures, and diversify further into video games and theme parks. To the surprise of many, glitzy Warner Communications merged in 1989 with the conservative publishing company Time Inc. to form Time-Warner.

Strategic Threats

With the coming of television as a competitor to theatre movie distribution in the 1950s and 1960s, Warner made a difficult attempt at diversification into this emerging market. This was initially delayed by anti-trust issues, with concerns that Warner might become too dominant in the entertainment market. However, Warner finally achieved a foothold with early shows such as ***Maverick***, and television is now part of Warner's core business. In 1995, Warner and Tribune Media launched the WB Television Network, seeking to capture the niche market in teenage drama. Here, early programming included ***Buffy the Vampire Slayer*** and ***Charmed***, which lasted eight seasons and became the longest-running drama with female leads. More recently, continuing this strategic theme, in 2020 Warner Bros launched HBO Max its new streaming service which, as well as boasting a rich and diverse back-catalogue including ***Friends***, ***The Sopranos*** and ***Game of Thrones***, will become their main platform for innovative new offerings.

Innovation

As time passed, Warner Bros came to rely more on innovation to stay ahead of the competition. Examples of this included the first colour newsreel in 1948, and the introduction of Cinemascope in the 1950s. Then came the realization in the 1960s that the soundtrack to a film could be sold as a separate product, and so they began distributing their film soundtracks through the Warner Music Company, in effect creating a new market and making use of the synergies within Warner's company portfolio.

More recently, further synergies were found in the opportunities provided by linking the latest technology in special effects with the comic-book characters supplied by the Warner-owned DC Comics. Prior to the introduction of this type of technology, the comic-book world had been all but impossible to recreate satisfactorily for live-action film. This new strategy culminated in 2008 with the release of ***The Dark Knight***, the Academy Award winning Batman film that became the second highest grossing movie of all time. In the late 1990s Warner Bros obtained rights to the Harry Potter series of books and released the first feature film adaptation in 2001 and the last in 2011. This became the most successful film franchise of all time.

In an innovative change of strategic direction, in 2019 Warner Bros released ***Joker***, a standalone film featuring the most iconic villain from the Batman franchise. Rather than standard comic book fare, this movie features a dystopian society with the hero a cackling, disturbed psychotic figure seemingly all but bereft of redeeming features. Though a strategically risky venture, ***Joker*** received critical acclaim and grossed over $1 billion at the box office, the first (and to date only) time an R-rated film has done this. Though, somewhat surprisingly, at the time of writing, four of the six highest grossing R-rated films are all comic book spin-offs. At the 92nd Academy Awards ***Joker***'s lead actor, Joaquin Phoenix, won Best Actor while the film received 11 nominations, ironically breaking the record for most nominations for a comic book adaptation, previously held by ***The Dark Knight***.

Looking Forward

Ahead of the 2023 centennial anniversary of the studio's founding, Warner Bros unveiled a new logo featuring a streamlined version of its classic 'WB' shield and it also released a new version of its mission statement, which reads 'To be the world's leading creator and distributor of extraordinary entertainment by partnering with the world's most inspiring storytellers'.

Sources: www.timewarner.com; www.boxoffice.com; C. Warner-Sperling and C. Milner (1999) ***Hollywood Be Thy Name: The Warner Brothers Story.*** University Press of Kentucky, Lexington, KY.

Introduction

Throughout its history, Warner Bros has been forced to shift strategic direction because of changes in technology – with the introduction of sound, technicolor, CGI (computer-generated imagery) and digital streaming; the competition – with the rise of television and internet-based entertainment platforms; and consumer taste.

One cynical interpretation of the Warner Bros story is that it has been a series of managerial knee-jerk reactions: discrete decisions taken at points in time in response to opportunities and situations that emerged. Another interpretation is that each decision was part of a larger strategy that was coherent and clear, designed to pre-empt changing conditions and so sustain and grow the company. In reality the true situation lies somewhere between these two extremes: a mixture of planned action and necessary reaction. The company today is vastly different in size and scope from that which was born nearly a century ago. The journey is of course not complete, with further reshaping already planned and under way.

This case is not unique: all firms undergo some form of evolution during their lifetime. While this case describes a company larger in scale than most, the changes and the situations that made the changes necessary, exist to varying degrees for all companies.

The concern of this book is operational rather than strategic, with a focus on the activities that generate the product or service that the customer 'buys', but in today's organizations the operational and the strategic cannot be fully separated. The organization must have an operational 'engine' that is capable of executing the business that it strategically chooses to undertake and conversely, the organization must understand its operational capability in order to decide which strategies to pursue.

Think of this as a journey. The company strategy will dictate the destination and the overall direction, whereas operations will be the vehicle that takes the company there. The vehicle must be appropriate to the journey: there would be little point in using a boat to cross a desert. While Warner Bros diversified a number of times, operational capability was required to make these strategic moves successful. This is a rather long-winded way of saying that a company's operations cannot be considered separately from its strategy.

The purpose of this first chapter is to create an understanding of strategic management against which the operational activity of the organization can be placed. This will then provide the foundation for the material on Operations Strategy that is contained in Chapter 2 that explains how operational activity can be aligned with strategic direction. This chapter also deals with influences in the market, such as competition, and political and economic conditions, and how these affect strategy making.

Chapter 2, p55

This chapter begins by presenting a method that will help you define and understand your business. It then explores the characteristics of strategic decisions, and how these can lead to some kind of advantage over the competition. The language of strategy is then described, this is the terminology that allows us to understand strategy, and communicate it easily. Different ways of approaching strategy are then introduced, dealing with such issues as what the company should be good at to be successful, and how this fits in with what the market wants. Finally, the role of operations in contributing to business strategy is examined and this material provides link to the operations strategy content in Chapter 2.

Chapter 2, p55

What Is Strategy?

Defining our Business

Strategy can be daunting, both to implement within the business and to study as a subject. This is due to the numerous concepts and terms that are involved in the academic treatment of the subject; the ever-increasing complexity of organizations, products and business environments; and the difficulty in finding a useful starting point. It is therefore best to start by defining what your business is about.

At its simplest, a business can be defined by the model shown in Figure 1.1. Here there are only three sets of strategic considerations:

1. Who the customers are – what the market is, what customers exist within it and how they are grouped
2. What the customer wants – what they value and will therefore pay to receive
3. How the company can deliver a product or service that will meet and satisfy the customer want.

All other strategic thinking comes as a result of addressing these three basic areas.

This model is a mix of questions that are *external* to the organization – the 'what' question and the 'who' question, and *internal* to the organization – the 'how' question. Simply speaking, strategy is the process of decision-making that provides the answers to these questions. Figure 1.2 illustrates the use of this model with an example from the banking industry.

Expanding on this simple view, strategy has been defined by Johnson *et al.* (2005) as:

> *the direction and scope of an organization over the long-term which achieves advantage in a changing environment through its configuration of resources and competencies with the aim of fulfilling stakeholder expectations.*

Figure 1.1 The business definition

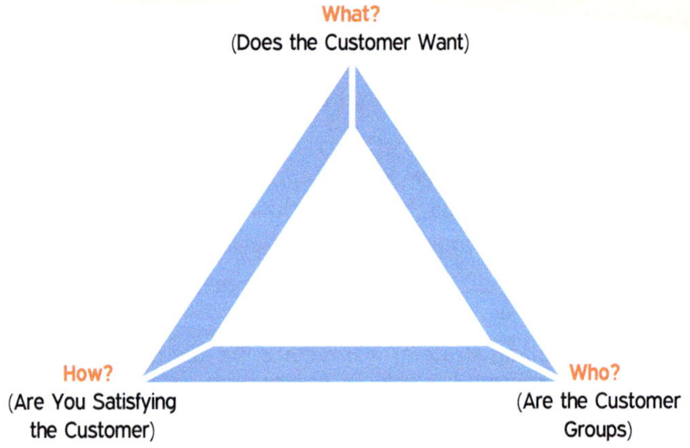

Source: Abell (1980).

Figure 1.2 The business definition of a bank

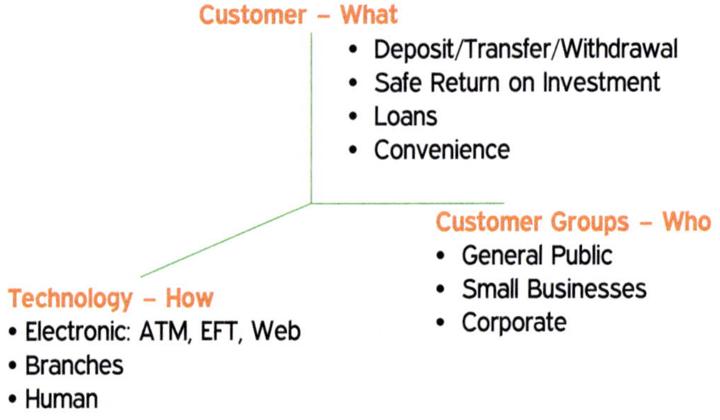

Therefore decisions are made with the aim of:

- Providing a product or service that the customer wants in preference to competitor products
- Guiding the organization throughout its lifetime by defining its scope of activity
- Configuring resources to carry out the required activity and so achieve greater market share and profits to satisfy those with a stake in the business.

Importantly these decisions must be taken within a changing social, political, economic and technological environment.

The point of this is to show that strategy need not be complex; it can be approached by answering some fundamental questions about the business. Jack Welch, Managing Director of the General Electric Company for many years adopted a similar approach to strategy. He described it as simply:

- Understanding where the business is
- Creating a clear view of where it wants to be
- Working out how it will get there.

Making Strategic Decisions

The decisions to be made that follow from these fundamental questions are rather conveniently termed *strategic decisions*. These decisions tend to differ from operational decisions in the following ways.

- *Time horizon:* Strategic decisions are concerned with the long term – maybe years or decades – whereas operational decisions tend to be more immediate – maybe weeks or months. What 'long term' means though is specific to the industry and the organization. Within the aircraft and defence industries, for example, projects tend to last for many years: so for companies such as Airbus or Boeing, strategic timescales may be measured in decades. For smaller companies strategic timescales may be measured in single years or even months.
- *Scale of consequence:* Strategic decisions may fundamentally alter the direction of the entire business, and therefore have an impact on all areas of the organization, whereas operational decisions may be limited to only one department, process or activity. For Warner Bros the strategic decisions taken have altered the shape of the company and the content of its product portfolio.
- *Scope of activity:* Strategic decisions tend to define the areas of activity and the geographical locations that the organization should concentrate on. Operational decisions are concerned with how the activities should be carried out, including the processes, tools and skills required. For Warner Bros the portfolio of activity has changed, in relation both to the markets operated in, with the acquisition of games companies, and to the activities undertaken, with the move into, for example, music production. Many companies will operate within a more limited scope than this, but all companies need to define where the boundaries of their activity lie.
- *Level of complexity:* Strategic decisions will be concerned with a multitude of diverse and seemingly unrelated factors, including the organization's capability, competitors' activities, the customer's needs, and the political and economic landscape. Throughout Warner Bros history several factors in the environment have changed; technology modified the products; fashion and culture altered customer taste; and economic trends reshaped the competitive environment. All companies, regardless of size, need to understand and manage many seemingly random, interacting factors.
- *Level of certainty:* To take strategic decisions managers rely on information. However, often this information is incomplete. This is partly because the vast and complex industrial landscape makes it difficult to construct a complete picture. But it may also be because the required information simply cannot be found as companies will guard against disclosing any details that might be of strategic significance to their competitors. Also, strategic decisions are highly speculative in nature. They tend to rely on 'guesses' about the future because it is impossible to know for certain what the world will be like in years to come. Prior to the invention of the microchip, who would have guessed that films based on computer-generated images, such as *Toy Story,* would be so successful, becoming more popular than traditional hand-drawn animation?

SHORT CASE 1.1

Drawing the Future of Animation

Source: ©Aaron Lim/Shutterstock

Andy's toys are fearful of being replaced when his birthday comes along. Woody, his favourite toy, a pull-string cowboy, discovers that Andy has been given a new toy, Buzz Lightyear, the latest, greatest action figure, complete with pop-out wings and laser beam. Woody's plan to get rid of Buzz backfires, and he finds himself lost in the world outside Andy's room, with Buzz as his only companion. Together they must try to find their way back home.

Made in 1995, and produced as part of a partnership between Disney and Pixar, ***Toy Story*** was the first animated feature generated completely on computers. But it was not the first movie to use CGI; this honour is held by 1973's ***Westworld***, starring Yul Brynner. From this inauspicious start the use of CGI grew in the 1970s and 1980s, featuring in sci-fi films such as the ***Star Wars*** trilogy and the ***Star Trek*** series. In the 1990s CGI hit the mainstream with ***Forrest Gump*** and ***Jurassic Park***, when the technology had matured to the point where it could be inserted seamlessly into live action scenes.

By the mid-1990s, though, the only film to have utilized CGI as the dominant medium was ***Tron*** in 1982, and it had been a commercial flop. The strategic decision to invest in a fully CGI film therefore was high-risk, made contrary to the current wisdom, much like Disney's decision to create the first full-length animated feature ***Snow White and the Seven Dwarfs*** over half a century earlier.

By the early 2000s computer-generated imagery had become the dominant form of special effect, with films based entirely on this technology routinely achieving box office success and all major studios using it. More recently, CGI has matured to such an extent that this technology is being used to entirely replace human actors who are no longer available. This was most famously done in 2016 in ***Rogue One: A Star Wars Story*** where Peter Cushing, who died in 1994, rather surprisingly reprised his role as Grand Moff Tarkin, the Commander of the original Death Star.

Questions

1. In relation to the concept of the business definition, what customer groups do you think CGI technology is targeted at?
2. Do you think at the outset this technology was filling a gap in the market or creating a new market?

Sources: www.disney.co.uk; S. Watts (1997) ***The Magic Kingdom: Walt Disney and the American Way of Life***, Houghton-Mifflin, Boston, MA.

If strategic decisions are taken correctly, initially they will help in defining the business model that is to be adopted, and then they will help in crafting the strategy that will support its implementation.

For example, consider Polaroid's business definition:

> *Perfecting and marketing instant photography to satisfy the needs of more affluent US and West European families for affection, friendship, fond memories, and humor.*

From this simple sentence, Polaroid's business can be understood from a strategic viewpoint.

- Question: what are the customer needs (or what is being satisfied)? Answer: affection, friendship, fond memories and humour.
- Question: who are the customer groups (or who is being satisfied)? Answer: more affluent US and West European families.
- Question: how are customer needs being satisfied (or what are the technologies used and functions provided)? Answer: instant photography.

CRITICAL PERSPECTIVE

The Taxonomy of Decisions

In our drive to organize the world, we tend to want to categorize everything around us. Sometimes this is useful, for example when cataloguing plants, animals or rocks, but sometimes it is not. An example of this is the labelling of decisions as one type or another. Decision-making is the process of selecting one option from a range of options. Decisions get labelled variously as strategic or operational, high-level or low-level, long-term or day-to-day.

This labelling system can sometimes be misleading. For a small building firm, a high-level, strategic, long-term decision might involve a small shift from home extensions into loft conversions; it might only affect a handful of people, and be relevant only for a few months (or until the next request to build an extension comes along); and it might not be very complex at all. For a large multinational, an operational decision might involve much analysis of complex information and affect the activity of thousands of workers.

The key point is ...

that decisions, and their consequences in terms of timescale and scope of activity, should be evaluated in terms of the context that they exist in, rather than on any absolute scale that defines decisions as either strategic or operational.

Competitive Advantage

Many would argue that strategic decision-making is only about one thing, and that is the search for **competitive advantage**. Competitive advantage is what sets a firm apart from its rivals, making it the supplier of choice for customers within a particular market.

Competitive advantage: what sets a firm apart from its rivals, making it the supplier of choice for customers within a particular market.

To gain competitive advantage it is essential for an organization to understand the competitive environment within which it exists. Porter (1979) summarized the competitive environment in his Five Forces Model (shown in Figure 1.3).

The Five Forces Model was originally developed as a way of assessing the attractiveness of different industries, but it can equally well be used to identify the forces of competition within a particular industry. The key insight brought by this model is the expanded scope of competitive analysis.

Figure 1.3 Five Forces Model

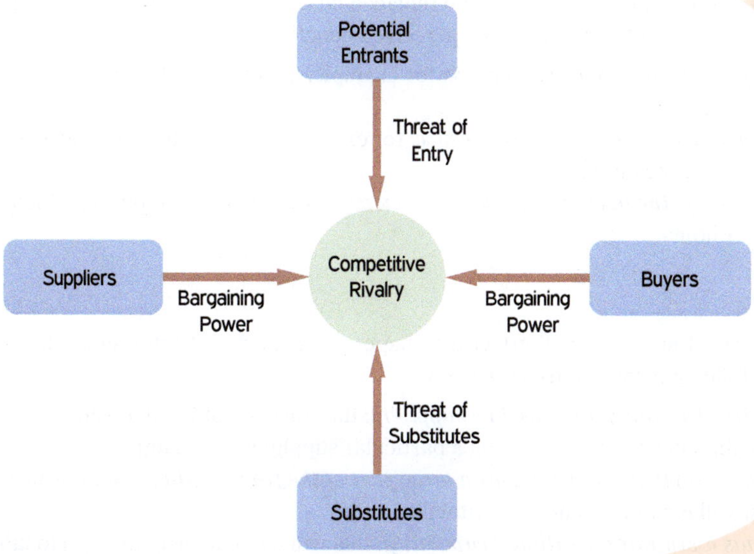

Source: Porter (1979).

In addition to direct rivals, Porter identifies four further factors or 'forces' that influence the competitive arena. The resulting five forces are explained below.

Direct Rivals

An organization's direct rivals are those with products or services that compete directly for a customer's business. The intensity of the competition between direct rivals tends to be shaped by the following factors:

- The *size and capability of competing companies:* similarity will tend to make competition more intense.
- *Market maturity* in terms of growth or decline in customer demand: in a growing market there may be enough business to support several competing organizations, whereas in a stable or declining market there may be more intense competition for the limited business available.
- *High fixed costs:* a large investment by a company in a particular product will leave it subject to greater loss if the venture is not successful. This therefore creates a greater motivation to succeed. Investment is effectively a barrier to both entry into, and exit from, a market.
- *Lack of differentiation:* this results in more intense competition, as no organization can gain an advantage purely as the result of product features.

Potential Entrants

The threat of other companies gaining entry to the market will shape the competitive environment. The size of this threat will depend upon the existence of barriers to entry into the market. If the barriers are high, then potential competitors should be less able to enter the market. Barriers to entry tend to be shaped by the following factors:

- *Size of investment:* the requirement for a large amount of up-front spend on tools, infrastructure or technology will deter potential competitors from entering a new market.
- *Specialist knowledge:* if this is difficult to acquire quickly, it will be difficult for a potential competitor to climb the learning curve and become effective in a new market.
- *Supply chain loyalty:* if those operating within a market are reluctant to deal with new companies, it will be difficult for a potential competitor to gain a foothold in a new market.
- *Legislation or quality approvals:* if these are cumbersome and extensive, it may be time consuming and costly to gain approvals, making it difficult for a potential competitor to become compliant in a new market.

These factors can exist in combination, so creating further barriers. For example, if profitable activity can be found only at large volumes, then economies of scale must quickly be obtained. Therefore a high level of investment, access to a robust supply chain and the necessary know-how must be in place at a very early stage.

Substitutes

These represent the threat that a product may be replaced by a different product that provides the same or better functionality and features, leading to increased perceived benefit for the customer. The substitution could be:

- *Product for product or service for service:* for example, the plane replaced as a mode of transport by the high-speed train.
- *Change of requirement through obsolescence:* for example, the car phone replaced as a mode of communication by the mobile phone.
- *Change of priority due to changing customer circumstances:* for example, a holiday abroad replaced by a holiday nearer home.

Suppliers

The bargaining power of suppliers will affect the shape of the market. Porter suggests that suppliers are more powerful when the following conditions are present.

- *There are a limited number of possible suppliers:* this means that it will be difficult to swap from one to another, resulting in greater reliance on a particular supplying company.
- *The cost of the supplied product forms a large part of the final product cost:* this means that an increase in supplier cost will result in reduced profitability.
- *A supplier has a similar operational capability:* this will make it easy for them to move up the supply chain and do business with the end-customer.

Buyers

The bargaining power of buyers (customers) will affect the shape of the market. Porter suggests that buyers are more powerful when the following conditions are present.

- *There are a limited number of possible buyers:* this means that the market is restricted, a condition that is especially difficult if there are a lot of competitor companies attempting to supply these few customers.
- *Products are relatively undifferentiated from those of rivals:* this means that the customer can shop around for the best deal on similar products.
- *A buyer has a similar operational capability:* this makes it easy for them to move down the supply chain and carry out the activities themselves.

WORKED EXAMPLE 1.1

Small-town Sandwiches: Eating Up the Market!

Small-town Sandwiches is a small, sit-in/take-out, food business with two outlets, both well placed: one in the main shopping area of Small-town and the other in the business district. Small-town Sandwiches specializes in freshly made sandwiches, salads, and fresh fruit products. It employs 30 people, all food is prepared daily within each shop, and most of the raw materials (fruit, vegetables, eggs, milk, etc.) are sourced locally from neighbouring farms. Small-town Sandwiches has enjoyed a relative monopoly throughout its 20-year history, due partly to its position as the first such business in the area, and partly to its good reputation as the 'local, quality, food supplier'.

Until recently Small-town was a relatively sleepy village, with little to recommend it to other food businesses. However, last year Big-city Broadcasting, attracted by low property values in Small-town, invested in a regional call-centre and administration office within the business district, bringing many new jobs to Small-town. With larger numbers of customers and consequent rising demand for fast-food, Small-town Sandwiches is currently benefiting from an increased volume of business. However, it is nervous of the likely effect that the arrival of Big-city Broadcasting will have on the food industry in Small-town. It therefore wants to carry out an analysis of its changing market.

Problem: *Use Porter's Five Forces Model to help Small-town Sandwiches understand the potential threats that these changes to its environment might bring.*

Approach: The competitive environment has changed. From a stable monopoly position, Small-town Sandwiches is now operating in a growing market, which may be attractive to other players. Porter's Five Forces Model can be used to help Small-town Sandwiches understand this changing market.

Solution:

Direct rivals: Until recently the market could not support another similar food business, so it currently has no direct rivals.

New entrants: With the increase in the size of the market, conditions may now be sufficiently attractive for other businesses to set up in the area. The Small-town Sandwiches business model is not difficult to replicate, as there are no intellectual property rights or protected supply, and set-up costs are relatively low. This means there are few barriers to entry to prevent either a new local rival or an existing franchise such as Subway from setting up.

Substitutes: The market here is for food of all types. Small-town Sandwiches has traded on quality and healthy eating, but other fast-food outlets such as McDonald's may see an opportunity, as the market requirement created by these new, more dynamic consumers may shift from quality to speed. The influx of new people to Small-town may bring a 'coffee shop' culture, where franchises such as Starbucks may further crowd the market with their brand of lunch and pre- and post-work offerings. In addition, with a growing population, Small-town may become attractive for the larger supermarkets, and this increased provision of inexpensive food may discourage consumers from buying pre-prepared take-out.

Suppliers: All produce is sourced locally, therefore the farms may consider moving up the supply chain by opening a shop and selling direct to the public.

Buyers: With a high volume of workers located in a single area, Big-city Broadcasting may consider providing its own food outlets, or inviting a franchise to operate directly within its site. Or someone that uses the service may decide to open up a shop of their own.

It is clear from this analysis that the change in the market will have considerable ramifications for Small-town Sandwiches.

Terminology Used in Strategy

So far we have looked at the definition of the business, the decisions that need to be made that will shape the direction of the business, and the issues in the competitive environment that the company needs to consider. We now turn our attention to the elements that make up a strategy, and how that strategy can be communicated to others. Some form of framework for organizing the outcomes of the decision-making process is necessary to allow these to be captured in a coherent way and be communicated to the rest of the organization. Terminology varies among books and authors, but the following terms provide a useful summary.

Mission Statement

This encapsulates the overriding purpose of the organization. It is a high level often relatively simple statement that informs stakeholders of what the company is about. An example could be: 'to provide quality cars to drivers who appreciate the ultimate driving experience'. This makes a statement both on the type of product produced, and on the customer that might buy it.

Vision

This is the desired future state to be achieved by the organization. Extending the automotive example, the associated vision statement might be 'to be the number one mass manufacturer of quality cars in the world'. This adds detail on the competitive positioning that is being sought.

Values

These are statements that guide how the organization will act while attempting to achieve the vision. 'Robust and safe engineering', 'fault-free construction', 'superior service' and 'environmentally aware' are phrases that guide the behaviour of staff and help shape the perception of the customer.

Strategic Objectives

These are statements indicating what needs to be achieved to meet the organizational vision. These objectives would tend to include something on finance such as: to return a profit of x% or to increase revenue by y% per year. They may also include something about the market such as: to become the number one supplier within a particular geographical area. They may also say something about the operational performance of the company – for example, to achieve error-free production.

While the aforementioned objectives are clear and directly linked to the traditional view of success in business it has become more fashionable recently for companies to set objectives that are a bit more vague and that relate to society as a whole. For example, Diageo states the very worthwhile objective of: 'reducing their environmental impact'. While British American Tobacco, somewhat peculiarly, states that it wants to 'create a better tomorrow for all its stakeholders'.

In short, strategic objectives can be set for anything that the company believes is important to achieving success.

Strategic Plans

These are high-level statements of how the company will achieve its strategic objectives. For example, a company may plan to develop a strong brand as part of its activity to meet its strategic objective of being number one in a particular market. Or, more operationally, a company may plan to implement a 'Lean' (see Chapter 10) manufacturing system to help it achieve its strategic cost reduction objective. Such strategic plans, although often broadly stated, should be specific enough to allow managers to create more detailed activity plans that can be implemented within the organization. Each of these plans forms a piece of the jigsaw that leads to the achievement of the overall strategy.

Chapter 10, p323

Strategic Priorities

These are high-level guides to what the organization should concentrate on. If the business is large and complex, some sort of coherent action must be taken across divisions, business units and departments. Strategic priorities help focus the organization on achieving its strategic objectives. Setting priorities is a recognition that no organization can do everything at once. For example, an organization might prioritize growing the home market before going overseas or improving efficiency over increasing output.

Packaging a Strategy

Not all companies use the entire lexicon that we have discussed above to package their strategy. Most will use some carefully selected pieces of the terminology. The defence company BAE Systems, for example, uses three:

Vision: to be the premier international defence, aerospace and security company.

Mission: to provide a vital advantage to help our customers protect what really matters.

Strategic objectives:

- *Maintain and grow our defence businesses*
- *Continue to grow our business in adjacent markets*
- *Develop and expand our international business*
- *Inspire and develop a diverse workforce to drive success*
- *Enhance financial performance and deliver sustainable growth in shareholder value*

Strategy statements are not limited to the for-profit sector. Many types of organizations create strategies. However, some choose to package them in a different way. For example, the charity The Earth and Space Foundation relies on a simple vision statement:

The Earth as an oasis, cared for by a space-faring civilization.

Though simple, the vision is very clear and it is very easy to extrapolate from this useful objectives, plans and priorities.

> **Stop and Think**
>
> Strategy can be packaged in different ways, as the examples above show. Consider how the packaging of strategy will help to communicate the correct message to employees.

Where Is Strategy Carried Out?

Decisions are taken at all levels of the organization, but we tend to associate strategic decisions with the most senior managers, and operational decisions with those managers further down the hierarchy. The complexity of many organizations makes it difficult to determine the point in the hierarchy at which the strategic decisions stop and the operational decisions start. Moreover, some decisions that are taken for purely operational reasons have a significant impact on the organization's capability, and therefore take on a more strategic dimension. Some companies, especially large multinationals, may have extremely complex structures, such as that shown in Figure 1.4, but it is generally accepted that three levels of organizational strategic decision-making are sufficient to work with.

Corporate Level

BUSINESS INTEGRATION

This is usually the top level of the organization. It may be a board of directors representing shareholders, or the owner of the company and his advisers. The larger and more diversified the organization, the more general the strategy will be as it must be relevant to all the diverse divisions or business units and their individual markets. Within a large conglomerate, strategy at corporate level may be described purely by a mission statement that is supported by a vision, a set of values, and a set of objectives. Strategic planning will be concerned with shaping the portfolio of businesses that the corporation has interests in. The main activity may therefore be in the acquisition and divestment of businesses.

Although the size of the company is a factor in the strategic activity that is carried out at corporate level, the degree of diversity of business that the company undertakes is more significant. A more diverse business makes it more difficult for corporate decision-makers to create an overall strategy that is applicable to all of the business units. Companies with very streamlined businesses are able to be more prescriptive at the top level, with detailed statements that can be more readily translated into action.

Figure 1.4 An example of a complex organizational structure

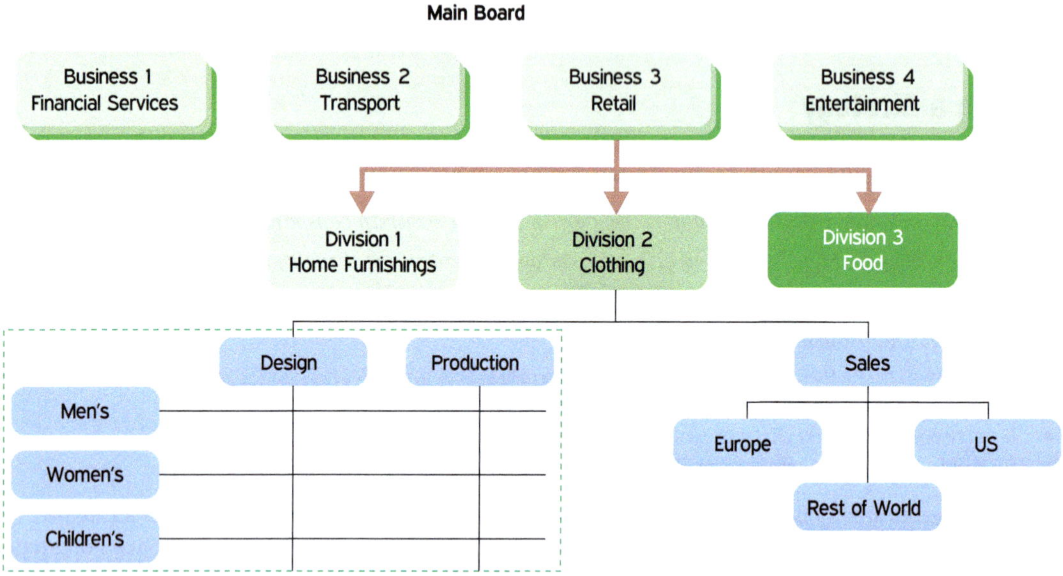

An example of a high-level corporate strategy statement that is generalized for a diversified business is that of the Babcock International Group:

> *Mission: to deliver high quality support services solutions through applying specialist knowledge, expertise and original thinking to the challenges of public and private sector customers.*

This company operates in a range of markets, including transport, estates management, marine and energy: therefore the corporate strategy must be relevant to all the divisions. Though broad it is easy to see how the component parts of this statement can be adapted in each business to help guide the activity and behaviour of all employees.

An example of a more specific corporate strategy is that of Google:

> *Mission: to organize the world's information and make it universally accessible and useful.*

This business is more focused, therefore the statement is clear and directly relevant to all activity.

Business Level

The next significant level is the business unit level, sometimes called the divisional level. The actual label does not matter; the key thing is that at this level decisions are made in relation to a discrete business, where strategy is applicable to the specific market within which the business is operating.

Another way to look at this is that corporate strategy defines what industries and markets an organization works within, whereas the business strategy will deal more with how the organization competes in these chosen industries and markets.

Like the corporate level strategy, the business level strategy will tend to have a vision statement, showing where the business wants to be in a specific period of time, and a set of strategic objectives to be met in support of that vision, which are aligned with the vision and objectives at corporate level (**strategic alignment**). Remember that the company's values and overall mission as defined at corporate level should apply equally at business level. The strategic planning carried out at business level will differ from that at corporate level, as it will be concerned more with taking decisions on specific market-based factors such as:

> **Strategic alignment**: the alignment of all decisions made at different levels of the organization with the overall strategic goals.

- The customers' requirements and what product or service should be provided to meet them
- The threat of competition and how to gain an advantage
- The changing nature of the market environment and how to stay ahead in it.

Figure 1.5 Time-Warner strategic levels

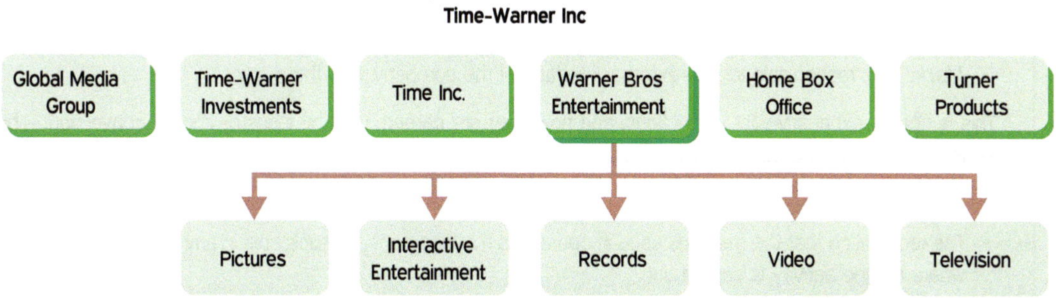

Like corporate strategy, business strategy is also concerned with the long term but it must provide enough detail and clarity to allow the organization to create processes and systems that support the achievement of the higher-level vision and objectives. This middle-level business strategy can therefore be thought of as providing a link between the corporate and the operational strategies.

Time-Warner is typical of a large multinational company with a complex structure, operating across a number of markets, and with many levels where strategic thinking may be carried out. Figure 1.5 illustrates the top three levels of the overall company. Each business has its own area of responsibility: for example, Time Inc. publishes magazines, and Warner Bros Entertainment is active across all current and emerging media and platforms, including feature film, television, video games and international cinema.

Here, for example, is the mission statement of its theme parks business:

> *To bring people together of all ages, cultures and backgrounds to enjoy the highest international theme park standards of quality, fun and entertainment.*

Operational Level

Within each organization there is an operational 'engine' that creates the product, or delivers the service. This may be a development laboratory, a production line, a set of retail outlets, a call centre or, more commonly these days, a combination of these. Whatever form the operation takes, decisions will need to be made as to how it is set up. These decisions will concern what equipment is bought and how it is utilized, how space is allocated, how processes are sequenced, and what skills are required. Operational strategy is concerned with the decision-making that ensures the configuration and utilization of resources that will most effectively support the achievement of the strategy.

Decision taken might concern the:

- Levels of automation required
- Layout of departments and work areas
- Degree of integration of IT systems
- Configuration of the supply chain.

These decisions provide a framework for and guidance on how things should be done on a day-to-day basis. In Chapter 2 we shall look at operations strategy in more detail.

Chapter 2, p55

CRITICAL PERSPECTIVE

The Scope of Operations

BUSINESS INTEGRATION

Once upon a time operations management was associated exclusively with the operations function. Operations functions were themselves associated mainly with manufacturing companies within which they might often be known as the production function. Operations functions existed as one of a number of functions that made up the organization. Other functions might have been:

- ***Human resource management:*** responsible for recruitment, training and selection of staff
- ***Engineering:*** responsible for the development of products and technology

- *Finance:* responsible for controlling the money
- *Procurement:* responsible for the control of suppliers
- *Marketing:* responsible for the external interface of the company with the market.

This is not an exhaustive list – functions, and how they are named, vary by industry and by convention – but it serves to illustrate the demarcation lines that existed within the structures of companies. More recently, though, there has been a change in thinking due to a number of factors.

- The recognition that the methods used in operations management are applicable in any part of the organization where routine activity is carried out
- The development of management structures that emphasize integration rather than discrete functional activity
- The adoption of the term 'operations' by companies that are not production focused, and its subsequent application to a wide variety of activities, such as call centre work.

This has expanded the scope of what is considered to be operations and also the reach of operations management. Some would argue that the term 'operations function' is redundant as operational activity happens across the organization.

It is difficult to generalize about what operations management is considered to be across industry sectors, but what can be stated with certainty is that our understanding of what operations management is has changed in recent years.

BUSINESS INTEGRATION

The key point is ...

that the scope of operations will vary, depending upon the industry sector and the company, therefore for managers it is more useful to think of the type of operational activity and how it is carried out, rather than how it is labelled within the functional and departmental structure of the company.

Stop and Think

As operations have grown in scope to encompass other organizational functions, consider how this affects the job of the operations manager.

SHORT CASE 1.2

Operations in the Finance Industry

As you read this press release from The Royal Bank of Scotland (RBS), consider how the terminology of operations has become commonplace in the finance industry.

Source: ©Jevanto Productions/Shutterstock

RBS to Locate Global Banking Operations Centre in Amsterdam

The Royal Bank of Scotland Group today announced that it would locate a new Global Banking Operations Centre in Amsterdam as part of its investment in the Netherlands if the RBS-led consortium banks are successful in completing their bid to acquire ABN AMRO. The centre will act as a hub for the enlarged RBS Group's international cash management and euro-currency processing.

The new centre would form the hub for a number of functions critical for the success of the combined RBS/ ABN AMRO group. The new centre is expected to become the base for the international cash management and euro-clearing activities for the combined RBS/ABN AMRO group worldwide, and be a centre of excellence for euro-denominated treasury functions.

A key component of RBS euro-denominated middle and back-office activities, supporting the enlarged RBS Global Banking and Markets business, and complementing its existing global operating model.

In addition to the set-up of 'operations centres', companies in the finance industry have gone further and adopted the language of operations management labelling the items they sell, such as mortgages, loans and investments, as 'products'.

Question

1. How much further does the financial sector need to go for its products to meet the quality and level of performance achieved by the best engineering and manufacturing companies?

Sources: www.rbs.co.uk; RBS press release, 25 September 2007.

Strategic Alignment

Table 1.1 summarizes how each level of strategic decision-making fits in. Note the change in emphasis from the more philosophical 'why' questions at the corporate level to the more practical and detailed 'what', 'how', 'who' and 'when' questions further down. This changing emphasis helps to create some degree of vertical strategic alignment through the organization.

BUSINESS INTEGRATION

While the business-level strategy can be thought of as the link between the corporate goals and how these are met, the operations-level strategy can be thought of as the link between the business strategy and the activities that are carried out to achieve it.

Table 1.1 Summary of strategy levels

Strategy level	Questions	Purpose	Concerns
Corporate	Why does the organization exist? What should the organization do? Where does the organization do it?	Set overall mission vision and purpose	Building a successful corporation Ensuring a balanced portfolio of businesses Creating synergies between businesses Satisfying the shareholders
Business	What should the business do? Where does the business do it? How does the business do it?	Create a business that is aligned with the corporate strategy	Building a successful business Ensuring the business unit contributes to corporate goals Responding to changing market conditions Maintaining a competitive product or service portfolio Coordinating the various operational groups
Operational	How does the operation do it? Who within the operation does it? When is it done?	Provide and sustain the competencies that result in a competitive advantage.	Setting up systems and processes that are efficient and effective Maintaining resources that are fit for purpose

Strategy begins at the top, and progressively adds detail at each of the lower levels. This layering is crucial, because:

- The vague principles defined at the top level need to be made clear so that they can be implemented, and this is more effectively done progressively, in a series of small, logical jumps rather than a single leap.
- The diversity of the business means strategy must allow for different conditions in each area of the business, and this incremental process of translation makes this possible.
- The strategy is not implemented at any single level but involves all levels.

Alignment is therefore the key feature. This is easiest to see at the operational level: if each department or function is working in isolation, they will not achieve the integration necessary to operate effectively. For example, if the procurement department are working to a different schedule than the production department problems will ensue. Alignment is also important at the business and corporate levels too: if each business unit is taking a different direction to the others, then the corporate goals will never be achieved. A poorly aligned organization is like a set of cottage industries working autonomously, neither contributing directly to the overall goals nor achieving any of the benefits of being part of a larger unit.

How Is Strategy Approached?

External (Market-Based) and Internal (Resource-Based)

Market-based view: the strategic approach that prioritizes what the market wants in its decision-making.

Resource-based view: the strategic approach that prioritizes the capability of the firm in its decision-making.

There are two overall approaches to strategy:

- The external **market-based view** which encourages understanding of all aspects of the external or market environment in an attempt to guide the firm safely through the terrain
- The internal **resource-based view**, which concentrates on the firm's capability, and how it can be configured and used to achieve success.

These schools of thought approach strategy-making from opposite directions. Regardless of which approach is preferred, some understanding of the other is necessary to a balanced, decision-making process.

The concern of this book is operational and therefore the internal resource-based view, and the management of the firm's resources to create a competitive advantage would seem more relevant. However, first we shall consider the market-based view, because resources must be managed against the backdrop of the external environment.

The Market-Based View

The market-based view or marketing-inspired strategic thinking provided the dominant paradigm in the early days of strategic management. Here, strategy content was (mostly) formulated in terms of satisfying customers (Biggadike, 1981). This approach prioritizes market conditions in the strategic decision-making process. Two levels of analysis are important: identifying the features in the macro-environment that may affect how a specific market behaves; and identifying the factors that are directly related to a company's operation.

Porter's Five Forces Model is one tool that we can use to analyse a single market, but for the wider environment we need a broader approach.

PESTEL Framework

GLOBALIZATION

The PESTEL method of analysis considers six factors in the macro-environment that might affect an organization.

- *Political factors,* including changes in government and associated ideologies:
  - Financial priorities – tax and spending
  - Global stability and inter-country relationships
- *Economic factors* that affect the cost of operations and the spending patterns of potential customers:
  - Exchange, interest and inflation rates
  - Economic cycles in geographical regions and industry sectors

- *Social factors,* including demographic and cultural aspects that affect patterns of customer taste:
  - Population structure, including factors such as age and ethnic mix
  - Lifestyle trends, such as health awareness, increasing leisure time and changing attitudes towards work
- *Technological factors* that can reshape markets, products and modes of production:
  - New discoveries and developments and rates of obsolescence
  - New purchasing mechanisms such as the Internet
  - IT and automation which create new modes of production and service delivery
- *Environmental factors* that shape the way business is done:
  - Global warming and pollution
  - Energy consumption
- *Legal factors* that set the framework that businesses have to operate within:
  - Trade regulation such as barriers, tariffs and quotas
  - Industry regulations such as quality and safety standards.

These factors are not independent of one another; they interact. For example, a politically motivated decision may have an effect on the economic situation or on the legislative framework. Investigating each of these areas and relating the findings to the immediate market context will unearth a range of things that may have a significant impact on strategy.

In addition to PESTEL, there are three more factors that can be used that will add to the utility of the analysis. These are:

- *Novelty:* the degree to which the environment presents the organization with new things
- *Predictability:* the degree to which things happen in a random and unforeseen way
- *Dynamism:* the speed (or rate of change) of the environment.

These factors can be added to the PESTEL to make the analysis less static and better able to cope with the time dimension.

The Customer Value Proposition

Customer value proposition: statement of precisely what the customer values and will therefore buy in the form of a product.

When you have defined your market, have identified the significant factors in the wider environment, and understand the influence they have on your company, the key thing that the market can tell you is the customer need.

To create a product or service that will sell, it is critical to understand what the customer's values are, and to do this we must understand what value means from a customer perspective.

A model first proposed by Gutman (1982) to define how customers categorize products in their memory has been adapted by Woodruff and Gardial (1996) into a hierarchy that defines what customers prioritize in terms of value. The hierarchy has three levels. From top to bottom, they are:

1. Goals that the product or service may help them achieve. For example, a package holiday may be about meeting new people, or finding a partner.
2. Desired consequences in use situations that will have an impact on goal achievement. A large number of nightclubs in a holiday resort will consequently provide more opportunities to socialize.
3. Desired product and service attributes that will contribute to the desired consequence. The provision of cheap alcohol and intimate atmosphere in the nightclub will provide customers with the chance to get to know each other better (and may lay the groundwork for an unwelcome surprise in the morning).

This thinking is drawn from the domain of marketing, but it is important to understand the process by which customers arrive at their understanding of value before we decide how the operations system will deliver it.

Customer value elements: factors that, when combined, define the value proposition.

Sheth *et al.* (1991) proposed a more practical model that relates mainly to the consumer market. It identifies five value elements that influence customer choice, as described in Table 1.2: functional, social, emotional, epistemic and conditional value. Different markets will place different importance on each of these **customer value elements** or, more commonly, a combination of elements, as a proxy of value.

Table 1.2 Customer value elements

Value	Definition	Example
Functional	Based on physical performance; measured on choice attributes	Automobile, based upon fuel economy and maintenance record
Social	Achieved through association with particular demographic group	Clothing and jewellery worn for others' attention
Emotional	Acquired when product arouses emotional states	Certain foods associated with particular settings
Epistemic	Refers to the seeking of new varieties of offerings arousing a sense of novelty or interest	Trying a new brand of product, moving away from the familiar
Conditional	Utility received based upon the result of a specific set of circumstances	Seasonal products such as Christmas cards or popcorn at the movies

Regardless of the nature of your customer – be it a government, another company, or a consumer group – it is essential that you understand what they value. Only by understanding this can your product or service offering be defined.

The Resource-Based View

Penrose (1959), first proposed that what happened inside the firm was as important as what happened outside it. It is generally agreed that the resource-based view (RBV) was initially conceptualized by Wernerfelt (1984). Over the last 30 years or so, it has been argued the RBV has risen to the pre-eminent position in strategy research (Locket *et al.*, 2009).

The RBV describes the firm as a collection of assets or resources that are tied semi-permanently to it (Wernerfelt, 1984). The definition of resources is necessarily wide. Daft (1983) defines them as assets, capabilities, organizational processes, firm attributes and knowledge controlled by the firm that enable it to conceive and implement strategies that improve its efficiency and effectiveness. Although such a comprehensive definition should be applauded, it is a little broad to be of much use from an operational perspective. Table 1.3 includes some examples of what can be considered as resources.

From an operations point of view, resources can be either tangible or intangible. Tangible resources are those that can be seen or touched or formalized, such as plant and equipment, systems and processes. Intangible resources are more difficult to define, they might include culture, skill and experience.

Table 1.3 The resources of the organization

Resource category	Tangible	⟷	Intangible
Physical	Plant and equipment Geographical location Access to raw materials		
Human			Skill and experience Judgement and insight Intelligence and creativity Relationships
Organizational	Systems and processes	Management structure	Culture

Resources should be thought of as 'potential to create value for the customer', and ultimately they contribute to competitive advantage. Tangible resources tend to be easiest to manage in support of the value creation, but intangible resources will be more difficult for competitors to replicate. The mobilization of these resources, and how they can be made to support the organization, is termed operational strategy, and will be explored further in Chapter 2.

Chapter 2, p55

Stop and Think

Tangible resources may be easier to manage than intangible resources, but which resource type has the potential to make the most impact on operational performance?

Resources and Competitive Advantage

For a resource to have the potential to result in some sort of competitive advantage it needs to have four attributes. These attributes were originally expressed by Barney (1991) as *valuable, rare, imperfectly imitable* and *non-substitutable* (VRIN).

A resource must be valuable, in that it enables the firm to implement strategies that improve its efficiency or effectiveness. A valuable resource is one that will help the firm exploit opportunities or neutralize threats. For example, possession of a source of a particular material will be of value only if this material is necessary for the particular business that is being undertaken. For a whisky company, access to a particular source of water is a very valuable thing because it is very much a part of their formula and their brand, but to most other companies water is cheap and widely available.

A resource must be rare, in that not many, or preferably not any, other companies have access to it. The more abundant the resource, the less valuable it will be, and so the less it will contribute to competitive advantage. How rare must the resource be to remain valuable? This is a tricky question. If the resource is unique, then it is easy to see that it will provide a considerable advantage, but the effect of its availability to some other companies will depend on the competitive environment existing in the market. To put it another way, as long as the number of firms who possess this resource is small enough to prevent the occurrence of perfect dynamic competition within the sector (Hirshleifer, 1980) then the resource is still rare enough to be useful. In the whisky example, if the source of water was plentiful, and the recipe and process for distilling the whisky were freely available, then the market would be 'flooded' with equivalent products, making any individual company's product less valuable. As it stands, the whisky industry is crowded with products that are differentiated by the subtleties such as water source.

For a resource to remain rare, it must either be imperfectly imitable (or in simpler terms difficult to imitate) and non-substitutable. This may be the case if the resource:

- Has been obtained through unique historical conditions, for example, a scientific breakthrough leading to intellectual property that can be protected, or the location of a factory in a geographical position that subsequently turns out to be uniquely valuable
- Is intangible, for example, a strong organizational culture that is difficult to formalize, leading to unique social relationships, such as a particularly strong management team
- Is made up of several resources in combination, for example, an organization with a strong R&D function that is composed of people, processes and infrastructure. The discrete resources, such as the scientists, their skills and their relationships, and how they use the processes and tools, will be difficult to duplicate.

The degree to which a resource can be imitated or substituted is always difficult to determine. The key thing to consider is not how similar the equivalent resource is, but what it can create in terms of competitive advantage for a rival that may erode or neutralize your own market position. History is littered with examples of substitute products such as the replacement of the horse by the car, the vacuum tube by the transistor and more recently the cathode ray tube by the liquid crystal display. These days the same is happening to services, for example retailing web-based shopping is replacing high street shopping.

We can think of these VRIN distinctions as a filter:

- First, does your resource neutralize a threat or exploit an opportunity?
- If so, is it rare enough that it is available either only to you or to a small enough number of competitors that the advantage it provides is not marginalized?
- If so, how long can this advantage be protected? Or, put another way, how long before it is imitated or substituted?

If this timescale during which the advantage can be protected is significant in terms of the industry life cycle and a company's strategic horizons, then the competitive advantage gained may be sustainable.

Using this system, and referring back to Table 1.2, we can see that resources that are more intangible, such as skills and culture, will tend to be more difficult to imitate. Tangibles such as equipment and tooling tend not to be key resources, as they can be bought and sold with relative ease.

CRITICAL PERSPECTIVE

Sustainable Competitive Advantage

CSR

A firm is said to have a **sustainable competitive advantage** when it is implementing a value-creating strategy that is not simultaneously being implemented by any current or potential competitors. For this advantage to be sustained two things must apply:

- The resources within a market, and available to the firms competing within it, are not equally spread
- These resources are not mobile: that is, they are company specific in some way, and are likely to remain that way.

Sustainable competitive advantage: based on a valuable, rare, imperfectly imitable and non-substitutable resource that is specific to the company, and cannot be transferred.

Therefore the resources must not only be VRIN for a short period; they must stay VRIN for an undefined, and possibly indefinite, period.

Some authors have suggested that an advantage is sustainable simply if it lasts for a 'long' period of time. This suggestion is attractively simple, but it is unsatisfactory, because it raises the question: how long is long enough for a firm to be sure that competitive advantage is safe, and can be sustained? The answer will vary by industry and by sector. To attempt to define a time period it is necessary to understand the product life cycle.

Others have suggested that competitive advantage is sustainable only if it continues to exist after all efforts to duplicate it have ceased. This is a bit more useful as it does not rely on the specification of a time period, but it requires complete knowledge of what the competition is doing.

The key point is ...

that while competitive advantage might be easily achieved, the perpetuation (sustainability) of this advantage over time is more difficult. So, it is important to predict how long an advantage might last, while at the same time working on its replacement.

Competences: Bundling of Resources

So far we have dealt with resources mainly as discrete entities. But although some resources may create a competitive advantage on their own, such as a unique supply of a raw material (water in the whisky industry) or a piece of intellectual property (a formula for a drug), it is more useful to think of resources in combination. Resources working together create a more useful capability, which is more likely to lead to a competitive advantage.

This bundle of resources is commonly called a *competence* (Hamel and Prahalad, 1990).

A competence in organizational terms might be the combination of its human resources, such as the skill and knowledge within a production department, and its physical resources, such as the IT infrastructure and the process tooling that allow the company to manufacture a product or deliver a service within a particular market. Or it might be the combination of the skills of kitchen staff in producing a certain type of food, the abilities of customer-facing staff and the décor of the restaurant (the infrastructure) that create a certain type of themed dining experience for a particular customer group.

Defining the scope of a competence – how many resources it comprises, or how much of the organization it encompasses – is not an exact science. The general rule is that it should be more than just one resource, but less than all the resources of the entire organizational system.

To unpack this concept further, we can understand competencies better in terms of their relationship with competitive advantage. Over the past few years a hierarchy of competencies has emerged from the literature that helps to define the nature, and more importantly the value, of competencies – that is, how much a particular competence contributes to competitive advantage.

Threshold Competencies

At the basic level are **threshold competencies**. These are competencies that allow the firm to exist and operate, but provide no competitive advantage. Without these competencies no level of operation is possible. Returning to our restaurant example, threshold competencies would be the basic package of resources that, when combined, allow the basic production and serving of food.

In the VRIN framework, at the threshold level competencies will provide little value, because all companies in the market should be able to do these basic things.

Threshold competencies: allow the firm to exist and operate, but provide no competitive advantage.

Core Competencies

At the next level exist what are termed **core competencies**. Hamel and Prahalad (1990) propose that for a competence to be core to the business, it must:

- Provide open access to a variety of markets
- Contribute significantly to performance
- Be difficult to imitate.

Core competencies: contribute directly to business goals.

This adds some clarity, but Eden and Ackerman (2005) further propose that, unlike a threshold competence, a core competence contributes directly to the business's strategic goals.

First, the resources must be identified and bundled together to create such a core competence. Then some differentiation must be created so that this core competence also leads to a competitive advantage.

SHORT CASE 1.3

Korry: We Package Light

Source: ©lightpoet/Shutterstock

One of the basic technologies mastered by early humans was harnessing the power of fire, and the light and heat it provided. Arguably, this was the single most significant event in the history of technological development. Now artificial light surrounds us – one of the most taken-for-granted features of modern life. Since early human beings created the first candle, the act of creating light has moved through many levels of sophistication, and now embraces many complex and diverse technologies.

Korry Electronics was founded in 1937 by Boris Korry to manufacture and distribute his invention, the first front-relampable, illuminated indicator for aviation. This led to the first illuminated cockpit controls for the developing military and commercial aircraft industry.

Today, the Korry product team continues this tradition as it develops the crew station of the future, providing state-of-the-art switches, cockpit controls, night-vision filters, and high-performance displays. Most recently it developed the first overhead touch screen display for the Gulfstream G500 aircraft which entered service in 2018.

Korry's competence is in the 'packaging of light' for specific applications. This competence comprises expertise in optics, electronics and software, mechanical packaging, mechanism design, and human factors.

Questions

1. What attributes would a customer value in a supplier such as Korry?
2. What is the key resource that supports Korry's core competence?

Source: www.korry.com

Distinctive Competencies

The term 'distinctive competence' has been coined to describe a competence that is so valuable, rare, inimitable and non-substitutable that it creates a clear competitive advantage. Quite simply, a competence is distinctive if others are unable to emulate it.

Distinctive competencies: competencies so unique that they create competitive advantage.

Distinctive competencies are sometimes difficult to understand, so this idea is probably best explained by an example. WL Gore and Associates is possibly best known to the general public for its brand Gore-Tex, the waterproof and breathable (and eye-wateringly expensive) fabric that is seen as the industry standard in high-performance garments. Gore, however, sees its core competence as being the development of fluoropolymer-based technologies. This competence allows it to operate in many diverse product markets, including medical devices and electrical cable assemblies, as well as the well-known clothing market. From this general core competence sprang the distinctive competence that is the ability to manufacture the Gore-Tex fabric, and the range of garments that this product is used in.

It could be argued that Gore-Tex is the perfect product. The manufacturing process is so rare that it is unique to WL Gore; it generates enormous value in the form of revenue to the company; although there have been many imitators, none has come close to breaking the Gore-Tex dominance; and it is difficult to think of a product that will replace clothes in most of the applications that Gore-Tex is used in.

Competencies in Service Provision

In this chapter we have proposed that most companies deliver a combination of physical products and services. Therefore we need to look further into the characteristics of core competencies in relation to service delivery.

There are several factors that make the operation of delivering a service different from that of producing a product:

- *Simultaneity of production and consumption.* A service cannot be inventoried or stored; it is created and consumed at the same time. For example, a theatre show is performed and viewed at the same time; the next show is a different service episode. This means that a service generally has no shelf life. If a ticket is not sold on a particular night, the show will take place anyway; there is no subsequent opportunity to sell that ticket.
- *Presence of the customer in the conversion process.* Most manufactured products are made in a factory, isolated from the view of the eventual customer. Most services are delivered in the presence of the customer: therefore there is little insulation between what the customer sees and what the delivery process does. In a theatre show, if a mistake is made (in operations terms, a quality error) this cannot be corrected before the service is dispatched to the customer.
- *Intangibility of services.* Unlike a physical product, service features are not easily defined, as they cannot be 'touched'. Also, each customer may have a slightly different perception of the service experience. Some customers may enjoy the theatre show, while others may be more ambivalent, but all have experienced the same service.

Companies that provide products must develop competencies in engineering and manufacture, generally within a closed environment. The elements of competencies here may include:

- The possession of intellectual property
- The achievement of process excellence
- The ability to manipulate technology.

By contrast, Van Looy *et al.* (2003) have suggested that competence in services is all about developing a *customer orientation.* This concept is perhaps more abstract than competence in the production environment, and the elements that make it up are consequently more difficult to define, but here are some suggestions:

- The capacity to understand the customer's priorities
- The ability to speak the customer's language

- The ability to empathize with the customer
- The ability to show consideration for the customer
- The ability to de-risk the customer's business.

As has been argued, most companies are a combination of product and service providers. They must therefore develop some form of customer competence, in addition to their product-based competence. The importance of this service-based competence – whether it is threshold, core or distinctive – will depend very much on the nature of the business.

Dynamic Capabilities

The resource-based view (RBV) that we have been discussing assumes that resources are heterogeneous, and can be sustained over time. Indeed, the whole concept of sustainable competitive advantage is based on a static view of the market (Locket *et al.*, 2009).

The RBV and competence literature therefore does not really address the dynamic nature of markets, or how current resources can be refreshed or future resources created to meet the changing environment. But change is a characteristic of most markets and, it could be argued, is becoming more prevalent as markets become increasingly competitive. If long-term market equilibrium does exist at all, it is limited to some specialized markets such as the whisky industry, or to luxury markets such as jewellery, where product life cycles are so long that change is slow to happen. For most companies, however, this benign state does not exist, so developing new resources and competitive advantage are critical concerns for managers.

Teece and Pisano (1994) and Teece *et al.* (1997) were the first to move beyond the established RBV when they proposed that it couldn't explain how some firms demonstrate timely and rapid reaction to changing market conditions. They coined the term **dynamic capability** to describe a firm's ability to integrate, build and reconfigure competencies to address rapidly changing environments. A dynamic capability is not a reactive, problem-solving event in spontaneous response to a stimulus: it is intentional, planned and deliberate. A dynamic capability is a process that impacts upon resources or bundles of resources (competencies) to change them to meet a perceived future state.

Dynamic capability: a firm's ability to upgrade and reconstruct its capabilities in response to the changing environment, therefore attaining and sustaining its competitive advantage.

Ambrosini and Bowman (2009) state that dynamic capabilities comprise four main processes:

- *Reconfiguration:* the transformation and recombination of assets and resources. This may occur after a merger or acquisition, where the new shape will realize new synergies that previously didn't exist
- *Leveraging:* the replication of processes or systems across operational units
- *Learning:* the increase in effectiveness and efficiency that is the outcome of reflection on failure and success
- *Integration:* the pulling together of resources to create new competencies.

They also give some examples:

- The R&D process, where the effective use of creativity and innovation can continually alter the nature of the game
- The strategic acquisition process, where the acquisition of other businesses can both refresh the resource portfolio and change the shape of the competitive environment
- The knowledge deployment process, where the effective use of knowledge assets can leverage competencies
- The organizational restructuring process, where the reconfiguration of the firm can release previously untapped capability.

Dynamic capabilities can therefore be seen as those that enable firms to keep pace with their changing environment, by developing resources and competencies that will continue to 'hit a moving target'.

It could be argued that dynamic capabilities exist at the opposite end of the continuum from sustainable competitive advantage, as they enable a firm in a fast-moving market, where sustainable advantage may be impossible to achieve, to gain advantage by achieving a series of temporary, short-lived advantages.

Contemporary Thinking: Industries and Ecosystems

Rethinking Industry

Possibly one of the most overused terms in the management lexicon is 'industry'. It is a term that most people are familiar with and because of its ubiquity very few stop to question its meaning or relevance.

An industry tends to be defined as a group of companies that are related based on their primary business activity. This is at first glance a simple statement. However it leads to the question; what is a company's primary business activity? Often a single company will carry out many activities and produce a diverse range of products and services.

In practice a company's primary business activity tends to be thought of as that which produces the largest source of revenue. A very simple example of this might be an automobile manufacturer that gains 90% of its revenue from sale of goods produced, in this case cars, and 10% of its revenue from other activities. However, it is obvious that while this logic may be simple to apply to small companies that may specialize in a single product or service, it may not apply so easily to all companies, particularly those that have many diverse interests.

The word 'industry' when employed in common parlance is actually rather flexible. It is used, often quite arbitrarily, to refer to a wide range of things. Some use it to refer to a market segment, for example the 'Fast Moving Consumer Goods Industry' or the 'Defence Industry'. Others use it to refer to a product group such as the 'Car Industry' or the 'Financial Services Industry'. Still others refer to it in relation to an activity set such as the 'Mining Industry' or the 'Fishing Industry'.

On close inspection 'Industry' is, to all intents and purposes, a rather slippery term that means different things to different people. Yet somewhat curiously, despite this ambiguity, it is used in many activities where clarity of thought and precision of language are crucial. Strategy-making is one such activity.

Classifying Industries

Despite the attendant ambiguity, governments use the concept of the industry as the basis for their Standard Industrial Classification (SIC) systems. These systems were introduced in an attempt to bring some degree of control and order to the sometimes bewildering assortment of economic activity that goes on in the world. This form of classification provides a framework for the collection and analysis of data. Its use promotes uniformity and it is valuable as a way of classifying economic activity into a common structure. While there are many versions of the SIC system throughout the world they all tend to follow a similar logic.

CRITICAL PERSPECTIVE

Standard Industry Classification: Bringing Order to Chaos

Standard Industry Classification was first introduced to the UK in 1948. Since then it has been revised seven times with the most recent in 2007. Revision is necessary because over time new products/services emerge and shifts of emphasis occur within existing classifications. The UK SIC (2007) is a hierarchical five digit system. At the top level it is divided into 21 sections, each allocated a letter from A to U. The letters of the sections can be uniquely defined by the next level, the divisions (denoted by two digits). The divisions are then broken down into groups (three digits), then classes (four digits) and, in several cases, sub-classes (five digits).

At the risk of oversimplifying things, the flow-down logic broadly moves from the top level defined by activity such as manufacturing or construction through levels of detail until the product or service that the activity is 'done to' emerges. For example, 'Section M - Professional, Scientific and Technical Activities' becomes 'M69.20/3 – Tax Consultancy'.

Close study of the SIC system suggests that a lot of thought has been applied to generating the logic behind it. The document 'UK Standard Industrial Classification of Economic Activities 2007' (UK SIC 2007) issued by the UK Government's Office for National Statistics (ONS, 2016), contains everything that you need to know (and admittedly a lot that you don't) about this system. The logic behind it is both sophisticated and complicated. In fact the section within this document entitled 'Rules for Classifying Statistical Units' runs to 20 pages and contains 132 items. For example, Item 7 outlines the foundational logic. It states:

The main criteria applied in delineating groups and divisions concern the following characteristics of the activities of production units:

– the character of the goods and services produced

– the uses to which the goods and services are put, and

– the inputs, the process and the technology of production.

Which is then followed by Item 8 which clarifies that:

In the case of the character of the goods and services produced, account is taken of the physical composition and stage of fabrication of the items and the needs served by them. Distinguishing categories in terms of the nature of goods and services produced provides the basis for grouping production units according to similarities in, and links between, the raw materials consumed and the sources of demand and markets for the items.

And so it goes on.

Despite the lengthy and detailed exposition of these rules there is still a number of ways that they could be interpreted. For example, this excerpt from Page 7 of the latest revision indicates a significant change to the logic of part of it:

Repair and installation of machinery and equipment, formerly classified under manufacturing of the corresponding type of equipment, is now identified separately in division 33 (Repair and installation of machinery and equipment). All specialised repair activities are now classifiable separately in SIC, although no high-level aggregate for 'Repair' has been created.

The key point is ...

that even within a system as elaborate as the SIC there is much scope for interpretation and, as economic activity becomes more complex, such systems may become so contrived as to be made meaningless.

While the SIC system provides a useful set of categories to enable consistent economic data to be gathered and analysed it also demonstrates the fundamental issues in attempting to use the concept of the industry to classify such diverse and complex activity as that which takes place in a global economy. These issues are broadly threefold.

First, some companies manufacture parts that are used in a variety of products which themselves occupy a number of market sectors. A long-established example of this is SKF who manufacture bearings used in products including bicycles, aeroplanes and medical equipment. In fact, any product that has a rotating assembly will contain a bearing of some sort. Some estimates boast that every household contains between 100 and 200 bearings buried within appliances of all types.

Second, some companies that once focused on a core product are now diversifying into ancillary, and often very different, activity related to that core product. Returning to the aforementioned automobile industry, until fairly recently car manufacturers concentrated on manufacturing cars with the ancillary activities such as financing, insuring and supporting dealt with by companies that specialize in finance, insurance and vehicle repair. Now car manufacturers often engage in all of these activities.

Third, increasingly there are many activities and products that span what we have traditionally thought of as industry boundaries and in doing so make meaningless any conceptualization we may each hold about what an industry is. Mobile phones are a good example of this. They no longer inhabit only the communications space but can be thought of as a platform (or toolbox) to enable a wide range of activities, only one of which represents the original function of facilitating verbal, person-to-person communication. The architecture and application of the technologies that enable the functionality that mobile phones provide and the diverse range of companies that are involved makes it difficult to argue that this conglomeration belongs to a single industry.

These are only three examples which highlight the need to question the traditional concept of what an industry is and how it can be used to inform our strategic thinking. Yet many of the methods and models we currently use for strategic thinking are still based on the centrality of the industry.

From Industry to Ecosystem

Because of these issues, some thinkers have started to question the concept of the industry as a useful lens for strategic analysis proposing that strategy must extend its reach beyond what goes on within the traditional boundaries of an industry (Adner, 2017). They argue that claiming any sort of coherence using traditional thinking about how industries are structured is problematic, therefore a new language and conceptualization is needed. As an alternative, Teece (2014) suggests that for performing strategic analysis 'the concept of ecosystem might substitute for the concept of industry'.

The term ecosystem was coined in the 1930s by Roy Clapham, an eminent British botanist, to denote the physical and biological components of an environment considered in relation to each other as a unit. In biology an ecosystem is made up of plants, animals, rocks and minerals, indeed anything that inhabits a common environment. The elements interact as a self-sustaining system and are linked to one another via nutrient cycles and energy flows. The key attribute in an ecosystem is complementary interdependence.

Taking the ecosystem concept and applying it to business would indicate that an ecosystem would consist of providers of products and services that may not exist in the same industry, as it is traditionally conceived, and may not be bound either by traditional supply chain relationships or market-based logic but have significant complementary interdependence nonetheless (Jacobites *et al.*, 2018).

Here the ecosystem takes into consideration the links that the single company has to all stakeholders that affect, or are affected by, its actions. This conceptualization therefore creates a broader analytical canvas which can include all actors within a particular environment. Crucially, ecosystems – unlike industries – tend not to be hierarchically organized, therefore in an ecosystem it is less likely that a dominant firm will control the entire supply chain.

It is clear that the concept of the ecosystem as explained to this point is rather broad and some further definition must be added to make it useful to us for the purposes of strategic analysis. Jacobites *et al.* (2018) helpfully summarize an ecosystem as a community of interacting actors where the activities of each affect all of the others. The ecosystem therefore represents the environment that each actor must be aware of and react to. They then identify two forms that an ecosystem might take.

First, an ecosystem built around a focal innovation. Here the ecosystem is a collaborative arrangement where firms combine their individual offerings to create a customer-facing value proposition. Again the innovation may be relevant across a number of what were traditionally conceived industries. Here the innovation activity that is driving the evolution of battery technology is a good example. The lithium-ion battery is now creating an ecosystem that spans many product types and therefore industries.

Second, an ecosystem built around a specific platform. Here, the ecosystem consists of the platform plus all providers of the complementary products and services that make the platform more valuable to the customer. This type of ecosystem can be identified in, for example, gaming where platforms such as games consoles create an ecosystem that many games producers and suppliers of supporting equipment can become part of.

Of course research on ecosystems theory is still very much in its infancy so other types of ecosystem may become evident as further work is done.

Strategic Analysis and Ecosystems

It is worth emphasizing that the ecosystem does not fully replace the industry as a lens in strategic analysis. However, it can provide an alternative to it, particularly if you are working within a company that suffers from what could be termed 'industry ambiguity'. Also, a further note of caution is necessary and this is that ecosystem theory is itself prone to criticisms of ambiguity. We employ the concept of an industry to help us simplify and make sense of complex phenomena: we employ the concept of an ecosystem for the same reason. While the concept of the ecosystem may be more flexible than the concept of the industry, it cannot be treated as a panacea. In some cases viewing activity using the lens of the ecosystem may provide a more useful analytical unit; in other cases the concept of an industry may suffice. Also, as explained, there are different types of ecosystem and it may not be clear which is relevant to you so often work must be done to customize this concept for use with a particular company.

The important point, though, is to broaden strategic horizons and provide an additional lens which releases strategists from the constraints of industry-based thinking.

SHORT CASE 1.4

'Smarter' than the Average City

Source: ©Elnur/Shutterstock

Mega-City One is a huge post-apocalyptic conurbation that covers the Eastern Seaboard of the United States. Most of the population are unemployed and violence is common.

First appearing in 1977 in the second edition of the science fiction comic ***2000 AD***, Mega-City One formed the main backdrop to a series of adventures starring the anti-hero Judge Dredd. Here in the early 22nd century urbanization has run amok. In this dystopian vision of the future, Mega-City One has a population of 400 million. It is a dictatorship and control is maintained using a combination of sophisticated technology, automation and human law-enforcers called Judges.

Representing a common theme in mid-to-late 20th-century science fiction, Mega-City One is an example of a genre that explored the problems of overcrowding. In 1977, when ***2000 AD*** was first published, a city with a population of 400 million was indeed the stuff of science fiction, now in 2020 this notion seems much less fantastical. New York, the original inspiration for Mega-City One, had a population of 96,000 in 1810, by 2010 it had climbed to 8.2 million. Yet, somewhat alarmingly, today New York does not even feature in the list of the top 10 most populated cities in the world. To gain this dubious honour it would need to increase its population by a staggering 250%. According to the Geographical Association it took 10,000 years to achieve the first billion urban dwellers, but only 25 years to achieve the second!

While large cities packed with people living lives controlled by computers were commonly featured in dystopian sci-fi, the writers of these stories were noticeably silent on the technical detail of how this control might be achieved. More recently, in an unexpected about-face, the coming of age of several technologies has allowed science fact to overtake science fiction.

Recent innovations such as 5G and the Internet of Things are enabling levels of connectivity and control that the science-fiction writers of the late 20th century could not have imagined. This maturation of digital technologies is providing access to more information, more quickly and in much more usable forms than ever before. This is forcing us to rethink how the infrastructures we rely on are configured.

Due to this reframing, the expression 'Smart Cities' has now entered the popular lexicon. Itself still evolving as a term, Smart Cities has a range of definitions, but the current consensus is that Smart Cities utilize sensors, actuators and communications technology to connect components across infrastructure. Data can be captured from almost everything. Sensors track all aspects of life and upload this data to be processed and used. Empty parking spaces can be identified and this information passed directly to internet-enabled vehicles; flows of people can be monitored; power consumption measured.

While a number of technologies are required to enable this functionality, sensors are at the root of these systems.

JWF Group is a UK-based company established in 1962 that specializes in instrumentation for measuring and metering. JWF provide all manner of sensors which can monitor such things as temperature, pressure and flow-rate. They operate in a number of market sectors including oil and gas, energy, pharmaceuticals, and food and beverage. In fact, JWF could be of use in any system where processes require measurement!

JWF have moved with the times with mechanical, manually monitored, sensors being replaced with electronic, remotely monitored sensors. It is difficult to classify JWF in the traditional industry sense. They design and supply solutions which are hardware-based systems supported by an expert service. Packaging this combination of elements into a customer-friendly offering is part of their distinctive competence.

The emergence of the recent enabling technologies that make Smart Cities possible provides a huge strategic opportunity for JWF. A new technologically enabled order is emerging that relies on the gathering of data using all forms of sensing equipment. JWF has built its reputation in what could be called traditional engineering applications. It is now poised to enter a new era where its products and services become key parts of an emerging system. Within this system they will be required to operate as part of processes that are still evolving and interface with technologies that are still maturing.

To succeed in this new order JWF must think beyond the confines of the traditional 'industry' and embrace ecosystem thinking where the platform provided by the Internet of Things will enable new systems to be established and new requirements to be created.

Question

1. Within a Smart City what ecosystems may be identified?

Sources: www.ec.europa.eu; www.geography.org.uk; www.urbantide.com; www.worldeconomicforum.org; www.worldpopulationreview.com; www.jwfltd.com

Summary

In this chapter, we have provided some tools that can be used to aid in your strategic decision-making. Strategy making has been presented from two viewpoints: the market-based view, which suggests that the route to success is in aligning the offering with market need, and the resource-based view, which suggests that if the organization concentrates on what it is good at, a market will be found. We have proposed that in most cases a mixture of both types of thinking is most useful.

The strategy process can be summarized as follows. First, using the business definition model, define what the nature of your business is. Second, drawing from the market-based view, investigate your overall market environment using PESTEL, characterize your immediate competitive position using Porter's Five Forces and investigate what your customer wants by identifying the value proposition. Third, drawing from the resource-based view, define what you need to be good at and from this definition you can develop competencies. These competencies may lead to competitive advantage. If so, analyse the nature of your competitive advantage and plan how your competencies must change over time to ensure your competitive advantage is sustainable.

Finally we proposed that building your strategic analysis within the context of the industry model may not always be useful to you and we have introduced the concept of ecosystems as an alternative.

The next chapter will continue broadly within the theme of the resource-based view by looking more closely at what can be done at the operational level to build and shape capability to achieve competitive advantage.

Key Theories

The key theories discussed in this chapter were:

- **Competitive advantage** – gained by being better than the competition in key areas of performance that are important to the customer.
- **Porter's Five Forces Model** – a framework that helps to identify the influences that shape competition in an industry sector. These forces come from immediate rivals, new entrants, substitute products, buyers and suppliers.

- **Market-based view** – an external-facing view of strategy-making that prioritizes the needs of the market in the strategic decision-making process, so shaping the operation to meet these needs.
- **Resource-based view** – an internal-facing view of strategy-making that prioritizes the capabilities of the organization as the most important factors in achieving competitive advantage.
- **Organizational competencies** – the activities and processes through which the organization deploys its resources effectively to ultimately achieve competitive advantage. These can be classed as threshold, core and distinctive.
- **Customer value proposition** – a combination of the attributes of the product or service that the customer values and the processes that they use to decide what to buy.
- **Dynamic capabilities** – the organization's ability to sustain competitive advantage by developing and changing competencies to meet the needs of the rapidly changing environment.

Suggested Answers to Stop and Think Questions

1. **Strategy packaging:** This issue is context specific. In large companies with large numbers of employees who do not have an overview of the business or are not knowledgeable enough to understand the concept and process of strategy, a simple and straightforward message communicated informally may be useful. In smaller, more knowledge-based companies, such as professional practices, the mission and vision statements may be more sophisticated, containing more information designed to provide direct guidance to employees.
2. **The job of the operations manager:** In the past, the operations manager was concerned purely with scheduling, logistics and production matters. Now the job has grown to include other areas such as design and development and the supply chain. It also requires knowledge of peripheral functions such as recruitment and training, and the sales and marketing processes. The operations management job has therefore broadened and now includes a greater degree of integration with other parts of the organization.
3. **Resource impact:** Most would agree that the sources of organizational capability are the intangible resources, in other words the people in the organization and their knowledge and creativity. However, to be most effective, the people must be provided with the resources they require in the form of tools and information and they must exist within a culture that is positive and supportive. While as operations managers, we tend to concentrate on the tangibles in our organizations such as machinery and equipment; finding a balance between the mechanistic and the organic elements is the key to achieving high performance.

connect

Review Questions

1. Explain how the time horizon, level of complexity and scope of strategic decisions will differ between a large multinational and an SME.
2. For your local rail company analyse the competitive environment using Porter's Five Forces model.
3. It has been proposed that ecosystems come in two types. Explain the key features of both of these types.
4. Explain the difference between threshold competencies, core competencies and distinctive competencies.
5. Explain what dynamic capabilities are.

Discussion Questions

1. Using the vocabulary introduced – mission, vision, objectives, priorities, etc. – create a corporate strategy package for an organization that you are familiar with.
2. For a highly diversified company such as the Virgin Group, discuss how the top level of the company can implement strategic control over each business unit.
3. Consider and discuss how, as the scope of the operations function increases, the relationship between marketing and operations should be managed.
4. The resource-based and market-based approaches to strategy-making are often considered as opposites. Which is more aligned with operations management?
5. Conduct a PESTEL analysis for a large company that operates in your local area.

Further Reading

Augier, M. and Teece, D.J. (2007) 'Dynamic capabilities and multinational enterprise: Penrosean insights and omissions', *Management International Review*, **47**(2), 175–192.

Di Stefano, G., Peteraf, M. and Verona, G. (2014) 'The organizational drivetrain: A road to integration of dynamic capabilities research', *Academy of Management Perspectives*, **28**, 307–327.

Fitzsimmons, J. A. and Fitzsimmons, M. J. (2006) *Service Management: Operations, Strategy, and Information Technology*, McGraw-Hill, London.

Griffiths, D. A. and Harvey, M. G. (2006) 'A resource based perspective of global dynamic capabilities', *Journal of International Business Studies*, **32**(5), 597–606.

Helfat, C. E., Finkelstein, S., Mitchell, W., Peteraf, M., Singh, H., Teece, D. and Winter, S. (eds.) (2007) *Dynamic Capabilities: Understanding Strategic Change in Organizations*, Blackwell, Oxford.

Kapoor, R., and Agarwal, S. (2017) Sustaining superior performance in business ecosystems: Evidence from application software developers in the iOS and Android smartphone ecosystems, *Organization Science*, **28**(3), 531–551.

Langlois, R. N. (2003) 'The vanishing hand: The changing dynamics of industrial capitalism', *Industrial and Corporate Change*, **12**(2), 351–385.

Whittington, R., Regner, P., Angwin, D., Johnson, G. and Scholes, K. (2020) *Exploring Corporate Strategy*, Pearson, UK.

References

Abell, D.F. (1980) *Defining the Business: The Starting Point of Strategic Planning*, Prentice Hall, Englewood Cliffs, NJ.

Adner, R. (2017) Ecosystem as structure: An actionable construct for strategy, *Journal of Management*, **43**(1), 39–58.

Ambrosini, V. and Bowman, C. (2009) 'What are dynamic capabilities and are they a useful construct in strategic management?', *International Journal of Management Reviews*, **11**(1), 29–49.

Barney, J. (1991) 'Firm resources and sustained competitive advantage', *Journal of Management*, **17**(1), 99–120.

Biggadike, E. R. (1981) 'The contributions of marketing to strategic management', *Academy of Management Review*, **6**(4), 621–632.

Daft, R. (1983) *Organisation Theory and Design*, West, Cengage, OH.

Eden, C. and Ackermann, F. (2005) 'Discovering core competences: Working with patterns of distinctive competences and competences', *Proceedings of the British Academy of Management Conference*, Oxford (CD-ROM).

Gutman, J. (1982) 'A means-end model based on consumer categorization processes', *Journal of Marketing*, **48**(2), 60–72.

Hamel, G. and Prahalad, C.K. (1990) 'The core competence of the corporation', *Harvard Business Review*, **68**(3), 79–91.

Hirshleifer, J. (1980) *Price Theory and Applications*, 2nd edn, Prentice Hall, Englewood Cliffs, NJ.

Jacobites, M. G., Cennamo, C. and Gawer, A. (2018) 'Towards a theory of ecosystems', *Strategic Management Journal*, **39**, 2255–2276.

Johnson, J., Scholes, K. and Whittington, R. (2005) *Exploring Corporate Strategy*, 7th edn, FT/Prentice Hall, Harlow.

Kaplan, R. S. and Norton, D. P. (2004) *Strategy Maps: Converting Intangible Assets to Tangible Outcomes*, Harvard Business School Press, Cambridge, MA.

Locket, A., Thompson, S. and Morgenstern, U. (2009) 'The development of the resource-based view of the firm: A critical appraisal', *International Journal of Management Reviews*, **11**(1), 9–28.

ONS (2016) 'UK SIC 2007', https://www.ons.gov.uk/methodology/classificationsandstandards/ukstandardindustrialclassificationofeconomicactivities/uksic2007

Penrose, E. T. (1959) *The Theory of the Growth of the Firm*, Wiley, New York.

Porter, M. E. (1979) 'How competitive forces shape strategy', *Harvard Business Review*, March/April, 86–93.

Porter, M. E. (1980) *Competitive Strategy: Techniques for Analyzing Industries and Competitors*, Free Press, New York.

Sheth, J. N., Newman, B. I. and Gross, B. L. (1991) 'Why we buy what we buy: A theory of consumption values', *Journal of Business Research*, **22**(2), 159–170.

Teece, D. J. (2014) Business ecosystems. In M. Augier and D. J. Teece (eds.), *Palgrave Encyclopedia of Management*. https://doi.org/10.1057/9781137294678.0190

Teece, D. J. and Pisano, G. (1994) 'The dynamic capabilities of firms: an introduction', *Industrial and Corporate Change*, **3**(3), 537–556.

Teece, D. J., Pisano, G. and Shuen, A. (1997) 'Dynamic capabilities and strategic management', *Strategic Management Journal*, **18**(7), 509–533.

Van Looy, B., Gemmel, P. and Van Dierdonck, R. (2003) *Services Management: An Integrated Approach*, 2nd edn, FT/Prentice Hall, Harlow.

Wernerfelt, B. (1984) 'A resource based view of the firm', *Strategic Management Journal*, **5,** 171–180.

Woodruff, R. B. (1997) 'Customer value: The next source for competitive advantage', *Journal of the Academy of Marketing Science*, **25**(2), 139–153.

Woodruff, R. B. and Gardial, S. F. (1996) *Know Your Customer: New Approaches to Understanding Customer Value and Satisfaction*, Blackwell, Oxford.

2 Operations Strategy

Learning Outcomes

After reading this chapter, you should be able to:

- Define the term 'operations strategy'
- Develop and implement an operations strategy
- Explain how operations strategy can contribute to strategic success
- Discuss how operations strategy can enhance operational performance
- Explain how the product life cycle might inform operations strategy
- Discuss the utility of generic operations strategies

IMV Imaging – Looking Inside the Animal Kingdom

Source: ©magnusdeepbelow/Shutterstock

The most popular pet owned in the United Kingdom is the dog, with 25% of people owning one. Pet ownership is on the rise across the world with more money being spent on pets and pet-related products than ever before. The trend towards treating pets like one of the family is growing – remarkably some owners even buy their dogs Valentine's Day cards (and no doubt expect one in return). However, the danger of treating pets so much like one of the family is that they will come to face the same lifestyle-based health issues as people do. Because of this, issues such as animal obesity are beginning to appear. Veterinarians in the UK report that currently 45% of the dogs they see are overweight. Conversely, some studies suggest pet owners have lower blood pressure, cholesterol and allergy levels. So, rather ironically, while pet owners report an increase in overall well-being, the pets themselves appear to be suffering the opposite effect.

Also somewhat ironically, though the population of domesticated animals seems to be increasing, some forms of human activity, such as habitat destruction and poaching, is having the opposite effect on wild animals. Many of the planet's most well-known animals such as the gorilla, the elephant, the orang-utan and the sea turtle are now considered endangered.

These phenomena of increasing numbers of domestic animals and decreasing numbers of wild animals, though entirely separate, have one thing in common. Whether the aim is to treat animals to ensure their continued health or to study creatures we know little about to ensure their continued existence, the provision of the right equipment to facilitate this work is critical to its success.

Throughout the history of biological research the key to progress has been the ability to 'look inside' and IMV imaging helps researchers and medics to do just that.

IMV imaging provides 'Your Complete Animal Imaging Solution'.

IMV imaging is the dedicated veterinary diagnostic imaging arm of the IMV Technologies group. In December 2017, BCF Technology and ECM (Echo Control Medical) merged with IMV Technologies, to create IMV imaging. Combining the expertise of both BCF Technology and ECM, IMV has over 35 years' experience in providing cutting-edge imaging technology to the veterinary market. It now operates across the globe with offices in the USA, India, China, Italy, The Netherlands and South Africa. IMV are specialists in all forms of veterinary imaging leading the market in ultrasound, X-ray, computerized tomography and magnetic resonance imaging (MRI).

For example, IMV imaging were the first to develop a water resistant, wearable bovine ultrasound scanner that allowed users to view the image on a head-mounted display. The market is constantly changing, requiring scanners that are more capable and rugged but at the same time smaller and lighter, allowing users to wear them comfortably all day within a variety of often challenging environments.

It is IMV imaging's strategic goal to be the world leader in the invention, development and provision of animal diagnostic imaging equipment. To meet this goal they pursue a corporate strategy that is very much a mixture of resource-based and market-based thinking. They closely follow developing markets, providing equipment that can deal with diverse applications from pet hedgehogs to wild cheetahs. They also rely heavily on their resource-base which itself rests on technologies developed and improved during their 35-year history. Technological innovation is at the core of their resource-based approach.

Did you know that the giant manta ray (***Manta birostris***), the largest of the three recognized species of manta ray, is listed as threatened under the US Endangered Species Act (1973)?

The giant manta ray is threatened by a number of factors that are human in origin. While its few natural predators such as large sharks and killer whales do not attack often, humans are almost always involved in the accidental injury or untimely death of these fish. Their primary threat is fishing, as they often become entangled in fishermen's nets. Once inside the net, the manta ray might suffocate because it becomes difficult for it to obtain oxygen from the water. This is particularly unfortunate as the commercial value of a manta ray is low due to the unpleasant taste of its flesh. Despite their lack of value as a foodstuff, manta rays are also fished on purpose as their 'gill-rakers', which they use to filter plankton, are prized in traditional Chinese medicine and are used to produce remedies for various diseases, including chickenpox and cancer. Even more tragically, as is often the case, there is no scientific basis to endorse the effectiveness of these remedies. Manta rays face other man-made threats. Destruction of their habitat caused by pollution, which changes the chemistry of the water and reduces their food supply, global warming which increases sea temperatures and changes their geographical habitat, and collisions with ships, all serve to deplete their numbers.

One of the keys to saving endangered species is to understand how they reproduce and, unfortunately with manta rays, very little is known about this. While many marine animals suffer from the consequences of human activity, manta rays are particularly vulnerable due to their slow reproductive rate – they birth only one or (rarely) two offspring at a time, with births occurring every 2–5 years. To learn more about these animals, scientists needed to look inside. Previously the only way to scan a live fish would be to remove it from its natural habitat while accepting all the associated risks. Obviously when dealing with an endangered species there is a good chance this rather intrusive and distressing activity could turn out to be somewhat counter-productive.

The challenge brought to IMV imaging was to conduct an internal 3D scan of a fully conscious female manta ray at depths of up to 30 metres without imposing any stress on the animal. The equipment therefore had to be portable enough to be easily used underwater in poor lighting and in strong currents. It also had to communicate wirelessly with a viewing device, itself underwater, and most importantly it needed to do all of this without coming into physical contact with the animal.

The development of this equipment represented a very special project. It was not only technically challenging with the potential to provide an exciting new product, but more importantly, if successful, it would contribute to the global sustainability agenda. IMV imaging worked with partners such as Manta Trust and Cambridge University to find a solution to this challenge. The innovative product that they designed was the 'Duo-Scan: Go Oceanic' which was released in May 2019. This was the first fully underwater veterinary scanner.

While IMV imaging successfully combines market-based and resource-based considerations, their operations strategy is also key as in this business there are many complex operational considerations. Here, operations strategy must guide the development of sophisticated technology and its embodiment within complex products. It must facilitate the efficient operation of a high-variety/low-volume production system and, more recently, with increasing numbers of products in the field and increasing customer expectations of support, it must also inform the development of a robust servitization strategy.

Sources: www.imv-imaging.co.uk; www.pfma.org.uk; www.mantaray-world.com; www.biologicaldiversity.org

Introduction

Unlike Warner Bros described in Chapter 1, IMV do not rely fully on corporate strategy and methods such as diversification into new product markets to find success. IMV has tended to stay within one arena, basing its strategy on its core competence in the design, production and support of imaging equipment.

Chapter 1, p23

Therefore it could be argued that IMV prioritizes operational strategies over corporate ones, embracing a resource-based approach that emphasizes the building and strengthening of core competencies. But this is not the whole story. More recently, this internal focus has been supported by a market awareness that informs its deployment of these products into many different niches. Indeed, IMV's market awareness extends beyond simply expansion into new geographical regions and increasingly diverse applications. IMV recognized that selling a service is seen by much of the market as far more valuable than selling the physical product alone. They are therefore developing an operational strategy based on a **servitization** model. Servitization (described later in the chapter) is an operational strategy that draws on both market- and resource-based thinking. This case serves to illustrate that there needs to be a balance found between different views of how strategy is made.

Servitization: the addition of services to complement the sale of a manufactured product

The purpose of this chapter is to pick up where the previous chapter ended and investigate how the operational systems and processes are conceived that will support the company in reaching its strategic goals. The treatment of operations strategy in this chapter will set the context for your study of the more detailed processes and systems that are the concern of the remainder of this book, as without an understanding of operations strategy to guide you, it may be difficult to piece together each aspect of operations management theory and method into a coherent whole.

This chapter will begin by detailing how operations strategy is generated and how it can contribute to and support the overall corporate strategy. It will continue by discussing how operations strategy is related to the overall performance of the organization. It will then look at more generic operations strategies that can be adopted to simplify the decision-making done when generating operations strategy.

The Role of Operations Strategy

What Is Operations Strategy?

Operations strategy is about decision-making. Like decisions made in relation to corporate strategy, the decisions made in relation to operations strategy must focus on the achievement of a common purpose, and the 'signposts' that inform the decision-making process may be formalized in statements, such as a vision or a mission. Unlike decisions made in relation to corporate strategy, the decisions made in relation to operations strategy tend to be short term and tactical, concerned more with the initiation and directing of action at the lower levels of the organization.

Operations strategy: the set of major decisions about core competencies, capabilities and processes, technologies, resources and key tactical activities necessary in the function or chain of functions that create and deliver product and service combinations.

Lowson (2002) proposes that operations strategy can be defined as:

> *Major decisions about, and management of: core competencies, capabilities and processes, technologies, resources and key tactical activities necessary in the function or chain of functions that create and deliver product and service combinations and the value demanded by the customer.*

This statement nicely captures the various elements that operations may call upon to support corporate strategy; it highlights the tactical level of operations; and it emphasizes the integration of activity into a single entity that works in an efficient and effective way to meet the goals of the organization.

How Is Operations Strategy Made?

Revisiting Corporate Strategy

The academic literature contains several approaches to generating operations strategy (Platts and Gregory, 1990; Hill, 1993; Slack and Lewis, 2017). These approaches are in many ways similar. The approach presented here uses elements of each to create an integrated view that is firmly linked with the concepts discussed in relation to corporate strategy in Chapter 1. In Chapter 1 we introduced what are arguably the two fundamental views that inform the generation of corporate strategy: the market-based view and the resource-based view.

Chapter 1, p23

Figure 2.1 Operations strategy making

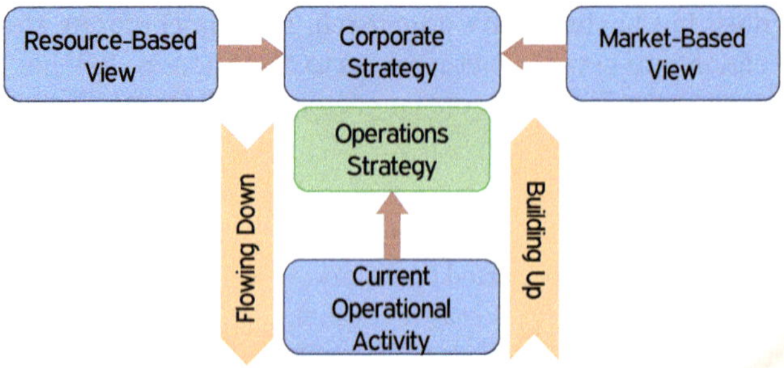

We outlined the macro-factors that may be taken into consideration when developing corporate strategy from a market-based view and these included the political, social, economic, technological, environmental and legal factors that exist in the wider environment. We indicated that customer value elements such as functional, social, emotional, epistemic and conditional would need to be understood and these in combination would represent the customer value proposition. Likewise we stated that from a resource-based viewpoint manufacturing firms must find their competitive advantage in valuable, rare, inimitable and non-substitutable capabilities.

Adopting a rather binary interpretation it could be argued that the market-based view assumes that operational capability is fully adjustable, in other words it assumes that operations can produce what the market wants regardless of what that is, and the resource-based view assumes that as long as operations is capable, a market will always be found for whatever is output.

Of course neither of these positions is entirely correct. In reality most organizations will consult both views while developing their corporate strategy and therefore most companies will settle on a strategy that in some way matches their resources, or aspirations for what their future resources will be, with the market requirements, or their view of what the future market will look like.

Therefore the corporate strategy that results from this thinking positions the organization in two ways. First, it positions the organization in the external environment by setting objectives about such things as product type, geographical positioning and financial performance. And second, it positions the organization internally by defining what competences the company must build and deploy.

Chapter 1, p23

So following this logic, Figure 2.1 contains the main elements to be considered when developing an operations strategy. It illustrates that in developing corporate strategy, organizations often use a mixture of both resource-based and market-based thinking. It recognizes, again as mentioned in Chapter 1, that strategy is hierarchical and indicates that operations strategy is subordinate to, but also must be aligned with and supportive of corporate strategy. The nature of this support will be discussed later in this chapter. More importantly though, from an operations management perspective, Figure 2.1 also illustrates that the current operational activity that is ongoing within the organization at any point in time will also play an important role in influencing the decisions made while making operations strategy. This recognition of the importance of ongoing activity is often an aspect that is missing from higher-level strategic thinking.

Operations Strategy – Flowing Down versus Building Up

It is clear that while corporate strategy is influenced by both resource-based thinking and market-based thinking, developing an operations strategy is about finding a balance between what the corporate strategy is asking to be done and what the operational activity that is being carried out suggests can be done.

Figure 2.1 illustrates this duality and indicates that both approaching operations strategy from the top and working down and from the bottom and working up recognize the hierarchical nature of strategy-making. Starting from the top with the corporate strategy prioritizes the importance of the objectives set at the corporate level and attempts to alter the operational capability to meet these. Starting at the bottom prioritizes what is happening operationally and attempts to alter the corporate strategy to better utilize these. Beginning with the corporate strategy is in many ways the more orthodox approach as it fits more easily with the model of rational decision-making that many believe should be adopted while developing corporate strategy. And because of this emphasis on rationality it provides a neat solution in the form of a clear set of information that can 'flow down' to the operational level.

The simplest way to enable this flow-down is to translate the output of the corporate strategy-making process, which will have been packaged as mission, vision and objectives as discussed in Chapter 1, into similar operational statements such as the:

Chapter 1, p23

- *operational vision,* which articulates the desired end-state that the operation wants to achieve
- *operational objectives* that define the level of performance that needs to be attained to meet the vision; this might be in terms of quantifiable targets, such as units of output or quality standards to be met
- *operational plans,* which are detailed sequences of activity that if undertaken will lead to the objectives being met and, ultimately, the vision being achieved
- *operational priorities* that bring focus to the operation by defining what is important in the short term as the plans progress.

The information collectively captured in these statements is a 'signpost' that ensures that operations stay aligned with the overall corporate strategy.

Beginning at the bottom, on the other hand, represents what some would argue is a more realistic approach in that it recognizes that often organizations develop competencies in a much more organic way. As activity is undertaken new ideas for products are generated, skills are developed and processes are improved and modified. This leads to benefits that may not have been planned or foreseen. This may result in new capabilities emerging and combining to form a new competence that may in itself become part of the operational strategy and so in turn may influence how the company sees its corporate strategy.

CRITICAL PERSPECTIVE

How Does Current Operational Activity Influence Operations Strategy Making?

In both Chapter 1 and this chapter we present strategy-making as a purposeful process of planning based on a set of rational decisions. This school of strategizing can broadly be labelled as 'strategy by design' and is associated with the rationalist approach. Where operations strategy is concerned, this approach to strategy-making seems a rather uncomfortable fit. Often capabilities cannot be planned, it is very difficult to 'force' the development of a new competence. There is another approach termed 'strategy as process' and this approach is useful when thinking about operations strategy. Strategy as process is best thought of as a process of emergence. This tends to be associated with incrementalism, setting an initial direction and continually adjusting, often by trial and error, until some idea emerges. With this approach there is some planning involved but this is subordinate to, and is expected to be changed by, the learning that emerges along the way. Lately a school of thought termed 'wayfinding' (Chia, 2017) has been proposed, which pushed this idea of emergence a step further. Wayfinding represents the view that 'strategic coherence can emerge inadvertently from local coping actions and decisions taken on the hoof' (Bounty ***et al.***, 2019: 1). Here there is no initial direction set; insights emerge from the ongoing operational work of the organization. This is a useful way to think about operations strategy making from the 'bottom up'. In reality this type of emergence has been characterized before in the 'continuous improvement' philosophy as operations improves and adapts organically.

The key point is …

that this thought-provoking view seeks to characterize the way strategy emerges unplanned from other forms of organizational activity. It suggests that the interweaving of seemingly unrelated actions may produce a useful outcome: a phenomenon that organizations would do well to take note of and exploit.

Operations Strategy: Decisions on Details

Having defined the operations strategy, we must plan the individual parts that make up our operational competence. Finding answers to the following questions will help with this.

- How is the conversion actually carried out – a mix of technology and human labour?
- What are the basic operations principles of the system – leanness, flexibility, etc.?

- What competencies will form part of the system – extent and use of supply chain?
- What are the limits of the system – capacity and time?
- Where is the system located – proximity to suppliers or customers?
- How is the system organized – layout and arrangement for movement of parts and/or people?
- How is quality ensured – what methods are to be used?

Making such decisions at this stage will help in guiding the design of the individual processes. The detail of how to design these processes is dealt with in Parts 2 and 3 of this book.

The tactical decisions around the shape of the conversion process now need to be supported by similar decisions on the support infrastructure. Decisions should be taken here in the following areas:

- *Management structure:* hierarchical, flat or matrix
- *Management system:* autocratic or empowered
- *Job design:* tasks highly divided and deskilled, or craft based
- *Enterprise control system:* discrete systems for inventory, accounts, manufacturing, etc. or all integrated within a single business system
- *Automation:* level and type of technology employed
- *Shape of the supply chain:* suppliers used, and how they are managed.

CRITICAL PERSPECTIVE

CSR

Operations Management: 'RESPECTing' the Worker

Operations management, at its core, is all about creating the correct product or delivering the correct service as efficiently as possible. The key drivers of efficiency are cost of labour, material and utilities. In the 1970s and 1980s efficiency levels tended to be driven by increasingly progressive management and engineering practices, such as 'Kaizen' (continuous improvement) and 'Lean' manufacturing.

However, since the turn of the century the emphasis has changed. There has been much debate about the ability of the 'high-cost' economies of the West to compete with the 'low-cost' economies of the emerging nations. The lower cost of labour in places such as China, India and South America has resulted in many high-profile companies such as Mattel and Apple taking strategic operational decisions to outsource the manufacture of their products to these countries. Although this has resulted in cheaper costs to produce, and therefore lower consumer prices, there are increasing concerns about the control of these factories and the working practices adopted. Often low cost is achieved by compromising on health and safety, with workers forced to work long hours in poor conditions, leading to ill health and accidents. Child labour is common, with workers as young as six years of age toiling for long hours in factories. While many industries have been associated with unethical practice the clothing industry has emerged as arguably the most recognizable face in this scandal. Nike were the original 1990s poster-boy for unethical practice with the term 'Nike sweatshop' entering the popular lexicon. More recently Inditex (owner of the Zara brand) have stolen this particular position, becoming associated with poor ethical practice with the high profile exposé in 2019 of worker exploitation in a Turkish garment factory where, rather ironically, the workers were producing a hooded sweatshirt emblazoned with the word RESPECT.

The key point is ...

that decisions in operational strategy are not always based solely on the practical aspects; they must also consider the ethical and social aspects of the factory system.

Sources: https://cleanclothes.org/news/2019/what-does-zara-mean-by-respect https://www.theguardian.com/fashion/2015/may/12/zara-owner-inditex-fines-brazil-working-conditions-claim

Operations Strategy and Performance

Generic Performance Objectives

One of the key purposes of developing an operations strategy is to define the required performance of the operation. Without this definition an operations strategy would have little purpose. While there are many different aspects to performance, or to put this another way, many different ways to define what criteria operational performance should be measured against, there are five generally accepted 'generic performance objectives' that all operations, regardless of the activities that they undertake, should consider. These are quality, cost, speed, dependability and flexibility. While a convention has emerged among operations managers and academics that asserts these are the fundamental attributes an operation must be measured against, these objectives do not represent all aspects of performance. How these five objectives can be expanded on will be discussed in Chapter 12. Despite their limitations they do provide a good overall starting point when working at an operationally strategic level. It is also important to recognize that while these five objectives can be applied to any operational system they need to be interpreted specifically for use in the industrial context in question.

Chapter 12, p391

Quality

Although possibly one of the most recognizable words in the lexicon of operations management, quality is also one of the most slippery. To simplify things, there are two points that need to be clarified when we talk of the performance of an operation in relation to quality.

The first point to note is that quality is thought of in two fundamental ways:

- **product quality**, or in other words, the quality of the output of the operation, whether it is a tangible product or an intangible service
- **process quality**, or in other words, the integrity of the operational system that creates the output.

Product quality: the quality of the output of the operation, whether it is a tangible product or an intangible service.

Product quality is generally defined as 'conformance to specification', or in simpler language, how well the product meets the requirements that have been set out in the product specification. Assuming the specification accurately reflects what the customer wants and the product meets the specification then product quality should be acceptable. Of course there are issues in relation to how accurately specifications represent what the customer wants and also how the customer might judge the product or service that is delivered against the specification. But these will be dealt with in more detail in Chapter 13.

Process quality: the integrity of the operational system that creates the output.

Process quality is generally thought of in relation to its reliability, repeatability and consistency (as described in the Introduction). In simpler language this means how efficiently the operational system produces the product or service it is set up to produce. Low yields, manufacturing defects and service delays are examples of how performance might be compromised in relation to process quality.

Chapter 13, p429

So when discussing the performance of an operational system with reference to the quality objective, both process and product quality must be considered. If the process meets the required standard in relation to output and the product meets the specification then the performance of the operation is acceptable from a quality point of view.

The second point to note is that quality is often not a singular objective that is separate from the other generic objectives. This point is particularly true in relation to the delivery of services. Quality may often be assessed in relation to three of the other generic performance objectives, namely speed, dependability and flexibility. For example, if you were to order a takeaway meal you may consider the quality of the food by reflecting on how good it tasted, and the quality of the delivery staff by reflecting on how courteous they were. However, if the agreed-upon delivery time was 15 minutes after order placement and the order was in fact delivered 30 minutes late then you would consider that you had received poor quality service when judged against the objective of speed. If the order did not arrive at all you would consider that as poor quality service when judged against the objective of dependability. Or if, after you placed the initial order, you changed the address that you wanted the meal to be delivered to and the delivery firm were unable to accommodate this change you would judge that as poor quality service in relation to the objective of flexibility.

This simple example illustrates that quality is often a composite comprising a number of aspects. For some this may seem a rather semantic point. However, when generating an operations strategy the importance of fully defining the nature of your performance objectives cannot be stressed highly enough.

Cost

Cost is possibly the most straightforward objective to define. This is simply the financial cost incurred by a company in providing its output. Standard accounting practice also helps to simplify things here as it provides a standard regulatory framework that specifies how costs must be gathered and reported. And, rather handily, this is also supported by a profession dedicated to this task. As such, this is the only performance objective that has this level of institutionalized structure. As a result, the cost objective tends to be easier to conceptualize than, for example, the dependability objective, as there is less need for additional contextual definition. Costs tend to fall into standard categories such as labour, materials, infrastructure and utilities. However, although costs can be collected across different industries in a standardized way, the proportionality will be different; in other words, money will be spent in different ways. Manufacturing firms tend to spend more on material than labour. However, highly automated, process-based manufacturers such as chemical producers may spend much more on infrastructure and utilities than either material or labour. A professionalized service company such as a legal practice, on the other hand, will see the majority of its cost as labour.

The key thing when considering cost is to clearly set the target for each unit of output whatever that might be. This unit could be a billing hour of legal advice or a tin of beans. Some argue that cost is the most important objective. This thinking is supported by the Product Life Cycle model that is introduced later in this chapter and also by Porter's work on generic strategies, where cost-based competitive activity is highlighted as an individual strategy. However, any form of ranking of performance objectives in this way is fraught with danger as there are many contingencies that affect how each of these objectives should be prioritized in any market.

Speed

Speed is another relatively straightforward objective to define. It simply represents the time elapsed between the beginning and the end of an operations process. The key consideration here is in defining the scope of the operations process that you are setting the performance objective for. As we discussed above, in food delivery, from the customer's point of view, the process start-point would be the time of order placement and the end-point would be time of order delivery. This is the service level that the supplier would commit to. For the chef, for example, the process would start when s/he receives the order from the front-office and end when s/he finishes cooking the meal.

It can be useful to think of speed in relation to responsiveness. When a patient arrives at the Accident and Emergency department of a hospital, speed would be measured in relation to the time taken for each stage of treatment. Time for triage to happen, time taken for treatment, and time for discharge. When reflecting on the service experience the patient may think in terms of speed of response.

Dependability

This objective is less tangible than either speed or cost and therefore a bit more difficult to make sense of. Broadly, dependability means meeting the commitments that you have made to your customers reliably, repeatably and consistently. However, there are many ways to commit to a customer. In manufacturing it may simply be meeting a single or a recurring delivery commitment. In transport, such as a bus or train service, it may mean sticking to a prearranged timetable, here it may be thought of in terms of punctuality. Whereas for a taxi service it may mean arriving after being called and not leaving a customer stranded. In retail it may mean ensuring that the same range of produce is available all the time regardless of season, or time of day, or day of the week.

In knowledge-based work such as financial or legal services it may mean providing robust and correct advice consistently. In this form of service work, for customers dependability may be thought of in terms of trustworthiness.

Flexibility

Here again, some work must be done to define exactly what flexibility means. Broadly, flexibility means the ability of an operational system to change the nature of its output. This alteration might be to the volume of product or to the variety of product. A more flexible operations system would therefore be able to change to a greater degree within a shorter period of time than a less flexible operations system.

While this general definition is useful, some further work must be done within each context to define what this means for each operation. In manufacturing companies the logic of economies of scale tells us that production of high volumes of a single product leads to more efficient systems and, consequently, a lower unit-cost per product. The most efficient operations systems were therefore set up for a specific configuration of product and a specific volume of output. To add flexibility, manufacturers began modifying their production systems to handle different volumes and varieties of output while attempting to retain efficiency. They did this by introducing more capable machinery which could be reconfigured quickly and simply and a more adaptable workforce that could be easily transferred to work on several product types.

It is generally agreed that there are a greater range of types of service system than manufacturing systems. Hospitals, banks, airports and supermarkets are all examples of service systems. Each produces very different outputs, and each has its own requirements in relation to flexibility. For hospitals, flexibility in relation to variety may be thought of in terms of range of ailments that it can treat; or in the case of banks, it may be the number of financial services it can provide. Like manufacturing systems, service systems need to consider flexibility in relation to volume and this is generally measured in terms of how customer throughput changes over time. So flexibility is therefore linked to volume and variety both in service delivery and in manufacturing.

Order-Winning and Order-Qualifying Criteria

While it is important to define the overall performance of an operation, often some performance measures are more important than others. A good way to determine what operations should concentrate on is to distinguish between **order-winning criteria** and **order-qualifying criteria** (Hill, 1993).

Order-winning criteria: the key reasons to buy a product or service.

Order-winning criteria are features that the customer regards as key reasons to buy the product or service. Improving these elements will directly affect the business that is won. Order-qualifying criteria may be less important to winning business, but will play a big part in *losing* it. In other words, if parts of these criteria are not present then this may prevent the product or service from being considered by the customer. Linn Products, described in Short Case 2.1, is a good example of a company that understands what it takes to win in its market. At each iteration of technology Linn clearly identify the products that are required, whether analogue turntable or a fully integrated digital media centre, and take time to fully understand the level of performance required.

Order-qualifying criteria: the required standards that, if not achieved, will disqualify a product or service from consideration by the customer.

Performance Prioritizing

To help understand the performance levels that are required in each of the elements above, Slack and Lewis (2017) extend this model by creating a performance matrix that also takes the competition into account. This is a more complex model, but it also provides an understanding of which factors need the most work. It can therefore help in prioritizing operational effort, in relation both to the order-winning criteria and to which elements are most deficient in relation to the competition. This model is shown in Figure 2.2.

Figure 2.2 Performance prioritizing

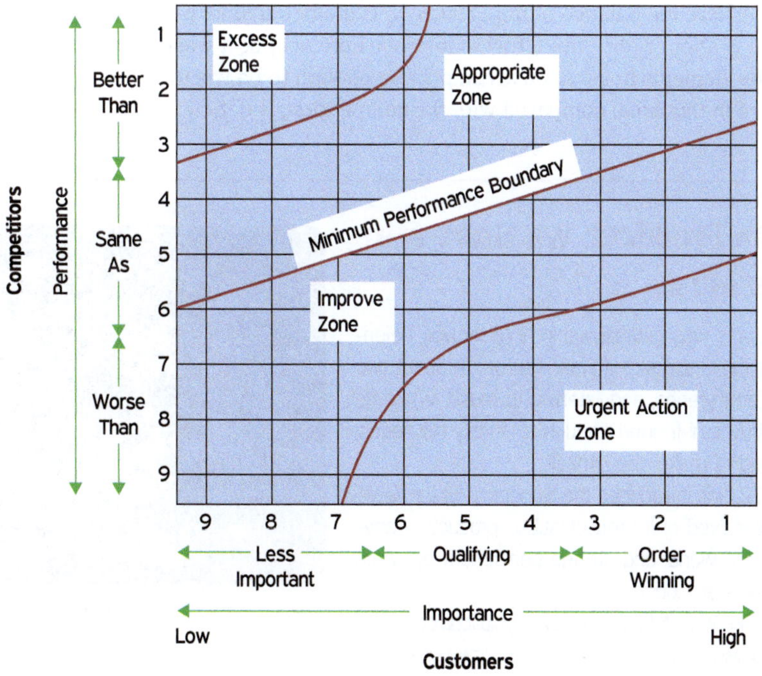

Source: Slack *et al.* (2007).

Table 2.1 Performance criteria

	Performance against competition	Importance to customer
1	Considerably better	Provides a crucial advantage
2	Clearly better than	Provides an important advantage
3	Marginally better	Provides a useful advantage
4	Sometimes better	Needs to be above industry standards
5	Same	Needs to meet industry standards
6	Slightly worse than some	Needs to be on par with competition
7	Worse than most	Not important but may become so in future
8	Worse than all	Rarely considered by customers
9	Considerably worse than all	Never considered by customers

This model has four steps:

1. Define the elements of the product or service that are important to the customer.
2. Plot these in the matrix in relation to competition and customer by assigning a score to each as defined in Table 2.1. For example, if an element is a 1 on 'importance to customer' but a 9 on 'performance against competition' then urgent action is needed to move it above the competition.
3. Prioritize the action areas by analysing the gaps between the performance of your company and the required performance.
4. Formulate plans to change the performance for each element to meet the required performance target.

There are four zones in the matrix:

- *Appropriate:* here the balance of importance to customer against performance as compared with the competition is about right. Any effort to improve here may be a waste of resources.
- *Improve:* the elements in question are important enough to be worthy of consideration, and the performance in this area, compared with the competition, is deficient enough to warrant action.

SHORT CASE 2.1

BUSINESS INTEGRATION

Linn Products: We Start with the Music . . .

Linn Products was established in 1972 by Ivor Tiefenbrun. Born in Glasgow, he was passionate about two things – engineering, and listening to music. When he couldn't buy a hi-fi good enough to satisfy his needs, he decided to make one himself.

In 1972 Linn introduced the Sondek LP12 turntable, the longest-lived hi-fi product still in production anywhere in the world, and still the benchmark by which all turntables are judged.

Source: ©Igor Bulgarin/Shutterstock

The Linn Sondek LP12 turntable revolutionized the hi-fi industry, proving categorically that the source of the music is the most important component in the hi-fi chain. Linn then set out to make the other components in the hi-fi chain as revolutionary as the first, setting new standards for performance over the years with each new product.

Today, Linn is an independent, precision-engineering company uniquely focused on the design, manufacture and sale of complete music and home theatre systems for customers who want the best. Linn systems can be found throughout the world – in royal residences, and on board super-yachts. In recent years Linn have followed the market, developing the technology to deliver the best equipment in digital streaming with their DSM network music player that can 'stream everything and connect everything'. Although operating at the cutting edge of digital technology Linn also continue to produce their award-winning range of analogue turntables which they proudly boast have been 'unmatched for four decades'.

At Linn, operations is an integrated process, from product development through to after-sales service. All aspects of Linn's products are designed in house, and all the key processes are controlled by Linn people. Linn believes that everything can be improved by human interest and attention to detail. So the same person builds, tests and packs a complete product, from start to finish. They take all the time necessary to ensure that every detail is correct.

Only then will the person responsible for building the product sign it off and pack it for dispatch. Every product can be tracked all the way from that individual to the customer, anywhere in the world. Linn systems are sold only by selected specialist retailers who have a similar commitment to quality products and service.

Question

1. In the production of its goods, Linn does not embrace a traditional Fordist production line philosophy, where numerous workers do very small pieces of the process in a highly controlled environment. Linn relies on skilled, empowered workers, who take responsibility for all aspects of build and test. What are the advantages and disadvantages of this production method?

Sources: www.linn.co.uk; in-company research.

Stop and Think

Most organizations strive for excellence in some way or other. Consider the operational challenges in actually becoming and remaining a world leader.

- *Urgent action:* these elements are critical to the customer, and the competition has a significant advantage, so action must be taken immediately.
- *Excess:* elements in this zone are performing well, but if the importance to the customer is sufficiently low, it may be that excessive effort and resource are being expended. Perhaps some reduction in performance could be accepted, with the associated reduction in cost.

Contingencies in Operations Strategy Generation

Trade-offs

When creating an operations strategy, it must be kept in mind that an operations system can be designed to do some things well but at the expense of others; one element of performance must be traded off against another. This has parallels in other pursuits. For example, in athletics, to achieve a certain speed over a long distance a good marathon runner must trade off the additional strength to be gained from greater muscle mass in favour of lowering the weight to be carried. Or to achieve supersonic flight a jet fighter trades off fuel efficiency in favour of maximum speed.

In operations systems, possible **trade-offs** are:

Trade-offs: factors that cannot exist concurrently in their best state; the optimization of one necessitates a compromise in another.

- *Low cost against available variety:* systems that have to operate at low cost will normally be set up to produce a single (or small number of) variant(s) of a product at high volume. Here the requirement to change the configuration of the production line to manufacture a different variant of product adds cost. This cost may then have to be passed to the customer as an increase in price.

- *Personalized attention against volume of customers:* a call centre, for example, may set time limit targets for its operators. These may specify a maximum call length. Under pressure for time, the call handler may be dismissive with the customer as s/he tries to meet the target, and in acting this way may therefore compromise the service experience from the customer's perspective.

Trade-offs are impossible to ignore. There are, however, two broad views on how to deal with them. The first view accepts the premise of the trade-off. Here effort is applied to gain an understanding of where the operational focus should rest, and then ensure that the element being compromised on is much less important to the customer than the element being prioritized.

The second view rejects the premise of the trade-off and attempts to increase the effectiveness of the operation to allow strong performance on both elements. In our manufacturing example above this may mean reducing the time and cost of the activity required to reconfigure the production line to the point where it has negligible effect on the product's unit cost. This tactic would allow the operation to offer a larger variety of inexpensive products. In our service example this may mean analysing call trends and more effectively harmonizing capacity. In this case, closely matching the number of call-handlers with customer call volume.

The Contribution of Operations to Strategy?

Linking Operations Capability with Strategic Impact

We have proposed that operational activity is the engine that drives the business. Extending this analogy, if 'operations' is the engine, the organization is the vehicle, and strategy is the map and destination, then the performance of the organization is based on the efficiency of the engine and how effectively it drives the organization towards the strategic destination. The efficiency of this operational engine is the concern of Parts 2, 3 and 4 of this book. The concern of this chapter is how effectively the operation aligns with strategy and therefore drives the organization. It is therefore worth spending some time understanding how operations can help the organization to pursue and achieve its strategy.

Figure 2.3 separates operational activity into four categories, each representing a different level of contribution that the operational engine makes in support of the business strategy.

Stage 1: Internal Neutrality

At this basic level, operations does the minimum to support the business. It is not aware of the overall business strategy or of its performance in relation to comparable operations in other organizations or to overall industry

Figure 2.3 The contribution of operations to strategy

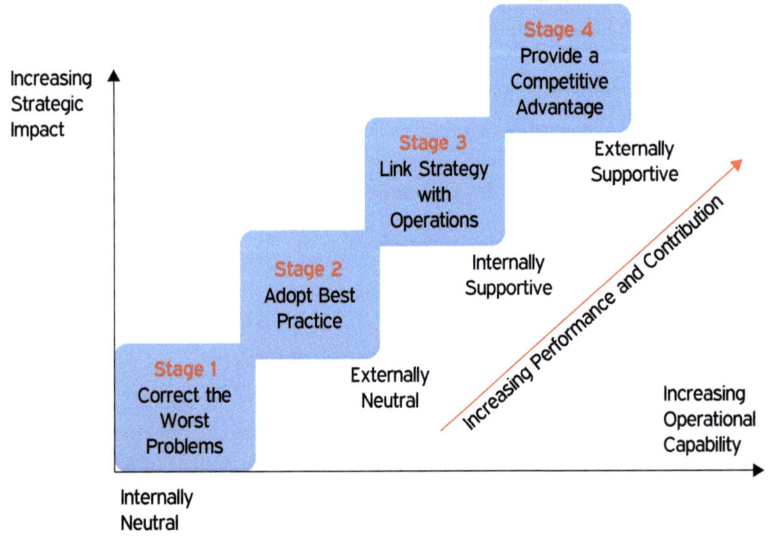

Source: Hayes and Wheelwright (1988).

standards. It is internally facing, aware of neither the environment external to the company nor the other parts of the company. There is little attempt to improve performance, and the view of the rest of the organization is that operations is a source of problems rather than of solutions. Any success achieved by the organization is in spite of operations rather than because of it. From a resource-based viewpoint, a company with an operational engine working at this level has no foundation upon which either to plan or to implement strategy. The perception of senior management when questioned about operations would be that it is inefficient, ineffective, isolated and uncooperative. Operations is an unconscious incompetent, it is performing poorly and is not even aware of it. It is, in effect, preventing the company from achieving its goals.

Stage 2: External Neutrality

To move on from Stage 1, the operational engine must become self-aware, conscious of its own performance limitations. It will do this by gaining an external perspective, and so begin to compare itself with other similar operational units that exist in other companies within the market. This awareness, coupled with management determination to change, will begin to move the operation to a higher level of performance. Initially operations will be consciously incompetent, where performance is poor but recognized as such. Importantly, though, there is a will to change, and a level of performance to aim for. The perception of senior management when questioned about operations would be of a group making some effort and achieving some level of improvement. At this stage operations is neither contributing to, nor detracting from, the achievement of the strategy of the company.

Stage 3: Internally Supportive

Here operations has achieved a level of excellence in terms of the activities that it carries out. It is efficient, and can be relied upon. The key thing is alignment, because at this stage operations has become aware of the business strategy and has aligned itself with it. Operations is effectively mobilizing its now considerable capability in pursuit of the overall business goals. Operations is a conscious competent: good at what it does, and aware of what it needs to do to sustain and improve. Operations will begin to generate its own strategy to guide it in the execution of the activities that are required of it in pursuit of the overall company strategy. It may be that some competitive advantage is achieved. Senior management will be confident in the ability of operations to support the direction that the business takes.

Stage 4: Externally Supportive

This stage resonates most clearly with the resource-based view. Here operations has moved further. The change in state from that achieved in Stage 3 is a subtle but significant one. The level of performance reached at Stage 3 has made it best in class, achieving a competitive advantage, but now at Stage 4 operations is innovating, proactively driving forward towards future markets by creating products and services that are one step ahead of the competition. Here senior management is so confident of operations that it can base future business strategy around it: operations is truly in the driving seat.

! Stop and Think

Corporate strategy should never be developed without taking operations management into consideration. Think about this statement. Do you agree with it?

Operations Contribution and Competencies

BUSINESS INTEGRATION

From a resource-based perspective it is critical that the maturity of operations is clearly understood, because it will be impossible to build a strategy around the creation of operational competencies if the operations of the company are not performing at least at Stage 3 of the Hayes and Wheelwright model. In the language of competencies, Stage 2 can be likened to threshold competencies, where just enough is being done for the organization to be present in the market. Stage 3 moves these threshold competencies forward to become core and perhaps even distinctive. Then, at Stage 4, competitive advantage should be gained, with distinctive competencies achieved that may be coupled with some degree of dynamic capability. All parts of the business are 'joined up', and operations now has the flexibility to alter its shape in response to, or in anticipation of, changing market conditions.

SHORT CASE 2.2

Teekay Corporation: The Marine Midstream Company

Source: ©G-Valeriy/Shutterstock

When you turn on a control on your cooker, gas will flow and ignite on the ring. When you insert the nozzle of a petrol pump into the filler of your car and pull the trigger, petrol flows into the tank. The journeys taken by these fuels from deep underground to kitchens and garage forecourts are generally invisible to us unless an ecological disaster and the resulting news story forces it onto our TV screens. Without energy, though, society would be unable to function. Energy powers industries, fuels transportation systems, and generally improves the quality of our lives. But first, that energy must be moved from where it is produced to where it is consumed. You will probably not have heard of the Teekay Corporation, but it is an essential link in the global energy supply chain. Teekay was founded in 1973 by Torben Karlshoej, whose initials provided the Teekay name. Teekay helps its customers link their upstream energy production seamlessly to their downstream processing operations. Teekay's vision is 'to bring energy to the world'.

Teekay's reputation for safety, quality and innovation has earned it a position as the world's leading marine service company; the strength and flexibility of its fleet create a significant competitive advantage for the corporation, and for its customers. At the heart of operations, multi-functional ship teams are fully responsible for the day-to-day operations of the fleet, with each team focused on a dedicated group of vessels. Every team is equipped to efficiently deliver the entire service process of vessel operations. Supporting these teams are dedicated competence and performance management systems, including centres of excellence with expertise focused on ensuring compliance, continuously improving performance and developing innovative projects and programmes for every aspect of operations, including marine and technical services, health, safety, quality and information technology.

These systems are the foundation of Teekay's service to its customers. Teekay is a company where success is built upon a core competence in seaborne transportation of fuels. For Teekay the performance of its operations must be externally supportive of the overall company strategy. Every effort is therefore made to achieve operational excellence in everything that the company does.

Questions

1. Operational flexibility is often mentioned as something that is desirable to organizations. In the context of the marine shipping operational system what would you consider 'flexibility' to mean?
2. Would speed or dependability be more important to Teekay's customers?

Sources: www.teekay.com; in-company research.

Simplifying Operations Strategy

Generic Strategies

What is clear about strategy-making, at both the corporate and operational levels, is the number and complexity of the decisions that need to be made. Michael Porter (1985) proposed a shortcut in the form of three *generic strategies* that firms could use to achieve competitive advantage:

- *Differentiation:* an emphasis on providing products and services that are different from and more desirable than those offered by the competition
- *Overall cost leadership:* an emphasis on providing a comparative level of utility at a lower cost than the competition
- *Focus:* an emphasis on serving niche markets

These strategies have been criticized somewhat as they are not totally discrete. Each must contain elements of the others: for example, low price alone will not sell a product or service, and a differentiation strategy may result in a greater focus on specific markets. However, although these proposals may break down under scrutiny, from an operations point of view it is useful to think of them as an overall guide to the emphasis that operations must adopt when creating the conversion process.

Value Disciplines

Porter's strategies were developed as a tool to assist higher-level strategy-making, but work has been done to translate similar ideas into the operational arena. Treacy and Wiersema (1993) approached the idea of generic strategies from the viewpoint of value for the customer. They argued that a value proposition is a combination of the elements that the customer wants and will pay for.

Treacy and Wiersema propose three generic operations strategies, or *value disciplines,* that inform the set-up of the operation: operational excellence, product leadership and customer intimacy.

Operational Excellence

The focus here is on the lowest overall cost to the customer. The key point is that the overall cost to the customer does not consist only of the price paid; it includes other intangible costs that the customer may experience, such as the inconvenience levels that result from problems with the product, or the wasted time associated with a poor service. The concept of operational excellence is based upon efficiency. As a result, products and services are standardized, with little variety, as this would have a detrimental impact on the efficiency of the organization.

Operationally the aim is to reduce waste, driving out cost at all opportunities within the conversion process. Growth comes from a constant steady volume of business, companies may also discover new ways to use existing assets, or identify opportunities to deploy their capability into new markets. Operational excellence tends to be at the heart of many service businesses, where high volumes of customers are routinely dealt with. Transport companies such as train operators understand this: customers often prioritize reliability and speed above the aesthetic appeal of the train and the track, and they seldom hold allegiance to one company over another. Banks and other companies that use call-centre-based operations also operate with this model. If the call centre does not work well, frustrated customers will consider taking their business elsewhere.

SHORT CASE 2.3

Serving up a Change: From Production Line to Humanized Robot

BUSINESS INTEGRATION

Source: ©Stefano Mazzola/ShutterStock

It's fair to say we live in a technological age – the latest gadgets, such as iPhones and iPads, dominate the world. The food industry has kept pace with modernity, embracing trends such as fast food and designer meals. However, 'S Baggers restaurant in Nuremberg, Germany, has taken things a step further, by incorporating the latest technology in the process of food delivery.

The proprietor of the restaurant, Michael Mack, decided to remove waiters and staff from the front of house, allowing the humans in the operation to focus on preparing exceptional food. 'S Baggers was the world's first fully automated restaurant. At 'S Baggers you don't need waiters to order food. Customers use touch-screen TVs to read the menu and select their meal. The dishes are delivered over a patented, gravity-fed, conveyor belt system. The inside of the restaurant resembles a theme park rollercoaster ride, with tracks running all the way from the kitchen high up in the roof down to the tables, twisting and turning as they go. The food whizzes down the tracks in little 'cars' to the customers' tables.

Unlike fast-food outlets, in the kitchen it is man, not machine, that makes the food. Everything is prepared from fresh ingredients, with high-quality dining in mind. When it is ready, the meal is given a sticker in a colour to match the customer's seat, and dispatched downhill to the correct table. As an operations strategy this allows 'S Baggers to combine the quality inherent in a meal prepared by a fully skilled chef with the low cost and convenience associated with a fully mechanized delivery system.

While at one time production line automation such as that used in 'S Baggers seemed newfangled and exciting, in the last 10 years restaurants have moved beyond this type of automation and are now deploying humanized robots to deliver the food. One of the first of these is the Dalu Robot Restaurant in Jinan City in China which opened in 2010. In Robot Restaurant robot waiters never get tired, bored or annoyed, they always deliver a reliable, repeatable and consistent service experience.

Questions

1. What do you think are the disadvantages of removing people from the process of serving food?
2. Do the advantages of the low-cost mechanized system outweigh the disadvantages?

Sources: www.sbaggers.de; www.designboom.com.

Product Leadership

The focus here is on the ability to make products and deliver services that customers quickly recognize as superior. Innovation is key and this relies on the talents and creativity of employees. Therefore, research and development is the operational focus in the pursuit of the next breakthrough.

Markets must be educated when breakthrough products and services are developed because customers must realize their potential value before they can be expected to buy them. Once educated, customers are willing to pay premium prices for these products. Intangible value here may be found in the social acceptance gained from buying a leading brand or the lifestyle that is associated with owning the product or using the service. From an operations perspective a flexible structure, with the ability to focus resources on the most successful projects is key. High-technology offerings, such as the iPhone or the latest games console, must be the leading product in their arena or the discerning customer will move on to the 'next big thing'. High-quality items such as Rolex watches or branded jewellery must similarly be seen as the 'best-in-class', or the customer will move on to another class.

Customer Intimacy

The aim in this value discipline is to offer a total solution to the customer. The value is therefore primarily in the overall service offered, of which the product may only be a part. Customer-intimate organizations form strong relationships with their customers. They focus on learning as much as possible about their customers' business, and ensure that they can serve them in the most effective way. The services on offer are tailored to customer requirements, to ensure that the client feels that they receive the best experience available. Such organizations exploit their customer relationships to ensure that they achieve the full revenue potential from each client. In some cases the customer may become dependent upon a supplier organization for their service. The development of such relationships results in these organizations taking on the responsibilities of their clients, with the aim that the two parties will achieve mutual success.

Operationally, all departments must be aligned to provide a total solution, as employees are required to adapt to the changing needs of the customer. All companies have some sort of relationship with their customers, but supply chains in some industries lend themselves more easily to this strategy. For example, large engineering and construction companies have recently discovered the utility of this strategy – partnering arrangements between governments and large engineering contractors in the procurement of defence equipment such as planes and submarines create a seamless relationship. Here success is based on knowing their customer better than they know themselves, predicting new requirements, managing their risks, and proactively solving their problems.

Value Matrix

Martinez and Bititci (2001, 2006) developed the value disciplines further in their model called the **value matrix**. This is based on the proposal that there are organizations that have the same value proposition (operational excellence, product leader or customer intimacy), but differ in their operational configuration.

Value matrix: a framework of generic operations strategies called value propositions that informs the set-up of the operation.

The value matrix therefore introduces *hard* and *soft* factors that provide further focus on how the overall operational strategy can be implemented by the organization. Hard characteristics are based on the technology used whereas soft characteristics are based on intangible activities (Table 2.2).

- *Innovators:* invest significantly in the R&D function of the business in their pursuit of breakthrough products. Operationally, they aim to reduce the time-to-market of their products, and dedicate resources to educating their potential markets. The customers of innovative organizations are prepared to pay premium prices for such products, expecting them to be technologically superior to any other comparable product.
- *Brand managers:* invest in the brand of their products by creating a status that becomes associated with their brand name. They achieve this with a mix of physical and non-physical attributes. The operational focus of brand managers is the market, developing streamlined distribution channels and fast delivery. The markets of brand managers often pay premium prices to gain the status that accompanies the product, so achieving social acceptance or recognition.
- *Price minimizers:* aim to offer products to their customers at the lowest price. They do so by operating a low-cost facility that is dedicated to optimizing efficiency. The customers of such organizations focus primarily on the price, combined with a just acceptable offering of product functions and features, when making purchasing decisions.
- *Simplifiers:* attempt to make the buying process accessible and convenient for their customers. This involves the coordination of production and distribution activities. Here it is about removing the 'middle-men'. Customers who buy products from simplifiers seek a purchasing process that is straightforward, and requires little input.
- *Technological integrators:* tailor their offerings to customer requirements. They have a wide variety of skills as it is their capability that allows them to adapt to consumer demands. These organizations tend to have selection criteria for their customers on the basis that they will form long-term relationships with them, presenting the potential for repeat business.

Table 2.2 The value matrix

	Hard	Soft
Product leadership	Innovators: • Customers buy new products never seen before, and value advanced technology applied in new devices • Google and Tesla	Brand managers: • Customers pay a premium for the status brought by the product, and value the feelings of superiority and well-being that it brings • Rolex and Mercedes
Operational excellence	Price minimizers: • Customers buy ordinary products, and value adequate performance at low prices • Kia and Aldi	Simplifiers: • Customers buy convenience at a relatively low price, and value easy-to-do business transactions. • Ryanair and Amazon
Customer intimacy	Technological integrators • Customers buy tailored products and services configured to their needs; they value total care • IBM and Cisco Systems	Socializers: • Customers buy flexible service, and value good relationships • Automobile Association and First Direct Bank

Source: Martinez and Bititci (2001).

- *Socializers:* offer a flexible service to customers, who have confidence in the ability of the organization. The customer seeks a reliable service and trusts the organization to deliver its offering, fulfilling the standards set by previous experiences of the organization and so perpetuating the relationship.

Although the value disciplines, like Porter's generic strategies, could be criticized for being rather vague in scope, they are useful when making decisions about operations strategy. Externally they help us to focus closely on a single market segment or customer group and how they expect to be treated, and internally they inform our thinking about the configuration of operational activity needed to deliver this treatment.

CRITICAL PERSPECTIVE

Value for All

Operations strategy, by its nature, is narrower in scope than corporate strategy. Indeed, until very recently the operations function was considered to be totally inward-facing, concentrating completely on what went on 'within the factory', with little concern about the external environment, because what went on in the outside world was the domain of the external-facing functions such as marketing. The increasing scope of what is considered operations, and the dominant role that operational activity now plays within the firm, necessitates some consideration of the impact of the way operations does its work. The matrix shown in Table 2.3 demonstrates that operations must be responsible for more than just the creation of value for the customer in the most efficient way, as the generation of the value proposition must necessarily take into account the concept of value for all.

Table 2.3 External value matrix

	Financial	Strategic	Social
Country	• GDP impact	• Employment • Intellectual capital	• Environmental impact
Investors	• Return • Growth	• Sustainability	• Ethics
Employees	• Wages • Pensions	• Career progression • Lifelong learning	• Personal development • Working conditions

Source: Adapted from Livesey (2006).

The key point is ...

that organizations have responsibilities for adding value to society as a whole, and this must be taken into consideration within the process of generating operations strategy.

Product life cycle: generalized model of the buying behaviour of customers over time; used to predict demand for a product or service.

Product/Service Life Cycle Model

Similar to the previously mentioned generic strategies and value disciplines the product life cycle model allows us to simplify operations strategy making. However, in this case simplification can be found by looking at how markets change over time.

The **product life cycle** model, originally formulated by Vernon (1966), and illustrated in Figure 2.4 is an attempt to generalize customer behaviour over the lifetime of a product. From an operations perspective, it is important to have some appreciation of how the life-cycle plays out in your market. As we can see from Table 2.4, at each stage the operations strategy may have to alter to concentrate on specific order-winning criteria as they change throughout the duration of the life-cycle.

Figure 2.4 Product life cycle

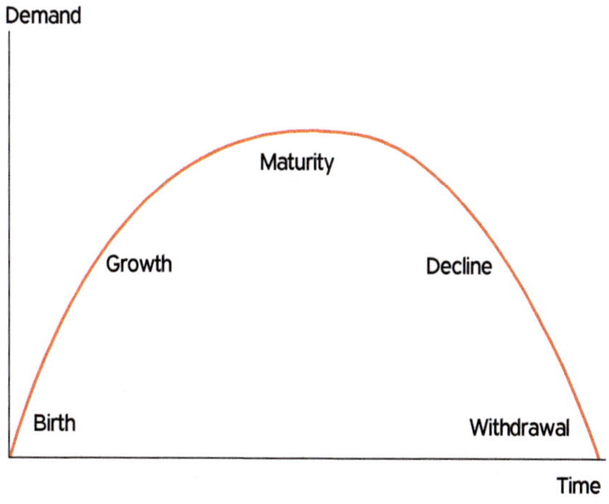

Table 2.4 Product life-cycle: common features at each stage

	Birth	Growth	Maturity	Decline
Description	Product/service just introduced to market	Product/service gains acceptance	Market saturates with product/service	Alternatives become available
Volume	Low	Increases rapidly	Level	Declines rapidly
Order winners	Functionality, capability and reputation	Availability and quality	Cost and dependability	Cost
Customers	Innovators	Early adopters	Main market	Late adopters

Contemporary Thinking: Servitization

The concept of operations strategy, or manufacturing strategy as it was known initially, was born out of work done by Skinner (1966, 1969, 1971, 1974) as he attempted to understand what was wrong with US manufacturing firms as they struggled to compete in the international market. Broadly, Skinner concluded that production performance in the US was sub-optimized in two ways. First, it was fixated on Taylorist methods which, although useful, were becoming outdated and somewhat inflexible, and second, it rarely tied in neatly with the overall strategy of the firm.

As time moved on and the tools and techniques that are associated with operations management became increasingly common in arenas other than manufacturing, the terminology changed in favour of the label operations strategy: a phrase more easily applicable to all industry sectors.

Though still traditionally associated with the manufacture of tangible products, the tools and techniques of operations management are now recognized as equally applicable to the delivery of intangible services. Furthermore, we now recognize that products and services are not discrete, they lie on a continuum with tangible products occupying one end and intangible services the other. This 'product-service continuum' shown in Figure 2.5 has forced manufacturing firms to rethink how they structure and compose their value propositions.

Most companies exist somewhere in the middle of the continuum between pure product and pure service. Pure service companies do exist, for example professional practices such as legal and accounting firms. Most companies these days are a combination of product and service provider. A restaurant is considered as a service, but it is supported by the manufacture of food products; and the entertainment experience provided by a cinema would not be possible without the production of a film. Most consumer goods are products that are wrapped in a service package. Ironically, pure product companies are the most difficult to define, because most products need some form of service and support.

Figure 2.5 Product service continuum

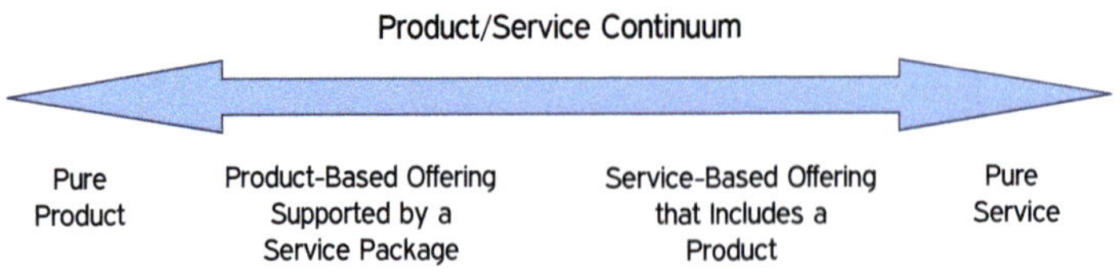

In business-to-consumer relationships, examples of products that don't need support might be fully disposable products such as razor blades, for example, or a child's balloon; here the support element is limited to disposal, an activity that is often taken care of by societal infrastructure rather than the supplying company. In business-to-business transactions all physical products, even relatively simple ones such as machined parts, must be supported by some sort of repair or replacement service as defined by legislation and encouraged by accepted quality management practice.

The historical convention has been for manufacturing firms to regard services as add-ons with end-user value generally considered to reside in the features and functions of the physical good (Gebauer and Friedli, 2005). Vandermerwe and Rada (1988) introduced the term 'servitization' to describe how manufacturing firms began to recognize the need to provide extra value in the form of add-on services such as maintenance, support and financing. This can be seen most easily in the automotive industry where consumers increasingly buy transport solutions. The car, which is now rarely owned by the customer, is only a part of a solution that includes a finance package, a maintenance programme, a roadside assistance scheme and (often) options on insurance.

Servitization is now an operations strategy in itself. Recent studies (see Kindström and Kowalkowski, 2015) have suggested that manufacturers may even be adopting servitization as a business model moving from basic product-oriented services toward more customized, process-oriented ones, and ultimately to the provision of end-to-end solutions based on product-service bundles. A servitization strategy can therefore help manufacturers avoid cost-based competition especially when differentiation can no longer be achieved through aspects of the tangible product.

However, for servitization to succeed as an operations strategy for manufacturing firms, changes must be made to how they work. Operationally, a firm's service activity must change from simply making sure the customer uses their tangible product properly, to making sure the product-service bundle fulfils the customer's needs. Commercially, the relationship must move from a product-orientated, often short-term, transactional arrangement to a solutions-oriented, longer-term, strategic arrangement.

Studies have classified three different types of servitization strategy (Cusumano *et al.*, 2015). The addition of 'Smoothing' services helps to regularize and control sales. The addition of 'Adapting' services expands the functionality of the product or assists customers in using the product in new ways. And finally the addition of 'Substituting' services makes the outright purchase of the product unnecessary.

Manufacturers are motivated to servitize for a number of reasons. These include competitive pressures that stem from the need to differentiate a mature product by adding services; demand-based forces driven by customers who may want to outsource some non-core activities; and economic factors such as the need to find a new source of revenue by accessing the often more profitable service market. Martinez *et al.* (2017), when studying how servitization as a strategy is generated, found that it was an emergent process with both market and resource-based considerations contributing to the eventual shape of the solution.

Servitization therefore both highlights another step in the evolution of operations management and illustrates the importance of a robust process for generating operations strategy.

Summary

In this chapter we have built on the content of Chapter 1 by relating strategic thinking to the operations management of organizations. We have defined what operations strategy is and presented a model that can be used to make sense of the activity required to generate an operations strategy.

We have proposed that one of the main purposes of generating an operations strategy is to define the required performance of the operation and we have introduced five generic performance objectives, quality, time, cost, dependability and flexibility, that will help guide thinking in relation to this. Further, we proposed that performance must be considered in relation to the market's order-winning and order-qualifying criteria. When considering the performance of operational systems we explained that often it is difficult to optimize all aspects of performance and therefore trade-offs are required where one aspect of performance needs to be compromised in order to optimize another.

We then went on to explain that conceptually the operations capability of an organization must be optimized to deliver the best strategic impact to help the firm meet its overall objectives.

Finally, we suggested that operations strategy-making could be simplified by following one, or a combination, of generic strategies and value propositions.

The intention here is to present strategic activity as a seamless process connecting the objectives set at the highest level with the activity that occurs at the lowest. Only by achieving this linkage can the organization take full advantage of its competencies, and achieve the standard of performance that it needs to create and maintain competitive advantage.

Key Theories

The key theories discussed in this chapter were:

- **The five generic performance objectives** – those aspects that customers value most and therefore must be delivered by the operation. These include quality, speed, cost, dependability and flexibility.
- **Order-winning and order-qualifying criteria** – those features that customers see as the key reasons to buy or not to buy a product or service.
- **Performance profiling and prioritizing** – the process of measuring the performance of the operation against that of the competition to identify what improvements must be carried out to create an advantage.
- **Operational trade-offs** – the prioritizing of important performance objectives over those that are less important.
- **The product life cycle** – the five stages that a product will pass through from the point of introduction to the point of withdrawal. These are birth, growth, maturity, decline, and withdrawal. Each stage requires a change of emphasis in operations strategy.
- **Value propositions** – those generic operations strategies that help focus the process of strategy-making to create competence in specific areas. The six propositions introduced are innovators, brand managers, price minimizers, simplifiers, technological integrators and socializers.

Suggested Answers to Stop and Think Questions

1. **World-leading operations:** Most markets are occupied by numerous companies, all attempting to gain the greatest share. The pace of technological change creates a challenge, because it is making it increasingly difficult to gain a leadership position and, more importantly, maintain it because a new process or device may soon be invented that will displace the previous best, either by direct replacement or by substitution. Communication and information availability creates a challenge as it helps to distribute best practice, and so creates a more level operational playing field: for example, Japanese manufacturing methods are no longer confined to Japan. Another challenge is presented by mobility of labour, as this means that companies can bid for the best people regardless of location, so removing the employee skill and knowledge advantage.
2. **Corporate strategy:** It could be argued that no corporate strategy should be devised without a good understanding of the core operational competencies of the business, and how well they are executed. The resource-based view prioritizes core competencies, arguing that a company should develop capability and then find markets that will allow them to succeed, whereas the market-based view prioritizes finding a market, and then working out how to be successful in it. Whichever way strategy is approached, little success will be gained without an efficient and effective operational engine driving the business.

connect

Review Questions

1. Explain what each of the five generic performance objectives represents.
2. Explain the difference between order winners and order qualifiers.
3. In relation to the product life-cycle describe some characteristics of the operational system used to produce a product in its mature phase.
4. Explain how flexibility of service and speed of service might require a trade-off decision.
5. Briefly describe the four stages in the Hayes and Wheelwright model of operations contribution.

Discussion Questions

1. Reflect on the value disciplines – do they seem relevant to the companies that you are familiar with?
2. In relation to a company that you are familiar with define how each of the five generic performance objectives might be used.
3. Consider Hayes and Wheelwright's four-stage model – how could this be used to shape a performance improvement plan for your operation?
4. Consider the concept of trade-offs. What trade-offs might a police force have to think about when planning its operational activity?
5. Discuss the product life-cycle model – do you think it is as relevant today as it was when it was first conceived in the 1960s?

Further Reading

Hayes, R., Pisano, G., Upton, D. and Wheelwright, S.C. (2005) *Operations Strategy and Technology: Pursuing the Competitive Edge,* Wiley, Hoboken, NJ.

Mirzaei, N. E., Fredriksson, A., & Winroth, M. (2016). Strategic consensus on manufacturing strategy content: Including the operators' perceptions. *International Journal of Operations & Production Management,* **36**(4), 429–466.

Rajala, R., Brax, S. A., Virtanen, A., & Salonen, A. (2019). The next phase in servitization: Transforming integrated solutions into modular solutions. *International Journal of Operations & Production Management,* **39**(5), 630–657.

Skinner, W. (2007) 'Manufacturing strategy: The story of its evolution', *Journal of Operations Management,* **25**(2), 328–335.

Treacy, M. and Wiersema, F. (1996) *The Discipline of Market Leaders,* HarperCollins, London.

Waters, D. (2006) *Operations Strategy,* Thomson, London.

Wortman, B. (2005) 'Value changing behaviour: getting the habit', *Journal of Business Strategy,* **26**(4), 38–45.

References

Bounty, I., Gomez, M.L. and Chia, R. (2019) 'Strategy emergence as wayfinding', *Management,* **22**(3), 438–465.

Chia, R. (2017) 'A process-philosophical understanding of organizational learning as "wayfinding": process, practices and sensitivity to environmental affordances', *Learning Organization,* **24**(2), 107–118.

Cusumano, M.A., Kahl, S.J., and Suarez, F.F. (2015) 'Services, industry evolution, and the competitive strategies of product firms', *Strategic Management Journal,* **36,** 559–575.

Gebauer, H. and Friedli, T. (2005) 'Behavioural implications of the transition process from products to services', *Journal of Business and Industrial Marketing,* **20**(2), 70–80.

Hayes, R.H. and Wheelwright, S.C. (1988) *Restoring our Competitive Edge: Competing through Manufacturing,* Wiley, New York.

Hill, T. (1993) *Manufacturing Strategy: Text and Cases,* Macmillan, London.

Kindström, D. and Kowalkowski, C. (2015) 'Service-driven business model innovation: organizing the shift from a product based to a service-centric business model', in N. Foss and T. Saebi (Eds.), *Business Model Innovation: The Organizational Dimension,* Oxford University Press, Oxford.

Livesey, F. (2006) *Defining High Value Manufacturing,* University of Cambridge Institute for Manufacturing, Cambridge.

Lowson, R.H. (2002) *Strategic Operations Management: The New Competitive Advantage,* Routledge, London.

Martinez, V. and Bititci, U. (2001) 'The value matrix and its evolution', *Proceedings of the 8th International EurOMA Conference: What Really Matters in Operations Management,* Bath, UK, pp. 118–130.

Martinez, V. and Bititci, U. (2006) 'Aligning value propositions in supply chains', *International Journal of Value Chain Management,* **1**(1), 6–19.

Martinez, V., Neely, A., Velu, C., Leinster-Evans, S. and Bisessar, D. (2017) 'Exploring the journey to services', *International Journal of Production Economics,* **192,** 66–80.

Platts, K.W. and Gregory, M.J. (1990) 'Manufacturing audit in the process of strategy formulation', *International Journal of Operations and Production Management,* **10**(9), 5–26.

Porter, M.E. (1985) *Competitive Advantage: Creating and Sustaining Superior Performance,* The Free Press, New York.

Skinner, W. (1966) 'Production under pressure', *Harvard Business Review,* November/December, 139–146.

Skinner, W. (1969) 'Manufacturing – missing link in corporate strategy', *Harvard Business Review,* May–June, 136–145.

Skinner, W. (1971) 'Anachronistic factory', *Harvard Business Review,* (January), 61–70.

Skinner, W. (1974) 'Decline, fall, and renewal of manufacturing plants', *Industrial Engineering,* **6**(10), 32–38.

Slack, N. and Lewis, M. (2017) *Operations Strategy,* Prentice Hall, Upper Saddle River, NJ.

Slack, N., Chambers, S. and Johnston, R. (2007) *Operations Management,* Prentice Hall, Harlow.

Treacy, M. and Wiersema, F. (1993) 'Customer intimacy and other value disciplines', *Harvard Business Review,* **71**(1), 84–94.

Vandermerwe, S. and Rada, J. (1988) 'Servitization of business: Adding value by adding service', *European Management Journal,* **6**(4), 314–324.

Vernon, R. (1966) 'International investment and international trade in the product cycle', *Quarterly Journal of Economics,* **80**(2), 190–207.

3 Innovation

Learning Outcomes

After reading this chapter you should be able to:

- Define what innovation is within the context of operations management
- Identify different types of innovation
- Distinguish between the process of innovation and the outcome of the innovation process
- Discuss where innovations come from
- Appreciate the importance of innovation to contemporary organizations

Four Revolutions of Innovation

The 1st Industrial Revolution

The term Industrial Revolution can be traced to 1799, when it was used in a letter by French envoy Louis-Guillaume Otto, announcing France had entered the race to industrialize. However, it wasn't until 1881 that the term was popularized by the English historian Arnold Toynbee in reference to the economic development of Britain in the late-18th and early-19th centuries.

Source: ©a-image/Shutterstock

Technological Innovation

The Industrial Revolution was driven by innovation. Product innovations such as the steam engine provided the power to mechanize. The steam engine was itself the result of a number of innovations. In 1712, British ironmonger Thomas Newcomen combined the ideas of engineer Thomas Savery and physicist Denis Papin, to invent a steam powered engine for use in mines. In the 1760s James Watt, a Scottish instrument maker, improved on Newcomen's engine with four innovations; a separate condenser allowing the engine to work constantly without pausing to reheat the cylinder; the double-action piston that delivered power on both downward and upward strokes; gearing to translate the 'to-and-fro' motion into rotary motion; and finally a centrifugal governor that maintained a constant engine speed despite varying loads. Interestingly, this governor marks the early beginnings of automation, as it results in an engine that is essentially self-regulating.

Steam power enabled rapid industrialization. Textiles became the dominant industry of the time. In the 18th century in Britain, cotton output overtook that of wool. This was partly due to production advantages such as ease of washing and colouring but mainly due to innovations in spinning technology where the main challenge had been to create a subtle mechanized device for pulling and twisting the cotton fibre just the right amount to create strong thread. The invention of the Spinning Jenny by James Hargreaves in 1764 solved this problem.

Did you know: Though one of the first to modernize, the textiles industry is actually one of the oldest in the world. It is thought that the Indo Saraswat civilization started cultivating cotton around 2500 BCE.

Social innovation

While technology and manufacturing are most often commented on, the Industrial Revolution also laid the foundation for the subsequent spread of capitalism and its emergence as the dominant logic for organizing economic activity. Capitalism refers to an economic system based upon private ownership of the means of production. During the 1st Industrial Revolution factory owners rapidly became rich and, with a large working population that felt exploited under these few wealthy capitalists, social tensions gradually increased. These tensions fed the innovative thinking that resulted in socialism. Socialism, as a system of economic organization, advocates shared ownership of the means of production. The most influential socialist thinker was undoubtedly the German economist and philosopher Karl Marx. Marx spent time in England critiquing the capitalist system that the Industrial Revolution had created. His ideas challenged the foundations of the capitalist world, inspiring uprisings against this model.

Did you know: Karl Marx is buried in London's Highgate cemetery: a cemetery that, ironically, charges an entrance fee. Would this form of capitalism see Marx turning in his grave?

Climate damage

Unfettered capitalism allowed firms to shape the landscape and this had a detrimental effect on the environment. Mechanization required energy and fossil fuels were burned, resulting in air pollution. Forests and farmlands were cleared to make room for infrastructure. Chemical discharge and untreated waste were dumped in waterways leading to early environmental catastrophes like the Great Stink of 1858 when hot weather exacerbated the smell of untreated effluent on the River Thames.

Reassuringly, interest in preserving our planet is not new; increasing political pressure from the emerging urban middle-class led to innovative legislation in the form of the first environmental laws, such as Britain's Alkali Acts (1863), to regulate air pollution.

Did you know: As industrializing economies mature, their CO_2 output tends to reduce as service industries replace manufacturing.

2nd and 3rd Industrial Revolutions

An economic recession occurred from the late 1830s to the early 1840s when the adoption of the original innovations of the 1st Industrial Revolution slowed. Economic growth began again around 1870 driven by a new group of innovations in process, such as mass production, and infrastructure, such as electrical grid systems. It could be argued that this, what is termed the 2nd Industrial Revolution, continues today as process innovation is still central to modern industry.

Then, later in the mid-20th century, another epoch began with the invention of electronics. The transistor, invented in the Bell Laboratories in 1947 (based on principles patented by Austro-Hungarian physicist Julius Lilienfeld in 1925), evolved into integrated circuits at Fairchild Semiconductors and was then embodied in the first commercial single-chip microprocessor, the Intel 4004 in 1971. These innovations brought the age of computers and telecommunications. This 3rd Industrial Revolution produced further automation in production thanks to three further innovations: programmable control, robotics and information technology.

Did you know: The first Intel 4004 microprocessor had around 2,300 transistors; today, microprocessors can be manufactured with many billions.

4th Industrial Revolution

It could be argued that the 1st Industrial Revolution used water and steam to mechanize manufacturing, the 2nd used electricity to create mass production and the 3rd used electronics and information technology to automate all aspects of business. Each had profound effects on society. Today, a 4th Industrial Revolution is underway that is characterized by the merging of technologies and the blurring of lines between the physical, virtual and biological, leading to combined impacts that are even more exciting than the capabilities any single technology represents. Artificial intelligence is augmenting processes and skill, neuro-technology is challenging the frontiers of human biology and smart materials are redefining how we perceive the physical world.

This latest revolution has the potential to be the most impactful yet, driven not by a small number of core innovations but characterized by a multitude of concurrent and interlinked innovations. Product life-cycles are shortening as new technologies are being developed and implemented at an increasingly rapid pace. Is innovation spiralling out of control? Is there a general sense of anticipation of forthcoming disaster? If innovations in the traditionally conservative and established service industries such as finance and law have already led to crises such as the credit crunch, what other catastrophes may be coming along?

Previous industrial revolutions have had both positive and negative impacts on humanity. Nations have become wealthier and technologies have helped reduce disease and create safer societies. However, the inability to fairly distribute economic benefits and to anticipate unintended consequences has resulted in global challenges. Economists Erik Brynjolfsson and Andrew McAfee have suggested the 4th Industrial Revolution could yield greater inequality. The substitution of automation for labour in activity beyond purely manual work might exacerbate the gap between social classes. However, it is also possible that this displacement will result in an increase in better paid and more rewarding jobs.

Are we, the stewards of the 21st century, in a position intellectually and socially to shape this current Industrial Revolution? Are we better equipped to maximize the benefit and minimize the harm than those in the late 18th century? Our responsibilities to one another and our ability to positively affect society are bound to and shaped by the innovations of the 4th Industrial Revolution. This revolution is an opportunity to unite, to create economies that are stable and to reduce inequality. Will society be the victim? Or can we develop and govern technologies in ways that nurture a more sustainable society built around a shared understanding of the common good and a commitment to inter-generational responsibility? Do we control innovation or does it control us? This is the core question that overshadows the 4th Industrial Revolution.

Introduction

A stand can be made against invasion by an army; no stand can be made against invasion by an idea.

Victor Hugo, *History of Crime* (1852)

Innovation, it would seem, is a poor fit with operations management. The term 'managed innovation' reads as almost oxymoronic. Operations management is concerned with creating order, reducing variation, ensuring reliable, consistent and repeatable process. Innovation, by its nature, is chaotic and random. Ideas are unpredictable and difficult to plan and when they come, they are difficult to control.

Most of what we see in our society is in some way a product of innovation. For most of history the act of innovating has been disordered: chance discoveries leading to inventions that emerged from a process of disjointed activity. Yet innovation is arguably one of the few sources of competitive advantage left to companies, and to harness it they must develop processes to help them innovate as efficiently as possible. So, despite the apparent uneasy fit, responsibility for innovation lies very much in the arena of operations management. Therefore the challenge that operations managers face is to shape the inherent randomness associated with innovation into a consistent and robust innovation process.

The Industrial Revolutions are packed full of stories of innovation in technology, product and process. More recently, disordered and isolated innovative activity has made way for innovation that has appeared as the managed product of integrated teams working within funded research groups. However, throughout history, the common theme has been a combination of customer-driven market pull and technology-driven industrial push.

The purpose of this chapter is to briefly explore the nature of innovation, investigate how it happens and examine how it can be encased within frameworks that allow us to manage effectively and (hopefully) efficiently as part of our operational activity.

This chapter will begin by defining what innovation is, before exploring where innovation comes from. It will go on to analyse the role of innovation within the organization, the factors that encourage it, and the processes that can be used to manage it.

CRITICAL PERSPECTIVE

Innovation out of Control

It could be concluded that the first industrial revolution set us on the path to climate catastrophe and subsequently many high-profile climate-bothering innovations have reached the market that, quite simply, should not have. One of the most prolific innovators of the 20th century is a man most people may never have heard of. Thomas Midgley Jr (1889–1944) was an American mechanical engineer turned chemist. It could be said that Midgley has had more negative impact on the atmosphere than any other single organism in Earth's history. Midgley held over 100 patents, one of his most 'successful' being chlorofluorocarbons (CFCs), the ozone-layer-depleting chemicals that found their way into most aerosols and many other applications. As if this gigantic mis-step was not enough, and with an astonishing talent for the unfortunate, Midgley also developed the tetra-ethyl lead (TEL) additive to gasoline that creates highly toxic exhaust fumes. He was celebrated at the time for his discoveries, but today his legacy is seen as a bit more mixed.

However, there is something of a cautious happy ending developing in relation to the CFC debacle. The international treaty 'The Montreal Protocol on Substances that Deplete the Ozone' was signed in 1987 by 24 countries. To date it has been signed by 197. Activity in line with it is gradually eliminating the production and consumption of ozone depleting substances and it is considered by many to be the most successful environmental global action to date. Due to this phasing out of CFCs it is predicted that by 2050 the hole in the ozone layer above Antarctica will reduce to pre-1980 levels. Does this provide hope that mankind can solve the growing crop of current environmental issues such as CO_2 emissions and plastic waste?

The key point is ...

that it is important to harness and control the innovation process, without unnecessarily strangling it, or the law of unintended consequences may prevail.

The Nature of Innovation

Capital isn't so important in business. Experience isn't so important. You can get both these things. What is important is ideas. If you have ideas, you have the main assets you need, and there isn't any limit to what you can do with your business and your life.

Harvey S. Firestone (1868–1938)

Although this chapter deals with an operational process, it is different from most of the others in this book in that it is concerned with a concept that is immediately recognizable in some way to us all. We are constantly confronted with innovation in our daily lives. It is everywhere. It is a lazy salesman's first and last choice of label for all 'new' products and services. The word is almost made valueless by its ubiquity.

Most people, if asked what innovation is, would probably say something like 'the act of coming up with something new'. This definition is close to what is contained in most dictionaries. For our purposes, though, more precision is necessary, and we can find it in this early definition provided by Van de Ven (1986: 591):

Innovation is a new idea, which may be the recombination of old ideas, a scheme that challenges present order, a formula, or a unique approach which is perceived as new by the individuals involved.

It is worth considering this statement further. Innovation is closely associated with the idea of newness, but we need to look at what 'new' actually means. 'New as the recombination of old ideas' is possibly the most common manifestation of innovation today. The engineering used to design and produce cars has evolved over the last 100 or so years, but much recent innovation has been in the mixing of existing technologies into different packages that can be used in the automotive application. The satellite navigation system is a good example of this. Although it was considered innovative when it was introduced by car-makers in the early 21st century, there was little that was actually new. The silicon chip and database software that provide the memory had been common for many years in IT applications; the liquid crystal display used for information presentation had been around in many audio-visual products; and the satellite system that provides the positional information had been operating in the aerospace industry since the late 1970s. Indeed the electric cars that are currently being developed with so much enthusiasm are in fact based on principles that date back to the 1830s.

For industry a broader and more practical understanding, which takes into consideration the popularity of 'repackaging', has been helpfully provided by the UK Department of Trade and Industry's Innovation Unit in 2004: it simply states that 'innovation is the successful exploitation of new ideas'.

To achieve this exploitation, operations managers Isaksen and Tidd (2006) add that innovation must be concerned with the organizational systems and tools necessary to translate ideas into new processes, products, services or businesses.

Innovation: Strategy, Process and Outcome

Now that we have a grasp of the term 'innovation', we need to consider how it is embodied in organizations. There are three separate concepts that we need to understand when thinking about how innovation happens:

- *Innovation as a strategy:* the decisions that are made about the development of capabilities that allow the organization to exploit gaps in the market or identify new market niches
- *Innovation as a process:* the sequence of steps and activities that need to happen to generate an idea and turn it into something that can be sold for profit
- *Innovation as an outcome:* the feature that is new and different that can be sold as a differentiator. These **innovation outcomes** can be categorized in four ways: *product, process, paradigm* and *position.*

Innovation outcome the output that is new or different.

Innovation as a Strategy

Chapter 2, p55

In Chapter 2 we looked at how operations strategy can be thought of as a pattern of decisions that shape the long-term capability of the organization. Here, more specifically, we are dealing with those decisions that are taken as part of the making of operations strategy that pertain to the organization's capability to innovate. From a strategic perspective three rather broad factors tend to influence an organization's capability to innovate. First, the external system that supports innovation within which the organization is embedded. This is important as the extent and structure of this system largely determines the resources that can be called upon by the organization. Short Case 3.5 describes the system that is being built within the UK to support innovation. Second, the internal resources that the organization contains. These resources tend to be thought of as tangibles such as process and knowledge, however, Isaksen and Tidd (2006) also identify intangibles such as inspirational and inclusive leadership and a creative and open climate. Third, the organization's position within its value chain(s) or, more specifically, how much power does it hold in relation to other participants. This is important as it determines its ability to exploit external resources and sources of innovation. Working collaboratively with external stakeholders is becoming more important and this will be discussed in more detail later in this chapter.

Innovation as a Process

In simple terms this can be viewed as a filter where ideas are gathered, channelled and focused before those ideas with potential are selected. This is shown in Figure 3.1. The beginning of the process is the generation of an idea, and this stage is necessarily random and disordered (the source of ideas will be discussed later). The key here is to create order from this randomness as quickly as possible. To do this, resources and effort are applied to these high-potential

Figure 3.1 The general process of innovation

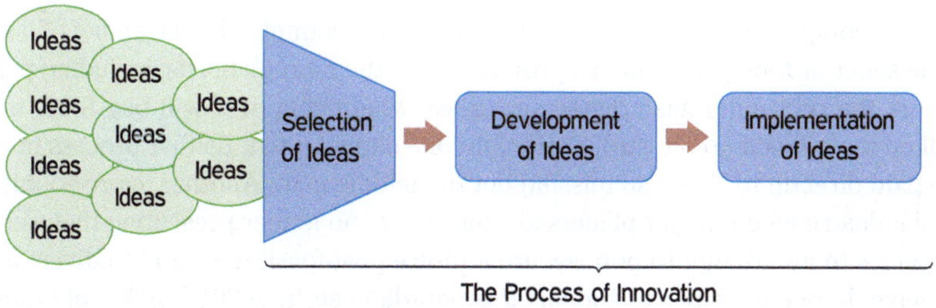

Source: Developed from Tidd and Bessant (2009).

ideas to develop them into something that can be sold as a differentiator. Each idea must be assessed for its practicality, in other words can it be done? And for its commercial potential, in other words, will it make money?

The high-potential ideas are then selected for further work. These 'lucky' selected ideas will go through a process of design to develop the concepts further. If this is successful, and no problems are encountered, the ideas can be implemented within the company's portfolio of offerings.

The same process steps will always occur, but their duration and complexity will vary, depending on the idea and its potential application. For example, an idea for a new product based on a new technology may require a high level of R&D effort to bring it to the point of market implementation, whereas an idea for repositioning an existing product in the market may require only a refocused sales effort.

Outcomes of Innovation: The Four Ps

Product Innovations

These are changes in the things that the organization offers for sale. We said in Chapter 1 that products can be either physical goods, such as cars and phones, or intangible service offerings, such as finance or transport. An innovation in a physical product would be a change in a function or feature, for example the incorporation of a global positioning system in a sports watch such as the Garmin Forerunner to allow accurate speed and distance to be measured when training. In relation to a service, it might for example be the incorporation of the facility to check in online for a flight. Such innovations enhance the utility of the physical product or the service offering, making the customer more likely to buy them.

Chapter 1, p23

Process Innovations

These are changes in the processes that create the product that is sold. An innovation here might be the addition of a self-service checkout at the supermarket, where customers can scan their own purchases using a barcode reader; or it might be a web-based account management system to allow customers to control their personal finances. In the design and manufacturing processes for products, innovations might take the form of computer-aided design software that allows products to be designed on-screen, without the use of prototypes or physical models; or new tools and equipment that lead to higher-quality, more efficiently produced products.

Position Innovations

These are changes in the way the product or service offering is targeted. Put another way, it is the targeting of a product or service at a different use or customer base. For example, Lucozade was once thought of as a convalescence drink for sick people, but it has subsequently moved market position and been retargeted as a sports drink for fit and healthy people. This repositioning strategy then led to product innovations in terms of flavouring and composition – for example, to drink as an energy source or for rehydration/electrolyte replenishment.

Another example of extreme repositioning is in the automobile market, where large, thirsty and cumbersome four-wheel-drive vehicles were once considered off-road workhorses. They have now become fashionable as on-road, safe (for passengers though possibly less so for other road users) family cars for picking up the kids from school.

Paradigm Innovations

These are changes in how companies might frame what they do – for example, the reframing of a supermarket such as Tesco from a simple seller of food products to a provider of all the family's needs, including petrol, clothing and financial products. Here the reframing has created synergies, where shoppers will buy food, then go for petrol, and then pay for it all on their Tesco credit card. This might one day lead to a further process innovation whereby your salary could be paid directly to Tesco so missing out the middle-man. Another, more sophisticated example, can be found in the oil industry where major players are reframing, no longer presenting themselves as oil companies but energy companies in an attempt to both secure a future post-fossil fuels and to divert the negative press that oil producers receive. In one example, to support this paradigm shift, in 2017 BP bought a major stake in the company Lightsource Renewable Energy subsequently renaming it Lightsource BP.

Types of Innovation: Radical and Incremental

Not all innovations are the same in terms of scale and scope. Some, such as the internal combustion engine and the microprocessor, have fundamentally changed society. Others, such as the fabric Gore-Tex or the ballpoint pen, while very successful, have made less of an overall impact.

It is difficult to classify innovations in terms of their impact. Many innovations, although very sophisticated, may have a low impact due to how they are applied, what they are replacing, or when they come along. For example, the development of a practical hydrogen-fuelled car as a replacement for the fossil-fuelled car might be a radical technological leap, but fundamentally it would change very little about the way we drive. There might be an incremental change but not much more. The Honda FCX Clarity is the first such car, and part of its appeal is that it drives very much like a normal car. However, in terms of the environment, the widespread use of this and other zero emissions technologies may have a significant impact. So for drivers the innovation is incremental, but for environmentalists the innovation would be considered radical.

So why is this important for us as operation managers? The point here is that innovations are not all the same in terms of scale, scope or impact; the same innovation can have a different impact depending on how it is framed. We as managers must assess the innovation's commercial potential in terms of revenue, profitability and risk before investing large amounts of capital in its development. It is therefore useful to categorize innovations along a scale from *radical* (those innovations that have a large impact) to *incremental* (those that have a smaller impact).

A review of commercialized innovations can tell us whether an innovation was incremental or radical, and what impact it has had, but this historical analysis is not forward-looking, and therefore is not particularly useful for us as managers. We need a method for carrying out a more proactive assessment, to understand how the pursuit of an innovation will affect our organization. Here it is useful to return to the strategy that we studied in Chapter 1: specifically the resource-based view, and the theory of competencies. If we assume that all firms have developed a range of competencies to undertake their business, and that it would be useful to understand the radical–incremental continuum in relation to these, then we can draw up Table 3.1.

Chapter 1, p23

As managers, we can use this table to categorize the potential innovation, and decide how we may have to revise our internal competence. If the innovation does not require significant change to our competencies it is probably incremental, and so is less risky to implement and less costly to pursue. But, as with many low-cost, low-risk ventures, it may not yield a large return. If we need to revise our competencies significantly, or engage with totally new markets, then we can consider the innovation as radical.

The innovations highlighted within each of the industrial revolutions indicate that, after a few early, **radical innovations**, **incremental innovation** has taken over, and has produced a large number of smaller improvements.

Radical innovation extreme, game-changing progress.

Incremental innovation change that moves things on in small steps.

It could be argued that, these days, most innovation is incremental. In service delivery it may be doing something a little differently and a little better. With physical products it may be a small improvement in performance, or a small increase in functionality.

Innovations can be radical or incremental in each of the four Ps, as indicated in Table 3.2, and as managers we must consider each innovation in these terms if we are to understand its full potential.

Where Do Innovations Come From?

Eureka Moments

It is thought that the word 'eureka' is derived from the Greek word *heúrēka* (εύρηκα), meaning 'I have found it', made famous by the ancient Greek thinker Archimedes, who is believed to have shouted it while jumping into a bath of water. The reason for this strange behaviour was that his observation of the displacement of water resulted in

Table 3.1 Competence and Innovations

Core competence	Potential innovation
Largely preserved	Incremental
Destroyed or requires significant rework	Radical

Source: Developed from Westland (2008).

Table 3.2 Innovation outcomes and types

	Incremental	Radical
Product	Turbocharger fitted to an internal combustion engine	Electric motors replace internal combustion engines
Process	Banking carried out by phone, rather than face to face in branch	Internet banking replaces human contact completely
Position	Under Armour as a sports clothing brand introduces a new range of clothes	Under Armour re-positions itself as a digitally enabled fitness brand
Paradigm	Music sold physically on analogue media such as vinyl being replaced with digital media such as compact disc	Music with no physical form being rented (rather than sold) through streaming services such as Spotify

Stop and Think

We are surrounded by so-called innovative products. Consider everyday items such as the iPod or the mobile phone. Use Table 3.2 to try to identify the radical innovations that made the technology possible, and the incremental innovations that matured the product to its current level of sophistication.

CRITICAL PERSPECTIVE

A Patently False Patent Myth

Is innovation and creativity limitless? For more than a century a story has periodically appeared in print about an official of the US Patent Office who, in the 19th century, resigned his post because he believed that all possible inventions had already been invented. Did a patent official really resign because he thought nothing was left to invent? This mystery was investigated by the D.C. Historical Records Survey. The investigator, Dr Eber Jeffery, published his findings in the July 1940 *Journal of the Patent Office Society*.

> *Jeffery found no evidence that any official or employee of the US Patent Office had ever resigned because he thought there was nothing left to invent. However, Jeffery may have found a clue to the origin of the myth. In his 1843 report to Congress, the then commissioner of the Patent Office, Henry L. Ellsworth, included the following comment: 'The advancement of the arts, from year to year, taxes our credulity and seems to presage the arrival of that period when human improvement must end.'*
>
> **Source:** Adapted from *The Skeptical Inquirer*, 13 (spring 1989), pp. 310–313.

Although the language used in the above excerpt may be somewhat impenetrable and difficult to follow, what is being discussed is the view that, given the acceleration in scientific and technical achievement that began around 300 years ago, we may come to a point quite soon where there is, quite literally, nothing left to invent.

Although this famous and rather attractive myth seems to have been proven to be false, it does raise questions for industry about the continuous and perpetual nature of innovation. It could be argued that, as technology progresses, each additional advance will be more difficult to make. The Moon is relatively easy to reach in comparison with Mars, which in turn is relatively easy to reach in comparison with the nearest star. Indeed, it may be impossible to reach the nearest star, no matter how innovative we are.

At a more practical level, mobile phones can only become so much smaller or be packed with so much more functionality, before the law of diminishing returns sets in. Many would argue we have gone past that point already, with phones able to do far more than anyone would ever need. A phone that fits in your palm may be better than a phone the size of a house brick (all the rage back in the 1980s), but would we really need one the size of a thimble?

There is a limit to the speed at which a service can be provided. Twenty years ago it might have taken a week to set up a mortgage; these days it can be done in a matter of hours. Would there really be any benefit to being able to do it in a matter of minutes? Customers and markets can only be served so well, or in so many different ways.

Does this mean that in future there will be less radical innovation and more incremental innovation? Or less product and process, and more position and paradigm? Put another way, will innovation be less about substance and more about how we view things? In current entertainment a recent so-called 'innovation' is in talent shows such as *The X Factor*. But, in reality, these shows are little more than a reinvention of the holiday camp talent competitions that have existed for as long as we can remember.

Each show has a similar format, and each strives (and often fails) to differentiate itself from the others, more often than not resorting to cheap shocks and revelations as opposed to real substance and true creativity. Are we on the verge of an era of the 'emperor's new clothes' where very little is actually new?

The key point is ...

that some time soon, innovation may not be the key to the strategy of product and service differentiation that it once was.

an insight on how to measure the purity of gold. This was a problem given to him by King Hiero of Syracuse, who was worried about the authenticity of his crown (and evidently the trustworthiness of his crown-maker). Regardless of the truth of this, the word 'eureka' has since come to be associated with the act of having an idea.

The classic view of innovation is the eccentric inventor, often of pensionable age, being struck by an impromptu idea – frequently accompanied by the famous shout and a lot of excited arm-waving before running off to spend the next couple of years in the garden shed, developing this brilliant idea into a working prototype. While this might have been the case in times gone by, these days innovation is usually the product of considerable investment in capital, manpower and equipment within the auspices of a large company's R&D department or a university laboratory.

There are famous cases of genuine 'eureka' moments, though. Probably the most famous is Percy Shaw's idea for the road safety device, which occurred when he noticed how light reflected from a cat's eye. Although simple in concept, this idea underwent a process of design and development before becoming the innovative product that we all know today. A more recent example is described in Short Case 3.1.

SHORT CASE 3.1

Chaining together Product and Process Innovation

Rehook was created after dropping a chain, and turning up late for a meeting, covered in oil.

Wayne Taylor, Creator of Rehook

In 1817 Baron Karl von Drais invented a walking machine, a kind of pre-bicycle, to help him get around his royal gardens. This early invention embodied design principles that have endured until today: two same-size, in-line wheels, mounted in a frame that is straddled by the rider. However, this device was propelled not by pedalling but by vigorously pushing one's feet against the ground. Then, after a short detour into the rather dangerous cul-de-sac that saw pedals attached directly to the front wheel on machines such as the Penny Farthing, in 1898 the German Diamant Bicycle Company invented the roller-chain. So, rather fortunately, from this point most bicycles were fitted with the chain that forms the basis of the propulsion system we know today. While the history of bicycle design is packed full of innovation resulting in the carbon-fibre framed, technology-packed steeds ridden today, it took well over 100 years for someone to invent a tool to help in the sometimes irritating, often time-consuming and always mucky process of resetting the chain should it become dislodged from its gears. Rehook is a simple but very effective tool that solves this problem.

Created by inventor Wayne Taylor and launched in 2016 at the Cycle Show in Birmingham's NEC, Rehook gained national attention in 2019 due to its appearance on the BBC's *Dragons' Den* programme. Made from plastic reinforced with graphite this lightweight tool allows the rider to re-seat the chain in as little as 3 seconds. The launch product was 3D printed with the latest 'Laser Sintering' technology. This technique allowed prototypes to be produced rapidly and enabled production parts to be manufactured and the market to be tested without a large initial investment. Demand soon outstripped the production capacity of the 3D printing technique (around 400 units per month) and, using the funding gained from Dragon Deborah Meaden, the company invested in injection moulding tooling to build a higher capacity production line. By the end of 2019 over 18,000 units had been sold.

Source: ©TORWAISTUDIO/Shutterstock

With, by some estimates, over 1 billion bikes currently on the road, although over a century in the making, it does seem as though there will be a healthy market for Rehook for some time to come.

Questions

1. With over a century of cycling and many millions of cyclists, why do you think it took so long for someone to spot the gap in the market?
2. After the initial idea, consider the steps required to turn the idea into a saleable product.

Source: www.rehook.bike

Despite the attraction of romantic and inspirational stories of unlikely individuals with brilliant ideas overcoming all odds, in reality the eureka moment is only one of a number of ways in which innovation can occur. Figure 3.2 illustrates the main sources that may trigger the innovation journey for an organization. In addition Figure 3.3 illustrates how the resource-based and market-based approaches are complementary and, again as explained in Chapter 2, often companies will use an approach that is a combination of both.

Chapter 2, p55

Figure 3.2 Sources of innovation

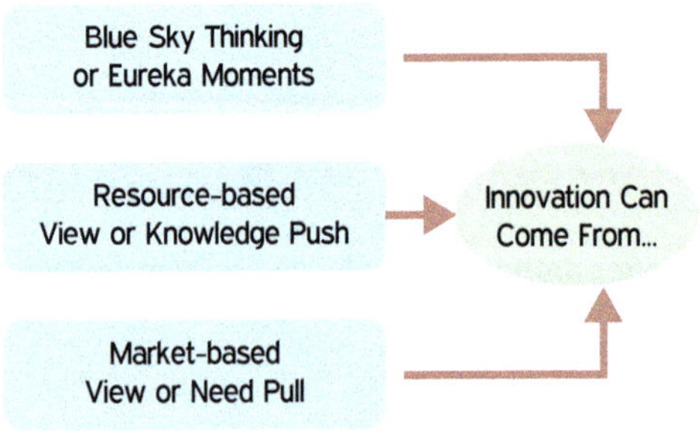

Figure 3.3 Push and pull innovation

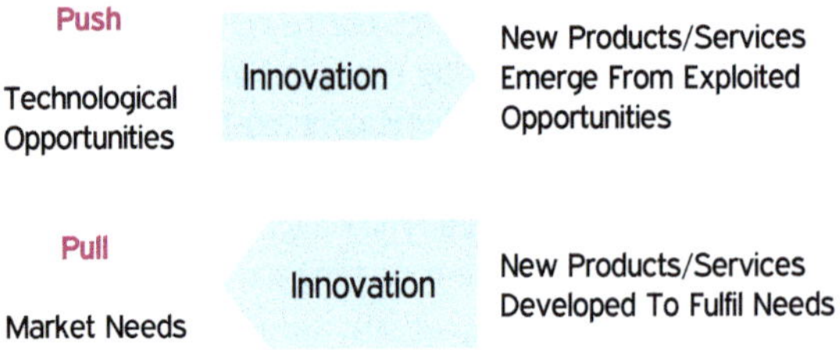

Knowledge Push – The Resource-Based View

Apart from eureka moments, the most obvious source of innovation is the laboratories that conduct formalized scientific research. History conjures images of individual laboratories, but these days, increasingly, it is large companies investing in networks of research and development centres that yield the most innovation. Some companies, such as ICI, DuPont, Apple and more recently Tesla, have made their reputation through the public's acknowledgement of their commitment to innovation.

These days innovation is less the result of freewheeling ideas generation, and more the result of a systematic commitment of specialist staff, equipment and facilities to solving specific problems (**knowledge push**).

Knowledge push innovation driven by advances in technology that create new products.

To produce consistent innovation, it is critical to specialize. Dupont, for example, has 14 technical centres. The European Technical Center in Meyrin, Switzerland, is its global R&D centre. Here, leading researchers support polymer and advanced materials innovation from early development through commercialization, using a range of processing and prototyping technologies, and testing expertise.

The important thing to note here is that the resources are generally focused on one or a small number of complementary areas of expertise, so the key thing for managers to do is to define the scope of the research, and develop it as an organizational competence.

Need Pull – The Market-Based View

The complement to creating an innovative new product is finding a gap to fill in the market (**need pull**). There is little point in investing significant resources in finding a solution to a problem that doesn't exist. Sometimes, though, the application of products is difficult to assess. Digital music players and lightweight headphones have for many years been an essential part of a runner's or cyclist's training kit. Until recently this method of combatting boredom was unavailable to swimmers. However, with the invention of lightweight waterproof music players which fit securely into the ears and, more excitingly, bone-conduction technology, this option is now becoming commonplace.

Need pull customer identification of gaps in the market that provide an opportunity to innovate and create a product.

Many products we see in the market today were inconceivable a few short years ago. It is logical that the typewriter would pave the way for a product such as Microsoft Word, However, it is less conceivable that it would lead to a product such as PowerPoint. Similarly, the home phone is clearly part of the lineage that led to the mobile phone, but has little relationship with the functionality embodied in the smart phone.

There have been some notable marketing failures, such as the Sinclair C5 electric vehicle for single person transportation. Despite this misfire, it has been followed more recently by (slightly) more successful innovations such as the Segway people transporter, a two-wheeled, self-balancing electric vehicle invented by Dean Kamen and produced by Segway Inc. While never achieving mass appeal, the Segway has found a market niche within some applications such as tourism and warehousing.

It is important to be aware of the driving forces in the external environment that may yield an opportunity.

Technological innovations, such as those noted above, do not always lead to a single product exploited by a single company. Technology spreads like a virus. There are many examples of this, but possibly the most ubiquitous in recent years has been touch-screen technology, which has found its way into all kinds of products such as mobile phones, cameras and iPads. Awareness of what the market is doing with technology application is therefore critical.

Scanning the market by analysing what competitor products exist may be useful, but there are other, more specific, external areas that may yield the opportunity for an innovative product or service.

Regulation Changes

We are surrounded by regulation. We live our lives within frameworks that seem to become more sophisticated and all-encompassing as time goes on. Regulation can restrict, but it can also trigger innovation by mandating change. Environmental legislation on pollution, for example, has paved the way for innovation in the development of renewable forms of energy – an industry that was for many years neglected because of the dominance of fossil fuels. On a smaller scale, the drive for reduced speed and greater safety on our roads has led to the development of speed cameras and airbags. Ironically, the Gatso road safety camera was originally invented by a rally driver, Maurice Gatsonides, to help him increase his speed around corners.

As well as direct opportunities resulting from the passing of laws, legal changes have also paved some elliptical paths to innovation. Tobacco use has not yet been directly regulated against, but the new focus on health, combined with

SHORT CASE 3.2

Spreadshirt: Innovative E-commerce

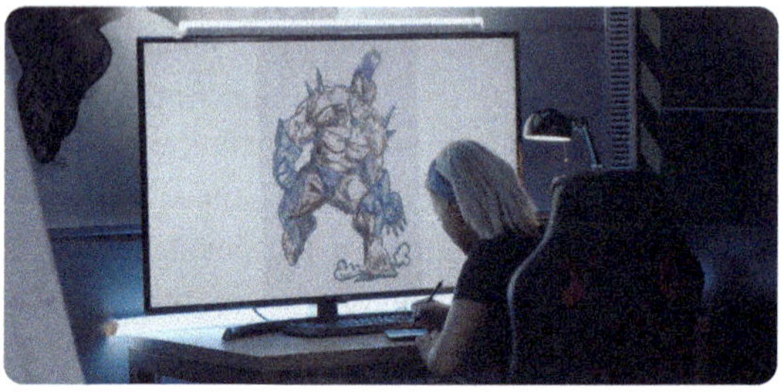

Source: FrameStockFootages/Shutterstock

Founded in Leipzig, Germany, by graduate students Lukasz Gadowski and Matthias Spiess, Spreadshirt is an online platform for apparel merchandising that allows Internet site operators to create their own online shops for free, and sell customized products. Spreadshirt lets anyone integrate these online shops with their own websites. These shop partners can then earn commissions on each sale through Spreadshirt. Requirements for using Spreadshirt are minimal: you need only an Internet connection, and design/logo graphic files for products. Spreadshirt does the rest by handling the production, shipping, payment processing and customer service. For people who just want to create and order personalized shirts with a design and text of their choice, Spreadshirt also has the Spreadshirt Designer shop available on its website. Since its origination in Germany, the company has expanded its market to the rest of Europe and the US. It has received acclaim globally, winning the Hewlett-Packard Innovation Award in 2004, and being named in ***Business Week***'s Europe Top 500 Growth Companies.

Question

1. Do you think that the growing sophistication of technology and its implementation in information systems such as the Internet is making society and individuals more innovative; or do you think that technology-based applications are purely an additional outlet to channel the output of existing innovative individuals?

Source: www.spreadshirt.co.uk

legal restrictions in advertising and lawsuits against tobacco companies, has forced the larger companies to devote increasing resources to creating innovative, 'safer' products, such as the Philip Morris Accord cigarette holder and the RJR Eclipse cigarette. Ironically, these attempts at product innovation have caused some difficulties for the tobacco companies, because the introduction of a cigarette that is 'safe' represents an implicit admission that the previous products were 'not safe' – an admission that (amazingly enough) tobacco companies are still reluctant to make.

So we can see that understanding the legal and social climate can produce a handy signpost to where new products and services may be needed in the future.

Accidents and Unplanned Events

Many innovations have been the result of an 'accident' in the lab, such as Alexander Fleming's discovery of penicillin, or alternative applications for discoveries such as 3M's reuse of 'sticky but not too sticky' adhesive in Post-it notes. We mentioned the Segway above. The innovative gyro that makes it possible was developed in the defence labs of BAE Systems before it found application in this alternative market.

Unplanned events such as terrorist attacks have also paved the way for innovation in safety and security products. Biometric scanning devices represent one such industry that has benefited from this unfortunate opportunity. Applied Biometrics Products is a company with a core technology that combines proprietary software and hardware designs to produce portable biometric scanning devices. But this is only part of their offering, as they use it in combination with their expertise in assessing the needs of a customer to provide a service developing innovative customized security solutions to meet those needs.

One of the largest service industries in the world – personal insurance – developed around the need to guard against unplanned events. From the initial innovation that set up Scottish Widows, the first Scottish personal insurance company (see Short Case 3.3), the insurance industry has continued to innovate, and now covers almost everything that one can think of. Famous insurances include Bruce Springsteen's voice and Jennifer Lopez's bottom. Lloyd's of London is said to have sold insurance against werewolf attacks and vampire bites. How much do you think it would cost to insure Jennifer Lopez's bottom against a vampire bite?

SHORT CASE 3.3

Dying to Be Innovative . . .

In 1906 the German insurance expert Alfred Manes defined insurance as:

> *an economic institution resting on the principle of mutuality, established for the purpose of supplying a fund, the need for which arises from a chance occurrence whose probability can be estimated.*

Source: ©Hugh Threlfall / Alamy Stock Photo

Two Church of Scotland ministers, Robert Wallace and Alexander Webster, are given credit for inventing the first true personal insurance fund based on correct actuarial and financial principles in 1743. This fund, the Scottish Ministers' Widows Fund, was set up to take care of the widows and children of deceased clergymen. There were two innovations here: first, the creation of a fund with premiums that were profitably invested to ensure a growing value; and second, the use of mathematics to allow projections to be made (with surprising accuracy, as it turned out) on the future finances, such as rate of growth of the fund.

Within a few years similar funds were springing up, using the same model, all over the English-speaking world spreading throughout the professions. One of these funds was conceived in 1812, when a number of eminent Scotsmen gathered in Edinburgh, to consider setting up a general fund for securing provisions to widows, sisters and other females. As a consequence of this, the Scottish Widows Fund Life Assurance Society – Scotland's first mutual life office – opened for business in 1815. It is a curious fact about this industry that the most insured people tend to live in the safest places and be least at risk from unplanned events.

Questions

1. Where do you think the next innovation will come from in the insurance industry?
2. Do you think most innovations in finance are radical or incremental?

Source: www.scottishwidows.co.uk

The insurance industry, old and stuffy as it may seem, still continues to innovate, with the latest incarnation being the infamous hedge funds that are a method of insuring against negative movements in the investment markets. Other technologies such as the Internet, and particularly its ability to enable fast marketing of services in facilities such as price comparison sites, is driving further innovation in this industry.

Users as Innovators

Users are sometimes viewed as passive recipients of innovation, but they can also be a useful source of ideas. When a product is in the market, there is potential for everyone who buys it to find a new application.

There are three categories of users who are particularly important for innovation:

- *Lead users:* people who not only use the product but also help in its development. Indeed, like Michelle Mone (see Short Case 3.4 below), they may even be the innovator who has an idea after using a similar product, and develops it into a competing and more successful product.
- *User communities:* groups of users who congregate around a product or product platform such as iTunes and find new and innovative ways to use it.
- *Extreme users:* users who push products to their limit, creating a need for improved performance. The story of the bicycle is an example of this, with the relentless drive for more durable and higher-performing machines. The modern clockwork radio is another example. It was designed and patented in 1989 by British accountant Trevor Baylis using existing technologies. He envisaged it as a radio for use by people in developing countries without access to batteries, or electrical supplies.

SHORT CASE 3.4

Comfort and Joy

Source: ©Featureflash Photo Agency/ Shutterstock

Michelle Mone grew up in Glasgow, Scotland. She began her career as a model, and later moved into sales and marketing. In October 1996, while attending a dinner dance wearing a very uncomfortable, cleavage-enhancing brassiere, she decided that she could design something that was more comfortable and better looking, but would still create the all-important enhanced cleavage.

MJM International Ltd was set up in November 1996, and three years of research, design and development resulted in the patented Ultimo bra, which achieved the aims Mone had set out to accomplish.

Once patented, the Ultimo bra then launched at Selfridges department store in London in August 1999. Selfridges sold the pre-launch estimate of six weeks of stock within 24 hours, and 20 years later this is still known as the biggest ever bra launch in the UK, where photographers and camera crews from all over the world were in attendance. In April 2000 Mone won the World Young Business Achiever Award in the Epcot Centre, Florida. Ultimo subsequently expanded into the United States, and in May 2000 Ultimo was launched at the Saks Fifth Avenue store in New York.

In September 2003 MJM launched another invention – the Ultimo Miracle Body. Mone said that she was given the challenge from her celebrity customers to create a backless and frontless bra. Her technical team said it was impossible – 12 months later it was achieved, and the product was aptly called the Miracle Body.

Question

1. Research this case further. Do you think that product innovation is the important success factor here, or is it the marketing of the brand that has created this success?

Sources: www.ultimoco.uk; MJM Limited; Wikipedia.

Innovation and Operations Management

The Innovation Life Cycle

It is clear that it is important to identify innovation opportunities, either by utilizing internal knowledge resources or by finding external gaps in the market. To help in this, Abernathy and Utterback (1978) have identified how innovation opportunities in relation to products may change over time, as shown in Figure 3.4.

Stage 1: The Fluid Phase

Initially, as a new technology emerges or a new idea for a product begins to take shape, there is a lot of uncertainty about its ultimate utility. This uncertainty can be categorized in two ways; the *target* – what the application of the technology will be, and the *technical* – how the technology can be harnessed to meet this application. The operational activity within the fluid phase will be characterized by extensive experimentation and will end when the dominant design emerges, or, put another way, when the configuration emerges that will characterize the product for most of the remainder of its life cycle.

For example, the dominant design that emerged for a family car is: four wheels, one at each corner, with engine in the front, steered by hand using a wheel, and clutch, brake and accelerator operated by foot, and arranged from left to right.

Figure 3.4 The product innovation life cycle

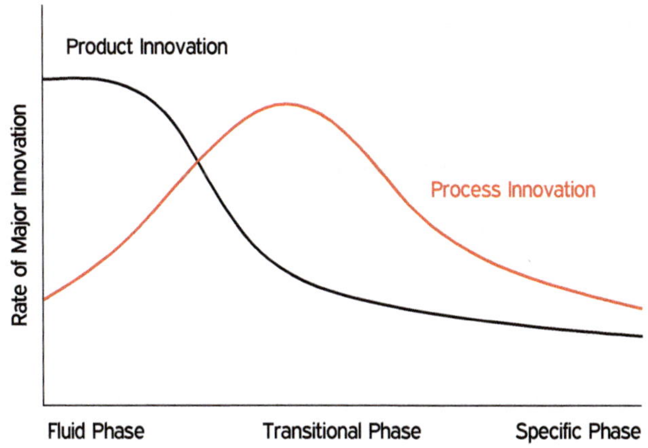

Source: Adapted from Abernathy and Utterback (1978).

At the end of the fluid stage the target will be defined, and the technical issues in relation to reaching that target should have been (mostly) overcome. The focus of innovation in this stage is very much on the technology and its application.

Stage 2: The Transitional Phase

Here operational activity becomes less random and more planned, with the product configuration becoming ready for sale. The focus of activity is on maturing the product platform by finalizing functionality, and improving quality and reliability. Innovation in product and technology is becoming more incremental, aimed at squeezing in as much functionality as possible, and achieving the greatest degree of differentiation in the market. This is evident in the automobile, where the configuration is now standard, but manufacturers are 'packing in' features and additional functionality, such as in-car entertainment systems and navigational aids. Innovation in process becomes more important, as the ideas generated here will define the production and service delivery processes.

Stage 3: The Specific Phase

Operational activity at this stage is focused on optimizing the production and service delivery processes, realizing economies of scale and improving efficiency. The aim is to drive down cost. The product is considered mature in the market, and, as time passes may only retain its position with a combination of historical customer loyalty and low price. Even though sales may still be strong, at this stage the product will be ripe for replacement by a newer offering. The manufacture of consumer goods is a prime example of this, as the mass production systems used are among the most efficient in the world.

From a product development point of view, as time progresses, innovation will move from the radical to the incremental, with each successive innovation becoming less and less impactful as the 'well of innovation' dries up. Similarly, from a process point of view, as the product becomes more mature the innovations that squeeze the final few drops of efficiency out of the manufacturing process may become more incremental. Therefore the emphasis of innovation changes over time, not only in terms of type (radical or incremental) but also in its emphasis on the process of manufacture as opposed to the technology embodied in the product.

Stop and Think

How might the focus of an organisation's innovative activity change in the fluid phase of the Innovation Lifecycle?

BUSINESS INTEGRATION

The Four Ss: Organizational Factors in Managing Innovation

The need to innovate is clear, but an organization's ability to innovate must be developed. Smith *et al.* (2008) have defined the features of the organization that will impact on the effectiveness of the process of innovation. These have been distilled here into four Ss: *strategy, style, structure* and *support.*

- *Corporate Strategy:* Above all, a corporate strategy must be developed and cascaded down from the top to communicate shared vision and goals (Jager *et al.*, 2004). If the organization is relying on innovation as part of its competitive advantage, then the strategy must state this explicitly, so that all employees will be encouraged to behave in the correct way.
- *Management Style:* The management team must act on the strategy, to reinforce its effect on the employees. A 'facilitate and empower' style will foster innovation better than a 'command and control' style; employees who are empowered and autonomous will act more innovatively than those constrained by organizational regulation (Muthusamy *et al.*, 2005). It would seem logical that, to be innovative, employees need to be given sufficient resources and the space to allow ideas to emerge. So there is a delicate balance to be struck here between controlling employees and empowering them, particularly with employees who are working within a process-dominated environment such as a production line or a call centre.
- *Organizational Structure:* This generally dictates the nature of jobs, and must be coherent with the management style used within the organization. Division of labour and extreme specialization of tasks are detrimental to innovation. Task variety and cross-functional communication are advantageous. Although lone employees can be innovative, teams of employees working together are likely to be more successful over the long term.
- *Technology and knowledge management Support:* Technology directly affects employees, as it is commonly used as a facilitator of knowledge transfer, drawing together fragmented knowledge resources to develop a single knowledge repository (Jantunen, 2005). Information technology can be used to pull together and centralize data from many sources making it easier to find and use. This means that employees can quickly and easily gain access to the information they need to support their innovative activity. Supporting the organization with the correct IT system results in a more integrated approach to the development of new ideas.

When considering the four Ss, it is clear that innovation is better supported in an integrated business, where all parts are aligned, and innovative employees are working to a *strategy* enabled by the appropriate management *structure,* facilitated by the correct management *style,* and *supported* by the provision of the best tools, equipment and information.

The Innovative Workforce

Enabling innovation within organizations is all about taking maximum advantage of employees as innovators – not only those who are directly employed for this purpose, but all workers, regardless of their role. 'With every pair of hands a brain comes free' was the mantra of the 'new' management of the 1980s and 1990s. The philosophy behind this was that all workers have the capacity to have ideas and many of these ideas will be useful and the accumulation of these ideas can, over time, bring significant rewards.

The wider management narrative over the last few decades has made much of employee participation. This initially emerged with the 'quality miracle' of the Japanese manufacturers, which was enabled by the system of *kaizen* or *continuous improvement* (Imai, 1986). Employees were encouraged to question work processes and identify incremental improvements resulting in better product quality and operational efficiency. Although re-energized by the Japanese, employee participation schemes are not new – indeed, Denny's Shipyard in Dumbarton, Scotland, implemented a suggestion scheme back in the mid 19th-century – but the more systematic and proactive approach of the Japanese was a key factor in their success. Kaizen has since been joined by other systems, such as total quality management (Bounds *et al.*, 1994), lean manufacturing (Womack and Jones, 1996) and six sigma (Pyzdek and Keller, 2018) – all of which are discussed in later chapters. While approaches differ, the key success in all these systems is in getting employees involved in the thinking behind the operational processes, and encouraging them to generate ideas that lead to improvements that ultimately benefit the performance of the company (Tonneson, 2003).

Continuous Innovation

'Traditional' continuous improvement is still useful for improving operational efficiency, but there are now some who propose that something more is needed and that companies must move beyond continuous improvement and develop a competence in continuous innovation. Boer and Gertsen (2003) define two areas in which a company must continuously innovate:

- Operational effectiveness – the ability to satisfy today's customers' demands in terms of cost, quality and functionality. This they term *exploitation*.
- Strategic flexibility – the capability to find and develop new configurations of products and markets. This they term *exploration*.

They argue that competence in only one area is sub-optimal, because a firm that specializes in exploitation will only become better and better at 'sweating' an increasingly obsolete technology, while similarly a firm that specializes in exploration will never realize the full advantage of its discoveries. A combination of both is crucial to a firm's survival, and this is what is meant by *continuous innovation*. The challenge is therefore to build an organization that can simultaneously exploit and explore on an ongoing basis.

There are two ways to do this. First, geographical separation where exploitation and exploration activities can be done in different parts of the organization, for example R&D located separately from production. Second, time-based separation where the organization reconfigures itself as required. There are two ways this can be achieved.

- The ambidextrous model – where the organization behaves organically in an empowered, flexible and creative way when the situation needs radical innovation to come up with new ideas, and then more mechanistically when the situation requires incremental innovation to realize increased efficiency.
- The punctuated equilibrium model – where the organization plans for a period of radical innovation in the development of a product, and then reforms for a longer period of incremental change as the product of the technology is exploited.

Continuous innovation is closely related to dynamic capabilities (discussed in Chapter 1). Both are seen as solutions to the challenges brought by the increasingly competitive environment that organizations find themselves in.

Chapter 1, p23

CRITICAL PERSPECTIVE

Freedom or Constraints

The goal of operations management is to achieve operational excellence. This is traditionally defined in terms of efficiency, measured as a ratio of some form of output to some form of input. Simplistically this could be x number of widgets produced using y number of labour-hours: more widgets for fewer hours means greater efficiency. Traditional thinking shows us that the path to efficiency is through repetition, conformance to a fixed system, and reduction in variation. Even in new product design, efficiency is the goal, with project management techniques put in place to measure the achievement of time, cost and scope. Efficiency is easy to measure in manufacturing, and possible (but not so easy) to measure in product design, but it is almost impossible to measure when radical or breakthrough innovations are being worked towards, because this type of innovation includes more substantial components of 'newness, uncertainty and ambiguity' (Magnusson *et al.*, 2009).

The need to balance innovation and efficiency is not new, and was once labelled 'the paradox of administration' (Thompson, 1967); but today's competitive landscape requires firms to reach new levels of performance. This results in them being forced to reach a delicate compromise between longer-term exploration – with its demands for the development of new ideas, and the flexibility this requires – and short-term exploitation, with its needs for efficiency and profitability that can be optimized only within the constraints of an operational system. Indeed, the attempt to systematize innovation may be counterproductive. Styhre (2008), in his analysis of R&D in the pharmaceutical industry, indicates that providing the time and space for employees to 'play' may be a factor in the innovation process. He further suggests that advanced scientific exploration can be a process of skill and chance as much as of method and management. For operations managers this raises the obvious question: how do we create a process for play?

The key point is ...

that when managing innovation, where new ideas and blue sky thinking are the output, then traditional operations management techniques may not apply. Sometimes the advantages gained by tightly controlling a process may be outweighed by the advantages of allowing a team of creative people free rein to generate ideas.

Contemporary Thinking: Open Innovation within Networks and Ecosystems

Henry Chesbrough coined the term 'Open Innovation' to describe 'the use of purposive inflows and outflows of knowledge to accelerate internal innovation, and expand the markets for external use of innovation. . .' (Chesbrough et al., 2006: 1).

Open innovation is a broad concept, and while some question what 'openness' actually means (Sydow et al., 2016), here we consider it to be innovation that is not limited to one organization but that takes place in collaborations that involve a number of organizations.

Initially the dominant models were the 'outside-in' approach where organizations draw ideas in from other places and the 'inside-out' approach where partially developed ideas are pushed to external organizations (Chesbrough et al., 2006). This collaborative activity allows ideas – that might have otherwise stagnated – to be fully developed and commercialized. This conceptualization of openness describes the relationship direction or the flow of knowledge. This thinking is further developed by Gassmann and Enkel (2006) who add that openness may also be conceptualized as a 'coupled' model, with innovations seen as co-created between complementary actors.

While these models are well established in open innovation studies, recent thinking has challenged their simplicity, highlighting the more complex nature of innovation that can take place in networks where a number of firms form alliances to innovate and in wider ecosystems where firms and other stakeholders, such as governments and universities, may create an environment that is open to any that wish to participate (West et al., 2014). Short Case 3.5 describes such an attempt to create a robust innovation environment at a national level.

SHORT CASE 3.5

GLOBALIZATION

Catapults – Investing in Networks of Innovation

Ten years into the 21st century, and with shock-waves from the financial crash still reverberating, the UK Government resolved to deliver a 'step' change in industrial performance. It understood that innovation was to the 4th Industrial Revolution what steam was to the 1st. They also realized that where innovation was concerned the UK had to raise its game!

CATAPULT

Source: catapult.org.uk

A report by entrepreneur and technologist, Dr Herman Hauser (2010), identified a need to 'close the gap between universities and industry through a "translational infrastructure" to provide a business-focused capacity and capability that bridges research and technology commercialisation.'

The report addressed an issue that had dogged the UK for many years: its failure to capitalize fully on the commercial potential of its world-class science and research base. In short, the UK was good at inventing but bad at commercializing.

In response, a nationwide-network of innovation centres named 'Catapults' was proposed, their collective aim was to harness British innovation and boost productivity.

Initially the key question was: Where should we focus resources? Proposals for these 'embryonic' Catapults were judged against four criteria: (1) Are the potential global markets accessed through each Catapult predicted to be worth billions of pounds a year? (2) Does the UK have world-leading research capability in the area? (3) Does UK business have the ability to exploit the technology, capture a significant share of the value chain and embed the activity in the UK? And (4) Is the proposed Catapult closely aligned with, and essential to achieving, national strategic priorities?

This led to ten Catapults. Eight were initially set up; these focused on High Value Manufacturing, Offshore Renewable Energy, Energy Systems, Cell and Gene Therapy, Transport Systems, Future Cities, Digital and Satellite Applications. Then Medicines Discovery followed in 2016 and finally Compound Semi-conductor was added in 2018.

The Catapults are tasked with delivering a paradigm shift in how market-worthy ideas are identified, nurtured and delivered. Rather excitingly they are mandated to 'creatively destroy obstacles to success'.

Over the years they have done just that, creating thousands of new collaborations between academia and industry while taking on challenges ranging from the mass production of graphene, the atom-thick 'wonder material', to shaking up the energy industry and putting the UK at the forefront of the Internet of Things. The Catapults operate facilities worth £850 million, providing open access to state-of-the-art resource and expert support that would normally be beyond the means of all but the biggest companies. While based in the UK they are active in over 24 countries around the world, developing markets for British ingenuity and attracting inward investment from leading international companies.

The achievements of the Catapults are not due to the discovery of some secret industrial success formula, but are due to the way they combine clarity of vision with ambition and commercial pragmatism.

Question

What do you think is the biggest issue with the Open Innovation model that may deter companies from engaging with it?

Source: www.catapult.org.uk

There are a number of decisions to be made when engaging in open innovation. Possibly the most important of these are taken to define the nature of the relationship. The relationship can be based on processes that are either formal or informal. Formal processes are based on 'tight' contractual agreements between organizational actors, and conversely, informal processes are based on 'looser' arbitrary agreements between organizational actors. Relatedly there is the often thorny problem of intellectual property (IP). Traditional models of IP protection stress its retention within the firm and go to extreme lengths to suppress knowledge 'leaks'. In the open innovation model, a firm's IP is available to external actors to create value within the network. This makes the management of IP and the appropriation of value, in the form of profits, by each network actor more complex. Huizing (2011) stresses the need for firms to find a way to capture value in collaborative networks when formal IP protection mechanisms are no longer relevant.

As thinking in relation to open innovation has developed, how organizations deal with it has changed. It is now more about the friction-less management of knowledge flows across boundaries, between organizations with complementary business models who are searching for shared value. Non-financial motivations are equally as important as financial in the open innovation model.

Current conceptualization of open innovation are more nuanced with the latest research exploring new contexts, appropriation regimes, and measurement practices while paying increasing attention to the contingencies of the market (West et al., 2014). Trott and Hartmann (2009) have noted that while innovation has very rarely been 'closed' it would now seem that innovation has never been more 'open'.

Summary

In this chapter we have defined innovation as both the creative process of coming up with a new idea and the operational process of implementing it and producing a product that can be sold in the market. We have shown that, as managers, we must distinguish between:

- innovation strategy – the overarching approach that the organization is taking to innovation
- innovation process – the series of steps taken to produce an innovative outcome
- and the outcome itself – the embodiment of innovative features or functions in a product or service offering.

Further these innovation outcomes can be embodied as:

- New *products* or changes to existing products
- Improvements in *processes* of manufacture or service delivery
- Changes in the market *position* of a product to increase sales
- Changes in company *paradigms* to open up new markets.

For each of these forms of outcome, innovation can be either radical, (game-changing), or incremental (smaller or more subtle).

We have demonstrated that innovations can come from three sources:

- Genuine eureka moments gained as the result of blue-sky thinking
- Resource-based 'knowledge push' generated internally within the company
- Market-based 'need pull' identified externally to the company.

We then went on to outline some methods that can be used to manage innovation in the organization. Innovation is subject to a life-cycle, with highly creative processes characterized by uncertainty and randomness, and aimed at producing new ideas, being replaced by more manageable processes, aimed at defining the product or service offering and then exploiting its potential. In addition, features of the organization such as its competitive strategy, its structure, its management style and its support systems can be configured to produce a more creative environment where employees can be encouraged to behave innovatively.

We then suggested that successful companies need to excel at both exploration (identifying and developing innovative ideas) and exploitation (extracting as much from them as possible). The critical success factor for these companies will be in developing operational systems that are effective at both.

Finally, we proposed that currently innovation is increasingly being carried out within ecosystems composed of collectives of organizations with a mutual interest. In this open innovation model, organizational boundaries are becoming less important; self-interest is being replaced by an emphasis on the creation of network value enabled by joint activity.

Key Theories

The key theories discussed in this chapter were:

- **The four Ps of:**
  - Product innovation: the changes in the things that the organization offers for sale
  - Process innovation: the changes in the process that creates the product
  - Position innovation: the changes in the way the product is offered or targeted
  - Paradigm innovation: the changes in how a company frames what it does.
- **'Knowledge push' or 'need pull':** where innovation is driven by advances in technology that create new products and markets where none existed before, or where customers identify a need and companies strive to fill the need.
- **The innovation life cycle:** a time-based representation of how innovation is carried out, from the discovery of a new technology until it becomes mature and fully developed.
- **The four Ss of facilitating innovation:**
  - Strategy: innovation is explicitly called for in the corporate strategy
  - Structure: roles and jobs are defined to aid in innovative behaviour
  - Style: management empowers the workforce to behave innovatively
  - Support: IT systems are available to support innovative behaviour.
- **Continuous Innovation**
  - Exploitation – the capability to satisfy today's customers' demands in terms of cost, quality and functionality
  - Exploration – the capability to find and develop new configurations of products and markets.
- **Open Innovation:** Innovative activity carried out within ecosystems composed of collectives of organizations with a mutual interest.

Suggested Answers to Stop and Think Questions

1. **Incremental and radical:** All electronic devices are made possible by the radical invention that was the transistor, followed by the radical repackaging of a large number of these in the microchip configuration. Incremental innovation is then the use of the microchip in different applications. In electronics technology the process of miniaturization that makes the density of functionality within a small product possible could be considered an incremental improvement. It may be useful to think of the radical innovation as the invention of the technology and the incremental as the steps in its application to products.
2. **Innovation lifecycle:** In the Fluid phase, the emphasis is on the product, therefore the focus will be on developing and improving the features and the functionality that it embodies. In the Transitionary phase, the emphasis is on the process of production and delivery, therefore the focus is on how efficient and effective these processes are.

connect

Review Questions

1. With reference to the 4Ps model that describes the 'Outcomes of Innovation', briefly explain what each P represents.
2. What do you think efficiency means in the early 'fluid' stages of the innovation life cycle?
3. Explain the difference between a radical innovation and an incremental innovation from the perspective of a company's operations strategy.
4. Explain the difference between 'continuous improvement' and 'continuous innovation'.
5. Describe how an organization might engage in open innovation.

Discussion Questions

1. Discuss the disadvantages of creating an innovative organization where all employees are encouraged to be creative and produce new ideas.
2. Examine the innovation lifecycle and discuss the way that operations management within the organization might deal with each stage.
3. Open innovation is an attractive idea. Many organizations coming together to share resources provides a much easier route to accessing the resources each needs. Discuss the issues involved with open innovation networks.
4. 'Innovation in the last century was based on finding a market need that was not filled, and then using innovation to fill it. In the 21st century, innovation is increasingly about creating needs that have never been thought of before.' Discuss this statement.
5. Think of a product or service for which users have driven innovation in its development. Discuss how the product started, and where it may be heading.

Further Reading

Benner, M.J. and Tushman, M.L. (2003) 'Exploitation, exploration and process management: the productivity dilemma revisited', *Academy of Management Review*, **28**(2), 238–256.

Brito, C.M. (2018) 'Promoting the creation of innovation ecosystems: the case of the University of Porto', *Journal of Innovation Management*, **6**(3), 8–16.

Burns, T. and Stalker, G.M. (1961) *The Management of Innovation,* Tavistock, London.

HBR's 10 Must Reads on Innovations, (2013), Harvard Business Review Press, Boston, MA.

Johnsson, M. (2017) 'Creating high-performing innovation teams', *Journal of Innovation Management,* **5**(4), 23–47.

Satell, G. (2017) *Mapping Innovation: A Playbook for Navigating a Disruptive Age,* McGraw Hill, New York.

Tidd, J. and Bessant, J. (2013) *Managing Innovation: Integrating Technological, Market and Organisational Change,* 5th edn, Wiley, Chichester.

References

Abernathy, W. and Utterback, J. (1978) 'Patterns of industrial innovation', *Technology Review,* **80**(7), 40–47.

Boer, H. and Gertsen, F. (2003) 'From continuous improvement to continuous innovation: a (retro)(per)spective', *International Journal of Technology Management,* **26**(8), 805–827.

Bounds, G., Yorks, L., Adams, M. and Ranney, G. (1994) *Beyond Total Quality Management: Toward the Emerging Paradigm,* McGraw-Hill, New York.

Catapult Network (2017) *Fostering Innovation to Drive Economic Growth,* https://catapult.org.uk/news/catapult-network-fostering-innovation-to-drive-economic-growth/

Chesbrough, H., Vanhaverbeke, W., & West, J. (Eds.). (2006). *Open Innovation: Researching a New Paradigm,* Oxford University Press, Oxford.

Gassmann, O. and Enkel, E. (2006) 'Constituents of open innovation: three core process archetypes', *R&D Management,* **39**(4), 311–316.

Hauser, H. (2010) *The Current and Future Role Technology and Innovation Centres in the UK,* https://catapult.org.uk/wp-content/uploads/2016/04/Hauser-Report-of-Technology-and-Innovation-Centres-in-the-UK-2010.pdf

Huizing, E. (2011) 'Open innovation: state of the art and future perspectives', *Technovation,* **31,** 2–9.

Imai, M. (1986) *Kaizen: The Key to Japan's Competitive Success,* McGraw-Hill, New York.

Isaksen, S.G. and Tidd, J. (2006) *Meeting the Innovation Challenge: Leadership for Transformation and Growth,* Wiley, Chichester.

Jager, B., Minnie, C., Jager, J. and Welgemoed, M. (2004) 'Enabling continuous improvement: a case study of implementation', *Journal of Manufacturing Technology Management,* **15**(4), 315–331.

Jantunen, A. (2005) 'Knowledge processing capabilities and innovative performance: an empirical study', *European Journal of Innovation Management,* **8**(3), 336–349.

Magnusson, M., Boccardelli, P. and Börjesson, S. (2009) 'Managing the efficiency–flexibility tension in innovation: strategic and organizational aspects', *Creativity and Innovation Management,* **18**(1), 2–7.

Muthusamy, S.K., Wheeler, J.V. and Simmons, B.L. (2005) 'Self-managing work teams: enhancing organisational innovativeness', *Organisational Development Journal,* **23**(3), 53–67.

Pyzdek, T and Keller, P. (2018) *The Six Sigma Handbook,* McGraw-Hill, New York.

Robertson, T.S. (1967) 'The process of innovation and the diffusion of innovation', *Journal of Marketing,* **31**(1), 14–19.

Smith, M., Busi, M., Ball, P. and Van Der Meer, R. (2008) 'Factors influencing an organisation's ability to manage innovation: a structured literature review and conceptual model', *International Journal of Innovation Management,* **12**(4), 655–676.

Styhre, A. (2008) 'The element of play in innovation work: the case of new drug development', *Creativity and Innovation Management,* **17**(2), 136–147.

Sydow, J., Schüssler, E., & Müller-Seitz, G. (2016). *Managing Inter-organizational Relations: Debates and Cases,* Palgrave, London.

Thompson, J.D. (1967) *Organisations in Action,* McGraw-Hill, New York.

Tidd, J. and Bessant, J. (2009) *Managing Innovation: Integrating Technological, Market and Organisational Change,* 4th edn, Wiley, Chichester.

Tonnessen, T. (2003) 'Continuous innovation through company-wide employee participation', *The TQM Magazine,* **17**(2), 195–207.

Trott, P. and Hartmann, D.A.P. (2009) 'Why open innovation is old wine in new bottles', *International Journal of Innovation Management,* **13**(4), 715–736.

Van de Ven, A.H. (1986) 'Central problems in the management of innovation', *Management Science,* **23**(5), 590–607.

West, J., Salter, A,. Vanhaverbeke, W. and Chesbrough, H. (2014) 'Open innovation: the next decade', *Research Policy,* **43**(5), 805–811.

Westland, J.C. (2008) *Global Innovation Management: A Strategic Approach,* Palgrave Macmillan, Basingstoke.

Womack, J.P. and Jones, D.T. (1996) *Lean Thinking: Banish Waste and Create Wealth in Your Corporation,* Simon & Schuster, New York.

Zaltman, G., Duncan, R. and Holbek, J. (1973) *Innovations and Organizations,* Wiley, New York.

PART 2 Designing

Contents

WANTED

An operations manager is needed to head our growing business. As part of a global organization delivering products and services to businesses you will need to be dynamic and resourceful.

You'll have the ability to draw on experiences from most business functions but particularly new product/service development, purchasing, logistics and operations. You should have a strong first degree, relevant professional qualifications and at least a proven 10-year record of delivering successful strategic change.

What does it take to become an Operations Manager?

We speak to Steven Barsanti, General Manager at GC Aesthetics to find out about managing operations in the Medical industry.

How did you get into Operations Management?

As a mechanical engineer originally, I was interested in designing and making things, I found the same skills were useful when designing operational processes. Operations management then became a natural career progression as I moved through various engineering and research and development roles.

What about the career attracted you?

The principle of transformation is very interesting to me: creating a value proposition from a set of inputs. Operations management also provides the opportunity to work with a broad range of people up, down and across the organisation. This in turn exposed me to organisational culture and introduced me to leadership. Working in operations also provides the opportunity to continually learn and adapt.

Do you think operations management provides a good grounding for higher level general management roles?

Absolutely and unequivocally. Operations management gave me the opportunity to 'touch the sides of the organisation' and get involved with all aspects of the business. This experience has given me a great platform to now lead the UK site in my current role as the General Manager. Having a solid background from my operations management role and a deep knowledge of how the 'engine' of the business operates certainly enables me to make better-informed decisions and engage with staff in a collaborative way.

Describe how your product ranges are managed. For example how do you decide when a new product is required or a change in technology would be useful?

We have recently introduced new processes to manage our products through their product life cycle. Firstly we review our existing product offering. There are products that have been in our portfolio for many years and are very mature and we assess the value of these products across different elements such as return on investment, supply chain complexities, duplication, voice of customer and maturity. This process has recently led us to discontinue a number of products in an attempt to optimising our portfolio of offerings.

Secondly, we are continually considering the introduction of new products. On approval of a new product we would set-up a development project that would be managed by our Engineering department using a stage-gate process. We take a collaborative approach as a number of different functions throughout the organisation are involved.

Can you briefly explain the main challenges involved in designing a product to meet the exacting standards of the medical industry.

Today, designing medical device and bringing it to market is changing with the introduction of the new Medical Device Regulation. The main challenge here is the need to provide primary clinical data for a new product. Historically clinical efficacy could be demonstrated using a clinical equivalence route (of a similar product currently on the market). That route is now no longer possible in many products. The design process of a medical device is fairly standardised but it must be done in a disciplined way using a clear set of design control procedures. A clear clinical user-need for the new product must be presented; the product must go through a rigorous pre-clinical test program (technical/physical testing, chemical testing, biocompatibility testing, sterilisation validation, etc.) and clinical data must be presented to support the safety of the device. On completion of all design and technical documentation we embark on a regulatory approval process on a global scale dictated by the marketing strategy for the product.

How do you go about choosing your suppliers – for example what vetting processes do you undertake?

We have critical (primary) suppliers and non-critical suppliers. Critical suppliers are those that provide raw materials/components that are directly used in, or come into contact with, the product or form part of the packaging of the product. Each supplier must demonstrate the necessary competence and knowledge and compliance to regulatory standards. We also carry out or own assessment and conduct a quality system audit to ensure they have the necessary controls in place to meet good manufacturing practices.

As we are positioned somewhere in the middle of the supply chain (if we consider the end-user to be the patient) we are also a supplier. In the UK market we operate in a B2C environment, supplying directly to the clinics and hospitals, whereas outside of the UK we operate in a B2B environment, supplying either subsidiaries within the organisation or through a third-party distributor network.

Irrespective of whether we are a supplier or a customer it is key to maintain good relationships with our supply chain partners.

4 Designing Products and Services

Learning Outcomes

After reading this chapter you should be able to:

- Explain the new product development process
- Discuss the role of platform strategies in managing product variety
- Assess how products can be mass-customized
- Identify key issues related to the organization of services
- Identify key operational activities related to the management of product innovation and service designs

The First Generation of Chrysler Jeep's WIPERs

Source: ©Khairil Azhar Junos/Shutterstock

As you read this case, please consider how a new product is created, and the various processes the designers have to go through in order to meet the customer's requirements.

The Jeep Grand Cherokee was first introduced in the US in 1993 as a high-end, sport utility vehicle (SUV). The commercial success of this new family of Jeeps was uncertain, as it had numerous new concepts and innovations that were not present in former Jeeps (i.e. the Cherokee and Wrangler). Moreover, a large portion of the development responsibilities for these innovations was outsourced.

For example, both the design and manufacturing of the wiper controller module (co-named WIPER) was outsourced to Motorola. The WIPER system links the switch (which is connected to the steering wheel) to the motor, wash pump and wiper blades. It translates the driver's command into the desired wiper mode. Although this is a simple function that many drivers take for granted, the new system took three years to progress from concept development to production.

The Concept

The controller used by older Jeep families applied relay-based technology, which made a 'clicking' sound when switching from ON to OFF – an annoying feature that Chrysler wanted to eliminate. Just imagine driving a car in rainy weather for hours, with the wiper controller clicking at you continuously! So Chrysler asked Motorola to develop a 'quiet' WIPER controller using Six Sigma quality principles. One plausible technical solution was to create a fully electronic controller. Because there were no radical innovations involved in the process, the development of the electronic 'el-WIPER' was carried out independently of Chrysler's involvement.

Challenges

Motorola faced some challenges. Not only was it working with Chrysler for the first time, but it had a tight budget and short development and manufacturing lead times. Although all the modules of the wiper system (i.e. motor, wiper arms, blades and wiper switch) had predetermined specifications set by Chrysler, how they would function as an integrated wiper system as part of the rest of the vehicle was not known. At this stage this was a new design and there were no cars available for testing the concept, so the designers had to rely on lab testing. New assembly lines were built so design and production engineers could work concurrently to ensure that the el-WIPERs were manufactured with Six Sigma quality. The final challenge Motorala faced was when Grand Cherokees were available for testing: el-WIPERs would catch fire when tested under certain conditions, even though they worked flawlessly in lab simulations and tests.

Learning from Failure

Because of these failures, interface specifications and compatibility issues had to be re-examined. As a consequence, the design team went back to the drawing board and started redesigning the system from scratch. Several solutions were assessed. This process provided Motorola and Chrysler with a valuable learning experience. Everybody gained a much better understanding of the windscreen wiper system as a whole, in terms of its functionality and interfaces with other elements of the vehicle. Most importantly, a great deal of the el-WIPER's specifications for the Grand Cherokee Jeep were redefined. This step was made possible through an active collaboration between Motorola and Chrysler to share and solve technical problems. Face-to-face meetings and daily phone calls became a habit.

What could the design team do to solve this problem as quickly and effectively as possible without having to change the manufacturing processes that were already in place? The ideal solution was to redesign the el-WIPER with a 'silent' relay. One of the advantages of relay-based technology for this application was that it would increase the robustness of the el-WIPER. The only problem was that all the relays available at the time were considered very 'noisy', as they all made clicking sounds. As a result, major relay suppliers in the world were invited to develop a silent relay, based on detailed technical requirements specified by Motorola. An innovation competition took place among the suppliers.

Solution

In less than a year, around 15 prototypes were tested and evaluated. In the end, a Japanese manufacturer was chosen as the sole supplier, because it was able to offer the best-performing silent relay at the most competitive price. The silent relay proved to be the key factor for economies of scale and scope, as it could also be used with other Jeep families (such as Cherokee and Wrangler). This meant that one common silent el-WIPER could be mounted on any Jeep without degradation in functionality and performance, and additional savings could be gained from economies of scale of components, universal tooling, and common assembly and manufacturing processes. This also meant that the silent el-WIPERs could be incorporated into future generations of Jeeps seamlessly with Six Sigma standards.

Source: Hsuan (1999)

Introduction

As we can see from the Jeep Grand Cherokee's experience, there were various uncertainties Motorola had to face when designing the WIPER system. Although the design concept was a simple one, the transition from lab test to on-car test added other dimensions of complexity and uncertainty. Even with a well-devised concept, a design that worked well at one stage of development (in the lab) had to be abandoned because of problems at the next stage (on the car). This highlights the pressure that the design team had to face in terms of lead times, cost and design options. As the case shows, the amount of money already invested in the design and manufacturing did not allow the team to redesign the el-WIPER system from scratch. They had to find solutions within the existing design. When introducing new designs to an existing systems it is important to test how the innovation performs with the rest of the system. Another issue that many manufacturers have to consider is how to create economies of scale from the innovations. This silent el-WIPER system ended up replacing the Wrangler and Cherokee's wipers systems too, effectively standardizing the system across the product range.

There is increasing pressure for firms to be competitive in the marketplace. They have to bring out products and services faster and offer the customers a wider range of choices. For instance, mobile phone makers must introduce at least two new models each year, with an array of new functionality such as more capable cameras and faster internet access.

Firms need to respond to the challenges of introducing new products and services into the market before their competitors, making sure they are defect-free and guaranteeing the desired level of service. So how should firms organize their development strategies? This chapter will begin by taking a look at the *New Product Development (NPD)* process, where product concepts are created and turned into designs. We shall learn about the product design strategies that firms pursue in order to achieve a balance between cost and performance. These strategies include product platforms, modularization and mass customization. Next, we link NPD processes to the management of manufacturing and services. Here we learn about how products and services are interlinked. We shall also learn about how services can be designed and the implications for an organization's front- and back-office processes.

The New Product Development Process

It often takes a long time for new products to be developed, evaluated, tested, manufactured, marketed and then sold into the market. Positive return on investment may not show up in the corporate accounting books until many years later. Take mobile phones, for example. The first commercial portable cellular phone, Motorola's Dyna TAC8000x, took more than 10 years to develop, with an investment of over $100 million.

Research and Development

New product development is often regarded as a part of the *Research and Development (R&D)* process (see Figure 4.1). **Research** is often referred to as a scholarly or scientific investigation. It is generally categorized as either basic or applied. In natural sciences, for instance, the main activity of *basic research* is to obtain a more complete understanding of the subjects under study (for example, superconductivity, the properties of chemical reactions, quantum physics or materials science), often with no implications for commercial applications. *Applied research* is directed primarily towards a specific practical aim (commercially or scientifically), with the goal of finding possible applications for the existing basic research. For example, silicon can be found in both semiconductors and cosmetic implants.

Research scholarly or scientific investigation or inquiry; generally categorzied as either basic or applied.

In many industries the goal of research is to apply scientific knowledge to a company's business, enabling it to lay the technological foundation for the development of new products or processes. Not all firms have the capability or resources to undertake research, and these companies tend to seek cooperation with universities and research centres.

The **development** (D) part of R&D, also referred to as *experimental development,* involves systematic but non-routine technical work that is often directed towards producing new or improved materials, products or services. Development also seeks to shift product or process concepts through a series of stages to prove, refine and ready them for commercial application. Many firms do not see a distinction between applied research and NPD, as many undertake both of these activities.

Development activity that involves systematic but non-routine technical work directed towards producing new or improved materials, products or services.

The high degree of uncertainty and risk inherent in R&D and NPD projects poses enormous decision-making difficulties for managers. Furthermore, R&D activity often includes other members of the supply chain and so requires cross-company collaboration. These factors make it extremely difficult to assess the return on investment of NPD projects. The transition from research to development can be incredibly challenging, as listed in Table 4.1.

Figure 4.1 Relationship between R&D and NPD

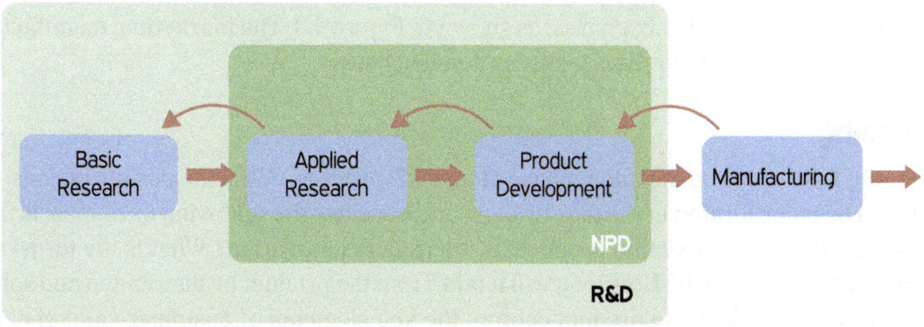

Source: Adapted from Hsuan (1999).

Table 4.1 Management challenges of research and development

	From research .	. . . to development
Cooperation	Informal	Formal
Knowledge	Tacit	Explicit
Criteria	Qualitative	Quantitative
Evaluation	Subjective	Objective
Business goal	Strategy alignment	Operational feasibility
Risk focus	Risk	Payback period
Cost focus	Opportunity costs	Cash flow
Financial focus	Option value	Contribution margin

Source: Adapted from Nixon and Innes (1997).

Figure 4.2 Drop-out rates for R&D projects

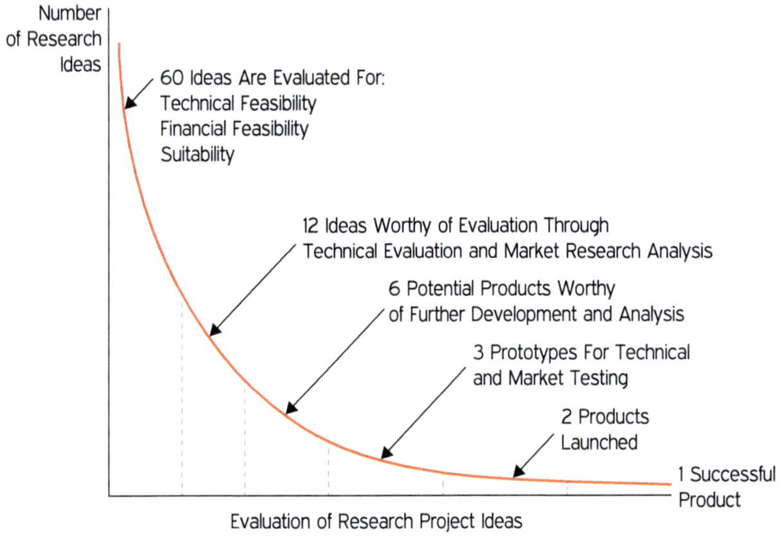

Source: Babcock (1996).

It is not surprising that the success rate of R&D projects tends to be low. Out of 60 ideas, typically only one project passes through all the NPD hurdles – technical evaluation, market research analysis, development, prototyping and product launch – a success rate of 1.67%. Figure 4.2 illustrates this drop-out rate for R&D projects.

Phases of Development

The NPD process can be divided into six phases, as shown in Figure 4.3. The marketing, manufacturing and finance departments are also involved with various tasks, as detailed below.

Phase 0: Planning

Planning is generally referred to as the initial phase of an NPD process. Often the designers consider the amount of innovation that is to be incorporated in the new product and consider the following questions: is the product simply an upgrade of or increment to an existing product? Is it a radical innovation? What is the target market? Does the firm have the capability to develop it? How long will it take? Can the product be distributed and sold with the current supply chain? To what extent does the product capture the key elements of customer value (i.e. functional, social, emotional, epistemic and conditional)?

At this stage, marketing activities usually include the articulation of market opportunities and the definition of market segments. Manufacturing identifies production constraints and sets up the supply chain strategy. In addition, the R&D department provides an overview of available technologies and the finance department provides the financial goals. Most importantly, the general manager, and sometimes the chief executive officer (CEO), is likely to allocate resources to the project.

Phase 1: Concept Development

Concept development is the phase when the designers investigate the feasibility of product concepts, develop industrial design concepts and build and test experimental prototypes. At this stage, the marketing department is in charge of collecting customer needs and identifying lead users and competitor products. This means that manufacturing costs need to be estimated and production processes checked for feasibility. Moreover, the finance department has to facilitate economic analysis, while the legal department investigates patent issues.

The early stages of NPD can be messy and are often referred to as the *fuzzy front end*. One of the main challenges during this stage is to understand how to capture and integrate customer requirements. This can be a daunting task, as the customers can have many roles in the NPD process (Figure 4.4), including customer as a resource, co-creator or user.

Figure 4.3 The new product development process

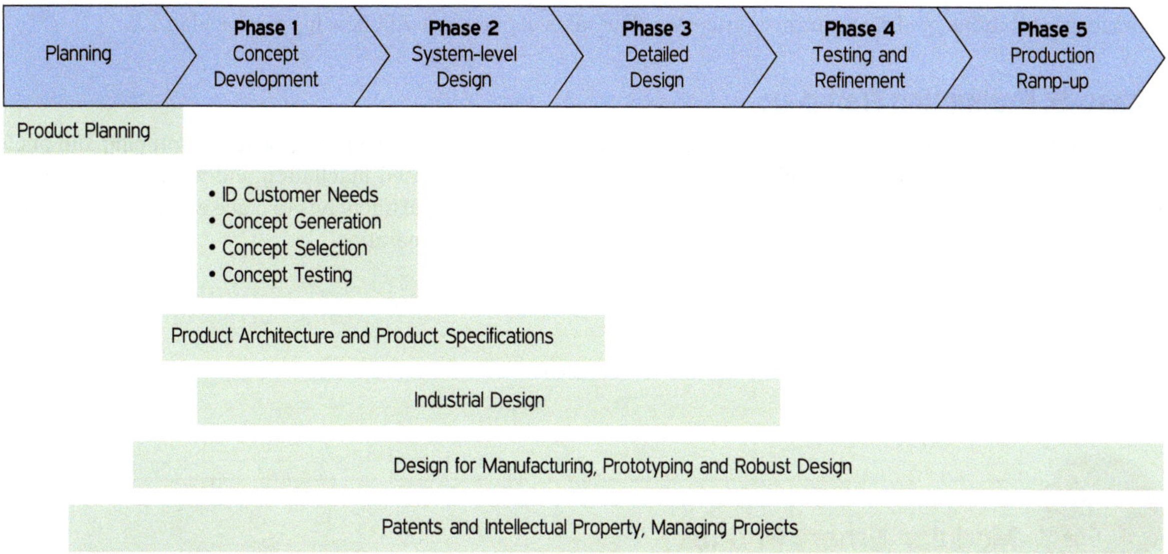

Source: Ulrich and Eppinger (2008).

Figure 4.4 Customer roles in NPD

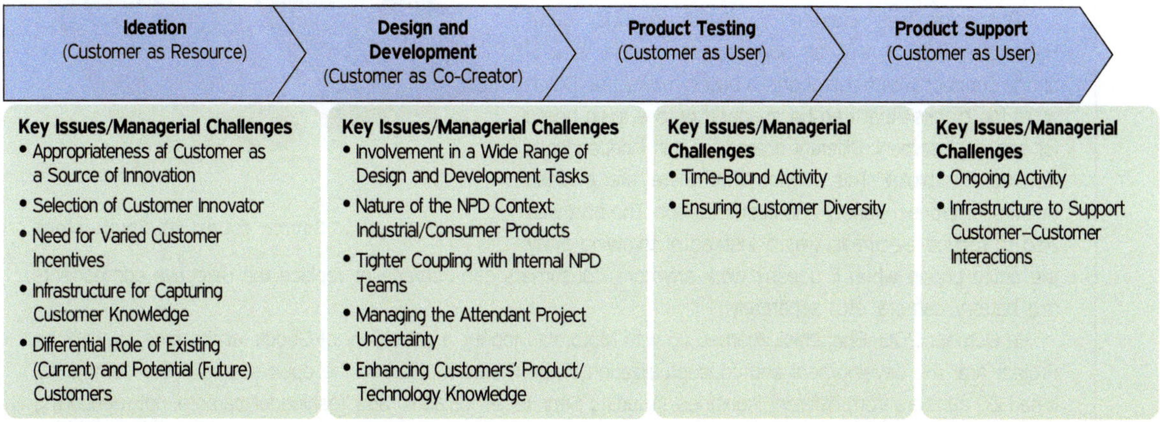

Source: Adapted from Nambisan (2002).

Phase 2: System-level Design

In the system-level design phase the designers typically generate alternative product designs and systems. The marketing department is usually responsible for developing marketing plans for product options and extended product families. The procurement department is responsible for deciding whether it would be more cost-effective to make key components in-house or to source them from external manufacturers, and for identifying suppliers for outsourced components. The manufacturing department will define final assembly schemes and set target costs.

Phase 3: Detailed Design

In the detailed design phase the designers define each part, choose materials and assign specification limits for the components. This means that, at this stage, the manufacturing department has to define piece-part production processes, design tooling, define quality assurance processes and begin procurement of tooling.

Phase 4: Testing and Refinement

In the testing and refinement phase, the designers typically have to perform reliability, life and performance tests. They are also responsible for obtaining regulatory approvals and implementing design changes. Concurrently, the marketing department has to develop promotion and launch materials and facilitate field testing. In addition, the manufacturing department has to facilitate supplier ramp-up, refine fabrication and assembly processes, train the workforce and refine quality assurance processes. The sales department will develop a sales plan.

Phase 5: Production Ramp-up

In the production ramp-up phase, production methods are likely to change from small-scale prototyping and pilots to higher-volume production methods, often requiring expensive dedicated machinery and workers. The design department has to evaluate early production units and the marketing department has to place early promotion with key customers. This is when the entire production system starts its full operation.

Stop and Think

Why do good designs sometimes become bad products?

SHORT CASE 4.1

Modular Smart Phones?

Source: ©AlexLMX/Shutterstock

Imagine that you can customize your smart phone any way you like it. You can personalize how it looks and how it functions, and you get to make the upgrades and repairs seamlessly.

Phoneblok was created by Dutch designer Dave Hakkens in 2012. It was an open-source modular smartphone concept where the phone is built in 'bloks' (the Dutch word for 'blocks') that can be snapped onto a main board for easy replacement. Different companies can independently develop the bloks. This means that there are endless options for product variety and customization. The goal was also to reduce electronic waste. Instead of throwing away the entire phone when it doesn't work anymore, consumers can upgrade or replace the defective components (e.g. battery, camera, etc.) separately.

In October 2013, Phoneblok teamed up with Motorola Mobility, a subsidiary of Google at the time, to work on Project Ara. The development and conceptualization of the modules relied on the open-source online community. It had 20 partners from different industries, including Sennheiser for audio and Toshiba for camera, not mentioning smartphone users in general, of which there are approximately 5 billion. With open source, the users can build and fully customize the smartphones through the Ara Configurator.

In 2015, prototypes of different versions of the phone were pilot tested in Puerto Rico, in compliance with US telecommunication laws. Google had planned to ship a new model called the 'Developer Edition' in late 2016 with subsequent consumer launch of Project Ara in 2017. Sadly, despite its potential and the efforts put into the development of modular smartphones for three years, in September 2016, Google suspended Project Ara. The project might have become too costly and complex for Google to manage, given the number of partners involved in the project and technological advancement of the modules.

Following Project Ara, start-ups all around the world began to replicate the concept of modular smartphones. Fairphone, another Dutch company, for instance, designs smartphones with social ethical supply chains in mind. Fairphones are designed with six modules: display, camera, battery, core, top and bottom. The modular architecture of the phones makes it possible for the phones to be disassembled and reassembled easily. This means that the modules can be easily isolated for upgrade, repair and recycling. Its online shop offers a selection of spare parts supplied with repair instructions, encouraging the users to do the repair themselves. Another service is recycling. When modules become obsolete, the users can return the whole phone or the modules to the company or third-party partners for recycling. In order to encourage recycling, users get a refund of €40 for Fairphone 1 or Fairphone 2 or €20 for any phone (as long as it can be turned on) towards a Fairphone 3 order.

Questions

1. To what extent do modular designs add value in making sustainability possible?
2. What are the challenges of modular designs?
3. What could Google have done to continue the development of Project Ara?
4. What can Fairphone learn from Project Ara?

CSR

Source:
https://www.cnet.com/news/project-ara-everything-we-know-about-googles-modular-phone/
https://*shop.fairphone.com/en/spare-parts/*
https://www.dezeen.com/2013/10/19/phonebloks-mobile-phone-concept-by-dave-hakkens/

Product Platforms

GLOBALIZATION

Product life cycles are getting shorter for many products, such as mobile phones, cars and video games, and many firms are relying on their NPD capabilities to develop products quickly and to cover a wide range of markets. These products have to be designed to function as specified and meet all regulations of the target markets. One strategy that can help firms to achieve this goal is by creating a **product platform**.

Platform strategy is basically a foundation for designs that can be used to build a large variety of products. It forms a structure from which a stream of *derivative products* can be developed. With a platform strategy, designs can be shared and reused, so that the designers don't have to start from scratch each time they create a new product. One of the first successful companies to pursue platform thinking on a large scale was Sony. Between 1980 and 1990, Sony introduced more than 160 variations of Walkman, a portable cassette player, based on a platform strategy. Sony continues to apply a platform strategy in its current products.

Product platform set of interconnected subsystems that form a common structure, from which a stream of derivative products can be developed and produced.

In car manufacturing, the platform shared between different car models might be a set of common designs, engineering and production processes. Major components, such as chassis, steering and suspension, are shared across models. For example, the platform for the Audi A4 is the basis for the VW Golf, the new Beetle and the Bora product families (Lung *et al.*, 1999). The Volkswagen Group also applies a platform strategy to support its brand strategy with different strategic objectives: see Figure 4.5. The brands are segmented according to cost strategy or differentiation strategy in relation to the product price, which can range from low to high. The Skoda Oktavia, for instance, has a low price tag and is produced based on cost leadership. Conversely, the Audi TT is expensive and highly differentiated.

Figure 4.5 VW inter-firm product platform development

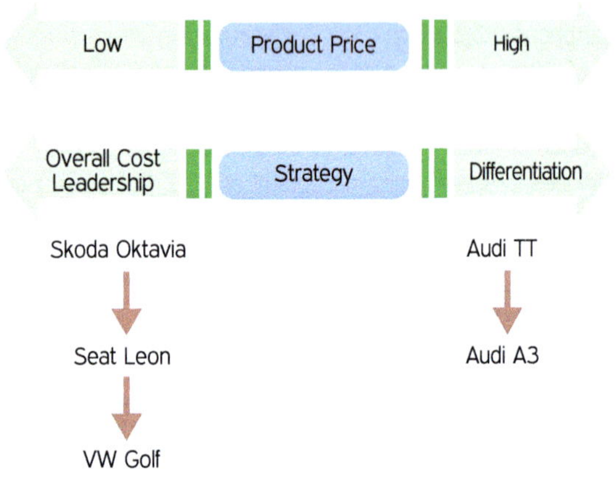

Source: Adapted from Trott (2008).

Platform strategy originated from the quest for product design simplification in the early 1990s. Many firms were facing tremendous pressure to reduce manufacturing costs, shorten product development lead-time and bring products to the market faster than before. There are many advantages associated with platform strategy, including:

- Reduced development and manufacturing costs
- Reduced incremental costs of addressing the specific needs of a market segment
- Reduced fixed costs of developing individual product variants
- Reduced development time
- Reduced systemic complexity
- Improved ability to upgrade products
- Lowered investment risks
- Greater degree of component and subsystems reuse
- Increased responsiveness of partners and suppliers
- Higher product variety offered to customers.

As the product life cycles of many products, such as mobile phones and computers, get ever shorter – new models are being introduced to the market much faster than before – many firms find that implementing platform strategies can be extremely difficult. This means that they have to be able to capture customer needs and market changes faster than before. One strategy to tackle this challenge is to increase the number of product variants, so that customers have more options to choose from. But too much product variety can create coordination problems for the firm. As a consequence, many firms are shifting their strategy towards reducing the number of platforms while increasing the number of derivative models and products.

This trend tells us that derivative products will be developed from fewer platforms. Reducing the number of platforms, while increasing the number of product variants (i.e. more options for customers to choose from), requires that there be components that can be shared with other platforms. Some of the key considerations when configuring platforms include:

- How to make sure that the platform is compatible with complementary products
- How to create technology competencies that prevent imitation
- How to share components and designs effectively
- How to maintain platform leadership – that is, how to maintain its market leadership in its core technical area.

WORKED EXAMPLE 4.1

Platform Reduction Decision

Yamaha has £500 million to invest in new models of motorbike for the next 10 years. It knows it costs £100 million to develop a platform and then £10 million to develop each separate model from the basic platform.

Problem: *If Yamaha needs 10 new motorbikes (or new models) to sell over the 10 years, how many platforms would you advise it to develop?*

Approach: Start by working out the total development cost for all 10 motorbikes, then work out how many platforms Yamaha can afford to invest in.

Solution:

$$\text{Development cost of 10 new bikes} = (\text{100 new bikes}) \times (\text{£10 million to develop})$$
$$= \text{£100 million to develop 10 new bikes}$$

$$\text{Investment left for platforms} = \text{total investment} - \text{development cost of new bikes}$$
$$= \text{£500 million} - \text{£100 million} - \text{£400 million}$$

$$\text{Number of platforms} = \frac{\text{Investment left for platforms}}{\text{Development cost per platforms}} = \frac{\text{£400 million}}{\text{£100 million}} = 4 \text{ platforms}$$

Yamaha needs to develop four platforms.

Modularization

One of the main factors that influence the management of platforms is how to simplify the complex processes related to the platform. This process is called *modularization* and it starts by partitioning the complex processes into simpler processes so that each portion can be dealt with separately. For instance, a mobile phone platform has both hardware and software and it would be much easier for the designers to be able to work on the development of these two processes independently. They can specialize in their own knowledge area, hence making the design and production processes more efficient. This can shorten the NPD cycle and reduce manufacturing costs.

Many people don't even bother to upgrade their computers any more; they just buy a new one. This is made possible because IBM-compatible PCs are modular systems that comprise key modules (operating system, keyboard, mouse, monitor, etc.) that can be easily mixed and matched. These modules are manufactured by various suppliers. As long as the interfaces of the modules comply with the industry standards, so that when they are plugged together the PC works, any company can make and sell them in the market.

Virtually all systems can be modularized. The first step to understanding how modularization works in a system is to identify how the system can be decomposed – that is, how it can be broken down into simpler, smaller portions. This process of simplification is referred to as *modularization*. For example, an automobile (a much more complex system than a PC) can be decomposed into four levels of complexity (Figure 4.6):

1. *System* – this is the level before deconstruction starts. For example, automobile systems can be passenger cars, sports cars, vans, etc.
2. *Subsystem* – the automobile system can be broken down into various subsystems, such as windshield wiper system, braking system, intelligent transportation systems (ITS), anti-lock braking system (ABS), engine, etc.
3. *Module* – each subsystem is further decomposed into modules. For example, the windscreen wiper subsystem is decomposed into wiper motor, motor, wipers controller, etc.
4. *Component* – each module is further decomposed into components. For example, the wipers' controller is made of various components, such as nuts, bolts, capacitors and resistors.

There may be many layers of decomposition, depending on the complexity of the system, but the component level is considered the lowest level of decomposition, as a component is a discrete item that cannot be broken down further.

Modular Product Architectures

Modular product architectures enable firms to minimize the physical changes required to achieve a functional change. The design of the furniture (like IKEA furniture) in Figure 4.7 illustrates an example of modular design. The physical components, such as the internal rails and hooks, shelves, doors, drawer unit, sides/bases/tops, and top, each have independent functions. Changes made to one of the components should not affect the function of the other components. For instance, the purpose of internal rails and hooks is to support hanging items. Making changes to the rails and hooks does not affect the function of the other components, such as the doors (to protect from dust and sun).

Figure 4.6 Modularization levels in automobiles

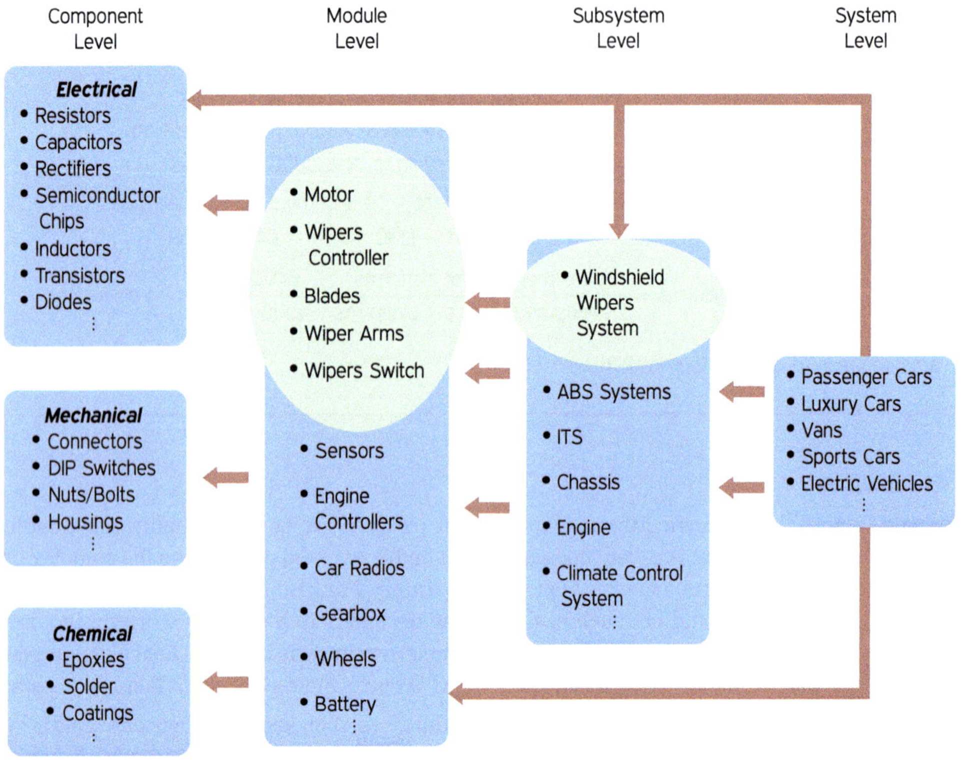

Source: Adapted from Hsuan (1999).

Figure 4.7 Example of modular design

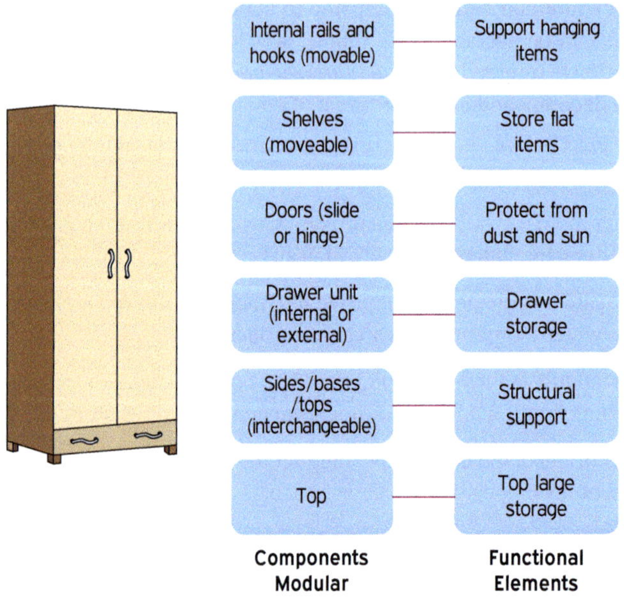

Source: Adapted from Ulrich (1995)

Modular product architecture designs provide the foundation for flexible platforms, as they allow for product variations. These designs intentionally create independence between components by standardizing interface specifications. That is, the components can be disassembled and recombined into new configurations. Product variants can be realized with less difficulty, as changes in one component do not lead to changes in other components. Physical changes can be implemented more easily without adding complexity to the manufacturing system. Consider another product such as personal computers, there is a wide range of screens, keyboards and mouses in the market you can choose from and simply plug-and-play into the PC without affecting its functionality.

The motivation behind this strategy is to gain cost savings through economies of scale from component commonality, inventory and logistics, and to introduce technologically improved products more rapidly. It also allows the firm to easily make product changes such as upgrades, add-ons, product line extensions and cosmetic adaptations. This in turn enables the firm to make use of customer feedback and alter its systems accordingly by substituting some components while retaining others. Other examples of products with modular product architectures include LEGO toys, bicycles, elevators and mobile phones.

Integral Product Architectures

With *integral product architectures,* modifications to any single component cannot be done without the redesign or reconfiguration of the other components, which can be expensive and time consuming. Figure 4.8 provides an illustration of an integral design approach to the furniture example. This piece of furniture is very expensive and inflexible to use, and is hand built by a traditional furniture builder. In contrast to the modular furniture design, the integral design does not exhibit a one-to-one relationship between components and the functional elements. In other words some components are involved in more than one function and some functions require more than one component. For instance, the function of structural support is dependent on three components: fixed middle structure, structural fixed external chassis, and structural top. If changes are made to fixed middle structure, it will affect the functionality that; allows the user to store flat items, that protect contents from dust and sun, and that ensures robust structural support.

Examples of integral designs include Formula One cars, satellites, the human body and even computers. The Apollo computer of the 1980s, for example, was considered more integral than IBM PCs or Sun Microsystems. High performance was emphasized and the workstation was designed with a proprietary architecture based on Apollo's own operating and network management systems. Much of the hardware was designed in-house. Apollo's designers believed that it was necessary for various parts of the design to be highly interdependent in order to achieve high levels of performance in the final product (Baldwin and Clark, 1997).

Managing Product Architectures

Similar systems produced by different companies undoubtedly have different product architectures, as a result of different design and technology choices. For instance, although Sony's and Philips' high-definition TVs are similar, the way they are designed and manufactured is specific to each company, dependent on the firm's NPD and manufacturing strategy, as well as on how its relationships with suppliers and customers have evolved over time. Depending on market needs and the technological core competencies of the firm, the trade-offs between modular and integral architecture strategies should be assessed carefully. Some trade-offs are summarized in Table 4.2.

Figure 4.8 Example of integral design

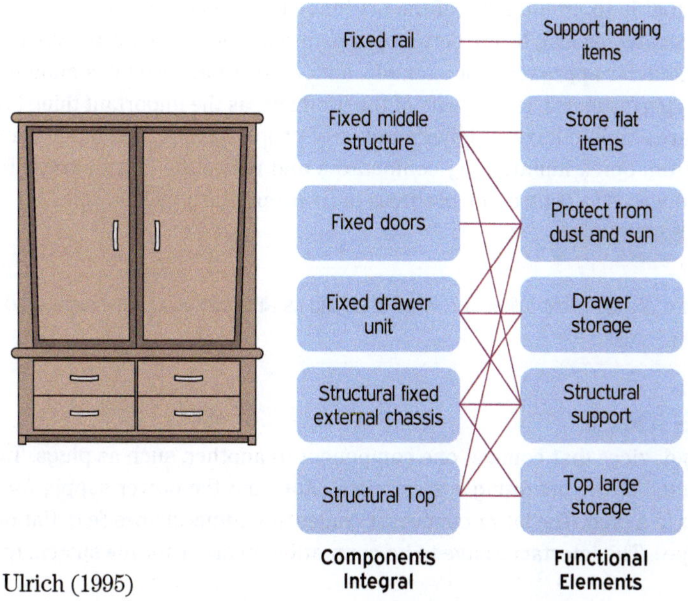

Source: Adapted from Ulrich (1995)

Table 4.2 The trade-offs between modular and integral designs

Benefits of modular designs	Benefits of integral designs
• Task specialization	• Interactive learning
• Platform flexibility	• High levels of performance through proprietary technologies
• Increased number of product variants	• Systemic innovations
• Economies of scale in component commonality	• Faster access to information
• Cost savings in inventory and logistics	• Protection of innovation from imitation
• Lower life cycle costs through incremental improvements such as upgrades, add-ons and adaptations	• High entry barriers for component suppliers
• Flexibility in component reuse	• Craftsmanship
• Independent product development	
• Outsourcing	
• System reliability due to high production volume and experience curve	
Examples: elevators, mobile phones, IBM PCs, LEGO toys	Examples: Formula One cars, Apollo computers, satellites

Source: Adapted from Mikkola and Gassmann (2003).

If the firm's goal is to reach as many customers as possible with many product variants, then it should follow a modular product design strategy. Modular architectures try to use as many standard and generic components as possible. These components allow the firm to gain from economies of scale in component commonality, as the same components can be shared with other products. This leads to cost savings in inventory and logistics, as components can be bought and shipped in large quantities. The modular nature of the design allows specialization of individual tasks to take place independently of other tasks (e.g. software development does not have to be carried out together with hardware development). Modular products typically rely on manufacturing processes that can support the production of high volumes of products.

If, however, the firm's goal is to create state-of-the-art innovation, where performance is the key criterion, then integral product design strategies may be the better option. Integral design tends to avoid the compromises that are required when using a modular approach. For example, a module or part used in a number of products may not be optimized, in terms of its performance, for any one of the products, as the important thing is that it works in them all. Also, integral architectures tend to have a higher number of proprietary technologies than modular architectures. This protects the firm from quick imitation by competitors and raises the entry barrier for component suppliers, especially when the firm wants to control the progress of its proprietary technologies.

! Stop and Think

What kinds of challenge might a firm face when changing its NPD strategy from integral product design to modular product design, or vice versa?

The Role of Interfaces

Interfaces are basically devices that connect one component to another, such as plugs. Take the PC, for instance. The keyboard is connected to the operating system via a cable and the power supply for the operating system is connected to the outlet via a plug. The latter connector comes in various shapes (e.g. flat pins for the US and round pins for mainland Europe). The interfaces have to be compatible in order for the system to work.

Interface specifications define the protocol for the fundamental interactions across all components of technological systems. The setting and development of interface specifications have a huge impact on setting industry standards. Consider, for instance, the smartphone industry. Virtually all handset manufacturers in the world (e.g. Apple, Samsung, Huawei, Sony and others) are developing devices based on the 4G standard, fourth generation of broadband cellular network technology. The next-generation technology based on 5G standard will make data communication much faster and enable seamless coverage, hence opening up possibilities for development of new services.

Interface specifications define the protocol for the fundamental interactions across all components constituting a technological system.

The 5G standard has a strong influence in shaping the competitive landscape of the wireless communication industry. The technological development of the mobile devices, in terms of platform and product architecture design, has to comply with industry standards and specifications. This means that interfaces linking different systems with the 5G standard have to be specified and standardized in order to ensure compatibility. Standardization of interfaces allows the makers of components to concentrate their capabilities narrowly and deeply, and thus to improve their part of the system independently of others. It encourages supplier specialization and hence fosters the emergence of network organizations. The rate at which interface specifications change influences the way product architecture is controlled and therefore impacts on how firms organize within the industry, to compete or cooperate around the new set of interface specifications.

Organizing Product Designs for Manufacturing

During a product's design, its manufacturing processes must also be considered. Some simple products are made from just one part – a drinking glass, for example. However, most products are made from many parts, where each part in turn might itself be made from many parts. For example, consider all the different materials needed to make a swivel chair. A product design must include a **bill of materials (BOM)** listing all the materials and components needed to make the product and the quantities required. The BOM may also be referred to as the *product structure* or *product tree.*

Bill of materials (BOM) file (or product structure or product tree file) lists the description of the product (such as the material, components and quantity) and the sequence in which the product is to be assembled.

Figure 4.9 illustrates the product structure of a swivel chair, portraying its product hierarchy, from the lowest level (Level 4) to highest level (Level 0) of assembly order.

- The swivel chair (Level 0) needs one seat and one base (Level 1).
- The seat is assembled from one back, one frame, two arms and one button (Level 2).
- The back is assembled with moulded back and padded back cushion (Level 3).
- Finally, the padded back cushion comprises one batting, one fabric and three buttons (Level 4).

Figure 4.9 Product structure for a swivel chair

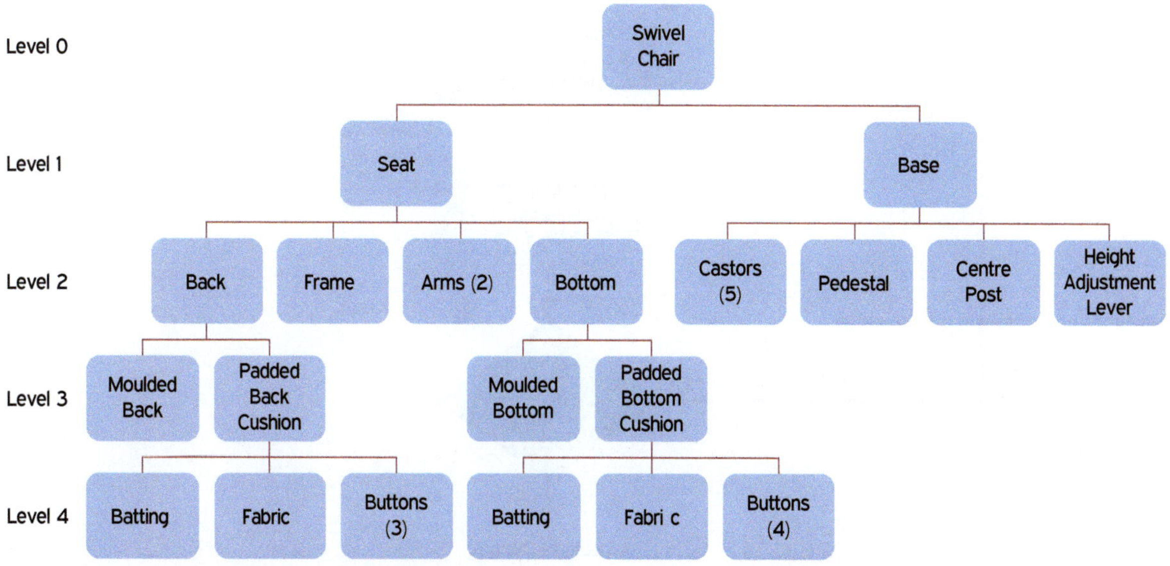

Source: Adapted from Davis and Heineke (2005, p. 548).

Similar logic applies for the base (Level 1) and the bottom (Level 2) and its subassemblies in Levels 3 and 4.

Each of the components in level 0 to level 4 is considered a Stock Keeping Unit (SKU), hence has its own part number. For a standard chair, like the swivel chair, the design is modular where all the components are generic. For a chair with integral design, the BOM would have fewer levels of decomposition.

The BOM provides the foundation for linking the final product design to the design guidelines or methods for other processes – what is known as the *design for X* (DFX). Here X denotes the various criteria that affect the characteristics of a product, such as reliability, robustness, serviceability, environmental impact, assembly or manufacturing. The design guidelines provide methods and information that help designers and managers to make decisions in order to control and improve the characteristics of a product. The most common DFX method is *design for manufacturing* (DFM), as it provides the information for estimating the manufacturing costs directly. The decision process of the DFM method is illustrated in Figure 4.10.

Contemporary Thinking: Product Design for Sustainability

The volume of waste electrical and electronic equipment (WEEE) continues to grow at an alarming rate, at 3–5% per year in the EU (Eurostat, 2019). If not treated properly after disposal, the various substances in WEEE can cause serious health and environmental risks. As products reach End-of-Life (EOL), what are the choices producers have to ensure proper disposal or recovery of the products? The producers have a few options for recovery

Figure 4.10 Decisions related to the DFM method

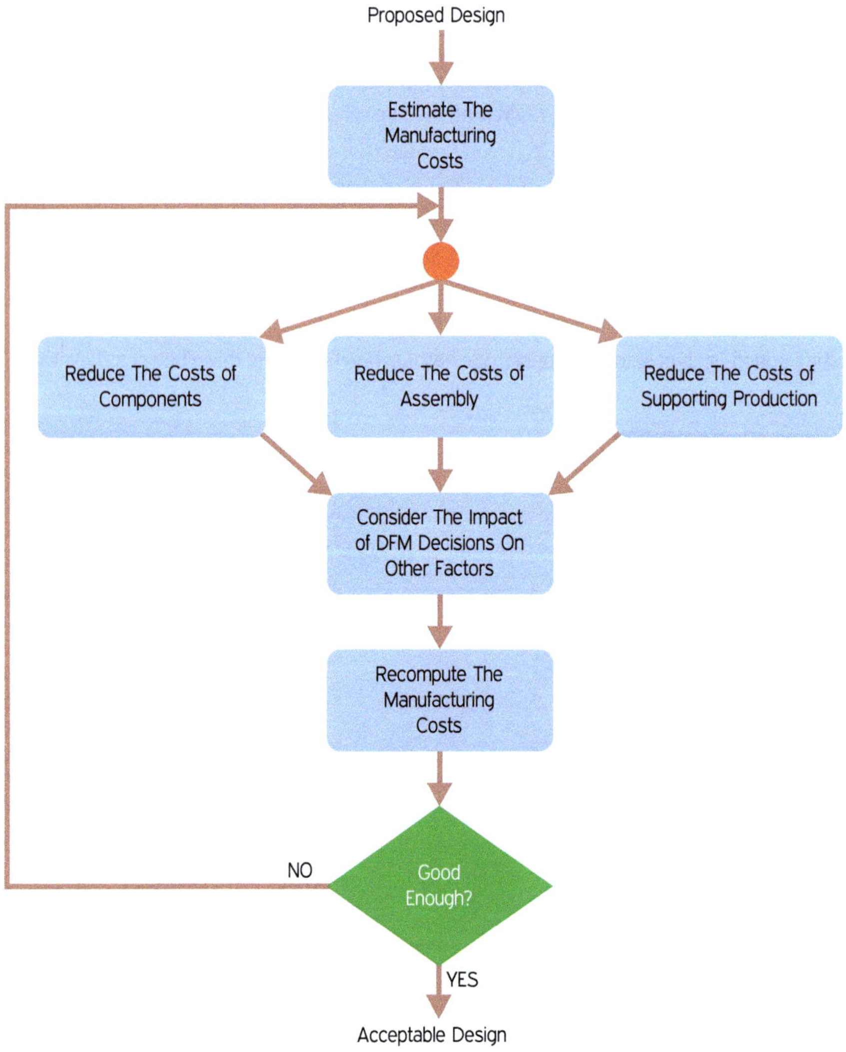

Source: Ulrich and Eppinger (2008, p. 213).

(De Britto and Dekker, 2002): product, component, material or energy recovery. In product recovery, the products are recycled or sent to a secondary market. In component recovery, the products are dismantled and the recovered components can be reused. In material recovery, the recuperated material is recycled into new material. In energy recovery, the products are incinerated to create energy.

As well as minimizing the amount of waste sent to landfills, increasingly companies are making efforts to increase recycling by trying to find ways to recover as many components and materials as possible from EOL products. While some components can be reused as-is, others have to be recycled and remanufactured.

Responsible companies are considering how to ease recovery already at the R&D and NPD stages through a concept called Design-for-Disassembly (DFD). The DFD method is deployed during the NPD stage and focuses on minimizing the complexities of disassembly. It typically aims at minimizing the number of parts and maximizing the use of common materials.

The key point is …

that 'green' product designs take a product's EOL and its disposal into consideration and as part of this the ease of disassembly is thought about during the early stages of design.

Stop and Think

How can you apply modularity concepts in Design-for-Disassembly?

Mass Customization

BUSINESS INTEGRATION

Mass customization emerged as a concept in the late 1980s. Generally, it emphasizes the need to provide products that can meet customers' individual needs through unique combinations of modular components. The goal is to produce customized products (to achieve economies of scope) at low costs (to gain from economies of scale). It allows companies to penetrate new markets and capture customers whose special needs could not be met with standard products. Da Silveira *et al.* (2001) identified six success factors of mass customization:

- *Customer demand for variety and customization:* successful mass customization depends on the trade-offs between the potential sacrifices that the customer makes and the firm's ability to produce and deliver customized products
- *Appropriate market conditions:* being the first to develop a mass customization system can provide competitive advantage for the firm
- *Value chain readiness:* successful mass customization depends on the willingness and readiness of suppliers, distributors and retailers to match the demands of the firm (mass customization is discussed in Chapter 8)
- *Technology availability:* the implementation of advanced manufacturing technologies (AMTs) is fundamental to enable the development of mass customization systems
- *Customizable products:* successful mass-customized products must be modularized, versatile and renewable
- *Shared knowledge:* successful mass customization depends on the firm's ability to translate customer demands into new products and services. The implementation of mass customization involves product configuration, value chain network, process and information technology, and the development of a knowledge-based organizational structure.

Chapter 8, p249

Product variety is driven by customer demand. The capability to design and produce products in collaboration with customers provides mass-customizing firms with the ability to capture valuable new knowledge. Mass customization strategy has been implemented with computers, Levi's jeans, bicycles, Nike shoes, Smart cars and many other products. The National Bicycle Industrial Company (NBIC) of Japan, for instance, has focused on its manufacturing competence to create customized bicycles. Over 11 million combinations were available, with production times ranging from 8 to 10 days. The company was able to produce 50 to 60 semi-customized bikes per day (Bell, 1993).

WORKED EXAMPLE 4.2

Product Complexity

Customers of a car dealer were given a free choice of combining 15 paint colours, four interior fabrics, three engines (4, 8 and 12 cylinder), a choice of manual or automatic gearbox, and a list of 10 different optional extras that could be chosen independently of each other.

Problem: *How many different options can the customers choose from?*

Approach: Each choice can be combined with other options independently: hence, the total number of options is the arithmetical product of the number of option choices.

Solution:

$$\text{Number of options} = (15 \text{ paint colours}) \times (4 \text{ interior fabrics}) \times (3 \text{ engines}) \times (2 \text{ gearboxes}) \times (10! \text{ Optional extras}) = 1{,}306{,}368{,}000$$

(Note: 10! is the factorial of 10:

$$10! = 10 \times 9 \times 8 \times 7 \times 6 \times 5 \times 4 \times 3 \times 2 \times 1 = 3{,}628{,}800)$$

Mass customization can be realized in many ways (Pine, 1993), as shown in Figure 4.11:

- Create products and services that are customizable by customers by involving them in the design phase
- Modularize components to customize end-products and services (e.g. postponed manufacturing involving design, manufacturing and distribution phase)
- Provide quick response through the supply chain (involving the distribution phase)
- Customize services around standard products or services (involving the distribution and sales phase)
- Provide point-of-delivery customization (involving the sales phase).

By using mass customization, firms can exploit their capabilities in NPD through market intelligence, so that customers' needs can be translated into individually tailored products.

Stop and Think

- What happens to the conventional analysis of the 4Vs (volume, variety, variation in demand and visibility), when the product is mass customized? Can you still achieve efficiency?
- What happens to the number of SKUs when greater product variety is introduced to the production process?

Approaches to Mass Customization

Gilmore and Pine (1997) proposed four approaches to customization (Table 4.3): collaborative, adaptive, cosmetic and transparent.

Figure 4.11 Methods for achieving mass customization

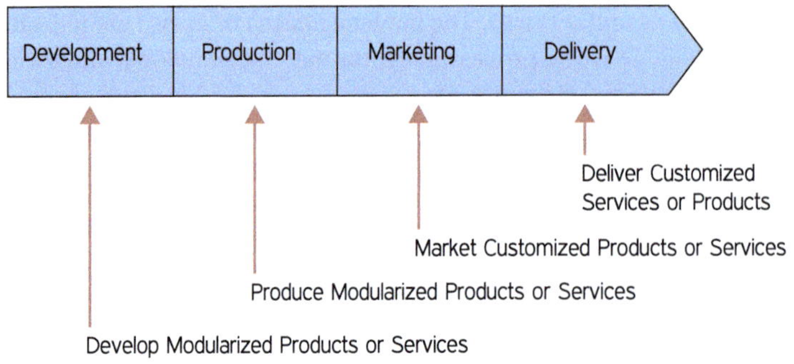

Table 4.3 Four approaches to customization

Type of customization	Product		Representation	
	Change	No change	Change	No change
Collaborative	X		X	
Adaptive		X		X
Cosmetic		X		
Transparent	X			X

- *Collaborative customization* helps the customers to articulate their needs and to identify the precise offering that fulfills their needs, such as with cars and kitchens.
- In *adaptive customization*, the product is designed so that users can tailor, modify or reconfigure it themselves to suit different occasions. For example, we can customize mobile phone features ourselves (ring tones, address lists, display patterns, etc.)
- With *cosmetic customization*, a standard product is presented differently to different customers, such as with the design of promotional items, where the individual customer's name is printed on the product.
- In *transparent customization* the individual customers are offered unique goods or services from a standard package. For example, based on a customer's previous purchase records, Amazon.com is able to recommend books and gifts that the customer might consider buying.

WORKED EXAMPLE 4.3

Mass Customization

You have just been hired as the product-marketing manager of a fashion jeans company. In order to increase customer satisfaction, the company is devising strategies to create customized jeans for individual customers. Your job is to figure out how to create unique value for the customers through mass customization.

The company sells three types of jeans:

- High fashion jeans: low sales volume, supplied directly by fashion factories, no option to make changes in stores
- Standard design jeans: high sales volume, supplied by the company, final tailoring added at the stores (e.g. name printing, special graphics printing, special buttons, final tailoring)
- Tailored jeans: varied sales volume according to season, supplied by the company, customers can order the jeans to their specific designs

Problem: *Apply the product–representation matrix in Table 4.4 to define the type of customization needed. What type of customization should you adopt?*

Approach: The first step is to classify the jeans according to the right customization strategy. Consider whether each type of jean can be customized by a change to the product and whether it can be customized by a change to how the product is represented.

Solution:

Table 4.4 Approaches to customization

	Product		Representation		
	Change	No change	Change	No change	Type of customization
High fashion jeans	X		X		Adaptive
Standard design jeans		X			Cosmetic
Tailored jeans	X			X	Collaborative

High fashion jeans fit best with adaptive customization, as there are no options to change the design of the jeans from the supplier (the product) or their visual appearance (the representation). The customers, however, can add accessories and make alterations themselves.

Standard design jeans fit best with cosmetic customization, as there are no options to change the design of the jeans (the product), but the final design of the jeans is tailored to customers' individual needs at the stores during the final purchase (the representation).

Tailored jeans call for collaborative customization, as there are changes both in the design of the jeans (the product) and in how the jeans should look (the representation). Customers need to articulate their design requests and needs before the jeans are produced.

There is another opportunity for the company to satisfy its customers through transparent customization. Although not practised by the company at the moment, it is possible for the company to offer new designs of jeans to its preferred customers based on their previous purchasing records.

Stop and Think

Consumers might be pleased to know that there is a wide range of product variety to choose from when purchasing a product, but what kinds of problem could they face when there are too many options? What kinds of problem does it present for the producers and retailers?

SHORT CASE 4.2

Oticon's Sumo Hearing Aid

Source: ©Pixel-Shot/Shutterstock

Most people with severe hearing problems tend to be conservative and stick to the same instrument for as long as possible. Some users are still wearing 30-year-old hearing instruments, as it takes a long time for the brain to adapt to new sounds and patterns.

Oticon, a Danish-based company, designs and manufactures a full range of hearing aids and fitting systems. Its most powerful behind-the-ear instrument is the Sumo, based on an analogue design, which has better power performance than a digital design. This is especially important for one niche of customers: those with profound hearing loss.

The development lead-time for the Sumo (from concept generation to final production) was a little over three years. The Sumo has been in production since 2002 and its product life cycle is estimated to be between 10 and 15 years, complemented with new versions approximately every 18 months. The trend in hearing aids, however, is changing from analogue to digital, so Sumo will probably be Oticon's last analogue product.

People have different shapes of ears and hence cannot all wear the same style of hearing aid. Hearing aids have to perform as specified, but also have to be adapted for each individual. Oticon applies the platform approach, with as many standardized components as possible. However, standardization needs to be balanced with innovation, as it is crucial for the company to prevent competitors from copying its innovation.

Questions

1. In what ways can the organization of NPD processes shape and influence the success of Sumo?
2. What type(s) of mass customization strategy is/are pursued with Sumo?
3. What kinds of process are involved in mass-customizing the SUMO?
4. How should Oticon plan for the future generations of its hearing aids?

Source: Juliana Hsuan, Copenhagen Business School, adapted from Mikkola and Skjøtt-Larsen (2006).

Product Service Systems

BUSINESS INTEGRATION

The service sector is becoming ever more important in industrialized economies. Service industries continue to dominate the UK economy. In 2017, 70.93% of the UK's GDP was generated by the services sector (STATISTA, 2020). Virtually everything we do, from buying goods to eating in restaurants, has service elements in it. When we buy a high-end video camera, for instance, we want to make sure we learn how it works. Sometimes the instruction manual is not clear enough. We also want to have access to a virtual help desk and other services. Inevitably, firms need to extend intangible aspects of products in order to satisfy various customer needs. Similarly, service providers such as restaurants, consultancies and banks are becoming increasingly dependent on products (especially with the help of new technologies) to enhance the perceived quality of the services offered.

Can services be designed so that they look like products? One of the biggest challenges of selling services is that they are intangible and heterogeneous. Services can't be touched, smelled, tasted or tried before purchase. Customers' requirements and needs also differ. *Productization* of services attempts to make intangible services more tangible. For example, a professional consulting firm might enhance its services to its clients by packaging the services with product documentation, such as executive materials, templates, worksheets and other tools. With service productization, the consulting firm can provide differentiation of its services and establish credibility with new clients.

Products should be designed with services in mind, and vice versa. The convergence process of creating products with a higher service content is referred to as **servitization of products**. Conversely, the convergence process of developing services to include product content is referred to as the **productization of services**. Together, servitization of products and productization of services form the *product–service system*.

Servitization of products the process of convergence of products with service content.

Productization of services the process of convergence of services to include product content.

CRITICAL PERSPECTIVE

Value propositions and customer expectations

Servitization is essentially about competing through value propositions that integrate services with product offerings (Avlonitis *et al.*, 2014). There are different types of value propositions depending on customer expectations, as shown in Table 4.5 (Avlonitis *et al.*, 2014, p. 10; adapted from Smith *et al.*, 2014).

Table 4.5 Types of value proposition and customer expectations

Type of value proposition	Customer expectation	Example
Selling an asset	Quality and performance of equipment	Offer customized product
Providing recovery of an asset	Minimum disruption in case of equipment failure	Repair of equipment after notification
Maximizing the availability of an asset	Fault free equipment	Provide remote and preventive maintenance
Offering outcomes for the customer	Assisting customers to achieve their goals	Take over customer functions and activities

The key point is ...

that the design of products and of their associated services have to be interlinked.

Service Design

Now that we have a better understanding of how products can be developed and designed for mass customization, let's find out about the role of service design.

Service any activity or benefit that one party can offer to another that is essentially intangible, and does not result in the ownership of anything.

A **service** is any activity or benefit that one party can offer to another that is essentially intangible and does not result in the ownership of anything. The production, delivery and consumption of services all take place at the same time. Services are also perishable: that is, they cannot be stored. When a service is designed, managers need to be aware of how it affects customer contact, the front- and back-office activities, its management processes and the bottom line.

A characteristic of many services is that they are extended, with elements or modules of the service consumed consecutively over a period of time. Examples of this type of service include air travel and sea cruises. In such services there are more complex relationships between elements of the service. An airline may provide different services for its coach class passengers and its business class passengers. On a cruise liner, passengers may choose which services to use and when to use them over the course of the cruise.

Whether the services are extended or consumed consecutively, all the service system elements must be designed in a way that creates a consistent service offering that achieves the strategic service vision of the organization. The service delivery system design considers three interrelated elements (Roth and Menor, 2003), as illustrated in Figure 4.12:

- Strategic service design choices
- Service delivery system execution, renewal and assessment
- Customer-perceived value of the total service concept.

The strategic design choices include choices related to structural, infrastructural and integration aspects of the system. Structural choices involve decisions related to the physical aspects of the delivery system, including facilities and layout, technology and equipment, aggregate capacity planning, and service product/process interfaces. Infrastructure choices relate to the people, policies, practices, processes and performance aspects of service design. Integration choices are concerned with issues related to operations organization and coordination, service supply chains, integration technologies, and learning and adaptive mechanisms aspects of the service design.

The strategic choices, in turn, influence how the realized service delivery system is executed or converted into customer-perceived value of the total service concept. These choices also impact on the possible gaps that might exist between the service delivered and customer perception of the service delivered.

Customer contact refers to the physical presence of the customer in the system, or the percentage of the time that the customer is in the system relative to the total service time.

Customer Contact

Because services involve **customer contact**, there are two elements that organizations need to consider when designing new services: the customer, and the communication channel with the customers. The *degree of customer contact* refers to the physical presence of the customer

Figure 4.12 Elements of service delivery systems

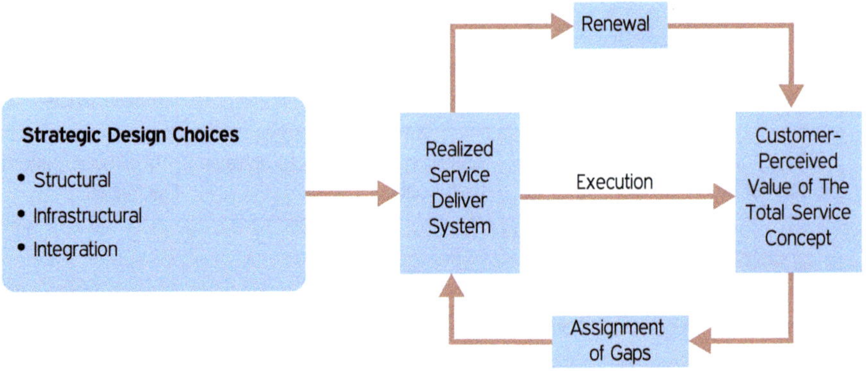

Source: Adapted from Roth and Menor (2003).

in the system or the percentage of the time that the customer is in the system, relative to the total service time (Fitzsimmons and Fitzsimmons, 2008):

$$\text{Degree of customer contact} = \frac{\text{Percentage of time the customer is in the system}}{\text{Total service time}}$$

In high-contact services (e.g. reception at hotels), the quality of service is determined by the perception of the customer's experience, as the customer participates directly in the process. In low-contact services (e.g. maintenance of trains), the customer has very little or no influence on the production process. Table 4.6 lists the major design considerations that an organization should consider in high- and low-contact systems.

Table 4.6 Major design considerations in high- and low-contact systems

Decision	High-contact system	Low-contact system
Product design	Both the environment and the physical product define the nature of the service	Customer is not in the service environment, so the product can be defined by fewer attributes
Process design	Stages of production process have a direct, immediate effect on the customer	Customer is not involved in most of the process steps
Capacity planning	To avoid lost sales, capacity must be set to match peak demand	Storable output permits setting capacity at some average demand level
Production planning	Orders cannot be stored, so smoothing production flow will result in loss of business	Both backlogging and production smoothing are possible
Forecasting	Forecasts are short term, time oriented	Forecasts are long-term, output-oriented
Facility location	Locations must be near the customer	Operations may be placed near supply, transportation or labour
Facility layout	Facility should accommodate the customer's physical and psychological needs and experience	Facility should enhance production
Scheduling	Customer is in the production schedule and must be accommodated	Customer is concerned mainly with completion dates
Worker skills	Direct workforce constitutes a major part of the service product and so must be able to interact well with the public	Direct workforce need have only technical skills
Quality control	Quality standards are often in the eye of beholder	Quality standards are generally measurable
Time standards	Service time depends on customer needs and therefore time standards are inherently loose	Work is performed on customer surrogates (e.g. forms) and time standards can be tight
Wage payment	Variable output requires time-based wage systems	'Fixable' output permits output-based wage system

Source: Adapted from Chase (1978).

Front and Back Office

Front-office activities activities where there is direct customer contact, whether face to face, or by email, telephone, or letter.

Back-office activities activities that are hidden from the customers.

The impact of customer contact on a service delivery system is often conceptualized in terms of front-office and back-office activities. **Front-office activities** are those where there is direct customer contact, whether face-to-face or by email, telephone or letter. **Back-office activities**, on the other hand, are activities that are hidden from the customers. The back office can also be interpreted as a platform from which many different front-office services can be managed. Front-office services will have a higher degree of customer contact than back-office services. The line of customer visibility separates the front- and back-office activities. Figure 4.13 provides an example of front- and back-office activities in processing a retail loan. Soliciting a loan application usually requires customer contact in the form of an interview. After the loan interview is completed and the application form filled out, a significant amount of back-office work is required to process the application. After the application process is checked, there is customer contact again as the customer is invited back to sign the document. Once the document is signed, the back-office proceeds on the post-loan processing activities.

Degree of variation the variation in the provision of a service, where customization for and interaction with customers are common sources of variation

Relative throughput time the interval of time between availability for use and completion of the service encounter

Service Process Matrix

The *service process matrix*, developed by Schmenner (1986, 2004), is a classification of service industry firms based on the characteristics of their service processes in terms of degree of variation versus the relative throughput time (Table 4.7). The **degree of variation** describes the customer's ability to affect the nature of the service being delivered. The **relative throughput time** describes the interval of time between availability for use and completion of the service encounter, measured for a service transaction as compared to others in the industry.

SHORT CASE 4.3

Kongsberg's Digital Platform Kognifai

Kongsberg Gruppen, head quartered in Kongsberg, Norway, is a diversified supplier of high-tech solutions for aerospace, marine and military operations. Following a consolidation of all IT activities under a new unit dubbed Kongsberg Digital, Kognifai, a new digital platform was launched in 2017 that creates a common infrastructure for all IT systems in the company. The Kognifai platform complements a variety of digital initiatives including the development of autonomous vessel navigation systems. Although the company has worked with real-time data analysis for a decade, the knowledge was dispersed within different business units. Kognifai instigates a common architecture for the company while also providing a range of open resources on GitHub platform.

Source: ©Red ivory/Shutterstock

Accompanying Kognifai was the release of APIs (application program interfaces), SDKs (software development kits) and a dedicated developer portal to allow for innovation via third-party complements. Offerings, or the apps available, are very diverse, ranging from cost control systems, simulation for digital twin technologies, to dry docking management and continuous data monitoring of different parameters. Applications available on the Kognifai platforms have been developed by Kognsberg in-house, by customers or other third-parties.

Questions

1. To what extent do digital platforms shape the integration of front- and back-office activities of Kongsberg?
2. What kinds of new services can potentially be developed through Kognifai?

Source: Viktor Avlonitis and Juliana Hsuan, Copenhagen Business School.

Figure 4.13 Activities in processing a retail loan

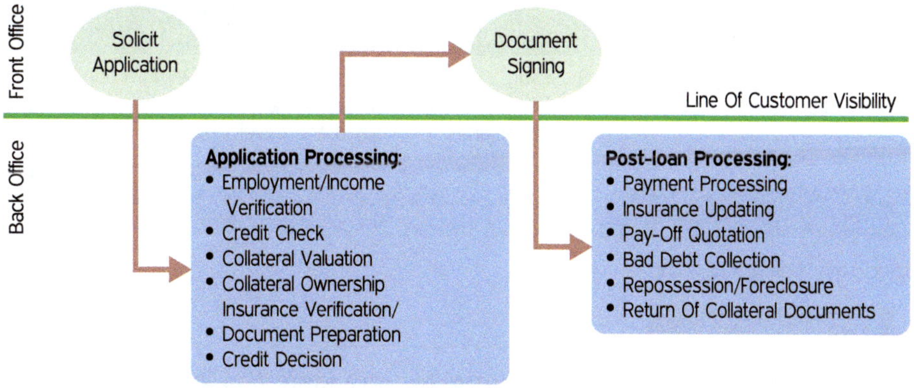

Source: Adapted from Metters and Vargas (2000).

Table 4.7 Service process matrix

Service type	Relative throughput time		Degree of variation	
	Low	High	Low	High
Mass service		X	X	
Service factory	X		X	
Service shop	X			X
Professional service		X		X

The service process matrix provides four classifications of services: *mass service, service factory, service shop* and *professional service.* The traditional tax accountant, for example, is classified as a professional service where customization and interaction is high (i.e. high degree of variation) and order-to-delivery time is high (i.e. high relative throughput time). In comparison, with firms such as H&R Block, the relative throughput time is much less and there is less interaction and customization.

Most services change over time. As the degree of variation and relative throughput time change over time, managers encounter new challenges. For instance, a Dutch network of care providers for the elderly delivers a variety of care and service packages, with three kinds of service: a basic service common to all customer groups; a set of services that can be configured by customer segment; and a set of services that allows for customization at an individual level (de Blok *et al.*, 2007).

Contemporary Thinking: IT (ERP) Implications: Virtual Service (e-Service)

With the increasing application of Internet technologies, virtual services are becoming a major competitive strategy for many service organizations. **e-Service** is the provision of service using online media, which can be delivered in a virtual environment with little or no human interaction (Voss, 2003). A range of services with respect to *customer relationship management* (CRM) is portrayed in Table 4.8. CRM can vary between e-service, such as the provision of pure services (e.g. computer services) and e-commerce, which is the sale of physical goods, such as CDs, through an environment such as Amazon. Other CRM includes selling information (e.g. infomediaries – intermediaries for information transaction), selling value-added service (e.g. online travel agents) and selling a bundle of service and goods (e.g. PCs).

e-Service the delivery of service using online media, which can be delivered in a virtual environment with little or no human interaction.

Table 4.8 A spectrum of virtual service strategies

e-Service <<<< The Internet and services >>>> e-Commerce				
Providing pure service – free or with service contract, e.g. computer service, status information	Selling information, e.g. infomediaries	Selling value-added service, e.g. online travel agent	Selling a bundle of service and goods, e.g. PCs	Selling goods, e.g. CDs
<<<< Customer relationship management >>>>				

Source: Adapted from Voss (2003, p. 89).

Stop and Think

Recall an experience you had when you were dissatisfied with a service. What caused it, and who was to blame?

Contemporary Thinking: New Service Development

Stages of Service Development

Although services and products differ in many aspects, the process of *new service development* (NSD) is not very different from that of NPD. Recall that the NPD process of physical products goes through six phases: planning, concept development, system-level design, detail design, testing and refinement, and production ramp-up. Figure 4.14 shows that the NSD cycle also goes through similar stages: design, analysis, development and full launch (Menor *et al.*, 2002).

The NSD cycle shows that the service design process is iterative and non-linear. When new services are being designed, the organization needs to focus on the formulation of new services objectives, idea generation and screening, and concept development and testing. During the analysis stage, managers need to analyse the business and obtain project authorization. After the analysis stage, the actual development of the service starts. During this stage the new service is designed and the related processes are tested. Organizations also need to train the personnel to deliver the service. Full launch does not happen until all the processes from the design stage are in place.

New services can also represent either a radical or an incremental upgrade on previous services, as described in Table 4.9. For instance, major service innovation is needed when the services are intended for markets that have

Figure 4.14 New service development process

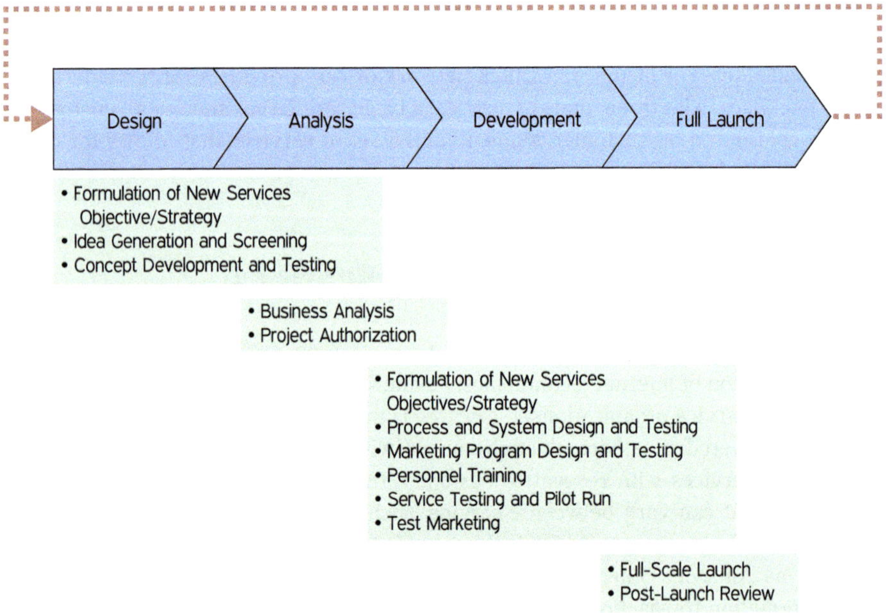

Source: Based on Menor *et al.* (2000).

Table 4.9 Levels of service innovation

New service category	Description	Example
Radical innovations		
Major innovation	New services for markets as yet undefined. These innovations are usually driven by information- and computer-based technologies	Wells Fargo Internet banking, launched in May 1995
Start-up business	New services in a market that is already served by existing services	Mondex USA, a subsidiary of MasterCard International that designs and distributes smartcards for retail transactions
New services for the market currently served	New service offerings to existing customers of an organization (although the services may be available from other companies)	Freestanding bank branches or kiosks in supermarkets or other retail establishments (e.g. Wells Fargo kiosks in Starbucks coffee shops)
Incremental innovations		
Service line extensions	Augmentations of the existing service line, such as adding new menu items, new routes or new courses	Singapore Airlines' first-class airport check-in in a special, exclusive lounge
Service improvements	Changes in features of services that are currently being offered	Delta Airlines' use of ATM-like kiosks to distribute boarding passes to passengers
Style changes	The most common of all 'new' services, these are modest forms of visible change that have an impact on customer perceptions, emotions and attitudes. Style changes do not change the service fundamentally, only its appearance	Funeral homes, such as Calvary Mortuary in Los Angeles, now offer abbreviated ceremonies that celebrate life instead of mourn death, full-service flower shops, and facilities with more pastels, brighter walls and more windows and lights

Source: Fitzsimmons and Fitzsimmons (2008, p. 66).

not been defined, such as with Wells Fargo's Internet banking that was launched in 1995. Since then the evolution of Internet banking could be described as incremental.

Service Architecture

New service development can be designed using the principles of product modularity. If we view a set of services as a system (just like a product system), then a service system can be broken down into different levels of complexity. What we have now is a service architecture instead of a product architecture. A service system can be decomposed into four levels of analysis:

Level 0: Industry

Level 1: Service company/supply chain

Level 2: Service bundle

Level 3: Service package/component

The holiday industry provides an apt illustration of the four levels of service architecture decomposition (Figure 4.15):

- Level 0 features the various players in the industry, such as cruise ship operators or airlines.
- Level 1 is the company in the supply chain. A firm, such as Independence of the Seas, may operate a number of cruise ships and has marketing services and port operations services, as well as back-office, procurement and other services. Some of these services may be outsourced, building a service supply chain.
- Level 2 reflects the service bundles offered in the ship. Each ship has an architecture consisting of a variety of guest services such as swimming pools, restaurants, night clubs and cabins. There are further

Figure 4.15 Decomposition of sea cruise services

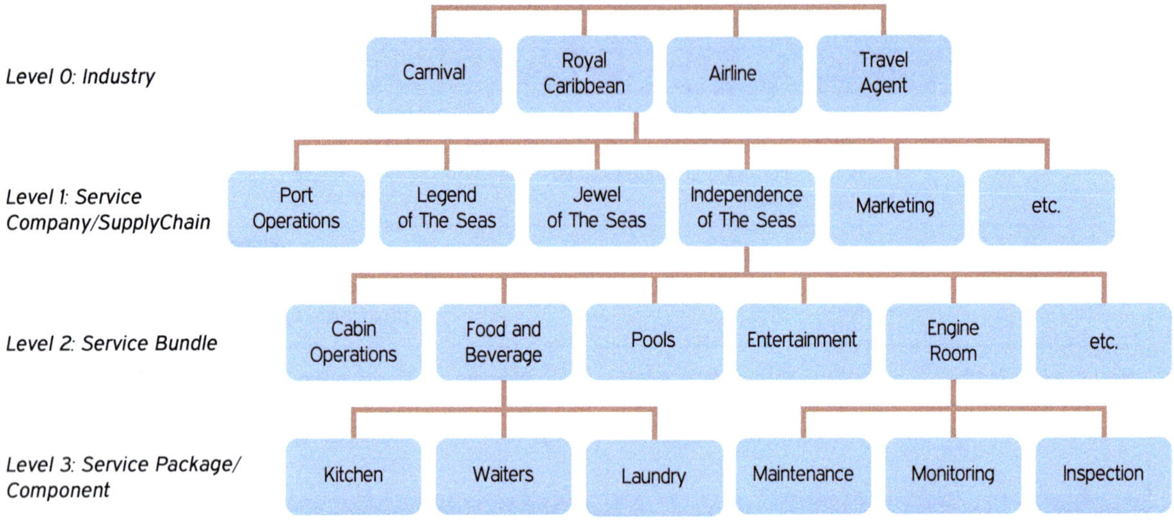

Source: Adapted from Voss and Hsuan (2009), used with permission.

services associated with the running of the ship and its interface with shore visits, and so forth. These guest services may be standardized and thus easily replicated across all the ships of the fleet or they may be custom-designed for that ship. Further, these services may be unique to the company and not easily imitated or they may be standard – that is, similar across all firms operating in the industry.

- Finally, at Level 3 is the service package and component level, as each of these services can be broken down into a further set of service components such as the individual elements of cabin operations, from cabin design to specific service personnel.

The key point is …

that service systems can also be decomposed into simpler pieces (modules).

SHORT CASE 4.4

Volvo Construction Equipment: Becoming a Solution Provider

Source: ©Maksim Safaniuk/Shutterstock

Among original equipment manufacturers (**OEMs**), equipment sales are considered first priority followed by sales figures, with a strong focus on spare parts sale. The emphasis is on growing the volume of the spare parts business while the risks and the potentials remain modest. However, OEMs are now expanding their business model into more advanced customer services. These services will challenge the reseller and OEM with increased financial exposure, more complex processes and systems, and the requirement for different skills.

Volvo CE has a wide range of equipment, each specially designed and optimized for performing defined tasks in the value chain of road construction, landscaping, gravel production, and so on. As Volvo CE explores the options of expanding their business model into new types of customer services, like production process optimization, a holistic and consultative approach must be incorporated in the service offering. This type of offering requires objectivity and focuses on total output across all equipment types, functionality and brands; in a few cases identified improvements could potentially reduce or even exclude its own products in the customer's production process. It also runs the potential risk of cannibalizing its own products by decreasing sales of parts and services.

However, quantifying production process improvements can sometimes be challenging. In a recent customer pilot project potential savings of around 4–5% of the total production cost were identified. Despite the strong value proposition, the project was a challenge because of the complexity of measuring progress and goal achievements in financial terms. Delivering this type of service requires analytics, lean methodology and industry skills that many traditional resellers struggle to meet.

This is a major obstacle; however, it can be mitigated by extensive channel development or with partnerships. But most importantly, it requires a radical shift in mind-set, competence and business model.

original equipment manufacturer refers to a company that develops or manufacturers a component or product that is sold by another company

Questions

1. How can value propositions and service offerings be incorporated in NSD and NPD?
2. What kinds of new services can be developed with partners?

Source: Christer Karlsson, Copenhagen Business School, Adapted from Karlsson *et al.* (2018).

Stop and Think

Are there major differences between innovation in services and innovation in products?

Customers' Input in Service Development Process

Customer satisfaction is one of the most important goals when developing new services, as we have learned that customers can act as resource, co-creator and/or user during the NPD process. Similarly, because services are consumed immediately after production, it is possible for customers to participate during the NSD process, as listed in Table 4.10.

SHORT CASE 4.5

Hotel Guldsmeden

Hotel Guldsmeden is one of the first hotel chains in Denmark to embrace the concept of ecology and high-quality organic foods and products. The hotel offers services tailored to environmentally conscious and health-conscious customers. One of its hotels has recently become a member of Green Globe, an international certification organization with the strictest standards in environmental tourism.

The hotels recycle as much as possible. For instance, the organic coffee scrub used in the spa is made of the coffee grounds left over from breakfast, mixed with Epsom salt and essential oil. The keycards are made of 100% biodegradable and sustainable materials, such as corn and other plant materials. In order to save energy, soon there will be solar panels installed on the roofs of the hotels.

At its hotels located in Denmark, there are no plastic bottles with water in any of the rooms and cafes. Instead, there are reusable glass bottles with the inscription 'Great water straight from the tap'.

Everything else in the hotels is organic, including the food, drinks, sanitary products, beauty and health products, cleaning products, linen and towels. The hotel chain promises that every single item of the food it serves to its customers is 95% organic.

Questions

1. In what ways do the services provided by Hotel Guldsmeden differ from ordinary hotels?
2. What challenges does Hotel Guldsmeden face in its new service development process in order to be the leader in providing an ecological and organic experience for its customers?
3. How could Hotel Guldsmeden involve its customers in the development of its services?

Source: www.hotelguldsmeden.com

Table 4.10 Customers' input in the NSD process

NSD processes	Activities performed by customers
Strategic planning	• Provide feedback on financial data
Idea generation	• State needs, problems and their solutions, criticize existing service • Identify gaps in the market • Provide a wish list (service requirements) • State new service adoption criteria
Idea screening	• Suggest rough sales guide and market size • Suggest desired features, benefits and attributes • Show reactions to the concepts • Provide input on liking, preference and purchase intent of all the concepts • Help the producer in go/kill decision
Business analysis	• Provide feedback on financial data, including profitability of the concepts, competitors' data
Formation of cross-functional team	• Join top management in selecting team members
Service design and process system design	• Review and jointly develop the blueprints • Suggest improvements by identifying fail points • Observe the service delivery trial by the firm personnel
Personnel training	• Observe and participate in mock service delivery process • Suggest improvements
Service testing and pilot run	• Participate in a simulated service delivery processes • Suggest final improvements and design change
Test marketing	• Provide comments on the marketing plan • Provide detailed comments about their satisfaction with marketing mixes • Suggest desired improvements
Commercialization	• Adopt the service as trial • Feedback about overall performance of the service along with desired improvements, if any • Word-of-mouth communications to other potential customers

Source: Adapted from Alam and Perry (2002).

CRITICAL PERSPECTIVE

Service-Dominant Logic

In contrast to goods-dominant logic (GDL) that has a product orientation, service-dominant logic (SDL) has a service orientation, where service is the process of providing benefit to products. SDL is a marketing concept that argues that effective competing through services is more than adding value to products. Customers are co-creators and producers of value (Vargo and Lusch, 2004). In other words, the customer is always involved in the production of value. Successful co-creation can be attained via joint and personalized value creation through experiences, as shown in Figure 4.16.

There are two types of resources:

- *Operand resources:* static and usually tangible resources that must be acted upon to be useful, such as materials and assets used in producing a good.
- *Operant resources:* dynamic resources such as competences (skills and knowledge) that are fundamental source of competitive advantage.

SDL is grounded in nine foundational premises (Vargo and Lusch, 2008, p. 7), as shown in Table 4.11.

Figure 4.16 Co-creation in SDL

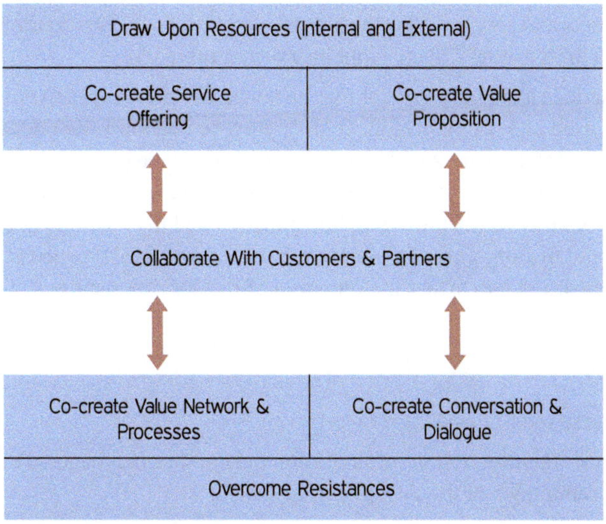

Source: Adapted from Lusch *et al.* (2007).

Table 4.11 SDL foundational premises

FPs	Foundational premise
FP1	Service is the fundamental basis of exchange
FP2	Indirect exchange masks the fundamental basis of exchange
FP3	Goods are a distribution mechanism for service provision
FP4	Operant resources are the fundamental source of competitive advantage
FP5	All economies are service economies
FP6	The customer is always a co-creator of value
FP7	The enterprise cannot deliver value, but only offer value propositions
FP8	A service-centred view that is inherently customer oriented and relational
FP9	All social and economic actors are resource integrators
FP10	Value is always uniquely and phenomenologically determined by the beneficiary

Summary

In this chapter we introduced some theories and tools for managing the design of products and services. Understanding the new product development (NPD) process provides the foundation for the development of innovative products and services. One current competitive strategy pursed by many firms is platform development, which enables them to offer higher product variety to customers at lower costs. How a platform is configured, in terms of the technology composition and organization, is dependent on product architecture design strategies (which can range from modular to integral).

One purpose for devising modular designs is to create flexibility and changeability of product configurations. If the product strategy is to offer a wide range of products at the lowest cost possible (such as mass customization), then modular product architecture designs might be the right strategy. The best way to achieve mass customization is with modular components – that is, with components that can be mixed and matched and configured into a wide variety of new products and services. However, if the goal is to be the best in the market in terms of performance, then integral product architecture design might be a better approach.

Development of services is equally crucial for the survival and competitiveness of the firms. We highlighted some key issues related to service design, such as how to measure the degree of customer contact and the value created by the front- and back-office activities. The service process matrix is a tool to assess the degree of interaction and customization with respect to degree of labour intensity. The design and development of new services go through several stages similar to those used in designing products. However, with services, the customers become the key part of the new service design (NSD) process and whether they are involved in the design process or not can affect the outcome of the service system.

Key Theories

The key theories discussed in this chapter were:

- **Platform design** – the creation of a foundation design that can be used in a number of products and upon which the remainder of the design can be based.
- **Modularization** – an approach to organizing complex products and processes efficiently by decomposing complex tasks into simpler portions to allow the tasks to be managed independently and yet work together as a whole without compromising performance.
- **Mass customization** – a strategy that emphasizes the need to provide outstanding service to customers in providing products that meet their needs (through maximizing individual customization) at a low cost (e.g. through modular components).
- **Service process matrix** – a framework that provides a classification of service industry firms based on the characteristics of a firm's services processes, in terms of degree of interaction and customization versus the degree of labour intensity.

Suggested Answers to Stop and Think Questions

1. **Good designs; bad products:** It takes a long time for good design ideas to become commercialized. The various NPD stages that any product has to go through make the success of the product even more uncertain. During the NPD journey, there are numerous trade-offs to be considered. Once in production, engineering changes cannot be made without lengthy procedures. When the product reaches the market, it becomes completely impossible for firms to control how the customers use the product. Often the final product sold in the market is very different from the concept idea. Firms typically discover that the real needs of their customer are not met with what the product is intended for (e.g. sleek mobile phones with touch pads – high tech, but unusable for blind people or people with big fingers). In other instances, customers may find innovative ways to use the products that the firms did not think of (e.g. using a cheese slicer as a vegetable slicer or using a cooking spatula as an ice scraper). These end up being perceived as bad products.
2. **NPD strategy:** The challenges can be discussed from many perspectives: organizational, manufacturing and supply chain management.

   Challenges from an integral design to a modular design: how to decompose the system. Once the product is decomposed, the management has to consider how to change the manufacturing processes and job designs accordingly. The manufacturing process has to be able to accommodate high-volume production and repetitive processes. The management has to consider how to divide the labour so that each design unit can work independently. If outsourcing is the motivation for pursuing a modular design strategy, then sourcing decisions have to be devised (i.e. low cost versus partnership strategies).

   Challenges from a modular design to an integral design: how to integrate the various modular components of the product to create a new product so that the firm can gain control of its technology.

The manufacturing process has to be redesigned to accommodate lower volumes. The management has to think about how to create synergy among the team members across various departments so that they can work harmoniously. The supply chain managers have to consider how to share knowledge of specialized technology with key suppliers or to integrate vertically.

3. **Product variety:** Psychological studies suggest that humans are able to process only up to nine different types of information in short-term memory. Too many options cause the consumer to become sidetracked from what they really want from the product. They may get lured away by options that they do not really need.

   For the retailers and producers, high product variety could create forecasting problems related to consumer preferences. Coordination problems in the supply chain might arise from stockouts, overstocking and product return policies. Overstocking translates into high inventory costs.

4. **Design-for-disassembly:** When you design products with modularity principles, the components can be designed and manufactured by various suppliers as long as the interface the components (or modules) comply with industry standards. When modularity concepts are applied in design-for-disassembly, designers includes specification of components for ease-of-disassembly, such as minimizing the number of SKUs and maximizing the use of common materials.

5. **Product complexity:** The goal of mass customization is to produce customized products to achieve economies of scope, at low costs to achieve economies of scale. This means high volume (from economies of scale) and high variety (from economies of scope). The variation in demand might also become higher as the required number of products differs from day to day (or week to week). When customers can do the customization themselves, visibility becomes higher. The BOM lists the SKUs of all the materials and components needed to make the product, including the required quantities. For modular products, the components are generic, which means product variety can be added into the production without drastic changes in the processes. However, as each new variant of the component (e.g., different colors of the same component) are added into the production, a new SKU has to be assigned, hence increasing the number of SKUs.

6. **Service quality:** The perception of service quality varies from person to person. A bad service for one person can be a good service for another. In order to understand the service delivery process and customer satisfaction, we need to look at the number and types of services delivered. The scale and scope of the services delivered are the outcomes of how the service system is designed, linking the front-office and back-office activities together. As customers, we are in contact only with the front-office part of the service system. However, the back-office activities provide the support and foundation for the success of the front-office activities.

7. **Innovation:** Basically there is not much difference between innovation in services and innovation in products, apart from the fact that services are intangible and consumed at the same time as they are produced, and products are tangible. We can apply the theories of innovation to analyse innovation in services. In most cases, though, service innovation cannot take place without products, and vice versa. The degree of integration between services and products can be analysed from the servitization of products and the productization of services perspectives.

Review Questions

1. Describe the current market situation of the music industry. How do innovation and standardization of technological development influence the way music is distributed and sold?

2. Check the mobile phones you and your colleagues have. Which brands do they have? Do they have the same functions? What are the common and distinct features of phones within the same brand? How can you apply the new product development and platform design theories to answer these questions?

3. Your brother is having a barbeque party at his house to celebrate his birthday. You want to buy something fun to wear for the party. At the shopping centre you saw a t-shirt shop that can print any kind of picture and photos on the shirts and one can add different types and colours of sleeves. Next day, you go back to the shop and buy 2 shirts (one for yourself and one for your brother) with the picture of family dog printed on it. Describe how customization of generic t-shirt can be realized.
4. You have just opened a restaurant in a posh area of your city. Through market research and your knowledge about the area, you decided that you are going to offer fusion food. Furthermore, the menu will be changed once a month. How would you organize its activities in: a) front office and b) back office
5. Your country is devising a new ticketing system for its trains. How would you design the service system? What kinds of challenges do you expect to encounter?
6. You noticed that more and more manufacturing companies have service offerings that are coupled with the products. As the product manager you started to wonder what value propositions you could offer to your customer base to improve the competitiveness of your company. Before you approach your top management, you have to explain the notion of servitization and types of value proposition. How would you proceed?

Discussion Questions

1. Discuss why it is important for firms to be at the forefront of technological development. Where do ideas for new product development come from?
2. Think about the last holiday you took. Which services impressed you most? Discuss the link between front- and back-office activities that might have taken place.
3. Consider a job that requires high levels of customer contact. Discuss how the management could design the service to create a great experience for the customers and job satisfaction for the workers.
4. You have just been hired by the health care director of a major hospital. The hospital wants to provide better care for its patients, such as the quality of the treatment received, and the sophistication of medical equipment used in the care. Discuss the factors you need to consider to make this process a success, through the perspective of the product–service system.
5. Imagine you are working for an IT company that is expanding into new markets. Discuss how you would design the service and whether the customers should be involved in the process.
6. You have just been hired as a R&D manager for a large manufacturer of an electronics corporation that is implementing a corporate social responsibility strategy to reduce the volume of electrical and electronic waste (WEEE). What would you need to consider to achieve this strategy for the corporation?
7. As the marketing manager for a large high-tech company, you have been working closely with the new service development (NSD) team. You want to emphasize to the team that customer satisfaction is an important goal. How can customers participate in the NSD process?

Problems

1. Philips's R&D department has been approved an investment of £800 million to develop new models of its smart home entertainment system for the next 5 years. The different models are to be developed from a basic platform. The management estimates that it costs £220 million to develop a basic platform. It also costs another £17 million to develop each model that is derived from the basic platform. Philips wants to introduce 10 new smart home entertainment models per platform over the next 5 years. Calculate the number of basic platforms (for 10 models) Philips can develop.
2. A new, trendy furniture shop is offering customized sofas to its customers. The customers have the choice of combining two types of legs (wood or steel), three types of upholstery (suede, leather or fabric), and seven colours (black, brown, tan, beige, red, blue or gray). Customers can also add accessories (buttons, belts, bows, etc.) from a list of nine options that can be chosen independently of each other. Calculate the number of options the customers can choose from.

3. You are the supplier of hair care products (shampoos, conditioners, hair creams, etc.) to hair salons all over Europe. You have three main categories of customer:

   High-end beauty shops: these sell all kinds of beauty products, including the standard hair care bottles from your company.

   Professional salons in the UK: the hairdressers want two types of product – large bottles to be used on customers' hair and standard bottles that can be displayed and sold to customers.

   Professional salons in Nordic countries: the requirements for these are the same as for the hairdressers in the UK, expect that the bottles have to be translated into Nordic languages – Danish, Swedish, Norwegian and Finnish.

   Apply the product–representation matrix to categorize the type of customization needed to satisfy your customers.

4. You are a part of a team in charge of improving the tourism of your city. One of the main sources of attraction is the culinary options and choices there are in your city that can tailor to all types of customers, including the local residents. Before you can make a strategy you need to classify the services types of these restaurants. Apply the Service Process Matrix to classify the services in three types of restaurants: fast food, traditional, and gourmet.

Further Reading

Binder, M., Gust, P. and Clegg, B.T. (2008) 'Frontloading: a means to improving the competitiveness of R&D collaboration in automotive supply networks?', *Journal of Manufacturing Technology Management,* **19**(3), 315–331.

Cooper, R. and Kleinschmidt, E. (1994) 'Determinants of timelines in product development', *Journal of Product Innovation Management,* **11**(5), 381–96.

Menor, L.J., Tatikonda, M.V. and Sampson, S.E. (2002) 'New service development: areas for exploitation and exploration', *Journal of Operations Management,* **20**(2), 135–157.

Zomerdijk, L.G. and Vries, J.D. (2007) 'Structuring front office and back office work in service delivery systems', *International Journal of Operations and Production Management,* **27**(1), 108–131.

References

Alam, I. and Perry, C. (2002) 'A customer-oriented new service development process', *Journal of Service Marketing,* **16**(2), 515–534.

Avlonitis, V., Frandsen, T., Hsuan, J. and Karlsson, C. (2014) *Driving Competitiveness Through Servitization: A Guide for Practitioners,* Copenhagen Business School Competitiveness Platform, Copenhagen.

Babcock, D.L. (1996) *Managing Engineering Technology: An Introduction to Management for Engineers,* 2nd edn, Prentice Hall, Upper Saddle River, NJ.

Baines, T.S., Lightfoot, H.W., Evans, S., Neely, A., Greenough, R., Peppard, J., Roy, R., Shehab, E., Braganza, A., Tiwari, A., Alcock, J.R., Angus, J.P., Bastl, M., Cousens, A., Irving, P., Johnson, M., Kingston, J., Lockett, H., Martinez, V., Michele, P., Tranfield, D., Walton, I.M. and Wilson, H. (2007) 'State-of-the-art in product-service systems', *Journal of Engineering Manufacture,* **221**(10), 1543–1552.

Baldwin, C.Y. and Clark, K.B. (1997) 'Managing in an age of modularity', *Harvard Business Review,* (September–October), 84–93.

Bell, T.E. (1993) 'Bicycles on a personalized basis', *IEEE Spectrum,* **30**(9), 32–35.

Chase, R.B. (1978) 'Where does the customer fit in a service operation?' *Harvard Business Review,* **75**(5), 137–142.

Da Silveira, G., Borenstein, D. and Fogliatto, F.S. (2001) 'Mass customization: literature review and research directions', *International Journal of Production Economics,* **72**(1), 1–13.

Davis, M.M. and Heineke, J. (2005) *Operations Management: Integrating Manufacturing and Services,* 5th edn, McGraw-Hill, Boston, MA.

De Blok, C., Meijboom, B., Luijkx, K., and Schols, J. (2007) 'Modularity in health care: towards cost-efficient and client-focused service provision', *Proceedings of the 14th Annual EurOMA Conference,* Bilkent University, Ankara.

De Britto, M.P. and Dekker, R. (2002) 'Reverse logistics – a framework', Econometric Institute Report EI 2002-38, Eramus University Rotterdam.

Eurostat (2019) 'Statistics explained: waste statistics – electrical and electronic equipment'. https://ec.europa.eu/eurostat/statistics-explained/index.php/Waste_statistics_-_electrical_and_electronic_equipment

Fitzsimmons, J.A. and Fitzsimmons, M.J. (2008) *Service Management,* 6th edn, McGraw-Hill, Boston, MA.

Gilmore, J.H. and Pine, B.J. (1997) 'The four faces of mass customization', *Harvard Business Review,* **75**(1), 91–101.

Hsuan, J. (1999) 'Impacts of supplier–buyer relationships on modularization in new product development', *European Journal of Purchasing and Supply Management,* **5**(3), 197–209.

Karlsson, C., Stjernqvist, P. and Frandsen, T. (2018) 'Becoming a solution provider: Integrating in the customer process', Copenhagen Business School.

Lung, Y., Salerno, M.S., Zilbovicius, M. and Dias, A.V.C. (1999) 'Flexibility through modularity: experimentations with fractal production in Brazil and in Europe', in *Coping With Variety: Flexible Productive Systems for Product Variety in the Auto Industry,* Y. Lung, J.J. Chararon, T. Fujimoto and D. Raff (eds), Ashgate, Aldershot, pp. 224–257.

Lusch, R.F., Vargo, S.L. and O'Brien, M. (2007) 'Competing through service: insight from service-dominant logic', *Journal of Retailing,* **83,** 5–18.

Menor, L.J., Tatikonda, M.V. and Sampson, S.E. (2002) 'New service development: area for exploitation and exploration', *Journal of Operations Management,* **20**(2), 135–157.

Metters, R. and Vargas, V. (2000) 'A typology of de-coupling strategies in mixed services', *Journal of Operations Management,* **18**(6), 663–682.

Mikkola, J.H. and Gassmann, O. (2003) 'Managing modularity of product architecture: towards an integrated theory', *IEEE Transactions on Engineering Management,* **54**(1), 57–69.

Mikkola, J.H. and Skjøtt-Larsen, T. (2006) 'Platform management: implications for new product development and supply chain management', *European Business Review,* **18**(3), 214–230.

Nambisan, S. (2002) 'Designing virtual customer environments for new product development: toward a theory', *Academy of Management Review,* **27**(3), 392–413.

Nixon, B. and Innes, J. (1997) 'Research and development performance measurement: a case study', paper presented at the 1997 R&D Management Conference, Manchester, 14–16 July.

Pine, J. (1993) *Mass Customization: The New Frontier in Business Competition,* Harvard Business School Press, Boston, MA.

Roth, A.V. and Menor, L.J. (2003) 'Insights into service operations management: a research agenda', *Production and Operations Management,* **12**(2), 145–164.

Schmenner, R.W. (1986) 'How can service business survive and prosper?', *Sloan Management Review,* **27**(3), 21–32.

Schmenner, R.W. (2004) 'Service businesses and productivity', *Decision Sciences,* **35**(3), 333–347.

Smith, L., Maull, R. and Ng, I.C.L. (2014) 'Servitization and operations management: a service dominant-logic approach', *International Journal of Operations & Production Management,* **34**(2), 242–269.

STATISTA (2020) 'United Kingdom: distribution of gross domestic product (GDP) across economic sectors from 2008 to 2018'. https://www.statista.com/statistics/270372/distribution-of-gdp-across-economic-sectors-in-the-united-kingdom/

Taylor, F. (1911) *Principles of Scientific Management,* Harper, New York.

Trott, P. (2008) *Innovation Management and New Product Development,* 4th edn, Financial Times/Prentice Hall, Harlow.

Ulrich, K.T. (1995) 'The role of product architecture in the manufacturing firm', *Research Policy,* **24**(3), 419–440.

Ulrich, K.T. and Eppinger, S.D. (2008) *Product Design and Development,* 4th edn, McGraw-Hill, New York.

Vargo, S.L. and Lusch, R.F. (2008) 'Service-dominant logic: continuing the evolution', *Journal of the Academy of Marketing Science,* **36,** 1–10.

Voss, C. (2003) 'Rethinking paradigms of service: service in a virtual environment', *International Journal of Operations and Production Management,* **23**(1), 88–104.

Voss, C. and Hsuan, J. (2009) 'Service architecture modularity', *Decision Sciences,* **40**(3), 541–569.

5 Process Design

Learning Outcomes

After reading this chapter you should be able to:

- Use the concept of systems thinking for process improvement
- Appreciate the value of the process perspective over the functional perspective
- Decide which type of process is best suited to a particular type of operation
- Use process mapping tools effectively to design and redesign processes
- Appreciate the use of technology in processes
- Design a suitable layout for a particular process

Take a Welcome Break

Source: ©Wozzie/Shutterstock

Driving long distances can be arduous at the best of times. The Bolt family were driving from Manchester in the north-west of England to Paris, France, via the Channel Tunnel and the Eurostar train. The weather was bad, the roads were snowy and the journey had been slow. They had already had to queue and pay for tunnels and toll roads, and needed to stop for a break after four hours of driving. As the family travelled frequently, the four of them knew the 'pit stop' process well.

As they came into the service area just off the main highway they were filtered into the 'cars' lane away from the 'trucks long-stay parking' and the 'fuel only' lanes. Once they had parked, the first things to do were to find the toilets and then some food. As these particular services were new, the layout of the facility was very efficient: there were lots of clean toilets with the latest 'cyclone' hand-drying machines, automatic taps and automatic flushing toilets. The food and shopping court had been designed so that people wanting to eat different foods – fast-food burgers or healthier snacks – could sit together. After eating, the two children went to the nearby indoor play area to get some exercise; Mr Bolt logged onto the Internet using the free WiFi connection to catch up on his emails and then used the ATM to get some cash. Meanwhile Mrs Bolt went to do a spot of shopping to buy gifts for the family they were visiting.

Outside, the snow was falling thick and fast and Mr Bolt was keen to get going as the traffic bulletin boards in the food court were warning of potential road closures. They all got back into the car, and after Mr Bolt had checked that the car was safe to drive, he drove to the on-site fuel station a few hundred metres away to fill up and get some de-icer for the windscreen. Once the car had been sorted out they tried to set off. Unfortunately the snow had worsened so, changing plan, Mrs Bolt suggested that they abandon the journey for now and check into the on-site Days Inn hotel before it filled up with similarly minded people. Mr Bolt thought this was a good idea, as he could use his loyalty card and earn points by staying there. It would also be quick and easy, as he knew this hotel had an express check-in-and-out and an 'open all hours' self-service breakfast bar, which meant they could get going as soon as possible in the morning.

The process that the Bolts had followed was similar to that of any other visiting family. Other types of customer, such as truck drivers or lone business travellers, would follow different paths through the services to meet their differing requirements. Truck drivers might wish only to use the showers and the overnight 'park and sleep' facility. Business travellers, on the other hand, might just want to stop for a quick coffee, or use the free WiFi lounge to send some urgent work messages, or even use the on-site 'pay by the hour' business conference facilities.

Introduction

The opening case demonstrates that we experience operations and operational processes every day, whether through travel, work or leisure. We experience so many that we often forget that they are operations and operational processes and that someone, somewhere, has consciously designed them and is responsible for managing them. This chapter will demonstrate the importance of operations and operational processes for an organization, how they are designed and how they are managed.

The design and management of processes are fundamental to establishing any operation. Common practice is to innovate, standardize and then optimize a process before beginning again with any new requirements. Process thinking is a radical departure from traditional thinking, which is more concerned with optimizing business functions and is known as *functional thinking*. Process thinking is more about optimizing **business processes** that cross functions within an organization and deliver goods and services for the end customer. Functional thinking can be an inefficient and ineffective practice. Process thinking can replace functional thinking and make organizations work better from the customer perspective.

Business process sequence of tasks to get things done.

Effective process management is the basis for many modern operations management practices, such as quality management and lean thinking, and therefore it is important to fully understand it. Process-oriented thinking is also the basis for successful supply chain management, which is the practice of joining up the processes of different organizations as seamlessly as possible.

This chapter begins by briefly outlining systems thinking in the context of process management. It then explains the different generic types of process and order, and the different sorts of process mapping used to support process design. It finishes by discussing the implications that physical layouts have for operations.

Systems Thinking

In order for us to discuss processes in a meaningful way, we need to briefly turn our attention to *systems thinking*. Simply defined, a **system** is a complex whole, the functioning of which depends on its parts and the interactions between those parts. We can easily think of many different types of system: natural systems, such as rivers and waterways; biological systems, such as living organisms or ecosystems; designed complex product systems, such as ships and IT networks; and human activity systems, such as businesses and organizations. Understanding how these systems work is known as *systems thinking*.

System a complex whole, the functioning of which depends on its parts and the interactions between those parts.

All too often, studies of systems are too reductionist. *Reductionism* sees the parts of a system as more important than the whole. However, the whole emerges from the interactions between those parts. A good understanding of the whole system cannot be gained from studying each of the parts in isolation, but must be gained by studying the whole system, and how its parts work together. The alternative to reductionism is **holism**, which is endorsed by those who use systems thinking (which is also known as **holistic thinking**). Holism considers a system to be more than a sum of its parts. This type of thinking is used widely in philosophy, biology, engineering, physical sciences, and

Holistic thinking/holism considering a system to be more than a sum of its parts.

Figure 5.1 Systems properties

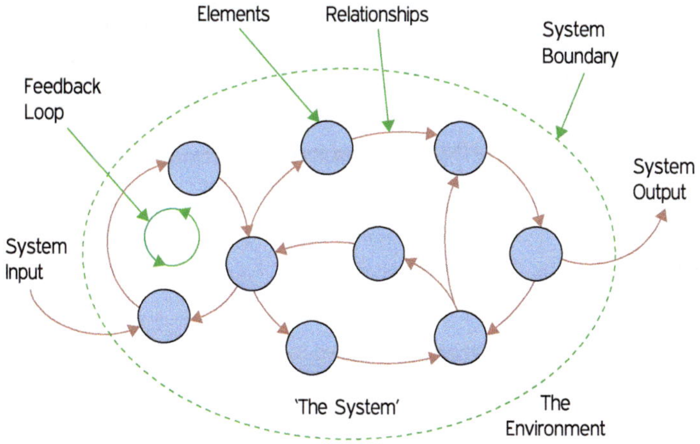

organizational and management theory. In this chapter we are interested in using holistic systems thinking for the design and management of business processes.

Figure 5.1 shows the essential parts of a system. Notice that a boundary separates the system from the wider environment. There is a defined route for inputs into the system and another for its outputs. Also, the elements interact with each other in different ways: some react with just a few other elements, some with many and some are involved in feedback loops.

Table 5.1 provides an example of how both a service provider (a high street bank) and a manufacturer (of washing machines) can be viewed as a system. Systems thinking should underpin all that operations managers do, if an operation is going to work well. It is possible to think of countless other operational examples and apply systems thinking to them. The opening case was an example of one such system.

Many techniques for process design and improvement are derived from systems thinking and learning these techniques is rather like learning a modern language. In contrast, learning systems thinking is like learning the root language from which they are derived (e.g. Italian and Spanish, which are both derived from Latin). Therefore, appreciating systems thinking can help one to understand process improvement tools better. It is useful to keep the systems thinking perspective in mind throughout this chapter, because all business processes and operations are systems.

Stop and Think

How do you think operations management would benefit if everyone applied systems thinking to it?

Processes

Processes are typically designed and operated to perform transformations; a transformation (or conversion) is something that adds value to the entity being processed (e.g. materials or people). A process is normally designed around two major factors; the *volume* (high or low) and the *variety* (small or large) of what needs to be delivered.

Figure 5.2 shows an input-output diagram, which is a very simple representation of a process: there are inputs, a transformation and outputs, which all need to be controlled and resourced. This representation can be used for a whole company, for part of a company or even for a single task.

BUSINESS INTEGRATION

Different stages (or tasks) in a process are often the responsibility of different functional areas (departments or business units) within an organization. Functions such as marketing, operations and finance are important for internal purposes – such as setting budgets, career development and measuring performance. But external customers are rarely interested in the internal structure of an organization; they are far more interested in performance factors that affect them directly, such as speedy delivery, cost, good quality, dependability, flexibility and sustainability.

Table 5.1 Systems properties in service and manufacturing processes

	Organization	
	High street bank	**Washing machine manufacturer**
System	Customer relationship management (CRM) system	Production system
System inputs (resources to be transformed, e.g. people, items or information)	New customers with no profile	Sheet metal
Feedback loops (keep the system in control)	Data-mining techniques to check the effectiveness of marketing promotions	ISO 9001 quality procedures, ISO 14001 environmental regulations, total productivity maintenance, shareholder meetings, health and safety regulations
Elements Transforming resources – those that do not become part of the final product or service but are used to make and deliver them Transformed resources – those that are being processed and may end up as part of the final product and service	People – marketing department; financial – employee incentives; tangible – computer hardware; intangible – intellectual property, CRM software Personalized and updated customer profiles to facilitate a more personalized service	Human – machine operatives; financial – working capital; tangible – machines; intangible – operating procedures Parts, materials and sub-assemblies to make finished products for the consumer
Relationships between elements (these make activities occur)	Customers (system inputs) are transformed by employees (who are a transforming resource): e.g. customer profiles are updated by the CRM software every time a transaction is made	Tangible materials (system inputs) are transformed by humans and machines (transforming resources): e.g. people use machines and materials to make other machines
System boundary (establishes authority and influence)	Limit of channel interfaces with customers and bank that can produce valuable communication	The interface with suppliers at one end, the interface with customers at the other end
Environment (to link a system with the rest of the world – which is itself made up of other systems)	Competition, and regulation of the high street banking sector	Competition, and regulations (e.g. health and safety, European laws)
System outputs (the creations of the systems – which are hopefully value-adding)	Transformed resources – e.g. loyal customers with a fully customized profile	Transformed resources – e.g. parts and materials become washing machines

Figure 5.2 A process: input–output diagram

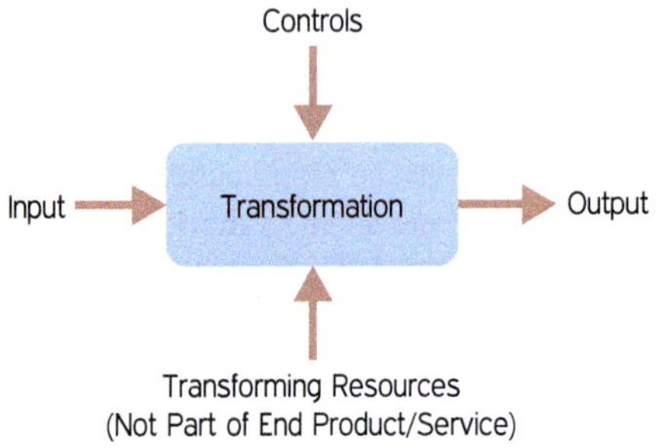

Table 5.2 Factors in process management

Process Performance Factors	Service (e.g. road service station)	Manufacturing (e.g. making a washing machine)
Time	Reduce time waiting for food, no queues	Reduce lead time from order to delivery
Cost	Reduce cost of food	Keep parts and labour costs down
Quality	Increase cleanliness of facilities, free fast WiFi	Error free manufacturing
Dependability	Always open and have fuel	Able to make to order without problems
Flexibility	Range of different service options for different tastes	Process can make a reasonable range of products and volumes
Sustainability	Recycling facilities, electric car charging points	Made without energy and material waste and designed for reuse and recycling

It is factors such as those in Table 5.2 that can be improved by taking a process view of an organization rather than a functional view. Figure 5.3 shows the functional view of the organization, with the vertical columns representing marketing, operations and finance.

In Figure 5.3 the business process is represented by the horizontal red line, going from left to right across the organization, that links together various activities carried out by different functions. This represents the path that a transformed item (e.g. people, data or material) would take through an organization. For example, the red line might be a business process for planning and executing a 'buy one, get one free' sales promotion in a brewery.

Figure 5.3 shows that processes often have *hand-offs* between one function and another; these are marked by the responsibility for the process activity changing. Because of these, time and information can be lost and costs can increase. In some cases, the number of hand-offs is immense and an organization performs badly as a result. For instance, a US study into the manufacture of a fighter aircraft revealed huge wastes as 'the typical sub-assembly goes through four plants, four states and 74 organizational "hand-offs" between engineering, purchasing and fabricating operations. It goes 7,600 miles and takes darn near forever' (Deming, 1999, p. 123).

Types of Process

There are five main types of process: continuous, assembly line, batch, job shop and project. In manufacturing, the product flow will be the same as the flow of materials, since materials are usually being converted into the end product. In services, it is more usual to have a flow of information or people – customers or clients – that are being processed.

Figure 5.3 Processes and functions

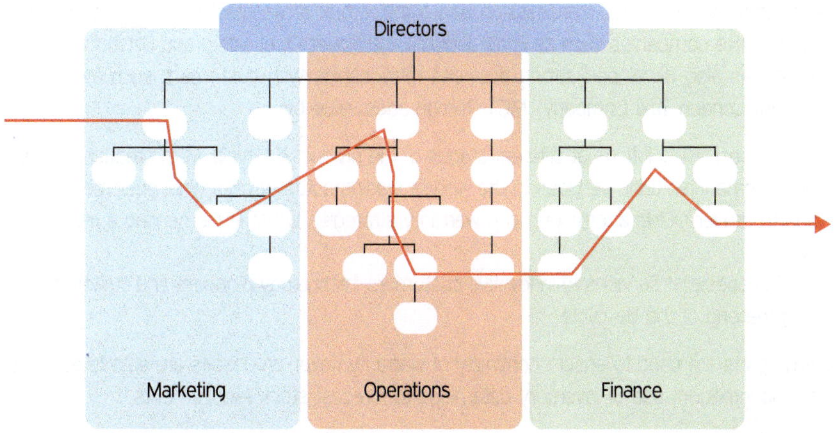

SHORT CASE 5.1

Sustainable Processes Performance Factors

Business processes are used to design, manufacture and remanufacture products and the service elements of these are essential for successful delivery. As resource depletion and energy conservation become more important to global businesses, new business value propositions are formed as part of the circular economy; these propositions focus on reducing, reusing, remanufacturing and recycling.

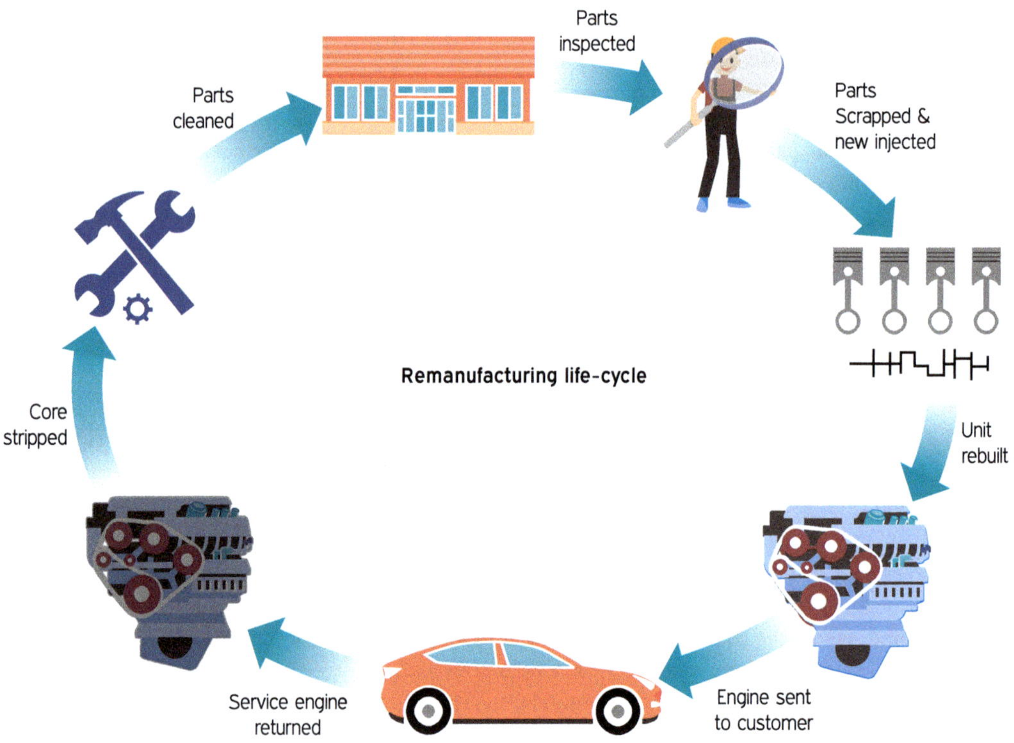

Source: mctreman.com

Remanufacturing is a process of bringing used products to a 'like-new' functional state with warranty to match. The practice is regarded as a more sustainable way of manufacturing as it causes less harm to the environment than conventional manufacturing and is more profitable. Products generated through a high standard, remanufacturing process have comparable quality to equivalent new products but require 50–80% less energy to produce. Remanufacturing can also provide 20–80% cost savings in comparison to conventional manufacturing. Remanufactured engines now account for 35% of total engine output.

MCT ReMan Ltd are experts in the remanufacture of transmissions, final drive assemblies and engines; they have been in business for over 40 years and demand for their services is growing. The company is a leading provider of aftermarket engine, transmission and transfer box remanufacturing services to many of the world's leading automotive companies such as Ford, Jaguar Land Rover, Opel, Volvo and Mitshubishi. In more recent years MCT ReMan has also developed strong business relationships with customers such as VW Heritage & Unipart Group (3PL for London Taxi Company). MCT Reman adds value by:

- providing specialist solutions at different stages of the product life-cycle, from product development to disposal
- providing remanufacturing services to the world's leading automotive original equipment manufacturers (OEMs)
- helping to deliver OEMs aftermarket and warranty strategies whilst implementing a more sustainable business model
- supporting specialist services to innovative customers, technology pioneers and customers who have products nearing the end of the life-cycle.

Genuine parts are used to ensure continuity of warranty cover, processes are able to deliver single units within 24 hours and intelligent use of inventory data helps to forecast stock requirements.

As a testimony to its quality, the company has been awarded the following industry accreditations: Ford Q1, ISO14001, ISO9001, and have recently transitioned from TS16949 to IATF16949.

Question

1. Use the process performance factors in Table 5.2 to critique MCT Reman Ltd's core processes. Where are their strengths and opportunities for future improvements?

Source: Ian Briggs, MCT ReMan Ltd, and Ben Clegg, Aston Business School.

Continuous

Continuous processes are most applicable to so-called *process industries*. Process industries are those in which products or services are made continuously and they tend to be highly standardized and automated, with very high volumes of production. Examples are fertilizer, steel, paper, oil and the production of electricity. Production may run 24 hours a day, seven days a week. Delivery may stop only for maintenance activities. For example, a nuclear power station may run without stopping for 50 years. It is often very hard to differentiate the product or service from that of competitors, and low cost becomes the order winner in an unregulated market. For instance, a house owner will usually choose the cheapest power supplier for their electricity and gas, as the product will often only be distinguishable by the associated service. That is, consumers may not measure the quality of their electricity supply but may be annoyed by the poor quality of its billing services.

Continuous operations tend to be highly automated, have high set-up costs, operate at very high volumes, and usually produce non-discrete products such as liquids (water or petrol), semi-solids (paint or concrete) or services such as cloud-based computing services and on-demand television applications. It is often very difficult to change over quickly from delivering one type of service or product to another. For these reasons a high demand, degree of certainty and predictability are needed for it to be worth setting up a continuous process.

Assembly Lines

Source: ©Ivan Azimov 007/Shutterstock

Assembly lines are characterized by a predefined sequence of operations which move items from one step to the next. Assembly lines are set up to deliver discrete products such as cars, washing machines, computers and mobile phones. The transformed resources (parts) are often moved from one step to the next in a semi-automated way on mechanisms such as conveyor belts or automatic guided vehicles (AGVs).

Traditional assembly lines are designed to be very efficient and produce high volumes of fairly standardized products; this is often referred to as *mass production*. The main advantage of an assembly line process is efficiency. The downside of an assembly line is that it can be difficult to change from delivering one type of output to another and so flexibility needs to be built into the line if possible. For instance, it can take weeks to change over from producing one type of car to another on a car assembly line if the product and process is not designed with production flexibility in mind. The changeover time is wasted (non-value-adding) time, as during changeover the operation does not produce any saleable output.

Batch

Batch flow processes are characterized by batches (or 'lots') of work being produced together (e.g. a particular customer order or a particular product or service derivative). Batches of work typically move between different functions or *work cells* throughout a process.

Work cells are particularly useful for batches, because they are relatively flexible and can achieve acceptable economies of scale. For instance, a large fairground ride can process a specific group of people, a baker's oven can bake batches of specific varieties of bread or cakes, and a clothes factory may have a work cell to make a certain type of clothing. The people and equipment in a work cell should be set up to handle batch sizes that match the demands of customers.

Batch flow allows more flexibility than an assembly line, as its machines and people are more adaptable – that is, they have lower task specificity. However, batch processing is difficult, because it requires careful *layout* of the work cells and *sequencing* of activities.

Batch operations are most useful when an organization has many different products that are processed similarly and are required frequently at relatively low volumes. In such situations the batch operation is the most economical type of process and incurs the least risk. Other examples of products made in batches are ceramic crockery, fashion clothing, wooden furniture and boats, as these are all products with high variety, made in relatively low volumes.

Job Shop

The *job shop* is a very adaptable and highly skilled work cell that may deliver an entire product by itself. In a job shop the output will still be made in batches, but it will be customized to specific customer orders (or '*jobs*'), which are typically received intermittently. Like batch processing, the job shop uses standard equipment but will have higher flexibility to deliver a variety of products and volumes of production. Costs are generally higher, since the volume of output and degree of standardization are lower and the labour resource more highly skilled. Typical products manufactured in a job shop are machine components, remanufactured goods or prototypes. Typical services delivered in a job shop include revision sessions for university courses and monthly drop-in clinics at doctors' surgeries for mothers and babies.

Project

The *project* type of process is typically used for large, unique products and services. Examples of service-based projects are concerts and large sporting events; examples of product-based projects are the construction of bridges, hospitals and stadiums. Technically speaking there is little product flow in a project, since materials and labour are brought to the project site and the project itself is at a fixed location and stationary. The unique nature of projects means that they are characterized by complex planning and scheduling, they are hard to automate and they need highly skilled and motivated staff to work on them.

In a project-type process each delivery is often made individually and is differentiated from other deliveries. Projects often result when a customer requires large amounts of customization and uniqueness. Generally speaking, the cost of unit production for projects is high and sometimes difficult to control. This is because projects are often difficult to define fully at the beginning and changes commonly occur during their delivery – which can have negative implications for timescales and cost.

Table 5.3 summarizes the different types of process and their characteristics, as described above. A process should ideally have characteristics that are suited to the nature of the product or service that it is delivering; if it does not, then this may result in process inefficiencies, high costs and loss of competitive advantage.

Volume and Variety

> **Volume and variety model** Hayes and Wheelright (1979) developed a model stating that volume carried out by an operation and variety or choice offered to customers is linked and results in the types of operation such as project, batch and mass production.

Figure 5.4 provides an overview of the five process types, differentiated by **volume and variety** demands – which are, arguably, the two most important factors determining process design. Note that job variety, process flexibility and unit cost are highest for a project, and get progressively lower moving from project processes towards continuous processing. Conversely, volume of output is lowest for a project, and gets progressively higher, moving towards continuous processing. Note, too, that all these types fall along a diagonal. The implication is that the diagonal represents the ideal choice of process for the given set of circumstances. For example, if the goal is to be able to process a single job involving a unique output (e.g. building the London Eye), then a project management process is most appropriate. However, for more volume, a job shop or a batch process would be more suitable, and so on. Note that any combinations too far from the diagonal should not normally be considered. For instance, using a job shop for high-volume and low-variety jobs may result in long lead times; or using a continuous processing process for low-volume and high-variety jobs could result in higher-than-necessary costs due to the number of slow changeover times the process needs to be reconfigured to make a different product.

Often, the processes shown in Figure 5.4 do not exist in their 'pure' form. Instead, hybrid processes that have elements of different process types embedded in them are usually found. For instance, organizations that operate primarily in a repetitive mode, or a continuous mode, will often have specialist *repair shops* (i.e. job shops)

Table 5.3 Summary of types of process, layout and order explained throughout this chapter

Process characteristics	Process type				
	Continuous	Assembly line	Batch	Job shop	Project
Description	Highly standardized goods or services	Standardized goods and services	Partly customized outputs to customer requirements	Made to order, custom-made specification	Highly customized and often unique output
Output	Continuous flow	Discrete	Discrete	Discrete	Discrete
Advantages	Very efficient, very high volume	Low unit cost, high volume, efficient	Flexibility	Able to handle a wide variety of work	Dedicated adaptable team and resources
Disadvantages	Very rigid, lack of variety, costly to change, very high cost of downtime	Low flexibility, high cost of downtime	Moderate cost per unit, moderate scheduling complexity	Slow, high cost per unit, complex planning and scheduling	High risk and cost uncertainty, takes time to establish
Cost estimation	Routine	Routine	Fairly routine	Specific costing – but relatively simple	Specific costing – simple to complex
Cost per unit	Low	Low	Moderate	High	Very high
Equipment used	Dedicated	Dedicated	General purpose	General purpose	Varied
Fixed costs	Very high	High	Moderate	Low	Varied
Variable costs	Very low	Low	Moderate	High	High
Labour skills	Low to high	Low	Moderate	High	Low to high
Marketing	Promote standardized goods and services	Promote standardized goods and services	Promote flexibility	Promote capabilities	Promote capabilities
Scheduling	Routine, interdependent and sequential	Routine, interdependent and sequential	Moderately complex	Complex	Complex, continually subject to change
Work in process inventory	Low	Low	Medium to high	High	Varied
Longevity of operation	Ongoing and indefinite	Ongoing for whole product/service life cycle	Short individual deliveries – repeated often	Fixed duration – short to medium	Agreed defined duration – medium to very long
Probable type of order	MTS (make to stock)	MTS/ATO (assemble to order)	ATO	ATO/MTO (make to order)	MTO
Probable type of layout	Product-service dominant	Product-service dominant	Process dominant	Work cell	Fixed position

Figure 5.4 Volume and variety: the impact upon process definition, with service and manufacturing examples

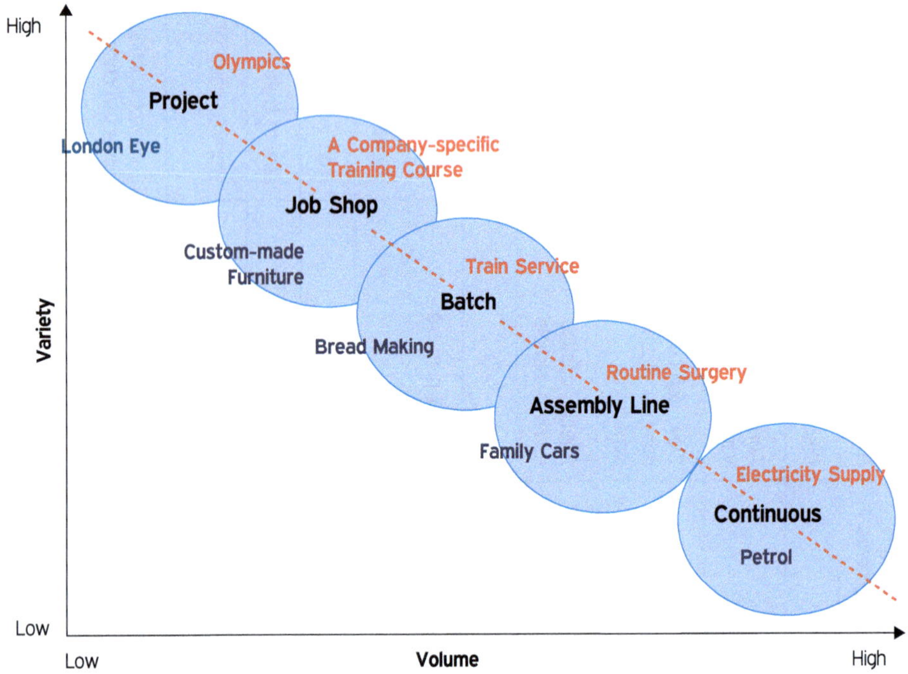

Source: Adapted from Hayes and Wheelwright (1979).

incorporated to be able to fix or make new parts for equipment that fails. Similarly, if a volume increases for some items, an operation that once began in a job shop or as a batch process may develop into an assembly line process. However, it is unlikely that any other type will evolve into a continuous process, as this process type tends to be suitable only for specific types of product and service with highly predictable demand patterns. Figure 5.4 shows examples of product (blue) and service (red) processes for each type.

Stop and Think

What happens if the process that you design falls into the 'dead zones' either side of the diagonal line in Figure 5.4?

Types of Order

A factor that greatly influences process design is the type of order. Orders can be fulfilled in different ways. The main types are *made to order* (MTO), *made to stock* (MTS) and *assembled to order* (ATO), which is an in-between hybrid of MTO and MTS. There are advantages and disadvantages to each practice. An MTS process can provide faster service to customers by taking a product from available stock, but there is an associated stockholding cost. The additional stockholding cost may be offset by a lower unit production cost, as the product will be manufactured in the most economical batch quantities. The MTO process will provide flexibility to customize the product or service to a customer's requirement and also avoid the cost of stockholding. The ATO practice attempts to use a process that has the best parts of MTO and MTS practices. The type of process most suited to each type of order is shown in Table 5.3.

Make to Order

In the MTO process, individual customer orders are identified during production. As each order is made to a particular customer specification, each job in the process is associated with a particular customer. For instance, when you buy a new BMW you will be given a unique number that will enable you to see your car being configured in the factory. BMW has even made this available to view on the Internet, using a webcam. One can always identify an MTO process by simply looking at who the job is for. In the MTO process the cycle of production and order fulfilment begins with the customer order, in this case from the car salesman in the BMW dealership. Only after receiving an order will the work begin – with the ordering of the necessary materials. Once the materials arrive, the order can be processed – assuming the necessary machines and people are available. When the order is complete, it can be delivered to the customer.

The key performance measure of an MTO process is the time it takes to design, make and deliver; this is referred to as the **lead time**. Although the idea of an MTO process applies mostly to products, an equivalent service would be something like a tailor-made personalized service – rather like having a chauffeur and limousine at your beck and call.

Lead time the time it takes to design, make, and deliver a product or service.

Make to Stock

The MTS process is a standard process used to make items that are put into inventory, which can then be used immediately to fulfil customer demand. Everything in an MTS process is geared towards having the right items in stock when a customer places an order, so that it can be fulfilled straight away. In contrast to MTO, MTS processes build products only for inventory stock, and the jobs in process are not linked to any particular customer. Classic examples are standardized homogeneous unseasonable products such as canned foodstuffs and small cheap consumer goods such as kettles.

The critical management tasks with MTS are forecasting, inventory management and capacity planning. The MTS process begins with the producer specifying the product or service. The customer then requests a product from inventory. If the product is available in inventory, it is delivered to the customer. If it is not available, a *back order* signal should be sent to production to make some more items to put into stock. In the MTS process, customer orders do not directly influence production; the production cycle is driven by the need to replenish stock. In other words, the customer-ordering cycle follows a completely independent cycle from the production cycle. Therefore what is being produced may have little bearing upon what is required by customers at any point in time.

Performance measures for an MTS process include the percentage of orders filled from inventory; this is called the *service level* and is typically targeted above 90%. Other measures are the length of time it takes to replenish inventory, inventory turnover, capacity utilization and the time it takes to fill a back order. The objective of an MTS process is to meet the desired service level at a minimum cost. Although the idea of MTS is applied mostly to products, the equivalent idea in services is to have a standard service that you may have to wait for, and which is non-negotiable – rather like having your car oil changed at a Kwik Fit garage or having customer service staff and spare capacity ready-to-go at a children's indoor play center.

Assemble to Order

Assemble to order (ATO) processes are a growing trend that has been facilitated largely by the use of Internet-based ordering systems that can make processes increasingly customer focused. The ATO process builds sub-assemblies in advance of demand and then puts them together to make the final product when a specific customer order is received. ATO is a hybrid of make to order and make to stock. Whereas the sub-assemblies are made to stock, the final assembly is made to order. When a specific order arrives, the sub-assemblies are taken from inventory and assembled to fill the customer's order. But, of course, the product must be designed in a modular fashion for ATO to be used. For instance, Benetton initially makes all its jumpers in an 'un-dyed' neutral color and then dyes them afterwards once an order has been received from a retailer. By doing this, Benetton is able to balance its inventory with customer demand better, while still providing quick 'final assembly' of the product and delivery to the customer.

There are other variations on ATO, including mass customization, in which every single product could potentially be different (explained in more detail in Chapter 4). For instance, Mattel offered Barbie dolls that could wear any item of clothing from a choice of thousands and any hairstyle from a choice of hundreds. Although ATO is usually applied to products, the service equivalent would be buying a package holiday and selecting different options to tailor your own holiday package (e.g. adding car hire, transfers, insurance etc.).

Chapter 4, p105

The differences between the three main types of order are described in Table 5.4.

The type of customer order determines the **customization point** in the ordering process. This is defined as the point where the product becomes linked to a specific customer order and the customer becomes involved in the process. There are three main points where customization can occur: these are shown by the shading in Figure 5.5.

Customization point the point where a process output becomes linked to a specific customer order.

For MTS the customization point is after the design and make is completed: therefore any customization has to be limited to delivery and packaging only. For ATO the customization point is after design, but before final assembly: therefore the ATO process gives the customer more choice, since the product is assembled after the order is placed. For MTO processes the customization point is during the design phase and may even include ordering in unique, bespoke parts (e.g. new materials for a tailor-made suit, new paint for an unusual car colour or a special gluten-free birthday cake for a celebratory restaurant meal). For MTO the maximum amount of customization is possible, but the lead time to the customer can be longer, and the product typically costs more.

Table 5.4 Characteristics of different order types

	Make to stock (MTS)	Assemble to order (ATO)	Make to order (MTO)
Product/service	Producer specified Low variety Inexpensive	Part customer and part producer specified Mid variety Mid expense	Customer specified High variety Expensive
Objectives	Balance inventory, capacity and service	Quick assembly – needs balanced inventory and quick delivery	Manage delivery lead times and capacity
Main operations problems	Forecasting, planning production, control of inventory	Designing products and services that are modular Flexible assembly line	Specification Quality levels Delivery time

Figure 5.5 Customer involvement in different types of order

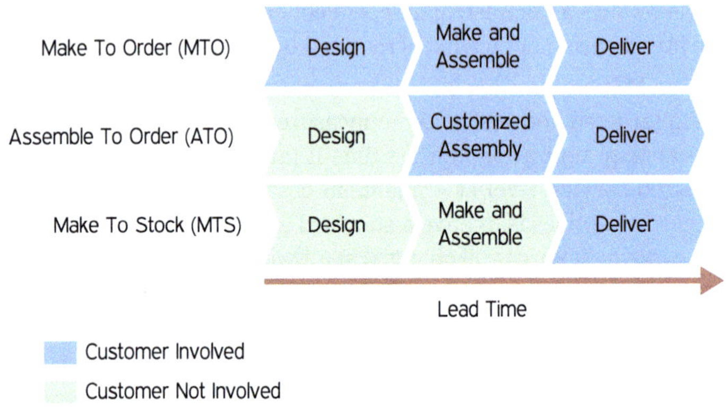

SHORT CASE 5.2

Diamonds Are for Ordering

Buying an expensive piece of jewellery such as an engagement ring can be a big decision and it is important to get it just right. For instance, mass-produced diamond rings can be bought in any high street jewellery chain, but if you want something more individual you have to go to a jeweller who can design and make bespoke items.

Online jewellery companies such as Blue Nile are an alternative. These e-retailers offer a choice of band shapes and styles, diamond cuts, shapes and quality, which can be selected and ordered over the Internet.

Source: ©Soniparag31/Shutterstock

Alternatively, one could also try renowned diamond centres such as Amsterdam, which have led customized jewellery design and manufacture for hundreds of years. There are many shops in such areas that possess the skills to design and make rings from scratch. Customers can have anything they desire . . . as long as they can afford it!

Questions

1. Which scenario is most likely to work on MTS, MTO and ATO ordering?
2. What implications are there for designing the manufacturing process?

Contemporary Thinking: Design for Mass Customization

BUSINESS INTEGRATION

Up to this point we have been discussing traditional process strategies and order types that map neatly onto Figure 5.4. However, there have been major developments in process and product technologies recently, such as computers, robotics and the Internet (e.g. the Internet of things, collection of big data and artificial intelligence for data analytics), which are facilitating a change in process thinking. New technologies have driven process strategy towards *mass customization*.

Mass customization is a process strategy that can repeatedly deliver products or services in very small batch sizes, often involving just one item or one service delivery. In the volume and variety figure (Figure 5.4) mass customization is placed in the top right-hand corner, which is a strategy that is not normally financially sustainable. This is because traditional mass production is built on *economies of scale*, delivering high volumes of standardized output with few options. By contrast, mass customization depends on *economies of scope*, which can provide a high variety of outputs from a single process. Consequently, mass customization has a common *process* rather than a common *product* or *service*.

Customization (or 'customer-ization') means making a different product for each customer (usually at high cost), whereas mass customization means delivering a different product or service for each customer at approximately mass production cost levels. Mass customization is difficult to do, though, as it requires the whole process to be flexible – from the order taking, through to assembly and delivery. For instance:

- The production process must be rapid, flexible and able to accommodate changes in specification. This means that batch (or 'lot') sizes of one are possible, such as pizza production at a takeaway pizza house.
- Inventory control needs to be tight and there should be no finished stock held and therefore no obsolescence; nobody wants yesterday's pizza.
- Delivery requires careful tracking and tracing of every order; there may be many different pizzas going to many different customers, all at the same time.

The key point is ...

that mass customization is difficult to achieve consistently, and requires mass collaboration along the supply chain. The advantages are that customers' demands are met quickly and forecasting errors and risks are reduced.

SHORT CASE 5.3

Mass Customization at Dell

BUSINESS INTEGRATION

Dell has recently become the number one maker of file servers in the United States (computers used to serve up files on a computer network – as found in a university library, for example) and holds the number two position worldwide. Dell builds servers efficiently and their customers know exactly where their server is during every step of the production process.

The production process begins when the customer orders the server. This information is placed in a production queue that itemizes every component to be built into the server. The required inventory is then sent to the assembly area to make sure that it is queued. Dell collaborates closely with its suppliers to provide them with real-time production data, so it can have inventory available on the loading docks connected to the factory floor. This allows Dell to keep only two hours' worth of inventory on the factory floor.

Assembly begins when the chassis, motherboard and memory are put together and moved to the 'kitting' area, where the other various internal components (such as drives, cards and connectors) from suppliers are added to the 'kit' tray. These kits are then moved to the assembly area, where they are automatically routed to the next available assembler. Each assembler can build a variety of servers (each is typically certified to build up to 15 different models). Once a server has been completed and tested, it is mechanically placed in a container and shipped out. Although production occurs very quickly, each server is customized specifically. The factory produces servers on a mass scale.

Questions

1. What is Dell's strategy and unique approach to order processing?
2. How has the design of its products helped mass customization?
3. What makes it possible to deliver high variation at competitive prices and lead times?
4. Why don't its competitors do the same?

Stop and Think

What other products or services can you think of that would benefit from mass customization? How could this become feasible, and why hasn't it already been done?

Process Mapping

BUSINESS INTEGRATION

When we design and analyse processes, we need to ask questions such as:

- Is the process aligned with organizational strategy in order to achieve competitive advantage in terms of differentiation, response or low cost?
- Has the process got any non-value-adding steps that need to be eliminated?
- Does the process maximize customer value as perceived by the customer?
- Will the process help win orders?

There are many tools that can help us understand the complexities of process design and redesign. Many of these build on systems thinking and focus on helping to develop a picture of the overall process; this is usually to help improve delivery of service, flow of information and management of materials. We shall now consider a few of these process-mapping tools, each of which has a slightly different purpose.

Flow Diagram

Flow diagram a drawing used to analyse the flow of people and materials.

A **flow diagram** is a general-purpose diagram or schematic used to map the flow of people, material or progress. Figure 5.6 shows a very simple example of a flow diagram, using standard flow chart notation, for ordering a new sofa.

The main purpose of a flow diagram is to create a logical flow of activities (the sequence in which things are done) and indicate what the inputs and outputs are between them so that an awareness of the 'big picture' of an operation can be gained.

Swim Lane Map

Another general-purpose process visualization technique is the *swim lane map;* this is so called because it looks a bit like a swimming pool with lanes. A swim lane map is very similar to a flow diagram, but with more structure, as it has a time dimension along the horizontal axis and a functional dimension along the vertical axis that shows organization 'hand-offs'. Figure 5.7 shows an example of a swim lane map for the same simple ordering process shown in Figure 5.6.

The swim lane map is most useful when we are looking at process problems associated with functional divisions and waiting time.

Process Chart

A *process chart* is a general-purpose table, rather than a diagram, that uses symbols, time and distance to provide an objective and structured way to analyse and record activities in a process. It allows us to focus on value-adding activities. For instance, the process chart shown in Figure 5.8 is about making deliveries. The advantage of process charts over flow diagrams or swim lane diagrams is that there is no artistry involved, as they are always one-page tables produced on a standard template.

The activities are listed in the left-hand column and a line (threading vertically through the symbols) joins up symbols on a standard template shown in the central vertical columns (ringed in the figure). Each symbol represents a different type of activity, as defined in the top left table. Other attributes and notes about the activities can also be added in the right-hand columns. Taken together, the information depicts a process that can be followed by operatives rather like an instruction sheet.

Figure 5.6 A flow diagram: ordering a sofa

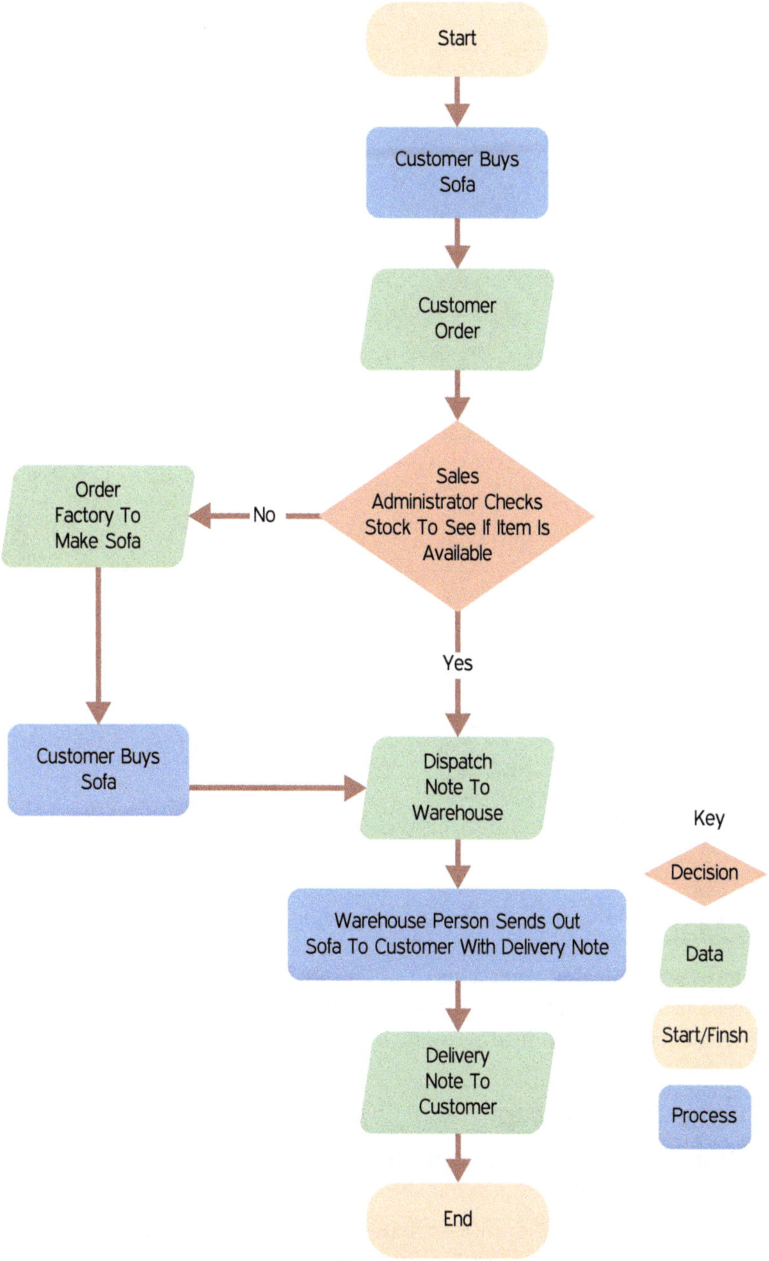

Service Blueprint

Processes with a high service element are best suited to *service blueprinting* (Shostack, 1984). Service blueprinting is a process analysis technique that focuses on the customer, the provider's interaction with the customer and on the activities of the provider. Service blueprints separate the service into physical evidence, customer/user actions, front-of-stage interactions (those actions by staff that interact directly with the customers or clients), backstage contact employee actions (those actions performed by customer-interfacing staff that do not involve the customer) and support processes that do not involve the customer. Figure 5.9 shows the service blueprint for the process of welcoming new students to a new course.

Figure 5.7 Swim lane map: ordering a sofa

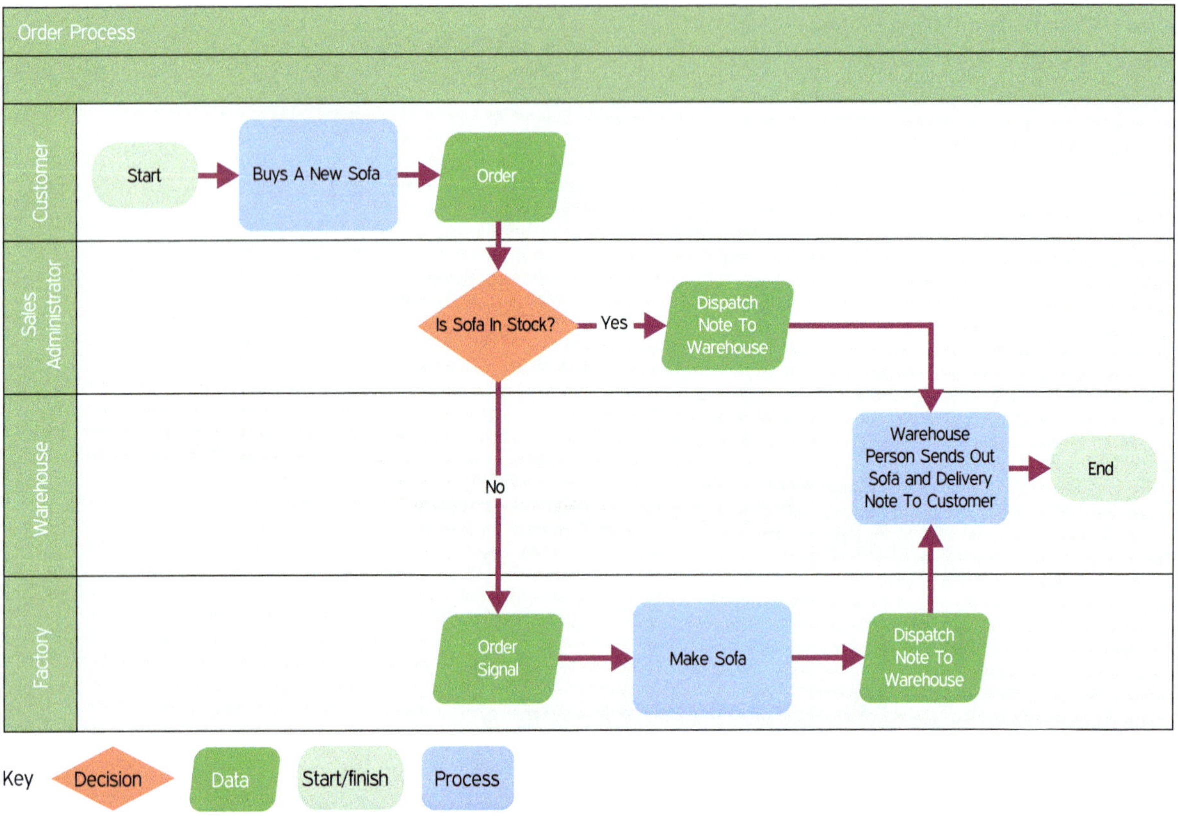

Value Stream Map

Perhaps one of the most sophisticated depictions of processes is the *value stream map* (VSM). A VSM requires a *current state* map to be produced, showing any present inefficiencies in the process, and a *future state* map that proposes how improvements can be made after waste in a process has been reduced.

Current State Value Stream Map

The current state VSM shows the process as it currently is, with all its inefficiencies. The most important icons used in this VSM are shown in Figure 5.10.

Figure 5.11 shows a simple example of a current state VSM for the ACME Company, which makes spare parts (brackets) for tractors. The operation is currently very inefficient, as there is a great deal of waste in it, and it needs improving.

A VSM always places the customer in the top right-hand corner and the suppliers are placed in the top left-hand corner. The tasks in the process are placed in white boxes with material flow going from left to right and data about each of the tasks are placed in *data boxes* beneath them. Between each of the tasks lies an arrow indicating the direction of material flow and a yellow triangle that indicates the amount of work in progress. Thick arrows between the tasks show material flow. Thin arrows are used to show information flow within a company and between its customers and suppliers. In the centre of the VSM at the top we show the method of production control. At the bottom of the diagram a *timeline* is calculated that shows all the waiting times and task cycle times in the process; these are summed up in the bottom right-hand corner.

The steps involved in producing a current state VSM are as follows:

1. Select a product or service family to focus on; this might be the food service in a hotel or a postal service to a particular area.

Figure 5.8 A process chart: making deliveries

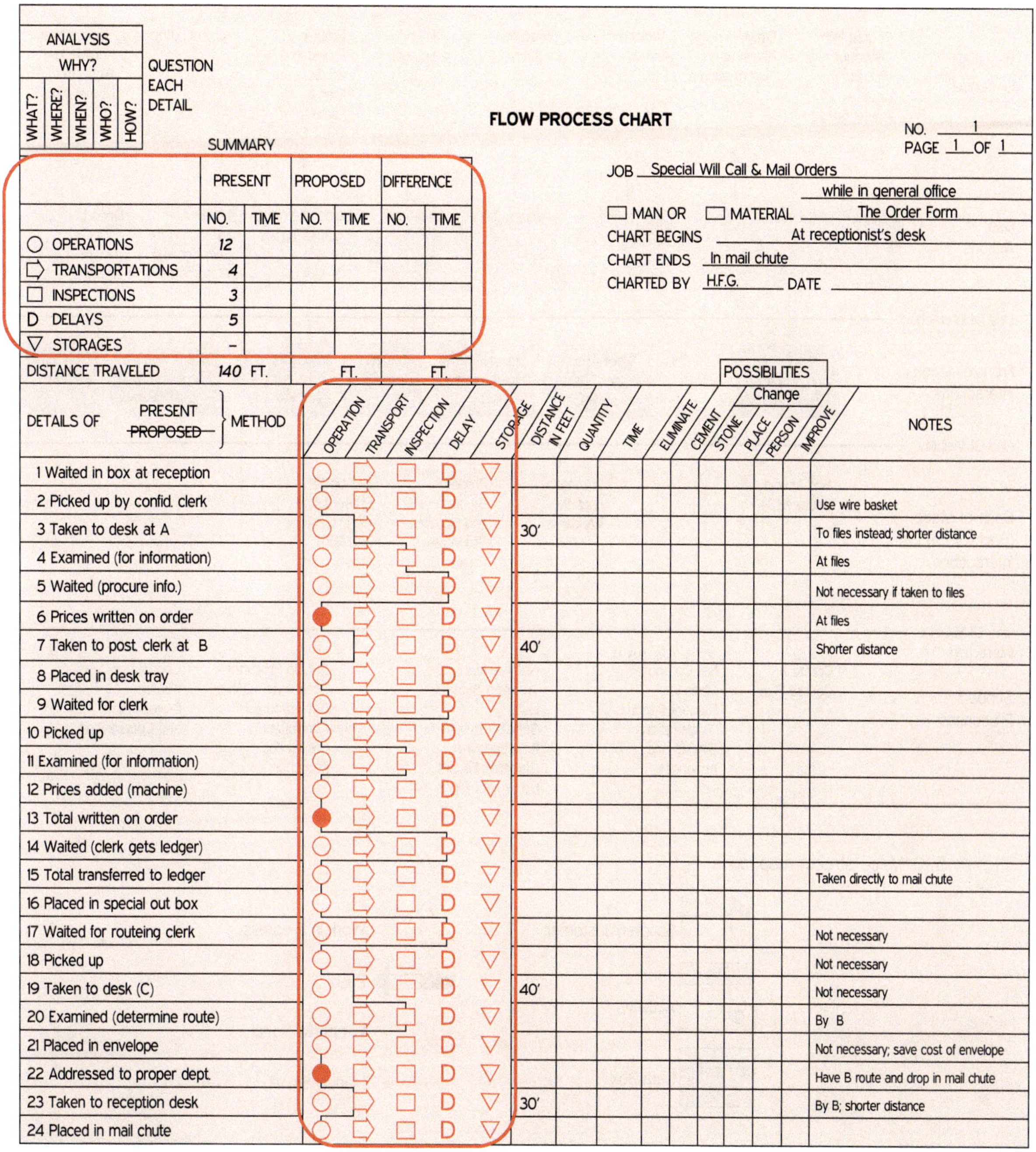

FLOW PROCESS CHART

ANALYSIS — WHY? — WHAT? WHERE? WHEN? WHO? HOW? — QUESTION EACH DETAIL

NO. 1 PAGE 1 OF 1

JOB Special Will Call & Mail Orders while in general office

☐ MAN OR ☐ MATERIAL The Order Form

CHART BEGINS At receptionist's desk

CHART ENDS In mail chute

CHARTED BY H.F.G. DATE

SUMMARY

	PRESENT NO.	PRESENT TIME	PROPOSED NO.	PROPOSED TIME	DIFFERENCE NO.	DIFFERENCE TIME
○ OPERATIONS	12					
⇨ TRANSPORTATIONS	4					
☐ INSPECTIONS	3					
D DELAYS	5					
▽ STORAGES	–					
DISTANCE TRAVELED	140 FT.		FT.		FT.	

DETAILS OF PRESENT ~~PROPOSED~~ METHOD	OPERATION / TRANSPORT / INSPECTION / DELAY / STORAGE	DISTANCE IN FEET	QUANTITY	TIME	POSSIBILITIES: ELIMINATE / CEMENT / Change: STONE / PLACE / PERSON / IMPROVE	NOTES
1 Waited in box at reception	○ ⇨ ☐ D ▽					
2 Picked up by confid. clerk	○ ⇨ ☐ D ▽					Use wire basket
3 Taken to desk at A	○ ⇨ ☐ D ▽	30′				To files instead; shorter distance
4 Examined (for information)	○ ⇨ ☐ D ▽					At files
5 Waited (procure info.)	○ ⇨ ☐ D ▽					Not necessary if taken to files
6 Prices written on order	● ⇨ ☐ D ▽					At files
7 Taken to post. clerk at B	○ ⇨ ☐ D ▽	40′				Shorter distance
8 Placed in desk tray	○ ⇨ ☐ D ▽					
9 Waited for clerk	○ ⇨ ☐ D ▽					
10 Picked up	○ ⇨ ☐ D ▽					
11 Examined (for information)	○ ⇨ ☐ D ▽					
12 Prices added (machine)	○ ⇨ ☐ D ▽					
13 Total written on order	● ⇨ ☐ D ▽					
14 Waited (clerk gets ledger)	○ ⇨ ☐ D ▽					
15 Total transferred to ledger	○ ⇨ ☐ D ▽					Taken directly to mail chute
16 Placed in special out box	○ ⇨ ☐ D ▽					
17 Waited for routeing clerk	○ ⇨ ☐ D ▽					Not necessary
18 Picked up	○ ⇨ ☐ D ▽					Not necessary
19 Taken to desk (C)	○ ⇨ ☐ D ▽	40′				Not necessary
20 Examined (determine route)	○ ⇨ ☐ D ▽					By B
21 Placed in envelope	○ ⇨ ☐ D ▽					Not necessary; save cost of envelope
22 Addressed to proper dept.	● ⇨ ☐ D ▽					Have B route and drop in mail chute
23 Taken to reception desk	○ ⇨ ☐ D ▽	30′				By B; shorter distance
24 Placed in mail chute	○ ⇨ ☐ D ▽					

Source: artoflean.com.

2. Capture the customer order requirements. For instance, how many of each type of service or item does the customer require and how often do they want them to be delivered? These are recorded in a data box, at the top right corner, under the customer.

3. Starting at the end of the process, define each of the separate tasks and measure their cycle time. The **cycle time** (C/T) is the *actual* time that it takes to produce a unit of output (sometimes known as *processing time*). Define the whole process by sequencing the separate tasks in the correct order.

Cycle time the actual time a process or task in a process takes to produce a unit of output.

Figure 5.9 Service blueprinting: welcoming students to a new course

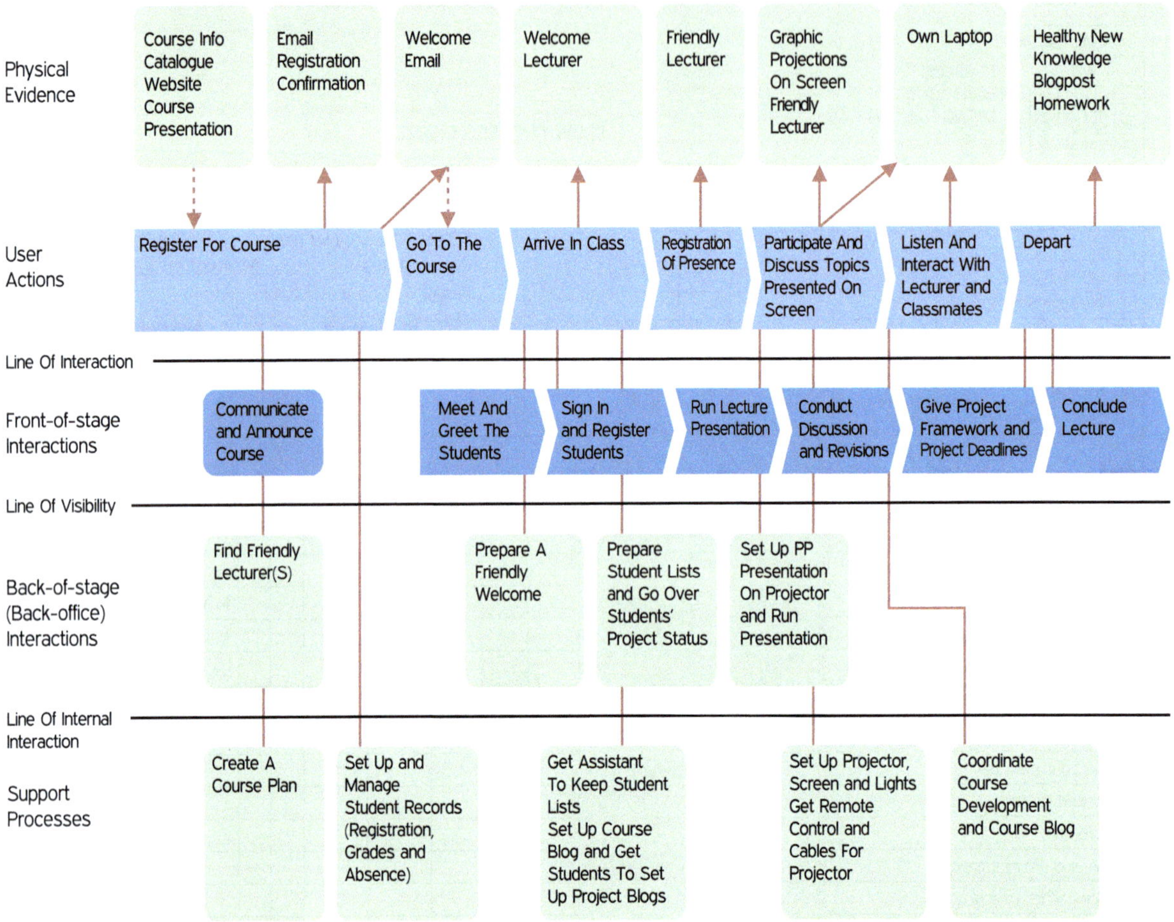

Figure 5.10 Value stream map icons

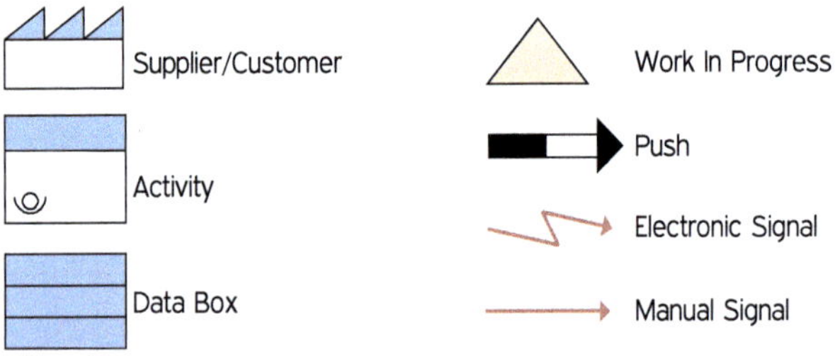

4. It is also useful to collect other performance measures in the data boxes, such as:
   - changeover time (C/O) – time taken to change between producing different kinds of output
   - uptime – the time a machine or person is available during a shift
   - number of people required for each task (this is shown at the bottom of each task box – for instance, stamping uses one person).

   These measures should be built into the calculation to help work out the *overall equipment effectiveness* (OEE) of a machine or the *overall professional effectiveness* (OPE) of a person in a task.
5. Define the information flows in the process. This will be in the opposite direction to material flows (right to left). It will include the reorder signal from the customer to the operation and the order the operations manager gives to people in the operations department; which could be via a manufacturing requirements planning (MRP) or enterprise resource planning (ERP) system (as described in Chapters 9 and 10), a kanban system, a manual instruction or a combination of all these.

Chapter 9, p289
Chapter 10, p323

Figure 5.11 A current state value stream map for ACME: brackets for tractors

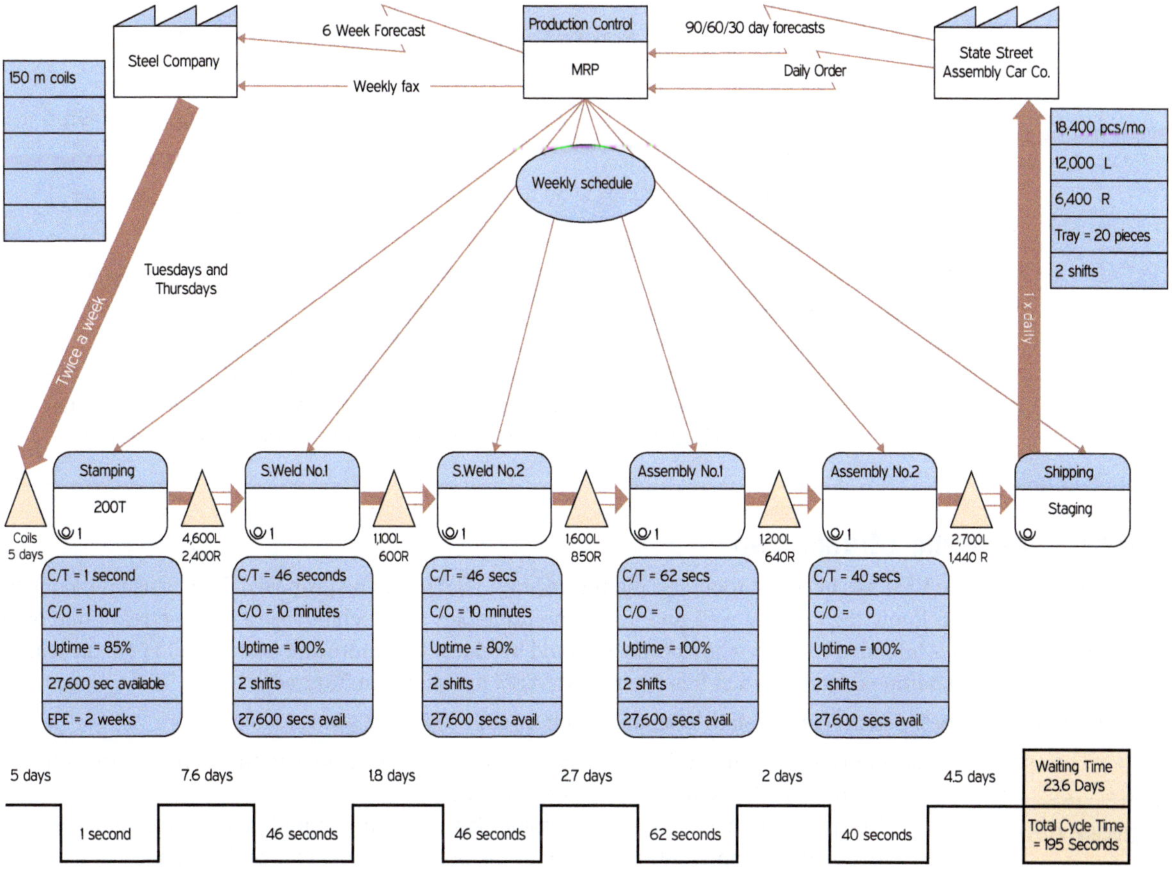

6. Measure the waiting time between each activity.
7. Work out the overall lead time in the process by adding up the cycle times of each task and the waiting times between each task.

Figure 5.11 shows an example that has a 23.6-day waiting time and only 195 seconds of value added time. This is very wasteful, but it is typical of many operations. It clearly shows that improvements can be made in terms of waiting time. It also shows that there is a lot of work in progress (WIP) between each of the workstations, which could also be reduced.

WORKED EXAMPLE 5.1

Interpreting a Current State Value Stream Map

Problem: *Figure 5.11 shows a simple completed current state VSM for producing tractor spare parts (brackets). See if you can read some information from it.*

(a) What are the customer's order requirements?

(b) What is the total cycle time for the tractor parts (in seconds)?

(c) What is the total lead time?

(d) Do you think that this is an efficient process? State why/why not.

Approach: Carefully re-read the diagram and the notes about how it was constructed.

Solution:

(a) 18,400 pieces per month are required, including 12,000 left-hand brackets (LH) and 6,400 right-hand brackets (RH). These are to be delivered in trays of 20 using two shifts

(b) Stamping (1) + weld 1 (46) + weld 2 (46) + assembly 1 (62) + assembly 2 (40) + shipping (0) = 195 seconds total cycle time.

(c) Total waiting time (in days) = 5 + 7.6 + 1.8 + 2.7 + 2 + 4.5 = 23.6 days. Therefore ACME total lead time = 23.6 days waiting time + 195 seconds total cycle time.

(d) No. This is very wasteful, but is typical of many operations. It clearly shows that improvement can be made in waiting time. It also shows that there is a lot of work in progress (WIP) waiting between each of the workstations, which can be reduced. Also, the current VSM example in Figure 5.11 uses an MRP-controlled system using 90-, 60- and 30-day forecasts from the customer, and places daily orders. The ACME Company passes a six-week forecast and a weekly fax order to its supplier. Signals are sent to all steps in the process simultaneously; this is not a lean or efficient process and should be improved.

Future State Value Stream Map

Once the current state VSM has been put together, the future state VSM has to be proposed. This is usually done by a team of people who know the process well and know the principles and techniques of value stream mapping. The future state VSM is intended to show what a process could be like in the future and how it could become leaner. The most important additional icons used in this future state VSM are shown in Figure 5.12.

The main differences between the current state VSM and the future state VSM here are as follows:

- The customer is sending a more regular demand signal with smaller quantities to the manufacturer – in other words, the demand pattern is less 'lumpy'.
- The production controller or customer is sending one signal (a kanban signal – as detailed in Chapter 10) to the end of the process to create a 'pull' system.
- Tasks have been consolidated and human resources reassigned to reduce waiting time. This results in the identification of the **pacemaker task**. This is the task that sets the pace of the overall process and receives a signal direct from the customer through continually flowing processes – in other words, without any WIP held between it and the customer.
- 'Stores' are used only to help balance the production mix and volume, and not because tasks are overly fragmented.
- The supplier makes more frequent deliveries that are in smaller quantities – in other words, the deliveries are less 'lumpy'.

Chapter 10, p323

Pacemaker task the task that dictates the speed of the overall process.

Takt time the time allowed by the customer for each unit of output to be produced.

Chapter 7, p213

The steps taken to create this are as follows:

1. Calculate the **takt time**. This is the time allowed by the customer for each unit of output to be produced; it is sometimes called the 'drumbeat' of the operation. It is calculated by using the following formula (which is explained further in Chapter 7):

$$\textit{Takt time} = \textit{Overall equipment effectiveness}/\textit{Average demand}$$

Figure 5.12 Further VSM icons

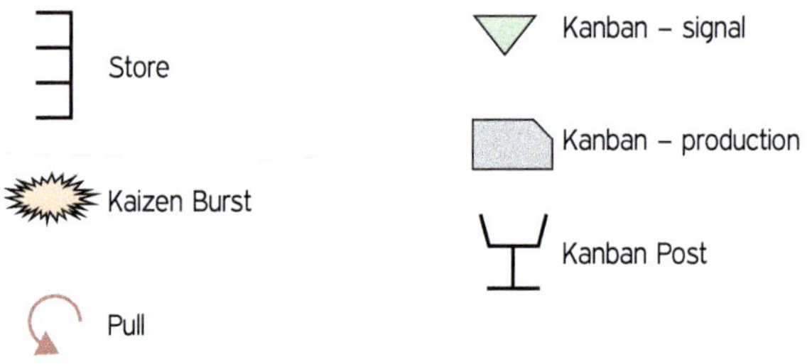

2. Develop continuous flow in the process wherever possible – which is pulled directly by the customer's demand signal. This means that work in progress (WIP) and waiting times should both be reduced.
3. Use 'stores' only if necessary to control production where continuous flow cannot extend upstream any further back from the customer.
4. Try to send the customer demand to only one task in the production process. This should be as close to the end of the process as possible, to ensure that a customer driven pull system is established.
5. Distribute the production of different products/services evenly over time at the pacemaker task. At the pacemaker task the production mix of parts needs to be 'levelled' so that the customer gets what they have asked for when they asked for it.
6. Create an initial pull signal by releasing and withdrawing small, consistent increments of work at the pacemaker task to level the production volume.
7. Develop the ability to make 'every part every (EPE) day', then EPE shift, then EPE hour, in tasks further upstream from the pacemaker process.
8. Recalculate total lead time. Most savings will be made in the amount of waiting time. Steps 1–8 enable an operation to produce the smallest batch (or 'lot') size possible in the correct sequence (as shown in Figure 5.13 for ACME).
9. Finally, VSMs can also be used to identify further areas of improvement and levelling within the process – these are shown by the yellow 'kaizen burst' stars in Figure 5.13.

Figure 5.13 A future state value stream map: spare parts for tractors

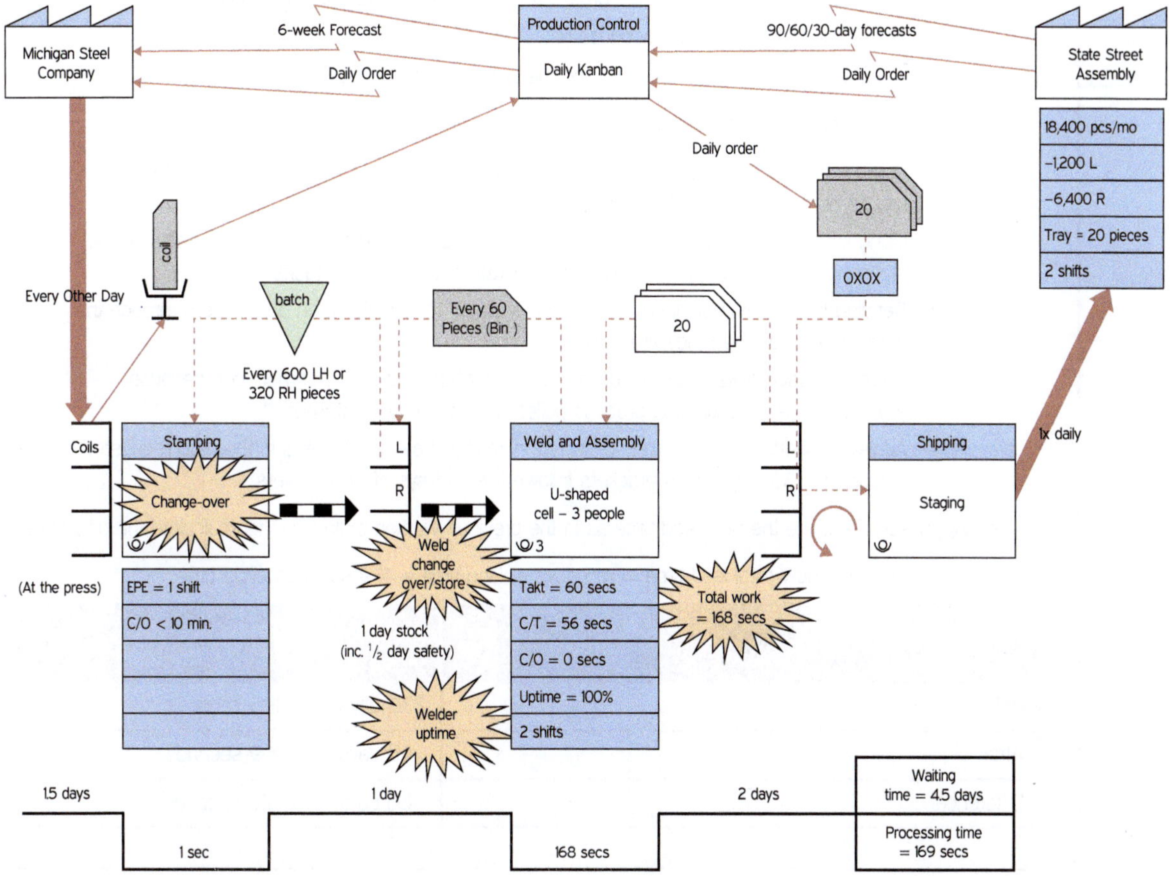

The main things to remember in relation to VSMs are that:

- An operation needs to work to the takt time set by the customer and not the cycle times defined by an operation's actual capacity and capabilities.
- The most dramatic savings are often made by reducing wasted time between tasks, rather than in the actual tasks themselves, which is not always apparent prior to the mapping exercise.

For further details on VSM, read the guides by Rother and Shook (1999) and Bicheno (2004).

WORKED EXAMPLE 5.2

Future State Value Stream Map for ACME Tractor Brackets

Problem: *Figure 5.13 shows a simple completed future state VSM for producing tractor spare parts (brackets). The waste in the process has been reduced. See if you can:*

(a) *Calculate the takt time.*

(b) *Describe some ways in which the process has been made leaner.*

(c) *Calculate how much better the new lead time is in comparison with the old lead time in Figure 5.11.*

(d) *Say what other things ACME could do in terms of kaizen burst to make the process leaner.*

(a) **Approach:** Use the formula takt time = OEE / average demand

Solution: Assuming that ACME has 100% OEE we have 27,600 seconds in a shift, and the customer wants 18,400 pieces per month. Also, assuming that ACME has 20 working days per month with two shifts per day, then it has:

2 shifts × 20 days = 40 shifts

18,400 brackets / 40 shifts = 460 brackets per shift

or 27,600 seconds in a shift / 460 brackets = one bracket every 60 seconds

Therefore the takt time is 60 seconds.

(b) **Approach:** Carefully re-read the diagram and the notes on how it has been constructed.

Solution: The process has been made leaner by:

- Joining together the two welding and the two assembly tasks and reducing the staffing requirement from four to three people
- Using kanban stores between the stamping and welding and assembly tasks, because the stamping machine works at a much quicker rate than any other tasks
- Sending the demand signal directly to the shipping task, which then pulls orders through the process as and when they are needed
- Creating a pacemaker task out of the newly created weld and assembly cell, because downstream is a continuous process pulled directly by the customer
- Achieving short production runs delivered in kanban trays of 20 parts in the ratio requested by the customer – 30 trays of LH brackets followed by 16 trays of RH brackets.

(c) **Approach:** Calculate the new lead time as in the previous worked example. Then calculate the difference.

Solution: ACME new total lead time = 4.5 days waiting time + 169 seconds cycle time

	Waiting time	Total cycle time (processing time)
Before	23.6 days	195 seconds
After	4.5 days	169 seconds
Difference	19.1 days	26 seconds

A significant improvement of 19.1 days waiting time and 26 seconds cycle time is achieved.

(d) **Approach:** Re-read the diagram and the notes on how it has been constructed.

Solution:

- Reduce changeover time and batch sizes at the stamping press and aim to produce every part every shift.
- Eliminate the stores between stamping and welding to give an overall continuous flow of mixed production.
- Make the operators more efficient by making the welders and assemblers 100% OPE; this might be through training, better working conditions or ergonomics.

Lean thinking and VSM is a contemporary method of looking at the relationship between process output, available capacity and time taken to perform a task. This relationship can also be calculated in more conventionally way by using **Little's Law** which states that:

Total process throughput time = No. of work-in-progress items × Item cycle time

Little's Law
Total process throughput time = No. of work-in-progress items x Item cycle time

Little's law does not, however, use lean thinking because it does not focus on the rate that the customer requires products and services to be delivered; it instead independently focuses on how much is being made or delivered and how long it will take to make, with no respect to actual demand. Therefore Little's Law is appropriate for make-to-stock processes but not for lean make-to-order or assemble-to-order processes. For example, if a university computer laboratory had 50 computers that each needed a software upgrade that took a single technician 10 minutes each, then the total process throughput time is 500 minutes (50 × 10 minutes = 500 minutes). If the laboratory is required to be used by students in 10 minutes' time then this would not be acceptable; this process would be known as a 'long-sequential' process and would be acceptable to do only before term starts in a make-to-stock type service. A quicker way to install the software would be for each student user to upgrade the software themselves at the beginning of class, which still has the same total process throughput time but has a lead time of only 10 minutes ((50 × 10 minutes)/50 people = 10 minutes). This second process would be known as a 'short-parallel' process delivering output much more quickly and accounts for the rate at which the customers (in this case students) require the service to be delivered. The first 'long-sequential' process has a takt rate of 1 computer per 10 minutes and the second 'short-parallel' process has a takt rate or 50 computers per 10 minutes. Therefore the second process would be leaner.

CRITICAL PERSPECTIVE

Is Process Mapping Scientific Enough?

Some will say that process mapping is the single best way to apply **lean thinking** in an operation. It is an approach that analyses material and information flows with a view to eliminating time wastage and reducing the overall duration of the process lead time. The use of it has grown significantly in recent years.

Lean thinking
extending lean production to broader ideas or philosophies. Based on five-step framework: concentrate on value for customers, appreciate the value stream, concentrate on improved flow, adopt pull, perfect quality.

Conversely, many people criticize process mapping for being too time consuming and for producing nothing other than numerous pretty pictures. But those who make such criticisms are not necessarily seeing the wider purpose of the exercise, as the main purpose of a process-mapping exercise is not the process map itself, but the team building and organizational learning that come from having conducted the exercise. Many people working in operations find it difficult to think about the philosophical approach of systems thinking and how to increase their process perspective on an operation; a process modelling or mapping exercise can help overcome these obstacles.

It is true to say that process mapping uses a combination of science and art. Measurements of process performance can be taken using scientific equipment, but the representation, design and improvement of processes often fall to the experience, creativity and 'artistry' of operations managers. The real choice comes in deciding which particular sort of process map is most suitable for a particular process. For instance, if you are looking at a customer service process, then a service blueprint map may be best, or if you want to omit creative drawing, then use a process chart. Alternatively, if a measure of throughput is explicitly required, a VSM may be the best option. Or if you are looking at a simple, low-volume process, a flow diagram may suffice.

The key point is ...

that whatever technique is used, process mapping must be a team exercise involving all the important stakeholders; process mapping is a tool to develop a collective vision for change and needs to take a holistic, systems thinking approach.

Physical Layouts of Processes

Layout the physical configuration of departments, work centres, and equipment in an operation.

Layout is a critical factor determining the long-term efficiency of an operation. Layout physically influences the organization's capacity, process operations, flexibility and cost, as well as the quality of work life, customer contact and image. Layout therefore has strategic implications: effective layout can help organizations achieve competitive advantage, whereas poor layout can have detrimental effects. Layout decisions include the best placement of machines (in production settings), of offices and desks (in office settings) or of service centres in hospitals, department stores or local government offices.

A good layout considers the following:

- *Materials handling equipment:* managers must make decisions about the equipment to be used, including conveyors, cranes, automated storage solutions and automatic vehicles. Materials handling costs should be minimized.
- *Capacity and space requirements:* only when personnel, machines and equipment requirements are known, can managers proceed with layout design and provide the necessary space for each part of the operation. Sometimes, though, extra space is used to create a feeling of opulence (as in the entrance to a bank, for example).
- *Environment and aesthetics:* factors such as air, noise, light, personal space, pollution and decor need to be considered. This is because a safe working environment is needed that keeps the morale of the workforce high.
- *Flows of information:* communication is important to any organization and informal communication can be hindered or facilitated by a good physical layout. Where face-to-face communication is not possible, information technologies such as email and Internet-based systems must be used to complement physical communication and help the flow of information.
- *Cost of moving materials between work areas:* there may be special reasons for locating certain work areas together. For instance, there may be a high degree of traffic between them (e.g. customs and baggage collection in an airport) or it may be very difficult and expensive to move items between them (e.g. moving trucks between a paint shop and an assembly shop).
- *Appropriate levels of customer and employee interaction:* for example, a theme park should have highly visible, presentable and helpful staff.

Layout decisions are strategically important from an operational perspective because they can require large investments of time and money, which can result in long-term commitments to a particular configuration of machines and workspace. However, as the pace of industry quickens and product life cycles shorten, layout designs need to be viewed as dynamic. To make quick and easy changes in product ranges and production rates, operations managers must design flexibility into factory and warehouse layouts. This means considering small, movable and flexible equipment – store displays need to be movable, office desks and partitions modular, and warehouse racks prefabricated and reconfigurable. To support this flexibility, managers must make sure their employees are multi-skilled, machinery is well maintained and equipment is movable.

Environmental and Social Legislation in Process Design

Legislation to protect our environment and society is constantly being developed that affects process design in the following ways:

- sources and types of inputs – for instance, they should be from sustainable sources (e.g. sustainable palm oil grown for liquid soap manufacture, and cacao beans for chocolate)
- amount of transforming resources used – for instance, amount of energy used in production processes (e.g. aluminium smelting) and amount of water used (e.g. for washing cars in automated car washers)
- waste output reduction – such as reduction of packaging, non-reusable and non-recyclable items. CO_2, heat emissions and harmful by-products should be reduced (e.g. chemical waste in tanning of leather)
- controls – such as the type of labour used (e.g. elimination of child exploitation and modern slavery practice), reduction in greenhouse gases emissions, fair-trade practices, health and safety practices, and data protection (e.g. the UK's General Data Protection Regulation (GDPR) Act in 2018).

There is often a trade-off between legislative requirements and operational performance metrics throughout a product or services life cycle.

Different Types of Layout

There are three broad types of layout:

- *Fixed position layout:* where all activities cluster around the product or service being delivered. This type is used mainly in large-scale projects such as buildings, roads or ships, or large-scale events such as festivals or markets.
- *Product-service-dominant layout:* established to deliver one closely related group of products or services very efficiently, such as processing people through customs and immigration in an airport or manufacturing LCD TV screens in a production facility. This layout type will deliver only one type of product or service and so a particular product or service dominates the layout decision.
- *Process dominant layout:* concerned principally with setting up a generic process able to deal with a high variety of outputs, such as a general practitioner's surgery or a mass customization production process. This layout type will deliver many different types of product and service and so the process takes precedence over any one particular product or service.

A hybrid version of the above three is known as a *work cell layout.* Work cells are typically used to help balance load requirements on a facility while increasing variety and establishing a process around the most common or routine elements (e.g. a repair shop for items returned under warranty). They tend to use highly flexible machines and multi-skilled staff in a *job shop.* Refer back to Table 5.3 to see a summary of how certain layouts are best suited to certain process and order types.

Fixed Position Layout

In a fixed position layout, the item being worked on remains stationary and workers, materials and equipment are moved around as needed. The nature of the product generally determines this kind of arrangement; weight, size, bulk or fragility will make it undesirable or extremely difficult to move the product. Fixed position layouts are used for large products such as buildings, bridges and ships. This layout is also used in services such as open heart surgery, theatres and restaurants.

In fixed position layouts, attention is focused on the timing of deliveries of materials, equipment and people to the 'site' so that it does not become too hectic. The main requirements are that the fixed position layout has adequate space for its needs, supply and collection, and minimal movement of materials and people. Lack of storage space at the site can present significant problems – for example, at construction sites in crowded urban settings or at banquets with large numbers of courses.

Because of the diverse range of activities carried out on large projects and the wide range of skills required, special efforts are needed to coordinate the activities. For this reason a project management process is often preferred, as for the 2012 London Olympic Stadium or a music festival such as the case described in Chapter 4.

Chapter 4, p105

Product-Service-Dominant Layout

Product-service layouts are used to achieve a smooth, rapid flow of high volumes of goods, such as making standard washing machines, or customers through a process, such as people entering a sports stadium. This is made possible by high standardization and repetitive processing. Work is divided into a series of standardized tasks, permitting specialization of equipment and division of labour. The large volumes handled by these systems usually make it economical to invest substantial sums of money in equipment and specific detailed job design.

Because only one (or a few closely related) product or service is being delivered by the process, it is possible to dedicate an entire layout to its processing requirements. For instance, if a portion of a manufacturing process required a sequence of cutting, bending and welding metal, the appropriate pieces of equipment could be arranged in that same dedicated sequence. Furthermore, because each item follows the same sequence of operations, it is often possible to utilize fixed-path material- or people-processing equipment, such as conveyor belts or moving walkways, between operations.

Product-service-dominant layouts are most applicable to continuous or assembly line processes (see Table 5.3 for a summary), such as car assembly. The main advantages with product-service-dominant layouts are efficiency and low unit cost. The main disadvantages are that they can create dull and repetitive working environments, require large capital investment, can be inflexible and can be susceptible to breakdowns due to the high inter-dependency of tasks. Often, preventive maintenance and worker incentive schemes need to be put in place to help reduce the chance of breakdowns, worker boredom and output variations occurring.

In manufacturing environments, the layouts are referred to as *production lines* or *assembly lines*, depending on the type of activity involved. In a service environment, where people are usually being processed, these layouts are not always explicit, unless there is a visible queue of people (e.g. at airport security). However, the concept and principles of product-service layouts are just as valid in service environments (e.g. in a large shopping and leisure centre).

Process-Dominant Layout

Process-dominant layouts are designed to process items or people that involve a variety of processing requirements. The variety of jobs requires frequent adjustments to equipment, such as retooling, and the use of operators with different skills. This causes a discontinuous (or discrete) workflow. Process-dominant layouts often feature departments or functional groupings.

A typical manufacturing example of a process layout is the machine shop, which has separate departments for milling, grinding, drilling, and so on. Items that require the same operations are usually moved in batches (or 'lots') to each departments in a sequence that varies from job to job. Consequently, variable-path materials-handling equipment (e.g. automatic guided vehicles, forklift trucks, hand carts) is needed to handle the variety of routes and items. The use of general-purpose equipment provides enough flexibility to handle the wide range of processing requirements. Workers who carry out the tasks and handle the equipment are usually skilled tradesmen.

Process layouts are also important for service environments. Examples include hospitals, universities, banks, garages, airlines, shops and public libraries. For instance, hospitals have departments specifically to handle surgery, maternity, paediatrics, physiotherapy, accidents and emergencies. Therefore, depending on the patient's condition, each one may take a specific route through different departments. Another good example is given by IKEA, which has a very cleverly designed layout. From the moment customers arrive, to when they leave, the layout is designed to force them all to travel around every department in the store, including the restaurant.

In summary, process-dominant layouts are a 'jack of all trades and master of none' type of layout, as they can be used for many different products and services, but are not tailored to any particular one. The advantages of process-dominant layouts are that:

- They can handle a variety of processing requirements.
- They are not particularly vulnerable to equipment failures.
- General-purpose equipment is often less costly than specialized equipment.
- There is little interdependence between successive operations.

The disadvantages of process-dominant layouts are that:

- Inventory costs are high, as batch processing is often used.
- Routeing and scheduling pose continual challenges.
- Equipment utilization rates are low, because of routeing and scheduling complexities related to the variety of processing demands handled.
- Materials handling is slow and inefficient, relative to product-service-dominant layouts.
- Job complexity results in high supervisory costs.
- Special attention is necessary for each product in relation to routeing, scheduling, machine set-up, etc.

Work Cell Layout

A *work cell* is a hybrid version of product-service and process-dominant layouts. A work cell brings together people and machines that would normally be dispersed across various departments into a group, often known as a *job shop,* so that they can focus on making a single product or group of related products. Cellular work arrangements are used when volume warrants a special arrangement of machinery, people skills and equipment. The advantages of work cells are as follows:

- Work-in-progress inventory is reduced, because the work cell is set up to provide one-piece flow from task to task or machine to machine.
- Less floor area is required, because less space is needed between machines and tasks to accommodate work-in-progress inventory.
- Employee morale is better, because they feel more involved with the overall deliverables.
- Equipment and worker utilization is increased, because of quicker material flow, better scheduling and more multi-skilled workers. This means that fewer machines and less capital investment are needed.
- Raw material and finished goods inventories are reduced, because reduced work in progress means more rapid movement of materials through the layout.
- Direct labour costs are reduced, because improved communication among employees, better material flow and improved scheduling are achieved.

The cellular production environment requires:

- Identification of families of products and services, often on the basis of shared processing equipment, parts or materials
- A high level of training, flexibility and empowerment of employees
- A self-contained facility with its own equipment, resources and quality.

A small restaurant could be considered a cell layout, where all the work is done in a specific area by a small team of people.

Designing Physical Layouts

Once the broad type of physical layout has been decided, the detailed design can take place. There are various techniques available, which are now discussed in more detail.

Fixed Position Layouts

In fixed position layouts, the location of resources will be determined by how often the transforming resources such as equipment and workers can access the product being worked on. The detailed layout of some fixed position layouts, such as a building site, can become very complicated, especially if the planned schedule of activities is changed frequently. Imagine the chaos on a construction site if heavy machinery from different suppliers was continuously crossing paths, or if storage areas were put in inconvenient places. Airbus use a fixed position layout to assemble large planes in its facility in Toulouse, France, where the delivery of sub-assemblies to each plane, such as wings, engines and seats must not interfere with the deliveries to other planes in the same facility.

Fixed position layouts will typically have clearly defined delivery areas for sub-assemblies, access paths, tactically placed lifting equipment, and areas where personnel put on and remove personal protective equipment.

Product-Service-Dominant Layouts

The goal of a product-service layout is to arrange workers or machines in the sequence in which they are needed for a specific product or service as efficiently as possible. The sequence is sometimes referred to as a *production line* or an *assembly line;* these can vary in length from short (e.g. making sandwiches) to long (e.g. making cars). The main benefit of assembly lines is the ability to divide work into a series of simple tasks, which may range from a few seconds to a few minutes. These tasks are typically bundled together and assigned to particular workstations and operators.

Deciding how to assign tasks to workstations is referred to as *line balancing.* The goal of line balancing is to obtain task groupings that represent approximately equal times. This minimizes the idle time along the line and results in a high utilization of labour and equipment. Idle time occurs if task times are not equal among workstations, as some stations will be able to complete tasks quicker than others. The faster stations will experience periodic waits for the output from slower stations or stand unutilized to avoid build-ups of work between stations downstream. Unbalanced lines are undesirable, as this situation leads to inefficient utilization of labour and equipment. Morale problems can also occur, as some workers may perceive they are working harder or faster than others.

Lines that are perfectly balanced will have a smooth flow of work, as activities along the line are synchronized to achieve maximum utilization of labour and equipment. The main obstacle to attaining a perfectly balanced line is the difficulty of forming task bundles that have the same duration. One cause of this is that it may not be feasible to combine certain activities into the same bundle, either because of differences in equipment requirements or because the activities are not compatible (e.g. the risk of contaminating sensitive electrical equipment with dust). Line balancing can be achieved via calculation (see Chapter 10) or by value stream mapping.

Chapter 10, p323

Process-Dominant Layouts

The main issue in designing process-dominant layouts concerns the relative positioning of the departments involved. For example, some departments may benefit from adjacent location, whereas others need to be separated. For instance, a food preparation area should not be near a less sanitary area such as a packing bay. Conversely, two departments that share the same equipment or have high interdepartmental workflows would benefit from being close together. Layouts can also be influenced by external factors such as the location of entrances, loading docks, elevators, windows and areas of reinforced flooring. In some situations, such as supermarkets or petrol stations, there may be a sufficient number of installations that a standardized layout will be defined.

Calculating a process-dominant layout requires the following information:

- A list of departments or work centres to be arranged and their approximate sizes
- A projection of workflows and communication required between centres or departments
- An understanding of the distance between work centres or departments and the cost per unit of distance to move loads between locations
- The size of the facility and the amount of money to be invested in it
- Any special requirements, such as operations that need to be together or kept apart
- The location of key utilities or shared facilities such as access and exit points, toilets or loading docks
- The sequence of flows.

If high-volume interactions or long distances are involved, for example moving thousands of items (or people) across a large site every day, the layout should be calculated mathematically using the formula:

$$\text{Total cost of moving} = \text{Unit cost of moving} \times \text{Number of items to be moved}$$

WORKED EXAMPLE 5.3

Moving Items in a Process-Dominant Layout

A bakery has two sites in a large town and part-made food items have regularly to be moved between them to be finished and packaged. Every tray of items that needs moving costs €20 (in time and petrol) to move. In an average day 100 trays are moved.

Problem: *How much does it cost the bakery per week to move these trays around?*

Approach: Total cost of moving = Unit cost of moving × Number of items to be moved

Solution:

$$€20 \times 100 = 2{,}000$$

€2,000 per day is incurred

Note: Perhaps the bakery should think about relocating its sites onto a single site to save this cost.

If low volumes and small distances are involved, it often comes down to a heuristic management decision (i.e. an educated estimate or 'rule of thumb' decision). If a process-dominant layout is more complicated then a proximity grid can be used to help determine which parts should be located close to another and which can be more remote. This is shown in Worked Example 5.4.

WORKED EXAMPLE 5.4

Proximity Pyramid: How to Layout a Process-Dominant Operation

If there are eight different departments in a clothing factory, decide which should go next to one another in order to make operations run smoothly.

Problem: *The Clothing Company has eight different departments to fit into a new building. You must take into account non-quantifiable factors and decide where to put each department in relation to one another to make operations as effective as possible.*

Approach

Collect information about frequencies and purposes of visits between different departments and if there are any departments that must be kept away from each other. This information can be displayed as below in a 'proximity pyramid'.

Figure 5.14 Proximity pyramid: proximity logic for The Clothing Company

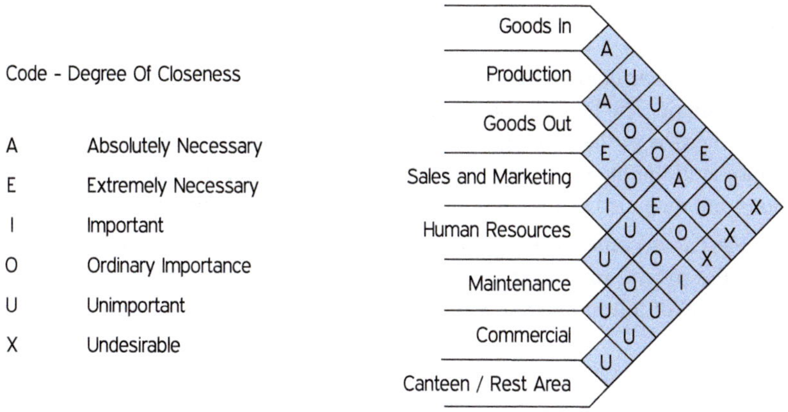

Solution

Draw a schematic of the layout in respect to the importance priorities and adjust them to fit the size and shape of departments and the new building taking into account non-quantifiable factors.

Figure 5.15 Layout solution for The Clothing Company

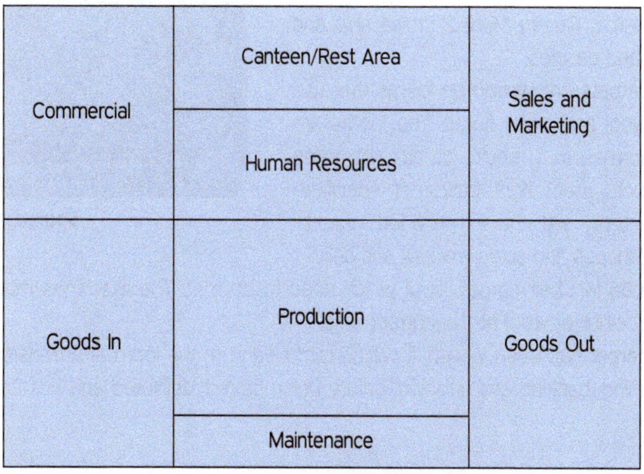

Layout will not only be determined by distance travelled and volumes moved but by other softer factors such as health and safety, culture, noise, cleanliness and external access. Also the peculiarities of the building need to be taken into account, thus newly purpose-built or regular-shaped buildings tend to be easier to fit layouts.

Figure 5.16 Work cell layouts: (a) straight; (b) U-shaped

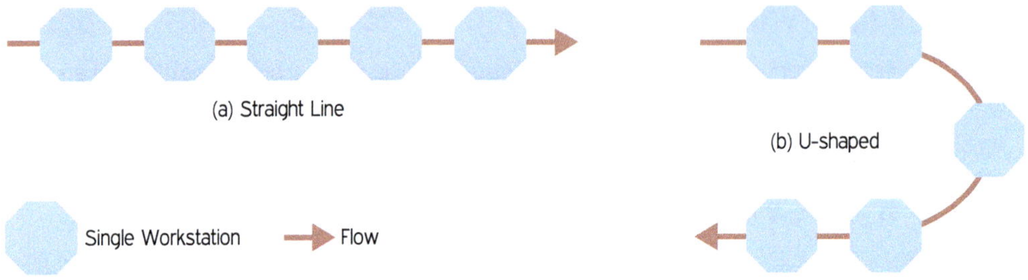

In reality layout decisions will be a combination of quantifiable measures of distance and volume (as in Worked Example 5.3) and other more subjective factors (as in Worked Example 5.4).

Work Cell Layouts

The detailed design of cellular layouts first involves getting the right people and machines together and then laying them out in the right shape. The basic variants for cell layouts are straight or U-shaped; see Figure 5.16. The main difference between these is in the placing of exit and entrance points, which may be influenced by the size and shape of the facility, and the overall operations that they are part of. U-shaped cells make it easier for people to share workstations and may also be adapted into S-shaped or circular layouts.

Sometimes work cells can become large and these are often referred to as *plants within a plant;* although these are an integral part of the overall organization, they may be capable of existing outside their parent organization, owing to their high level of autonomy and capability. Sometimes they may even be spun off to become separate new companies.

SHORT CASE 5.4

Lay Out the Carpet

Source: ©JeanLucIchard/Shutterstock

Brintons Carpets has been a world-leading supplier of carpets to households and industrial clients across the world for over 200 years. Recent prestigious industrial clients include Changi Airport in Singapore, Cunard's *Queen Mary 2* cruise ship and leading hotels and casinos.

Brintons' carpets are woven on looms that use a mixture of wool and other fibres. The looms are big, heavy machines that require careful set-up so that the products meet tight customer specifications. Each client will have provided exact specifications (shapes and sizes, colours and delivery requirements) for their carpet, all of which need to be met. The machines must be supplied with exactly the right type and colour of wool at the correct time.

After the carpet has been woven, it will be removed from the loom and transferred to another department for checking, trimming, backing and finishing, before being stored, delivered and installed at the client's site.

Questions

1. What type of process do you think Brintons uses for: (a) its domestic customers; (b) its industrial clients?
2. What types of order do you think Brintons typically gets?
3. What types of layout do you think Brintons uses during the design, manufacture and delivery of its carpets?

Stop and Think

What would be the consequences of using the wrong layout for a particular operation?

Technology in Processes

BUSINESS INTEGRATION

Operating a process will usually require the use of supporting technology. Whether it is a scanning machine for a hospital, a production robot for a factory or a new IT system for an office, the decision to adopt the technology will need to consider cost, quality, capacity and flexibility. To make this decision, operations managers must carefully identify the necessary capacity, size, robustness and tolerances for the technology, as well as its ongoing maintenance requirements.

The correct selection of equipment for a particular type of process can provide competitive advantage for an organization. Many organizations develop unique process technologies to give added *flexibility,* lower cost or higher quality. Innovations and equipment modification may also allow for a more stable production process that requires less adjustment, quicker change-over times, less maintenance, and operator training.

Production Technology

In this section we shall introduce you to a range of production technologies. These are machine technology, automatic identification systems, process control, vision systems, robots, automatic storage and retrieval systems, automated guided vehicles, flexible manufacturing systems and computer integrated manufacturing (CIM). It is common to find one or more of these technologies being used together in an integrated system.

Machine Technology

Machinery used for operations such as cutting, pressing and stamping, milling and drilling has made dramatic improvements in recent years. New machinery can cut metal components accurately to one micrometre (about 1/100th of a typical human hair) and assemble tiny *nano-machines* that can be used to operate inside our bodies. At the other end of the spectrum we have large powerful machinery, such as water-jet cutting tools so powerful they can be used to cut steel or pneumatic hovering platforms so large that they can be used to move vehicles such as tanks along assembly lines. Machinery of the 21st century is considered to:

- Be five times more productive than that of previous generations
- Save more space and power
- Use more environmentally friendly materials and allow for more recycling
- Be easier to control and operate quicker and more precisely
- Be connected to the Internet of Things (IoT) to be operated. monitored and upgraded remotely.

Digital data is becoming easier to generate, cheaper to store and easier to analyse. We are thought to be digital age where '*big data*' is an asset core to competitive advantage and '*artificial intelligence*' is used to analyse it.

Automatic Identification Systems and RFID

Most new processing technology (from manufacturing machinery to automatic teller/transaction machines) is controlled by digital signals. The challenge for operations management is to get data relating to physical items, materials and geographic locations accurate and up to date in computer systems.

Until recently, data on physical things has been matched up manually with information in information systems; this can result in delays and errors. The first major advance in this area was the use of *bar codes* (labels with patterns that can be read by computers), which are attached to items or people. Typical applications have been stock control of materials, point-of-sale records in shops and patient monitoring in hospitals. Bar codes require a visible line of sight between the reader and the object being read.

More recently, advances in technology have enabled *radio frequency identification* (RFID) to be used. RFID tags use integrated circuitry with their own aerials to send radio signals over a limited range (usually a few metres) to RFID readers. These tags can provide unique identification, which enables the tracking and monitoring of parts, pallets, people and pets – virtually anything that moves. Unlike a bar code reader, RFID requires no line of sight between the tag and the reader. Examples of RFID use include:

- The matching of records to patients, by including an RFID tag in their ID bracelet
- Tags on cars to locate where they are stored and their product configuration and recycling history (e.g. as used at Jaguar Land Rover)
- Tagging aircraft parts to monitor their history
- Finding out what is in a transportation container.

Process Control

Process control is the use of information technology to monitor and control a physical process. For instance, process control technologies can be used to measure the accuracy of printing, as printed material (such as stamps) can move over sensors at hundreds of metres per second to be automatically checked. Process control is also used to determine and control temperatures, pressures and qualities in petroleum refineries, cement plants, steel mills, nuclear reactors and other process focused facilities. Process-controlled systems operate as follows.

1. Sensors periodically collect data such as size, colour intensity and moisture.
2. This data is transmitted to a computer, which analyses it and looks for variations in outputs and deviations from acceptable tolerances.
3. The output from the computer analysis may be a warning message on a computer screen or a text to a personal digital device.

Process control is important to make sure that problems in the process are detected quickly.

Vision Systems

Vision systems combine video cameras and computer technologies, such as face, colour and shape recognition software. Visual inspection is an important task in most processing and manufacturing industries, but can be extremely monotonous, tedious, error prone and even hazardous for humans to do. Vision systems enable visual inspection to be automated. Examples include inspecting the insides of brewing vats for beer making, gas pipelines and parcel sorting on mail delivery systems.

Robots

Robots are mechanical devices controlled by computers. Today, robots can perform very complex tasks, at high speeds, very efficiently. They are best suited to highly repetitive, high-volume tasks that are monotonous, heavy, dangerous or can be improved by the substitution of human effort. For example, Toyota uses robots to do welding on car bodies.

Automated Storage and Retrieval Systems

Warehouses can be computer controlled; computer and machinery can be used together to automatically store, record and retrieve items. These systems, known as *automated storage and retrieval systems,* often work without any human intervention. Such systems are operated by large logistic suppliers in their warehouses.

Automated Guided Vehicles

Automated guided vehicles (AGVs) are electronically controlled carts that are used to move parts and equipment around large facilities. They are used in car factories to move parts, in mail-sorting depots to move packages, and in hospitals to move meals around. They are often part of a wider automated system.

Flexible Manufacturing Systems

When a central computer is used to instruct each workstation and the materials handling equipment (which moves material between stations), the system is known as a *flexible manufacturing system* (FMS). An FMS is flexible because both the materials handling devices and the machines themselves are controlled by computer programs. Operators simply load new programs to manage different processes and produce different products. The result is a system that can economically produce low volumes and high varieties, as the cost associated with low utilization and changeover is substantially reduced. FMSs bridge the gap between product-service-dominant layouts and process-dominant layouts.

Computer-Integrated Manufacturing

Flexible manufacturing systems can be extended into the engineering and design, and inventory control departments. FMSs can also be electronically extended into the warehousing and shipping departments. In this way, *computer-aided design* (CAD) can generate the necessary electronic instructions to run a robot or an FMS. In a computer-integrated manufacturing environment, a design change to a part initiated at a CAD terminal can automatically result in changes being made to what is being manufactured on the shop floor in a matter of minutes. When this capability is integrated with inventory control, warehousing and shipping as part of a flexible manufacturing system, the entire system is called a *computer-integrated manufacturing* (CIM) system.

FMSs and CIM are reducing the distinction between low-volume/high-variety and high-volume/low-variety production. Information technology is allowing FMSs and CIM to handle increasing variety while expanding to include a growing range of volumes. Through the use of technology, mass customization is made possible.

Service Technology

Service technologies have also changed dramatically in recent years. Service technologies include diagnostic equipment at garages when cars are being serviced, security scanners at airports, and automatic machines in banks, hotels and restaurants. These are all aimed at either increasing flexibility or reducing costs. We can see self-check-in machines in low-priced hotels, self-service counters in fast-food restaurants and many different types of self-service machine in banks.

Many of the fundamental technologies used in services are the same as in production, although their use is usually focused more on moving people (e.g. the customers) and information around, rather than parts and products. Table 5.5 summarizes some typical examples of service technologies.

Table 5.5 Technology in services

Service industry	Example
Financial	Debit cards, electronic funds transfer, cash machines (ATMs), Internet-based transactions (e.g. stocks and shares, mortgages), paying-in machines, electronic cash (e.g. Paypal)
Education	Online journals, newspapers, virtual learning environments (VLEs) such as Blackboard, classroom technology (e.g. classroom voting)
Utilities and government	Online tax payments (e.g. car, company, TV), flood warning systems, congestion charges, variable road speed systems, public utility vehicles
Restaurants and foods	Wireless ordering, table booking and payment systems, robot butchering, air-conditioning, milking machines for cows, rotating tables or conveyor belts to access food
Communications	Electronic publishing, interactive TV, mobile devices (e.g. smart phone, tablet devices)
Hotels	Express check-in and out, automatic room billing, swipe cards
Wholesale/retail trade	Point-of-sale recording, e-commerce sites, use of bar codes and RFID tags, visual observation systems, e-pay systems (e.g. Apple Pay)
Transportation	Public transport, automated toll booths, satellite navigation devices
Health care	Online patient health (e.g. blood pressure) monitoring
Airlines	Ticketless travel, Internet purchases, self-check-in, moving walkways, scanners for baggage and people
Leisure	Gym machines, wireless hotspots to access the Internet (e.g. social networking sites), video games, health monitoring apps

We take many of these service technologies for granted, as they have become embedded into processes that we use all the time (there are many examples of service technologies in the opening case).

SHORT CASE 5.5

How the Mighty Amazon Flows

Jeff Bezos founded Amazon in 1994 in Seattle, USA. Since then Amazon has become one of the leaders in Internet-based shopping. Many people see Amazon as purely an online company that provides shopping services, but much of its success has been due to its extensive investment in technology – both front-end web technology and back-end process technology. This is essential for Amazon, as it predominantly retails physical products that need to be physically moved.

Amazon has software development centres, fulfilment and warehousing centres based all around the world, as well as many business partners, such as logistic carriers. Its online ordering process has to link seamlessly to its picking, packing and shipping operations. This requires it to have advanced information technology that drives the whole order fulfilment process.

Other companies, such as Webvan (a USA online grocery company), were not originally successful, as they did not anticipate the scale and complexity of the offline operations investment, and they went bankrupt quickly. Amazon learned quickly how to utilize process technology effectively and has grown through research, development and implementation of new process technologies, as well as by partnering with other technology companies (e.g. print-on-demand book suppliers such as Lightning Source).

Questions

1. Could a company like Amazon have existed before Internet-based technology?
2. Which process technologies do you think Amazon uses for competitive advantage?
3. How do you think Amazon should use process technology to position itself against online competitors such as eBay or retailers with stores such as Tesco?

Stop and Think

How many process technologies do you use in an average day that provide you with some kind of value?

Summary

The content of this chapter is fundamental to every operation, as it describes the process of how work gets done – or, to put it another way, how things become transformed from inputs into outputs, using various transforming resources along the way. The chapter initially focused on designing processes to match the types of order they receive and to ensure that they use the correct layout. Systems thinking is fundamental to good process management, because all processes are systems that need to be carefully integrated and controlled.

When designing and managing processes, factors such as volume, variety, order type, layout and the extent of mass customization all need to be taken into account. Often the best way to design or improve a process is to map it out using a process-mapping technique. These are used to develop group consensus, visualize the process and debate future improvements.

Processes utilize people, knowledge and technology. How they are put together requires a mix of scientific principles, artistry, experience and technical know-how – all of which can have a fundamental impact on how well organizations perform.

Key Theories

- **Systems thinking** – a system is a complex whole, the functioning of which depends on its parts and the interactions between those parts. We can easily think of many different types of system: natural (e.g. river systems), biological (e.g. living bodies), designed (e.g. cars), abstract (e.g. religions), social (e.g. families) and human activity (e.g. business and organizations). Thinking about these systems is known as systems thinking. Operations management is founded upon systems thinking, as all processes are systems.
- **Volume and variety** – this is a simple but fundamental idea. It states that for an operation to work effectively and efficiently it must either be high-volume/low-variety or high-variety/low-volume. Any other combination, unless supported by advanced management thinking and technology, is likely to fail.
- **Order type** – the three basic order types are make to order, make to stock, and assemble to order. Each type is suited to different types of physical layout and process management. Each order type fundamentally changes the way that the operation is run and the philosophical approach of the managers. Mixing different types of order successfully is difficult to do and requires careful planning.
- **Process layout** – there are three basic process layout types: fixed position, product-service dominant, and process dominant. Each of these is suited to a certain type of order and process management approach. Getting the layout wrong can cause inefficiency.

Key Equations

$$\text{Takt time} = \frac{\text{Overall equipment effectiveness}}{\text{Average demand}}$$

$$\text{Total cost of moving} = \text{Unit cost of moving} \times \text{Number of items to be moved}$$

Little's Law

$$\text{Total process throughput time} = \text{No. of work in progress items} \times \text{Item cycle time}$$

Suggested Answers to Stop and Think Questions

1. **Systems thinking:** Operations would become better. This is because a business operation is a complex organizational system that has many different elements, which cannot create value by themselves. It is important to ensure that all the parts work together, so that their total value is greater than the sum of their individual parts. This requires combining functional and process thinking to give a holistic, systems perspective, rather than a reductionist perspective that will tend to produce sub-optimal thinking.
2. **Dead zone:** If the process falls into the top right-hand corner, the chances are that it will be very complicated and far too expensive to operate cost-effectively, unless a mass customization approach is adopted. This is because of the high-volume and high variety combination. If the process falls into the bottom left-hand corner then the chances are that scales of economies are not being met, owing to low volume and low variety, resulting in a high unit cost. The organization should either remain as a low-volume operator and offer more variety, or keep to low variety and increase volume.
3. **Mass customization:** Generally speaking, any product or service that has a high propensity for customers to want to tailor the specification to their own requirements and to be willing to pay for that, is able to use a mass customization approach. Services might include, online shopping, wedding reception organization, car maintenance or home help services, for example. Products could include car, shoe, or clothing manufacture. Product-service systems may include take-away food making and delivering (e.g. Deliveroo or Just Eat). These are made feasible by using advanced IT (e.g. Internet-based systems that link up with 'back end' manufacturing and service operational systems and devices,

known as the Internet-of-Things), computer-controlled production machinery (e.g. assembly robots and electronic packing and sorting systems) and advanced operations management practices. Often mass production has not been adopted because one or more of the above factors is not known about or present.

4. **Wrong layout:** Using the wrong layout type could result in an inefficient process, producing poor quality output. At best this could result in wasteful practices, overcrowding, confusion, etc. At worst it could endanger the people (employees and customers) who work in the operational layouts.
5. **Process technologies:** Start with any typical morning: there will normally be a process that you follow (e.g. get up, get dressed, eat, travel to college or work, etc.). This will probably use both stand-alone technologies (e.g. toaster, car, shower) and more complicated systems (e.g. TV, Internet, railway, satnav). Without process technologies, our lives would be hugely different.

connect

Review Questions

1. What is holistic thinking?
2. Name one product and one service that is suited to each of a (a) continuous, (b) assembly line, (c) batch, (d) job shop and (e) project type of production process, and state why they are suited.
3. Name one product and one service that is best delivered via (a) make to stock, (b) assemble to order and (c) make to order type of process. State why they are suited.
4. Name one product and one service that is best suited to (a) a product-service-dominant layout, (b) a process-dominant layout, (c) a work cell and (d) a fixed position layout. State why.
5. Describe what happens at the 'point of customization'.
6. List the reasons for conducting a process-mapping exercise.
7. What challenges are present when designing operational layouts?
8. State how different sorts of technology can help manufacturing and services operate more efficiently.

Discussion Questions

1. Discuss what would happen in an organization if there were no clearly defined operational processes.
2. (a) Think of an organization that you are familiar with (e.g. airport, college, or manufacturing workplace) and then think of a particular product or service it supplies. Use Table 5.3 in this chapter to try to characterize the process that is used. Do you think it is effective? If not, how should it be improved? (b) Using the same organization, discuss the most suitable type of order, and state why it is suitable.
3. Have a go at sketching the layout of the organization you have used in question 2 and try to make it as efficient as possible. Discuss why you have sketched it as you have.
4. With the same organization state how new digital Internet-of-Things (IoT) technology can improve its (i) operations, (ii) sustainability and (iii) ethical practices.

Problems

1. A process has three tasks, A, B and C. A takes 80 seconds, B 20 seconds and C 10 seconds. The waiting time between A and B is 20 minutes and the waiting time between B and C is 4 hours. What is (a) the total cycle time, (b) the total lead time?
2. If a weekly shift is 4,800 minutes long and a customer requires 9,600 units to be produced, what is the takt time?

3. A large electronics company has a head office and a semi-autonomous manufacturing cell on a single, large site. Large amounts of components and finished product pass between them. One of the locations has to be removed and merged with the other. Every month 100 products are moved from the manufacturing cell to the head office, at a cost of €250 per 100 for final checking. Every week 500 components are moved between the head office and the manufacturing cell to help with the planning and production process, at €10 per 100. (i) If there were no other conflicting soft factors, on this information alone, would you recommend closing the head office or the semi-autonomous manufacturing cell in order to minimize travel and its associated costs? (ii) What soft factors might change your layout decisions?
4. (i) If a process had a total cycle time of 60 minutes and a customer required a takt time of 40 minutes, would this be satisfactory to the customer? (ii) If a process had a total cycle time of 60 minutes and a customer required a takt time of 100 minutes, would this be satisfactory to the producer?
5. A manufacturing facility requires a new layout design. Using the ratings given below assign departments to the shape of the new facility using the proximity pyramid technique. What will the solution look like on a 2 × 3 production section layout?
6. The diagram below shows a current state value stream map for a production process.

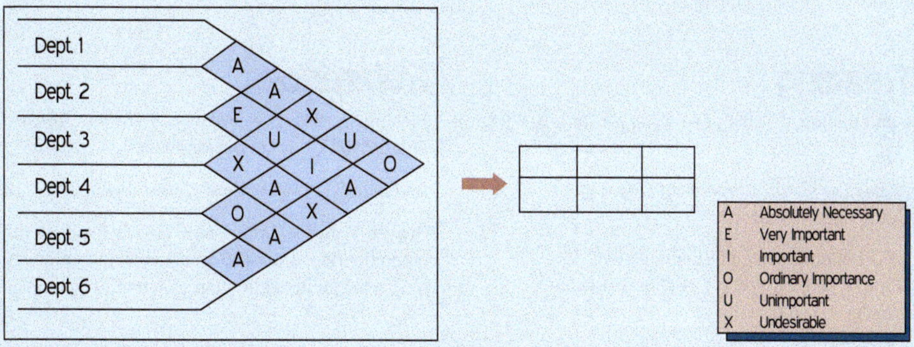

a) What is the total lead-time?
b) What is the value added time?
c) What is the least available workstation?
d) What is the longest change over time?
e) What is the longest cycle time?
f) What is the fundamental reason why this is not a lean process?
g) What would you do to change this to a leaner future state process?

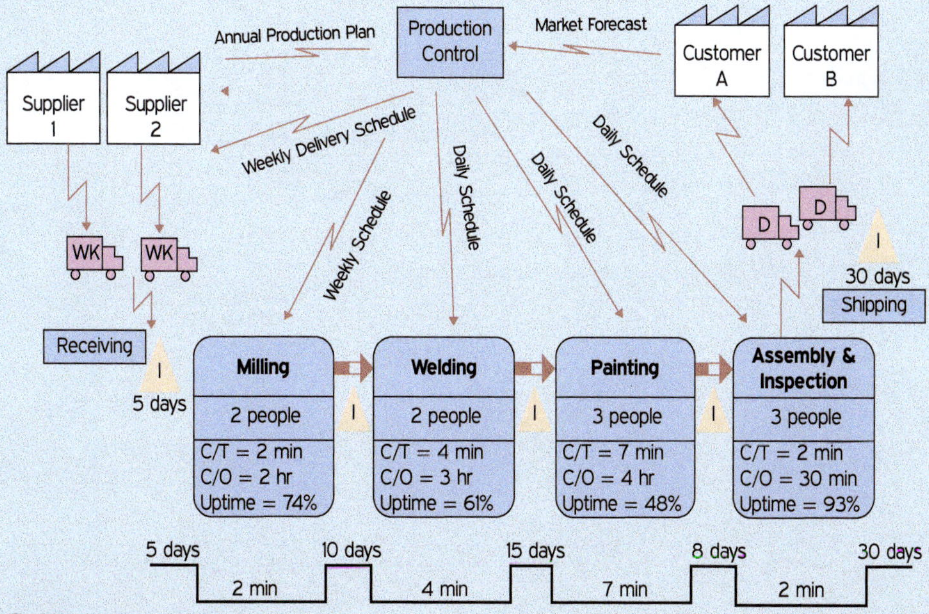

Source: www.epa.gov

A Learning Game: The Paper Airplane Game

connect

This paper airplane folding exercise demonstrates basic process design and the push versus pull aspect of lean manufacturing. The game can be played in a seminar room or even in a lecture theatre row.

The learning objective of this game are to illustrate the significant reduction in work in progress and throughput time using the pull system, to explain and illustrate the concepts of push and pull, bottleneck, cycle time, idle time, line balance, takt time, kanban, and to illustrate worker behaviour in an operational setting.

This exercise utilizes four assembly operators in an assembly line to build a paper airplane and a quality manager. Students first work in a standard push approach and each student works at their own comfortable pace as long as inventory is available, and they do not worry about inventory accumulation.

The second run requires a pull of one unit at a time. The reduction in inventory and throughput time is readily evident to all, and a useful discussion about process design can follow.

The full version of this game is available as part of the Instructor Resources on Connect.

Further Reading

Checkland, P.B. and Poulter, J. (2006) *Learning for Action*, Wiley, Chichester.

Goldratt, E.M. (2004) *The Goal: A Process of Ongoing Improvement*, Routledge, Abingdon.

Hammer, M. (1997) 'Beyond the end of management', in *Rethinking the Future*, R. Gibson (ed.), Nicholas Brealey Publishing, London, pp. 95–105.

Holweg, M., Davies, J., De Meyer, A., Lawson, B. and Schmenner, R. (2018) *Process Theory*, Oxford University Press, Croydon.

Pidd, M. (ed.) (2004) *Systems Modelling: Theory and Practice*, Wiley, Chichester.

Senge, P. (1990) *The Fifth Discipline: The Art and Practice of the Learning Organization*, Doubleday, New York.

References

Bicheno, J. (2004) *The New Lean Toolbox: Towards Fast Flexible Flow*, PICSIE Books, Buckingham.

Deming, W.E. (1999) *Metal Centre News*, **39**(6), 123.

Grover, V. and Malhotra, M.K. (1997) 'Business process reengineering: a tutorial on concept, evolution, method, technology and application', *Journal of Operations Management*, **15**(3), 193–213.

Hayes, R.H. and Wheelwright, S.C. (1979) 'Line manufacturing process and product life cycles', *Harvard Business Review*, Jan–Feb, 133–140.

Rother, M. and Shook, J. (1999) *Learning to See: Value Stream Mapping to Add Value and Eliminate Muda*, Lean Enterprise Institute, Brookline, MA.

Shostack, G.L. (1984) 'Designing services that deliver', *Harvard Business Review*, **62**(1), 133–139.

6 Supply Network Design

Learning Outcomes

After reading this chapter you should be able to:

- Define what a supply chain, a supplier network and a multi-organization enterprise are
- Appreciate how suppliers and their customers often work together in an increasingly integrated way
- Describe why and how outsourcing takes place
- Apply simple models to help locate an operation in respect of its suppliers
- Design an agile multi-organization enterprise based on the theories of the resource-based view of an organization, and transaction cost economics

More Power for More Passengers?

CSR

The Airbus A380 is the largest commercial passenger jet ever built. It was designed to meet new market requirements for an increasing number of longer haul flights between major airports while meeting more stringent security and environmental regulations. From an industrial perspective, the plane needed to save the ailing European large-passenger-aircraft industry by competing head to head with some of the most successful commercial aircraft ever built, such as the Boeing 747 Jumbo Jet.

Source: ©SpaceKris / Shutterstock

Arguably, Airbus and its then parent company EADS gambled the future of the company on this double-decker, monster-sized, 'super-jumbo' plane – which can carry up to 853 people. In contrast, their main competitor, Boeing in the USA, continued to invest in mid-sized passenger jets that are faster, cheaper and easier to own.

It was nearly seven years from the start of the project until operators got their first planes in 2007. Pre-orders for planes were essential for this huge project (estimated at €11 billion) in order to start generating revenue. Singapore Airlines, the first customer, formed a joint venture with Airbus to ensure that their planes were designed and built exactly to their requirements. Later Emirates became the biggest fleet operator of A380s with more than 100 in service.

In 2014 the total development costs were estimated to have reached approximately €20 billion and each plane sold for approximately €445 million, costing nearly this amount to manufacture. With used planes on the market, costing around half this price, it is debatable whether the plane would ever become profitable. In 2019 it was decided that production of the A380 would cease after current orders were filled. It seemed that the market favoured smaller planes with lower fuel consumption that were cheaper to operate and that the global market had become saturated, with around 251 being delivered.

BUSINESS INTEGRATION

GLOBALIZATION

Key suppliers were included throughout the design and manufacturing process. For instance, Rolls-Royce Aerospace Group was one of only two engine suppliers. Rolls-Royce built the new Trent 900 engines – one of the most powerful jet engines ever built. The other engine (the GP2700) was built by the American Engine Alliance (AEA), whose parent companies are General Electric and Pratt & Whitney. Rolls-Royce and AEA are the main partners in the joint venture, investing time, money and knowledge right from the beginning.

Rolls-Royce joined up with its key suppliers in risk- and revenue-sharing arrangements, where suppliers invested in the development of the new engine in exchange for a percentage of their sales revenue. Seven companies participated as risk- and revenue-sharing partners (from Spain, the USA, Italy, Sweden and Japan). Three other companies were included as programme associates (from South Korea and Japan). These companies had an input into some design decisions, but did not share in the overall risk-and-revenue partnership. In addition, hundreds more suppliers were engaged in conventional, openly competitive arrangements.

Much responsibility rested with the supplier management team at Rolls-Royce. They managed the huge network of global suppliers to try to ensure that parts and services were delivered on time, every time, at acceptable costs. This involved recruiting new suppliers, developing new processes, planning and scheduling, materials management, manufacturing, assembly, and final delivery to the customer. In short, the supplier team provided the links that kept the supply chain together. As a result, Rolls-Royce is now a major player in Singapore's aerospace industry, accounting for over 10% of the country's aerospace output via joint ventures with local industry. Eight out of the first 11 airlines to order the A380 chose the Trent 900 engine.

However, at around US$26,000 per hour or US$50 per seat-hour, the A380 has proven too costly to operate. Comparing this to a new Boeing 777 which costs just US$44 per seat-hour the A380 may be consigned to history if a new economically viable variant cannot be conceived. The A380 will remain in service until 2035 and respective maintenance and service contracts have to be honoured by all suppliers throughout that period; this is a big challenge for operators, manufacturers and servicing companies.

Introduction

Multi-organization enterprise: a group of different companies, or group of parts of different companies, working together to deliver a product or service in a highly integrated way.

This chapter focuses on how internal organizational and external competitive forces interact and influence the design and management of operations, and particularly on how organizations come together to form different types of supplier relationship. Supplier relationships can most simply be thought of as a *chain* of organizations working together. Or, if the relationships are more complicated, they can be thought of as a *network* of organizations working together. Sometimes, if relationships between organizations are highly integrated, they may be considered as a joint venture and may be delivered in a **multi-organization enterprise**.

A chain of suppliers is normally thought of as one organization supplying another in a simple, openly competitive set-up, such as a farmer supplying a grocery store, or a manufacturer of paper supplying a newspaper company. A network of suppliers is a collection of organizations that collectively deliver parts and services to an end customer. This arrangement can arise simply because an element of collaboration between organizations can often be better than purely open competition. A multi-organization enterprise arises when organizations work so closely together that it becomes hard to differentiate them; they may have shared capital assets, intellectual property and processes.

The opening case describes a sophisticated form of supplier relationship, best thought of as a multi-organization enterprise. Even Airbus itself is a collaboration of aircraft manufacturers, spanning a number of European countries. In this case supplier relationships have to work at all levels throughout the enterprise (i.e. strategic, tactical and operational). Relationships have been successfully forged with customers (e.g. Singapore Airlines) and with suppliers (e.g. Rolls-Royce), who work very closely with Airbus using their processes, working to their objectives, and sometimes sharing in their risks and rewards. In this case the types of relationship have arisen because the design and manufacture of the product (the Airbus 380) are too complex to be controlled by a single organization; they require the expertise and buy-in of many different partners at all levels.

Supplier relationships between organizations cover not only elements that are bought and sold, such as materials or services; they also include intangibles such as competencies, processes, decisions and strategies. Supplier relationships will usually focus on the delivery of a family of products, such as aircraft, or a group of services, such as package holiday and travel related services. Sometimes relationships are set up to encourage innovation, as a new product or service can often be created more easily than by a single company working alone.

Supplier relationships are an important part of the operational strategy (Chapter 2) of the organization. This chapter begins by looking at the basics of supplier relationships, including the terminology that is used. It will also look at why different types of supplier relationship arise, and at the decisions that are taken in designing effective networks.

Chapter 2, p55

Different Perspectives on Supplier Relationships

BUSINESS INTEGRATION

Three different views or perspectives on supplier relationships are introduced in this section. They range from a simple *supply chain,* through the more complicated but increasingly common *supplier network,* to the *multi-organization enterprise management* perspective.

Supply Chain Relationships

A 'supply chain' is a metaphor used to describe a simple, linear relationship between a series of different organizations such as a raw materials supplier, a product manufacturer, a distributor and an end customer. Supply chains are concerned with the flow of three things between participating organizations: information, money and materials. This is illustrated in Figure 6.1. Within each organization there are activities and processes related to each of these flows.

The flow of activities might be triggered by a customer order – for example, a bicycle from Halfords, a large UK retailer of bicycles and car accessories. The information about the order is transmitted to the distributor, in this case the Halfords warehouse; then to the manufacturer, which might be Raleigh, a UK based bicycle producer; and then, in turn, to the manufacturer's suppliers. As goods are moved along the supply chain, the firms involved incur transaction costs. These are the extra costs involved in buying goods or services (e.g. employing people to negotiate contracts, and the costs involved in moving items from one place to another). The management of these ongoing costs and activities are referred to as *supply chain management.*

Historically, business processes within individual firms in a traditional supply chain have operated relatively independently of each another. There was little sharing of information between the customers and the suppliers. Firms tended to rely on their immediate stakeholders for demand information, and therefore the information flow was slow and could be inconsistent. In order to make sure the supply chain operated smoothly, the stakeholders focused on maintaining buffers (excess stock) of materials, and held spare capacity, and lead times were based on forecast rather than actual demand.

Globalization, deregulation (the removal of government control), increasing customer demand and advances in both information and transportation technology have all contributed to make the design and management of supply chains increasingly complex. Shorter product life cycles and competitive pressures have forced firms to find new ways to work together, improve their operational efficiency, and make supply chains increasingly integrated. Figure 6.2 shows the contrast between traditional supply chains and integrated supply chains.

> **Supplier network:** loose group of organizations that collectively deliver parts and services to an end customer.

Supplier Network Relationships

A **supplier network** has a supply side and a demand side, as illustrated in Figure 6.3. On its *supply side* an operation has its suppliers of parts, information and services. These suppliers themselves have their own suppliers, who in turn may also have their own suppliers, and so on. On the *demand*

Figure 6.1 Stakeholders in a simple supply chain

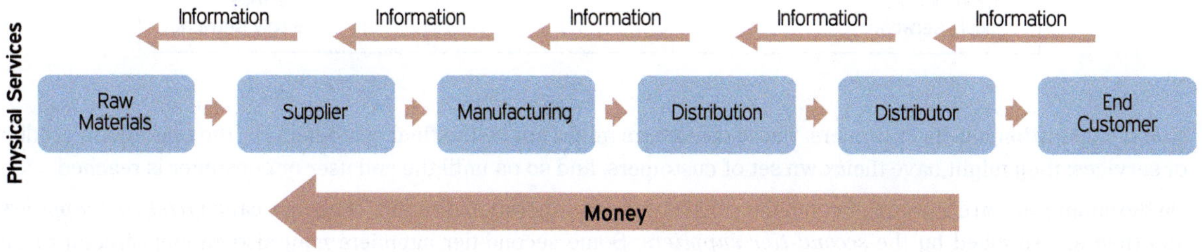

Figure 6.2 Traditional versus integrated supply chain

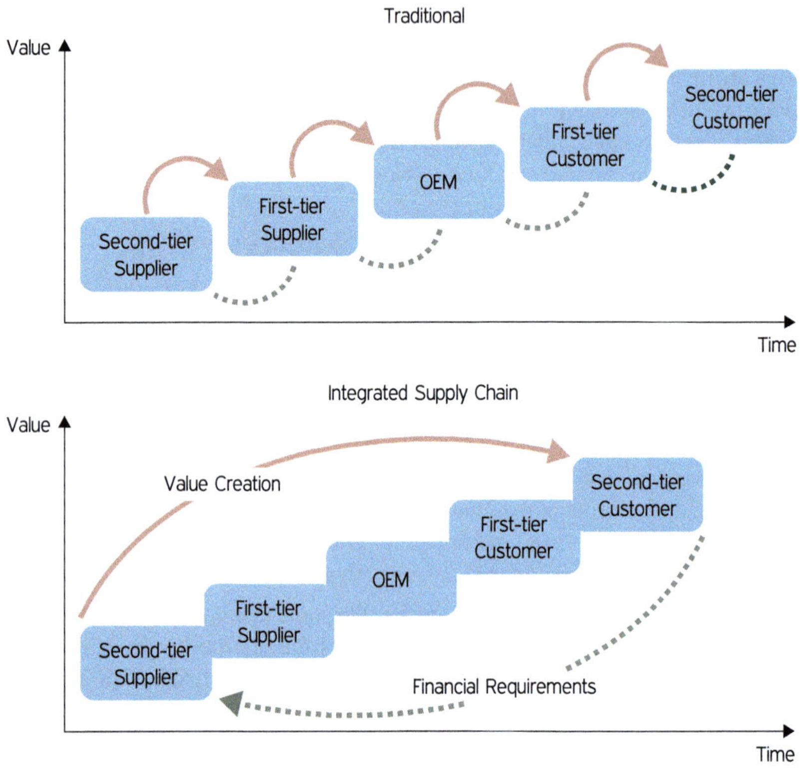

Figure 6.3 A simple supplier network

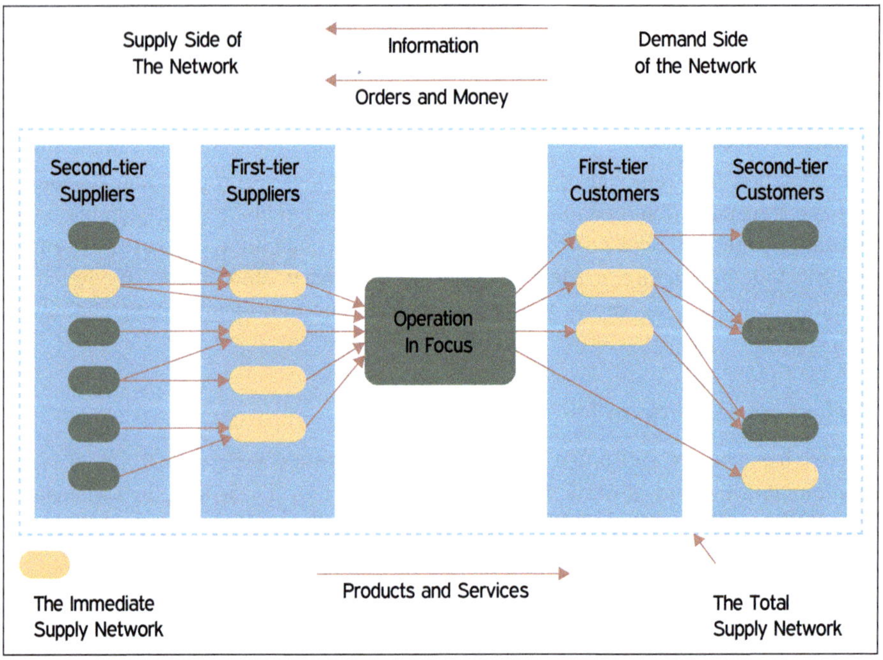

side the operation has its customers. These customers might not be the final customers for the operation's product or services; they might have their own set of customers, and so on until the end user or consumer is reached.

On the supply side are a group of companies that supply the operation directly. These are called *first-tier suppliers*, and they are supplied by the *second-tier suppliers*. Some second-tier suppliers may also supply directly to the company that sells to the end customer, thus missing out some tiers in the network. For example, a second-tier supplier of nuts and bolts might supply its product both to the first-tier supplier, which might be an engine manufacturer, and to the operation in focus, which might be a car maker.

Similarly, on the demand side of the network, *first-tier customers* are those that receive inputs directly from an operation. In turn, first-tier customers may also supply *second-tier customers*, and so on. Customers who receive inputs directly from an operation are referred to as the *immediate supply network*, and customers that receive inputs indirectly from an operation, are referred to as the *total supply network*.

Occasionally a second-tier customer may receive inputs from an operation directly, as well as from its first-tier supplier. If this practice is unplanned, it can cause confusion in the network (most often in relation to pricing), but if it is carefully planned it can be advantageous. For example, if the central operation were a golf club maker, its first-tier customers would include wholesalers, who in turn would supply retail outlets, the second-tier customers. However, it might also supply some retailers directly with made-to-order products, such as expensive custom-made clubs for professionals. On the supply side, most of the second-tier suppliers will provide only raw materials such as metal and rubber to manufacturers in the first-tier, who may carry out other work such as machining and assembly. However, occasionally they might also provide the golf club maker directly with simple products such as rubber hand-grips, or accessories such as golf-trolleys. Hence a network of supply and suppliers develops.

Along with the flow of goods and services in the network, each link in the network will feed back orders and information to its suppliers. When stocks run low, the retailers will place orders with the wholesaler or directly with the brand owner or manufacturers, who will in turn pass on these orders to their suppliers, and so on. It is a two-way process, with goods and services flowing one way – *downstream* – towards the end customer, and information, such as order quantities, and financial payments flowing the other way – *upstream* – towards the suppliers.

Enterprise Relationships

The European Commission (2003) defines an *enterprise* as:

> *any entity engaged in an economic activity, irrespective of its legal form. This includes, in particular, self-employed persons and family businesses engaged in craft or other activities, and partnerships or associations regularly engaged in an economic activity.*

Enterprise management is the management of these enterprises.

In its simplest form, an enterprise could be a single integrated organization, but enterprises are normally thought of as being made up of parts of different organizations, and so are therefore more helpfully referred to as multi-organization enterprises. The structure of a multi-organization enterprise will depend upon many different, business-related factors, and its success will depend on its ability to acquire *core competencies* and integrate them into its strategy and operations to deliver successful products and services. In other words, the peripheral activities of one organization should be a core competence of another organization within an overall multi-organization enterprise structure focused on delivering a particular family of products or services. However, even when a multi-organization enterprise has been set up, it may need to be reconfigured and adapted to meet changing needs. For example, the construction of the Channel Tunnel between France and the UK was carried out by a multi-organization enterprise that, throughout its lifetime, had many different structures and member companies, depending on the phase of work that was under way. For instance, when the tunnelling phase was complete, the tunnelling company left the multi-organization enterprise.

CRITICAL PERSPECTIVE

Different Supplier Relationships

The term ***supply chain management*** (SCM) was introduced by consultants during the 1980s, buts its roots can be traced back to the 1920s, when mass production philosophies began to dominate industry. In the 1970s supply chain management was known primarily as ***distribution***, which focused on the integration of warehousing and transportation within the firm. The focus was on ways in which firms could make internal changes that would reduce inventories and distribution costs.

In the 1980s the focus of SCM shifted towards re-engineering firms' supply chain processes in order to lower supply chain operating costs. This included a change in thinking, from ***pushing*** goods to customers towards being more market focused, and letting customers ***pull*** what they wanted, as and when they needed it, from their suppliers. This was achieved mainly through real-time interaction with customers, and having wider product ranges, with more emphasis on modular products and customization. SCM also made extensive use of computers and information technology in planning, delivery and control. By the end of the 1980s the goal of many firms had become reduction of SCM cost to improve customer service; this was often achieved by giving activities and responsibilities to other organizations.

In the 1990s new management concepts emerged, most notably that supplier relationships are best thought of as networks rather than as chains. This is because SCM also aimed to achieve better linkages and coordination between the processes of other organizations throughout the supply chain. From the 1990s the view was that SCM could become a strong competitive advantage for many firms. This would require a firm to align its SCM strategy (sourcing, demand flow, and customer service) with its business strategy.

With an increasing focus on services and satisfying customer needs, supply chain management had also become known as ***demand chain management***. Demand chain management emphasizes market needs and customers, while the supply chain focuses on suppliers. Together, demand and supply chain management are thought of as parts of the supply network. Since the turn of the 21st century the term ***multi-organization enterprise management*** has arisen: this is concerned with the management of companies that have become so closely integrated that it is difficult to think of them as networks of separate companies, or simple supply chains. Internet based digital technologies are widely used throughout supply operations and are vital to be competitive.

Contemporary thinking in operations management usually considers the supply chain or network metaphors to be an oversimplification. Supplier management theory is focusing increasingly on the multi-organization enterprise as an operational entity, rather than on the traditional concept of supplier networks. For those of us who like a straightforward view of the world, though, a multi-organization enterprise can be thought of as a group of different companies, or a group of parts of different companies, working together in a highly integrated manner to deliver a family of closely associated products and services to end customers.

The key point is ...

that different terms are used to describe the buyer-supplier relationships between companies. You must decide which one is most appropriate in any given situation. This will mostly depend on the complexity of the product and service being delivered.

! Stop and Think

Managers often use metaphors to help explain complicated ideas. Do you think these are helpful, or do they add to the complexity? Do you think new technology has changed supply management in the last ten years, if so how?

Transferring Activities to Suppliers

Outsourcing: process of giving part of your operations to another organization.

Outsourcing is the process of giving another organization the responsibility to deliver part of your products or services rather than doing it from within your own organization (known as *in-house* delivery). The term 'outsourcing' also means setting up a *procuring* and *purchasing* process for products and services, this can be seen in the Barclays 'Banking on Outsourcing' Short Case 6.1. By outsourcing, a company enters into a contractual agreement, typically with a supplier for the supply of a certain capacity that has previously been carried out in house. The ownership, responsibility and decision-making power are shifted – partly or wholly – to the supplier.

Outsourcing is typically used to improve an organization's financial position, operational productivity or structure. Financially driven reasons include improving return on assets, gaining access to new markets and customers, reducing overall costs, and turning long-term fixed costs into costs that are more variable in the short term. Productivity-driven reasons include improving quality, shortening cycle time, obtaining new expertise and

SHORT CASE 6.1

Banking on Outsourcing

Source: ©chrisdorney/Shutterstock

Barclays is one of the world's biggest banks. In the early 2000s Barclays Global Retail Bank was attracted to outsourcing and offshoring (i.e. moving work out of the home country in favour of another) to India, because of the low labour rates. According to David Skillen, Chief Operating Officer of Barclays Global Retail Bank, the original driver for outsourcing was labour arbitrage (i.e. taking advantage of different labour rates around the world), delivering as much as 40% savings compared with the UK. Barclays initially outsourced its non-voice back-office services (i.e. its Internet services) for both its commercial and retail banks to Intelenet in 2003. Skillen explains that 'There was no reason for us to own our servicing call centres, since they were really a commodity.' In addition to reducing labour costs, the ability to serve customers 24/7, 365 days a year, was another attraction. Also, outsourcing helped the UK call centre to balance its workload by providing more flexibility.

As the relationship evolved, Barclays learned how to manage it for best value. In the early days of offshoring, Barclays just sliced off the mechanical aspects of a particular process, such as data entry, and only outsourced that. However, it eventually came to understand that service providers can deliver more value at a strategic level if they control the whole process from start to finish. As trust and understanding grew, Barclays began to outsource the end-to-end delivery of its core processes, such as new information technology development, finance and accounting, and human resources management.

GLOBALIZATION

Around 2015 Barclays also handed over some of its post-trade processing and regulatory reporting obligations to SunGard, in a first-of-its kind deal that the IT service provider said would typically cut costs in the area by 20%. The news comes just days after Barclays' chief executive Antony Jenkins warned he was losing patience with its poorly performing investment bank and would make further cuts if profitability did not improve. 'Barclays is looking for cost savings across the entire group; this is one of, I'm sure, numerous projects going on', said Ray Kahn, of Barclays over-the-counter derivatives business, adding that the cost savings from the SunGard deal would be 'significant'. A new utility provider created by US based SunGard will begin carrying out some futures and over-the-counter derivatives operations and technology processes, as well as some regulatory reporting. Some of Barclays' staff will move to SunGard's new utility provider, which ultimately hopes to tap a $250 billion market across about 100 banks and brokers.

BUSINESS INTEGRATION

Banks have been outsourcing some IT functions for years, but SunGard and Barclays said this was the first time these types of activities had been carried out by a third party. Brian Traquair, executive vice-president of SunGard Financial Systems, said the utility will offer a more efficient way for banks and brokers to deal with the ever-increasing demands of regulation because SunGard could tap economies of scale. At industry level, banks and brokers have mounting reporting and processing costs after a wave of regulations including the Dodd–Frank Act in the US, the European Market Infrastructure Regulation and the Basel III package of global banking rules. 'SunGard's post-trade derivatives utility will help transform the cleared derivatives middle and back office across the entire industry, resulting in a more sustainable operating model and cost structure for the future', Mr Traquair said.

Alun Green, also of SunGard, said the company is in discussions with a 'large number' of other potential clients who already use SunGard for software services. SunGard is the primary software supplier for 85 of the 100 banks and brokers it is targeting. 'We're trying to focus on the areas that are common across all of the FCM (Futures Commissions Merchants) and not take over functions that would enable them to differentiate themselves', Mr Green said. Mr Traquair said post-trade cleared derivatives processing was an example of an activity that is 'highly commoditised, providing little differentiated value' to banks and brokers.

Barclay's Bank UK PLC 2018 Annual Report acknowledged the bank's dependence on suppliers, including internal suppliers such as Barclays Service Limited, for the provision of many of its services and development of its technology and it continues to be accountable for the risk arising from the actions of such suppliers. The report also states that failure to monitor and control suppliers could potentially lead to client information or critical infrastructure and

CSR

services not being adequately protected or available when required. Inadequately managing these risks could result in increased losses, inability to perform critical economic functions, customer detriment, potential regulatory censure, legal liability and reputational damage. Of increasing concern are cyber-attacks that have the capabilities and intention to cause harm, or to profit from attacks committed via network information systems, against us, our suppliers, or customers/clients. Cyber-security concerns have led to increased scrutiny of third parties.

Questions

1. How have Barclays and their suppliers built good relationships?
2. How can service providers add more value?
3. How can the risks of outsourcing be managed effectively?

Sources: http://www.outsourcing-center.com, 13 September 2010 FT.com (2020) https://www.ft.com/content/69190de0-c64c-11e4-add0-00144feab7de Barclay's Bank UK PLC 2018 Annual Report.

technologies, and reducing risks. Organizationally and structurally driven reasons include being able to focus on what the firm does best (i.e. its core competencies), increasing flexibility to meet changing demand patterns, helping to improve customer responsiveness, and joining up with other successful companies. These reasons are summarized in Table 6.1.

Offshoring is a specific form of outsourcing in which companies transfer some of their activities to other countries outside their country of origin. The main drivers behind offshoring have been access to new markets worldwide, and lower labour costs in developing countries. For example, the average salary in 2018 in Mexico was US$16.3k and for the USA it was US$63.1k; therefore the USA looks to use Mexican labour where ever possible. In the United Kingdom the average 2018 salary was US$44.8k, and for Germany it was US$49.8k; meanwhile the average salaries in the Slovak Republic and Poland were US$25.4 and US$29.1k, respectively, therefore a great deal of outsourcing and offshoring takes place from Western Europe to Eastern Europe (OECD, 2018).

The reverse of offshoring is known as *onshoring*. This is when organizations use suppliers from their home country to reduce risk or cost and increase supply certainty when political, economic and/or environmental conditions are unpredictable.

Single Sourcing

In *single sourcing* the buyer relies on one source for the supply of an item or service. The arrangement between the firms is like a partnership, and often results in a strong, durable and trusting relationship. Price will not necessarily be the most important criterion. Single sourcing often requires that the partners trust each other, especially

Table 6.1 Reasons for outsourcing

Financially driven reasons	• Improve return on assets by reducing inventory and selling unnecessary assets • Generate cash by selling low-return entities • Gain access to new markets, particularly in developing countries • Reduce costs through a lower cost structure • Turn fixed costs into variable costs (or vice versa) depending on the situation
Productivity driven reasons	• Improve quality and productivity • Shorten new product lead times and production cycle times • Obtain expertise, skills, and technologies that are not otherwise available • Improve risk management • Improve credibility and image by associating with superior providers
Organizational/structurally driven reasons	• Improve effectiveness by focusing on what the firm does best • Increase flexibility to meet changing demand for products and services • Increase product and service value by improving response to customer needs

Source: Adapted from Jacobs and Chase (2008, p. 189).

regarding the sharing of confidential knowledge about the outsourced products and services, which can be complex and specialized. The strong dependence, in turn, encourages more commitment and effort from both parties.

Single sourcing also has its disadvantages. The buyer might be more vulnerable to disruption if a failure to supply occurs. For instance, this can happen when a supplier files for bankruptcy, and has no means of fulfilling the contract. Too much dependence on a particular supplier also makes the firm vulnerable to price demands. The extreme version of this occurs when the supplier is the sole source of the product or service: there are no other suppliers with the capability to deliver it – a monopoly situation (e.g. the supply of piped water to homes in a particular area of the UK).

Multiple Sourcing

In order to avoid the supply risks associated with single sourcing, companies can use *multiple sourcing*, establishing a wide supply base, where the suppliers are encouraged to compete with each other – often on price. The buyer can then drive down the price by *competitive tendering*. Multiple sourcing strategies also allow the buyer to switch sources in case of supply failure, as well as tap into wider sources of knowledge and expertise. If such a practice becomes too adversarial, though, it can be difficult to encourage commitment from suppliers. They will also be less willing to invest in new technologies and processes if they know their customer may be sharing confidential details with their competitors.

Sourcing from two parties (or *dual sourcing*) combines the advantages of single sourcing and multiple sourcing by building strong relationships without the danger of a monopoly occurring. Some guidelines for sourcing decisions, adapted from Burt *et al.* (2003), are as follows:

Single sourcing is appropriate when:

- Lower total cost results from a much higher volume (economies of scale)
- Quality considerations dictate
- The buying firm obtains more influence or 'clout' with the supplier
- Lower costs are incurred to source, process, expedite, and inspect
- The quality, control, and coordination required with just-in-time manufacturing require a single source
- Significantly lower freight costs may result
- Special tooling is required, and the use of more than one supplier is impractical or excessively costly
- Total system inventory will be reduced
- An improved commitment on the supplier's part results
- More reliable, shorter lead times are required
- Time to market is critical.

Multiple sourcing is appropriate:

- To protect the firm during times of shortage, strikes and other emergencies
- To maintain competition and provide a backup source
- To meet local content requirements for international manufacturing locations
- To meet customers' volume requirements
- To avoid lethargy or complacency on the part of a single-source supplier
- When the customer is a small player in the market for a specific item
- When the technology path is uncertain
- In areas where suppliers tend to leapfrog each other technologically
- When political and economic relationships change (e.g. Brexit).

SHORT CASE 6.2

Did IBM Make the Wrong Move?

Until 1985, all of IBM's printed circuit boards (PCBs) were built in house. By the late 1990s it made only about 10% of its boards. Furthermore, it used to make 85% of the memory chips used in computers, but by 1999 the figure had dropped to 15%. IBM used to build its power supplies and keyboards, and assemble all of its own computers in house. Today, these tasks are outsourced to contract manufacturers, including PC assembly, manufactured notebook computers, lower-end servers and workstations, and mass storage devices. From 1986 to 1996 the proportion of IBM's revenue spent on outside suppliers increased from 28% to 51%. The economic outcome that resulted meant that IBM had reduced the overall costs by about 20% through outsourcing (Carbone, 1999). In 2005 IBM sold its PC division to Lenovo Group, the largest PC maker in China, formerly known as Legend.

Lenovo is now the preferred supplier of IBM branded products and IBM provides end-to-end client solutions, financing and maintenance services.

Source: ©Lukmanazis/Shutterstock

Questions

1. What had been the long-term effect of outsourcing for IBM?
2. What happened with the key suppliers of IBM components, such as Microsoft and Intel?
3. To what extent did this decision change the relationships IBM shared with its suppliers and customers?

Source: Based on Carbone (1999) and IBM website (2020) ibm.com

If organizations decide to outsource their products and services, and there is a choice between different possible suppliers, they need to decide which one to go for. The next section looks at choosing suppliers, based on their location.

Location Decisions and Supplier Relationships

It is often said that, when buying a house, there is nothing as important as location: the same might be said for locating a business or an operation. Unfortunately, not all businesses and operations have good reasons for their location choice. Often they are there for historical reasons, and find it difficult to justify the cost and disruption of moving unless compelled by very strong reasons. Strong reasons might include changes in demand for their goods and services, or in changes in their supply of inputs.

The Impact of Demand Changes

Demand changes can be driven by a change in the location of a customer, in frequency of purchases, or in the total number of customers in a particular area. For instance, if there is a boost in the construction activity in a particular area of a country – Beijing's new airport, for example – then a cement manufacturer may choose to locate there. Similarly, if there is growth in the student population in a certain area of a city, then more fast-food outlets may locate there.

Demand-based location is heavily influenced by the suitability of the site itself. For instance, luxury holiday hotels are often located next to a sandy beach in a beautiful bay. If a hotel were located in a back street industrial area, it would have little appeal, and demand for its service would inevitably be low. The same is also true for retailers, who compete for high-profile sites in the high street, where demand from passing traffic is high; such sites can fetch a premium price in comparison with back streets that have little passing traffic. Quite often a particular address is sought after, such as Wall Street in New York for trading companies, Harley Street in London for medical practices, or Sunset Boulevard in Los Angeles for swanky restaurants and boutique shops. At other times the site is determined by convenience: for example, public services such as fire stations, hospitals and schools have to be located near the population that will use them.

The Impact of Supply Changes

Supply changes can be driven by the cost or availability of inputs supplied to an operation. For example, a mining company or a forestry company may need to relocate as resources become depleted, or an energy company may need to relocate to where there is a plentiful and reliable supply of water to drive its hydroelectric turbines.

A manufacturing or software engineering company may choose to relocate to parts of the world where the labour force is relatively cheap, in terms of cost per hour of employment, or beneficial exchange rates, or lower overheads. (Overheads in this case refer to the extra costs of employing someone, e.g. pension, fringe benefits and sick pay.) Other labour-related issues include the availability of the right sort of labour. For example, science parks are often located close to universities because they hope to recruit the people that the university has educated.

A company may also choose to relocate to areas where land and business rates are cheaper, and so can be influenced by wider governmental, political, societal and economic forces.

Making the Location Decision

The aim of making a good location decision is to achieve an appropriate trade-off between the costs associated with the geographical location, the ease of making supply deliveries, the level of service an operation is able to deliver to its customers, and the potential the location has to generate revenue. In different scenarios some factors are more important than others. For instance:

- Commercial manufacturers are concerned mainly with minimizing the variable costs due to geographic locations associated with the transportation of supplies and finished goods, while maximizing their revenue and customer service levels
- Commercial service providers are concerned mostly with the direct costs of renting or leasing premises (such as offices, conference centres or retail units) and their potential to attract clients, as clients usually place a lot of weight in *where* they go for services such as a meal or a haircut
- Non-profit organizations are concerned mainly with a location's ability to provide an acceptable level of service to its customers, sometimes despite its costs of leasing, renting or any associated transportation costs to and from it. For instance, the location of a school is often chosen for easy access by its pupils and their parents.

The location decision for any operation is therefore determined by the relative strengths of its supply-side and demand-side factors.

Operations managers need to draw on their skills and experience when making location decisions, although there are some basic quantitative steps that can help rationalize the process. We describe two here: the **centre of gravity method**, which is most useful for transportation-based decisions, and the **weighted score technique**, which can be used to assess wider managerial factors in an outsourcing decision.

Centre of gravity method: approach that uses the physical analogy of a 'balancing point' to determine the geographical location of an operation relative to others that it has a direct relationship with.

Weighted score technique: used for comparing the attractiveness of alternative operational locations that allocates a weighted score to each relevant factor in the decision.

Centre of Gravity Method

Minimizing transportation costs for an operation is usually an important contributing factor in locating an operation. The **centre of gravity method** can be used to help minimize these costs. It is based on the idea that all possible locations can be scored and assigned a numeric value, based on the sum of all transportation costs to and from that location. The best location is the one that minimizes the overall transportation cost.

All locations are represented on a scale map that has square gridlines on it, rather like a standard road map. The centre of gravity of the map is found, and this represents the coordinates of the lowest-cost location for a site. The x and y coordinates of this location are calculated using the following formulae:

$$x = \frac{\Sigma x_i V_i}{\Sigma V_i}$$

$$y = \frac{\Sigma y_i V_i}{\Sigma V_i}$$

where x_i is the x coordinate of the source or destination i, y_i is the y coordinate of the source or destination i, and V_i is the volume to be transferred from source or destination i.

WORKED EXAMPLE 6.1

Putting the Centre of Gravity Method into Practice

A local authority operates four schools, which currently each have a small storeroom for their foodstuffs (e.g. tins, vegetables, milk). The local authority has decided to get rid of these small storerooms and build a large new central distribution centre to try to cut costs and create more space in the schools for the pupils. Each school is a different size, and needs a different volume of supply, and hence a different number of deliveries (i.e. trucks) travelling to and from them per week. Table 6.2 shows the volumes transported each week.

Problem: ***Where should the new distribution centre be located?***

Approach: The local authority region is sketched out on a grid – which is represented by the blue area in Figure 6.4. In the figure the schools' locations are also plotted, and the above formulae are applied.

The calculation is therefore:

$$x = \frac{(1 \times 5) + (5 \times 10) + (5 \times 15) + (9 \times 20)}{50} = 6.2$$

$$y = \frac{(2 \times 5) + (3 \times 10) + (1 \times 15) + (4 \times 20)}{50} = 2.7$$

This means that the minimum-cost location, or the 'centre of gravity', for the new distribution centre is at point (6.2, 2.7) – which is shown by the red cross on the map.

In practice the optimum location will also be influenced by other factors, such as the transportation network, congestion and low emission zones, or the geography of the land. So if the optimum location was at a point with poor access to a suitable road, in a restricted area, or at some other unsuitable location, such as in a river or in a graveyard, then the chosen location would need to be adjusted. Therefore this technique is used only as a guide, suggesting general locations.

Table 6.2 Weekly deliveries to the schools

	Deliveries per week
School A	5
School B	10
School C	15
School D	20
Total	50

Figure 6.4 Centre of gravity model for the local authority

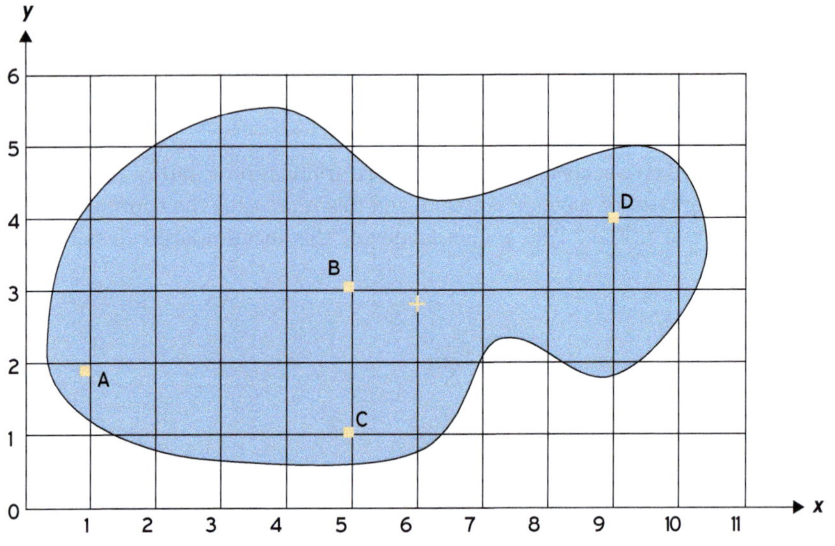

Weighted Score Technique

This technique involves:

1. identifying criteria (in addition to distance and frequency of supply) that can be used to evaluate different locations
2. assigning a weighting of relative importance to each criterion
3. scoring each location's suitability against each criterion.

This technique can also be extended beyond physical factors to wider management considerations, such as cultural fit, or the language capability of the population.

WORKED EXAMPLE 6.2

Putting the Weighted Score Technique into Practice

A UK Internet service provider (ISP) has decided to set up a new call centre, which could be either in Poland, South Africa or India. In order to choose the correct location, it has decided to evaluate them on the following criteria:

- The cost of acquiring the location (crucial)
- Cultural and language compatibility (very important)
- The site's access to the international airport (very important)
- Local taxation rates or subsidies (important)
- The availability of suitable skills in the local labour force (important)
- Time zone difference from UK Greenwich Mean Time (minor importance).

There are three sites to consider that may work. These are known as sites P (Poland), SA (South Africa) and I (India). After investigating each in detail, the operations managers allocate a score between 0 and 100 that they believe represents the usefulness of each site in relation to each criterion; this is shown in Table 6.3.

Problem: ***Where do you think the ISP should locate its new call centre, and why?***

Approach: Allocate a weighting between 1 and 5 to each of the criteria to indicate how important they are. Then multiply each usefulness score by the importance weighting. Finally add up the adjusted scores (Table 6.4).

Solution: The preferred outsourcing option is the South African site (see Table 6.4), as the weighted total score is the highest: (90 × 5) + (50 × 3) + (50 × 3) + (80 × 4) + (70 × 4) + (50 × 1) = 1,400.

Table 6.3 Usefulness scores for new call centre outsourcing decision

Criterion	Usefulness scores for sites		
	P	SA	I
Cost of the site	80	90	95
Rate of local property taxation	40	50	80
Availability of suitable skills in the labour force	50	50	50
The site's access to the international airport	50	80	25
Cultural and language compatibility	30	70	25
Time zone difference from UK Greenwich Mean Time	30	50	40

Table 6.4 Weighted usefulness scores for new call centre outsourcing decision

Criterion	Importance weighting	Weighted usefulness scores for sites		
		P	SA	I
Cost of the site	5	400	450	475
Rate of local property taxation	3	120	150	240
Availability of suitable skills in the labour force	3	150	150	150
The site's access to the international airport	4	200	320	100
Cultural and language compatibility	4	120	280	100
Time zone difference from Greenwich Mean Time	1	30	50	40
Total weighted scores		1,020	1,400	1,105

Using the same method, the Polish site has scored lowest, and the Indian site has achieved the middle rank.

Note: The ISP company can use this technique to reassess the scenario should any factors become more or less important; or if other factors need to be considered later on.

CRITICAL PERSPECTIVE

Digital disruptors of decision locations

Decision locations are of course more important when physical items are being transported. Once products become digitized transportation becomes much less of an issue. For instance, once books, music, learning materials, videos become digital their provider can move from a local product supplier to being a service provider located anywhere in the world (e.g. local shops become digital platforms). Many business who have not planned for this disruptive innovation are no longer in operation (e.g. Blockbuster video store) or have seen their businesses shrink (e.g. HMV music stores).

Supply Base Rationalization

Supply base rationalization: reduction of suppliers in order to become more efficient.

From the late 1990s onwards, supplier management practices have shown a strong trend towards increasing supplier integration, which in turn reduces the overall number of suppliers. This practice is often called **supply base rationalization**, and can be seen as a backlash to the tendency of organizations to outsource during the preceding decades.

The underlying purpose of supply base rationalization is simple: it involves working more closely with fewer suppliers. The practice builds on the idea that an individual organization has only a limited amount of resources, and by reducing the number of suppliers an organization has to manage *directly*, it becomes easier for it to focus its management efforts; this can be seen in the Sony Foxconn study in Short Case 6.3.

The financial effect of supply base rationalization can be demonstrated by looking at cost structures. Broadly speaking, there are three levels of cost:

- *Strategic costs* – which are best thought of in terms of commercial risks incurred and lost business opportunities. They are typically intangible overheads, indirect, and very hard to measure or attribute

Figure 6.5 The effect of cost on supply base reduction

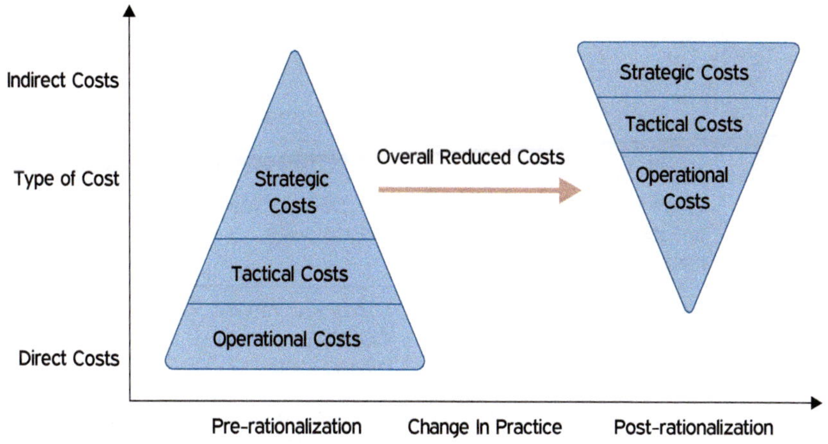

Source: Adapted from Cousins (2005).

- *Tactical costs* – which are management costs associated with things such as visiting suppliers, holding quality audits and supplier conferences. These are usually overheads that can be indirectly attributed to particular products production or service deliveries
- *Operational costs* – which are the direct costs of making the products or delivering the service, such as materials, and salaries of employees. Relatively speaking, these are direct costs and are the easiest to measure.

Chapter 10, p323

Although supply base rationalization may achieve short-term cost savings, and complement other practices such as *lean management* (as described in Chapter 10), it can bring its own organizational challenges. This is because quite often when organizations move from a large supply base to a smaller one, the cost structure seems to turn upside down, as demonstrated in Figure 6.5. Strategic costs increase relatively as the buying organization becomes increasingly dependent on fewer firms, and has more strategic activities to participate in, such as the co-development of new products and services. In contrast, operational costs *should* decrease relatively, because the overall number of transactions should decrease (e.g. moving from ten suppliers to one can mean raising ten times fewer purchase orders). The overall intention of supplier rationalization, by the dominant organization, is to reduce overall cost (as implied in Figure 6.5 by the smaller triangle post-reduction) and management complexity. This is achieved by reducing the number of suppliers managed, by either encouraging first-tier suppliers to merge, or encouraging some first-tier suppliers to manage other first-tier suppliers, who, as a result, effectively become second-tier suppliers.

We should treat the practice of supplier rationalization with caution, though, because it is difficult to demonstrate clearly *overall* cost savings, owing to the problems of measuring the indirect cost element accurately.

WORKED EXAMPLE 6.3

Costing Supply Base Rationalization at EuroCook

A large European industrial catering company known as EuroCook is looking to outsource some of its food production in an effort to reduce its overall supply costs and their variable cost component. EuroCook has five different non-meat food production lines that it wants to outsource (bread, cakes, pastries, biscuits and cereals), as it wants to concentrate on meat-based products, which will continue to be made in house. It has invited FoodFactory to bid for the work. The costs should be based on 1,000 units of output per month over a 12-month period, and need to be broken down and attributed to strategic, tactical and operational activities.

EuroCook's management accountants have calculated what it costs the company currently to produce its non-meat product lines; these are shown in the 'Pre-rationalized suppliers' column in Table 6.5. FoodFactory's accountants have costed the bid; their costs are given in the 'Post-rationalized suppliers' column in Table 6.5.

Table 6.5 Supply base rationalization for EuroCook's non-meat product lines

Level at which cost is incurred	Example	Supplier management costs	
		Pre-rationalized suppliers managed by EuroCook	Post-rationalized suppliers managed by FoodFactory
Strategic	Whole company (e.g. EuroCook or FoodFactory) on an annual basis	€100,000 per year variable costs	€300,000 per year fixed costs
Tactical	Particular production line (e.g. bread) on a monthly basis	5 lines × 12 months × €10,000 per month variable costs	5 lines × 12 months × €5,000 per month fixed costs
Operational	Unit of output (e.g. one tray of bread)	1,000 units per month × €1.2 cost per unit variable	1,000 units per month × €0.8 cost per unit variable

Problem: *Will it be cheaper for EuroCook to keep managing its non-meat product lines in-house, or let another company (e.g. FoodFactory) manage them?*

Approach:

Pre-rationalized suppliers' total annual costs (€s):

$$= 100,000 + (5 \times 10,000 \times 12 \text{ months}) + (1,000 \times 1.2 \times 12 \text{ months})$$
$$= 100,000 + 600,000 + 14,400$$
$$= €714,400$$

Post-rationalized suppliers' total annual costs:

$$= 300,000 + (5 \times 5,000 \times 12 \text{ months}) + (1,000 \times 0.8 \times 12 \text{ months})$$
$$= 300,000 + 300,000 + 9,600$$
$$= €609,600$$

Solution: It can be seen that at 1,000 units of production per month it is far cheaper (€714,400 – €609,600 = €104,800 savings per year overall) to let FoodFactory manage its suppliers.

Note: Rationalization means that EuroCook is effectively dealing with only one supplier (FoodFactory) for all its non-meat products, rather than with many individual suppliers. This should make management of suppliers simpler. This decision will also reduce its risk, as some of its variable costs have been turned to fixed costs, which makes budgeting and financial planning easier.

The key point is ...

that, by practising supply base rationalization, an organization has costs that are arguably more certain, and easier to measure and manage.

Stop and Think

If you were a senior manager in a small organization supplying a large organization that was conducting a supplier rationalization programme, what steps would you take to ensure that your company was not adversely affected?

SHORT CASE 6.3

Supply Base Rationalization at Sony Contributes to the Rise of Foxconn

Source: ©Michael Vi / Shutterstock

GLOBALIZATION

BUSINESS INTEGRATION

Sony makes innovative products such as LCD televisions and the PlayStation game consoles. It has built a valuable global consumer brand. However, in the financial year ending 2009, the Japanese company made its first annual loss in 14 years (nearly £0.5 billion) as it was hit by declining global demand, a strong Chinese yuan, and reducing product prices. In response Sony halved the number of its parts suppliers to reduce its costs by 20%. This was achieved because it was less costly to manage fewer suppliers. Sony therefore reduced the number of its parts makers from about 2,500 to about 1,200 in a single year

After supplier rationalization, Sony became more focused, improved its efficiency, boosted its earnings and profits, expanded its demand-side distribution network, and increasingly shared its parts makers' processes with its suppliers. Furthering this strategy by 2011, 80% of Sony's TV sets were manufactured externally, with 40–50% of them coming from the Taiwanese company Foxconn, and other large and significant suppliers including Wistron and Compal. Outsourcing to large scale electronic manufacturing contractors such as Foxconn has accelerated their growth and they are fast becoming some of the largest device manufacturers in the world, even though they do not have well-known consumer brand names. In 2018 Foxconn employed 250,000 people with sites in Taipei, Suzhou, Mexico City, Madrid, Cleveland and more, with most volume production being done in China; it had revenue of over US$152 billion. The role of Foxconn according to their CEO Terry Gou is to 'provide low cost mechanical and electrical parts to drive down the overall cost of electronics worldwide'.

Another closely related issue for Sony was that the various internal divisions of Sony needed to work together better. Their CEO at the time, Howard Stringer, said that their business units often didn't communicate well with each other, and even hinted that they were territorial. Stringer said that 'we must transform Sony into a more innovative, integrated and agile global company', which is an essential step to take before rationalizing the external supply base. Subsequent steps have proven to be even more radical – Sony recently sold some of its manufacturing capability and capacity to Foxconn.

Foxconn also does contract manufacturing for other companies such as Apple, Dell, HP, Samsung and LG.

Questions

1. What further steps could Sony take to save supply costs?
2. What would you do if you were a contract manufacturer such as Foxconn?
3. What are the downsides to the supplier reduction that Sony is implementing?

Source: Adapted from ***Fortune Magazine*** (2009), https://archive.fortune.com/2009/06/24/technology/sony_digital_transformation.fortune/index.htm (accessed January 2020); Forbes (2019), https://www.forbes.com/search/?q=foxconn#55b47ec9279f (accessed January 2020).

CRITICAL PERSPECTIVE

Why Do Organizations Outsource and Rationalize?

Outsourcing is concerned with finding alternative external supply sources for an organization, and supply base rationalization is about ensuring that the organization does not have too many external supply sources. If an organization has too many suppliers, this can generate a burdensome overhead and unnecessary complexity.

Often businesses go through cycles of outsourcing followed by periods of supplier rationalization, which is then repeated as organizations drop certain suppliers and subsequently look for new ones. Although this may be seen as wasteful and iterative, it often stops an organization from stagnating, by bringing in fresh ideas and approaches.

The use of shared processes and Internet-based information systems, perhaps provided by third parties, helps managers from different organizations achieve more comprehensive operational integration.

The key point is ...

that an organization must make sure that it has enough external suppliers to keep costs and internal bureaucracy down and innovation up, but not so many that they begin to become burdensome and counterproductive.

Multi-Organization Enterprises for Closer Supplier Relationships

Multi-organization enterprise management is an emerging idea about how organizations are designed, structured and managed. Contemporary thinking sees an enterprise as an inter-organizational structure that links the operations of separate companies very closely.

There are three basic types of multi-organization enterprise:

- **Virtual enterprise (VE)**: a short-term temporary group of (parts of) organizations exploiting a specific short-term, often high-risk opportunity
- **Extended enterprise (EE)**: a semi-permanent group of organizations working towards joint strategic objectives
- **Vertically integrated enterprise (VIE)**: an almost permanent and extremely well-integrated group of organizations; similar to a single legal entity.

These three types exhibit different characteristics and are suited to different operational contexts, as described in Table 6.6.

In a multi-organization enterprise there is always one dominant – most strategically influential – organization, known as the **enterprise integrator** or **orchestrator** (Brown *et al.*, 2002). This organization is predominant in the design of the multi-organization enterprise, and it is critical that operations managers within this organization understand suppliers' motives, capabilities and structures, in order to be able to design an appropriate *multi-organization enterprise structure*. The multi-organization enterprise should contain the most useful parts of the most suitable organizations. This requires managers in the integrator organization to combine an 'outside, looking in' view, known as an *exogenous view*, of each partner with an 'inside, looking out' view, known as an *endogenous view* of their own organization. This is based on the resource-based view of an organization described in Chapter 1 and the theories of transaction cost economics described in the section below.

Chapter 1, p23

Endogenous theories or views and **exogenous theories** or views should be used to complement one another; excessive focus on either one can result in a poor operations strategy. For instance, too much internal focus can mean that an organization does not develop strong enough links with its suppliers and customers, implying that it might be hard for it to buy or sell products and services easily. Conversely, too much external focus can mean that the organization may not develop internal skills and resources adequately, implying that it risks losing its unique competitiveness, competences or innovative features. We shall now build on these ideas to show how multi-organization enterprises should develop over time.

Transaction Cost Economics

If you bought a new coat, you might spend time and money choosing it, and have to pay delivery costs if you bought it through the Internet, or pay petrol and parking costs if you drove to a shopping centre. These costs are all **transaction costs**. Another example would be buying a house: where as well as the purchase cost of the house, there is the time spent with estate agents, fees to estate agents and legal solicitors fees, tax to the government and the costs of moving, which are all transaction costs of house buying.

Virtual enterprise: temporary group of organizations exploiting a short-term, high-risk opportunity.

Extended enterprise: semi-permanent group of organizations working towards joint strategic objectives.

Vertically integrated enterprise: almost permanent and extremely well-integrated group of organizations; very similar to a single legal entity.

Enterprise integrator/orchestrator: organization that takes the lead role in transforming a loose supply network into a tightly integrated enterprise.

Endogenous theories: theories about an organization that focus on the organization and its links to the business environment.

Exogenous theories: theories about an organization that focus on its internal workings, resources and skills.

Transaction costs: the price associated with buying or selling goods or services.

Table 6.6 Multi-organization enterprise types: virtual, extended, and vertically integrated

	Virtual multi-organization enterprise	Extended multi-organization enterprise	Vertically integrated multi-organization enterprise
Philosophy	Have a quickly adaptable strategy (e.g. be agile)	Need to be adaptable *and* reduce waste (e.g. be lean and agile)	Reduction of waste dominates (e.g. use lean thinking)
Foundation of relationship	Based mainly on technical competence features; emphasis on high innovation; allocation of resources depends on competitive and comparative advantage	Based mainly on social competence features; past relationship experience important; emphasis on strategic sourcing of critical products	Based mainly on efficiency factors; emphasis on transaction costs (e.g. prices)
Core competencies	Newly emerging, speculative, untested, high risk, requires many members to spread risk; high asset specificity; high transaction costs	Tested to some extent, medium risk, understood by innovators; medium asset specificity; medium transaction costs	Mature, well-accepted, tested and widely usable; low asset-specific investments; low transaction costs
Scope of relationship	Project-based activities that exploit specific opportunities across organizational boundaries; present a unified face to externals; partners involved in many other collaborative activities simultaneously to lessen their risks	Mid-term strategic thinking; often spans whole product life cycle across organizational boundaries	Standardization, high production volumes and corporatization of structures; focus on scales of economies rather than on scope of economies
Longevity of relationship	Short-term temporary alignment of operations	Medium to long term	Foreseeable as permanent (as long as competitive)
Proximity and depth of relationship	No stability; dynamic and unpredictable environment; collaboration improves agility and flexibility; low degree of interdependence and integration	Strategic collaboration; relationships, technology and knowledge management become critical; medium degree of interdependence and integration	Tend towards industrial dominance; emphasis on removal of IT legacy systems; high interdependence and integration
Governance of relationship	Loose and flexible; temporary and reactive to emerging trends; right balance of control and emergence (i.e. co-opetition)	Strategic sourcing and partner development; design and implementation of co-owned processes; proactive governance aiming for efficiency	Single command and control; focused on monitoring and control through standardization and corporatization
Strategic role of enterprise integrator	Incubator; scouting for potential value members; initiates collaborative activities	Integrator; coordination of collaborative activities; supports value members in competence development	Incumbent; in-house development of proprietary systems; relying on power and authority
Strategic role of value members	Innovative suppliers; deploying specific competencies for innovating new technologies and solving complex R&D problems	Integrator; integrating parts to more complex systems and managing and coordinating sub-supplier base	Volume production; value creation through cost-efficient making and delivery of parts to high quality
Main collaboration points	Mainly new product and service planning and concept design	Mainly concept, early delivery design and mass delivery planning	Mainly high-volume design and delivery

Transaction cost economics (TCE) has emerged as a *de facto* economic explanation for the existence and scope of a commercial organization. Nobel Prize Laureate Ronald Coase (1937) stated that commercial organizations exist because of these 'transaction costs' – in other words, they are the price of using the open market mechanisms. An organization has to use this thinking all the time when buying new products or services. For example, buying new computer services for students' residences or a university library will incur transaction costs. These may include the time taken to do research (e.g. spending time researching what type of server is needed, and who provides them), bargaining (e.g. spending time negotiating with potential suppliers) and enforcement (e.g. maintenance of the servers, and extra costs for fixing problems). There will be similar costs involved for the computer service provider (e.g. time putting together a proposal, delivering a sales pitch, etc.). Bringing capabilities in-house can be one way to try and reduce transaction costs.

TCE is based upon the interplay of four behavioural assumptions: bounded rationality, opportunism, asset specificity and uncertainty.

Bounded rationality is the assumption that, although most human behaviour is intended to be rational, it is often limited by knowledge, behaviour and language (Simon, 1957). For instance, we may try to choose the cheapest or most waterproof coat we can, but we have no sure way of knowing this for sure, as we cannot check *every* coat that is for sale.

Opportunism is the assumption that 'actors' (organizations or individuals) will try to improve their own standing in comparison with others. For instance, if we saw a coat that was fashionable and good value, and we really wanted it, we would buy it regardless of any other actors' needs or desires. Opportunism could be described as 'self-interest seeking with guile' (Williamson, 1975). This is self-centred behaviour, and is often how free markets operate. However, it is difficult to distinguish between those who act like this deliberately, those who act like this from bounded rationality, and those who may actually want to collaborate. Higher competitive pressures and levels of mistrust between organizations will cause more opportunism.

Asset specificity considers how specialized assets (e.g. core competencies for design, manufacture or branding) are dedicated to delivering certain products or services. In successful times these are often the source of competitive advantage. These specialized assets are risky to own, though, as they cannot be fully utilized if the particular application for which they were acquired is no longer required. This is because they cannot be easily transferred to another application. For example, a general-purpose sewing machine that is used to make coats will have low specificity, because it can easily be used for making a variety of other clothing, whereas a machine that can be used for only one task (e.g. a fabrication plant for PC processors) will have high specificity, as it will have expensive retooling and changeover costs. The four main types of asset specificity are *location* (e.g. restriction to a particular place), *physical properties* (e.g. speed of a machine), *human limitations* (e.g. limited skills) and *degree of dedication* (e.g. the amount of different things that can be done at any one time). In adverse conditions, assets with highly specific properties are believed to increase the opportunism, or, if conditions allow, may result in organizations collaborating.

Uncertainty relates to the business environment, and the behavioural limitations of organizations and individuals. Organizations facing high levels of uncertainty in their markets and the external environment will tend to seek to develop their own internal resources, and look for low-risk projects and organizations to work with (e.g. hospitals often have their own back-up power plants to ensure that they always have a reliable source of electricity). However, such risk aversion usually means more expense, and slower rates of innovation.

The key point is ...

that all the above assumptions affect transaction costs. If other factors are favourable, then when an organization's overall transaction costs with external organizations are higher than its internal transaction costs, it will often grow. This is because it is cheaper and easier to do activities in house. Conversely, if internal transaction costs are higher than external transaction costs, an organization can benefit from downsizing or outsourcing noncompetitive parts of its operations, because it is cheaper and easier to get another organization to perform these activities.

TCE is often criticized for:

- Failing to explain clearly situations when suppliers should collaborate as partners in jointly strategic relationships
- Focusing too much on cost minimization rather than on value maximization.

Resource-based View

Chapter 1, p23

As explained in Chapter 1, the *resource-based view* (RBV) traditionally focuses on the internal resources of a single organization. We also saw how the traditional RBV has, more recently, been extended to recognize that resource bases vary over time and require collaboration with different organizations, leading to the *dynamic capabilities view* (DCV) of organizations (Teece *et al.*, 1997) discussed in Chapter 1. The main difference between the DCV and the RBV of organizations is that DCV considers a number of simultaneously collaborating organizations working towards joint business objectives, instead of individual organizations being purely opportunistic. This is also recognized by the managers of multi-organization enterprises.

The core competencies of an organization (which are endogenous resources) are difficult to transfer, because of high transaction costs, dependence on tacit knowledge, and high asset specificity. Because of this, core competencies can usually only be deployed effectively internally within single organizations. However, under certain conditions organizations may prioritize development of their core competencies over and above the minimization of transaction costs – for instance when engaging in a new collaborative venture (such as a long-term research project with a university to develop a new artificial intelligence technology for manufacturing). This challenges the notion of competitive advantage, and suggests that *cooperative advantage* or *collaborative advantage* (Dyer and Hatch, 2004) can sometimes be more appropriate. Collaboration should occur when the minimization of operational transaction costs has become less significant than gaining new external core competencies in new collaborative enterprises.

In other words, to remain competitive, new meta-core competencies (those that are a property of the whole multi-organization enterprise, rather than just one company) need to be built by the multi-organization enterprise integrator alongside existing traditionally valued ones to reconfigure operational competencies and organizational structures. The enterprise integrator's role is assumed by the most significantly influential member of the enterprise. For example, the Canadian company Magna Steyr attempted to acquire parts of the former European General Motors as it almost became strategically and financially more dominant than GM, the original equipment manufacturer (OEM).

SHORT CASE 6.4

CarFest: Serious Fun

Source: ©Shutterstock/Natalya Kokhanova

CarFest (or car festival) is a groundbreaking car, music and gourmet food and drink festival, as it was one of the first of its kind to be delivered at two different UK venues – Laverstoke Park in Hampshire and Bolesworth Park in Cheshire. Originally, the festival was the brainchild of the British celebrity radio and TV presenter, Chris Evans, who wanted to have two live festivals, one at the beginning and one at the end of the summer, one in the north and one in the south of England. The festival contrasts with other big summer music festivals, such as Glastonbury, that are held over a longer period, focus mostly on music and not on cars, and are held at a single location.

The event is a cooperation organized by Brand Events Ltd and the BBC (British Broadcasting Corporation) who is a principal partner that helps to promote the festival. The planning also involves many other different types of organization such as caterers, other broadcasting stations, website engineers (ASP), online ticket agencies (SeeTickets.com), the Press, engineers, sanitation providers, security, emergency services and, of course, the musical artists, car companies and car clubs. Plus many individual volunteers. They come together for a short time span to deliver a service to paying festival-goers and then part until, perhaps, participating again in the southern festival later in the summer, or in festivals in the following year.

BUSINESS INTEGRATION

CarFest is principally run to make money for UK children's charities and is a not-for-profit organization. It generates money mostly for the BBC's Children in Need (who take 50% of net income) and others such as the Ellen MacArthur Cancer Trust, Teenage Cancer Trust and the Rainbow Trust.

CSR

What makes this festival so successful is that the key partners in it have a shared long-term vision for philanthropic activities, and know how to deliver it whilst having fun. Even the short-term stakeholders (e.g. the food stalls, and the artists) become part of the bigger picture as they must buy into the ethical ideals of this festival which include: zero waste to landfill, compulsory use of reusable cups, no single use plastic, canned water not plastic bottles, 75% use of LED lighting and being carbon neutral on primary emissions by 2020. This is done by reducing emissions and carbon offsetting by planting 1,000 trees. Since 2012, CarFest has raised over £16.5 million for UK children's charities.

Questions

1. Who do you think are the most influential organizations and or people in this enterprise, and what core competencies do you think they have?
2. Name aspects of the festival that have high and low transaction costs.
3. Are there any advantages to be gained from having multi-site festivals?

Source: Ben Clegg, Aston Business School.

Stop and Think

Why don't organizations cooperate all the time, if there are potential gains to be made from doing so?

Contemporary Thinking: Collaborative Multi-Organizational Enterprise Governance

Collaborative enterprise governance: method of controlling parts of many different organizations simultaneously, in order to deliver products and services with agility and efficiency.

Designing and integrating collaborative enterprises is rather like putting together a jigsaw puzzle where each piece is owned by a different organization. **Collaborative enterprise governance** (CEG) is an approach to designing multi-organization enterprises. It considers multi-organization enterprises to be made up of parts of different companies (i.e. the pieces of the puzzle), known as *enterprise modules*, where each individual enterprise module is built around highly specific core competencies belonging to an individual organization. For instance, an enterprise module could be the engines on a ship such as the *Queen Mary 2*, or a military vessel such as the new BAE Systems Astute Class nuclear submarine; or the provider of ticketing services for a train company such as Eurostar.

Often the enterprise module provider gives a unique and valuable proposition distinct to the rest of the enterprise, such as an in-house design and engineering specialism, or is a provider of additional capacity, such as an additional assembly plant in another country. The core competencies of any enterprise module are combined with other less specific resources, such as communication technology, cooperative contracts, and shared processes (which are relatively easy to share), to form a multi-organization enterprise structure with economically acceptable transaction costs.

Enterprise integrators help overcome the traditional adversarial view, and help promote the ideas of intercompany collaboration instead. This means connecting enterprise modules (parts of one organization) with other enterprise modules (parts of another organization) to create *agile enterprises*. These agile enterprises often meet the demands of rapidly changing business environments, while operating with acceptable costs, more easily than single large traditional organizations. The role of enterprise integrator is often fulfilled by companies such as information technology consultancies, which provide the skills and technology to design shared processes and technology (e.g. companies such as SAP, Capgemini or Accenture). Sometimes, if it is necessary and if the enterprise is agile enough, the jigsaw can be remade with different pieces, to create a new picture (e.g. a new multi-organization enterprise). The four main stages of CEG are shown in Figure 6.6, and are explained below.

Stage 1: Mapping the Enterprise

First we have to decide on a particular product or service family on which to focus the enterprise, and then map the enterprise using the *enterprise matrix* shown in Figure 6.7.

Figure 6.6 Collaborative Enterprise Governance

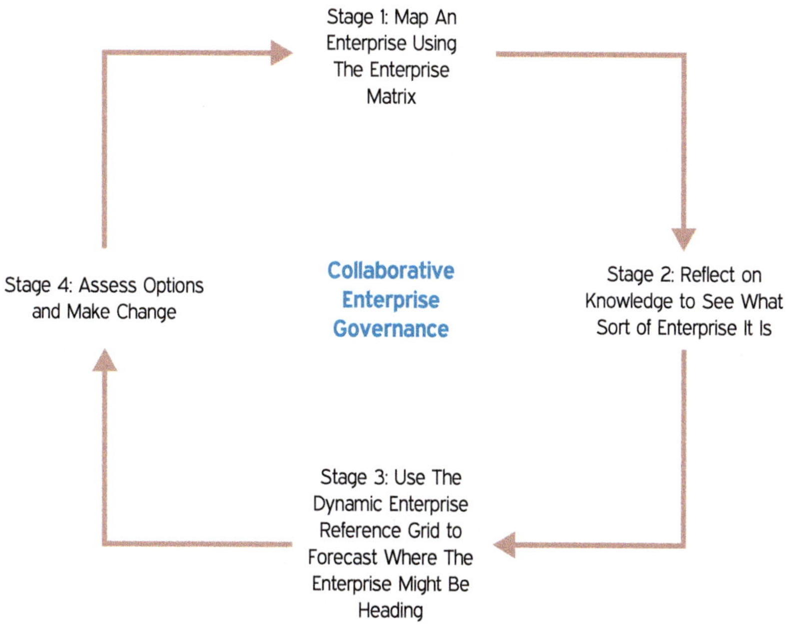

Figure 6.7 The enterprise matrix: a mapping tool

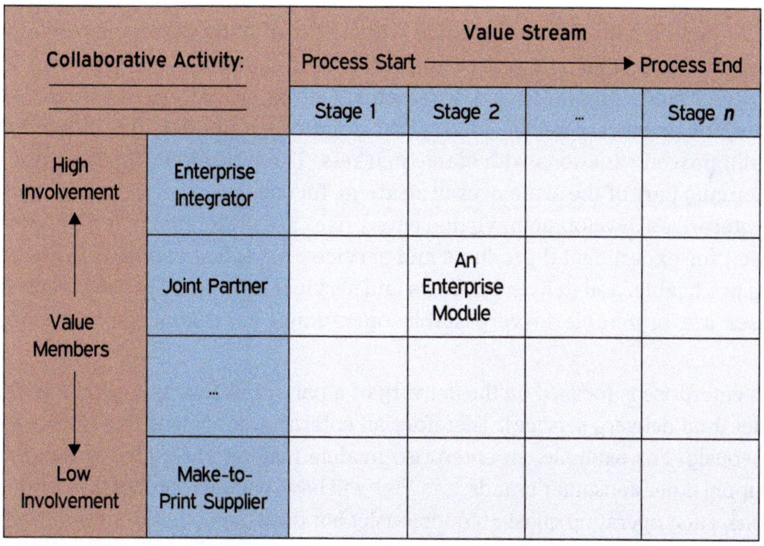

The members of the enterprise, who create value for it in some way or another, should be listed on the vertical axis; they are listed in order of significance, from the most important at the top to the least important at the bottom. There can be any number of these value members, which may reach into the hundreds for a complex product such as an aircraft or a complex service such as a long-distance luxury air flight. But the different types of value member can usually be classified into just a handful of different types, in order of the most significant: enterprise integrator, joint partners, design-make-and-deliver, and make-to-print suppliers:

- An *enterprise integrator* will be the most influential, as it brings all the other companies together (like Airbus in the opening case study).
- A *joint partner* will usually have made some up-front investment in the project, and will share in the revenues and losses of the multi-organizations enterprise (like the Rolls Royce Aerospace Group in the opening case study).
- *Design-make-and-deliver suppliers* could be employed by the enterprise integrator or joint partner to design and deliver items or services, and so are skilled members (like the programme associates in the

opening case study), and will usually be hired through an invited competitive tendering process to participate.

- *Make-to-print suppliers* are relatively low-skilled organizations, delivering standard low-risk and low-value items that are easily available.

Design-make-and-deliver and make-to-print suppliers are likely to get paid whether the multi-organization enterprise is successful or not (as long as it does not become bankrupt), as they have not invested in it up front, and do not share directly in its profit.

Value Stream: sequence of activities designed to create value and eliminate waste

Each stage of the **value stream** in the multi-organization enterprise is then mapped along the horizontal axis, with the first stage on the left-hand side and the last stage on the right-hand side. There can be any number of stages, but the whole value stream can usually be described adequately in a few key stages (e.g. 7 plus or minus 2).

What each member of the enterprise does at each stage of the value stream is then described in the appropriate place in the enterprise matrix. This is a description of:

- What the enterprise module has as specific assets, and how they differentiate it from the others
- What processes it uses, and what they deliver
- How its performance is measured
- How it can be efficiently linked with other modules
- The transaction costs that are incurred by using it.

By describing the parts like this, we can begin to understand how the whole multi-organization enterprise is built and governed.

Stage 2: Reflecting on Knowledge

This stage compares practice with theory to decide which sort of enterprise structure a particular scenario is currently best suited to. Table 6.6 characterized the three main types of multi-organization enterprise: *virtual enterprises* (VEs), often found in research and development situations; *extended enterprises* (EEs), often found in knowledge transfer and product or service derivation situations; and *vertically integrated enterprises* (VIEs), found in commercially proven situations with stable markets. These different types do not result from different strategies, but are actually part of the same overall strategy, focused on inter-organizational collaboration at different times of the enterprise's development. Virtual enterprises are preferable in rapidly changing environments, and are typically used for experimental products and services; extended enterprises are preferable in environments that are fairly predicable, and deliver products and services with some proven track record; and vertically integrated enterprises are preferable in very stable operational environments, when organizations compete mainly on cost.

Remember that each enterprise is focused on the delivery of a particular family of products or services (e.g. mobile phones, or an Internet food delivery service). Therefore an enterprise module is likely to be part of many different enterprises simultaneously. For example, an enterprise module making parts for Samsung mobile phones is also likely to be able to supply other consumer brands; and Visa will have payment-processing modules operating in many different organizations, each operating quasi-autonomously, but drawing upon the same specific competencies. It is therefore useful to perceive multi-organization enterprises as a collection of quasi-autonomous modules, where each module is simultaneously able to contribute value to a number of coexisting multi-organization enterprises.

Stage 3: Using the Dynamic Enterprise Reference Grid

Engageability: the ability to attract partners and the means to deliver value.

It is important to recognize that competencies are strategic resources which need to be developed and managed. The number and type of enterprise engagements for any organization depends on the value placed on its enterprise modules by other companies and, the capability to deploy them; this is known as an enterprise module's **engageability**. The engageability of a module may increase over time as value members become more integrated, transaction frequency increases, and costs reduce (exogenous factors). In a similar way, the low marketability of a new competence (exogenous factor), due to its untested market value, will initially result in low attractiveness and low engageability. However, this may change through further development of the competence, leading to higher maturity and less risk.

Figure 6.8 Dynamic enterprise reference grid (DERG)

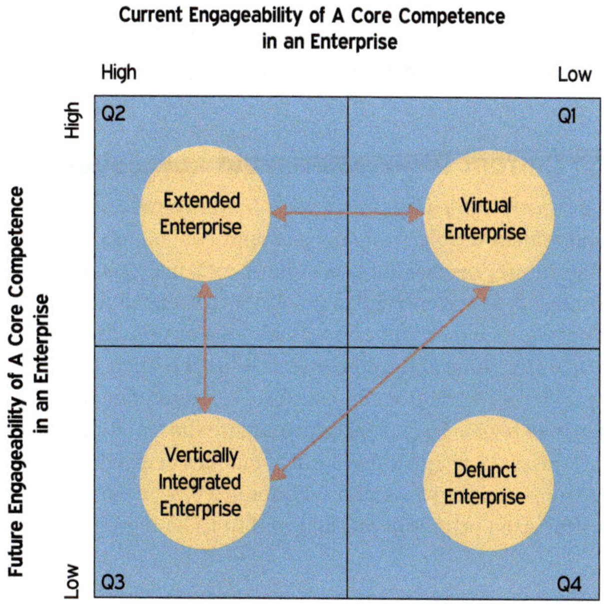

Figure 6.8 shows the *dynamic enterprise reference grid* (DERG). It summarizes the four main types of enterprise and their engageability, ranked simply as 'high' or 'low'. In each of the quadrants, the most suitable enterprise structure is shown. The DERG is important because it is the basis of how dynamic changes in a multi-organization enterprise can occur. Below we give a description of each of the quadrants (Q) of the DERG, with examples.

Quadrant 1 (Q1): Low Current Engageability but High Future Potential Engageability

Enterprises in this quadrant are managed and governed 'virtually', and show a prevalence of modules with competencies that have low current but high future engageability potential. This is because they usually have many newly emerging competencies – for example, the initial enterprise that developed the prototype Bluetooth short-range, hands-free communications protocol for mobile devices, which at the time was untested on consumer markets. In this situation, the enterprise governor and the value members will be reluctant to make long-term plans and investments until they start to produce revenue. So, here, collaboration arrangements will often be temporary, intended to exploit market opportunities and spread the risk over many different value members. In addition, the cost of collaborating may be very high, owing to the fragmented resource base, the high specificity of the competencies, and the high transaction costs. These are all characteristics of a *virtual enterprise*. In a virtual enterprise it is usual for value members to deliver very specific and limited value to the overall value stream. The selection of value members is based on their ability to solve complex technological problems, and their capability to bring them to market quickly. A current example of this would be the use of crypto-currencies in online payments, a capability still perceived to be high-risk and high-uncertainty.

Quadrant 2 (Q2): High Current Engageability and High Future Potential Engageability

Multi-organization enterprises in this quadrant are governed as extended enterprises, and show a prevalence of competencies that are currently highly engageable, owing to their relatively mature nature and market success; this makes them highly attractive to other value members. eBay, an Internet site that has proven ability to sell products, or an ability to deliver a market-ready Bluetooth chip for mobile devices, are good examples. Such competencies involve relatively low levels of uncertainty and risk during their deployment. They are also perceived to have high potential engageability in the future, based on an ever-increasing universal application of their value proposition. In this situation the enterprise integrator will seek a more stable, medium- to long-term co-developmental supply strategy with value members in order to minimize commercial opportunism. This decreases the costs of collaboration, and increases the ability to integrate these competencies into efficiently operating multi-organization enterprises. These are characteristics of an *extended enterprise*. In an extended enterprise the value members tend to be involved in collaborative activities spanning many steps of the value stream. Their selection is based primarily on their good interface capabilities, making it relatively easy to use their competencies in an increasing number of different enterprises at relatively low transaction costs.

Quadrant 3 (Q3): High Current Engageability but Low Future Potential Engageability

Enterprises are governed in a *vertically integrated* way; they are currently highly engageable, thanks to their mature, well-established and widely usable competencies and capabilities. However, on the downside, they may become less attractive in the future, because of fears that profit margins are eroding, or that their technologies may become obsolete. This may cause the enterprise governor to seek whole-ownership of capabilities to minimize transaction cost. This leads towards a merging of organizations or permanent acquisitions of enterprise modules within a *vertically integrated enterprise*, and a control-based governance structure. An example of this is Chinese auto manufacturer NAC's purchase of MG Rover's Longbridge production plant. By taking this course of action, the once collaborative enterprise begins to closely approximate the traditional vertically integrated organization. In vertically integrated enterprises a single significant member (or small number of significant members) will cover most of the value stream in order to maximize economies of scale and standardization. In this situation, the selection of value members is based primarily on their ability to be highly efficient, and not necessarily on their ability to be innovative.

Quadrant 4 (Q4): Low Current Engageability and Low Future Potential Engageability

Multi-organization enterprises found in this quadrant have a prevalence of enterprise modules that are perceived as undesirable for current and future engagement. The enterprise integrators seek to disengage them from the rest of their organization before an unrecoverable commercial situation is reached. For example, IBM sold the major shareholding in its PC manufacturing enterprise in 2004 to a Chinese company (Lenovo Group). Recovery from this situation is possible by simultaneously developing other new virtual engagements, such as Hewlett-Packard partnering with management consultancies so that they can provide high-value IT business services. Another example is Apple, who allow software development companies to become 'app' providers for their hardware devices. In this way, if an innovative new software application becomes highly successful, a new collaborative enterprise governance cycle may begin again, as Apple may look to acquire part or whole ownership of them.

Stage 4: Assess Options and Make Changes

This stage occurs when enterprise managers need to redesign and implement changes to a multi-organization enterprise, based on new understanding of any given context. The dynamic enterprise reference grid shown in Figure 6.8 indicates how one enterprise structure may change into another as a result of different factors acting upon it. This is a two-way dependency, as the chosen multi-organization enterprise structure will affect the development of future potential competencies, just as the development and deployment of competencies will influence the emergence of enterprise structures. Proactive strategies are shown in Figure 6.8 by the arrows, and are based largely on controllable endogenous factors.

It is important to note that all enterprises are at risk of becoming defunct, and could fall into Quadrant 4 if their managers do not closely monitor internal and external factors, act upon changes affecting them, and proactively seek to modify the multi-organization enterprise type to best suit their situation. This may lead to the break away and subsequent sale of previously integrated parts of an organization. The above multi-organizational dynamics are explained in the Smart Car study in Short Case 6.5.

The key point is ...

that at different points of a product and service life cycle different enterprise structures and methods of governance are required.

SHORT CASE 6.5

A Smart Car Needs a Dynamic Enterprise

BUSINESS INTEGRATION

The Smart car is one of the most innovatively designed and produced cars of recent years. Production of the Smart car was initially a temporary collaboration, with weak ties between parts (enterprise modules) of Daimler-Benz (DC) and SMH, manufacturer of Swatch watches, to exploit market opportunities for very small cars. As the market grew the relationship strengthened, and it became longer term and more permanent.

Source: ©Robert Churchill/E+/Getty Images

These changes were accompanied by a change in the role of DC, which grew from a coordinator of manufacturing and logistics operations (relationship and technology management) to include the coordination of strategic information (knowledge management). DC began to act as the enterprise integrator. These changes saw the enterprise move from a virtual enterprise (Q1) into an extended enterprise (Q2).

Because of problems of achieving further market penetration for the Smart car, tension between DC and Swatch grew, and led to the buyout of the two-seater Smart car from Swatch by DC. This signified a transition from a extended enterprise (Q2) structure towards a vertically integrated enterprise (Q3) as major parts of the know-how and competencies of the venture became 're-insourced' into parts of DC. DC became an overwhelmingly dominant force, controlling the collaborative relationship that once had been a virtual and then an extended enterprise.

As a vertically integrated enterprise (Q3) DC also deployed its core competencies in other directions, which gave birth to the production of the new Smart Forfour car jointly designed with Mitsubishi, in another separate inter-company enterprise where parts would be supplied by Mitsubishi and the engines by Mercedes-Benz. This initially formed a new virtual enterprise (Q1) that quickly became successful and moved towards an extended enterprise structure (Q3). And so the cycle goes on.

Unfortunately, neither the new Forfour or original Fortwo cars sold in sufficient numbers. An experimental SUV was developed but not built and the roadster version was discontinued. By 2006 DaimlerChysler bought the development companies outright and operated it under the Mercedez-Benz car division. The next generation was the electric version launched in 2009 available in markets around the world to either lease or through car-sharing services (e.g. Car2go in San Diego and Amsterdam). The lithium battery in the Smart Fortwos is provided by Tesla Motors. New versions have more power batteries and greater range. Around 2 million units of the Smart car in numerous variants have been produced and can be seen around the world.

The Smart car is the result of effective collaborative enterprise management, and by being proactive the enterprise has avoided becoming defunct and continues to make innovative new variants.

Questions

1. Using the collaborative enterprise governance concept, describe how careful enterprise management has helped the Smart car's evolution.
2. Why do you think these changes have helped effective innovation and efficient production?

Source: Ben Clegg, Aston Business School and OSV (2020).

WORKED EXAMPLE 6.5

Using the Enterprise Matrix

Isobel has chosen to do her dissertation on medieval history, and urgently requires a rare book that is currently out of print for her research. She finds it on the website of a popular online bookseller, who promises to print and deliver it within 24 hours by using their on-demand print supplier. The enterprise for the on-demand print company is mapped out using the enterprise matrix, as shown in Table 6.7

Table 6.7 The enterprise matrix for an on-demand book-printing service

Value members	Book-printing value stream				
	New process development	**Scheduling**	**Printing**	**Finishing**	**Delivery**
Publishers (customers)	Electronic data links				
On-demand printing company	Electronic data links	On-demand electronic data links scheduling	High-technology printing	Binding and finishing	
Development partner	Company that co-develops the printing machines		Contract maintenance		
Strategic/dual-source supplier		Paper suppliers			
Open-source supplier				Other materials (e.g. glue and card)	Logistics company

Problem:

Using Table 6.7:

1. ***State how many key steps there are in their value stream, and how many different types of value stream members they have. What does the 'development partner' do?***

2. ***What sort of enterprise do you think it is? Who is the systems integrator? Why?***

Approach:

Read the above section (Collaborative enterprise governance) carefully, and then refer to the enterprise matrix example in Table 6.7.

Solution:

1. Table 6.7 shows five key stages in the value stream, starting with new process development and ending with delivery. It also shows five main types of supplier/value member: the most significant are the customers, and the least significant are the open-source suppliers. The development partner is responsible for making the special printing machines and making sure they are well maintained.

2. One might consider the printer to be the systems integrator in this extended enterprise. This is because using a print-on-demand system for books (i.e. they do not begin to make the book until it has been sold) requires a highly integrated process. To deliver this requires a collaborative and competitive enterprise strategy, developing strong semi-permanent links with their immediate customers (the publishers), a good understanding of their end customers' needs (i.e. Isobel, the buyer and reader of the book), access to a large distribution of wholesalers, retailers and booksellers, and unprecedented inventory control via electronic links (Internet and electronic data interchange).

Stop and Think

From your experience, can you think of other examples that the collaborative enterprise governance concept could be applied to?

Summary

This chapter has focused on how supplier relationships are formed. It started by providing a background to different ways of thinking about supplier relationships – chains, networks and multi-organization enterprises – and emphasized that these give us metaphors and models to help us understand different types of relationship. It showed how these relationships can change and evolve due to internal and external factors.

It then examined how operational activities can be transferred to and from firms by outsourcing, and outlined the advantages and disadvantages of doing this, and also the benefits and costs of using multiple-source and single-source supply chain strategies. Decisions on site location were considered with two tools – the centre of gravity method and the weighted score technique – introduced to help in making these decisions. Finally the characteristics of multi-organization enterprises were studied in more detail, and a method of designing them (collaborative enterprise governance) was explained.

Outsourcing is not a panacea for all operations management problems; too much uncoordinated outsourcing can itself cause problems. Sometimes in an industry or company there is a trend to rationalize, and bring the supply base back into control, which can mean a reduction of suppliers overall, or the use of other organizations to manage suppliers for you.

Key Theories

- **Transaction cost economics (TCE)** – an economic explanation for the existence and scope of a commercial organization. TCE is based on the interplay of four behavioural assumptions; *bounded rationality, opportunism, asset specificity* and *uncertainty.*
- **Resourced-based view (RBV)** – an organization theory that focuses on the internal resources of a single organization. RBV explains how competitive advantage within organizations is achieved and sustained over time. RBV assumes that each organization (i.e. a single legal autonomous entity) is thought of as a bundle of resources in its own right.
- **Multi-organization enterprise management** – the management of companies that have become so closely integrated that it is very difficult to think of them as networks of separate companies, or simple supply chains.
- **Supply base rationalization** – management practice that reduces the number of suppliers an organization has to deal with. The objective is often to reduce management costs and complexity.

Suggested Answers to Stop and Think Questions

1. **Management metaphors:** There probably is no easier way of doing this, although managers sometimes develop metaphors, models, frameworks and formulae to help develop generic principles for managing. Most metaphors need to be treated with caution, though, as they will only get you so far before they fail. The use of digital technology, especially Internet based, has accelerated the possibilities of the virtual enterprise because scope for innovation grows and opportunities to collaborate widen.
2. **Combatting supplier rationalization:** Seek to 'move up the value chain' by becoming a module supplier rather than a component supplier, develop meta-competencies of integration yourself in addition to traditional ones, seek to understand the end customer better, and cease competing only on a cost basis.
3. **Cooperation:** Cooperation and collaboration between organizations are suitable only when complementary competencies are being used. At other times, when similar competencies are being used, organizations will be in competition with one another, unless there is excessive demand for their goods and services. Sometimes there is a grey area between these juxtapositions that require organizations to work together within strict legal arrangements (e.g. UK train operating companies); these often focus on the delivery of specific products and services.

4. **Collaborative enterprise governance:** The concept could be applied to the delivery of any complex product or service that uses competences from a variety of different organizations. It is especially relevant where the business environment, role and membership of the multi-organization enterprise are rapidly changing. For instance, services would include air flights, Internet service provision, online payment systems, online accommodation rental (e.g. Airbnb) and mobile phone services; products would include big budget films, large buildings and construction projects.

connect

Review Questions

1. Can organizational relationships be accurately explained using a simple 'chain' metaphor, or is this an oversimplified view? If so why?
2. Why is it important for companies to work together more closely than before?
3. What are outsourcing, in-sourcing and offshoring?
4. Under what circumstances would you practise supply base rationalization?
5. What are TCE and RBV? What are they used to explain?
6. What is a multi-organization enterprise, within the context of supplier management? What different sorts of multi-organization enterprises are there, and how do they differ?
7. What does supply base rationalization try to achieve?
8. What risks are associated with too much outsourcing?
9. What is an example of a value proposition?

Discussion Questions

1. What effects do you think good supplier–buyer relationships have on an industry overall? How can they be encouraged?
2. Map out a supply network for a product such as a car or aircraft, or a service such as hotel accommodation. State and discuss the complexities that you come across in trying to do this. What do you think are the success factors?
3. Try to map a multi-organization enterprise for a product or service that you are familiar with, using the enterprise matrix. State who you think are the relatively major and minor members of the enterprise, and what their roles are. Using the dynamic enterprise reference grid, describe what you think are the dynamic changes occurring in it.
4. What factors affect the location of a supplier?
5. What are the characteristics of a dual source supply chain in comparison to other sourcing policies?

Problems

1. A County Council is proposing to build a new waste processing plant to serve three small towns – Alphatown, Betatown and Gammatown. These are located at coordinates (20, 50), (10, 30) and (90, 50) respectively. Taking into account how many people may travel from each town per day (V) to the waste site the County Council wants to minimize the total distance travelled to the new waste processing plant. Using details for each town and frequency of visits, as given in Table 6.8, find the best location for the new waste processing plant.

Table 6.8 Locations of Alphatown, Betatown and Gammatown and the potential frequency of visits to the waste processing plant

Town	Location		Frequency
	x	y	V
Alphatown	20	50	100
Betatown	10	30	50
Gammatown	90	40	75

Required: *Using the centre of gravity method, find the best place for the new waste processing plant.*

Use the following formulae:

$$x = \frac{\sum x_i V_i}{\sum V_i}$$

$$y = \frac{\sum y_i V_i}{\sum V_i}$$

where x_i is the x coordinate of the source or destination i; y_i is the y coordinate of the source or destination i, and V_i is the frequency of journey between source and destination i.

2. A UK marketing company is thinking of setting up a new sales office in mainland Europe. It needs to take into account:

- Number of local customers (crucial – 5)
- Rent of the site (very important – 4)
- Availability of suitable English speaking staff in the area (important – 3)
- Accessibility from the home nation by air, sea and rail (minor importance – 1)
- 5G connectivity for conference calls (very important – 4)

The marketing company is considering three sites, one in Paris (P), one in Berlin (B) and one in Zurich (Z). After some research, the company allocates usefulness scores (out of 100) to each potential location, shown in the following table. The company also allocates a weighting to each factor, as shown in Table 6.9.

Table 6.9 Weightings for each factor

Criteria	Importance Weighting	Usefulness scores for sites		
		P	B	Z
Number of local customers (crucial)	5	80	50	50
Rent of the site (average)	2	20	50	100
Availability of suitable English-speaking sales staff in the area (important)	3	10	50	90
Accessibility from the home nation by air, sea and rail (minor importance)	1	50	80	80
5G Connectivity for conference calls (very important)	4	30	75	80

Required: *Using the weighted score technique, calculate which site you think the marketing company should choose for its new offices, and why.*

Table 6.10 Cost comparisons for two possible outsourcing solutions for Chickfest

Level at which cost is incurred	Example	Supplier management costs		
		Pre-rationalized suppliers	Supply Chain Management Company ONE	Supply Chain Management Company TWO
Strategic	Whole-company costs on a annual basis	€2,000,000 Fixed costs	€1,750,000 Fixed costs	€600,000 Fixed costs
Tactical	Different product lines: (e.g. burger, wings, drumsticks, etc.) on a monthly basis	2 lines × 12 months × €400,000 per month variable costs	2 lines × 12 months × €200,000 per month fixed costs	2 lines × 12 months × €300,000 per month fixed costs
Operational	Unit of output: (delivery of 100 meals)	500 units per month × €200 cost per unit variable	500 units per month × €60 cost per unit variable	500 units per month × €100 cost per unit variable

3. A fast food restaurant 'Chickfest' wants to rationalize the number of its suppliers, as it believes there are too many, and thus creates unnecessary complexity and costs in the supply network. It is considering outsourcing the management of all its suppliers to specialist companies: Supply Chain Management Company ONE or Supply Chain Management Company TWO. Table 6.10 shows the current supplier management costs in the 'Pre-rationalized suppliers' column and bids from the potential alternative options in the other two columns.

   Required: *Using the supplier rationalization approach described in the chapter, and a planned output of 500 units per month, calculate whether Chickfest should continue to manage its own suppliers, or rationalize them by giving the management of them to Company ONE or to Company TWO, on the premise that this will reduce their overall annual supply costs.*

Further Reading

Baldwin, C.Y. and Clark, K.B. (2000) *Harvard Business Review on Managing the Value Chain,* Harvard Business School Press, Boston, MA.

Binder, M. and Clegg, B.T. (2010) *Sustainable Supplier Management in the Automotive Industry: Leading the 3rd Revolution through Collaboration,* Nova Science Publishers, New York.

Christopher, M. (2016). *Logistics and Supply Chain Management,* 5th edn, Pearson Education, Harlow, UK.

Doz, Y.L. and Hamel, G. (1998) *Alliance Advantage,* Harvard Business School Press, Boston, MA.

Dyer, J.H. (2000) *Collaborative Advantage: Winning Through Extended Enterprise Supplier Networks,* Oxford University Press, Oxford.

Fine, C.H. (1998) *Clockspeed: Winning Industry Control in the Age of Temporary Advantage,* Perseus Books, Reading, MA.

Fung, V.K., Fung, W.K. and Wind, Y. (2008) *Competing in a Flat World: Building Enterprises for a Borderless World,* Wharton School Publishing, Philadelphia, PA.

Hamel, G. and Prahalad, C.K. (1994) *Competing for the Future,* Harvard Business School Press, Boston, MA.

References

Brown, J.S., Durchslag, S. and Hagel III, J. (2002) 'Loosening up: how process networks unlock the power of specialization', *The McKinsey Quarterly, Special edition: Risk and Resilience,* 59–69.

Burt, D.N., Dobler, D.W. and Starling, S.L. (2003) *World Class Supply Management: The Key to Supply Chain Management,* 7th edn, McGraw-Hill/Irwin, Boston, MA.

Carbone, J. (1999) 'IBM to suppliers: how are we doing?', *Purchasing Magazine,* 18 September, 52.

Coase, R. (1937) 'The nature of the firm', *Economica,* **4**(16), 386–405.

Cousins, P.D. (2005) 'The alignment of appropriate firm and supply strategies for competitive advantage', *International Journal of Operations and Production Management,* **5**(3), 143–155.

Dyer, J.H. and Hatch, N.W. (2004) 'Using supplier networks to learn faster', *MIT Sloan Management Review,* **45**(3), 57–63.

European Commission (2003) 'Commission recommendation of 6 May 2003 concerning the definition of micro, small and medium-sized enterprises', *Official Journal of the European Union,* C(2003) 1422, L124/36–41.

Gartner, C.A. (2004) 'Offshoring in the service sector: economic impact and policy issues', *Economic Review – Federal Reserve Bank of Kansas City,* **98**(3), 5–37.

Green, A. (2019) 'Delia Smith: the original influencer?' National Science and Media Museum, 20 November, https://blog.scienceandmediamuseum.org.uk/the-delia-effect/

Jacobs, F.R. and Chase, R.B. (2008) *Operations and Supply Management: The Core,* McGraw-Hill/Irwin, New York.

OECD (Office for Economic Co-operation and Development) (2018) *Employment and Labour Market Statistics.* https://data.oecd.org/earnwage/average-wages.htm#indicator-chart (accessed 4 February 2020).

Siklos, R. (2009) 'Sony: lost in transformation', *Fortune Magazine,* 26 June, https://archive.fortune.com/2009/06/24/technology/sony_digital_transformation.fortune/index.htm (accessed January 2020)

Simon, H.A. (1957) *Models of Man: Social and Rational,* Wiley, New York.

Teece, D.J., Pisano, G. and Shuen, A. (1997) 'Dynamic capabilities and strategic management', *Strategic Management Journal,* **18**(7), 509–533.

Telegraph, The (2009) 'Delia effect strikes again', 3 December, https://www.telegraph.co.uk/culture/tvandradio/6709518/Delia-Effect-strikes-again.html

Williamson, O.E. (1975) *Market and Hierarchies: Analysis and Antitrust Implications,* Free Press, New York.

PART 3 Managing

Contents

JOBS

WANTED

Director of Operations

We are currently undergoing a period of rapid growth and have ambitious plans for the future. As Director of Operations, you will play a central role in growing the business and controlling operational activity. Leading a team of operations experts, your key challenge will be to create additional capability in our world-class manufacturing and service delivery.

This position has total responsibility for all operational activity including:

(1) The translation of corporate strategy into operational activity while setting and meeting performance targets

(2) Developing core competences and world-class operational processes

(3) Management of all operational staff in design, production, supply chain and service delivery areas

The right candidate will have at least 10 years of proven success driving business improvement, experience of managing large budgets, and knowledge of current operations management methodologies and principles. Most importantly, you will be an inspirational leader, capable of motivating, coaching and getting the best from your team.

What does it take to become an Operations Director?

We speak to Allan Gowans at Walker Group to find out about managing operations in an engineering company.

How did you get into Operations Management?
I joined the Walker Group in January 2020 after working with Rolls-Royce for 22 years. I began my career in Rolls Royce as an engineering apprentice and progressed from there. My last role with Rolls-Royce was Head of Operations within the Maintenance Repair and Overhaul business. It was a role in which required delivery of schedule, the management of unit cost, and leadership of over 300 employees. I have managed various different operational systems including low volume/high variety and high volume/low variety.

What was the most useful experience that prepared you for your current role?
One of the most useful experiences that prepared me for my current role was relocating a Rolls Royce operations facility. This was achieved without impacting production output. Within 18 months thousands of machine tools were relocated, commissioned, productionized and millions of parts co-ordinated all while maintaining customer satisfaction. When delivering a programme of such complexity it is imperative that you have a robust plan with clear actions, and identified owners. In addition a high level of engagement with all the workforce was required to ensure the success of the project. Communication is key in managing operations and it is the most important tool in your kit

What is a typical day of a Group Director of Operations?
A typical day starts with a 'stand-up' meeting with the extended leadership team, discussing the main elements of the operation system, quality, supply, delivery and cost. Then daily meetings with the satellite facilities are carried out, there are various planning meetings covering load and capacity, work in progress as well as engagement meetings with the workforce. The day finishes with a meeting with the executive board members and delivering a daily communication to the workforce.

What aspects of the job do you enjoy most?
I love being challenged, having to change and adapt and bringing order out of chaos. The key to Operations Management is to remove the variation from all processes. Doing all these things, creating a change and watching how people grow from it is what I enjoy the most.

What are the biggest challenges in the role?
In industry it is important to 'stay ahead of the curve'. Walker Group produce some very complex, machined components manufactured to extremely tight engineering tolerances. Building new capability and improving operational processes is key to being competitive and efficient. My first task when I started my current role was to appoint a Chief of Future Programmes. The purpose of that role is to understand how technology is evolving, and what we could do with this new technology. This appointment has already paid off in reductions in unit cost and process time and improvements in efficiency (all of which are related).

What do you consider the ideal skills for your job/ role?
I believe the key skills are to lead through trust and the ability to simplify things, like your vision and your operations system, this can be done using KPIs. It is important to be able to develop a strategy outlining where you want your organization to be in the next 6 months to 5 years then engage with the workforce to gather support for that vision. This is critical in making it a success.

7 Capacity Planning and Management

Learning Outcomes

After reading this chapter you should be able to:

- Define and measure capacity, and appreciate the factors that influence it
- Assess the difficulties of matching capacity to demand
- Evaluate and apply the different strategies for matching capacity with demand in the short, medium and long term
- Analyse the impact of constraints and bottlenecks on a process, and consider the theory of constraints
- Appreciate yield management as a tool for profit maximization with limited supply
- Outline the different strategies available for both manufacturing and service operations
- Explain and apply some key forecasting techniques, and understand the circumstances in which each method is appropriate

Waitrose and the Delia effect

Source: ©Adisa/Shutterstock

The supermarket industry has regularly used advertising and special offers to increase both overall demand for its stores and also demand for individual and seasonal products.

Waitrose and Partners, the high-end supermarket chain, recently abandoned its policy of not working with celebrities to endorse its products, by signing two world-famous celebrity chefs on a three-year deal. Delia Smith, a recipe writer, leading author and TV presenter joined forces with Heston Blumenthal, a maverick chef, famed for egg and bacon ice cream, cooking with dry ice, and other such inventive creations in the kitchen, to front the advertising campaign.

The campaign involves Smith and Blumenthal filming a series of television advertisements, as well as appearing on billboards and in magazine features. The advertising strategy for Waitrose and Partners is to demonstrate a number of seasonal products being used in a recipe every week, in television commercials, backed up by a poster campaign and in-house special offers. Most of the ads are short cookery programmes, with one or both of the cooks demonstrating the various recipes; some ads last the whole advertising break of three and a half minutes. Richard Hodgson, Waitrose and Partners' commercial director, said: 'Every week will be a totally amazing new idea. Sometimes it will be a recipe, sometimes visiting a supplier or farmer, maybe even demonstrating a kitchen utensil.' He promised that viewers would not be bombarded with some of Blumenthal's more wacky recipes. 'Don't worry; we won't start selling snail porridge or liquid nitrogen. But I don't see why Heston couldn't demonstrate how a blowtorch can be used to get the top of crème brûlée crispy.'

Ocado, Waitrose and Partners' distribution supplier, has restructured its website to allow customers to order products direct from the online recipe. Waitrose and Partners has allocated prime locations on the end of the refrigerated aisles, with all the ingredients for the week's campaign grouped together and on a special offer price.

It has not all been plain sailing, though. The campaign received criticism for the timing of a particular ad for Delia Smith's rhubarb and ginger brûlée. The ad was screened so early in the year that British rhubarb growers were unable to meet the resulting demand. The well-known phenomenon of the 'Delia effect' meant that Waitrose and Partners sold enough of the plant for 61,000 desserts in four days alone, or the same quantity that it usually sells in 12 weeks. British growers said they simply could not meet the spike in demand. Much of Britain's rhubarb is grown in a small area of West Yorkshire between Bradford, Wakefield and Leeds, known as the Rhubarb Triangle. Early in the year growers 'force' it by growing the plant in heated sheds, but there is limited capacity. Janet Oldroyd, of the Yorkshire Rhubarb Growers' Association, said this season's crop had been delayed by cold weather, further reducing output. A Waitrose and Partners spokesman said that sales of rhubarb were 'so extreme' following the recipe being published online that it had to source from abroad.

A Delia recipe for fish risotto caused a backlash even from diehard Delia fans, when it was described as 'vile' on the discussion section of the Waitrose and Partners website. One customer wrote, 'I bought the very expensive ingredients for the seafood risotto, expecting to lay on a treat for my family. We all had one mouthful and gagged. It was disgusting, to say the very least. The entire meal went in the bin, and we all had toast instead.' Following the initial reactions to the recipe from news programmes, Waitrose and Partners appeared to be left with excess stock of the ingredients.

There is a requirement when planning these campaigns for Waitrose and Partners to have a greater understanding of what might impact upon supply of the products, and how much is likely to be demanded. This must be done within the supply chain, and the supermarket may need to be flexible within this plan to prevent further problems. Overall, however, Waitrose and Partners has seen an increase in demand for its products, and is encouraging customers to be more seasonal with their selection of goods. This enables the suppliers to meet the supermarket's demand more easily.

Sources: 'Delia Smith: The Original Influencer', https://blog.scienceandmediamuseum.org.uk/the-delia-effect/, 20 November 2019; 'Delia Effect Strikes Again', https://www.telegraph.co.uk/culture/tvandradio/6709518/Delia-Effect-strikes-again.html, Daily Telegraph, 3 December 2009.

Introduction

The case demonstrates how complicated it can be to deal with the unpredictability of demand, and how difficult it can be to match this to the supply of goods and services and still have an efficiently run operation. The difficulty of meeting customer shopping patterns (**demand**) with what the suppliers and therefore the supermarket can provide (**capacity**) is a complicated timing issue (**forecasting**). Providing the right amount of product at the correct time requires careful planning and investment decisions.

Demand the quantity of goods and services demanded by consumers.

Capacity the maximum goods or services that an operation can produce.

Forecast predicting the future, normally based on historical data with some interpretation.

There are three things an operation must consider when looking at production of goods and services:

- *Capacity:* How much can it make?
- *Demand:* How much does the market require?
- *Forecasting:* How can the operation match what is required with what it can make, without wasting resources?

These factors all impact upon each other. In order to fulfil the requirements of a market, an operation must be able to evaluate what capacity it can provide, and the options it has to increase or decrease this.

It is not just a case of offering the amount of goods or services wanted; it is also important to time when they are required. This can give an operation several problems when attempting to plan capacity.

An operation may experience many changes and fluctuations in the demand for its products or services, and must be able to maximize the opportunities of demand without having excess capacity. For example, the daily demand for a restaurant often peaks in the evening, but this may not be the only pattern in demand; the weekend may be busier than a weekday, and there may be other events, such as Valentine's Day or the Christmas period, when demand may be expected to increase.

The provision of capacity is a decision that should not be taken lightly; once implemented it cannot easily be reversed, and the operation is then left to manage the choice it has made.

This chapter considers how capacity can be provided, adjusted and managed in order to satisfy the customer's demand and meet the operation's objectives, as efficiently as possible.

Capacity Management

Capacity management affects all areas of an operation. Capacity measures the rate at which the operation can transform inputs into outputs. Capacity is about the *quantity* of a product or service that can be delivered within a *given time period.* This could be, for example:

- The number of passengers per flight on an aeroplane
- The number of patients who can be seen in a surgery session at a doctors' practice
- The number of mobile phones that can be produced in a week by a factory.

Capacity is defined as the number of units (of goods and/or services) that an operation can produce over a given time period, under normal working conditions, without deploying additional resources.

Capacity is usually measured in convenient units, such as litres per hour or passengers per taxi. For instance, a domestic tap may be able to deliver 20 litres of water per minute; a bus may have a capacity of 53 passengers; a football stadium may be able to seat 50,000 spectators; or a branch of McDonald's may be able to serve 600 customers per hour.

Capacity may often be simple to calculate, but not always. More difficult questions might be, for example:

- How many fire engines should an airport have on standby?
- How many operations should a surgeon schedule?
- What service level should be offered to broadband customers?

When planning capacity, there are always two aspects to consider. First, there is the demand – the amount of the product or service that might be wanted. Second, there is the provision of the good or service. In providing products or services, the operation must evaluate the costs involved, and the trade-off between satisfying customers and the costs of production. Having too little capacity to respond to customer demand may mean missed opportunities and annoyed customers, but underutilized capacity is a waste of resources, resulting in higher costs.

Aggregate planning a top-level look at demand for the operation as a whole; does not differentiate between different products and services.

Long-term capacity plan a relatively high level plan covering strategic decision 1–3 years ahead.

Medium-term capacity plan a capacity plan covering tactical decisions 3–12 months ahead.

Short-term capacity plan an active and often reactive plan covering all the detail needed to carry out the operation.

Aggregate Planning

Capacity decisions happen at a series of different levels where, in descending order, each level represents a greater degree of refinement. At the highest level is **aggregate capacity** planning where overall numbers are used to develop new facilities or plan investments in equipment. For example, how many hotels should Hilton have globally in the next decade? This is a very strategic decision based on international financial outlook and global trends. The next level is to break this top level capacity down to think about how best to use the resources of the firm to meet this strategy. This is often called the **long-term capacity plan**. So Hilton would now have to decide for the next few years which regions are most valuable and how many properties to have in a certain country or city. We have moved from a top level aggregate plan where we added all the hotels together, hence aggregated, to think about how we should start to carry out the plan and make it happen. This plan will then be broken down to a more tactical level or **medium-term capacity plan**. For Hilton this is where they consider the detail of which brand of hotel to deploy and when to phase their opening and renovation over certain months or weeks as well as what staff to recruit or train.

These plans are even further broken down with more detail and consideration given to product mix and inventory in the **short-term capacity plan**. This also links into the daily management of the operation and is interrelated with the inventory plans discussed in Chapter 9. These represent how the firm carries out its daily operations. For example, within each hotel Hilton also has short-term capacity plans considering each day or week ensuring that there are enough staff rostered, towels provided or food available in the restaurant to keep the customers happy.

Chapter 9, p289

Source: ©Kim Lewis Photography/Shutterstock

Adjusting Capacity

Discrepancies between an organization's capacity and its customers' demands result in inefficiency, either in underutilized resources or in dissatisfied customers. The former may be a serious cost, but the latter may result in lost sales, lost customers and loss of reputation. The operation's ability to adjust its key resources will minimize these discrepancies.

Some capacity changes can happen almost instantly, such as asking employees for 30 minutes overtime at the end of the day to complete an order. But others, such as adding a new machine, may take longer to put in place as doing this takes time to develop the specification, purchase and install.

As a result, an operation's capacity is made up of a complicated mix of transforming resources. These resources are inputs to the process and changes to these allow capacity to be expanded or contracted. How flexible the resource is depends on how much and how quickly it can be altered.

Capacity can be increased by various methods that involve adjusting the resources and inputs into an operation, such as:

- Introducing new approaches and materials
- Increasing the number of service providers or machines
- Increasing the number of operational hours
- Acquiring additional facilities.

It is often more difficult and expensive to decrease capacity as an operation needs to sell or reduce resources as cost-effectively as possible. There are usually costs involved in reducing resources – for example, if the resource is staff, there may be redundancy costs; and closing facilities may incur demolition or selling costs.

Therefore the decision to alter capacity has to be taken carefully, in line with predictions of future demand, and is often difficult to quickly reverse.

Capacity Constraints

A **constraint** is a resource that is less capable of increasing or decreasing its throughput over a given time period when compared with other parts of the operation. For example, in a production line one machine may not be able to process as many units per hour as the others and so the line's capacity is constrained by this machine, or in the wind farm case the poor connection to the grid (see Short Case 7.1 for more information). We often say it creates a bottleneck in the process. It may be possible to increase the machine's capacity by adding additional resources, or replacing it with a better one. This will also increase the capacity of the whole facility.

Capacity is always constrained by the slowest or smallest capacity task in a process: an operation will always go 'at the pace of the slowest walker'. Identifying restrictions in the process, and adding resources that can increase the output of the constraint, will improve the overall capacity of the operation.

Constraint a restriction on the running of an operation.

To investigate the constraints of an operation we can consider the *resource mix* which is made up of the individual transforming inputs. The mix includes:

- *Staff/skill levels:* Staff can be trained over time to be more flexible in their contribution to the process. A new employee can become more efficient at a given process over time and therefore become quicker at his or her job which can increase the operation's capacity.
- *IT /technology:* Investment in IT can reduce process time, or even completely change the nature of the process itself. For example, the introduction of online banking has brought significant improvements to the finance sector by reducing the number of staff required to process individual transactions. This therefore increases the bank's capacity to deal with its customers.
- *Material availability:* A change in the supply of raw materials can affect the operation's capacity. Any restriction in the availability of materials or poor timing can reduce capacity. Once this is remedied the capacity is improved.
- *Product or service mix:* Adjustments in other products or services that the operation delivers can restrict its capacity. This is because different products and services use different resources and so changing the product mix can free resources to increase capacity.
- *Storage:* If an operation has the ability to store work in progress or finished goods it can improve the capacity of the process as fluctuations in demand can be more easily met. The ability to store products allows the full capacity to be utilized.
- *Working schedules and access to facilities:* Time available can also dictate capacity availability. A lecture theatre could operate beyond a standard working day to increase capacity, but both staff and students might be reluctant to support 6 a.m. or 10 p.m. lectures.

These factors can be addressed in varying time frames. Some can be easily dealt with in the short term, but others can only be addressed in the long term. For instance, a short-term strategy for expanding a café's capacity would be to put a few extra tables outside, or extend staff working hours. In the medium term the café owner would have more options available to increase capacity, such as hiring more staff, or installing additional cooking facilities in the kitchen. In the long term the possibilities can be much greater: the premises could be expanded, better equipment could be purchased, and more staff could be hired. The options available to an operation increase if there is more time to plan and implement them.

Theory of Constraints

The theory of constraints (TOC) was proposed by Eliyahu Goldratt (1984). TOC is a philosophy that suggests that any system always has *at least one constraint,* otherwise it would generate an infinite amount of output. The constraint also determines the pace of an organization's ability to achieve its goal, which is usually profit.

Goldratt emphasizes that constraints pose a significant threat to the well-being of an organization and must be identified. He suggests that constraints may be labour availability, staff skills, machine availability, and capital or time available – or they may be more difficult to identify, such as organizational policies, guiding principles or the rate of innovation.

There is rarely an equal flow of work within each work centre or task in a process. The constraint – the bottleneck – therefore controls the pace of the process. TOC reduces emphasis on maximizing all resources within a process, and instead prioritizes management of the bottleneck. Goldratt advocates a methodology he calls *drum–buffer–rope.* The bottleneck is the 'drum' that marks the time through the process. Because of insufficient capacity in this section this should be continually busy. The 'buffer' is required to make sure that the bottleneck is never short of work and therefore the front end of the process should stockpile inventory to maximize throughput. The 'rope' is the communication device that makes sure the front part of the process does not *over* produce.

Goldratt's Five Focusing Steps

TOC sets out a five-step process that an operation should follow in order to free the system from the bottleneck slowing it down:

1. Identify the system's bottleneck that constrains the process.
2. Exploit the system's constraints and establish the resources required to remove them.
3. Subordinate everything else to the above decision. This requires full management support to make sure the steps are followed.

Figure 7.1 The bottleneck point in a simple process

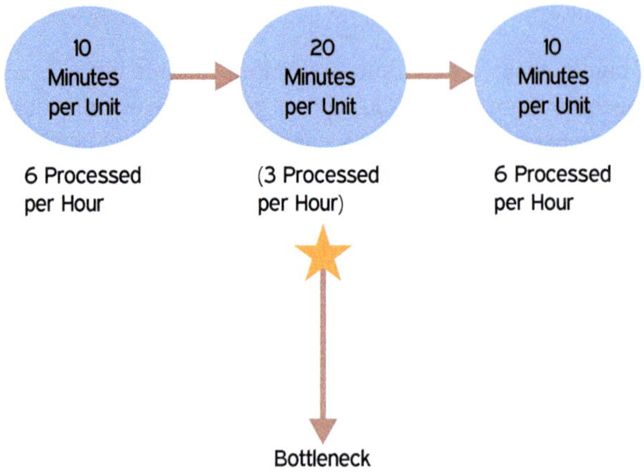

4. Elevate the system's constraints (identify the next constraint). Once this bottleneck is removed the next constraint in the process needs to be found.
5. If a constraint has been removed in a previous step, go back to step 1, but do not allow inertia to become the system's constraint.

By following these steps the operation identifies and clears a blockage. This moves the system constraint to a new bottleneck and the five steps can start again.

Goldratt advises that the identification of any constraint is only transitional. When this constraint is removed, another will appear in its place.

In Figure 7.1, the output of the process will be constrained by its slowest point. This is referred to as a *bottleneck* in the process.

It is not always possible to predict accurately how long each stage is going to take. A hairdresser, for example, may allocate 30 minutes for the haircut, 40 minutes for hair dyeing and 10 minutes for styling, but some individual customers may take more time and others less. In such processes with much variability it may not be possible to locate the bottleneck accurately.

This shows an important feature of capacity planning. In order to understand an operation's output, and hence plan the process, we need to make assumptions about what it is capable of, but often we find that these assumptions are inaccurate.

Constraint analysis is a subject far larger than the subject of capacity management, but it does offer an important perspective on the question 'Is all capacity equally important?'

SHORT CASE 7.1

Wind Energy: Where's the Constraint?

According to the China Wind Energy Association, the power output generated by wind farms in China has not met expectations. Less than 80% of the power created has reached the national grid. The reason given for this underperformance is that, although new wind farms and turbines have been set up and are working as planned, their output has not been reaching the grid effectively for around the first 3–4 months.

Differences in wind resources can partly explain the disparity, but insufficient investment in grid connections plays a key part. The problem appears to be that the regions where wind resources are most abundant

Source: ©Shutterstock/chaiviewfinder

tend to have the weakest grid connections. In addition, some wind farms are generating more power than initial estimates and their output is rejected by the local grid companies because of concerns that it would overload their systems.

Wind farms generally have smaller generation capacity than coal-fired power plants and their output is less stable as they are subject to variable wind speed. As a result, the return on investment from wind power is lower for grid operators. The utilization rate of mainland wind farms in China is currently much lower than that of comparable projects operating in the UK or USA.

Questions

1. What resources are needed to reduce or remove the current bottleneck?
2. Where could the next bottleneck occur if this bottleneck is reduced or removed?

Source: 'Wind power loses puff – infrastructure to tap captured energy is lagging headlong capacity expansion', *South China Morning Post*, 13 July 2009.

The key point is ...

a constraint will restrict the operation's capacity. If this constraint is reduced, or even removed, capacity will increase. A constraint can be reduced by increasing the resource in the bottleneck.

Measuring Capacity

When measuring capacity the unit of measure can be either an input to or an output from the process. The key is to take the unit that best reflects the operation's ability to create and deliver its product or service. If inputs are too complicated to measure, then output measures may be more suitable. For example, factories are more often measured on units produced per day than on machine-hours utilized; and retail units can be measured on takings per day rather than on staff-hours employed. A suitable unit of measure could be volume, size, or rate of throughput but the unit of output and timescale needs to be *consistent*, that is, if you start measuring your capacity in hotel *rooms* available it is not comparable to switch to number of *beds* available.

Input Measures of Capacity

Where the provision of capacity is fixed it is often easier to measure capacity by inputs, for example the rooms available in a hotel or seats at a conference venue. When using input measures of capacity, the measure selected is defined by the key input into the process. Input measures are most appropriate for small processes, or where capacity is relatively fixed, or for highly customized or variable outputs, such as complicated services.

Output Measures of Capacity

Output measures count the finished units from the process, such as mobile phones produced in a day, or cars manufactured per week. They are best used when there is low variety in the product mix, or limited customization.

Capacity can be measured by looking at the operation as a whole and then calculating the resources or facilities available and the process time. Table 7.1 shows examples of the alternatives that can be used for input and output measures.

Table 7.1 Examples of possible input and output measures

Process	Input capacity measure	Output capacity measure
Music festival	Square metres of land	Number of festival attendees
Hotel	Rooms available	Number of guests per week
Car-manufacturing plant	Machine capacity	Cars produced per month
Milk-bottling plant	Machine-hours available	Bottles filled per day
Lecture theatre	Number of seats available	Students on courses
Wedding planning service	Consultants available	Weddings per season

For example, the measure of output capacity could be cars per shift, or tonnes per hour, or customers per day. However, the capacity of a surgeon or a university professor may not be measured in this manner: in these cases, capacity could be shown in the form of working hours per week.

A simple formula for capacity is:

$$\text{Capacity} = \frac{\text{Time available}}{\text{Time needed for task}}$$

WORKED EXAMPLE 7.1

Calculating Output

A fitness instructor works an 8-hour day, takes two 15-minute coffee breaks, and has a half-hour lunch break. The time available for work is 7 hours per worker per day.

Problem: *If the instructor spends 60 minutes with each customer (10 minutes for the consultation and booking, and 50 minutes for the gym session), how many clients could the instructor process during a 5-day week?*

Approach

$$\text{Design capacity} = \frac{\text{Time available}}{\text{Time needed for task}}$$

where ***time available*** is the hours in the day for working (which excludes breaks), and the number of days worked in the week. The example has an 8-hour working day. The instructor works a 5-day week, so this is multiplied by 5.

The ***time needed for task*** is the number of minutes spent with each client, which in this case is 60.

Solution

$$\text{Number of clients per week} = \frac{(8 \text{ hours per day} \times 60 \text{ minutes per hour}) \times 5}{60 \text{ minutes per client}} = 40$$

The design capacity of the fitness operation can be expressed as 40 clients per week.

This is a simplified measure, because it assumes that the fitness instructor doesn't have time off sick, or do any other activities such as maintain the gym equipment, or diversify into other areas such as taking classes.

Most processes will not have just one activity; many will have interlinking processes, with different capacity constraints on each. In such cases management will have to consider the capacity of the whole process, rather than individual constituent processes..

Utilization actual output shown as a percentage of the operation's design capacity; demonstrates how well the operation is working to expectations.

Efficiency actual output shown as a percentage of the operation's effective capacity; demonstrates how well the operation is working to expectations.

Design capacity the expected output of an operation when there are no stoppages.

Defining Capacity

We can calculate an operation's **utilization** of resources, and the **efficiency** of its processes, by considering three categories of capacity: design capacity, effective capacity and actual capacity.

Design capacity is a theoretical number; it is not applied to the daily production of an operation. Design capacity is the output that an operation can produce continuously, at *maximum rate without stopping* for any shift changeovers, maintenance or other delays. It is what the process is capable of producing under perfect conditions. In some cases this might be interpreted as an operation's *maximum capacity.*

Effective capacity considers how the operation will run in the long term, how it will be staffed, and how it will be maintained. All *planned* stoppages in the normal working time frame are taken into consideration. It is also known as *available capacity.* The planned stoppages may include operational factors such as shift changeovers, lunch breaks and set-up times.

Figure 7.2 The proportions of capacity measures

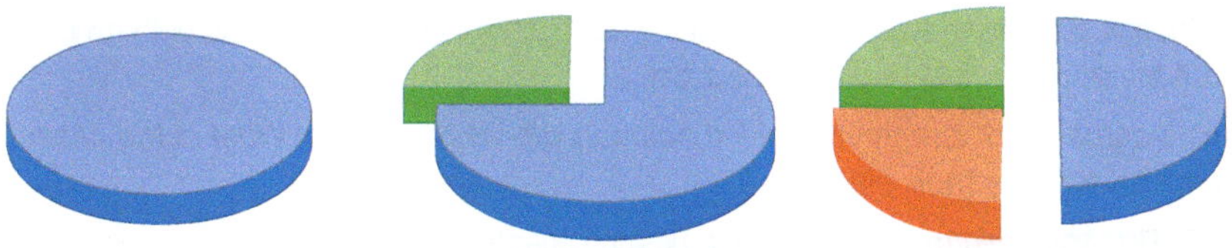

Actual capacity is the same as effective capacity but contains *unplanned losses* as well as planned ones. These could include poor work rate, absenteeism, or new staff training, for example.

Actual output plus unplanned losses is the same as effective capacity (see Figure 7.2). Therefore an operation that is working its assets efficiently is minimizing unplanned losses.

The *actual capacity*, when applied to individual machines or tasks, is sometimes known as the **overall equipment effectiveness (OEE)**. This tells the operation how well the equipment is being used. By using such measures the equipment can be evaluated, and its contribution assessed. A similar measure can be applied to the contribution of people, and is sometimes known as the **overall professional effectiveness (OPE)**.

Effective capacity the expected output of an operation considering planned stoppages for maintenance, shift changeovers etc.

Actual capacity the expected output of an operation, considering both planned stoppages and unplanned stoppages.

Overall equipment effectiveness (OEE) actual capacity when applied to individual machines; tells the operation how well the equipment is being used.

Overall professional effectiveness (OPE) actual capacity when applied to individual workers; tells the operation how well the employee is performing.

Efficiency and Utilization Calculations

The efficient use of the resources available is assessed by calculating output shown as a percentage of effective capacity:

$$\text{Efficiency} = \frac{\text{Actual output}}{\text{Effective capacity}} \times 100$$

In an operation that has been well designed, there will be minimal planned losses. This allows the resources to be used to the best of their ability. Capacity utilization is the measure of how much of the available capacity is used. Utilization is output shown as a percentage of the design capacity.

$$\text{Utilization} = \frac{\text{Actual output}}{\text{Design capacity}} \times 100$$

For example, if the fitness trainer in the previous example had only 24 clients who arrived at their appointments on time, the calculation would be:

$$\text{Utilization} = \frac{24}{40} \times 100 = 60\%$$

Therefore the utilization rate is 60%.

These measures of capacity can inform managers about how well resources are being utilized, and how efficient a process is.

WORKED EXAMPLE 7.2

Calculating Capacity Measurements

Imagine you are managing a group of 10 electricians. They undertake in-home servicing of electrical systems, and are called by telephone for either emergency or pre-arranged visits. They charge a minimum call-out fee that covers the first 15 minutes of their visit plus travelling time. Beyond the first 15 minutes they charge in blocks of 15 minutes, plus the cost of any materials that they need to complete the job. The average call-out takes 1 hour.

The electricians are usually available for 8 hours a day but, with two coffee breaks of 15 minutes each and a half-hour lunch break, they actually work a 7-hour day.

Problem: *If actual work is only 200 billed hours in the week then: (a) What is the capacity utilization of the team? (b) What is their efficiency?*

Approach: First you need to calculate (a) the design capacity and (b) the effective capacity. Then use the actual output given above to calculate the capacity utilization and efficiency.

$$\text{Design capacity} = \frac{10 \text{ workers} \times 8 \text{ hours per day}}{1 \text{ hour per customer call-out}} \times 5 \text{ days of a working week}$$

$$= 400 \text{ customers per week}$$

$$\text{Effective capacity} = \frac{10 \text{ workers} \times 7 \text{ hours per day}}{1 \text{ hour per customer call-out}} \times 5 \text{ days of a working week}$$

$$= 350 \text{ customers per week}$$

Note: 8 hours per day has reduced to 7 hours per day

(a) If actual work is only 200 billed hours in the week, then what is the capacity utilization of the team?

$$\text{Capacity utilization} = \frac{\text{Actual output}}{\text{Design capacity}} = \frac{200}{400} \times 100$$

$$= 50\%$$

Note: Actual output is 200 billed hours

Solution: The utilization of the process is 50%.

(b) If actual work is only 200 billed hours in the week, then what is their efficiency?

$$\text{Efficiency} = \frac{\text{Actual output}}{\text{Effective capacity}} = \frac{200}{350} \times 100$$

$$= 57\%$$

Note: Actual output is 200 billed hours

Solution: The efficiency of the process is 57%.

Takt Time and Cycle Time

In the above example, we suggested that the time taken to service each customer was 1 hour. This is often referred to as the *cycle time,* and can be applied to individual tasks or a whole process.

Takt time can be defined as the time allocated to each unit for making a product or providing a service in order to meet the customer demand. This is the rate at which the customer requires the product, and defines the speed of the manufacturing line.

Cycle time usually determines the output rate for manufacturing lines. For instance, in automobile manufacturing, cars are assembled on an assembly line, and are moved from station to station after a certain time: this is the cycle time. In a fast-food restaurant the service time for each order would also be called the cycle time.

Takt time can be used to compare with cycle time when balancing workloads. Ideally, the cycle time should be close to, but should not exceed, the takt time.

Takt time can be determined with the formula:

$$T = \frac{T_a}{T_d}$$

Where T is the takt time (e.g. rate at which work/unit should be produced); T_a is the time available to work (e.g. minutes of work/day); and T_d is the average (customer) demand (e.g. units required/day).

WORKED EXAMPLE 7.3

Calculating Takt Time

An assembly line has a total of 8 hours available time in a shift. The employees working the shifts have a half-hour lunch break and two 15-minute tea breaks in each shift. The machines also require 10 minutes per shift in basic maintenance. At the start of each working day, the supervisor spends 10 minutes talking to the staff, and setting goals for the shift ahead.

Problem: ***Calculate the available time to work for the line, and the takt time for 100 units per day.***

Approach: You will need to calculate the total time in the working shift, and then subtract the non-working time to determine the available time (i.e. the OEE or OPE).

Solution: 8 hours per shift is 480 minutes. Take away 30 minutes for lunch, 30 minutes for breaks (2 × 15 minutes), 10 minutes for a team briefing, and 10 minutes for basic maintenance work:

$$\text{The available time to work (i.e. OEE or OPE)} = 480 - 30 - 30 - 10 - 10 = 400 \text{ minutes.}$$

If output demand was for 100 units a day, and you were running one shift, then the line would be allowed to spend a maximum of 4 minutes to make a product in order to be able to keep up with demand of 100 units per shift.

The ***takt time*** would be 4 minutes.

The available time is the amount of time available for work to be done. This excludes break times and any expected stoppage time (e.g. scheduled maintenance, team briefings); this is also referred to as overall equipment effectiveness (OEE) or overall professional effectiveness (OPE) as in Chapter 5.

Chapter 5, p139

Capacity Planning

We have already seen how capacity plans can happen at different levels of aggregation from long to short term. In each of these an organization needs to decide how it is to manage its capacity and has several ways in which it can respond to the changes in demand with its provision of capacity. The decision to provide capacity depends upon the selected strategy, the ability to store the product, and the timeliness of service production. The timing decisions of how and when to provide capacity need to be determined in line with demand.

Capacity Planning Methods

The organization has three main choices:

1. It can provide capacity ahead of the forecast, so that it is ready to respond immediately. This is known as a *capacity leads demand* strategy.
2. It can provide capacity as demand changes, so that it expands and contracts its capacity to follow demand. This is a *capacity matches demand* strategy.
3. It can wait to see what demand is, and then respond after it is confirmed. This is a *capacity lags demand* strategy.

Capacity Leads Demand

It is possible to have excess capacity ready to react to an increase in demand as *ready and available* capacity. This is therefore an opportunistic strategy with the purpose of attracting customers away from competitors.

This capacity strategy offers the advantage that the operation is ready to satisfy customer demand and meet short-term opportunities. However, there is a risk of demand not rising, in which case the operation is left with unnecessary costs and excess unused capacity.

It is an expensive way of providing capacity as it requires investment to be made ahead of demand, but it is a useful strategy if the organization is trying to build market share and establish good customer relationships – these are benefits that can outweigh the cost of providing excess capacity.

An example of a capacity leads demand approach would be building an extension to a lecture theatre before increased student numbers were confirmed.

Capacity Matches Demand

This strategy is adopted for the provision of capacity in line with demand. Capacity is increased in measured amounts in response to changing demand in the market. This is usually accomplished with flexible resources.

This strategy relies heavily on forecasting and accurate information, as investment decisions are made in line with the forecast. Incorrect forecasting will cause missed opportunities or wasted resources.

This strategy is often used in services, where staff are the flexible resource; they can be brought in to cover peak demand, and then sent home in quieter times – a toy store catering to the Christmas rush, for example, or a restaurant expanding and contracting its staff in line with anticipated peaks and troughs in customer demand at different times of the day.

Capacity Lags Demand

Here increments of capacity are added after the demand has increased by providing capacity after the demand has risen. This allows the organization to provide capacity with certainty, and reduces the risk of unnecessary investment in capacity increases. However, this method does rely on the ability to provide products and services on short lead times, and assumes that the customer is prepared to wait.

This is less risky than providing investment ahead of demand. However, it has the disadvantage that customers may not be prepared to wait for the product or service, and opportunities can therefore be lost.

Capacity Timing

The ability to increase or decrease capacity can be planned over three time periods: short term, medium term and long term.

Short-term planning is predominantly reactive, and can be almost immediate, for example if capacity is adjusted on the same day, or may be over a period of up to 3 months (depending on the industry). Typically, only flexible resources can be applied to increase the capacity. It may be costly for the operation because the cost of adjusting the resources may be higher on short-term timescales. In many cases, employees are the most readily available resource. Examples of this might include overtime for existing staff, or having multi-skilled staff who can be reallocated to where a bottleneck has occurred. An example of the latter could be the call on the PA system in a supermarket, requesting 'all till-trained staff to report to the checkout' in order to increase capacity when queues are growing.

Medium-term planning changes are not implemented immediately; they typically have a horizon ranging between 3 and 12 months. In the medium term an operation has more time to make plans to adjust capacity, and therefore the changes tend to be more fundamental than short-term changes. They might include hiring or firing contract staff, or leasing additional facilities. For example, the postal service recruits temporary or casual staff to cover the Christmas period and starts this recruitment drive in the summer.

Long-term planning changes are typically over 12 to 18 months. Here the investment decisions tend to be more fundamental than the short or medium term, and will link to the organization's strategy. The changes will take a long time to implement, and may also be difficult to reverse. They could include new full-time staff, new faster processes, or investment in new machinery. A hotel chain, for example, may decide to build a new annex if it knows there is a new exhibition venue or tourist attraction opening in the town.

With each of these options the ability to make the adjustment depends on the nature of the individual process, and on the industry in which it is found. Some industries, such as the software industry, change very rapidly, and changes can be implemented much more quickly than in industries such as shipbuilding or oil production.

Staff training is another issue. A fast-food restaurant may be able to recruit and reassign staff easily as training is relatively simple for a new employee and investment costs are low. In comparison, a hospital may not be able to hire or reassign skilled surgeons as they take many years to train.

SHORT CASE 7.2

Etihad Stadium, Manchester

Source: ©Cosmin Iftode/Shutterstock

The stadium used by Manchester City Football Club was originally designed to be the central arena for the Manchester bid to host the 1996 Olympics. When the games were awarded to Atlanta, the City of Manchester refocused its efforts on the Commonwealth Games bid for 2002, which it won.

The stadium was originally planned as an 80,000-seat arena for the Olympics. This was revised down to a 60,000 capacity stadium for the Commonwealth Games. The Council's main concern, though, was that the stadium should have a sustainable future, and so the plan was revised down again to accommodate a future for the stadium as the new ground for Manchester City FC, to replace its Maine Road stadium in Moss Side. The revised plan meant that the capacity for the Games in 2002 was 38,000, which then rose to 48,000 in 2003 when the stadium was handed over to Manchester City FC and currently has a capacity of 55,097.

Construction of the stadium took 3,000 workers just over 2 years to complete, and it was handed over to the organizers four months ahead of the Games. The Commonwealth Games was a spectacular success, both for British athletes and for the City of Manchester. But no sentiment was shown when the bulldozers moved in, just hours after the closing ceremony. The track was removed, a third tier of seating was added, and the central pitch was lowered. The conversion costs of £30 million were met by the football club.

This plan was not without criticism, as there were many calls by leading athletes for a large athletics stadium to be retained, but there were parallels elsewhere: the stadiums from the Sydney and Atlanta Olympics became rugby and baseball grounds respectively. The City of Manchester Stadium has also been used as a concert venue, and has a capacity for 60,000 music fans, making it one of Europe's largest open air concert venues.

There are 2,000 parking spaces at the stadium, and a further 8,000 spaces provided locally. There are two train stations within a half-hour walk of the ground, and for concerts and special events a bus service is set up. The stadium is used twice weekly during the football season, and also hosts conferences, major sporting events, and even weddings.

Questions

1. How has long-term planning affected the final result for the City of Manchester Stadium?
2. Why was the original capacity for the Commonwealth Games stadium reduced from 60,000 to 38,000?
3. What other large facilities have changed use from their original purpose, and have they been as successful as the City of Manchester Stadium?

Sources: http://www.gameslegacy.co.uk/cgi-bin/index.cgi/30 http://www.football-rumours.com/manchester_stadium.htm

Anticipating Changes in Demand

Demand can be volatile; it is something that tends to happen 'to' an operation. It exists outside the organization, and is therefore difficult to control. It is subject to many influences, which are summarized in Figure 7.3.

- *Changing tastes* – these can be hard to plan for. Fashions change, and new ideas occur. For example, the gradual trend towards a more environmentally friendly lifestyle has resulted in a slow and steady evolution of products and services to follow this trend. There can also be sudden unpredictable swings or

Figure 7.3 The external factors affecting demand

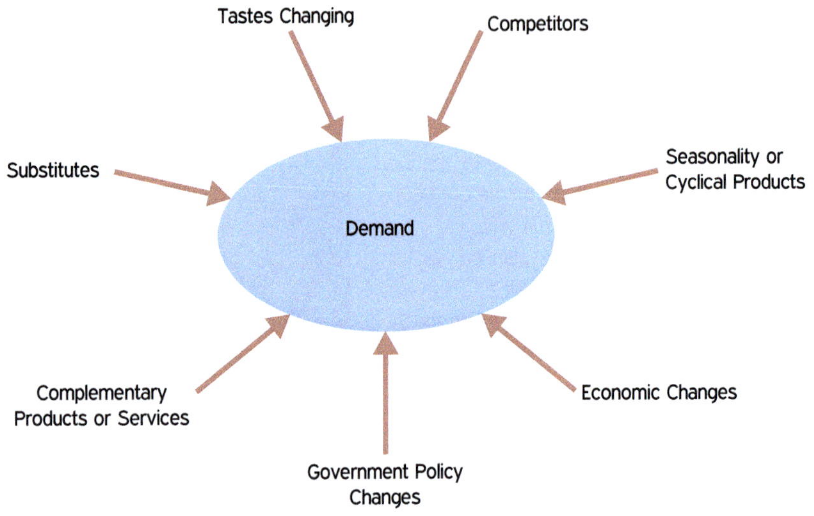

changes of fashion that it is virtually impossible to plan for: for example, an influential celebrity may be seen using a product or service which creates a sudden increase in demand.

- *Competition* – the demand for an organization's product or service will be highly dependent on the actions and reactions of its competitors. There may be a steady demand for the product the organization offers, but this can be severely affected if a competitor brings out a new, improved or even cheaper version of the product. The organization must be aware of its competitors, and how they may impact upon future demand.
- *Substitutes* – similarly, an alternative product may become available and divert the market demand for the product.
- *Seasonality* – many products are naturally seasonal. For example, ice cream, fireworks and fluffy St Valentine's day teddy bears all have a time period where demand will peak. The nature of this peak relates to the particular product or service, and demand for it at a given time. For example, sunscreen sales in the UK peak in June and July, with a lower demand during the rest of the year for travel abroad, whereas Christmas cards have only the short window of demand in the months up to Christmas, before dropping to insignificant levels until the following Christmas. With a seasonal event, the previous year's demand can be used as an indicator for predicting future demand patterns.
- *Cyclical events* are similar to seasonal demand peaks, as they are regularly repeating events, but they may not necessarily occur at specific calendar dates – for example, daily commuter demands on transportation systems, or weekly shopping cycles that place high demands on shop car parking at weekends.
- *Special events* are one-off unique events that have very little or no demand pattern or history, such as the Olympics, or the football World Cup, which while appearing cyclical are actually unique events as the locations are a key factor. They are the most complicated to plan or predict demand for.
- *The external environment* may also affect demand patterns, with influences such as change in laws and government policy.
- *Economic changes* such as tax or mortgage rates, for example, will have a significant impact on demand for goods and services and will affect buying habits and behaviours.

The key point is ...

. . . it is essential to try to understand demand patterns, and their predictability.

SHORT CASE 7.3

Unpredictable Demand

Source: © Ingrid Emilie S Hansen/Shutterstock

On 27 March 2007 the BBC's ***Horizon*** programme screened the results of a study of Boots' No7 Protect & Perfect Beauty Serum. A team of dermatologists, led by Professor Chris Griffiths, carried out an independent study into anti-ageing cosmetic products. The effect of No7 Protect & Perfect was compared with that of retinoic acid, a prescription drug used to treat severe photo-ageing of the skin, and the only product known to have a clinical effect on facial lines and wrinkles. The research revealed that in laboratory tests, pioneered by the research team, No7 Protect & Perfect Beauty Serum really could repair fine wrinkles damage associated with photo-aged skin.

In the days following the airing of the programme, the £16.75 Boots serum product sold out. Within 10 days of the show the sales volume – usually 1,000 pots of the lotion per week – reached 60,000. Ian Filby, the Beauty Director of Boots, said: 'We have been overwhelmed with the response following BBC's ***Horizon***, with women literally racing each other to get hold of the last product in stores. We are getting more stock out to our stores on an hourly basis to meet demand.'

To cope with the sudden increase in demand, Boots issued a policy of ***one product per customer*** in order to dissuade consumers from reselling product on auction sites. A waiting list was then introduced; approximately 50,000 customers signed up for the product, and orders were being received from as far afield as the USA and Australia. Despite Boots' efforts to control sales, the product was being sold on eBay for up to five times its original price.

It took several months for supply to be fully restored. Despite other less optimistic studies, the product continues to be a top seller for Boots, and the range is sold around the world. Protect & Perfect Beauty Serum remains the fastest-selling product in Boots' history.

Questions

1. What action did Boots take to cope with this unexpected surge in demand?
2. What risks were there for Boots when undertaking this reaction to demand?
3. Think of other products or services for which there has been an unexpected surge in demand. What have been the successes and failures of the operations dealing with these surges?

Sources: 'Early rush for anti-ageing cream' (http://news.bbc.co.uk/1/hi/uk/6623709.stm); Finch, J. (2007) 'Serum to tackle age-old problem is here. Prepare for mayhem' (http://www.guardian.co.uk/lifeandstyle/2007/may/03/shopping.science); Poulter, S. (2007) 'The £17 cream even scientists say can banish wrinkles' (http://www.dailymail.co.uk/femail/article-445488/The-17-cream-scientists-say-banish-wrinkles.

Forecasting

Forecasting is the prediction of future demand based on qualitative and quantitative measures. It is an attempt to predict the future and, as this is unknown, it is prone to being wrong. There are many different alternative forecasting methods but despite these, sometimes the unpredictability makes forecasts little more than educated guesses.

A forecast is selected by a scheduler in an operation, and needs to be based upon the short, medium and long terms. Many subsequent decisions are dependent upon the forecast:

- *Material purchasing and expediting:* bought-in goods need to be ordered and allocated in line with the forecast. An incorrect decision may leave the operation with excess stock to be stored, or with the costs of extra material that may have to be purchased hurriedly.
- *The product mix:* this defines which products or services are to be made and when they are to be made. If the forecast is incorrect, the operation may be left with unsold finished goods, or missed sales opportunities.

- *Staff levels and overtime decisions:* staffing levels are based on the forecast, and recruitment decisions are made in line with medium- and long-term plans. Operations with skilled staff need to make decisions to increase capacity well in advance of increases in demand, as it will probably take longer to recruit a specialist than an unskilled worker.
- *Capital investment decisions:* these include facility, plant, and research and development issues. These will be made in line with forecast information.

Decisions to expand or contract facilities are not without risk, when based on a potentially uncertain future. Forecasting, when accurate, allows for timely planning of facilities and resources. But when it is inaccurate it can result in missed opportunities, or wasted capacity, or extra costs in expanding capacity. Organizations may invest heavily in collecting or getting access to information that may be relevant to future demand patterns or volumes. For example, Zara the clothes company not only have real-time information about garment sales sent back to the HQ, but also have scanners at the changing room doors to track details on which products are taken in but not sold.

Forecasting Models and Techniques

Forecasting models can be used to help predict future demand patterns. By understanding how the forecasting information will be used, for example in work plans, investment or supply chain information, it is possible to appreciate the detail required of the forecasting models.

Questions that a manager should consider are:

- What is the time frame for the forecast? Is it for short- or medium-term decision-making, or for long-term planning?
- What decisions are to be based on the forecast?
- Who will be using the forecast?
- What is the risk exposure to the organization from an incorrect forecast?

Short-term plans are normally reliant on recent real data which can be quite accurate and a good reflection of the future, but longer-term plans almost always need to include more speculative forecast data and place more reliance on the expertise of the planner. For example, a scheduler responsible for production planning and capacity timing will often use known or planned orders for the short-term element of the forecast but for medium- and long-term time horizons the information is based upon estimated data. If a product has a four-week lead-time, then the materials already ordered are relatively fixed and the company tries to sell the products in the plan. Beyond this, though, the operation needs to decide what it is going to make, and this is where the management team will have to rely on a forecast to estimate future demand patterns, and plan capacity accordingly.

Methods of forecasting can be quantitative or qualitative. These two approaches can be used independently, but they are not mutually exclusive. Qualitative methods use appraisal, judgement and experience to estimate demand swings. These methods take into consideration factors that may be based on past experiences, opinions, or even hunches. Quantitative methods rely on data including factors such as previous sales, which can help in identifying future trends. When combined, these methods can be very effective.

Qualitative Methods

The three main approaches to qualitative analysis are:

- Market surveys
- Delphi methods
- Scenario planning

Market Surveys

Here customers are surveyed for their future buying habits. From the resulting data, inferences can be drawn regarding future demand.

Surveys are especially useful when there is no previous information that can be used, most likely with new products or services that do not have a tested market or customer base.

Market data need to be collected from a representative sample of the target market, but this can be difficult to identify. Also, the reliability of the consumer response may be questionable, as the survey will ask for opinions,

Figure 7.4 The Delphi method of forecasting

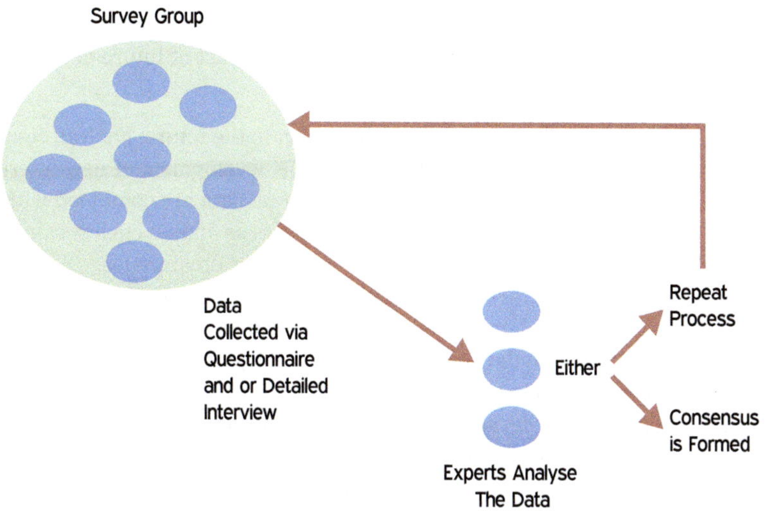

which may vary from person to person. Customer bias may be a problem if those surveyed customers tell interviewers what they think they want to hear rather than their actual perceptions and intended buying habits. Collecting data and carrying out detailed analysis of the responses can be time consuming and expensive.

For a new form of technology, such as a new feature for a mobile phone, market surveys can test the reaction of potential customers as to how they would use such a product feature and what they would value about it. This can give an indication of likely sales and whether the new feature would be considered to be significant enough to increase current production volumes.

Delphi Methods

These are detailed studies of the opinions of a panel of experts in a particular area. Individual opinions are collected anonymously via questionnaires, and the results are circulated to other members of the group for interpretation and comment. This process is repeated until a group consensus is formed. Figure 7.4 shows the Delphi method process.

This is a useful method because it evaluates different perspectives, and provides a wide commentary on collective opinion. The results from Delphi panels can be informative and provide useful insights into future demand. The method is likely to consider a wide range of ideas and intangible factors that may be missed in quantitative data.

The entire process can be very time consuming and expensive though. Also, it relies on a good selection of experts and these can be difficult to identify. Sometimes their opinions do not reach a consensus, and then the process is of less use.

Scenario Planning

This is a 'what if' approach. It considers the potential scenarios that an organization might face and then analyses the demand pattern that might result from each scenario. A range of alternative outcomes are generated and then the likelihood of each occurring and the risks involved are analysed.

This method can cover a wide range of possible futures, but there will always be scenarios that are not considered and some of these might be significant.

An example of a scenario plan might be to consider the potential impact on demand for a building company if a general election is due. The scenarios could be related to the relevant policies offered by the political parties related to funding of housing projects, should they win the election. This can give information to the organization regarding the potential impact on their volumes.

Scenario planning works well when there is an established product or service and when the variables and scenarios are understood. For new or emerging products there is too much that is unclear and unknown for this method to be of much value.

Quantitative Methods

Time series analysis is a mathematical model that uses past data to predict future demand. It attempts to establish a pattern from previous time periods, and then extrapolates into a forecast of future demand.

Demand can be classified into four identifiable types:

- *Trend:* a gradual change over time, which is then carried on to the future. Factors contributing to a trend might include the economy, legislation, globalization, or the development of new Internet technology.
- *Seasonal demand:* a regular, year-on-year pattern. When these data are combined with qualitative data, such patterns can be simple to understand. Seasonality occurs as annual cycles, causing peaks and troughs of demand such as the summer and winter impact on ice cream sales.
- *Cyclical demand:* a deviation from the trend line that might last for more or less than a year – it is the ebb and flow that is apparent. Cyclical demand may be affected by many factors, including economic or social conditions, fashion, and technology development. For example, fashions tend to swing back and forth between natural or man-made fibres in clothes.
- *Random variation:* an unexplained deviation from the trend line that follows no pattern or repetition. When all known causes for demand in a forecast that can be identified have been accounted for, then the remaining unexplained variations are referred to as *random* variations, error, or *noise*. Predictable variations fall into one of the previous categories, but may be classed as random if considered a true one-off event.

Figure 7.5 illustrates the demand pattern for each of the following elements: average demand for the period trend, seasonal demand, cyclical demand and random.

If the time period under consideration is short, the forecaster's principal concern may be with random variations, short-term cyclical patterns or errors, whereas over longer timescales trends become more detectable, and play a more important role.

Causal Relationship Forecasting

Causal methods are a form of mathematical analysis used when historical data are available and the relationship between the demand pattern to be forecast (referred to as the *dependent variable*) and other key related factors is known. The relationship between the variables is of interest because it is required in order to forecast demand based on it.

A **dependent demand** pattern is derived from such an association. This allows a level of predictability, and so demand isn't totally random. By contrast, **independent demand** means that there are few factors that can help in predicting demand patterns. The operator is almost 'working blind' as to the future, and has to take much more of a gamble when making future decisions. Examples of this could include the demand for umbrellas linked to rainfall, or the demand for New York City breaks linked to the exchange rate between the dollar and the pound or euro.

Dependent demand reasonably predictable demand, linked or associated with another factor, which may have a clearer future pattern.

Independent demand a less predictable demand pattern as it is not easily linked to other factors.

The first step in causal forecasting is to establish whether the relationship is actually linked, or whether occurrences are merely coincidental and unrelated. To discover this, the data need to be analysed for the irregular peaks and troughs in demand.

For example, the demand for baby essentials is closely linked to the *birth rate*. The dependent variable will be the demand for baby products. The independent variable will be the birth rate, for which there should be reliable current and past data. Figure 7.6 shows a simple relationship between baby products and the birth rate. The straight-line graph shown has been arrived at by analysing past sales data using a mathematical technique called *linear regression*.

Figure 7.5 Patterns of demand

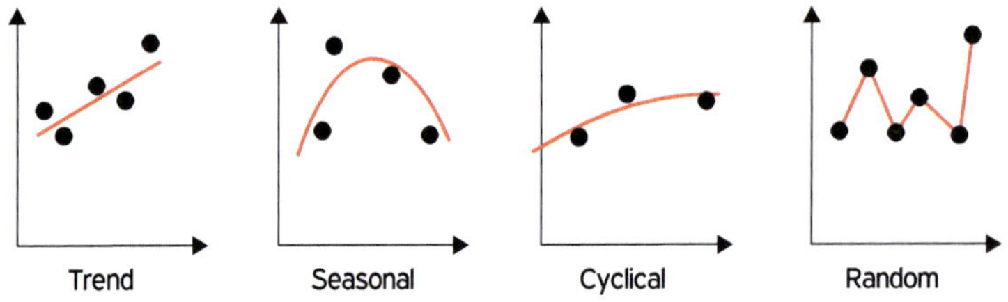

Figure 7.6 Relationship between baby products and the birth rate

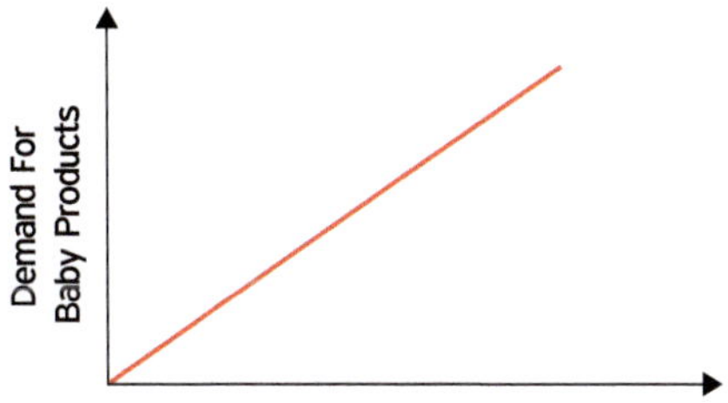

WORKED EXAMPLE 7.4

Forecasting

This worked example looks at the steps involved in forecasting future sales from historical data. It adopts a very simple approach to show the process. In practice forecasters use more advanced tools and methods to help them with their predictions.

Problem: *A shop owner in Latte-by-the-Sea looks at the past sales of coffee beans and wonders what next year's sales might be.*

Table 7.2 Past coffee bean sales (bags per quarter)

Year	2018	2019	2020
Quarter 1	100	120	134
Quarter 2	70	80	80
Quarter 3	60	70	70
Quarter 4	90	110	100

Approach

First look for any linear trend over the years to see if sales are growing or falling each year.

Solution

Calculate the total sales for each year.

Table 7.3 Total sales per year

Year	2018	2019	2020
Total Sales	320	380	384

It looks like the sales are increasing each year and so we should look at the trend to predict the sales for 2021. We can plot the values on a graph and then add a trend line to show what might happen in the future. Looking at the line drawn on the chart, it suggests the 2021 sales should be just above 420.

Another way is to use a linear regression or mathematical line fitting approach. This calculates the line which most closely fits the data. Easily accessible tools to help include the SLOPE and INTERCEPT functions in Excel or the more advanced LINEST routines. Using the Excel functions, the equation for the best fit line is shown on the figure along with the correlation coefficient (R^2) which shows how well the line fits the data. Using this the forecast value for 2021 sales is 425.

Figure 7.7 Sales with trend line and equation

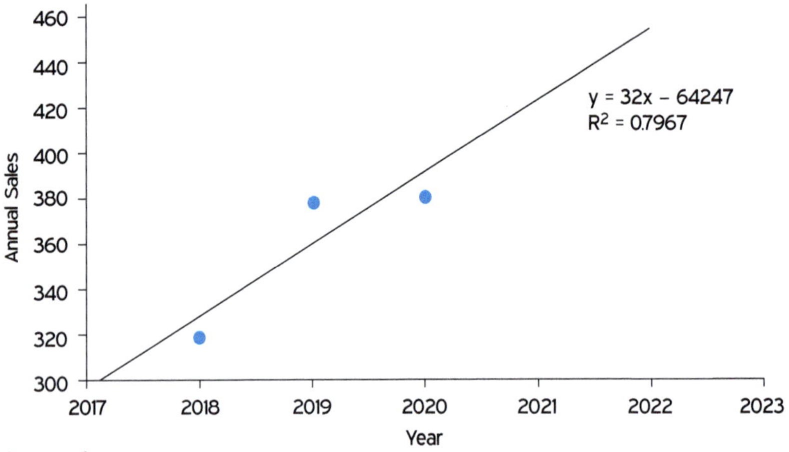

Approach

This helps the shop keeper with his total ordering, but the beans only have a short shelf life and he has to buy every 3 months. He is sure there are variations in each season and he wants to estimate the amount he should buy each quarter.

Solution

Calculate the average sales in each quarter and then work out the fraction of this to the average year.

$$\text{Weight of Q1 sales} = \frac{\text{Average Q1 sales}}{\text{Average quarter wales}} = \frac{(100 + 120 + 134/3)}{(320 + 380 + 384/12)} = 1.3063$$

$$\text{Weight of Q2 sales} = \frac{\text{Average Q2 sales}}{\text{Average quarter sales}} = \frac{(70 + 80 + 80/3)}{(320 + 380 + 384/12)} = 0.8487$$

$$\text{Weight of Q3 sales} = \frac{\text{Average Q3 sales}}{\text{Average quarter sales}} = \frac{(60 + 70 + 70/3)}{(320 + 380 + 384/12)} = 0.7380$$

$$\text{Weight of Q4 sales} = \frac{\text{Average Q4 sales}}{\text{Average quarter sales}} = \frac{(90 + 110 + 100/3)}{(320 + 380 + 384/12)} = 1.1070$$

These show the relative weights of each quarter over the year and can now be applied to forecast quarterly sales for 2021 to give an estimate of the sales in each quarter.

$$Q1\ 2021 = 1.3063 \times \frac{425}{4} = 138.8 = 140$$

$$Q2\ 2021 = 0.8487 \times \frac{425}{4} = 90.2 = 90$$

$$Q3\ 2021 = 0.7380 \times \frac{425}{4} = 78.4 = 80$$

$$Q4\ 2021 = 1.1070 \times \frac{425}{4} = 117.6 = 120$$

The values are an estimate and so it is sensible to round them to whole bags and also to the nearest 10 as this is likely to be the number which can be ordered.

Further Considerations

As these are estimates they are helpful for the shop keeper, but they need to remember that things not included in the forecast can influence the sales. For example, if a large office building is going to be built next door, they might imagine the sales would increase. They could add another 10% to the values above as a result..

Other Factors

Other factors need to be taken into account. One is the *product life cycle* (see Figure 2.4). Product demand typically follows four phases: birth, growth, maturity and decline. For products in the first two phases, longer forecasts are necessary – e.g. sales of ultra-high-definition TV sets or the Microsoft Windows 10 operating system – whereas products in the latter two phases require shorter, more specific forecasts, usually of staffing levels, inventory levels or supply chain calculations.

Business cycles also are taken into account. Market growth or recession provides a general backdrop for forecasting estimates and time periods.

When creating a forecast, each factor must be carefully considered and evaluated for its expected impact on future demand. See Chapter 8 for more about the product life cycle.

Chapter 8, p249

Capacity Strategies

Even after an operation has decided on the long-term capacity needed it must also think about how it will react to changes in demand. There are three general strategies that can be used in the medium term:

- Level production
- Chase demand
- Demand management

These strategies are not mutually exclusive and many organizations use a mix of them, but it is likely that one strategy will dominate. These are not reactions to small, daily swings in demand, but look at demand over an extended time frame and will require planning and investment.

Level Production

Level production largely ignores demand fluctuations and works on producing units efficiently, storing the finished goods and then satisfying demand from stock. See Figure 7.8. Basically, it allows an operation to manufacture efficiently and optimize capacity with a rigid production system which does not vary irrespective of the demand. There are two key conditions for this to work;

- The product must be suitable for storage, that is, not highly customized, and non-perishable or with a reasonable shelf life.
- Demand must be relatively reliable, to avoid the risk of large stock-outs or excessive stock levels which may occur if the demand is too far away from total production.

Level production capacity strategy in which the operation produces to a consistent level; unsold product is stored, and sold when demand peaks.

The level production strategy doesn't work for services as they cannot be made in advance and stored until needed.

This strategy forms part of a *cumulative plan*, where demand is satisfied over a period of time to suit the operation. Stockholding and selling from stock allow production to be effectively managed, allowing the operation to have the benefit of working to low levels of volatility.

Certain industries and products lend themselves to this strategy. For example, the demand for cigarettes is fairly consistent. Sales drop off in January and February as smokers make New Year resolutions to give up their habit, but demand returns to fairly consistent levels (as some fail to quit), and then peaks around Christmas time for the party season. The product is straightforward to store and has a reasonable shelf life. As demand is fairly consistent the operation can feel confident about following such a strategy.

Figure 7.8 The level production strategy produces units to a consistent rate

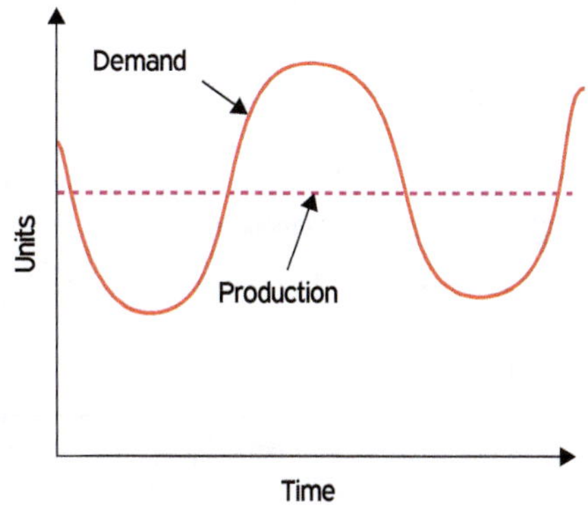

Figure 7.9 The level production strategy considers cumulative production ahead of cumulative demand

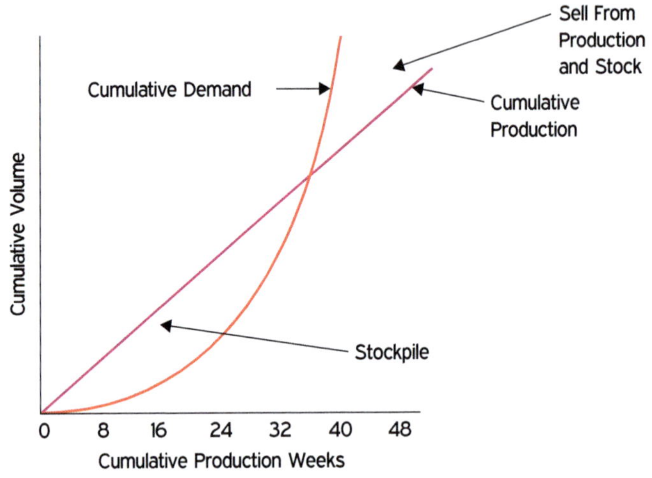

Aggregate planning a top-level look at demand for the operation as a whole; does not differentiate between different products and services.

In **aggregate planning**, forecasts are set to be as capacity-efficient as possible, yet the aim is still to match the demand. See Figure 7.9. This style of planning rises above the detail of the product or service mix and looks at capacity overall in line with the demand. It is a schedule that works in the medium term and makes decisions based upon staffing and stockholding levels or leasing decisions. This works as part of a level production strategy so that manufacturing is carried out to cover the current demand and stockpiles are built up for future demand. A risk is that if no stockpile has been created it cannot satisfy the demand to sell products as the warehouse is empty.

Chase Demand

Chase demand capacity strategy in which the operation expands and contracts its capacity to follow demand changes.

In a **chase demand** strategy the operation attempts to track changes in demand by expanding and contracting capacity (Figure 7.10). Some elements of capacity can only be adjusted over the long term, such as buildings or facilities, but there are also other elements which are more flexible. For example, adding overtime or contract working. By expanding and contracting these flexible resources the operation can minimize the costs of having excess capacity, yet still increase capacity to meet increases in demand.

The demand chasing strategy is often difficult to implement as it requires considerable planning to give process flexibility and needs complex staff training. The operation needs to consider the question 'If demand goes up and then falls, how are we going to expand and then contract our capacity without wasting money?' In order to expand and contract capacity efficiently the process needs to be adaptable. This can be achieved by designing a very simple process so that staff can be trained quickly as they are hired and fired, but may require highly trained multi-skilled staff. Flexible machinery or the ability to make other products in times of low demand, may help too. If a demand peak for one product can be combined with a demand slump in another, reallocation of resources can offset the expense of large changes to the operations.

Figure 7.10 A chase demand strategy has production following demand

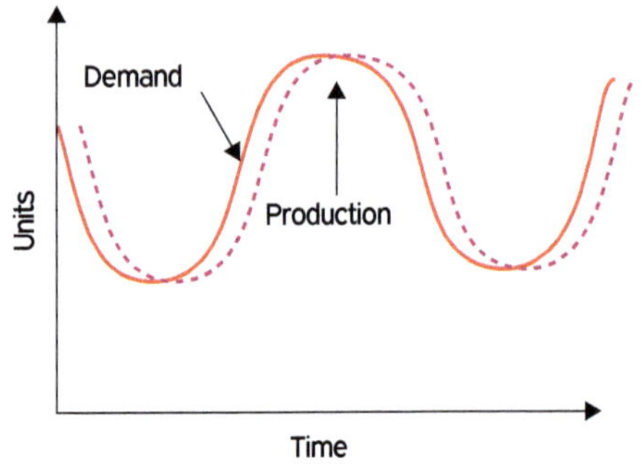

Figure 7.11 Demand management attempts to smooth demand fluctuations to allow a level production rate to be used

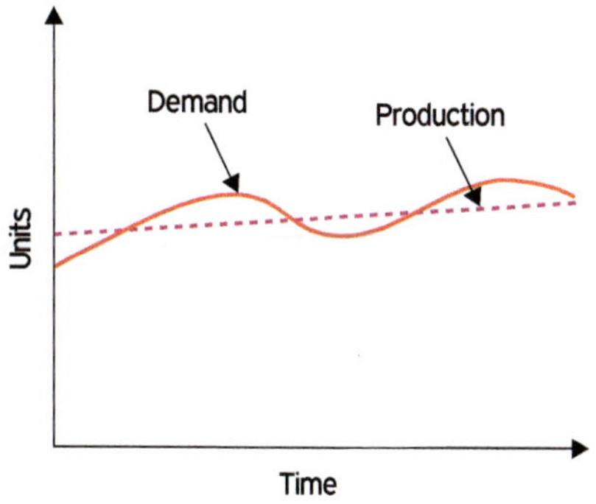

Demand Management

The level production and chase demand strategies are both supply-related solutions as they manipulate the production process. The alternative approach is to manage or control demand – **demand management**. (Figure 7.11).

Demand management capacity strategy in which the operation attempts to manipulate demand to smooth the peaks and troughs; used in conjunction with the marketing department.

The concept of manipulating or controlling demand may be unfamiliar to an operations manager, but it is possible to use marketing tools to smooth demand in line with the required forecast for certain products or services. Many of the tools may be short-term measures and it is important that the adjustments made do not damage the potential long-term demand. Some methods of demand adjustment include:

- *Varying the price.* A discounted price for a product with an elastic demand curve – a product where its demand is affected by price – can be a strong incentive for the consumer to buy more. Supermarkets do this regularly with price discounting and it can work well when combined with effective advertising.
- *Providing an incentive for off-peak services or products.* This works well with services to help smooth demand throughout a given time period. Good examples of this are an off-peak rate in the gym, or the early-bird diner menu. Both flatten the peaks in demand and increase utilization of wasted capacity at quieter times.
- *Additional marketing* can create awareness of a product that wasn't there before. This is most effective when combined with other methods, such as price discounting.
- Providing *alternative products or services.* Having additional products which customers can choose can reduce the impact of capacity constraints without too much financial loss.

Demand management practices often work in combination with the supply approaches mentioned above. It may not be possible to control demand to a constant level, but it can be useful in smoothing out the fluctuations of a chase demand strategy.

Contemporary Thinking: Yield Management

Yield management is widely regarded as an increasingly useful business tool. It is generally used in operations where the medium-term capacity is relatively fixed and there is no straightforward way to expand and contract it. This is often the case in services with high investment in facilities, where variable costs are low, and where fixed capacity prevails. Examples are hotels, with a fixed number of rooms, or airlines, with their fixed number of seats.

Yield management a group of methods that assist an operation with fixed capacity to maximize its revenue and utilize the capacity it has to best advantage.

Yield management, or *revenue management* (as it is sometimes known), was first introduced by airlines to maximize returns. Revenue management is founded in pure economics and is a result of understanding the behaviour of demand curves or the way prices influence customer activity. This relationship looks at historical trends, fixed capacities and revenues generated, and then forecasts the future demand, thus giving the business a set of rules to apply to its assets in order to maximize their financial potential.

Yield management involves a set of strategies that an operation can employ to maximize revenue either by charging individual customers as much as they are prepared to pay or by extracting as much revenue from a process as possible. It asks the question: if one customer is prepared to pay more for a good or service, is it possible to charge them a higher price than another customer?

At its simplest level companies using yield management sell their product to two distinct groups of customer knowing their demand reacts differently to changes in price. For example, business customers are willing to pay more for a flexible rate or at the last minute when their trip becomes necessary, whereas leisure customers are looking for the lowest price and normally book early. These two groups do not normally chase the same rooms or airline seats. An approach often used is to exploit this by offering a set amount of cheap, non-refundable packages for leisure travellers, this is designed to cover the operating costs of the hotel or flight. Once these costs are covered, the company looks to maximize the profit from the higher prices business customers are willing to pay for their last minute journeys. Determining how much to sell to each group, and at the prices that maximize the total revenue from the hotel or airliner, is the key.

Certain conditions enable companies to use yield management. They include:

- Fixed capacity in the short and medium term
- The ability to sell the service at different times to different customers, and in advance of the service being delivered
- A market that has diverse customer requirements
- A service that has some unique characteristics to avoid a homogeneous market (this might be the destination or timing of an airline flight, or the facilities or location of a hotel).

The three key strategies for maximizing revenue through yield management are:

- Overbooking
- Price discounting
- Varying the service type.

In *overbooking* the operation books more customers than it can accommodate on the presumption that there will be some no-shows. It has the rather obvious disadvantage caused if all the customers *do* turn up! A policy of overbooking is effective only if the take-up rate for the service is predictable and if the costs of compensating a customer if they are unable to have their booked service are not too high. The advantages for the operation include maximum revenue and full capacity. This has been a popular policy of many airlines which regularly overbook their flights. They have a large volume of data from previous flights to predict rates of no-shows on various routes; customers who miss flights because of this policy are then compensated with alternative flights and possible upgrades. However, recent legislation now requires airlines in many countries to compensate passengers financially as well as finding alternative flights and this extra cost has led many of the budget airlines to discontinue this policy.

Price discounting has the same characteristics shown in the demand management strategy, in that it is aimed at optimizing the capacity at non-peak times. The top price that can be charged is set for the time of highest demand and the price is then reduced for less attractive time periods. A high peak-time price may also be used to deter people from booking at peak times and so control demand. Price discounting helps smooth demand over a given time period and maximizes revenue. A good example of this is the holiday market: with a finite number of holidays available in Europe, peak times such as school holidays incur heavy premiums, and many bargains can be had 'off peak'.

Varying the service type allows an operation to 'grade' the services they are selling, and charge different prices accordingly. This allows them to justify charging extra from those who are prepared to pay more. Theatre seats are grouped with the dress circle seats being the best and most expensive, and the stalls being the cheapest. Upgrading a service can differentiate it from the standard service, and therefore higher prices can be charged. The advantage of this policy is that it is flexible in the short term; if an airline, say, has excess demand for economy class seats for a flight, but does not sell all its business class seats, then a business class seat can be 'converted' to an economy seat to maximize revenue. This is also a commonly used approach in selling on-demand software-as-a-service (SaaS) to businesses, or financial services to individual customers.

Yield management is also applied in retail situations where buyers decide the quantity of a product to purchase at the start of the year. There are two groups of customers with different sensitivities to price: those who buy full price and a different group during end of season sales. As such, the problem is similar to above and the calculation is trying to maximize the total revenue by identifying the optimum sales prices for each group. This determines the amount that the shop should buy at the start of the season to ensure they have sold everything at the end of the year.

Stop and Think

Today, some argue that this practice is not so much revenue management as price manipulation – altering the price that the business asks for a product or service at a particular point in time. It may help the company increase revenues, but is it always fair to customers who pay different rates depending on the time of purchase?

Queuing

Why Are We Waiting?

Several of the strategies for managing capacity described above require the ability to store products in order to follow demand. In times of low demand the product can be stockpiled; in peak times the rise in demand can be satisfied from stock.

Sometimes it is not possible to increase supply in advance, though. This is especially true of services: by their very nature, the production and consumption are simultaneous. In these cases *queuing theory* offers a more appropriate strategy. Queuing theory works on the basis that where the flow of consumers into a process is not regular, then there will be an element of waiting involved – customers have to queue.

This means that while some customers may be satisfied immediately, others may need to queue because the arrival times of customers at the start of the process is not controlled by the operation.

The waiting line or queue effectively regulates the flow of customers into the process, and turns uneven arrivals or demand into a manageable, consistent flow.

We can see a good example of this in a theme park. Customers are free to walk around the theme park and take a trip on any of the rides on offer. The customers will arrive at the rides in an irregular fashion and so there will be peaks and troughs in demand all day long. If a roller coaster can accommodate 50 passengers on a ride that runs for 2 minutes and takes 3 minutes to load and unload customers per ride then they will be processed in 5-minute batches of 50. If 1,200 customers arrive together the queue will take 2 hours to clear. However, the customers actually arrive in varying groups and batch sizes as they work their way around the park and so none will be waiting 2 hours.

The customers entering into the process are called the *calling population*. The number of customers may be known – where, for example, a quantity of tickets have been sold in advance, as for a theatre show – or they may be completely unknown, where there is no advance warning of arrival numbers – an example of this might be at a post office, where daily demand can be uncertain.

When arriving, a customer is not usually engaged in the process straight away. The customer is free to either join the queue or not: the latter is known as *baulking*. Or the customer may queue for a time, but then leave the queue: this is referred to as *reneging*. The operation itself can also prevent customers from entering the queue if there is too much demand for the service at the given time: in this case the customer is *rejected* by the queue.

Figure 7.12 shows a simple queuing system.

Figure 7.12 A simple queuing system

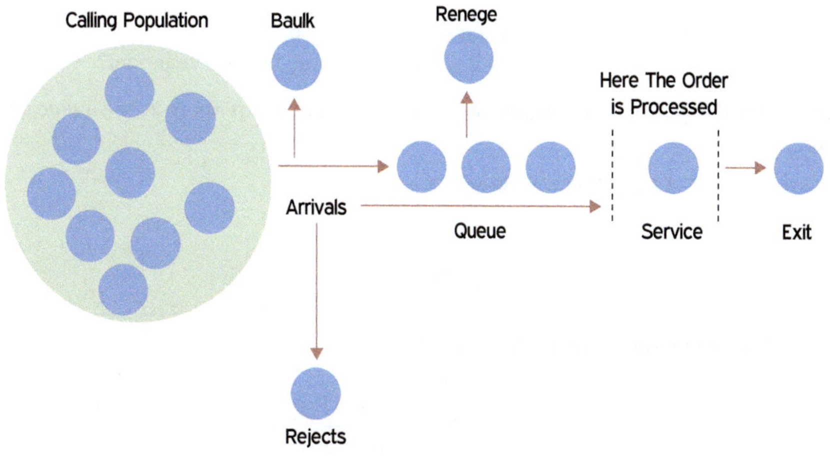

The Process Servers

Process servers the points of sale or stations at the front of the queue where the customer is served.

The point of sale, or **process server**, is where the queue is processed and there are several ways of designing the queue to feed the servers:

- *There can be one main queue, facilitated by several servers.* An example of this could be the security check at an airport. This has a single, central queue that filters off at the front to the next available scanning machine. This can result in a very long queue, but one that moves quite swiftly: a customer is not affected by a delay with another customer, as they are able to be seen by any available server.
- *Each server can have its own queue, and therefore there will be several queues side by side.* This is common in supermarkets with the till checkout system. Here the customer has to select a queue and estimate the process time in order to find the shortest one. In this case the consumer has control over their selection, but this can lead to frustrations for customers if other queues move faster than the one they are in.
- *Lastly, there can be a sequential queue.* This is where the customer joins a queue, is served, and then moves on to the next part of the process in a continuing queue. An example of this could be in an accident and emergency department in a hospital, where the patient will join the queue to be seen by a nurse; is then moved to the second part of the queue to be seen by a doctor; and then may move on to a queue for an X-ray. If all the treatments take the same time, then the queue will flow evenly; if not, a bottleneck will occur. More pressing cases can be moved up the queue as needed.

For a queue to be effective, it must have clearly defined rules and layout. Each customer needs to be aware of how they are expected to queue, and in what sequence they are to be served. Customers boarding an aeroplane may expect a *first come first served* basis, but may need to understand that there will be other passengers who are able to bypass the queue, such as disabled passengers or travellers with young children.

Customer involvement in the process can be part of queuing theory. If a customer queues, they wait to join the process, but if the queue becomes part of the process, then technically the customer is served sooner. Using the queue to collect information, such as pre-orders in a cafe queue, or collecting information relating to a process, such as personal details and requirements, engages the customer in the process, and may reduce reneging and frustration levels.

Queuing Calculations

There are many queuing *models* that can be used to calculate the effectiveness of a queuing system. The key factors are:

- *The population's source* – is it finite, where the potential customers are limited, or not finite, where arrivals are unrestricted?
- *The arrival rates and patterns of the calling population.* This is where the timing of customers arriving and how long it takes to serve each customer are variable, the system may be overloaded at times (hence the waiting): this is most often described using the mathematical model of the Poisson distribution.
- *The number of servers* – multi-server or single-server points.
- *The queuing discipline* – for example, is it a true first come, first serve model?

The most commonly used equations for a single-server distribution, where there is one queue and one service point, are shown below.

- The average number of customers waiting in a queue:

$$L_q = \frac{\lambda^2}{\mu(\mu - \lambda)}$$

- The average time a customer spends in the queue:

$$W_q = \frac{\lambda}{\mu(\mu - \lambda)}$$

- The server utilization, or the probability that the server is busy:

$$\rho = \frac{\lambda}{\mu}$$

where λ is the average arrival rate of customers per hour, and μ is the average number of customers served per hour.

WORKED EXAMPLE 7.5

Calculating Single-Server Queues

Problem: *A coffee shop has a single service desk, where customers order and pay for drinks and food. Throughout the day, customers arrive at an average rate of 40 customers per hour, and service times are distributed with an average rate of 55 customers per hour.*

Calculate:

(a) *The average number of customers waiting in the queue*

(b) *The average time a customer spends in the queue*

(c) *The probability of the barista being busy*

Approach: You will need to use the formulae to analyse the average time in the queue.

Solution:

$$\lambda = 40$$
$$\mu = 55$$

(a) The average number of customers waiting in the queue:

$$L_q = \frac{\lambda^2}{\mu(\mu - \lambda)}$$
$$= \frac{1{,}600}{55 \times (55 - 40)}$$
$$= \frac{1{,}600}{55 \times 15}$$

The average number of customers waiting in the queue is 1.9.

(b) The average time a customer spends in the queue:

$$W_q = \frac{\lambda}{\mu(\mu - \lambda)}$$
$$= \frac{40}{55 \times (55 - 40)}$$
$$= \frac{40}{825}$$

The average time a customer spends in the queue is approximately 0.05 hours (or nearly 3 minutes).

(c) The probability of the barista being busy:

$$\rho = \frac{\lambda}{\mu}$$
$$= \frac{40}{55}$$

The probability of the barista being busy is 0.73 therefore a 73% chance.

Customers' Perception of Waiting in Queues

The psychology of queuing, or 'waiting in line', is a much discussed topic. An organization needs to know how its customers will react to a queue and indeed whether having queues damages its operation in any way. Will customers switch to competitors who do not have queues, or whether it affects satisfaction and repeat purchasing? It is also important to understand how the disadvantages of queuing can be minimized by considering the feelings of the consumer towards queueing.

There are several common factors that can be identified from customers' perceptions:

- Time spent in a queue is seen as idle or wasted time. A consumer will make a judgement to trade off the time spent in the queue against the perceived value of the service.
- Some consumers are prepared to pay a premium to reduce or avoid queuing time. This can clearly be seen at airport check-in desks, where first and business class have their own server who does not support the main queue. Another example is paying for private health care instead of waiting for state-provided services.
- The perception of the queue depends on the type of queue, and on whether the end result is worth waiting for. For example, the queues for a theme park can be several hours long, but the ride is valued highly so there is a 'reward' for being in the queue.
- If the customer has information about the queue in relation to expected wait or position in the queue there is a much lower level of anxiety. Informing a customer of their situation enables them to make a rational decision as to whether to remain in the queue or leave. Passing on this information often uses technology: for example, automated call centre queues regularly inform customers of wait time and queue position.
- A customer queuing to start the process will feel more dissatisfaction than a customer who has already started the process. This can be seen in the accident and emergency queue, where once patients are seen by a nurse they are less stressed waiting to be seen by a doctor. This begins the process more quickly but does not necessarily shorten the wait time.
- Consumers have expectations for good service, and queues are often seen to detract from the quality of service.
- One of the lessons for operations managers is that customers dislike uncertainty. Waiting in a queue is an uncertainty.

Many things can affect happiness in the queue; it can be something as simple as good weather when queuing outside, to the mood of the individual customer in the queue. For example, an individual complaining loudly affects the mood of the whole queue.

It is important for an operation to be aware of and tackle frustration and irritation with the queue. Technologies have been devised to 'bust' queues: such as busy restaurants giving out 'buzzers' which hold the queuer's position so they can go away and look at something else knowing they will be called when a table is ready. Similarly, some shops use hand-held devices to take customers' orders while they are in the queue and then give them an order number. These types of system are sometimes used in large shoe stores where the customer order number – the paper ticket picked up by the customer when entering the shop – is entered into a hand-held terminal by an assistant with the selection and sizes of shoes the customer would like to try. When a qualified assistant becomes available the customer is then served; the shoes have, during the wait, been made ready for the assistant to collect from the store room. In this way customers are committed to the process, and are less likely to baulk or renege the queue. Many operations may take the customers' engagement in the process one step further, and provide entertainment in the queue: this can be an effective policy for queues for music concerts, sporting events or theme parks.

CRITICAL PERSPECTIVE

Are All Queues Bad?

Consumers are generally unhappy to wait for goods and services. As operations managers, we have come to see waiting and queuing as negatives in a process that involves customers. Queuing has become so much part of the life of a consumer that it affects the way they make choices, plan purchases and allocate time to activities – but it has an important role to play in decision-making:

- A consumer may be prepared to wait longer in order to get a lower price rather than pay a premium for a better service.

- A queue can also be an opportunity to encourage impulse buys which keeps the customer shopping for longer than they had initially intended.
- Queues can also act as a signal or give information to a consumer. A night club with a queue may indicate that there is a popular party going on inside rather than a half-empty club with no atmosphere.
- A queue may also be part of the anticipation for an experience. The queue for a theme park ride can allow customers to view the ride, and see what they are about to experience themselves.

The key point is ...

to consider what the customer expects from the queue, and aim to meet their expectations. A queue, in itself, isn't necessarily negative; but queues are negative if they are unexpected, there is a lack of information about the wait itself, or if they are particularly long.

SHORT CASE 7.4

Queuing for Wimbledon

As one of Britain's most popular sporting events, the Wimbledon Tennis Championships attract thousands of visitors a year. It is one of the few major events to offer a certain number of tickets to spectators for sale on the day, rather than in advance. There are around 500 premium tickets available for the 'show courts' and approximately 6,000 tickets for the grounds. The actual number varies according to previous sales, the weather, and the number of courts in play.

Source: ©SOPA Images Limited / Alamy Stock Photo

For a ground pass it is usually necessary to join the queue several hours before the grounds open. For a show court ticket, many people choose to queue overnight to maximize their chances of getting a ticket for the Centre, No. 1 or No. 2 Court. An area is created in Wimbledon Park for campers, and facilities are provided. In the early morning, campers are woken by stewards to pack up their kit and form a more regular queue.

There may be a wait of around 5 hours before the tickets then go on sale. Some members of the queue may be unsuccessful in their attempts and leave empty handed.

The queue at Wimbledon has become part of the Championships themselves, and is known for being good-natured and friendly.

Questions

1. What makes a queue for Wimbledon different from the normal approach to queuing?
2. What are the positive and negative aspects for a customer queuing for Wimbledon?

Source: http://aeltc2010.wimbledon.org/en_GB/about/tickets/queue.html

Summary

This chapter has introduced various approaches for dealing with everyday capacity problems. These should enable demand to be anticipated, and resources managed, in the light of actual variable customer demand.

Capacity management affects all areas of an operation. Capacity measures the *rate* at which the operation can transform inputs into outputs. Capacity is about the *quantity* of a product or service that can be made within a *given time period.* When measuring capacity, the unit of measure can be either an input to or an output from the process.

To assess the efficient use of the resources available, efficiency is calculated as output shown as a percentage of effective capacity.

In planning capacity, the organization has three main choices: to build ahead of a forecast (*capacity leads demand*); to provide capacity as demand changes (*capacity matches demand*); or to respond after demand (*capacity lags demand*).

Demand can be volatile, and is something that tends to 'happen to' an operation. It exists outside the organization, and is therefore difficult to control. Demand may change due to a number of factors or circumstances.

Methods of forecasting can be quantitative or qualitative. These approaches can be used independently, but are not mutually exclusive. Qualitative methods use appraisal, judgement and experience to estimate demand swings.

There are three general strategies that can be used in the medium term in planning capacity: level production, chase demand and demand management. These strategies are not mutually exclusive, and most organizations use a mix of the three, but it is likely that one method will dominate the strategy.

Where it is not possible to build a product in advance, *queuing theory* offers a more appropriate strategy. Queuing theory works on the basis that where the flow of consumers into a process is not regular, then there will be an element of waiting involved.

Key Terms and Theories

- **Resource mix** – this is the collection of inputs or resources into a process that can be adjusted to increase or decrease capacity.
- **Input and output measures of capacity** – it is possible to measure the capacity of an operation by analysing either inputs or outputs. Either method is correct; the selection of the method depends upon which measure is more logical. For example, the number of beds in a hospital is a logical input; barrels per day of oil from an oil rig is a logical output.
- **Design capacity** – is a top level and unachievable result as it presumes a 24/7 operation with no stoppages.
- **Effective capacity** – is the same as design capacity, but subtracts stoppages such as lunch breaks and maintenance.
- **Actual capacity** – is more of a working number; it looks at what is actually produced, and considers both planned and unplanned stoppages.
- **The theory of constraints** – created by Goldratt, suggests that capacity can be almost infinite if constraints or bottlenecks are identified and removed. The theory states that once a constraint is removed, capacity will increase, and another constraint will form.
- **Efficiency and utilization of capacity** – are ratios that show how well an operation is using its assets and resources to generate output. Efficiency looks at how much is produced, it considers what the operation would hope to make, taking into account planned stoppages. This allows the operation to establish how much unplanned problems are affecting the output. Utilization looks at output compared with design capacity, and demonstrates how well the processes are working.
- **Takt time** – is the rate at which a customer requires the operation to produce the product.
- **Yield management** – or revenue management, allows operations to maximize revenue if they have fixed capacity, by varying price from customer to customer depending on their willingness to pay. Higher-paying customers might receive additional features or benefits.

Key Equations

$$\text{Capacity} = \frac{\text{Time available}}{\text{Time of task}}$$

$$\text{Efficiency} = \frac{\text{Actual output}}{\text{Effective capacity}} \times 100$$

$$\text{Utilization} = \frac{\text{Actual output}}{\text{Design capacity}} \times 100$$

$$\text{Takt time, } T = \frac{T_a}{T_d}$$

The average number of customers waiting in a queue, $Lq = \dfrac{\lambda^2}{\mu(\mu - \lambda)}$

The average time a customers spends in the queue, $Wq = \dfrac{\lambda}{\mu(\mu - \lambda)}$

The server utilization, or the probability that the server is busy, $\rho = \dfrac{\lambda}{\mu}$

Suggested Answers to Stop and Think Question

1. To answer this question, consider what the advantages are to the customer who pays the higher price. A customer may benefit from a better view in the theatre, or a more comfortable seat on a plane. However, consider also the advantages to the customer paying the lowest price; they might not be able to afford the service if there was no differentiation in pricing, as the average price would most probably be higher.

connect

Review Questions

1. What would be the most effective measure of capacity for:

   (a) A car manufacturer?

   (b) A music concert?

   (c) An airport?

2. How could the capacity of a coffee shop be:

   (a) Increased in the short, medium and long term?

   (b) Decreased in the short, medium and long term?

3. When forecasting demand, what qualitative methods can be used? What are the advantages and disadvantages of these methods?

4. When an operation has a seasonal product such as chocolate, what strategies are available to it when planning capacity?
5. What must an operation consider when using historical data to predict future trends?
6. How can queues be managed effectively to reduce waiting time and customer frustration?
7. Using the theory of constraints, what are the most common constraints in:

   (a) A car manufacturing plant?

   (b) A post office?

   (c) Dentists?

Discussion Questions

1. How can having multi-skilled staff increase the capacity of a hospital? Discuss what factors must be considered when increasing or decreasing a hospital's capacity.
2. If an operation adopts a level production strategy, what features must the product have for it to be successful? When may other strategies be more appropriate?
3. Discuss how an operation might manage demand in a restaurant.
4. Why are capacity decisions critical for operations managers?
5. Which queue style would you recommend for a post office and why?

Problems

1. A computer firm has a group of 50 computer consultants. These individuals either visit firms in the area on pre-arranged visits, or are called in for emergency repairs.

   A call-out fee is charged that covers the first hour of their visit. Beyond the first hour they charge in minimum blocks of 30 minutes. The average call-out is 2 hours long.

   The working day is usually 8 hours long, but allows two breaks of 15 minutes each and a half-hour lunch break, leaving a 7-hour day. If holidays are accounted for at 25%, the 7 hours per day is actually a 5¼ hour day.

   Required: *If actual work is only 500 hours billed in the week, then:*

   (a) *What is the capacity utilization of the team?*

   (b) *What is their efficiency?*

2. A student registration line has a working day of 6 hours. There are 25 members of staff working during induction week. These employees have a half-hour lunch break and two 15-minute tea breaks each day. At the start of each working day, the process takes 20 minutes to set up.

   Required: *Calculate the total time available to work for the registration team, and the time that can be spent on each student application (the takt time) for 2,000 students per day.*

3. A beachside kiosk selling food has a single queue where customers order and pay for soft drinks and ice creams. On an average summer day, customers arrive at a rate of 160 per hour, according to a Poisson distribution, and the time it takes to serve each customer is distributed with an average rate of 130 customers per hour.

   Required: *Calculate:*

   (a) *The average number of customers waiting in the queue.*

   (b) *The average time a customer spends in the queue.*

4. Aculens produces contact lens cleaning solution for a big supermarket. The orders for the cleaner from January 2019 to November 2019 inclusive are presented in Table 7.4.

Table 7.4 Orders for cleaner

Period	Month	Orders
1	January	1,290
2	February	1,230
3	March	1,190
4	April	1,245
5	May	1,330
6	June	1,370
7	July	1,355
8	August	1,452
9	September	1,478
10	October	1,568
11	November	1,678

Required: *Help the company by estimating the sales in December either by plotting the data and drawing your best fit line or using the Excel functions SLOPE and INTERCEPT.*

5. A student union bar normally has customers arriving with a Poisson distribution of 50 per hour, and the time taken for each to be served their drink is distributed with an average rate of 80 per hour.

   Required: *Calculate:*

   (a) *The average number of customers waiting in the queue.*

   (b) *The average time a customer spends in the queue.*

   (c) *The probability of there being a queue at the bar.*

6. Holiday firm long-waits.com has set up a manual check on credit card payments on its website. Assume clearances arrive with a Poisson distribution of 20 per hour, and the time taken for each to be checked by hand is distributed with an average rate of 25 per hour.

   Required: *What is going to happen when this line starts operating? Think about how many can be processed in an hour compared to how many will arrive. What advice would you give to the manager to make this process work more consistently?*

7. A mobile phone refurbishment centre has a packing line that works 7 hours a day including a half-hour lunch break and two 15-minute tea breaks. It has 8 staff packing the refurbished phones to send out for shops.

   Required: *Calculate the total time available to work for the packing line, and the time that can be spent on packing each phone (the takt time) for 1,800 phones per day.*

8. The website bookings.org has recorded the orders from their customers between January and November inclusive. The orders are presented in Table 7.5.

   The company observes that there is a clear upward trend in the orders for the product and it decides to employ linear regression analysis to forecast future orders.

   Required: *Estimate the sales in December either by plotting the data and drawing your best fit line or using the Excel functions SLOPE and INTERCEPT.*

9. Monthly demand for new electric vehicle charging points in Futureville is shown in Table 7.6.

Table 7.5 Total customer orders

Period	Month	Orders
1	January	5,200
2	February	6,700
3	March	6,800
4	April	6,900
5	May	6,900
6	June	6,800
7	July	7,200
8	August	7,300
9	September	7,400
10	October	8,200
11	November	8,900

Table 7.6 Monthly demand for charging points

Month	2018	2019	2020
Jan	80	85	105
Feb	70	85	85
Mar	80	93	82
Apr	90	95	115
May	113	125	131
Jun	110	115	120
Jul	100	102	113
Aug	88	102	110
Sept	85	90	95
Oct	77	78	85
Nov	79	78	83
Dec	82	78	80

Required: *The expected future demand for 2021 is 1,200 in total. How many of these are likely to be in February?*

Further Reading

Aksin, Z., Armony, M. and Mehrotra, V. (2007) 'The modern call center: a multi-disciplinary perspective on operations management research', *Production and Operations Management*, **16**(6), 665–688.

Hyndman, R. J., & Athanasopoulos, G. (2018). *Forecasting: Principles and Practice,* 2nd edn, OTexts, Heathmont, Victoria.

Martin, K., & Osterling, M. (2014). *Value Stream Mapping: How to Visualize Work and Align Leadership for Organizational Transformation,* McGraw-Hill, New York.

Pinedo, M. (2014) *Planning and Scheduling in Manufacturing and Services,* 2nd edn, Springer, New York.

Sproull, R. (2020). *The Secret to Maximizing Profitability: A Business Novel on How to Successfully Combine the Theory of Constraints, Lean, and Six Sigma to Drive Profit Margins to New Levels,* Productivity Press.

Winter, H. (2019). *The Business Analysis Handbook: Techniques and Questions to Deliver Better Business Outcomes,* Kogan Page, London.

Reference

Goldratt, El. M. (1984) *Theory of Constraints,* North River Press, Great Barrington, MA.

8 Supply Chain and Supply Relationship Management

Learning Outcomes

After reading this chapter, you should be able to:

- Describe the management of supply chains
- Assess purchasing strategies for different types of item
- Identify key issues in managing supplier–buyer relationships
- Identify postponement strategies in supply chains
- Assess how demand uncertainties can be managed
- Compare various mechanisms for supply chain integration
- Compare different strategies for supply chain efficiency and responsiveness

BUSINESS INTEGRATION

GLOBALIZATION

Barilla: Managing Inventory

Barilla is the world's leading manufacturer of pasta products with 35% of the Italian and 22% of the European market, employing 8,358 people, selling 1.9 million tons in 125 countries and generating sales of €3.5 billion in 2018. Barilla was founded in 1877 when Pietro Barilla opened a small shop in Parma, Italy, selling his own bread and fresh pasta. It now owns over 20 brands selling 1,500 different products.

Source: ©Bokehboo Studios/Shutterstock

Manufacturing

Barilla has 28 production units throughout Italy and the rest of the world making pasta, bread, sauces, and various cakes and biscuits, as well as 10 flour mills producing much of the raw material. Making pasta is relatively straightforward, with flour, water and often eggs and spinach mixed together to form a dough. This is then rolled and forced through dies to shape before being cut to length. The pieces are then dried on a long conveyor in an oven where the conditions are carefully controlled for temperature and humidity to ensure quality. The drying process varies depending on the shape and size of the pasta, and so Barilla develops complex plans to ensure low set-up penalties. Barilla's plants specialize in terms of the type (flour and ingredients used), shape and size of pasta, and whether the product is fresh or dried. The largest plant can produce 900 tons of pasta a day.

Sales and Distribution

Barilla's products are sold in over 100,000 outlets in Italy alone. Dry products have a shelf life of around 2 years and make up 75% of Barilla's output, coming in approximately 800 different stock-keeping units (SKU) of different package sizes and products. Many of the biscuit products, about 200 SKUs, have a shelf life of 3 months, whereas fresh pasta lasts only 3 weeks. Fresh bread products have even shorter usable times of one day. As a result, Barilla needs different ways of distributing the products.

In Italy, fresh products are sent from the manufacturing units through two distribution centres which generally hold 3 days' supply. From here, the fresh products are sent out to 70 regional warehouses for distribution. The dry products are sold predominantly through supermarkets, and dispatched from the distribution centres to the supermarket's own distributors, called ***grande distribuzione*** (GD). The rest of the dried products go through the distribution centres to 18 Barilla depots before going out to independent distributors called ***distribuzione organizzata*** (DO) and eventually to shops.

Ordering and Inventory

The wide range of products at Barilla and the different handling and sales routes make it an interesting case to think about managing inventory – both the stocks of raw materials needed for manufacture and the finished products. For example, Barilla's raw materials and the GDs for the supermarkets have very regular and predictable demands, whereas the DOs need more reactive methods to cope with unpredictable events and consumption rates. There is no single way that can help Barilla and its distributors manage the ordering and delivery of products and raw materials. The demand at the DO stage is unpredictable, and managed on an ad hoc basis by local managers juggling the need for products in the shops. This is a different task from managing demand at Barilla and the GDs, where it is possible to predict accurately the amounts needed. This certainty means they can create a flow of materials and products to support a fixed production plan.

Sources: Barilla SpA (A) Harvard Business School case: 9-694-046, and Barilla website, http://www.barillagroup.com/, accessed 7 October 2019.

Introduction

The Barilla case shows how inventory management is vital to matching demand and supply of pasta and bread throughout the supply chain. Remember that in Chapter 6 we looked at how supplier relationships are formed, and explored the different types of supplier relationship that may result. In this chapter we explore how such collaborations, once set up, can be managed, by taking a closer look at the various processes that link the firm to its suppliers and customers.

Chapter 6, p177

We'll learn that, before procurement decisions are made, it is crucial that the organization classify the purchased items in terms of their impact on the business, as well as on the supply risk and market complexity. This subsequently impacts on the nature of the supplier–buyer relationship, which can vary from an arm's length relationship to a strategic partnership.

Effective relationships depend on the extent to which firms are willing to share information. It is challenging to manage supply chains when we don't know the variation in demand. We need to understand why information about a customer's actual demand gets distorted all the way upstream along the supply chain.

As innovative products and services are continuously introduced to the market, all parties in the supply chain need to collaborate in devising flexible and efficient channels. A firm may combine efficiencies from logistics (e.g. collaborating with third party logistics companies), manufacturing (e.g. postponing customization), or supplies (e.g. combining the best solutions from lean and agile supplies). All these processes are supported by coordination efforts and information technology.

This chapter covers the key concepts and strategies related to the management of supply chains. We shall investigate the management of activities and processes that take place when goods and services are produced by suppliers and provided to customers. We'll also learn about how firms can organize their supply chains for operational efficiency.

Supply Chain Management

In Chapter 6 we learned that the term 'supply chain' is a metaphor used to describe a simple linear relationship between a series of different organizations, such as a raw materials supplier, a manufacturer, a distributor, and the end customer. Supply chains are concerned with the flow of three things – information, money and materials – between participating organizations. **Supply chain management (SCM)**, then, is the management of activities, organization and processes involving all stakeholders, from the supplier that produces the raw material (upstream) to the end customers (downstream). In order for goods or services to reach customers, the various processes have to be integrated.

Chapter 6, p177

Supply chain management (SCM) the management of activities, organization and processes involving all the stakeholders, from the end customers (i.e. downstream) to the supplier that produces the raw material (i.e. upstream).

SCM is built on the assumption that a company's supply chain (internal as well as external) is a resource to be exploited for market position. Strategic use of this resource requires companies to pay close attention to understanding customer needs, and how to fulfil them. The companies also need to pinpoint the inefficiencies in their processes that hinder cross-functional relationships with suppliers and customers. Many contemporary SCM concepts have been developed since the mass production era, such as third party logistics (TPL or 3PL), enterprise resource planning (ERP), and collaborative planning, forecasting and replenishment (CPFR). These concepts will be explored in later sections.

Managing Supplier–Buyer Relationships

BUSINESS INTEGRATION

Once an organization has achieved an appropriate supply network, with the correct number and type of suppliers in the correct locations, it must then decide how best to procure products and services from them on an ongoing basis. The type of relationship an organization shares with the supplier will depend on the types of items purchased, and their impact on the business, as illustrated by *Kraljic's matrix* in Figure 8.1. The strength of Kraljic's matrix lies in its simplicity: it shows four purchasing *tactics* that are contingent upon a product or service's complexity, risk and impact if it fails to be delivered.

The vertical axis of Kraljic's matrix is concerned with the impact on profit or the value obtained from a transaction for a buyer organization. These are the factors internal to the purchasing company, whereas the horizontal axis is concerned with market and supply risks – that is, external factors.

The ideal type of procurement process will depend upon the four contexts: routine, bottleneck, leverage, and critical.

Figure 8.1 Kraljic's tactical procurement matrix

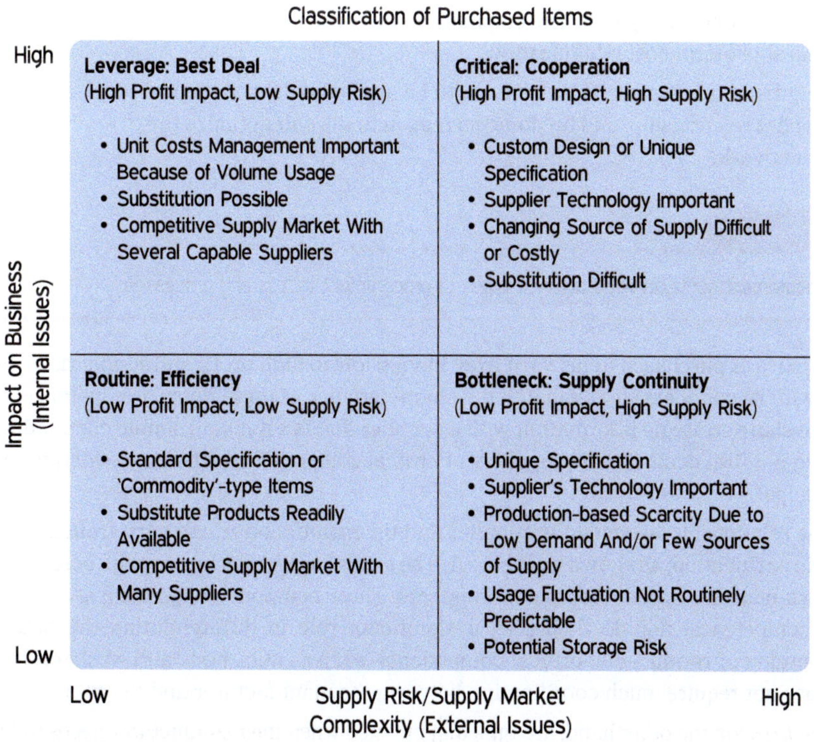

Source: Adapted from Kraljic (1983).

Routine: Efficient Process

When purchase items have a low profit impact and low supply risk, the procurement tactic should emphasize competition among suppliers to reduce transaction and unit costs. This requires high buyer power and multiple suppliers, competing primarily on a cost basis. Examples of this include low-value commodities such as nuts, bolts or rivets in manufacturing, or stationery for offices, or low-skilled, temporary labour for a building site.

Bottleneck: Reliable Process

When purchase items have low profit impact and high supply risk, suppliers tend to have very high power, because if supply is not available it will cause loss of production or service delivery to the end user. Examples could include processor chips for personal computers, or fuel deliveries to a petrol station, because without the supply of these products the end user has no product. To ensure constant availability, a long-term service contract is normally established between the buyer and supplier. In such cases it is normal to have a single supplier that makes very frequent and very reliable deliveries.

Leverage: Cost-effective Process

When purchase items have a high profit impact and low supply risk, the procurement tactic is often to liaise closely with a small number of suppliers to ensure that the product meets specifications and is sold at a reasonable cost. Consider, for example, the supply of seats for car manufacturers, or logistics providers for Internet-based retailers. These elements form a substantial part of the cost of the end product, which can often be tailored to customers' specific requirements. Leveraging can involve pooling together related products or services from within the buying organization (which may have previously been geographically dispersed) to increase the contract size and therefore the buyer's bargaining power.

Critical: Cooperative Process

Critical items have both high profit impact and high supply risk. Organizations often have key suppliers who account for the majority of the companies' purchasing costs, such as module engine manufacturers for aircraft manufacturers, or IT support for banks. This type of supplier is often single-sourced, and an in-depth, long-term relationship results, because the switching costs and the potential disruption to output if the product or service is not delivered would be extremely high. The emphasis in this case is on long-term collaboration and mutual dependence, rather than short-term cost minimization.

Despite the strengths of this matrix, it is designed to be applied only at a tactical level, and it seeks to optimize a single buyer–supplier relationship, and by doing so may actually sub-optimize the overall performance of an enterprise or supplier network.

The key point is ...

that different procurement contexts need different types of procurement tactics and processes.

As the characteristics of purchased items vary from having low to high profit and supply risks, the relationship that the firm shares with its suppliers should match the characteristics of these items. For instance, it would not be efficient for a firm to share strategic information with a supplier that is supplying simple commodity items. It would be equally damaging if a firm dealt with its suppliers of critical components without considering the long-term effects of their partnerships.

The nature of the relationship between the supplier and the manufacturer can vary from an arm's length relationship to a strategic partnership, as shown in Table 8.1. The *arm's length relationship* fits best when the manufacturer buys low-value, standardized products from its suppliers. These components typically are not related to the manufacturer's core competence, nor do they play a significant role in differentiating the buying firm's products. For example, sourcing of routine, non-critical components (such as nuts, bolts and washers) that can be bought in high volumes does not require much coordination between the manufacturer and the suppliers.

Strategic partnerships, on the other hand, are typically pursued when the manufacturer needs to have a close collaboration with its suppliers. This type of relationship tends to be pursued when the products are non-standard or unique,

Table 8.1 Characteristics of arm's length relationships and strategic partnerships

	Arm's length relationships	Strategic partnerships
Product/input characteristics	• Commodity/standardized products • Open architecture products • Stand alone (no or few interaction effects with other inputs) • Low degree of supplier–buyer interdependence • Low-value inputs	• Customized, non-standard products • Closed architecture products • Multiple interaction effects with other inputs • High degree of supplier–buyer interdependence • High-value inputs
Supplier management practices	• Single functional interface • Price benchmarking • Minimal assistance (minimal investment in inter-firm knowledge-sharing routines) • Supplier performance can be easily contracted *ex ante* • Contractual safeguards are sufficient to enforce agreements	• Multiple functional interfaces • Capabilities benchmarking • Substantial assistance (substantial investments in inter-firm knowledge-sharing routines) • Supplier performance on non-contractables (e.g. innovation, quality, responsiveness) is important • Self-enforcing agreements are necessary for optimal performance (e.g. trust, stock ownership)

Source: Adapted from Dyer *et al.* (1998).

with high-value inputs (e.g. rare materials, unique technologies, etc.), and critical items. Because of this, the supplier and the manufacturer both seek to enhance their capabilities. There is also substantial investment in fostering inter-firm knowledge sharing routines. The case study on Jeep's WIPER in Chapter 4, for instance, describes the strategic partnership shared between Chrysler and Motorola in order to make the silent-relay WIPER a success.

Chapter 4, p105

Suppliers and Product Life Cycle Effects

The strength of the relationship between members of a supplier network or enterprise changes over time, as shown in Figure 8.2, which illustrates the *partnership life cycle effect*. Initially, relationships may start off shakily but, if

Figure 8.2 Partnership life cycle effect

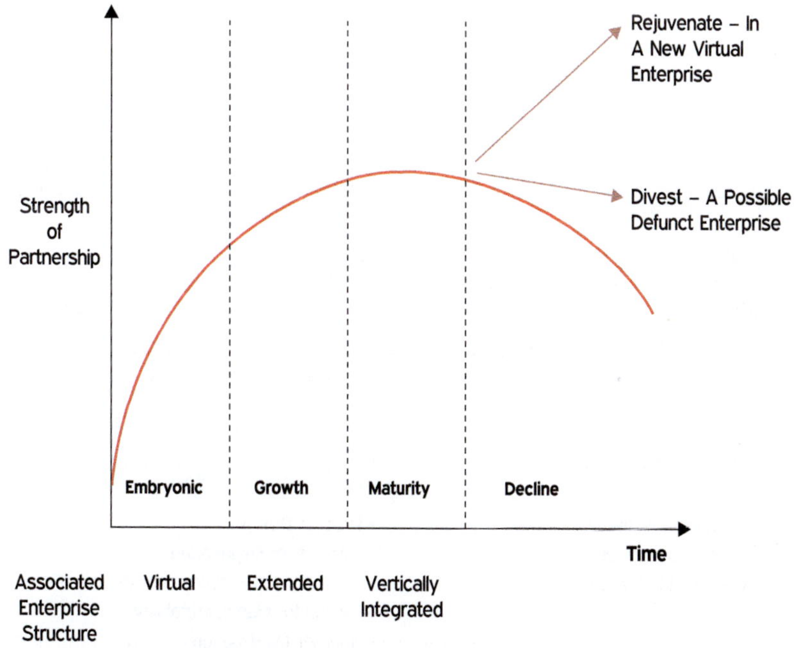

Source: Adapted from Sako (1992).

successful, move to a rapid growth stage and then into a mature phase as innovation and profitability wane. At this point, tough decisions need to be made. Successful relationships can have a strong effect on product life cycles, and can affect whether a company decides to invest in rejuvenation, chooses to divest selected products, or falls into decline.

The figure also shows how the strength of the relationship relates to the type of enterprise structure. As the enterprise moves from a virtual to a vertically integrated structure, the strength of the partnership shifts from weak, at the embryonic stage, to strong, at the maturity stage.

CRITICAL PERSPECTIVE

Early Supplier Involvement

BUSINESS INTEGRATION

Many firms are convinced that having a relationship with their customers and suppliers is an important source of competitive advantage. As many firms continue to reduce their supplier base and rely more on system integrators, ***early supplier involvement*** (ESI) becomes crucial. ESI refers to a form of co-operation in which manufacturers involve suppliers at an early stage of the product or service development process. It is a means of integrating a supplier's capabilities into the manufacturer's supply chain and operations. In doing so, the manufacturer might gain from reduced development costs, improved overall performance, reduced development lead time, and access to the supplier's technical expertise and capabilities.

But involving suppliers early in the development process also imposes challenges, such as trust between the parties and difficulties in matching technical capabilities. It can be hard to gain supplier buy-in at the early stages before there is any financial incentive, and both parties need to provide a substantial investment of time and resources to develop and manage their business relationship.

The degree of supplier involvement needed depends on the complexity of the product or service being developed. The timing of involvement and competitive pressures among the suppliers also need to be taken into consideration. The firm needs to decide whether the supplier should be involved from the beginning of the project, and whether the supplier has the expertise and capability required to support the project all the way. If, for some reason, the supplier cannot support the project, the firm needs to find another qualified supplier, which might be extremely difficult.

Suppliers can be involved in the planning, design and production stages (Figure 8.3). In the automotive industry, the planning phase is often referred to as the ***functional specification phase,*** whereas the design and production steps are often referred to as the ***detailed engineering phase*** (Clark and Fujimoto, 1991; Lamming, 1993). Involving suppliers requires that joint engineering processes be adopted (e.g. computer-aided design tools). Engineering expertise must also be shared.

Figure 8.3 Supplier involvement points in new product development

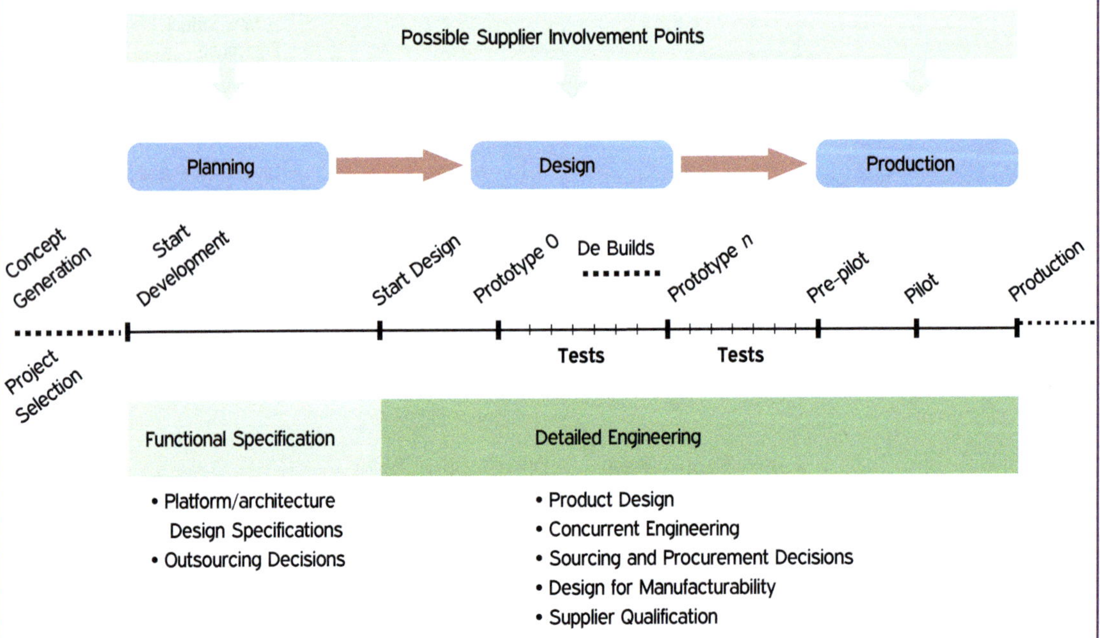

Source: Mikkola and Skjøtt-Larsen (2004).

The key point is ...

that most firms regard their ability to manage designs as their core competencies, and hence any involvement with the suppliers during the new product development process is carefully handled, often with strategic partnerships.

Challenges in Managing Supplier Relationships

Some factors have a negative impact on the success of supplier relationships. These might be:

- Changes in the supply base due to short-term, cost-oriented criteria rather than long-term value creation
- Late and insufficient involvement of suppliers in the development process
- Lack of open communication and information sharing.

These factors cause quality problems, increased costs and unforeseen changes, which can delay the start of production or service delivery (Binder *et al.*, 2008). The later changes take place, the more severe the impact will be.

Common reasons for switching suppliers change as a project matures. For example, during the early conceptual stages, technological and innovation issues are drivers for switching supplier. In the later stages, quality and time issues are more important. Ironically, this pattern increases time delays, quality problems and cost, which leads to a vicious circle of supplier switches and R&D ineffectiveness. Supplier managers believe this can be reduced by:

- Quick and early problem-solving through early collaboration
- Risk and reward sharing
- Less opportunistic behaviour through shared strategic thinking
- Increased communication and information sharing
- Joint definition of product and process specifications
- Clearly defined responsibilities and convergence of expectations
- Better responsiveness to critical issues through stronger integration.

Improving Supplier Relationships

Supplier relationships can be improved if *system integrators:*

- Make longer-term commitments to suppliers early on, with guaranteed return business for suppliers over a product's lifetime
- Encourage open-book accounting, where the target price of each product or service ensures a profit margin for suppliers, and is unaffected by renegotiations for unforeseen changes
- Endorse whole life-cycle costing rather than just the short-term, upfront research and development costs
- Endorse open source standards for information sharing for things such as design data, time schedules and production volumes
- Assume the role of leader and coordinator within inter-firm R&D projects
- Balance internal and external know-how, as success is based on the effective exchange of technical information and the social interfaces between the members
- Balance the supply base to consider product attributes such as complex systems, standards and commonality, as well as supplier attributes such as R&D competence, high quality and low cost
- Are aware of customer needs and requirements, and translate these into technical functionalities and specifications for suppliers
- Are boundary spanning, transforming the traditional role of purchasing into a more strategic sourcing function involving a cross-functional and inter-organizational R&D committee composed of all the key members.

Supplier relationships will also improve if *suppliers:*

- Take more ownership, playing a more active role during inter-company R&D projects, by making investments in testing and tooling, actively setting quality standards and prices
- Offer exclusivity to the systems integrators in return for early and long-term commitment with potential return business, instead of aiming to standardize parts and services to sell to others

- Are more open to organizational agility, adjusting organizational structures and processes to adapt to working in inter-organizational relationships
- Develop their own integration competencies to manage their sub-suppliers, because inter-organizational R&D collaboration is increasingly being carried out at system and module levels.

The key point is ...

that to develop sustainable supplier management and high-value outputs, a high level of trust is needed between all parties. This helps the transition from opportunistic behaviour in loose supplier networks to collaborative thinking in tight, strategically aligned enterprises.

Stop and Think

Preserving competition while encouraging cooperation is almost a contradiction. In addition to the above suggestions, how else can this be accomplished?

The Impact of Product Design on Supply Chains

The way a supply chain is configured has an influence on how a manufacturer of complex products organizes and coordinates design activity. Nokia's supply chain, for instance, handles 100 billion components, 60 strategic suppliers, and 10 factories worldwide. New product introductions and variations are also impressive: one phone can have 170 handset variations and 250 sales package variants. To manage the supply chain, Nokia nurtures value-based strategic partnerships with suppliers, which are based on information sharing and flexibility. Companies such as Nokia design their new products and services while taking into consideration their supply strategies, such as mass customization and postponement.

Chapter 4, p105

Chapter 5, p139

Mass Customization and Postponement Strategies

In Chapter 4 we showed how mass customization provides products that meet customers' individual needs through combinations of modular components. There are various ways in which components can be combined, stored and assembled in order to create the desired customization. In Chapter 5, we learned that mass customization is a strategy for delivering different products or services at approximately the same cost as mass producing them. It requires mass collaboration (in logistics, manufacturing, service delivery, etc.) along the supply chain.

Postponement delaying the timing of crucial processes in which end products assume their specific functionalities, features and identities

One central feature of mass customization is **postponement**. Postponement is about delaying the timing of crucial processes by which end products assume their specific functionalities, features and identities (Lee, 1998). It is a strategy that helps managers to achieve delivery of goods in a timely and cost-effective manner, by rearranging the production and logistics supply chains.

The logic behind postponement is that risk and uncertainty costs are tied to the differentiation of goods (i.e. form, place and time) that occurs during manufacturing and logistics operations, resulting in four types of strategy: full speculation, manufacturing postponement, logistics postponement, and full postponement (Figure 8.4).

Figure 8.4 The postponement and speculation matrix

		Logistics	
		Speculation *Decentralized Inventories*	Postponement *Centralized Inventories and Direct Distribution*
Manufacturing	Speculation *Make to Inventory*	Full Speculation Strategy	Logistics Postponement Strategy
	Postponement *Make to Order*	Manufacturing Postponement Strategy	Full Postponement Strategy

Source: Adapted from Pagh and Cooper (1998).

Full Speculation Strategy

The *full speculation strategy* is the equivalent of mass production strategy, in the sense that the goods are made to stock, and then dispatched to local warehouses according to the amount of local demand forecast (Figure 8.5). Holding stocks close to the customers ensures short delivery times. This also means that products are distributed through a decentralized distribution system, requiring high inventory investment.

Manufacturing Postponement

With *manufacturing postponement,* the product retains its standard form in the manufacturing process for as long as possible. The differentiation is delayed until the latest possible point – normally when a customer order has been received (Figure 8.6). The final packaging of mobile phones, for instance, is often carried out by a TPL provider (after receiving the customer order), who has an inventory of handsets, manuals, SIM cards and accessories. Afterwards the package is shipped directly to the customer.

Figure 8.5 Full speculation strategy

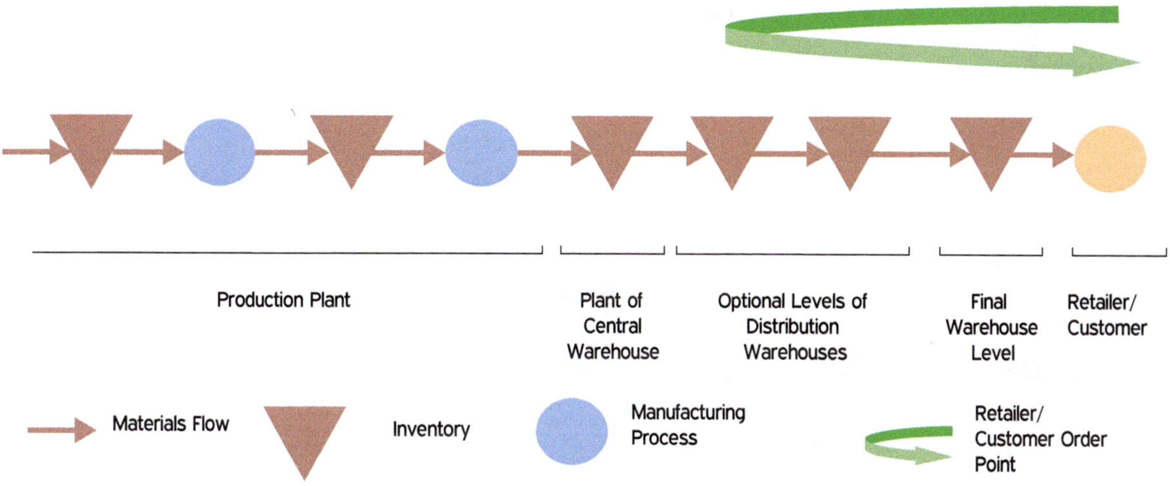

Source: Adapted from Pagh and Cooper (1998).

Figure 8.6 Manufacturing postponement strategy

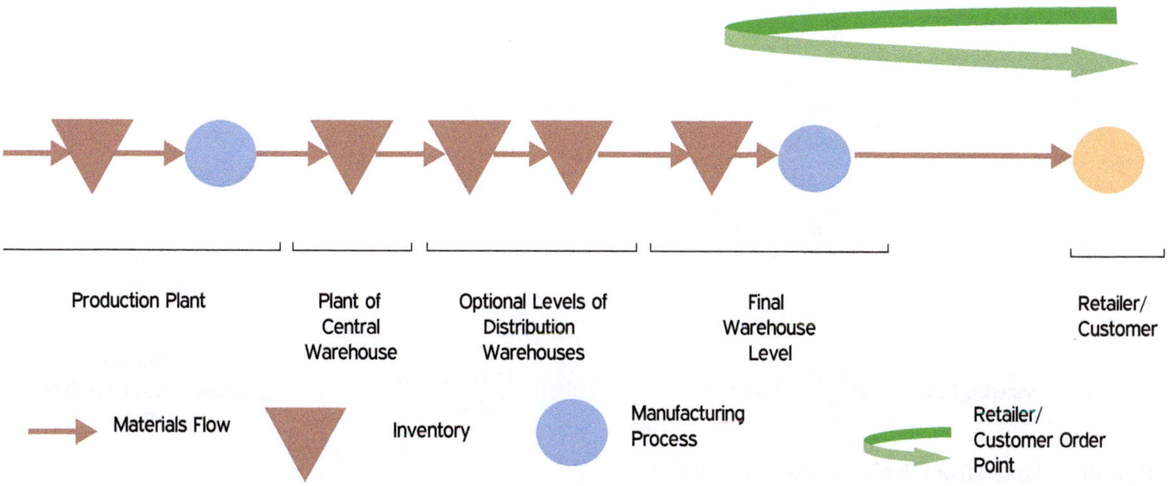

Source: Adapted from Pagh and Cooper (1998).

Logistics Postponement

With *logistics postponement*, a full line of anticipated inventory is stored at a few strategic locations (Figure 8.7). The changes in inventory location are delayed downstream in the supply chain to the latest possible point. The logistics operations begin after a customer order is initiated. For example, in order to improve the spare parts distribution for Ford, DB Schenker collects the required car parts from over 800 suppliers in Germany and Austria and brings them together in a consolidation centre in Cologne, where the car parts are repackaged and taken to the distribution centres of car factories.

Full Postponement

Full postponement takes place when both manufacturing and logistics activities, both customer order initiated, are postponed (Figure 8.8). For example, Bang & Olufsen, a Danish manufacturer of audio-video systems, can assemble, test and deliver customized products directly to the final customers in Europe within five days.

Figure 8.7 The logistics postponement strategy

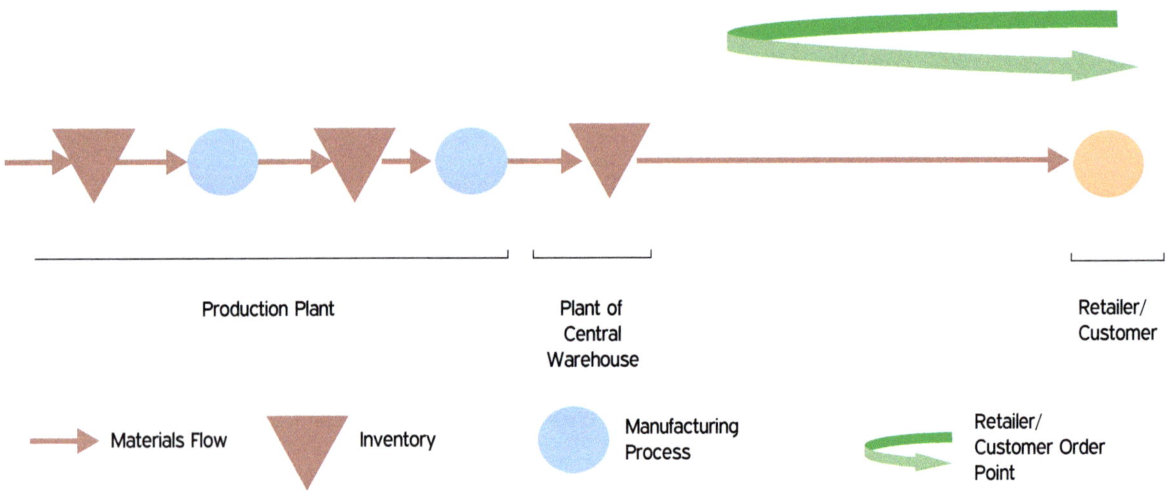

Source: Adapted from Pagh and Cooper (1998).

Figure 8.8 The full postponement strategy

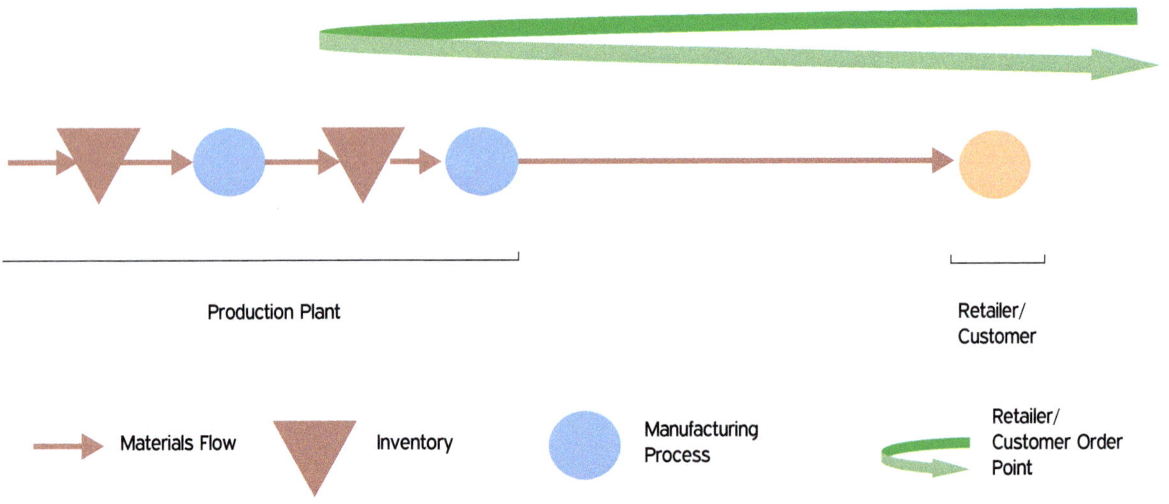

Source: Adapted from Pagh and Cooper (1998).

CRITICAL PERSPECTIVE

Component Design for Postponement and Mass Customization

Design for postponement refers to design of products or processes so that postponement is possible. It calls for a fundamental change of the product architecture, by using designs that standardize some of the components (hence changing the form of the product architecture) or process steps. In order for postponement to be successful, products or processes should be modular in structure (Lee, 1998). In other words, product modularity requires module interfaces to be redesigned so that they can easily be assembled and tested as a total unit. Furthermore, because postponement strategies involve many suppliers, collaboration becomes inevitable between multiple functions (e.g. cross-functional integration) and organizations (e.g. collaborative efforts among multiple firms).

One of the aims of the postponement strategy is to retain product commonality as far downstream in the supply chain as possible. Whereas the goal of mass customization is to produce customized goods at low costs, postponement strategy focuses on delaying customization as long as possible. The extent of customization and postponement of products is rooted in how modular the product architecture is. Taken together, postponement, mass customization and product modularity are dependent on supply chain strategies to facilitate assembly, logistics and outsourcing decisions.

Component design for postponement can take place in the following way (Figure 8.9). Let's assume that a mobile phone company sells two products, X and Y, to two markets: the US (market A) and Europe (market B). It needs to develop product specific components for each mobile phone – a component set for X and a component set for Y. The company then decides to redesign these products, and discovers with the advance of technology, that it is now possible to standardize the components for both phones X into one component set we can call Z. Now the company needs only to focus on producing one component set (Z) that can serve both markets A and B.

Figure 8.9 Component design for postponement

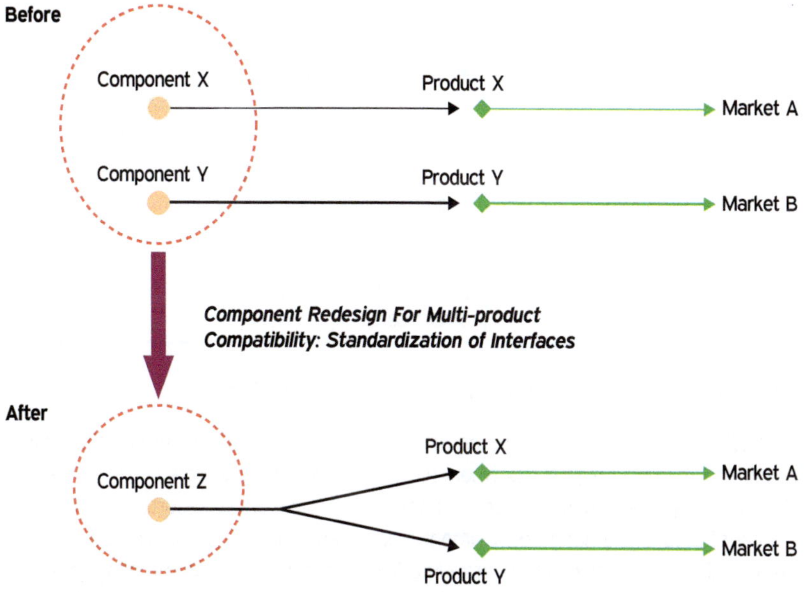

Source: Mikkola and Skjøtt-Larsen (2004).

Mass Customization and Postponement Supply Management

We have learned that mass customization strategies are closely linked with postponement and modularization strategies. The various points at which customers can influence the degree of customization also require that firms manage their supply chains according to how the product platform can be modularized. The comparison of mass customization and postponement supply chains with respect to a traditional mass production supply chain is illustrated in Table 8.2.

Table 8.2 Mass customization and postponement supply chains

Modularization elements	Traditional supply chain	Mass customization supply chain	Postponement supply chain
Interface compatibility effects	• Integrated vertical structure • Long development lead time	• Modular product architecture • Reduction of development lead time • Vertical coordination	• Customer decoupling points • Accurate and short customer response time
Component customization	• Design and manufacturing focus • In-house product development • Standardized components	• Autonomous innovation in NPD • Customer focus • Design for manufacturability	• Process design • Design for postponement
Value inputs	• Economies of scale • Exploiting advantages of market mechanism • Standardization of operations • Consolidation of outbound logistics	• Outsourcing • Flexibility towards specific customer's needs • Economies of scale and scope	• Reduced inventory costs and risks of obsolescence • Increased flexibility towards market needs and changes • Economies of scale and scope
Supplier–buyer interdependence	• Arm's length • Supplier involvement in development not critical • Multiple sourcing	• Early supplier involvement in NPD • Strategic partnership • Supplier as system integrator • High interdependence	• Customer relationship management • Involvement of TPL providers in final manufacturing and logistics • Direct deliveries to customers through merge-in-transit
Examples	Ford's Model T Generic bicycles Light bulbs Tyres	Dell computers HP printers Oticon's hearing aids Bang & Olufsen's audio-video systems Smart cars	

When modularizing a product platform for supply chain, the company should consider:

- ***Interface compatibility effects***, which refer to the degree to which component interfaces are specified and standardized. Mixing and matching is possible when interface compatibility effects are minimized. The push nature of a traditional supply chain does not see interface standardization as important, as it tends to have an integrated vertical structure, with long development lead times. Mass customization and postponement supply chains, on the other hand, seek to maximize interface standardization as a means to reduce development lead time. With standardization it is also possible to decide the decoupling points for postponement.
- ***Component customization*** refers to the extent to which a component can be customized. Customized components, as opposed to standard components, are often dedicated to specific applications. The traditional supply chain does not give too much importance to customization, as it often focuses on efficiency of design and manufacturing processes, dictated by the production of components in high volumes. The mass customization supply chain focuses on customer needs, and encourages the new product development (NPD) group to innovate independently, owing to the modular nature of the product architectures. The engineers also have to consider how to design the products so that they can be manufactured (i.e. design for manufacturability). The postponement supply chain considers how to organize a company's processes to support the products that are designed for postponement.

- ***Value inputs*** refer to the value-adding inputs that differentiate the buyer's final system. The relevance of added value is relative to the structure of supply chains, such as the number of tiers of suppliers. First-tier suppliers play a more prominent role in creating value inputs, as they are more willing to invest in product and process developments, and are also responsible for coordinating the required supply of inputs from the second-tier and lower-tier suppliers. Parts supplied by the key suppliers often have higher strategic value. The traditional supply chain focuses on economies of scale, and tends to exploit the advantages of the market mechanism (e.g. many tiers of suppliers). The value inputs are often gained from standardization of operations, and consolidation of outbound logistics. Mass customization and postponement supply chains seek to gain both from economies of scale (i.e. high volume production) and from economies of scope (i.e. product differentiation through customization). Postponement supply chains also focus on how to reduce inventory costs, and how to manage risks of obsolescence, such as when accidents take place, disrupting the flow of the supply of the components.
- ***Supplier–buyer interdependence*** refers to the degree of supplier involvement in product development that leads to capabilities benchmarking, trust development and creation of inter-firm knowledge. The traditional supply chain tends not to involve suppliers in NPD. Multiple sourcing and arm's length relationships with suppliers are often the policy. The mass customization supply chain, on the other hand, sees key suppliers as partners for the success of platform development, especially with the system integrators, and this close collaboration leads to increased interdependence between the partners. The postponement supply chain takes a focus on customer relationship management in terms of services and logistics efficiency, by involving TPL providers in the manufacturing and logistics processes.

The key point is ...

that when an organization is designing a new product, it should take supply chain strategies into consideration.

Stop and Think

Is there a limit to standardization?

Dynamics of Supply Networks

In Chapter 6 we learned how supply chain relationships can be organized. Here we present an alternative model, focusing on how products can be designed to shape the supply networks. As mentioned in Chapter 4, modular product architectures enable various specializations to take place independently of each other. This encourages innovation and technical advances to be developed in isolation. Any supplier can develop innovations, independent of other suppliers. This also means that suppliers compete with each other. Often the supplier with superior capabilities captures the market when its proprietary systems are established (such as Intel's microprocessor for IBM). Proprietary systems tend to encourage integration with other systems so that more value can be offered to the customers.

BUSINESS INTEGRATION

Chapter 6, p177

Chapter 4, p105

It is fair to say that it is extremely difficult for a firm to stay dominant in the marketplace for a long time. Vertically integrated firms are typically large corporations with hierarchical organizational structures, making them extremely rigid and unable to respond to rapid changes. These corporations face increasing competition from niche players that seek to have a share of the market. Eventually these corporations have to find ways to become more efficient, and be able to respond to market changes faster. The once-dominant integral product can no longer compete with the innovations from the niche players, either in price or in performance. This will force the company to modularize the product system (i.e. decompose the system into simpler portions). This will allow it to outsource portions of the system and have more supply options. When products become modular, and when there are many competing suppliers, the industry becomes horizontal.

Supplier relationships can change from a vertically integrated structure (with integral product strategies) to a horizontally fragmented structure (with modular product strategies), as shown in the *double helix model* in Figure 8.10.

Figure 8.11 provides an illustration of how the structure of the computer industry looked between 1975 and 1985. The industry was structured vertically with three main dominant players, each with its own integral product architectures and proprietary systems.

Figure 8.10 The double helix model

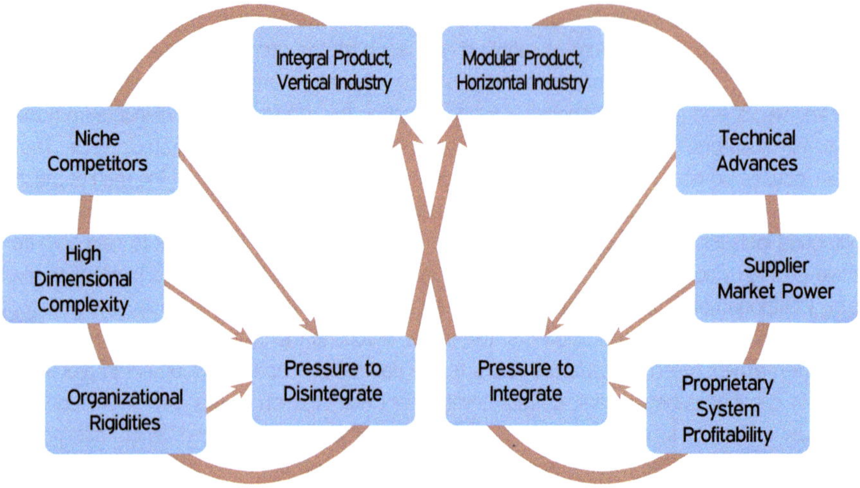

Source: Fine (1998).

With IBM's decision to standardize its PC platform, the computer industry suddenly became fragmented, with a large number of players dominating in specific parts of the computer system. The industry structure had become less vertically integrated, owing to the modularity of product architectures (Figure 8.12).

Figure 8.11 Computer industry structure, 1975–1985

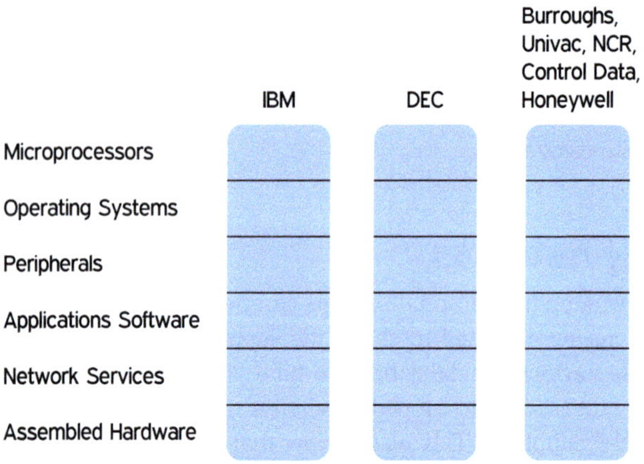

Source: Fine (1998).

Figure 8.12 Computer industry structure, 1985–1995

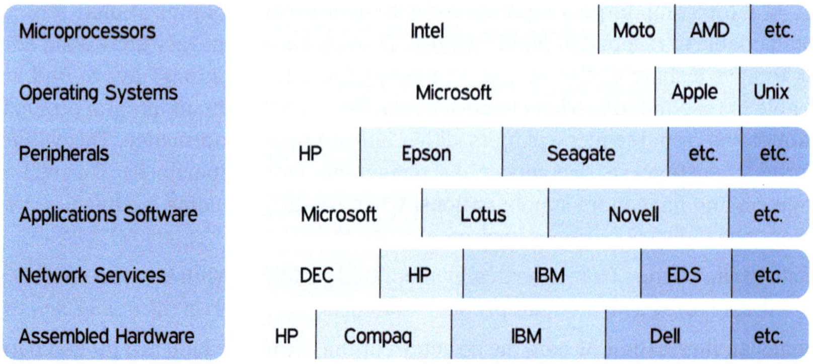

Source: Fine (1998).

The key point is ...

that whatever decisions a company makes in order to optimize its supply chain, one of the most difficult challenges is to predict how the supply chain structure might change over time.

WORKED EXAMPLE 8.1

Double Helix Model

There are twice as many bicycles as automobiles worldwide. Bicycles were introduced in the 19th century, and there have been few changes to its product architecture since then. The bicycle's inherently modular design allowed a large number of suppliers to compete in innovation as well as in price.

Shimano currently has approximately 50% of the market share in the global bicycle component market (such as drive train, brake, wheel and pedal components), and major control of the technological development of this industry. It gained this huge market share by integrating traditionally modular components into new components. For instance, the rear hub and cog set were integrated in a way that made other brands of cogs and hubs incompatible with Shimano's components. Shimano also integrated its shift levers into the braking system, requiring bicycle assemblers to purchase Shimano brake and shift levers as a single unit. Furthermore, bike makers that rely on Shimano parts also became distributors (Kerber, 1998).

Problem: *Apply the double helix model to describe the current bicycle industry, and predict what is going to happen in this industry. How might this affect Shimano's market share?*

Approach: Start by assessing whether the product architecture of the bicycle is modular or integral, and whether the industry structure is horizontal or vertical. In Figure 8.13, pick the starting point as either box 1 (modular product, horizontal industry) or box 6 (integral product, vertical structure).

Figure 8.13

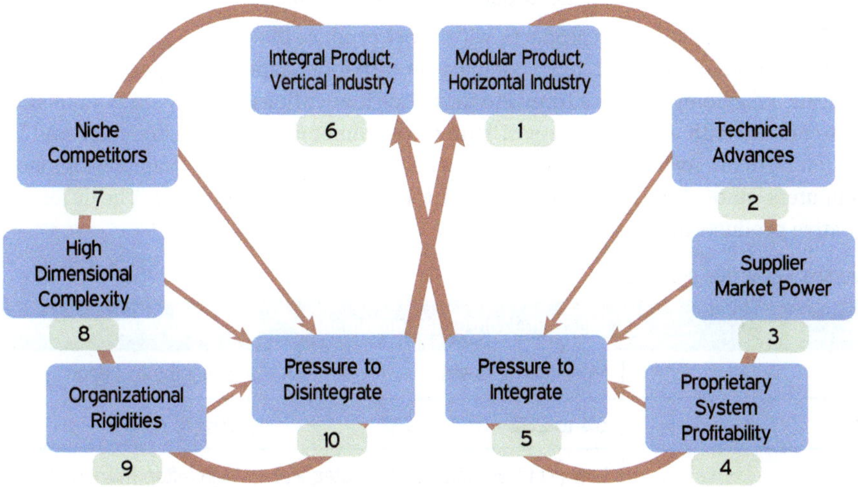

Solution:

Step 1 Start with box 1: The modular design of bicycles and the huge number of suppliers suggest that the current bicycle industry has a horizontal structure, and the product architecture is modular.

Step 2 The Double Helix Model predicts that the technical advances (box 2 – e.g. integration of rear hub and cog set), supplier market power (box 3 – e.g. requiring bicycle assemblers to purchase Shimano brake and shift levers as a single unit), and proprietary system profitability (box 4 – e.g. 50% market share) enjoyed by Shimano are going to change.

Step 3 According to the model, the bicycle industry will face significant pressure to integrate (box 5) into a vertical industry structure, with bikes that are characterized by integral product architectures (box 6 – e.g. electric-powered bikes or other innovative systems).

Step 4 When this happens, the various component makers and assemblers will face competition from their respective niche markets (box 7). This will introduce many new dimensions of complexity (box 8 – e.g. capacity for market expansion, technological imitation from competitors, control of the supply chain, etc.). As these companies grow, their organization structures become rigid (box 9): that is, the organizations become slow and inflexible to respond to market needs. This will exert pressure for the industry to disintegrate (box 10) again into a horizontal structure, with bikes having modular product architectures (box 1). The cycle starts all over again.

Tactics for Supplier Management

Functional Versus Innovative Products

Demand for products and services is difficult to predict, and supplier relationships are affected by this. In order to manage supplier relationships effectively, a company needs to understand the nature of the demand for the product or service it supplies. Uncertainties in demand for products can be better managed if we understand the type of product – that is, whether they are functional or innovative.

Functional products are products that have long product life cycles, low contribution margin, low product variety, and predictable demand. For example, fast-moving consumer goods sold in grocery stores typically have stable, predictable demand and long life cycles. The low product variety makes accurate forecasting easier. Certainly the nature of demand for toothpaste and toilet paper can be quite different from those for high-speed cameras. Toothpaste and toilet paper are products that satisfy our basic needs, which don't change much over time. They are staples, with long product cycles, that people buy in a wide range of retail outlets. Their demands are predictable and stable. Functional products tend to have stable supply chains, and the focus for operations is on increasing efficiency through lean thinking, which is explored more in Chapter 10, or on gaining from economies of scale through mass production.

Chapter 10, p323

Innovative products, on the other hand, are products with short product life cycles, a high contribution margin, high product variety, and unpredictable demand. In comparison with toilet paper, high-speed cameras have shorter product life cycles, because the companies are forced to introduce innovations to counteract innovations from the imitators. The market ends up with a large variety of innovative cameras. The short life cycle and large variety make demand prediction difficult. Average stock-out rates tend to be high too. Other examples of innovative products are high-end computers, state of the art semiconductors, and mass-customized goods. The differences between functional and innovative products are shown in Table 8.3.

Table 8.3 Functional versus innovative products

Aspects of demand	Functional (predictable demand)	Innovative (unpredictable demand)
Product life cycle	More than 2 years	3 months to 1 year
Contribution margin*	5% to 20%	20% to 60%
Product variety	Low (10 to 20 variants per category)	High (often millions of variants)
Average margin of error in the forecast at the time production is committed	10%	40% to 100%
Average stock-out rate	1% to 2%	10% to 40%
Average forced end-of-the-season markdown as percentage of full price	0%	10% to 25%
Lead time required for made-to-order products	6 months to 1 year	1 day to 2 weeks

* The contribution margin equals price minus variable cost divided by price, and is expressed as a percentage.

Source: Adapted from Fisher (1997).

Table 8.4 Efficient versus responsive supply

	Physically efficient process	Market-responsive process
Primary purpose	Supply predictable demand efficiently at the lowest possible cost	Respond quickly to unpredictable demand in order to minimize stock-outs, forced markdowns, and obsolete inventory
Manufacturing focus	Maintain high average utilization rate	Deploy excess buffer capacity
Inventory strategy	Generate high turns and minimize inventory through the chain	Deploy significant buffer stocks of parts or finished goods
Lead time focus	Shorten lead time as long as it doesn't increase cost	Invest aggressively in ways to reduce lead time
Approach to choosing suppliers	Select primarily for cost and quality	Select primarily for speed, flexibility, and quality
Product design strategy	Maximize performance and minimize cost	Use modular design in order to postpone product differentiation for as long as possible

Source: Adapted from Fisher (1997).

Services, too, face similar issues. For instance, standard services (such as those from McDonald's) can be more easily predicted than innovative services (such as Internet shopping for organic food).

Efficient Versus Responsive Supplier Relationships

In order to understand how to manage the supply chain for functional and innovative products, we need to understand the differences between efficient and responsive supply. Efficient supply is characterized by longer production lead times and larger batch sizes, which allow the firm to produce at a low unit cost. Responsive supply focuses on the ability to respond to wide ranges of quantities demanded, meet short lead times, handle a large variety of products, build innovative products, and meet a high service level. These characteristics are illustrated in Table 8.4.

Supply for innovative products should be responsive in order to deal with unpredictable demand – that is, innovative products should have a market-responsive supply chain. On the other hand, functional products require efficient and stable supply chains to maintain high utilization rates of manufacturing. Figure 8.14 shows the right match between products and supply chains.

Figure 8.14 Matching products with supply chains.

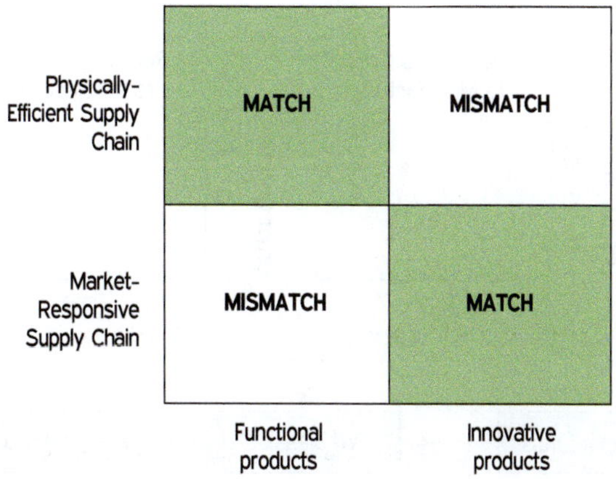

Source: Adapted from Fisher (1997).

Stop and Think

Do all functional products have stable and mature supply processes? Do all innovative products have evolving processes? For example, how have the distribution channels for USB memory sticks changed during the past 10 years?

The Bullwhip Effect

BUSINESS INTEGRATION

The *bullwhip effect,* also referred to as the Forrester effect, is a term used to explain why information about the final customer's actual demand gets distorted from one end of the supply chain to the other. Distortion of information occurs further upstream in the supply chain because each member in the supply chain makes ordering decisions based on the information it receives from its downstream member. Each member has its own ordering protocols and policies that are based on reorder points and order quantities. When there are disruptions in the ordering process, demand variability increases as we move upstream towards the supplier. Fluctuations in these cause distortion of information in the supply chain, leading to excessive inventory, out-of-stock, inefficient production schedules, and higher expediting costs. Figure 8.15 shows the amplification of order variability from consumers to the supplier.

It shows the order patterns faced by each intersection in the supply chain, consisting of a supplier, a manufacturer, a wholesaler, a retailer, and consumers. The retailer places an order on the manufacturer that is based on the consumer sales data. The wholesaler plans its production based on the order it receives from the retailer; the manufacturer plans its production based on the order it receives from the wholesaler; and, finally, the supplier plans its production according to the order it receives from the manufacturer. As each party makes decisions based on the information it receives from the downstream member, the demand information gets distorted. The figure shows that the retailer's orders to the wholesaler display greater variability than the consumer sales; the wholesaler's orders to the manufacturer shows even larger variability; and, finally, the manufacturer's order to the supplier has the largest oscillations.

Imagine you are playing 'Chinese Whispers' in a party with your friends. One person (consumer) whispers a word or a phrase into the ear of the person next to him or her (retailer). The person who gets the whisper passes it down to the next person, and so on, until the last person (supplier). The last person has to say what he or she thinks was whispered to him or her. There are always errors or misunderstandings during the retellings, and they accumulate as the whispers are passed: therefore the message received by the last person is often quite different from the message sent by the first.

There are four factors that *amplify* the bullwhip effect:

- *Inaccurate demand forecast updating:* forecasting relies on the order history from the company's immediate customers. When all parties in the supply chain add a percentage to their demand forecasts, the true customer demand becomes distorted.
- *Order batching:* customers place orders in batches at varying cycles. Some order daily, whereas others place orders weekly or monthly.

Figure 8.15 The bullwhip effect

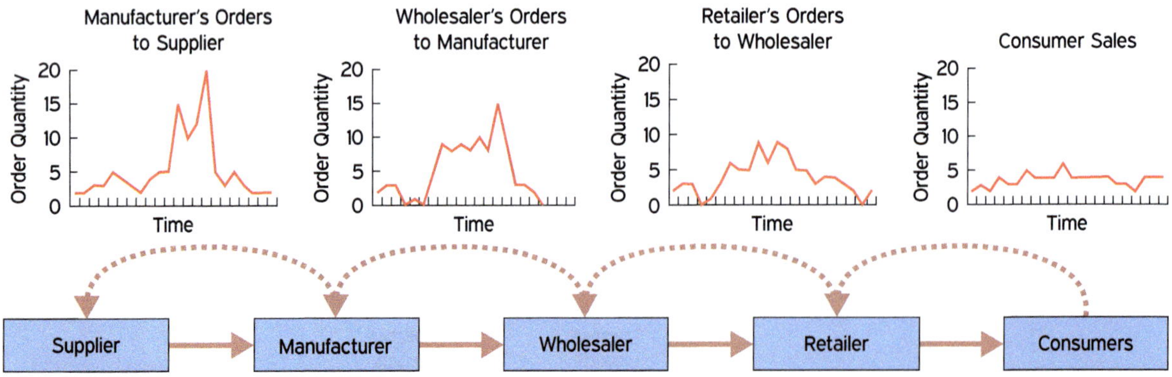

Source: Adapted from Lee *et al.* (1997).

Table 8.5 A framework for supply chain coordination initiatives

Cause of bullwhip	Information sharing	Channel alignment	Operational efficiency
Demand forecast update	• Understanding system dynamics • Use point-of-sale (POS) data • Electronic data interchange (EDI) • Internet • Computer-assisted ordering (CAO)	• Vendor-managed inventory (VMI) • Discount for information sharing • Consumer direct	• Lead time reduction • Echelon-based inventory control
Order batching	• EDI • Internet ordering	• Discount for truck-load assortment • Delivery appointments • Consolidation • Logistics outsourcing	• Reduction in fixed cost of ordering by EDI or electronic commerce • CAO
Price fluctuations		• Continuous replenishment programme (CRP) • Everyday low cost (EDLC)	• Everyday low price (EDLP) • Activity-based costing (ABC)
Shortage gaming	• Sharing sales, capacity, and inventory data	• Allocation based on past sales	

Source: Lee *et al.* (1997).

- *Price fluctuation:* distributors and manufacturers periodically offer special promotions such as price discounts, quantity discounts or coupons, in order to boost the order quantity. This encourages customers to buy in quantities that do not reflect their immediate needs. Often the customers will not place the next order until the inventory is sold.
- *Rationing and shortage gaming:* customers order more than they need when they know there will be a shortage in supply. Later, when demand is stabilized, excessive orders disappear and cancellations pour in. This 'game' that the customers play with the orders gives the supplier little information about the product's real demand.

Let's consider how the bullwhip effect can be controlled to improve supply chain performance. This requires the firms to find ways to coordinate the information flow and plan along the supply chain: namely, information sharing, channel alignment, and operational efficiency (Table 8.5). *Information sharing* is concerned with how demand information at the downstream site is transmitted upstream. *Channel alignment* refers to the coordination of pricing, transportation, inventory planning and ownership between the upstream and downstream sites of a supply chain. Finally, *operations efficiency* is concerned with activities that improve the performance of the supply chain.

Distorted information can lead to inefficiencies, such as excessive inventory investment, poor customer service, lost revenues, misguided capacity plans, ineffective transportation, and missed production schedules (Lee *et al.*, 1997).

WORKED EXAMPLE 8.2

Estimating Demand Fluctuations

You work as a supply chain manager of a large clothing retail store. One of the best-selling items at your store is the latest fashion bag from a Brazilian manufacturer called Gorgeous. You have always ordered 200 bags every 6 months (in March and in September). Now other retail stores have started to sell competing fashion bags. You notice that the sale of Gorgeous bags is declining, so you decide to reduce the order by 5%, to 190 bags. Assume that the supply chain of Gorgeous bags has four tiers: the retail store, the wholesaler, the manufacturer, and the supplier. Let's also assume that each tier keeps one period's worth of inventory.

Problem: ***Estimate the demand fluctuation across the supply chain due to the 5% drop in demand order. How many periods does it take until each tier is able to meet the new demand?***

Approach: Start by calculating the production stock needed for each tier in order to satisfy the consumer demand. This can be done with the grid shown in Table 8.6.

Period 1 is the base of your calculations, where there are no disruptions in the supply chain. Every tier is able to supply the 200 bags.

In Period 2, however, the drop of market demand to 190 bags requires the retail store (RS) to have a final stock [stock (f)] of 190 bags. However, RS still has 200 bags of initial (or starting) stock [stock (i)], which means that RS needs only to have a production rate of 180 bags (this becomes the demand rate for the wholesaler W).

The production rate is simply two times the demand (to account for actual demand in that period, and also assuming the same demand for the next period). This is because you need to keep one period's worth of inventory.

The production rate of W for Period 2 is 2(180) – 200 = 160 bags

Production rate of W = Demand for M = 160 bags

Follow the same logic for each period, until each tier is able to meet the new demand of 190 bags.

Solution: In this case, it took six periods. Graphically, the demand fluctuations (or the production rates) for the entire supply chain are illustrated in Figure 8.16. Notice how the fluctuations amplify towards the supplier.

Table 8.6 Demand order of Gorgeous bags

Time (period)	Supplier (S)		Manufacturer (W)		Wholesaler (M)		Retail store (RS)		Market demand
	Production rate	Stock (i) Stock (f)	Production rate	Stock (i) Stock (f)	Production rate	Stock (i) Stock (f)	Production rate	Stock (i) Stock (f)	
1	200	200 200	200	200 200	200	200 200	200	200 200	200
2	40	200 120	120	200 120	160	200 180	180	200 190	190
3	360	120 240	240	160 200	200	180 190	190	190 190	190
4	120	240 180	180	190 190	190	190 190	190	190 190	190
5	200	180 190	190	190 190	190	190 190	190	190 190	190
6	190	190 190	190	190 190	190	190 190	190	190 190	190

Figure 8.16 Demand fluctuation in the supply chain of fashion bags from Gorgeous

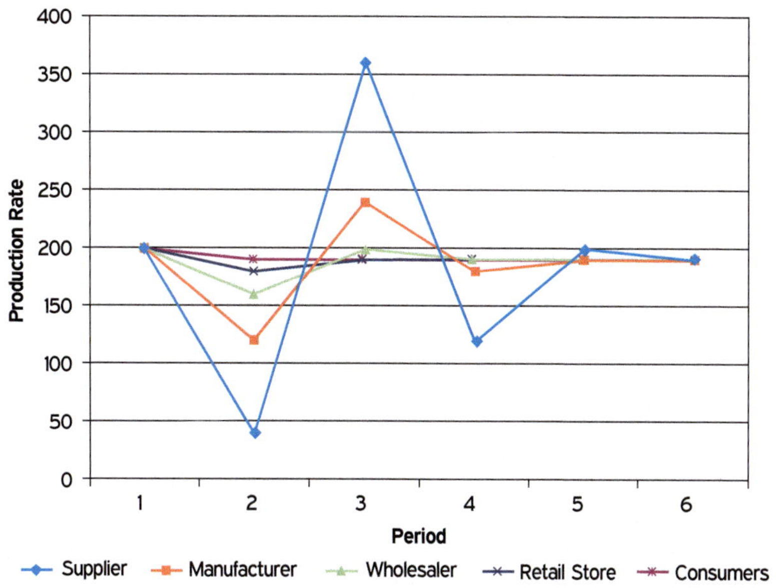

SHORT CASE 8.1

Measuring your body for online apparel shopping

Source: © MONOPOLY919/Shutterstock

In 2001, when IoT was just taking off, a forward-thinking American company called FitMe developed smart solutions for the apparel industry. It had size information on more than 300 brands of clothing. One of its products was Size Genie, which used web-based software that allowed individual shoppers to accurately determine their measurements. Its purpose was to enable consumers to purchase apparel with confidence. The Size Genie service was used by retailers who wished to offer clothing purchases online or at their retail stores. Its success was soon met with competitors, such as My Virtual Model and other app-based solution companies. In 2020, there is now a wide range of companies that provide even more sophisticated solutions, such as TD3D Studio's Scanatic from Taiwan, where you can have a 3D scan of your body.

With the increasing number of online retailers offering customized clothing, the information along the supply chain from the customer to the supplier should be as accurate as possible. Information technology and applications, such as Size Genie, My Virtual Model, and TD3D align the supply chain by providing more accurate and on-time demand forecast updates. They also reduce order-batching problems, as customers can place orders whenever they wish, and the information is transmitted directly to the supplier. Price fluctuations as well as rationing and shortage gaming are also reduced, as customers do not have to purchase larger quantities than they need. In short, information sharing and collaboration between all parties in the supply chain can help reduce the bullwhip effect.

Questions

1. In what ways can information technology influence the bullwhip effect?
2. How can TD3D make sure that its products have the right supply chain?

Leagile Supply

Leagile supply combination of a lean supply chain and an agile supply chain.

Lean supply seeks to develop a value stream to eliminate all waste.

Chapter 10, p323

Agile supply use of market knowledge and the virtual corporation to exploit profitable opportunities in a volatile marketplace.

We have learned that variation in demand can be difficult to predict, and that companies need to match their products with the appropriate supply channels. The supply channel for mass-produced goods, for instance, would not be effective if the company wanted to be flexible, and to be able to respond to unique customer demand quickly. On the other hand, firms also seek to achieve efficiency by eliminating waste. In fact, the ideal situation is to find the best way to be lean and to be agile. **Leagile supply** is the combination of a **lean supply** chain and an **agile supply** chain.

Lean Supply

If a supply chain is stable, the aim for operations is to make it as *efficient* as possible, that is, having an efficient supply. The focus of lean supply is on *minimizing waste* (see Chapter 10).

Agile Supply

When demand is unpredictable and changes quickly, it creates challenges for suppliers, as described above. But it also creates opportunities for those companies or enterprises that are able to respond quickly to changes in demand, that is, having a responsive supply. *Agile suppliers* use market knowledge and cooperation to exploit profitable opportunities in a volatile marketplace. The data shared between suppliers and buyers is increasingly based on information technology. In order to be agile, suppliers need to be *flexible* so that they can be ready for change.

A comparison of lean supply with agile supply is illustrated in Table 8.7. As elimination of waste is central to being lean, lead times and costs need to be minimized. Lean supply works best with products with predictable demand and long product life cycles. These products tend to compete on price, and hence have low profit margins. Agile supply chains, on the other hand, fit best for fashion- or technology-based goods subject to volatile market demand, where product variety is high and life cycles are short. Here, availability becomes the driver.

Matching supply and demand of the product leads to four supply chain strategies (Figure 8.17), depending on replenishment lead times and to what extent demand is predictable: (1) lean continuous replenishment; (2) agile quick response; (3) lean, planning and execution; and (4) leagile production/postponement.

Table 8.7 Attributes of lean supply and agile supply

Distinguishing attributes	Lean supply	Agile supply
Typical products	Commodities	Fashion goods
Marketplace demand	Predictable	Volatile
Product variety	Low	High
Product life cycle	Long	Short
Customer drivers	Cost	Availability
Profit margin	Low	High
Dominant costs	Physical costs	Marketability costs
Stock-out penalties	Long-term contractual	Immediate and volatile
Purchasing policy	Buy goods	Assign capacity
Information enrichment	Highly desirable	Obligatory
Forecasting mechanism	Algorithmic	Consultative

Source: Adapted from Mason-Jones *et al.* (2000).

Figure 8.17 Lean, agile and leagile supply chain

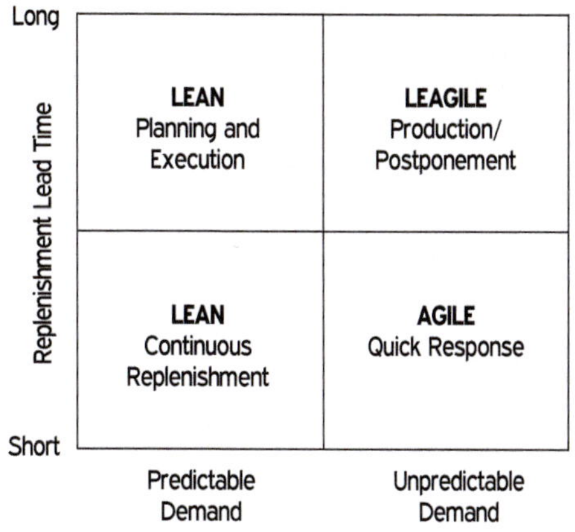

Source: Adapted from Christopher *et al.* (2006).

Combining Lean and Agile

It is possible to combine the best of both the lean and agile approaches. The challenge is to balance efficiency and flexibility. To find the balance between lean and agile processes in supplier management, all parties involved need to understand the market requirements, such as product variety and demand variability (Figure 8.18). Whereas lean processes focus on developing a value stream to eliminate all waste, agile processes use market knowledge to find the value provided to the customers. Balancing the two processes means finding the best combination of efficiency of lean processes (early in the supply chain) and flexibility of agile processes (later in the supply chain). The point in the leagile supply chain that links these two processes is called the *decoupling point.*

Decoupling Point

For optimal supplier relationship management, the *decoupling point* separates activities that are directly geared towards satisfying customer orders (i.e. pull strategy) from activities directly based on forecast demand (i.e. push strategy). With a 'pull' strategy, customer order information is acquired before production of the goods starts. With a 'push' strategy, on the other hand, goods are produced first and then sold to the customer, which means that an organization has to have plenty of inventory ready for shipment. In order for the items to flow efficiently, the push and pull strategies should be aligned.

The decoupling point is also associated with mass customization and postponement strategies as the point of differentiation. With make-to-stock products, products are pushed down the supply chain without differentiation to the retailer and distributor. With assemble-to-order and make-to-order products, customization and differentiation of the product takes place at the manufacturer and assemblers. With buy-to-order products, the customization of the product is not initiated until the order information is received up-stream, at the raw material supplier. For a detailed description of types of order, see Chapter 5 on Processes.

Chapter 5, p139

The decoupling point is where the buffer stock is held. This is to help safeguard against fluctuating customer orders, and simultaneously help to smooth production (Figure 8.19). It is also the point where product differentiation (from standardized goods into customized ones) takes place through postponement.

Figure 8.18 Lean, agile and leagile supplier management

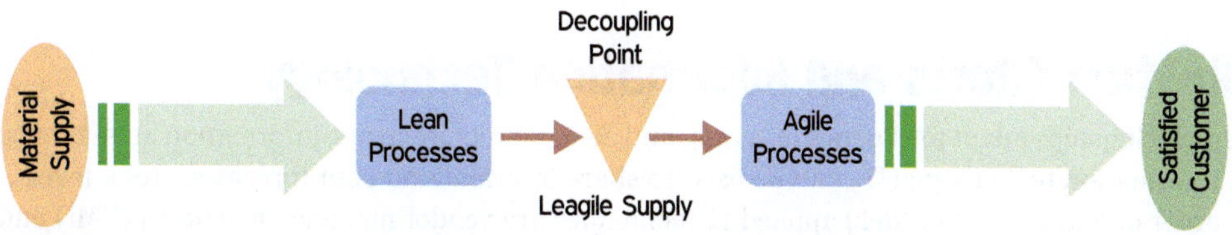

Source: Adapted from Mason-Jones *et al.* (2000).

Figure 8.19 Decoupling point

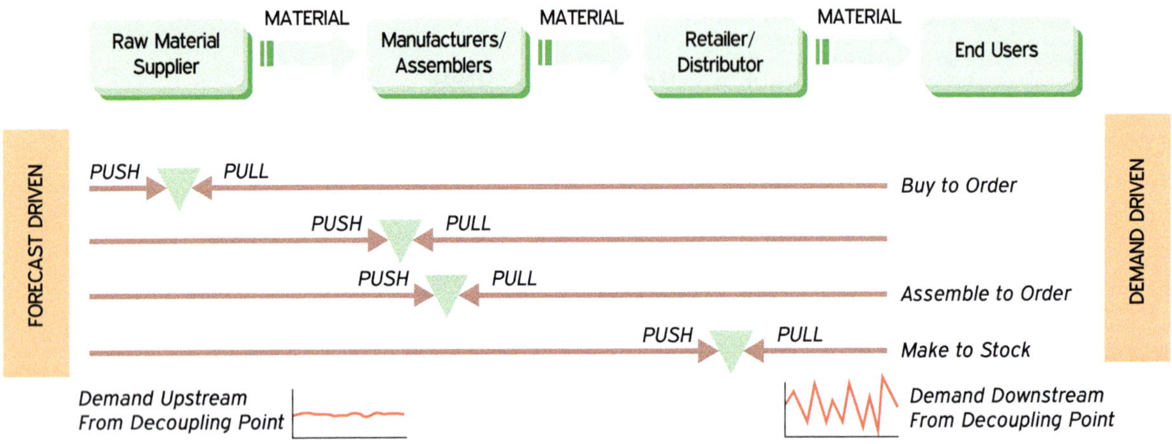

Source: Adapted from Mason-Jones *et al.* (2000).

Figure 8.20 Route map for integrating lean and agile supply chains

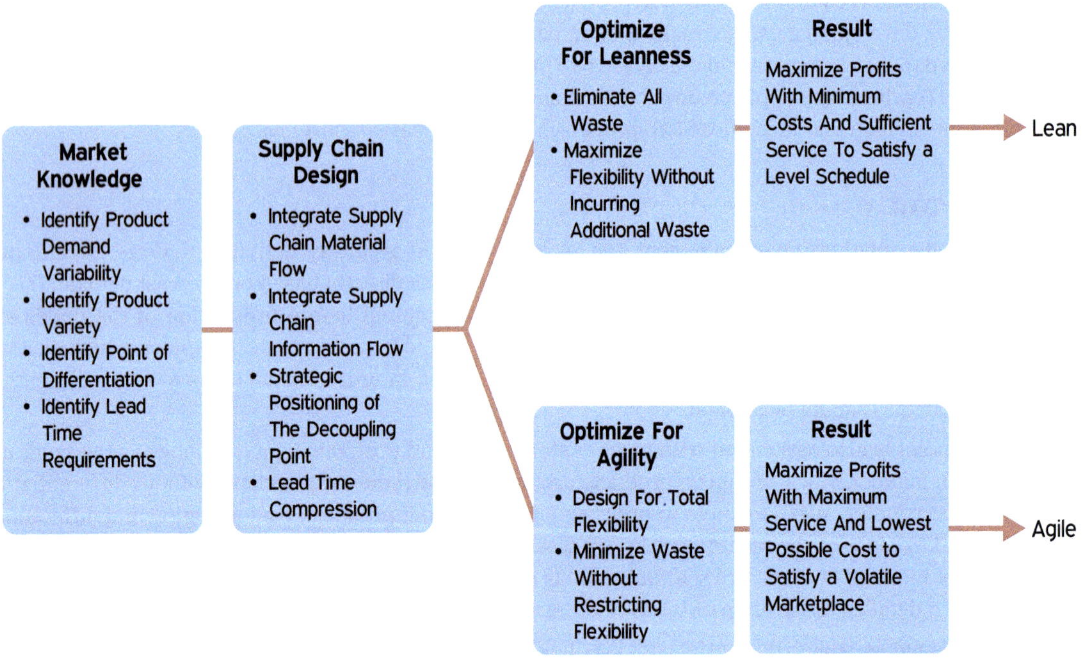

Source: Adapted from Mason-Jones *et al.* (2000).

A route map for integrating leanness and agility is illustrated in Figure 8.20.

BUSINESS INTEGRATION

GLOBALIZATION

Coordination Efforts and Information Technology

As supplier relationships adapt to changes in supply and demand requirements, information must be shared with all suppliers. Information technology (IT) can be used to share information about forecasts, stock levels, production plans and order quantities. Two widely applied IT techniques are vendor-managed inventory (VMI) and collaborative planning, forecasting and replenishment (CPFR).

Vendor-managed Inventory

Vendor-managed inventory (VMI) is inventory that is managed by a supplier on behalf of its customers. It is also known as *co-managed inventory*. The buyer shares its inventory information with its vendors (or suppliers), so that the vendors can manage the inventory for the buyer, dealing with such things as inventory replenishment decisions regarding order quantities, shipping and timing. The purchase order still has to be initiated by the buyer, though. With VMI, the buyer's transaction costs related to ordering and order fulfilment are transferred to the vendor. This reduces the supply-side uncertainty, and gives the vendor a better chance to coordinate its inventory with the buyer's. This is a practice used widely by leading grocery stores such as Tesco.

Some of the benefits of VMI partnership are (Angulo *et al.*, 2004):

- Reduced costs due to better resource utilization for production and transportation
- Improved service levels due to better coordination of replenishment orders
- Reduced lead times and increased inventory turns
- Reduced inventory stock-outs achieved by increasing inventory visibility
- Higher selling space productivity obtained by optimizing inventory.

SHORT CASE 8.2

P&G's Pampers

One of the best-selling items made by Procter & Gamble (P&G) is Pampers nappies. The logistics executives could not understand why its sales at the retail stores were fluctuating, when it is well documented that the customer demand for nappies does not fluctuate significantly. The executives discovered that P&G was faced with a substantial degree of variability in orders from its retailers. After a close investigation, P&G found that the primary causes of this bullwhip effect were the demand signals from its distributors, who would often place orders on an infrequent basis. Changes in prices by the manufacturer also changed the order demand. This was accentuated when distributors placing multiple orders were not certain that the manufacturer could meet the distributor's demand. Currently P&G employs VMI in its supply chain for nappies, starting with its supplier 3M and finishing with its customer Wal-Mart. This allows P&G to have access to the demand and inventory information from 3M and Wal-Mart, hence improving its demand forecasting.

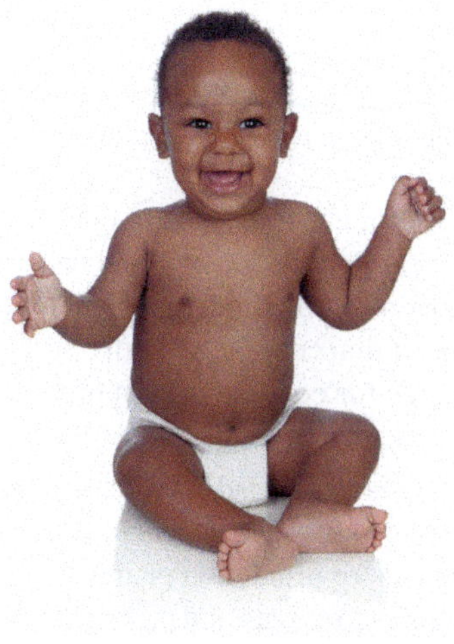

Source: ©Shutterstock/Gelpi

Questions

1. Should Procter & Gamble implement VMI for other products? Why?
2. How can Procter & Gamble, through VMI, improve its relationship with its suppliers and customers?

Source: Lee *et al.* (1997).

Collaborative Planning, Forecasting and Replenishment

Collaborative planning, forecasting and replenishment (CPFR) is a business practice that combines the intelligence of multiple trading partners in the planning and fulfilment of customer demand. It links sales and marketing best practices to supply chain planning and execution in order to increase availability, while reducing inventory, transportation and logistics costs (www.vics.org). It establishes guidelines for companies to integrate their planning processes across corporate boundaries. The CPFR model comprises four collaborative activities, each complemented by business-to-business tasks: strategy and planning, demand and supply management, execution, and analysis. *Strategy and planning* activities include establishing the ground rules for the collaborative relationship, determining product mix and placement, and developing event plans. *Demand and supply management*

Table 8.8 CPFR tasks

Retailer tasks	Collaborative tasks	Manufacturer tasks
Strategy and planning		
Vendor management	Collaboration arrangement	Accounting planning
Category management	Joint business plan	Market planning
Demand and supply management		
Point-of-sale forecasting	Sales forecasting	Market data analysis
Replenishment planning	Order planning/forecasting	Demand planning
Execution		
Buying/re-buying	Order generation	Production and supply planning
Logistics/distribution	Order fulfilment	Logistics/distribution
Analysis		
Store execution	Exception management	Execution monitoring
Supplier scorecard	Performance assessment	Customer scorecard

Source: Adapted from VICS (2004).

activities include projecting consumer demand, ordering and shipment requirements. *Execution* activities include placing orders, preparing and delivering shipments, receiving and stocking products on retail shelves, recording sales transactions, and making payments. *Analysis* activities include monitoring, planning and execution activities for exception conditions, aggregating results, calculating key performance metrics, and sharing insights and adjusting plans for continuously improved results. Each of these tasks is linked to respective retailer and manufacturer tasks, as summarized in Table 8.8.

The Düsseldorf-based Metro chain, for example, implemented the CPFR process with Metro Cash & Carry in Germany with its seven key suppliers of detergents and paper goods. The goal of the programme is to support joint workflow processes for promotion planning and promotional sales forecasting among the partners. Metro shares transactional data, sales forecasts and production schedules with its partners. This initiative has enabled a reduction of out-of-stock inventory and its end-of-promotion stocks. In 2012, it extended Metro Cash & Carry to smaller, local food producers globally to intensify direct cooperation to ensure more assortment, better quality and prices (Metro Group, 2011).

Stop and Think

If the benefits of embracing VMI and CPFR are so great, why aren't there more companies working with these concepts?

CRITICAL PERSPECTIVE

Disruptive Technology in Supply Chain – Near Field Communication

Technology has continuously offered tremendous benefits to the supply chain in terms of transparency, visibility, cost reduction and convenience for the customers (Druehl et al., 2017). Recently, near-field communication (NFC) technology is having a huge impact in the supply chain.

NFC is a set of communication protocols that enable two electronic devices, one of which is usually a portable device such as a smartphone, tablet or smart card, to establish touch and contactless communication in near proximity of each other. The information is transferred through a NFC reader and a NFC tag/card in close proximity, within 4 cm to 10 cm of each other.

The application of NFC is growing at an exponential pace in a wide range of industries, including food, healthcare, transportation, retail, to name a few. Examples of NFC applications include mobile payment services (e.g. mobile wallet), contactless ticketing (airport check-in for premium travellers), travel cards in public transportations, and so on.

NFC requires that SC members collaborate, particularly downstream as in consumer-to-business (C2B) and consumer-to-consumer (C2C). With C2B, online transfers use a secure platform where a consumer's own phone number is used at the online checkout. C2C transfer of money is possible, by linking credit card to a phone number. Transferring money is much like sending a text message to another phone number. The transfer of funds takes place instantly. In practice, it should speed up the process and potentially reduce the number of clerks, but the additional modes of payments might actually create the opposite effect (in the short run) as customers learn how to use the new technology.

Standardization of protocols for interoperability and compatibility for NFC devices determines, to some extent, how data is exchanged among devices, hence the infrastructure supporting NFC devices. Standardization invites anyone to compete in the NFC market, and as the standardization of NFC matures, there will be more specialized service innovation developed by third parties. As a consequence, there might be a surge of intermediaries (incumbents) in the supply chain, and potentially bypass the established organizations, risking supply chain disintermediation (Rossetti and Choi, 2005).

NFC devices are comprised of several components (i.e. tag, reader, mobile) involving stakeholders from diverse industries; NFC services cannot be offered by any firm alone. Stakeholders from different business sectors (e.g. retail, banks, customers, regulatory institutions) have to work together to ensure interoperability, which means new routines for services have to be developed and scaled up within and across the organizations.

Processes would need to be reorganized to ensure the performance of supply network and stakeholders are aligned. NFC technologies are developed in combination with different devices, therefore integration, adaptation and compatibility influence the speed and alignment of technological advancement of the devices. It is important to note that the user is active in the process, that is, the process is not activated until the customer starts the process. In other words, active participation of the customer is required, hence the service becomes interactive and the customer is the process owner; the service becomes interactive.

NFC has been quickly adopted in industry due to its easiness to use, share and exchange real-time data and information. The operational challenges for adoption and implementation of NFC are plenty. As NFC applications have different technical requirements (e.g. choice of technology, technology complexity) as well as use purposes (e.g. travel, payment, security) the price levels will vary. For instance, there are tradeoffs between price and security, as the more security prevention elements and options embedded in tags, the more expensive the tags. Volume and variety tradeoffs also influence the price, especially in applications where there are economies of scale (e.g. travel cards). Reliability of the data transfer might become problematic; if the NFC tag has a slow data transfer rate, the data might not be fully transferred in time. Hence, Interoperability, compatibility and standardization of the accepted NFC technology model are essential to achieve a good business model (Coskun *et al.*, 2013).

The key point is ...

is that the adoption of disruptive technologies requires that all members of the supply network collaborate to achieve standardization of protocols, interoperability and compatibility.

Service Supply Chains

Emerging technologies are shaping how new business models based on services are created, as evidenced by Uber in transportation services and Airbnb in hospitality services. Technologies such as 3D printing, virtual reality, autonomous vehicles, drones, and the Internet of Things (IoT) are ubiquitous, as they can be applied in many stages of the supply chain, and have huge impacts in the supply chain and provision of services (Figure 8.21).

Figure 8.21 Emerging technologies in the service supply chain

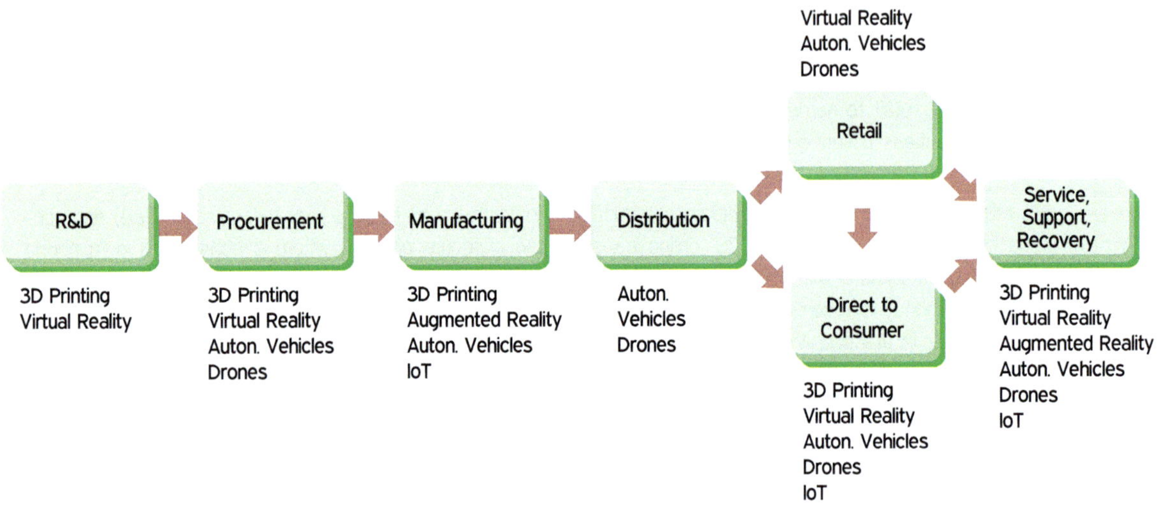

Source: Druehl *et al.* (2017).

- 3D printing is a process of building three-dimensional components and products directly from raw material and design data, enabling the production of designs in a single production step.
- Virtual reality and augmented reality are computer-generated environments, allowing for immersive customer feedback on designs without physical prototype or customer presence.
- Autonomous vehicles are driverless and self-driving vehicles such as trucks, cars and ships.
- Drones are essentially flying robots that can be controlled autonomously or via remote control.
- The Internet of Things (IoT) is a system of interrelated semi-autonomous devices that are interconnected via the Internet.

Stop and Think

Is supply chain of service different from the supply chain of physical products? In what ways do disruptive technologies enable the development of new services and influence the service supply chain?

SHORT CASE 8.3

Buying your car from a vending machine

Carvana is an American online used car retailer where customers can buy a car from its vending machines across 25 locations in the US. There are no dealerships involved. Everything is done online, from finding your car, getting financing, and purchasing. You can even take a virtual spin and inspect the features of the car with their patented 360-degree photo technology.

Source: ©Shutterstock/Jonathan Weiss

In 2018, Carvana was named one of the fastest growing used car dealers in the US. The vending machine business model has inspired other companies to replicate it. In China, Ford is partnering with Alibaba, the e-commerce giant, to open its first vending machine in the city of Guangzhou. With Alibaba's Tmall app, customers can book a test drive and time to visit the five-level vending machine.

Questions

1. How is digitalization changing the service supply chain?
2. Should the supply chain of the cars be reconfigured?

Source: www.carvana.com; Ward (2019).

Third-Party Logistics

Logistics refers to the process of planning and implementing the movement and storage of goods in the supply chain. As many companies expanded their operations to international markets, various logistics service providers began to emerge, often referred to as **third-party logistics** (TPL or 3PL) providers. In the EU market, the outsourced logistics operations is estimated to be €878 billion in 2012, with the top largest logistics service providers in the world located in Europe, including Deutsche post DHL and Maersk A/S (European Commission, 2015).

Logistics the process of planning and implementing the movement and storage of goods in the supply chain.

A TPL provider can be treated as an external supplier that performs some or all parts of a company's functions, especially logistics services. Examples of TPL services include facility management, transportation, warehouse management, call centres, and administration. The best-known TPL providers are UPS (United Parcel Service), FedEx (Federal Express), DHL and TNT.

Third-party logistics (TPL) a TPL provider can be treated as an external supplier that performs some or all parts of a company's functions, especially logistics services.

There are several advantages of using TPL providers (Simchi-Levi *et al.*, 2008):

- *Focus on core strengths:* it allows a company to focus on its core competencies, leaving the logistics expertise to the TPL providers.
- *Provide technological flexibility:* often companies do not have the time, resources, or expertise to update their technology and equipment, such as RFID (radio-frequency identification). Many TPL providers have the capability to constantly update information technology and equipment in a quicker and more cost-effective way.
- *Provide other flexibilities:* increasingly, suppliers are demanding rapid replenishment, which may require regional warehousing. The TPL providers will provide services for this warehousing, so that the supplier can meet customer requirements without committing capital and limiting flexibility by constructing a new facility or committing to a long-term lease. TPL providers can also bundle customized services to fit companies' specific needs.

Depending on the required skills shared between the parties, TPL relationships can be classified into four types (Halldorsson and Skjøtt-Larsen, 2004):

- *Market exchange:* almost no specific assets or integration exist between the parties. No specific skills are required from the providers (e.g. shippers who buy transportation and logistics services on the 'spot market').
- *Customized logistics solutions:* the clients can customize the desired package of solutions, which can be bundled together from a broad range of standard services, such as transportation and warehousing services.
- *Joint logistics solutions:* the collaboration is seen as a win–win solution, as the two parties collaborate to find unique logistics solutions. For example, some companies provide a 'one-stop solution' for their clients, acting as the single interface between the clients and the multiple logistics service providers.
- *In-house logistics solutions:* logistics is considered the core skill for the TPL provider. A broad range of management and value-adding logistics services is offered. The collaboration also involves knowledge about system integration and inter-organizational teams from different management levels.

Stop and Think

Would it be difficult for TPLs to provide customized services?

SHORT CASE 8.4

Lauritzen Bulkers

Source: ©Emagnetic/Shutterstock

Did you know that around 90% of world trade is carried by ships? Do you know what happens when a global transportation network is disrupted? Recall the disruptions in air space caused by the ash from the volcanic eruption in Iceland on 15 April 2010. The International Air Transport Association (IATA) estimated that, within a week, it affected almost a third of global flights, costing airlines about US\$1.7 billion of revenue.

Lauritzen Bulkers (LB) of Denmark operates around 85 vessels, which specialize in ocean transport of dry bulk cargo – that is, commodities such as coal, grains, bauxite, iron ore aggregates, food products and steel products. These goods are typically transported from the Americas, Australia and Africa to Asia and Europe. With self-loading and discharge capabilities, LB can readily respond to almost any market. It also has one of the youngest fleets afloat, with an average vessel age of 5–6 years. It makes about 500 voyages per year, equivalent to 22,000 vessel-days, transporting more than 20 million tons of over 45 different commodities.

CSR

While shipping bears the stigma of being a big polluter, it is actually the least damaging form of transportation. LB is committed to reducing CO_2 and other exhaust emissions, such as NO_x and SO_x. The new generation of LB's fleet is 25% more energy efficient than the 10–15 year old vessels it is replacing. Recently, LB introduced Lab-On-A-Ship™ (LOAS), an on-board system that can analyse fuel and lubricants automatically, making significant contributions to the engine performance of the vessels. It not only helps to make the vessels more reliable and efficient, but also ensures compliance with environmental standards.

Figure 8.22 Comparison of CO_2 emissions by different transport modes (European Shipowners' Association and International Chamber of Shipping)

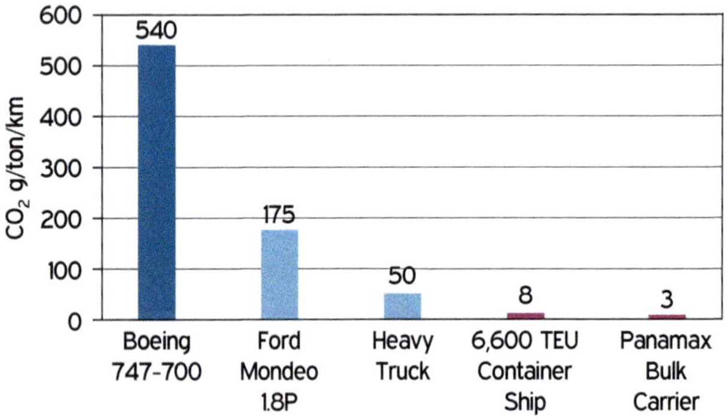

As explained by the Senior Technical Manager:

Having more efficient ships is more attractive for the customers. Our customers, the charterers, are the ones who hire our ships to freight cargo from A to B. Having lower operational costs in terms of fuel consumption is a plus. Energy conservation, and subsequently lower fuel consumption, reduces the overall operating cost and negative environmental impact. If we can show that we can operate the ships very effectively in terms of fuel consumption, it's a benefit for the charter, as they are typically the ones paying for the fuel. This eventually will have a tremendous impact on the environmental reputation of the company, and sustain a 'green image'.

Questions

1. Why do you think disruptions in one mode of transportation, such as air, impact on the supply of and demand for goods across the world?
2. How would you decide on the right supply chain strategy and mode of transportation for your goods?
3. How would new environmental regulations impact on the transportation of goods between regions?

Contemporary Thinking: Reverse Supply and Logistics

Reverse Supply

Supplier management traditionally charts the path of raw materials as they are transformed into goods and sold to end consumers. *Reverse supply* also includes processes related to retrieving used products from a customer, to either dispose of them or reuse them (Figure 8.23). Managing product returns is essential and mandatory for many industries. For instance, some goods, such as washing machines, computers, batteries and tyres, are typically managed by government agencies after disposal. Depending on the type of product, it might be repaired and reused, refurbished, recycled (with or without disassembly), or incinerated.

A great deal of manufactured products such as refrigerators and aerosols contain hazardous substances, such as mercury, lead and arsenic. This creates a huge burden for the waste management authorities. Many governments and environmental groups are encouraging *product stewardship*, making the manufacturers responsible for collecting, recycling and disposing of their products after consumers have finished with them.

The management of a reverse supply includes the following tasks (Guide and Wassenhove, 2002):

- *Product acquisition:* the task of retrieving the used product, as the quality, quantity and timing of product returns are crucial for creating a profitable supply.
- *Reverse logistics:* the process of transporting the retrieved goods to facilities for inspection, sorting and disposition.
- *Inspection and disposition:* the task of testing, sorting and grading the returned products.
- *Reconditioning:* the task of extracting and reconditioning components for reuse, or remanufacturing the product for resale.
- *Distribution and sales:* after reconditioning, the task of determining whether there is a market for the product.

Reverse Logistics

Forward logistics (or simply logistics) is a part of the supply chain process that plans, implements and controls the efficient flow and storage of goods from their point of origin to the point of consumption, in order to meet customers' requirements (Council of Supply Chain Management Professionals: www.cscmp.org). **Reverse logistics** reverses the flow of these activities. It addresses key issues related to how companies can become more environmentally efficient through recycling, reusing and reducing the amount of materials used (Carter and Ellram, 1998).

Many companies in the world have started to include reverse logistics in their supply management. Some are forced by legislation or environmental regulations to embrace reverse logistics; others do it to reduce operational costs. Kodak, for example, has recycled more than 310 million cameras, and remanufactures its single-use cameras after the film has been developed.

Reverse logistics addresses key issues related to how companies can become more environmentally efficient through recycling, reusing and reducing the amount of materials used.

Although forward and reverse logistics are concerned with similar activities, they are not necessarily the same. It is much more challenging to manage reverse logistics. The differences between these processes are listed in Table 8.9.

Figure 8.23 Reverse supply management

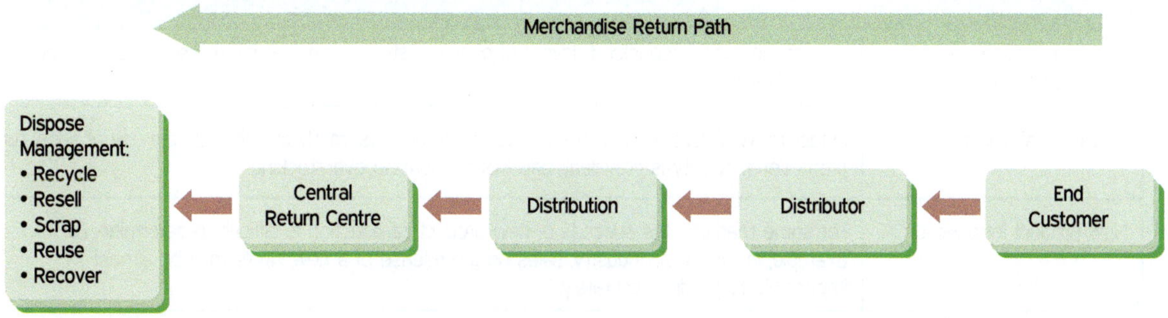

Table 8.9 Differences between forward and reverse logistics

Forward logistics	Reverse logistics
Forecasting relatively straightforward	Forecasting more difficult
One-to-many transportation	Many-to-one transportation
Product quality uniform	Product quality not uniform
Product packaging uniform	Product packaging often damaged
Destination/routeing clear	Destination/routeing unclear
Standardized channel	Exception driven
Disposition options clear	Disposition not clear
Pricing relatively uniform	Pricing dependent on many factors
Importance of speed recognized	Speed often not considered a priority
Forward distribution costs closely monitored by accounting systems	Reverse costs less directly visible
Inventory management consistent	Inventory management not consistent
Product life cycle manageable	Product life cycle issues more complicated
Negotiation between parties straightforward	Negotiation complicated by several factors
Marketing methods well known	Marketing complicated by several factors
Real-time information readily available to track product	Visibility of process less transparent

Source: Tibben-Lembke and Rogers (2002, p. 276).

It has been estimated that between 4% and 30% of products are returned by customers, and total UK retail returns are estimated to be valued at £6 billion per year. Despite the fact that it is costly and challenging to manage returns, they can have a significant impact on bottom-line performance as well as on environmental concerns. The major drivers for reverse logistics operations are listed in Table 8.10.

Table 8.10 Drivers of reverse logistics operations

Driver	Issues
Forecast accuracy and demand variability	One of the most recognized drivers of obsolete stock is caused by 'make to stock' or 'push' supply chains.
Promotional activity	In fast-moving consumer goods (FMCG) environments, marketing through the use of short-run promotional activity is prevalent, and this can lead to overstocking.
New product introduction	For some markets, the success of new product introduction is difficult to determine. For example, in the music industry, sales on the release of a new single may be almost impossible to predict accurately.

Product range and safety stock policy	Consumer expectations of choice mean that companies will provide a wide range of stock-keeping units (SKUs) within each product category. Brand extensions that drive additional SKUs require safety stock to be held for each SKU.
Product life cycles	Product life cycles are shortening, and the risk of obsolescence is becoming a major supply chain strategy for providing competitive advantages in markets such as electronics and high-technology products.
Logistics trade-offs	For some products the economics are such that the costs of manufacturing and logistics are low, compared with lost revenue from not having on-shelf availability. This can lead to excessive stockholding in retail outlets, which has to be returned at some later date.
Purchasing policies	Purchasing by placing large orders to obtain quantity discounts may result in obsolete stockholding, and the benefits gained through bulk buying may be offset by the cost of dealing with returns.
High on-shelf availability	On-shelf availability is a prime measure of supply chain performance for retailers. In order to achieve superior performance, some retailers may keep high stock levels at both the retail outlet and the distribution centre. This may lead to high returns of obsolete stock.
Legislative factors	Emerging EU legislation, for example WEEE (European Union legislation on electrical and electronic equipment), is likely to have a significant impact on organizations planning their returns management policy.
Cash flow management	The trading terms that exist between retailers and manufacturers will include the commercial arrangements for managing returns. Liberal terms may exist, and some retailers may take advantage by returning goods to manufacturers for credit to enhance their cash flow position.
Liberal returns policies and customer returns	A liberal returns policy may allow customers to return unwanted goods for a refund within a defined period of time. Customer returns will inevitably be in a condition that very often renders them unfit to be resold, either because the product has been removed from its original packaging, or because there is a quality problem.
Customer 'no fault' policy	A significant number of products that are returned by customers are found to have no problem. The problem is linked to the liberal returns policies that companies offer to customers. For many 'no fault found' items, the costs involved in taking the product back to grade A for resale are uneconomical, and therefore it will be sold at a significantly reduced price.

Source: Bernon and Cullen (2007, p. 47).

SHORT CASE 8.5

Fun with LEGO blocks

As you read this case, consider how LEGO toys are designed, distributed and sold internationally.

The LEGO Group is a Danish company, founded in 1932, which is globally known for its brick-based toys. As well as its strong brand name, it has a reputation for the product quality of its toys. In the past, the number of toys produced was based on demand forecasts from the retailers. However, the toy market is changing, and it has become more difficult to predict children's toy preferences. Consumers are shifting their preference to cheaper toys with added

Source: ©Brownstock/Alamy

innovations. Retailers, too, are demanding lower purchase costs with greater supply responsiveness, in order to reduce the risk of lost sales.

Ten years ago, the LEGO Group felt an urgent need to reshape its overall strategy. It started to restructure its production strategies with recognized platform designs and updated facilities, and began initiatives to create more exciting experiences for children, with new games, theme parks and other, virtual, stimulations.

New products and product lines of LEGO bricks have been the key design strategy. There are about 2,350 different elements and 52 colours that have been mixed and matched into more than 7,000 products offered. The company grew from producing only a small variety of LEGO bricks to a large array of different bricks. It also started to partner with external organizations to create innovative games. The partnership with Massachusetts Institute of Technology, for instance, resulted in the creation of the LEGO Mindstorms® family, allowing children to design their own robots. The package includes a computer, transmitter and receiver, software and sensor.

The company has production facilities in Denmark, the Czech Republic, Hungary and Mexico. Its products are sold in more than 130 countries via the LEGO Group's own sales channels, or through local distributors. Since 2006, a major part of the production has been outsourced to an external partner, Flextronics, in the Czech Republic. The new European distribution centre, also located in the Czech Republic, is operated by DHL. However, in 2008 the company started to in-source this operation, by taking over the Czech and Hungarian partners. The company also started to build a factory in Mexico.

Not only children are having fun with LEGO. Adults, too, can share the exciting experience. Now adults can design and showcase their creations through BrickLink (acquired by LEGO in 2019), the world's largest community of adult LEGO fans, with 1.1 million members from 70 countries as well as an online market place with 600 million LEGO items for sale and 10,000 sellers.

Another initiative is on sustainability. The company has plans to phase out plastic retail bags in all LEGO stores globally in 2020. LEGO has a partnership with World Wildlife Fund for Nature (WWF) to promote action on climate change as well as to reduce CO_2 emissions in manufacturing and supply chain operations.

How about the plastic bricks? LEGO has invested US$150 million in its Sustainable Materials Center in its headquarters in Denmark, to find sustainable alternatives for the bricks and packaging, including a plant-based alternative that is less harmful to the environment. For instance, one such plant is from the Brazilian sugar cane.

Questions

1. How should LEGO manage its relationship with the new partners in the supply chain to ensure sustainability initiatives?
2. What can LEGO do to enhance the services offered to customers?

Source: www.lego.com/ accessed 31 December 2019; Forbes, 30 October 2019, https://www.forbes.com/sites/sujatakundu/2019/10/30/lego-challenge-to-find-a-strong-sustainable-alternative-plastic/#62ad41603647

Summary

In this chapter we focused on supply chain and supply relationship management. We took a close look at the issues that firms should consider when integrating their processes and activities with those of their suppliers and customers.

We started by analysing how purchased items can be classified according to their impact on business and supply/risk complexity. We showed that the ideal type of procurement process depends on four contexts: routine, bottleneck, leverage and critical. As the characteristics and value of the purchased items vary, the relationship between the supplier and the buyer also varies. For instance, an arm's length relationship fits better when sourcing low-value, standardized products, but a strategic partnership is crucial when sourcing key components that require close collaboration with the supplier.

We looked at the role of third-party logistics (TPL) as an external supplier of logistics services. Depending on the required skills shared between the firm and the TPL supplier, relationships can range between market exchange, customized logistics solutions, joint logistics solutions, and in-house logistics solutions.

We also learned that the configuration of supply chains can influence how a manufacturer of complex products organizes and coordinates its design and distribution activities. We looked at how postponement strategies can be applied in order to achieve delivery of goods in a timely and cost-effective manner, by rearranging the production and logistics supply chains. It is also important to note that the product architectures of product systems can potentially shape the structure of supply networks. Through the lens of the double helix model, we saw how the industry structure can change between vertical and horizontal, influenced by the technological changes embedded in product architectures (i.e. modular and integral).

Demand for products and services is difficult to predict. We learned that whereas functional products should have an efficient supply chain, innovative products should have a market-responsive supply chain. Furthermore, it is important for firms to be able to estimate demand fluctuations, and understand why demand information becomes distorted. Various industries are applying IT to reduce the information distortion, including vendor-managed inventory (VMI) and collaborative planning, forecasting and replenishment (CPFR).

Finally, as firms become more socially responsible towards the environment, especially in terms of product return, reuse and recycling, the supply chain management of reverse logistics operations is becoming one of the competitive advantages for many firms.

Key Theories

The key theories discussed in this chapter were:

- **Postponement** – delaying the timing of crucial activities by which end products assume their customer-specific functionalities, features and identities.
- **The bullwhip effect** – a concept used to explain why information about the final customer's actual demand gets distorted from one end of the supply chain to the other.
- **Fine's double helix model** – this theory describes how supply structure can oscillate between vertical integration and horizontal disintegration with respect to product architecture strategies (i.e. modular versus integral).
- **Leagile supply** – the combination of lean supply and agile supply.

Suggested Answers to Stop and Think Questions

1. **Competition versus cooperation:** The answer to this is not simple. Often it can be achieved only through legal contracts and intellectual property rights (IPR) protection. Unfortunately, there are many unethical organizations that will pretend to be working collaboratively when they only want to steal ideas and practices. Another answer is to use open source agreements (e.g. the Linux operating system for PCs).
2. **Limit to standardization:** Standardization creates common operating procedures for suppliers of goods and services, which make it simpler for everyone to collaborate. Standardization fosters economies of scale, though, and forces the market competition to focus on prices rather than on performance. When this happens, many firms find it difficult to survive on low profit margins.
3. **Functional products:** We should always apply frameworks with caution. There are functional products with evolving processes. Let's think about functional products that have innovation in them, and which require a responsive supply chain. Examples of these types of product include vitamin-fortified yogurts and milk products, and ready-made organic soups. Similarly, there are innovative products with mature supply processes. In this case, think about innovative products that are supplied with efficient processes. Examples of these types of product include new versions of mobile phones, and new drugs. The dynamics of matching products with processes also change over time. The USB memory stick, for instance, was considered an innovative product when it was first introduced to the market. It required the market to be responsive. But, over time, it has become a standard product for data storage. Nowadays, USB sticks are considered functional products, with stable supply processes.

4. **VMI and CFPR:** The adoption of most process technologies tends to be slow, especially when they involve other parties outside the organization. VMI and CPFR allow the firm to share information with its suppliers. In order for both parties to access each other's systems, their systems have to be compatible. Compatibility issues are one of the most challenging barriers to manage. The firms also need to consider upgradability of the technology (i.e. one party cannot change its system without making sure it will not affect its supplier's system), the level of security, the costs incurred, the type of information to be shared with the other party (this means that there should be trust), and technology lock-in (once a particular VMI and CPFR system is adopted, it will be difficult and expensive to switch to another technology).
5. **Service supply chains:** Services differ from products in many ways. Services are essentially intangible and do not result in ownership of anything. Services are also perishable, which means they cannot be stored. The production, delivery, and consumption all take place simultaneously. In services, the customer becomes a part of the production and consumption process. As such, supply chain of services should be shorter than the supply chain of physical products. With disruptive technologies, product and service supply chains might become integrated where the point of production and consumption along the supply chain might be shifted in both directions, upstream and downstream.
6. **Customized TPL services:** It would be difficult if the TPL didn't understand its processes well. Before embarking on customization of services, it is crucial for the TPL to know how the information and services provided are being transformed across the supply chain. The type and amount of customization are also dependent on whether it is to take place in the upstream or downstream supply chain. Customization downstream (i.e. closer to the consumers) would be looking at how to optimize customization for increasing service variety. Customization upstream (i.e. closer to the suppliers), on the other hand, would have to take into consideration how the service is to be designed and configured.

Review Questions

1. Consider Short Case 8.5, the 'Fun with LEGO Blocks' case study, again after reading this chapter. How has customization changed the competitive landscape of toy industries? What issues (internal as well as external) should LEGO consider when implementing mass customization? Give examples.
2. You have been recently promoted to the position of purchasing manager. Your company designs and manufactures components to the automotive industry. Your job is to make a classification of components in order to decide what kinds of supplier-buyer relationships to consider. Apply Kraljic's tactical procurement matrix to classify the purchased items and related processes.
3. What supply strategies should product based firms consider when developing new products? Describe in terms of (a) functional products and (b) innovative products. What is the right supply strategy of these products?
4. How can a firm decide on how to balance between lean and agile supply strategies?
5. If you were a producer of standard bicycles, and decided to sell customized bicycles, how would you make this happen? How would you organize your suppliers?
6. You are in the fashion business, and it is extremely crucial that you have the latest fashion items in the retail stores. What can you do in order to match customer demand with production of fashion items?

Discussion Questions

1. Discuss the role of product design for supply chain management. Depending on the degree of technological complexity of the innovations, how should firms manage the relationships shared with suppliers and customers?

2. Consumers are becoming more health conscious. The number of organic products and dairy products with added vitamins is growing at an astronomical rate. Discuss the benefits and challenges a dairy producer may face with the farmers and the grocery stores as a result.
3. Companies are becoming increasingly dependent on IT to share information. Discuss the benefits of vendor-managed inventory (VMI) partnership for grocery stores.
4. You are the manager of a large grocery chain. The top management has decided to offer food delivery service to homes. You have been assigned to find a third-party logistics (TPL) provider that can take over some of the delivery functions. When assessing the TPL providers, what advantages will you consider?
5. Imagine you are the manufacturer of the world's most famous brand of customized tennis shoes. There are wholesalers and retailers in Asia, the USA and Europe. Discuss how and why the order information for this product could become distorted from downstream to upstream supplies.
6. Discuss why we sort our household waste into paper, glass, food, and so on. Where does the waste go? What would the reverse logistics look like for this example?

Problems

1. The mouse for your PC has just broken. You desperately need to use it, so you go to an electronics store to buy a replacement. At the store you have many brands and options to choose from, ranging from a simple plug-in mouse to fancy multifunction ones. The prices are affordable, too. On the way home, you start to wonder how it's possible for producers to survive and compete on such devices. It is obvious that there are many mouse producers, and that they compete on price. You also notice that the producers of keyboards and monitors face similar challenges. Apply the double helix model to describe the current structure of the PC industry. Can you predict what is going to happen?
2. You are the manager of a supermarket chain. You notice that the sale of organic products is increasing, which means that the sale of non-organic products is decreasing. You want to promote the 'healthy food' image of the supermarket chain, so you have started to buy less of certain types of non-organic product. One such product is ordinary spaghetti. You have always ordered 500 kg every month. With the 'healthy food' initiative, you decided to reduce the order by 10% to 450 kg. Assume that the supply chain of spaghetti has four tiers: the supermarket chain, the wholesaler, the manufacturer, and the supplier. Assume that each tier keeps one period's worth of inventory. Estimate the demand fluctuation across the supply chain due to the 10% drop in demand order. How many periods will it take until each tier is able to meet the new demand?
3. You have recently been hired as the production manager of a large manufacturer of smart phones. As the company is getting ready for the production of new smart phones with 5G technology, you are planning the procurement process of two components. You also want to know how such components can have an impact on profit impact and supply risk for the company.

   Component 1: newly developed module of integrated circuit with 5G technology, provided by a single-sourced Chinese supplier.

   Component 2: high-performance batteries.

   Apply the Kraljic's Matrix to classify the components and the ideal procurement process for Component 1 and Component 2.

Further Reading

Clark, K.B. and Fujimoto, T. (1991) *Product Development Performance: Strategy, Organization and Management in the World of Auto Industry*, Harvard Business School Press, Boston, MA.

Corbett, C.J. and Klassen, R.D. (2006) 'Extending the horizons: Environmental excellence as key to improving operations', *Manufacturing and Service Operations Management*, **8**(1), 5–22.

Fine, C. (1998) *Clockspeed: Winning Industry Control in the Age of Temporary Advantage*, Little, Brown and Co., London.

Halldorsson, A., Mikkola, J.H., Kotzab, H. and Skjøtt-Larsen, T. (2007) 'Complementary theories to supply chain management', *Supply Chain Management: An International Journal*, **12**(4), 284–296.

Hsuan, J., Skjøtt-Larsen, T., Kinra, A. and Kotzab, H. (2015) *Managing the Global Supply Chain,* 4th edn, Copenhagen Business School Press, Frederiksberg.

Lamming, R. (1993) *Beyond Partnership: Strategies for Innovation and Lean Supply,* Prentice Hall, New York.

Mikkola, J.H. and Skjøtt-Larsen, T. (2006) 'Platform management: implication for new product development and supply chain management', *European Business Review,* **18**(3), 214–230.

Sako, M. (1992) *Prices, Quality and Trust: Buyer Supplier Relationships in Britain and Japan,* Cambridge University Press, Cambridge.

Sampson, S.E. and Froehle, C.M. 82006) 'Foundations and implications of a proposed Unified Services Theory', *Production and Operations Management,* **15**(2), 329–343.

Selviaridis, K. and Spring, M. (2007) 'Third party logistics: A literature review and research agenda', *International Journal of Logistics Management,* **18**(1), 125–150.

Simchi-Levi, D., Kaminsky, P. and Simchi-Levi, E. (2008) *Designing and Managing the Supply Chain,* 3rd edn, McGraw-Hill, Boston, MA.

Stock, J.R. and Lambert, D.M. (2001) *Strategic Logistics Management,* 4th edn, McGraw-Hill, Boston, MA.

Wynstra, F., van Weele, A. and Weggemann, M. (2001) 'Managing supplier involvement in product development: Three critical issues', *European Management Journal,* **19**(2), 157–167.

References

Angulo, A., Nachtmann, H. and Waller, M. (2004) 'Supply chain information sharing in a vendor managed inventory partnership', *Journal of Business Logistics,* **25**(1), 101–120.

Bernon, M. and Cullen, J. (2007) 'An integrated approach to managing reverse logistics', *International Journal of Logistics: Research and Applications,* **10**(1), 41–56.

Binder, M., Gust, P. and Clegg, B. (2008) 'The importance of collaborative frontloading in automotive supply networks', *Journal of Manufacturing Technology Management,* **19**(3), 315–331.

Carbone, J. (1999) 'Reinventing purchasing wins the medal for Big Blue', *Purchasing,* 16 September, 38–62.

Carter, C.R. and Ellram, L.M. (1998) 'Reverse logistics: a review of the literature and framework for future investigation', *Journal of Business Logistics,* **19**(1), 85–102.

Christopher, M., Peck, H. and Towill, D. (2006) 'A taxonomy for selecting global supply chain strategies', *International Journal of Logistics Management,* **17**(2), 277-287.

Clark, K.B. and Fujimoto, T. (1991) *Product Development Performance: Strategy, Organization and Management in the World of Auto Industry,* Harvard Business School Press, Boston, MA.

Coskun, V., Ozdenizci, B. and Ok, K. (2013) 'A survey on near field communication (NFC) technology', *Wireless Personal Communications,* **71,** 2259-2294.

Druehl, C., Carrillo, J. and Hsuan, J. (2017) 'Technological innovations: Impacts on supply chains', in *Innovation and Supply Chain Management: Relationship, Collaboration and Strategies,* A. C. Moreira, L. M. D. F. Ferreira and R. A. Zimmermann (eds), Springer, Cham, pp. 259–281.

Dyer, J.H., Cho, D.S. and Chu, W. (1998) 'Strategic supplier segmentation: the next "best practice" in supply chain management', *California Management Review,* **40**(2), 57–77.

European Commission (2015) 'Fact-finding studies in support of the development of an EU strategy for freight transport logistics; Lot 1: Analysis of the EU logistics sector'.

Fine, C. (1998) *Clockspeed: Winning Industry Control in the Age of Temporary Advantage,* Little, Brown and Co., London.

Fisher, M. (1997) 'What is the right supply chain for your product?', *Harvard Business Review,* **75**(2), 105–116.

Guide, V.D.R. and Wassenhove, V.N.L. (2002) 'The reverse supply chain', *Harvard Business Review,* **80**(2), 25–26.

Halldorsson, A. and Skjøtt-Larsen, T. (2004) 'Developing logistics competencies through third party logistics relationships', *International Journal of Operations and Production Management,* **24**(2), 192–206.

Kerber, R. (1998) 'Bicycles: bike maker faces a tactical shift', *The Wall Street Journal,* 12 October, Sec. B, 1.

Kraljic, P. (1983) 'Purchasing must become supply management', *Harvard Business Review,* September–October, 107–109.

Lamming, R. (1993) *Beyond Partnership: Strategies for Innovation and Lean Supply.* Prentice Hall, New York.

Lee, H. (1998) 'Postponement for mass customisation: satisfying customer demands for tailor-made products', in *Strategic Supply Chain Alignment: Best Practice in Supply Chain Management,* J. Gattorna (ed.), Gower, Aldershot, pp. 77–91.

Lee, H.L., Padmanabhan, V. and Whang, S. (1997) 'The bullwhip effect in supply chains', *Sloan Management Review,* **38**(3), 93–102.

Mason-Jones, R., Naylor, B. and Towill, D.R. (2000) 'Engineering the leagile supply chain', *International Journal of Agile Management Systems,* **2**(1), 54–61.

Metro Group (2011) 'New sourcing strategy of Metro Cash & Carry strengthens small producers', https://archiv.metrogroup.de/en/press-releases/2011/03/04/new-sourcing-strategy-of-metro-cash-and-carry-strengthens-small-producers (accessed 20 April 2020).

Mikkola, J.H. and Skjøtt-Larsen, T. (2004) 'Mass customisation, postponement, and modularisation strategies in shaping supply chains', *Production Planning and Control,* **15**(4), 352–361.

Pagh, J.D. and Cooper, M.C. (1998) 'Supply chain postponement and speculation strategies: how to choose the right strategy', *Journal of Business Logistics,* **19**(2), 13–33.

Rossetti, C. and Choi, T.Y. (2008) 'Supply management under high goal incongruence: An empirical examination of disintermediation in the aerospace supply chain', *Decision Sciences,* **39** (3), 507–540.

Sako, M. (1992) *Prices, Quality and Trust: Buyer Supplier Relationships in Britain and Japan*, Cambridge University Press, Cambridge.

Simchi-Levi, D., Kaminsky, P. and Simchi-Levi, E. (2008) *Designing and Managing the Supply Chain*, 3rd edn, McGraw-Hill, Boston, MA.

Skjøtt-Larsen, T., Schary, P., Mikkola, J.H. and Kotzab, H. (2007) *Managing the Global Supply Chain*, 3rd edn, Copenhagen Business School Press.

Tibben-Lembke, R. and Rogers, D.S. (2002) 'Differences between forward and reverse logistics in a retail environment', *Supply Chain Management: An International Journal*, **7**(5), 271–282.

VICS (2004) 'CPFR – An overview', available from http://www.vics.org

Ward, J. (2019) 'The customer in control', *DHL Delivered. The Global Logistics Magazine*, **5**, 8–13.

9 Inventory Management

Learning Outcomes

After reading this chapter, you should be able to:

- Explain the different roles of inventory
- Explain the problems of excess inventory
- Apply the economic order quantity (EOQ) model
- Use the reorder level and cyclical review systems
- Use the ABC technique to determine stock control methods
- Define dependent and independent demand systems
- Describe the functions of a material requirements planning (MRP) system and the extensions that lead to MRP II
- Define the scope of enterprise resource planning (ERP) systems
- Appreciate the difficulties of dealing with reverse inventories for recycling and disposal

Amazon: Managing Inventory

Source: ©Mike Mareen/Shutterstock

Amazon is a leading **FANG (Facebook, Amazon, Netflix, Google) e-business**. Having started as an online bookstore and later selling CDs, Amazon now has a ubiquitous presence and is often seen as synonymous with internet commerce. Amazon's turnover in 2019 was $265 billion and it has a market capitalization of $756 billion, making it one of the world's largest corporations. It employs 650,000 people and has dedicated marketplaces for the United States, the United Kingdom, France, Ireland, Canada, Germany, Spain, Italy, Australia, Japan, China, India, Mexico, with new ones constantly being added.

FANG Collective term for e-businesses: Facebook, Amazon, Netflix, Google

Integration

One of Amazon's most striking traits is the way it differs its activities from other e-commerce giants such as e-bay and Ali Baba. Whereas most competitors focus on being a marketplace to bring suppliers and customers together without handling the resulting goods, Amazon chooses to control and have a hands on role in the complete procurement and selling process.

As such, Amazon owns and operates a huge network of distribution centres around the world which take in products, store them before sale, and then distribute the products, often using its own fleets of trucks and even airplanes. This means that Amazon is able to control all the steps of its business and so can maximize the efficiency of each operation.

Ordering and Inventory

However, Amazon does not own all the products itself as about half are called 'fulfilled by Amazon' where the products are held in Amazon warehouses for the sellers. It also has a seller fulfilled programme where larger partners can sell through the Amazon website, but ship their products direct to the customer without Amazon support. This has allowed Amazon to add 6 million extra products to its marketplace.

For most organizations, decisions about how many products to make or store and when to ship or produce are key business drivers. The aim is to try and match the supply of products to customer demand as closely as possible. Having too much wastes money and is costly on storage, whereas running out or poor delivery timing leads to dissatisfied customers.

Whilst Amazon and its suppliers have these normal business risks of managing their product availability they also have to work extra hard to cope with the way that the products can be sourced and delivered in several different ways – from Amazon stock, direct from suppliers by Amazon, or by the supplier using their own delivery system. Given that they offer two-day Prime delivery to subscribers, they also need to manage the timing of these deliveries more closely than most organizations. Being able to manage these processes and inventory levels effectively is one of the reasons why Amazon is such a global success.

Source: https://www.macrotrends.net/stocks/charts/AMZN/amazon/revenue

Introduction

Inventory management is about working out what to produce or deliver and when. As a result, it is a key topic in operations management because firms such as Amazon, with good inventory control, can expect consistent deliveries to their customers, whereas weak inventory management reduces customer satisfaction and adds cost. For example, according to its 2019 annual report Jaguar Land Rover has a materials bill of about £15 billion per year and so a 1% saving in this bill gives an immediate profit of £150 million.

In service operations inventory may be harder to identify, but is just as important. Running out of a particular drug in a hospital could mean the death of a patient; and in retail, the main assets are the products on the shelves – more people may be employed stacking shelves than dealing directly with the customer.

Inventory the materials and finished products that are present in the firm, and also in its supply chain. In general, inventory represents a waste, and should be avoided if possible.

Raw materials materials purchased but not processed.

Work in progress Work in progress (WIP) is inventory which is in the manufacturing process and so no longer raw material but not yet a finished product.

Finished goods inventory completed products awaiting shipment or built for stock.

Reverse logistics addresses key issues related to how companies can become more environmentally efficient through recycling, reusing and reducing the amount of materials used.

What Is Inventory?

Types of Inventory

Inventory represents the materials and finished products in the firm and supply chain. This includes:

- **Raw materials** – purchased but not processed
- **Work-in-progress** inventory – being worked on
- Maintenance/repair/operating supplies (MRO) – for the plant
- **Finished goods inventory** – completed and waiting shipment
- Goods in transit – to warehouses and customers
- **Reverse inventory** – materials being returned for recycling or disposal.

Stop and Think

Take a minute to think about an organization you know well. What represents its inventory, where is it kept and what might happen if it got out of control?

The Valuable Functions of Inventory

Inventory has various different roles, the most obvious being to satisfy immediately customer demand. For example, blood supplies must be stocked as they cannot be ordered when a patient needs a transfusion; and food can only be sold if it is on the supermarket shelf. In other examples, though, an immediate response is not always possible: BMW, for example, may expect us to wait for a car to be made if we want it in a colour that is not available on the garage forecourt. Here the inventory does not need to be immediately available. Therefore, as well as satisfying immediate demand, inventory has other roles in the smooth running of operations, as summarized in the following list.

The useful functions of inventory are:

- To provide immediate satisfaction for customer demand – some customers expect to walk in off the street and out again with the product
- To uncouple stages in the operation chain – inventory between manufacturing stages smooths fluctuations, allowing machines to operate independently
- To provide cover for uncertainty
  - Extra inventory prevents shortages which can otherwise cause operational problems and poor customer service
  - Inventory allows work to continue if there is a delay or breakdown elsewhere in the supply chain
- To reduce costs
  - It can be cheaper to buy things in bulk
  - Buying in advance can hedge against future price changes, but carries risk.

Problems Caused by Inventory

Despite the useful ways inventory can help a firm with its operations, the aim will always be to operate with the minimum inventory possible because excess stocks add cost and cause other problems, as summarized below:

- Inventory ties up working capital
  - What else could the firm do with the money invested in materials?
  - The firm will have interest charges if it borrows the money to buy the inventory
- Inventory takes up space
  - It costs money to store, monitor, document and manage the inventory
  - There is a lost opportunity of using the space, such as installing another machine
- Inventory is prone to:
  - Damage: if things are lying around then they can get broken
  - Pilferage: it can be stolen. For example, car makers used to install CD-radios at the factory, only to find them missing later. Now they are fitted just before delivery.
  - **Obsolescence**: changes in design may mean throwing away old parts, and other products, such as food, have a limited life.
- Inventory causes manufacturing errors to go undetected; reducing inventory can make it easier to see delays and uneven supply chains.

Obsolescence the state of becoming obsolete, or out of date.

Inventory turn the time taken for a firm's entire inventory to be used and replaced.

It is possible to measure firm performance with **inventory turn** – the time taken for the entire inventory to be used and replaced. The more efficient a firm, the faster its inventory turn. Accountants measure this as the ratio of annual cost of goods sold to annual inventory investment. Care should be taken when comparing these measures between firms within an industry as they are a very high-level and generalized guide because firms can have different scopes of operation. Comparisons of inventory in UK and Japanese car makers in the 1980s were sometimes made. However, because Japanese firms were not manufacturing high-value engines and gearboxes like their UK competitors, but instead only buying them from a supplier, the parts and assemblies that made up the inventory were not the same, resulting in an unfair comparison.

! Stop and Think

Before we go into how we can model inventory systems mathematically and arrive at optimal solutions, it is important that we reflect on the nature of inventory. Thinking about your local supermarket, identify three different types of their inventory and how they are useful to the company.

Service Inventories

Service inventory includes the steps that are completed before the customer arrives and allows resources to be buffered from variable demand. For example, processing an existing customer's application for an additional credit card can be improved if the credit check has already been completed. In many cases, service inventories offer an advantage to the firm as they store the service in advance, improving quality, speed and customization, and cutting costs, as shown in Table 9.1.

Inventory Management

Most inventory changes take place with regular patterns and therefore lend themselves to mathematical modelling. With a mathematical representation, managers can find solutions to minimize inventory cost. The simplest models order fixed amounts of parts and materials at fixed intervals but, in practice, variation – either in how much to order or when to order it – leads managers to use one of two different approaches, either ordering based on *fixed quantities* or ordering based on *fixed dates*.

A fixed order quantity approach, where the timing is adjusted and the quantity stays the same, is called a *continuous review* or *Q system*. The fixed date approach, where quantity is adjusted but timing stays the same, is called a *periodic* or *P system*.

Stock Time Charts

Figure 9.1 shows a useful inventory management tool, the inventory chart or **stock time chart**. This plots the changing inventory level of a part over time.

Stock time chart chart showing how the inventory of a part or component changes over time.

In Figure 9.1, items are used at a constant rate and delivered in bulk. The steady usage of items is shown as the line of constant value in the left-hand chart. This would happen on a production line needing a constant supply of materials. The peaks on the second diagram show the instantaneous delivery of a new batch of stock. The delivery rate is zero for long periods of time; then, when a bulk shipment of parts is delivered, it is very high; it then

Table 9.1 Reasons to build service inventories

Service attribute	Ways in which service inventory can improve performance	Reasons to build service inventory
Quality	Provides consistency Facilitates service recovery	Customers value transactional conformance Enables simple, standardized response to common service failures
Speed	Reduces the amount of work needed after customer arrival Allows provider to expand capacity Reduces handoffs	Allows for significant capacity expansion Eliminates need for handoffs
Customization	Applies standard process to individual inputs Allows greater customer control	Customers provide unique inputs to a standard process Customers value exercising greater control
Price	Facilitates self-service Allows use of cheaper resources Enhances resource productivity	Significantly reduces resource costs Increases staff productivity Allows higher resource utilization

Source: Chopra and Lariviere (2005, p. 95).

Figure 9.1 A basic inventory chart

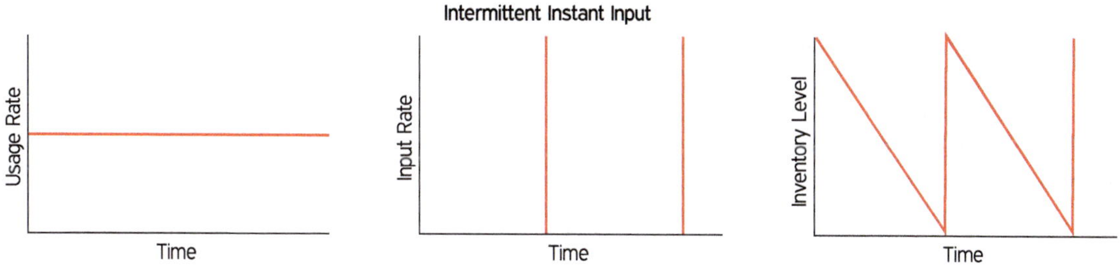

returns to zero until the next delivery. Plotting the combination of these two elements on the right-hand chart shows the changing amount of inventory. From the starting level, items are used at a constant rate and the level drops gradually. When a batch of new materials is delivered, the stock level returns to the starting level, and is again used at the same rate. Repeating the cycle gives the sawtooth diagram.

This is the simplest representation of inventory delivery and use: regular deliveries of materials at fixed times, with constant usage. In practice, the input and output often change unpredictably and so different patterns appear. As a result the stock charts can look very different and so correspondingly more complex mathematical models have been developed beyond the simple one.

Economic Order Quantity

One basic inventory management approach minimizes the costs associated with ordering fixed quantities of items (the Q-type system). Under the simple conditions shown in Figure 9.1 there is an optimum amount to order that minimizes the inventory costs. This is called the **economic order quantity (EOQ)**.

The total cost of the inventory system includes the holding cost plus the ordering cost, shown in Figure 9.2. These costs vary with the amount ordered and with the order size. Obviously, the goal is the cheapest total cost.

Economic order quantity (EOQ) fixed order (or production) amount that minimizes the total costs over a whole year.

Holding Costs: Pressure to Order Small Amounts

Figure 9.2 shows *holding costs* rising with order quantity. Ordering a large quantity of an item each time results in more parts being stored for longer, which costs money in terms of light, heat and security for the warehouse, especially on high-value items (e.g. precious stones) or items that are difficult to store (e.g. food). These costs vary depending on what we are buying and how it needs to be kept. In a small shop the ice cream in the freezer will cost more to hold than the biscuits, because of the electricity used for the freezer. Similarly, a jeweller's shop needs expensive security, which in effect can be considered a stockholding cost.

Often the main cost of holding an item is the interest incurred in borrowing the money to buy it. Thus holding costs are often calculated as bank interest on the stored items' value.

Holding costs encourage parts to be bought in smaller batches, so less material is stored.

Figure 9.2 The economic order quantity (EOQ)

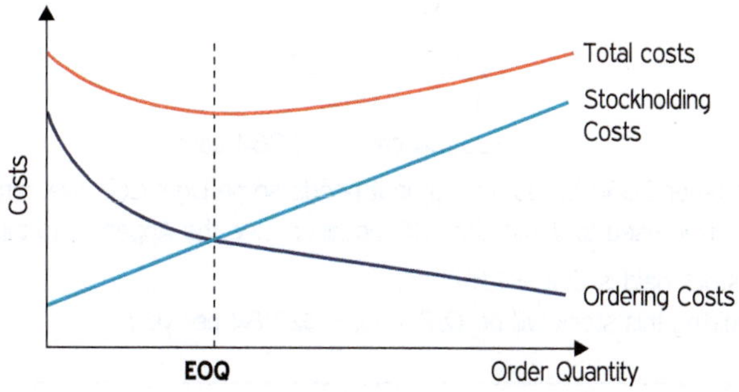

Ordering Costs: Pressure to Order in Bulk

Ordering costs are those charged by suppliers to process an order. This may be because they have to select, package and transport items from their own warehouse, or it may be that they need to change a machine from making their normal product to manufacture the one being ordered. This machine set-up takes time during which the machine is not producing. The longer it takes to set up the machine, the more the cost associated with machine downtime (unproductive time). Normally the set-up time (and its associated cost) is a fixed amount, which needs to be recovered equally from all the items produced in the batch. This encourages large numbers of parts to be ordered because, once the machine is set up, a long run reduces the cost assigned to each item in the batch.

Total Inventory Costs

The two costs above – holding and ordering – therefore seem to be pulling in different directions, but it is the *total cost,* calculated by adding the holding and order costs, which is important. The quantity to order that minimizes this total cost is the EOQ, and is given by the formula:

$$Q = \sqrt{\frac{2DC_s}{C_h}}$$

where Q is the economic order quantity, D is the demand, C_s is the set-up cost and C_h is the holding cost.

The EOQ states that the cheapest inventory costs will result if a firm orders this amount. Ordering more or less will cost more overall.

A good example of this formula in action is the amount of money you take out of an ATM. Your decision on the amount optimizes the frequencies of visits (the time you waste as the set-up cost of travelling to and from the ATM) against the risk of carrying too much cash (the holding cost of your taking extra care of the money).

WORKED EXAMPLE 9.1

Economic Order Quantity (EOQ)

The EOQ concept is very important and fairly easy to implement in many situations, as the calculation is straightforward.

Problem: *The Corner Convenience Store (CCS) gets its drinks delivered by a wholesaler. At CCS, Light Cola sells at a rate of 860 cans per day. (The shop is open 250 days of the year.) A six-pack of Light Cola costs CCS $1.20. Annual holding cost is 10% of the cost of the cola. It costs CCS $25 to place an order and this covers any delivery charge. What is CCS's EOQ?*

Approach: This calculation is simple, but take care to get the units consistent, such as using days or years, and cases or cans.

Solution:

$$D = 860 \times 250 = 215{,}000 \text{ cans/year}$$
$$C_h = 1.20/6 \times 10\% = \$0.02\text{/can/year}$$
$$C_s = \$25$$
$$Q = \sqrt{\frac{2DC_s}{C_h}}$$
$$= \sqrt{\frac{2 \times 215{,}000 \times 25}{0.02}}$$
$$= 23{,}184 \text{ cans or } 3{,}864 \text{ cases}$$

Therefore CCS should order 3,864 cases each time it needs some Light Cola. We can learn other things about this situation using the formulae used to derive the EOQ equation (see the Appendix to this chapter):

- The average stock held is $Q/2 = 11{,}592$ cans.
- The cost of holding this stock will be $Q/2 \times C_h = \$231.84$ per year.

- The number of orders they will place a year is $D/Q = 9.3$ times a year or every 39 days (365 days in a year divided by 9.3 orders).
- The cost of placing all the orders in a year will be $D/Q \times C_s = \$231.84$ per year (note: by definition, this is the same as the annual holding cost).
- The total cost of operating the inventory system will be $231.84 + $231.84 = $463.68 per year.
- CCS will spend $D \times$ Cost per can = 215,000 × 1.2/6 = $43,000 on buying the Light Cola per year.

CRITICAL PERSPECTIVE

Accuracy and the EOQ

In practice, we are unlikely to know the precise demand for an item or the exact holding/set-up costs, so we normally use estimates. Indeed, it is likely that any figures used are probably subject to variation as demand or other factors change. Luckily, the EOQ equation is relatively insensitive to any errors in our figures.

Look again at the EOQ equation. You can see that if any one of the estimated values (D, C_s or C_h) is out by 50%, the correct EOQ value would be out by only about 30%. (Try putting some example numbers into the equation to check this for yourself.)

The key point is ...

that as long as the values are close, it is unlikely to make a big difference to the EOQ value, which means it is acceptable to round the EOQ to some convenient value, such as the nearest hundred, or a multiple of a whole truckload or full box.

Extending the EOQ Model

Inventory management techniques can be extended to take account of different situations. The EOQ equation is used when an order comes from a supplier or for something we make ourselves. There is no difference mathematically, as identical set-up costs apply to our factory as apply to the supplier's factory.

An extension of the EOQ is the **economic production quantity (EPQ)**, sometimes called the **economic batch quantity (EBQ)**. This includes intermittent demand, where parts are consumed constantly but also produced in the factory at certain times. The stock time chart is slightly more complicated, but still cyclical and easily modelled. The EPQ generates an EOQ-type value that we can use to optimize the inventory costs of this system.

Economic production quantity (EPQ) extension of the EOQ that includes the effect of producing parts.

Economic batch quantity (EBQ) another name for EPQ.

Another example extending the simple EOQ idea involves price-break discounts on ordering above a certain amount. For example, printing your design on t-shirts cost £15 each if you order less than 200, but are only £12 each if you order more. The total costs have multiple values depending on quantity. In practice, therefore, we would calculate the EOQ at each different price range to find the cheapest overall.

Things get more complex when we adapt the model by adding statistical likelihoods to reflect variations in demand or production. Here we want to ensure that enough stock is available to meet any likely situations. Again, the EOQ model can be extended to reflect this variability and arrive at an optimal inventory model. However, these inventory models are all based on the EOQ.

The key point is ...

We should spend a little time thinking through the difference between the different models above, such as EOQ and EPQ. What are the major differences between the EOQ for bought-in items and those made in our factory? What other factors does the EPQ model take into account over the EOQ approach?

Inventory Systems in Practice

We have already noted two distinct main inventory control systems based on either fixed quantity (Q) or fixed period (P). These ideas are most often implemented as either:

- Q: the **reorder level (ROL)** system (sometimes called the **reorder point (ROP)**)
- P: the **cyclical review (CR)** or reorder cycle system.

Reorder level (ROL) the trigger level used in the reorder point inventory system (Q type), which generates the ordering of a fixed amount (normally the EOQ) with an irregular interval.

Reorder point level of inventory that indicates the time to order a batch of the EOQ in a reorder level system.

Cyclical review inventory review system that determines the amount to be ordered at set intervals.

Safety stock extra inventory used to cover uncertainty or delivery times so that the system can keep operating..

Stock-out When an organisation runs out of material this is often called a stock-out and can be expensive as the operations have to wait until more inventory is delivered.

The Reorder Level System

As an example, a simple reorder level system can be used for screws used on a production line. The bucket the screws are kept in has a line drawn around the inside to indicate the reorder level. When the level of screws in the bucket is down to the line, an order is placed, and there are just enough screws left in the bucket for the workers to use until the order is delivered. Normally there is a little extra (**safety stock**) in the bucket to cover any variation in the delivery time. The more safety stock, the less likely we are to run out. The cycle is then repeated, as shown in Figure 9.3.

The ROL system is sometimes implemented as the *two-bin system*. Instead of a line on one container, one bin is filled up to the ROL and the rest of the batch is put in the second bin. An order is placed when the first bin is empty, that is, when the ROL is reached.

One problem with the ROL system is that we need to keep track of how many parts we have in stock all the time. If we cannot use a simple visual tool, such as two bins or the line on a bucket, it can be expensive to track the stock level continually, which is necessary to identify when the ROL is reached.

The manager designing a ROL system tries to balance the costs of running out of materials (called a stock out) against the costs of holding unused extra stock. This can be worked out mathematically or may just be based on judgement if the cost of running out is small or the value of the parts is low. For example, if the **stock-out** cost involves sending someone off for two minutes to the warehouse, then the safety stock need not be accurate or large. However, if the items are very expensive or have a long lead time, such as the gearboxes in a car factory, then managers need to be as accurate as possible given the potentially high cost of getting it wrong. If the car factory runs out of gearboxes, the production line stops and stands idle until the delivery. A very expensive situation.

The Cyclical Review System

In the cyclical review (CR) system (an example of the P approach) inventory is reviewed at set intervals and an order is placed each time for the amount needed to bring the stocks back up to a set level. This means a different amount is ordered each time. Again, safety stock is needed to cover the time taken to deliver the order or for any likely delay. The main advantage of CR over ROL is that the firm does not need to have a costly system to keep track of how many parts are in stock, as they are counted each time an order is made.

Figure 9.3 The reorder point

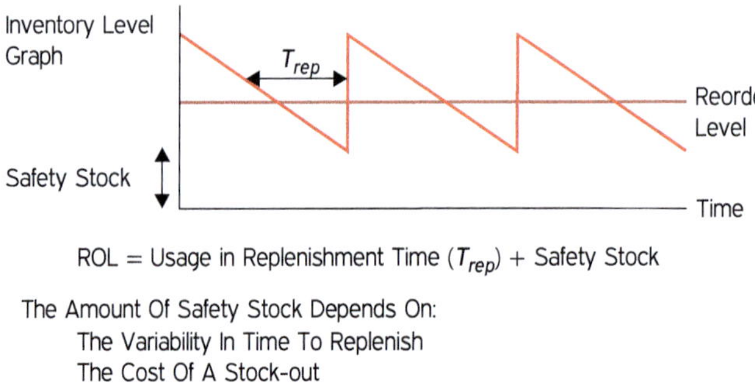

WORKED EXAMPLE 9.2

Reorder Level System

A college radio station records a copy of its five hours per day broadcast stream onto CDs. Each CD records one hour. The stationery firm delivers CDs exactly three days after an order is received.

Problem: *What is the ROL for the CDs, and what is the ROL when a safety stock of 1 day's worth of CDs is used for reserve?*

Solution: The ROL for the CDs is 15, as they need 5 CDs per day for the 3 days until the order arrives. Mathematically, we can say that:

$$\text{ROL} = \text{Demand (per day)} \times \text{Delivery lead time (in days)}$$

In practice the radio station will want to make sure it has a few CDs left in case of a delay or if a CD is faulty. A safety stock of one day's worth of CDs would be a sensible number as a reserve. The ROL is now 20 (15 to cover the normal usage for 3 days and another 5 for one day's safety stock):

$$\text{ROL} = \text{Demand per day} \times \text{Delivery lead time in days} + \text{Safety stock}$$
$$\text{ROL} = 5 \times 3 + 5 = 20$$

CR is often used when several items come from one supplier as the separate orders can be combined to cut costs. CR is common in retail where stocks are checked at the end of the month and enough is ordered to bring the level back to that at the start. This system is easily automated with electronic point of sale systems (EPOS) or smart tills, which report sales at regular intervals.

WORKED EXAMPLE 9.3

Cyclical Review

The chemists' shop on the high street uses a cyclical review system for its toothbrushes. Typically, the shop sells 3,300 toothbrushes a year. An order is placed each month to bring the stocks up to the average monthly demand for the toothbrush. It takes a week for the delivery to arrive and the chemists use a 10% safety margin to cover for any variation in demand.

Problem:

(a) *What is the target level of stock for the toothbrush?*

(b) *On counting the stock as part of the end-of-month review they find 120 brushes left on the shelf. How many should they order?*

Approach:

Start by calculating the target stock. In this case it is the sum of average sales, lead time cover and safety stock.

Solution:

(a)
$$\begin{aligned}\text{Target stock} &= \text{Average sales} + \text{Lead time cover} + \text{Safety stock}\\ &= \frac{3{,}300}{12} + \frac{3{,}300}{52} + \frac{3{,}300}{12} \times 0.1\\ &= 275 + 63.4 + 27.5 = 365.9\\ &= 366 \text{ brushes}\end{aligned}$$

(Note the rounding up, as this is a safety stock and we don't want less than the 10%.)

(b) When counting the 120 brushes left as part of the end-of-month review, the chemists need to order 246 (366 – 120) to bring the stock up to the target level. It appears they have had a bad month, and have sold less than the usual 275.

Which System: Reorder Level or Cyclical Review?

Choosing between ROL and CR depends on several things:

- *Accuracy:* ROL systems can be more accurate as they monitor the level constantly; but some ROL systems capture only changes, and can get out of step with reality. As CR is forced to count all the stocks at regular intervals, its values are accurate, if not always up to date.
- *Consolidating orders:* CR groups orders from a single supplier, resulting in lower transportation and ordering costs. ROL systems will order each part as the need arises, and combining orders is difficult.
- *Safety stocks:* safety stocks with ROL cover a relatively short and fixed period – the delivery time. In CR sufficient stocks are needed not only for the delivery time, but also to cover the time before the next review.
- *Implementation costs:* counting the level of stock every review period may cost more than monitoring the changes in an ROL system, particularly if there is an accurate way of recording usage. EPOS systems, for example, know by the minute how many of each item is in stock, and orders are generated automatically.

Greater accuracy is provided by ROL systems, as they operate with a monitoring system to track the level of stock. Cyclical review systems can be cheaper to introduce, but by their nature are less accurate, as the stock level is checked only once per period. This means that firms have a higher risk of either having too much inventory or running out.

Stop and Think

These systems are actually very simple to operate in practice, and a short exercise will show we knew them before we started this chapter. Can you think of any examples from your own home where you effectively use the systems above? Did you know you were practising inventory management?

ABC Inventory Classification: Choosing Inventory Control Methods

If we have only limited resources to manage our inventory, it makes sense to identify the parts that we should control closely with a sophisticated and accurate but sometimes expensive system, and separate them from those we can get away with controlling less accurately but more cheaply. **ABC** inventory classification analysis is a tool to help us do this.

ABC system for ranking inventory into parts to control closely and parts that don't merit undue effort in monitoring.

ABC analysis ranks inventory items to identify the amount of money that is spent on each during a year. This consists not only of how much the item costs, but also how many are used. The ABC ranking divides those we should control closely from those that are less important.

ABC produces a chart sorted by the cumulative annual usage value, as shown in Figure 9.4. Items are labelled A, B, C in accordance with their annual usage value, expressed as a percentage of the total annual usage value of all the items in inventory. Class A items constitute a small percentage of the items (normally about 10%) but contribute most of the total material spend (often around 80%). These can be high-value items with high unit costs or cheaper items used in large numbers. At the other extreme, class C items are plentiful (60%) but contribute only a very small amount (5%) of the total material bill. These tend to be small and cheap items such as nuts, bolts and washers, which we only use infrequently. Class B is typically 30% of items, costing about 15% of the total material spend.

Figure 9.4 ABC inventory classification

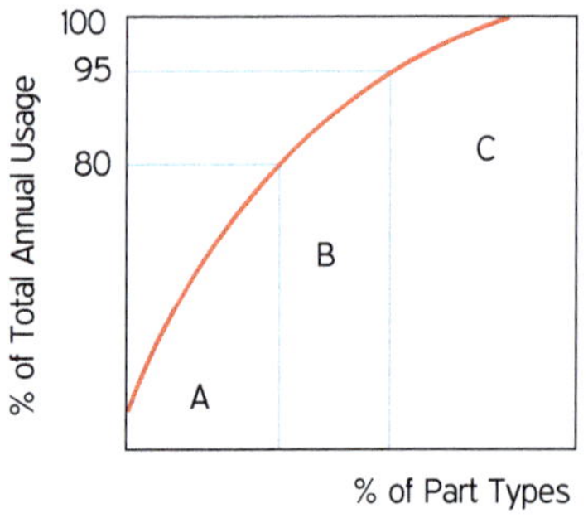

Class A items should be very closely controlled with an accurate system, such as ROL using real-time tracking and barcodes, whereas class C items need only cursory checks as holding excess inventory is not going to add much cost. They are ideal for a long-interval CR system. Type B is somewhere in between and managers need to decide for themselves how to control this class of inventory.

WORKED EXAMPLE 9.4

ABC Analysis

To perform ABC analysis, the first thing to do is calculate, for each item in the analysis, the annual usage value (how many we use and how much each costs):

$$\text{Annual usage value} = \text{Unit cost} \times \text{Quantity used per annum}$$

Then rank the items in order of annual usage value and plot the cumulative percentages on a graph to classify them.

Table 9.2 shows the bought-in price and annual sales of the set of different types of garments that are held in stock by a wholesaler.

Step 1 is to calculate the annual usage value, as shown in Table 9.3.

Next, put the items in descending order of annual usage value and work out the annual spend on each item as a percentage of the total (see Table 9.4). This is done because there could easily be thousands of parts and so using

Table 9.2 Item usage and value

Item type	Purchase price (£)	Annual sales (items per year)
a	8	1,250
b	18	450
c	30	75
d	25	10
e	3	280
f	4	80
g	18	45
h	7	250
i	12	150
j	26	30

Table 9.3 Annual usage values

Item type	Purchase price (£)	Annual sales (items per year)	Annual spend (price × number)
a	8	1,250	10,000
b	18	450	8,100
c	30	75	2,250
d	25	10	250
e	3	280	840
f	4	80	320
g	18	45	810
h	7	250	1,750
i	12	150	1,800
j	26	30	780

Table 9.4 Ascending percentage usage values

Item type	Purchase price (£)	Annual sales (items per year)	Annual spend (price × number)	Percentage spend (%)	Cumulative spend (%)
a	8	1,250	10,000	37.2	37.2
b	18	450	8,100	30.1	67.3
c	30	75	2,250	8.4	75.7
i	12	150	1,800	6.7	82.3
h	7	250	1,750	6.5	88.8
e	3	280	840	3.1	92.0
g	18	45	810	3.0	95.0
j	26	30	780	2.9	97.9
f	4	80	320	1.2	99.1
d	25	10	250	0.9	100.0
			26,900	100.0	

Figure 9.5 ABC chart showing classifications

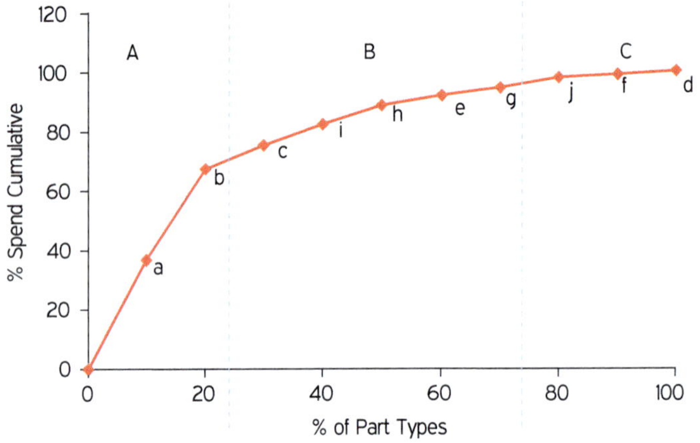

percentages allows comparisons with other studies. Also add each of these percentages, item by item, to give the cumulative spend. This column in the table is needed, as it is plotted on the chart to analyse the results.

From the table, plot the chart for the garments against the cumulative percentage of annual usage value (Figure 9.5). From this identify which to label A, B or C.

In this example we could use a strict rule, such as 'Class A are designated as the first 20%', but as we have only 10 items it is better to examine the values in the table to help identify items as A, B or C. Garments a and b are clearly very significant and should be type A. We could put c into type A as well, but its annual usage value is more similar to i, h, e and g, so it seems sensible to group these together as type B. Again j, f and d all have similar annual usage values and so they can be labelled type C. These divisions are shown on the graph. We can now find different inventory control procedures for each group.

- Type A items require very close monitoring and very tight inventory control procedures with real-time tracking and counting such as bar code scans and RFID.
- Type B items require formal inventory control, but less intense scrutiny and intervention than is the case with A items.
- Type C items require a minimum of formalized control. In manufacturing, type C parts are often provided on free issue and reordered in long lead time cycles.

SHORT CASE 9.1

ABC: Cathay Pacific's Spare Parts Inventory System

GLOBALIZATION

Cathay Pacific Airlines has an alternative application of ABC analysis in managing its spare parts. Cathay Pacific spent HK$9,401 million (£951 million) on spares and maintenance in 2018 and there is great pressure to reduce the bill. Managing airline spare parts is a highly complex task because of the time-critical nature of the business (it costs US$60 per minute to have an aeroplane on the ground), the large numbers of parts (Cathay Pacific has 380,000 spares coming from 2,300 different suppliers) and the special safety and quality regulations, which often vary from country to country.

Source: ©KITTIKUN YOKSAP/ Shutterstock

One tool that Cathay Pacific uses to analyse and manage its spares is to grade them based on criticality rather than rate of usage. The grading system is as follows:

1. No Go: must be replaced before the plane can fly
2. Go If: there is an alternative solution to the problem not requiring replacement
3. Go: the part is not critical and can be fixed later

Another ABC-type analysis that Cathay Pacific uses is to classify the spare parts for the cabin by the class of passenger they affect:

1. first class VIP
2. first and business class
3. economy class

The reason behind this is the potential loss of business and revenue from the passenger having a less than perfect experience on the flight. This does not mean that Cathay Pacific does not carry spares for economy class, but that the systems it uses mean there are higher levels of safety stock for the more 'valuable' passenger classes, so that a first class passenger should never have a poor experience of flying with Cathay Pacific.

Questions

1. What risks does Cathay Pacific face by prioritizing the spares using the ABC method?
2. Think of your own experiences and try and find a place where the ABC analysis would be useful. Perhaps you can think about the food you keep in your kitchen cupboards. Which would you like to monitor most closely to ensure you never run out?

Sources: Cathay Pacific website, https://www.cathaypacific.com/content/dam/cx/about-us/investor-relations/interim-annual-reports/en/2018_annual_report_en.pdf, accessed 20 October 2019; Hong Kong Aircraft Engineering Company Limited, www.haeco.com/about_haeco/group.html, accessed 20 July 2019.

Manufacturing Control Systems: Dependent Demand

In large organizations, with complex multi-part products, managers do not control inventory for single parts separately.

The ROL and CR approaches treat all items as having **independent demand**. This means that the demand for one item is not linked to or influenced by anything else happening in the firm. In most production lines, though, very few components or raw materials are independent.

Independent demand demand that is treated as unrelated to anything else.

In car assembly the plant runs at a predetermined capacity and so the materials planners will know how many parts they need. Making 3,000 cars in a week needs 3,000 engines, 3,000 gearboxes, 3,000 bodies, 15,000 wheels and 6,000 front seats. The parts demand is dependent on the number of cars produced.

When to place an order is also known, as it is based on the production lead time. For example, if it takes 3 weeks to make and ship an engine from the supplier to the assembly area, the plan for car assembly can be used to produce a schedule for ordering engines. Dependent demand and backwards ordering for a tractor is shown in Figure 9.6; it starts with the finished product and works back, adding the time needed for each sub-assembly step. The diagram also breaks the product down into the parts to be assembled into the finished product. A sensible plan would be to start placing an order for the gearbox 27 days before the finished tractor is to be delivered to the customer as this is how long the whole process takes.

The implication of dependent demand is that, with enough information, managers can determine which parts to order, how many and when, to make the products ordered by the customers.

Dependent demand demand for a part that is normally directly related to that for some others, and ultimately to the aggregate production plan.

Material requirements planning (MRP) a way of calculating the demand and timing for component deliveries in order to make the products listed in the master production schedule.

Enterprise resources planning (ERP) ERP systems are corporate-wide information systems that present data as if from a central single entity source.

Master production schedule (MPS) a formal list of the products to be sent to customers, plus detailed specifications and delivery dates; the start of the MRP calculation.

Bill of materials (BOM) file (or product structure or product tree file) lists the description of the product (such as the material, components and quantity) and the sequence in which the product is to be assembled.

Material Requirements Planning (MRP)

There are several manufacturing control systems which make use of dependent demand, but the most widespread is material requirements planning (MRP). This section explores MRP and then looks at how the idea has been expanded to make more complex manufacturing control systems MRP II and the more generally applicable Enterprise Resource Planning (ERP) systems which can be adopted by any enterprise to carry out its operations effectively.

The MRP Process

MRP works out the timing and quantities needed to meet a given production schedule, as shown in Figure 9.7. It uses three key pieces of information to generate a material plan: the master production schedule (MPS), the bill of materials (BOM) and inventory records. MRP is nearly always a computerized system as this is the only way that the complex steps can be carried out quickly and accurately.

Master Production Schedule

In developing a plan, MRP starts with a statement of the aimed outcome. This is the master production schedule (MPS), a formal list of the products to be made, including delivery dates. Ideally, this information is a list of customer orders that have already been paid for, but often it is a forecast of orders depending of whether the firm is make to stock or make to order. The MPS can also be derived from the aggregate capacity plan (Chapter 4).

MPSs normally have three sections of either fixed, firm or flexible depending on how far from delivery the order is. The fixed period looks not very far ahead and is needed as many parts have already been produced and so in the short term there is no chance to change plans. The firm part of the MPS can cope with limited changes, depending on what has already been ordered; and the flexible part of the MPS looks far enough ahead to allow changes to the plan without significant consequences.

Bill of Materials

Chapter 4, p105

The bill of material (BOM) lists, in a hierarchical structure, the individual parts and sub-assemblies needed to make finished products (Figure 9.8). It is a result of the new product development process as it formally records product design (Chapter 4). The BOM processor is a computer

Figure 9.6 The backwards time tracing approach

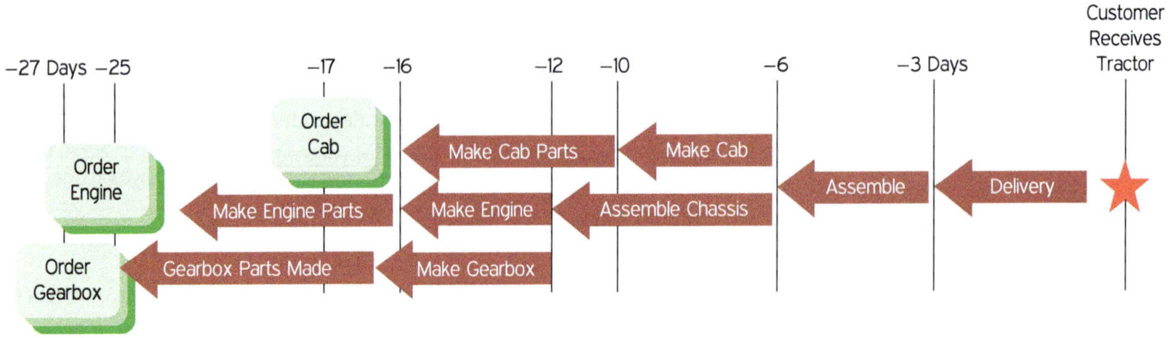

Figure 9.7 What is required to run MRP?

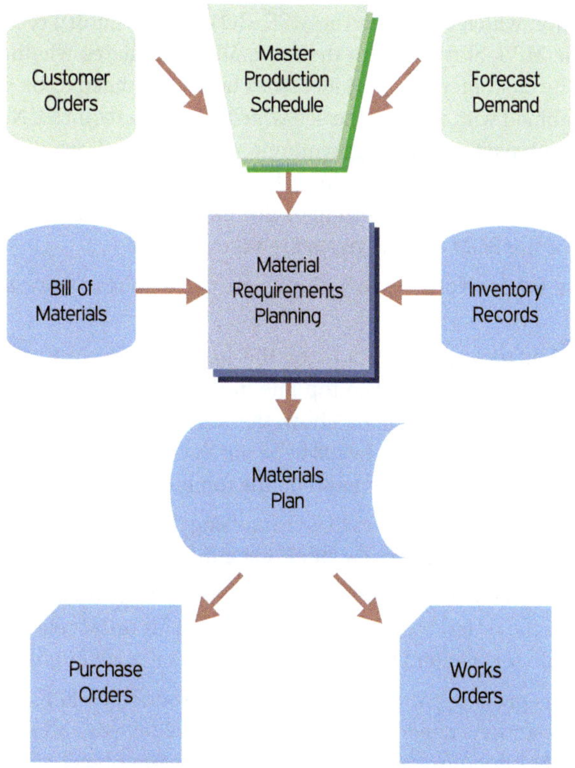

Figure 9.8 The bill of materials

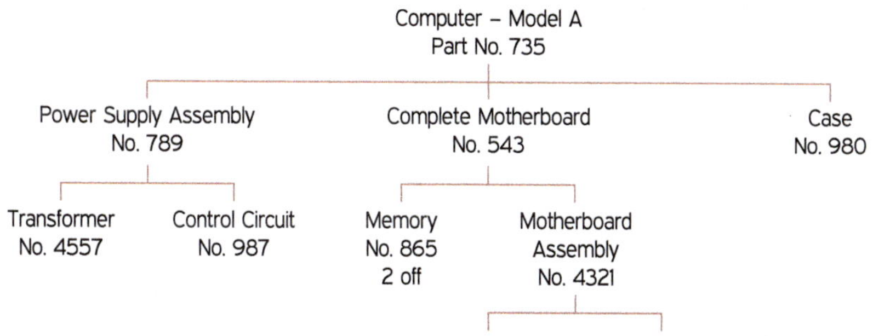

program for generating and maintaining the BOM structure for all the products in the company. One major task is to ensure that design modifications are updated in the BOM in an accurate and controlled manner as errors result in missing parts when it comes to production.

One important feature of a BOM for MRP is the way it is organized with all entries for the same part being shown on the same level. It could be that the same part is used in different products or sub-assemblies; if so, then it is easier to work out the total demand for the part if all its instances are on the same level of the BOM. The manager needs to only look across one row to find all instances of the part to calculate the total number to order.

Inventory Record File

Combining the MPS and BOM will give a list of all the parts needed but as some may already be in stock, or orders have already been placed, there is more information needed to work out what else needs ordering to satisfy the MPS plan. This is the role of the **inventory record file** which as well as recording the stock levels, introduces future demand not directly needed to satisfy the current MPS, such as orders for spares and service parts.

Make to stock (MTS) where production happens before an order has been received.

Make to order (MTO) where planning, procurement and production wait until there is an order from a customer before starting.

Aggregate planning a top-level look at demand for the operation as a whole; does not differentiate between different products and services.

Inventory records file information about the part, including sources, and the stock levels. A key part of the MRP calculation.

Running the MRP Calculation

At the core of MRP is a calculation which combines the MPS, BOM and inventory records to compute (or explode) the parts required to satisfy the MPS. Starting with the MPS, MRP calculates whether there are enough finished products in stock to supply to the customer. If not, it identifies how many need to be produced, and when. This list of products to make is then combined with the BOM to see which parts are required. Next the inventory records are examined to see how many of each part are already available, to determine how many more are needed. This tells us how many and when to start making (or buying) them. In practice the process calculates one layer of the BOM at a time as demand for higher level assemblies determines the demand for parts further down. This process is thus repeated through all the levels of the BOM until all parts are taken care of.

Figure 9.9 shows the BOM for a kettle. Note the way that some parts appear more than once, but always on the same line.

Figure 9.10 shows the MRP calculation in operation for the kettle: Figure 9.10a is the starting blank record, and Figure 9.10b shows it after the calculation. The top line in the table shows the week number and below this is the demand for the part. The two bottom lines show the stock situation at the beginning and end of the week respectively. The remaining rows show what needs to be purchased (or produced) and when the order needs to be sent out to allow delivery in time to meet the demand on the top line.

The MRP process completes the table by moving forward and assessing the number of parts required, compared with the current stock level. A shortfall leads to an order for new stock, but if there are enough parts in stock, none are ordered.

Lead time the time it takes to design, make, and deliver a product or service.

The 'Orders delivered' row gives the extra parts needed and the 'Orders released' row indicates when to place the order, based on the **lead time**. This order release information is the manufacturing schedule for the item (or the plan for orders if it is bought from a supplier).

Repeating this process for all the parts in the product, as in Figure 9.11 for example, gives a plan of all the actions needed to ensure we can achieve the MPS. Note the way that the orders released from a higher-level BOM item represent the demand for the next level and the need to incorporate how many of each part is required to make the one above it in the BOM. In this example, the orders released for the kettle become the demand for the body and base. Demand for the screws are two for each handle required, one each for the lid and base. These are added together to calculate the total number of screws needed in each week.

Figure 9.9 BOM representation for a kettle

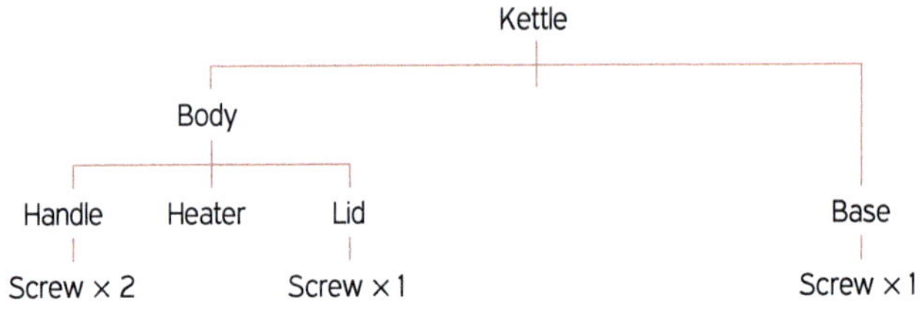

Figure 9.10 The basic MRP calculation in operation for the MPS (level 0 of the BOM)

Part: Kettle Week Number	23	24	25	26	27	28
MPS Demand	10	10	15	10	15	10
Orders Delivered						
Orders Released						
Starting Stock	45					
Balance of Stock	35					

Order Size = 30 Units, Lead Time = 1
(a)

Part: Kettle Week Number	23	24	25	26	27	28
Forecast Demand	10	10	15	10	15	10
Orders Delivered					30	
Orders Released				30		
Starting Stock	45	35	25	10	0	15
Balance of Stock	35	25	10	0	15	5

Order Size = 30 Units, Lead Time = 1
(b)

Figure 9.11 The complete MRP schedule for production of the kettle and all its sub-assemblies

BOM Level 0

Part: Kettle Week Number	23	24	25	26	27	28
Forecast Demand	10	10	15	10	15	10
Orders Delivered					30	
Orders Released				30		
Starting Stock	45	35	25	10	0	15
Balance of Stock	35	25	10	0	15	5
Order Size = 30 Units, Lead Time = 1						

BOM Level 1

Part: Body Week Number	23	24	25	26	27	28
Forecast Demand				30		
Orders Delivered				40		
Orders Released			40			
Starting Stock	20	20	20	20	30	30
Balance of Stock	20	20	20	30	30	30
Order Size = 40 Units, Lead Time = 1						

BOM Level 2

Part: Handle Week Number	23	24	25	26	27	28
Forecast Demand			40			
Orders Delivered			20			
Orders Released		20				
Starting Stock	30	30	30	10	10	10
Balance of Stock	30	30	10	10	10	10
Order Size = 20 Units, Lead Time = 1						

BOM Level 2

Part: Heater Week Number	23	24	25	26	27	28
Forecast Demand			40			
Orders Delivered						
Orders Released						
Starting Stock	100	100	100	60	60	60
Balance of Stock	100	100	60	60	60	60
Order Size = 100 Units, Lead Time = 3						

BOM Level 2

Part: Lid Week Number	23	24	25	26	27	28
Forecast Demand			40			
Orders Delivered			15			
Orders Released		15				
Starting Stock	30	30	30	5	5	5
Balance of Stock	30	30	5	5	5	5
Order Size = 15 Units, Lead Time = 1						

BOM Level 2

Part: Base Week Number	23	24	25	26	27	28
Forecast Demand				30		
Orders Delivered				30		
Orders Released			30			
Starting Stock	20	20	20	20	20	20
Balance of Stock	20	20	20	20	20	20
Order Size = 30 Units, Lead Time = 1						

BOM Level 3

Part: Screw Week Number	23	24	25	26	27	28
Forecast Demand		55	30			
Orders Delivered		30	30			
Orders Released	30	30				
Starting Stock	40	40	15	15	15	15
Balance of Stock	40	15	15	15	15	15
Order Size = 30 Units, Lead Time = 1						

Stop and Think

Why is it important to ensure a high degree of accuracy in the inputs to the MRP calculation?

Manufacturing Resource Planning

BUSINESS INTEGRATION

Early MRP systems were initially limited to planning first-level (finished product) requirements. These were then extended to other levels of the BOM, resulting in a materials plan for the whole 'tree' of parts. Increases in computing power led to MRP systems that could do more than just calculate future materials needs and more sophisticated systems were developed. These were called **manufacturing resource planning (MRP II)** and cover the planning and control of production, including the production operations in addition to the inventory and purchasing calculations. MRPII controls:

- Production routeing data
- Shop floor tracking and control
- Batch traceability
- Capacity planning
- Business planning
- Sales analysis and forecasting
- Supplier contract management
- Work tool management
- Design/engineering change control
- Cost control
- Links to existing finance systems such as ledgers.

These days it is rare to find a simple MRP system as firms make use of the extended MRP II functionality. Figure 9.12 shows a typical MRP II system, with top-level planning and detailed materials requirements (the original MRP elements we saw earlier), but with routines for **capacity planning**, and the tasks for subsequent monitoring and execution of the plan.

Manufacturing resource planning (MRP II) extension of MRP that not only identifies the amounts and times for delivery for components but also includes capacity checks, and extends the calculations to cover the scheduling of production.

Rough-cut capacity planning CRP applied at the aggregate level to try and ensure the plan is close to achievable with existing capacity limits.

Closed-loop MRP use of the MRP calculation to examine whether the plans it produces are achievable, given limits in capacity or supply times and other constraints.

Capacity requirements planning (CRP) MRP module that examines workloading on workstations to identify shortfalls.

Finite capacity scheduling advanced MRP II system including routines to try and solve any capacity problems.

Rough-cut capacity planning CRP applied at the aggregate level to try and ensure the plan is close to achievable with existing capacity limits.

Capacity Planning and Scheduling

The original MRP system assumed that there was infinite capacity in the system and scheduled items based on due dates. Often this produced plans that overloaded some workstations and so one of the first MRP II developments was **closed-loop MRP** approach shown in Figure 9.13. Here the designed capacity of the production system checks the plan to see if it is achievable at aggregate and rough-cut capacity levels. As computing power developed and the accuracy of MRP systems improved, **capacity requirements planning (CRP)** modules were developed that analysed production constraints at the individual part level. CRP identifies whether a work centre is going to be over- or underloaded and produces a *load report* that identifies where problems will occur.

Finite Capacity Scheduling

Finite capacity scheduling is a more advanced MRP II system which includes routines to try to solve the identified capacity problems. The computer reschedules the jobs in a structured and iterative manner, taking the available work centre capacities into account. Work is often rescheduled, giving preference to jobs with the earliest due dates, and so a better plan can be established. However, prioritizing jobs can be very complex, so few firms manage to make this work well. As a result, scheduling to infinite capacity, together with **rough-cut capacity planning**, and then adjusting the plan by hand when capacity issues are identified, is still common.

Figure 9.12 MRP II system elements

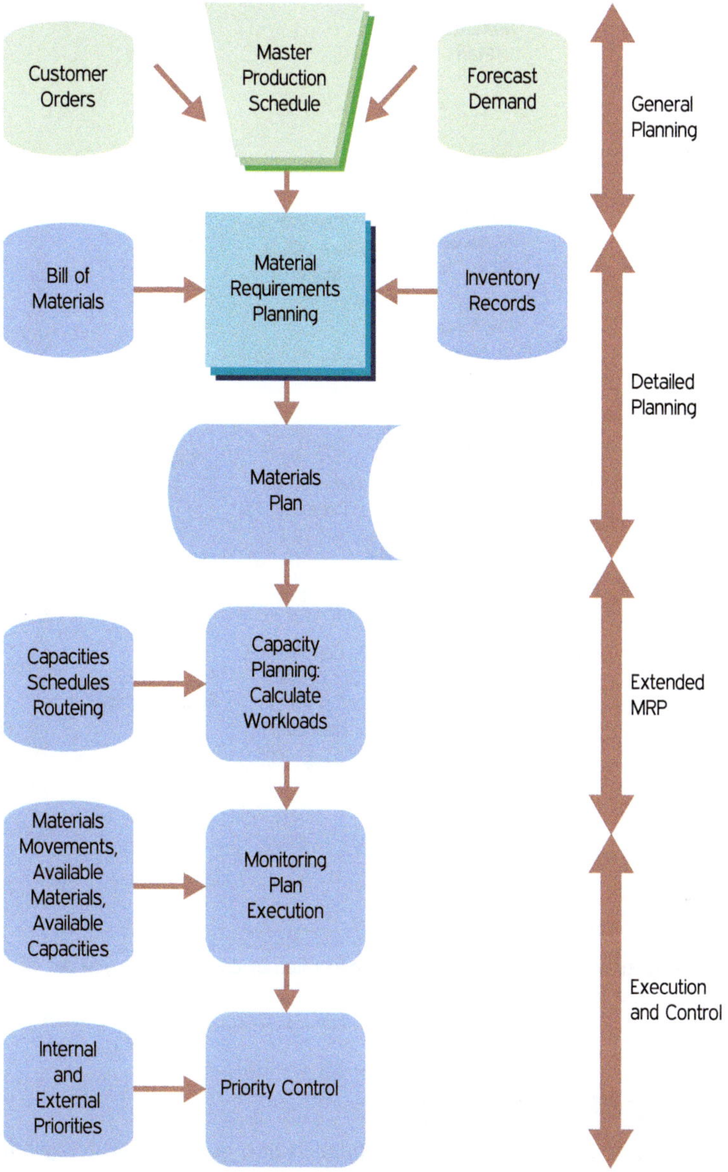

CRITICAL PERSPECTIVE

Evaluating MRP

MRP systems represent a way to schedule production and control inventory and are in use in most firms. However, introducing such large computer systems to an organization can lead to problems:

- Inadequate training of production control staff
- Inadequate preparation and maintenance of the database
- Inadequate understanding of the system purchased
- Difficulties combining the new system with existing ones.

The key point is ...

that the MRP system will only be as accurate as the data input, and the degree to which the resulting plan is followed.

Figure 9.13 Closed-loop MRP

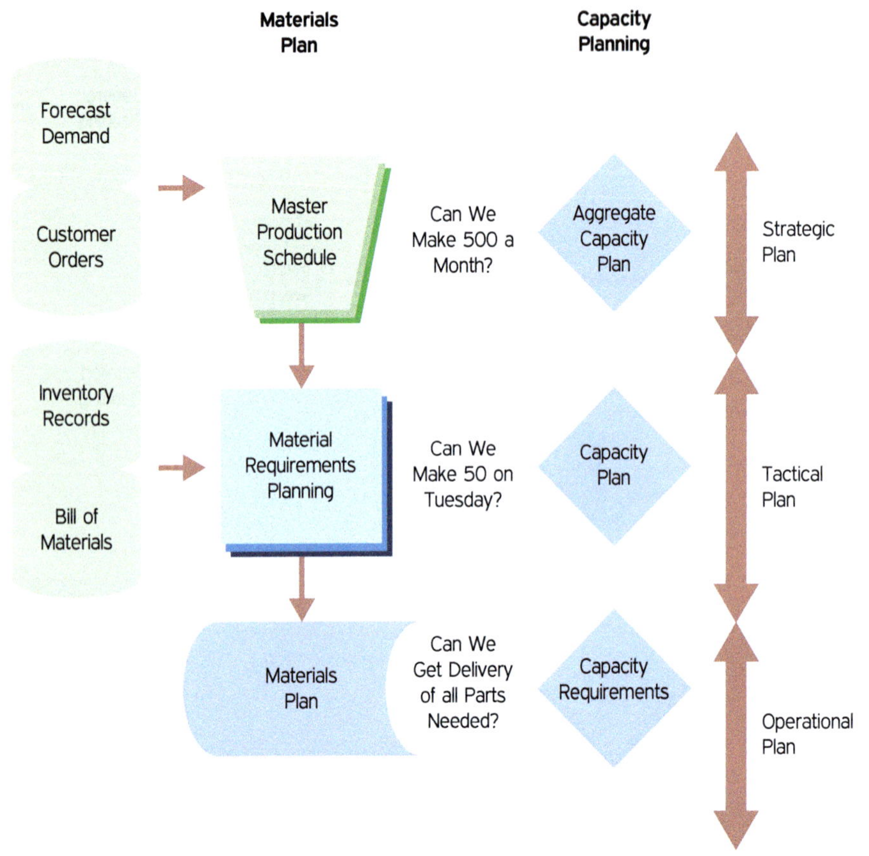

Stop and Think

As MRP II is an integrated planning process that is generated by computer, can you see how senior managers can direct and control the system?

BUSINESS INTEGRATION

Enterprise Resource Planning

Enterprise resources planning (ERP) ERP systems are corporate-wide information systems that present data as if from a central single entity source.

Supply chain management (SCM) the management of activities, organization and processes involving all the stakeholders, from the end customers (i.e. downstream) to the supplier that produces the raw material (i.e. upstream).

Recently MRP II systems have been expanded into corporate-wide systems that extend beyond production, called **enterprise resource planning (ERP)**.

Extending MRP II to ERP

Enterprise resource planning (ERP) systems are commercial software packages that integrate transactions-oriented data and business processes throughout an organization (and perhaps throughout the entire inter-organizational **supply chain**). Although ERP systems often have MRP II workflow and planning modules, their wide coverage, as shown in Figure 9.14, means they are equally applicable to service organizations.

One significant ERP improvement over MRP is a single central data store that allows commonality of information between different modules. Traditionally, when the data was held in separate sections for each task, sharing it between the modules needed specialized, very complex software which was prohibitively expensive to develop.

In addition, ERP systems have Internet interfaces that make it easy to link and share data, both internally and also with customers and suppliers. These often enter and manage their own information directly, such as updating a delivery address or placing an order online direct into another company's MPS.

Figure 9.14 ERP systems with central data stores and processing modules

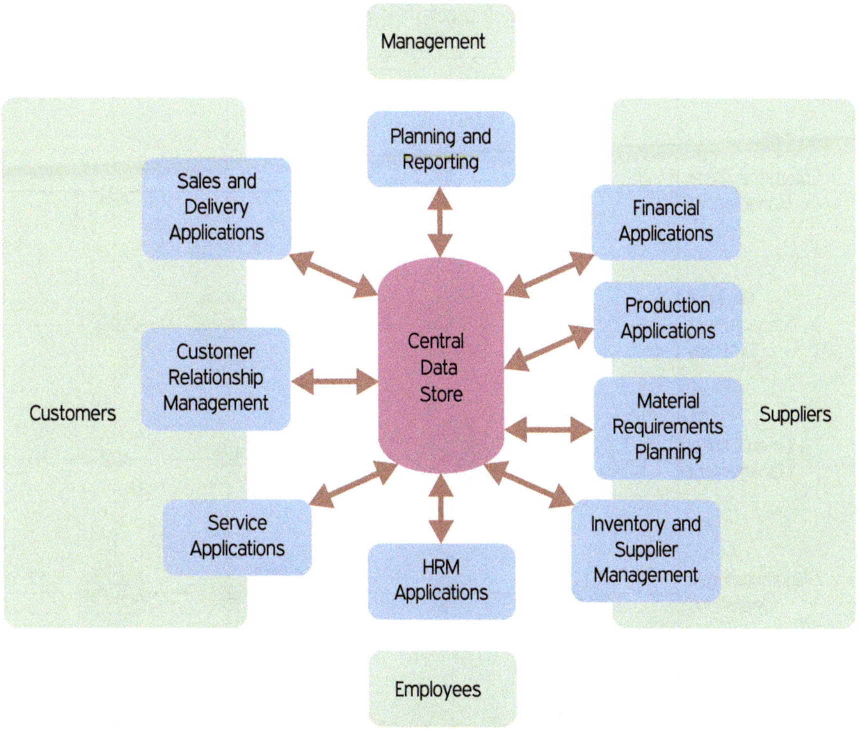

ERP can present data in a single application to whoever needs access. For example, in **customer relationship management (CRM)** all the relevant information about a customer – previous orders (from the sales data), current order status (production schedules), service calls (from after sales), payment history and creditworthiness (accounts data), and any other contact the customer may have had with the firm – is presented on one screen, giving better customer service and more efficient operations.

Customer relationship management (CRM) ERP tools where all relevant information about a customer can be presented in one place, thus offering a transparent way of supporting customers.

ERP Challenges

Successful ERP systems offer many benefits to the organization, including executive information systems to allow long-term planning, decision support applications for medium-term planning and control, and transaction processing. But there are problems, as ERP systems are normally purchased as standard packages and it is the task of the company to translate existing organizational processes into these predefined systems. This adaptation to the software adds considerable cost and risk to the adoption of ERP. However, as the systems are utilized within many firms, they can represent industry best practice, and so their adoption can lead to improved operational performance. Problems can also be caused by implementation issues, such as the management of the transition, the accuracy of data, people's resistance to change and the difficulties of integrating legacy systems. Current focus on ERP is on moving the system to a cloud based service.

Contemporary Thinking: ERP Players and Scope

The leading purveyors of ERP solutions are shown in Figure 9.15, together with their market shares. The players chose different sectors to target, offering sets of solutions tailored to particular industries based on their expertise, as can be seen in Figure 9.15.

The key point is …

that, as we saw in the discussion of MRP systems, the validity of the data and ensuring the systems are followed closely are very important to the correct running of ERP systems. There is also much choice in the market, and finding or developing a system that aligns closely with the firm's operations is a major factor in ensuring effective ERP.

Figure 9.15 Top ERP software firms and their relative market focus, 2018

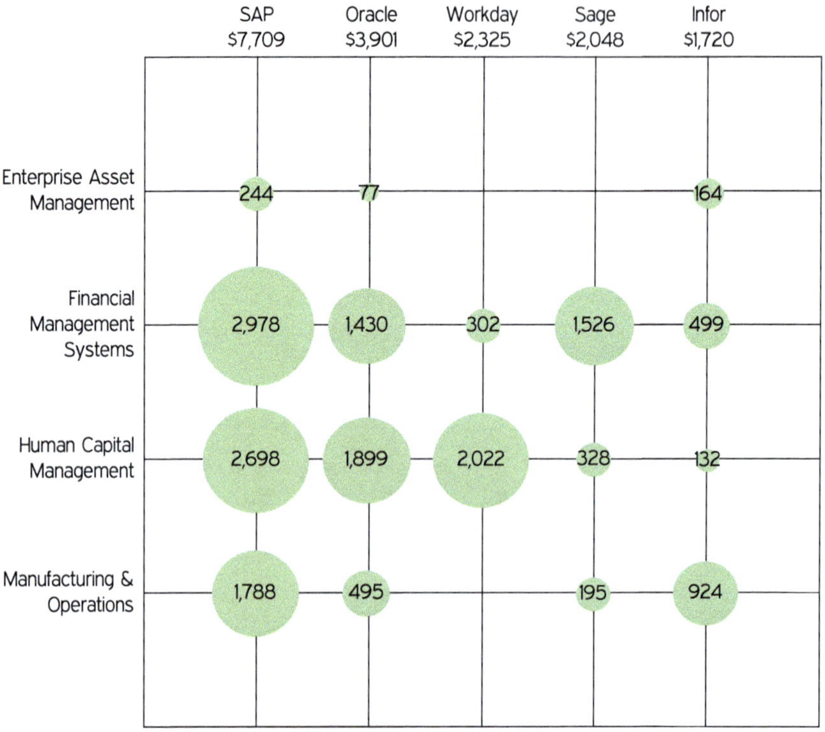

Note: The size of the bubble and value equal 2018 revenue (millions of US dollars) and the color coding equals positive or negative year-over-year change. A green bubble represents positive change, and a red bubble represents negative change.

Source: https://blogs.gartner.com/debbie_wilson/2019/04/19/erp-software-market-35-billion-40-years-making-still-growing-nicely-chris-pang/

Stop and Think

We can now see that the MRP-based ERP systems are very pervasive and employed in all areas of business, both services and manufacturing. But what gave the push for traditionally manufacturing-centred systems to be so widely adopted? Try the following question. How important do you think the Internet was for the recent explosion in ERP systems?

SHORT CASE 9.2

NIKE: ERP Implementation, from Failure to Success

Source: ©franz12/Shutterstock

One of the most-analysed examples of ERP introduction is Nike. Late 2001 saw an uncharacteristic 30% fall in profits, which Nike attributed to problems with a new ERP system introduced with i2 Technologies. The issues were a major worry for Nike and its shareholders, as the i2 system was only the first part of a move to adopt ERP based on SAP/R3.

The i2 system shortened the planning, ordering and production time of products, allowing real orders to drive the system rather than reliance on a forecast.

However, the i2 project, based on their established TradeMatrix Plan system for retail and supply, did not go well. One major issue that emerged was the high degree of customization Nike made to the i2 system, making it slow to update entries and difficult to track down and rectify errors. The customization problems were compounded by i2's lack of experience in clothes and shoes and Nike's changing operating conditions, which forced the adoption of the system before it was ready. When first used, the system had poor integration with Nike's other systems. Nike and i2 quickly found solutions to the problems, but had already over-ordered on some products, leading to heavy discounting, and under-ordered on others, leading to shortages of some top sellers.

Nike learnt from the project and the rest of the ERP programme with SAP has been far more effective. Nike now uses a third-party integrator to migrate data to new systems and has reduced system customization. Increased testing of the system before going live ensures it works as expected.

Nike now has a single-instance, apparel industry focused SAP/R3 system (i.e. all data is held only once in the database) that gives a competitive advantage as it now operates with firm orders from retailers, rather than having to rely on a forecast. Nike's and their partners' learning will help with the next steps, which includes plans to capture orders from end customers.

The case shows the problems and benefits of ERP, where firms effectively replace the entire operating systems at the core of the firm with one system. Such a large-scale change carries very high risks, but can also generate great rewards if done properly.

Questions

1. What advantage does Nike get from having its single-instance ERP system?
2. What advice would you give to other firms embarking on ERP programmes, given the experience of Nike?

Sources: adapted from Songini (2001); Davenport (1998).

Reverse Inventory Management

As environmental concerns grow, there is a particular problem that bothers many organizations, namely how to manage recycling or **reverse logistics**.

There is a growing need for firms to think about how they manage the flow of products back from customers. This could be as a result of warranty issues demanding correction or the desire to take back products and capture value from reusing or recycling the parts, or it may be the result of legislation demanding firms are responsible for the proper and safe disposal of their products when their **life cycle** is complete. Good examples of this process come from worldwide end-of-life legislation for vehicles and the waste electrical and electronic equipment (WEEE) rules introduced by the EU. Another push for this activity comes from firms looking to adopt **circular economy** ideas which focus on reusing resources wherever possible (Figure 9.16). This leads to lower costs and also less impact on the environment.

If we think about all the approaches we have so far proposed to manage the flow of materials in our supply chain, the focus has been on being either efficient or effective as captured in the ideas of **lean and agile (leagile) supply chains**. However, when we need to manage the flow back from the customer to the manufacturer, often termed **reverse logistics**, the same approaches cannot be used for many reasons. Primarily, it is almost impossible to predict the timing, volume, location and condition of the returned products. This means that in most cases the reverse logistics and subsequent inventories are nearly always managed separately from the forward logistics as it is too complicated to develop a system which can manage both together. One common solution is to employ **third party logistics (TPL)** firms to manage the reverse logistics.

The key point is ...

that reverse logistics and the resulting inventories are complex operations which do not easily fit into efficient forward logistics and inventory management systems. As a result, they almost always need treating independently.

Reverse logistics addresses key issues related to how companies can become more environmentally efficient through recycling, reusing and reducing the amount of materials used.

Product life cycle generalized model of the buying behaviour of customers over time; used to predict demand for a product or service.

Circular Economy When firms look at the resources they use and seek to keep re-using them rather needing more fresh materials.

Leagile supply combination of a lean supply chain and an agile supply chain

Third-party logistics (TPL) a TPL provider can be treated as an external supplier that performs some or all parts of a company's functions, especially logistics services.

Figure 9.16 The circular economy

Source: European Commission (2017).

Summary

Managing inventory is a very important task for all firms and there are many ways to ensure they tackle the problem effectively, such as ROL and CR. Although firms should normally try to reduce inventory whenever possible, they need to remember that inventory is not always a bad thing and has many uses, including uncoupling separate activities in the chain of operations.

We can apply mathematics to managing inventory levels and there are many refinements to the EOQ formula that take in ever more accurate representations or statistical ideas to improve the accuracy of the models.

By controlling the flow of material, we can control the activities of the organization. MRP II systems schedule the activities of the firm to meet the planned orders for finished products and so match output to demand. This can greatly reduce inventory and waste. Despite the claims of the systems providers, the complex ERP systems with their central data stores and web-integrated processes are an extension of MRP and are equally valuable to service firms as well as to manufacturers.

In summary, we have:

- Contrasted the different roles of inventory
- Explained when inventory is useful and when it is problematic
- Explored the use of reorder level and cyclical review systems
- Shown how the ABC technique can help classify parts
- Witnessed the power of EOQ models
- Defined dependent and independent demand systems
- Seen what is involved in an MRP system
- Described the extensions that lead to MRP II
- Defined the scope of ERP systems
- Explored the complexity of reverse inventory management.

Key Theories

- **EOQ** – economic order quantity (EOQ) is a fixed order amount that minimizes the total costs over a whole year.
- **Reorder level** – reorder point inventory systems (Q-type) tell us when we need to order a fixed amount (normally the EOQ).
- **Cyclical review** – cyclical review inventory systems (P type) determine the amount to be ordered at a fixed time.
- **ABC** – ABC ranking tells us which parts we should control closely and also those that we should not exert undue effort in monitoring.
- **Dependent/independent demand** – with independent demand, the demand for each part is treated as unrelated to anything else. Dependent demand makes use of the fact that demand for a part is normally related to that for others, or to the aggregate production plan.
- **MRP** – material requirements planning is a way of calculating the demand and timing for component deliveries in order to make the products listed in the master production schedule.
- **MRP II** – manufacturing resources planning is an extension of MRP that not only identifies the amounts and times for delivery for components, but also includes capacity checks and extends the calculations to cover the scheduling of production.
- **ERP** – enterprise resources planning systems are corporate-wide information systems that present data as if from a central, single source.

Key Equations

Economic order quantity:

$$\text{Economic order quantity, } Q = \sqrt{\frac{2DC_s}{C_h}}$$

Reorder level system:

$$\text{ROL} = \text{Demand (per day)} \times \text{Delivery lead time (in days)}$$

Reorder level system with safety stock:

$$\text{ROL} = \text{Demand (per day)} \times \text{Delivery lead time (in days)} + \text{Safety stock}$$

ABC inventory classification:

$$\text{Annual usage value} = \text{Unit cost} + \text{Quantity used per annum}$$

Suggested Answers to Stop and Think Questions

1. **Inventory control:** The answer depends on the organization you chose. In a hospital, say, the inventory would include the drugs, and losing control would mean that patients could not be treated if stocks were low. If inventory is too high, though, the costs can spiral and the hospital will have to throw some unused drugs away, as they will have passed their use-by dates. If you were thinking about a firm of builders, the inventory would be the materials they have at the yard. If they ran out of something, then they would need to get it in quickly and that would cost more than a normal order. If they had too much material in the yard, then it would be hard to find the right materials behind the piles of other stuff and there the firm would have too much capital tied up in inventory.
2. **Function of inventory:** The functions of inventory can be summarized as meeting demand (anticipation), protection against stock-out (buffer), cutting costs by ordering in bulk, flexibility

(buffer), covering delays (decoupling), taking advantage of price changes, and also as transit or pipeline, and cycle inventories. In a supermarket we can see the stocks on the shelves as anticipation (awaiting demand), decoupling in the materials held behind the counter whilst more are delivered and work in progress in the bakery ovens at the rear of the store.

3. **EPQ:** EPQ models add a level of complexity, in that they also consider the fact that parts may also be produced in the factory at a set rate and not arrive in the system by instantaneous delivery.
4. **Order systems:** Most of the foodstuffs we have in our homes effectively operate on some form of either reorder point or cyclical review. Some food we buy every time we visit the shops, such as milk and bread, and we decide how much to get, based on when we will next go shopping (cyclical approach). Others we only buy when the jar or packet is empty, or we notice we are getting low – in effect a reorder point approach. These are not as formalized as they are in a manufacturing firm.
5. **Data accuracy:** Accuracy of data in the files is a major area of concern when introducing MRP, as the outputs of the system are used repeatedly in other calculations. If any mistakes are not identified in advance, then the firm will either run out of materials it needs, or else carry excessive stocks.

   The Oliver Wight organization, which sells MRP consultancy, grades the implementations of systems in firms and one of the criteria for getting its A grade is 99% BOM accuracy. This is particularly hard when you remember that products are constantly being developed and changed. Quite complex systems exist to ensure that such engineering changes are managed and timed through the supply chain in a coordinated manner. If, for example, the old steering wheel and the new steering column are not compatible, but come from different suppliers with different lead times and order quantities, you can imagine the potential problems this could cause.
6. **Design of MRP:** Top managers have a very important role in ensuring that the system works correctly. Rather than chasing day-to-day issues, their new focus is on the strategic roles of implementing and developing the system. Their biggest input is not in how the plan is carried out, as it once was, but in designing the parameters of the system and thinking forward. For example, they need to be aware of future capacity issues and develop plans to alleviate them. At a more practical level, the managers are responsible for setting the MPS that drives the system; this can be a very delicate task, trying to keep an eye on CRP outputs and sales performance.
7. **ERP and the Internet:** The Internet and the evolution of ERP occurred at the same time. As IT systems were just evolving that could manage the complex data operations fast enough for the ideas of MRP extension to become reality, so too was the development of wide-area networks. As these became faster with the explosion of the Internet, so the ERP systems could be distributed. The development of ERP would probably have happened without the Internet, but this made it available to a much wider range of firms, who could not have invested in their own fast wide-area networks. The universal availability of the Internet also helped ERP systems, and their web-based front ends, to enable the sales force and customers to interact with the processes directly. It is likely that many of the truly useful elements of ERP would have been very slow to emerge if the Internet had not developed at the same time.

connect

Review Questions

1. What is the aim of inventory management and what targets should firms aim for?
2. List a few examples of when inventory can be useful to help operations managers.
3. Write down the equation to determine the EOQ for a product. Why is the EOQ concept significant for a shop manager?
4. What tools exist to help managers control inventory levels?

5. Describe the processes in MRP II systems, paying particular attention to the organizational issues of introducing the system to a company with little previous experience of computerized production systems.
6. Describe the steps in introducing ERP systems, paying particular attention to the organizational issues.
7. What is ERP, and how does it differ from MRP?
8. What is reverse inventory?

Discussion Questions

1. Use the internet to investigate the differences between the operations of Amazon and its Chinese rival Ali Baba.
2. Discuss, with examples from international firms, whether inventory is an asset or a liability.
3. How useful is the concept of EOQ to service operations?
4. Describe the difference between MRP and MRP II production control systems.
5. Giving examples, discuss the circumstances under which MRP systems are inappropriate. Also, discuss the choices that following such a strategy predefines.
6. With reference to theoretical frameworks, discuss whether firms can adopt MRP-based inventory systems for products with both low and high production volumes.
7. Discuss why reverse logistics is difficult to integrate with forward logistics.

Problems

1. Pay a visit to the college shop, or one nearby, and see if you can calculate the EOQ for a popular soft drink. (Be sure to ask the shop manager for permission before you start.) You will need to estimate the daily demand (you can always watch for 30 minutes and use that as an estimate), stock order costs (you could work out how much it would cost to send an employee to the wholesaler, including wages and van mileage), and holding costs (try a bank loan rate of 10%). When you are done, see what the manager thinks about your figures and find out exactly what stock control system they use.
2. As a more advanced task, you could try and work out the reorder level as well.
3. Look at the different stocks held in the library. There is probably a short or restricted loan section where books can be taken out for only a short time. How do you think the librarian knows which books to put in this section? How would you adapt the ABC method to help the librarian estimate better the books to hold on restricted loan? Perhaps you could see whether the librarian can find time to give you the information to help your calculations and whether they know about ABC analysis.
4. Using the Internet, try to identify the different competitive strengths of the ERP suppliers (as mentioned in the Contemporary Thinking: ERP Players and Scope section). The introduction to their annual reports would be a good place to look. Which sectors of the industry would you recommend as good pickings for a small, start-up company to make its first move?
5. The demand for Tasty-Lick snacks at the college shop is constant at 2,000 a month. The snacks sell for £1.99 each and the cost of placing an order with the supplier, Sticky Sweets Co. Ltd, is £10 an order (including delivery charges). The cost of storing items in the small storeroom is estimated to be £28 per snack per year.

   (a) How many snacks should the shop order in each delivery?

   (b) What is the total holding cost associated with Tasty-Lick snacks for the shop in a typical year?

   (c) Why is the EOQ concept significant to the shop manager?

6. The demand for cans of Bernard's Baked Beans at the Cold Storage Supermarket in Egham is constant at 9,000 a month. The cans sell for 55p each, the cost of placing an order with Bernard (which also covers the delivery by Man-n-Van Co.) is £75 and the cost of keeping a can in the storeroom is estimated to be £2 per can per year.
   (a) What are the most important limitations to the use of the EOQ formula in inventory management decision-making?
   (b) Describe how the EOQ is different from the EBQ (Economic Batch Quantity).
   (c) How many snacks should the shop manager order in each delivery?
   (d) What is the total holding cost associated with Bernard's Beans for the shop in a typical year?
   (e) Why is the EOQ concept significant to the shop manager and what might happen if the items needed special care, such as refrigeration?
7. The demand for Munch-u-Like snacks at the college shop is constant at 500 a month, the snacks sell for £1.50 each, the cost of placing an order with Jones Snacks Co. (which also covers the delivery by Securicor) is £60 and the cost of keeping a snack in the small store room is estimated to be £18 per snack per year. How many snacks should the shop order in each delivery?
8. The demand for 2GB memory sticks at the Computer Centre is constant at 500 a month. It takes 3 days for an order to the supplier to be delivered.
   (a) What is the reorder level for the memory sticks? (Note the units of days and months.)
   (b) If the IT consultants add a 10% safety stock, what is the new reorder level?
9. The petrol station sells 1,200 litres of unleaded fuel per day. It takes 15 days for an order to the refinery to be delivered. The EOQ is 30,000 litres.
   (a) What is the reorder level?
   (b) If the managers add a 10% safety stock, what is the new reorder level?
10. If it takes half a day to deliver an order of milk to Starbucks in the city centre and they use 20 bottles per day:
    (a) What is the reorder level?
    (b) If the managers add a 10% safety stock, what is the new reorder level?
11. The business school's stock of paper is operated using a cyclical review system and an order is placed every month.
    (a) If the school normally uses 64 packets of paper a day and it takes 4 days for the delivery, what is the target stock level it should aim for?
    (b) This month the business school finds it has 120 packets of paper left in stock. Using the information above, how many more should it order?
    (c) The office manager at the business school is worried that it might run out of paper and so adds a 10% safety stock. What is the new target level?
12. The supermarket uses a cyclical review system for its own-brand shampoo. Typically, it sells 4,500 bottles a week. An order is placed each week to bring the stocks up to the average weekly demand. It takes a day for the delivery to arrive and the supermarket uses a 10% safety margin to cover any variation in demand. What is the target level of stock for the shampoo?
13. A farmer keeps his chickens in a shed in winter, heated by special bulbs. If he needs to replace 6 bulbs a week and it takes 4 weeks for the bulbs to arrive, how many should he aim to have ready to use when he counts the spares every Monday morning?
14. The table below shows the bought-in price and annual sales of the set of different types of garment that are held in stock by a wholesaler.

Itemtype	Purchase price (£)	Annual sales (items per year)
a	4	2,250
b	47	1,950
c	148	85
d	75	200
e	11	580
f	129	115
g	67	15
h	201	150
i	69	310
j	78	900

(a) Should inventory be seen as an asset or liability? Ensure you justify your views.

(b) Construct an ABC chart for the items above.

(c) Suggest, giving clear reasons, which items should be treated as classes A, B and C.

15. The table below shows the bought-in price and annual sales of the set of different types of garment that are held in stock by a wholesaler.

Itemtype	Purchase price (£)	Annual sales (items per year)
a	24	2,250
b	54	950
c	90	95
d	75	20
e	9	380
f	12	120
g	56	155
h	21	550
i	36	310
j	78	90

(a) Construct an ABC chart for these items.

(b) Suggest which items should be treated as classes A, B and C, discussing why, and what this means.

16. The table below shows the purchase price and annual sales for various items of stock.

Itemtype	Purchase price (£)	Annual sales (items per year)
a	880	1,400
b	810	400
c	2,100	70
d	1,650	20
e	100	350
f	160	1,850
g	6,100	150
h	230	550
i	1,500	650
j	2,500	50

Construct an ABC chart for these items, showing which items you designated as class A, which as class B and which as class C.

17. SPG Ltd produces a range of household products. Its top-selling cordless kettle is made of five subassemblies: lid, handle, body, heater and base. The assembly process has recently been streamlined and now consists of push-fitting the heater into the body and then fastening the lid and handle using three screws. The bases are a complete unit and do not need any work before packaging with the assembled kettle.

It is Monday morning at the start of week 7 and the sales director has the following orders for the kettle.

Week	8	9	10	11
Orders	150	260	220	190

You have the following information on stock levels and delivery times.

Part	Current stock level	Delivery/assembly time (weeks)	Batch size
Kettle	190	1	50
Base	150	1	50
Body	450	2	200
Heater	170	2	200
Lid	200	1	90
Handle	30	1	90
Screw	3,000	1	1,000

(a) Given the description above, construct a table or diagram of the BOM (Bill of Materials) for the kettle.

(b) Generate the MPS of the top-level demand for the kettle.

(c) Using the MPS, run through the MRP calculation to identify whether there are any supply problems for the firm to satisfy the sales orders. If you identified any problems, what advice would you give to the firm?

18. TVS manufactures satellite dishes from sheet metal components. It controls its material supply using a manually based MRP system. Each dish (part A001) is made of two subassemblies: a reflector assembly (part B001) and a mount assembly (part B002). Each reflector assembly requires one dish (C001), one arm (C002) and four screws, and each mount requires one pole (C003), one mount (C004) and two screws. The reflector assembly and mount assembly are fastened together using a further two screws. All the screws are the same design (F500).

The latest information available from the sales department shows expected orders of:

Week number	Predicted sales of dishes
1	100
2	400
3	600
4	300

The current stock level and ordering information is:

Part	Opening stock for week 1	Delivery time from placing order with supplier (weeks)	EOQ
Dish (A001)	360	1	100
Reflector assembly (B001)	600	1	300
Mount assembly (B002)	600	1	150
Dish (C001)	500	1	50
Arm (C002)	1000	1	300
Pole (C003)	600	2	80
Mount (C004)	500	1	200
Screws (F500)	1000	2	1,000

(a) Draw a tiered representation of the BOM for an assembled dish (A001).

(b) Produce the MRP calculation requirements record cards for each part for the four weeks, including the demand, opening stock, closing stock, orders released and deliveries received.

(c) State whether the current production forecast is realistic. If you identified any problems, what might be done to solve them?

19. A company manufactures solid oak doors and controls its material supply using a manually based MRP system. Each door requires one solid oak door panel, two brass hinges and two brass handles. Each hinge is fastened to the door using three screws and each handle uses two screws of the same type as for the hinges.

The latest information available from the sales department shows expected orders of:

Week number	Predicted sales
1	70
2	20
3	40
4	30

The current stock level and ordering information is:

Part	Opening stock for week 1	Delivery time from placing order with supplier (weeks)	EOQ
Panels	90	1	50
Hinges	150	1	150
Handles	170	1	75
Screws	350	2	400

(a) Draw a representation of the BOM for an assembled door.

(b) Given the sales forecast, work out the weekly aggregate demand for each part used in the factory.

(c) Produce the requirements record cards for each part for the four weeks, including the demand, opening stock, closing stock, orders released and deliveries received.

(d) Identify whether the current production forecast is realistic. If you identified any problems, what might be done to solve them?

Further Reading

Bertsimas, D., Kallus, N. and Hussain, A. (2016) 'Inventory management in the era of big data', *Production and Operations Management*, **25**(12), 2006–2009.

Davenport, T.H. (1998) 'Putting the enterprise into the enterprise system', *Harvard Business Review*, **76**(4), 121–131.

Grant, D., Trautrim, A. and Wong, C.Y. (2015) *Sustainable Logistics and Supply Chain Management*, Kogan Page, London.

Grubbstrom, R.W. (2006) 'Analysis of standard ordering policies within the framework of MRP theory', *International Journal of Production Research*, **44**(18/19), 3759–3773.

Li, Y., Wu, F., Zong, W. and Li, B. (2017) 'Supply chain collaboration for ERP implementation', *International Journal of Operations and Production Management*, **37**(10), 1327–1347.

McCutcheon, D.M., Raturi, A.S. and Meredith, J.R. (1994) 'The customization–responsiveness squeeze', *Sloan Management Review*, **35**(2), 89–99.

Orlicky, J. (1975) *Material Requirements Planning; The New Way of Life in Production and Inventory Management*, McGraw-Hill, New York.

References

Chopra, S. and Lariviere, M.A. (2005) 'Managing service inventory to improve performance', *MIT Sloan Management Review*, **47**(1), 56–63, 95.

Davenport, T.H. (1998) 'Putting the enterprise into the enterprise system', *Harvard Business Review*, **76**(4), 121–131.

Appendix

Mathematical Derivation of EOQ

There are several ways to find the EOQ. They are all based on the following argument.

$$\text{Total cost} = \text{Total holding cost} + \text{Total ordering (or set-up) cost}$$

$$\begin{aligned}\text{Total holding cost} &= \text{Average number held} \times \text{Cost of holding one item per year}\\ &= \text{Average inventory} \times C_h\\ &= \frac{Q}{2} \times C_h\end{aligned}$$

To see why the average inventory in the cyclical behaviour is $Q/2$, look at the sawtooth diagram in Figure 9.17. See how the top halves of the triangles fit in the gaps to give the same as a flat line at $Q/2$.

$$\begin{aligned}\text{Total ordering (or set-up) cost} &= \text{How many times we need to order} \times \text{Cost per order}\\ &= \text{Number of orders} \times C_s\\ &= \frac{D}{Q} \times C_s\end{aligned}$$

(If we need D per year, and order them in batches of Q, then we shall need D/Q orders in a year.)

The next step is based on looking back at Figure 9.2 and observing that the optimum order quantity occurs at the point where set-up costs and holding costs are equal. Mathematically, we can write this down using the formulae above:

$$C_s \frac{D}{Q} = C_h \frac{Q}{2}$$

Rearranging this formula:

$$2C_s D = Q^2 C_h$$

$$Q^2 = \frac{2DC_s}{C_h}$$

And therefore:

$$Q = \sqrt{\frac{2DC_s}{C_h}}$$

Figure 9.17 Average inventory is Q/2

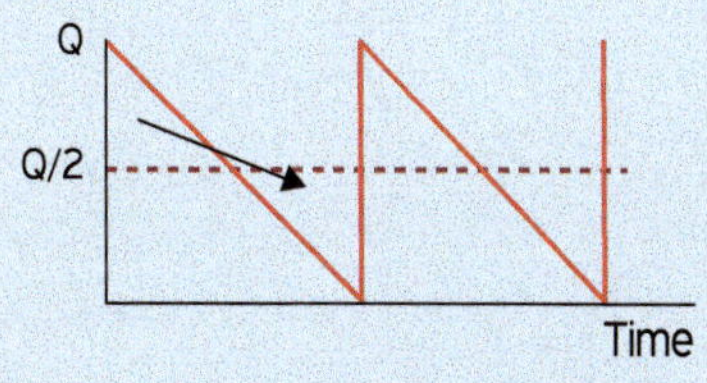

10 Lean Operations

Learning Outcomes

After reading this chapter, you should be able to:

- Classify push or pull systems
- Explain how kanban works
- Describe the factors that are needed to support lean systems
- Identify the limits of lean management
- Employ the volume and variety model to identify which production control system is suitable for which operating conditions

Subway: Sandwiches Just in Time

Source: ©Brent Hofacker/Shutterstock

We are all familiar with fast food, but perhaps we have never really looked at what is going on behind the counter. How can firms produce their products so cheaply and quickly and yet still offer high quality and the choice from the menu we want every time? The answer lies in the fact that fast-food restaurants have wholeheartedly adopted the ideas of lean production and just in time.

The Subway sandwich chain is a good example of the application of lean production to service provision. In 2019 Subway operated more than 42,431 restaurants in 87 countries and in America they had 17% more outlets than McDonald's. Part of this success comes from Subway's franchising approach, which means that local owners run the stores but use central advertising, design and logistics expertise. Subway plays on the current focus on health, quoting the healthy calorie and fat content of their food, and offering diet plans. Indeed the parent company is called Doctor's Associates, reflecting the founders who, in 1965, were a PhD and an aspiring medical student.

The lean production of sandwiches at Subway is driven directly by the customer, who first chooses the bread, then chooses a filling and choice of cheese, and then selects the 'veggies' and sauces. The sandwich is assembled along a counter and at busy times is passed from employee to employee (or 'sandwich artists' as Subway prefers to call them), who cut the bread, add one of the three elements and wrap the finished sandwich. A sandwich is made in less than 60 seconds and Subway holds regular competitions where artists race one another: Sara Tiegs from Pullman, Washington is the current champion with 49.85 seconds.

The choice on the menu may seem complicated, but it is actually simple and well thought out. For example, the bread is one of just five options: Italian, nine-grain wheat, nine-grain honey oat, Italian herb and cheddar, and healthy Italian. These are made of two base doughs but with different toppings added before baking.

Make to order (MTO): where planning, procurement and production wait until there is an order from a customer before starting.

So one key element of the lean system we can observe is late configuration of the product to **make to order (MTO)**.

The bread itself is delivered as frozen sticks and prepared (proved and baked) on the premises in small batches using special machines that closely control the oven temperature and humidity. The proving machines automatically rotate the loaves to ensure a high consistency. The bread is always fresh, not just because it is baked locally, but also because it is allowed to stand for (at most) only three hours before being discarded.

The meat is also closely controlled and comes pre-portioned in paper trays. This ensures the correct quantity and also speeds up the preparation process as the employee does not need to count the slices. When stocks of meat run low, another container is fetched from the cold store to replenish the counter stocks. Again, freshness is ensured as the meat is only out of the cold store for a short time. The Subway approach is based on a set of core values and aims that permeate the operations of the franchises. The important elements of the Subway system are:

- *Simplicity:* the system is kept free of complexity by having tight control on the options available to customers.
- *Control:* the system has built-in controls and material flow is fast, regular and very visible.
- *Made to order:* the customer is important not just as the source of cash, but also in defining the products to make.
- *Quality:* as the customer is impatiently waiting for lunch, there is no scope for Subway to make mistakes, run out of a filling, or provide substandard items.
- *Training:* the employees have clear instructions and direct training to ensure they operate the system exactly the way it was designed.

Sources: www.subway.com and www.ipcoop.com (Independent Purchasing Cooperative of Subway owners that runs the supply chain), accessed 8 November 2019.

Introduction

Chapter 9, p289

Lean production: highly efficient management approach with repeated focus on waste reduction, and based on the ideas of the Toyota Production System and JIT.

Just in time (JIT): the pull-based material control system used at Toyota, and the basis of developing the lean model.

In Chapter 9 we examined inventory management and saw how in most cases companies try to keep the levels of inventory as low as possible to reduce costs. One method of coordinating the supply of parts across the whole organization is to use dependent demand planning systems, such as MRP-based ERP (enterprise resource planning). These apply the EOQ (economic order quantity) to develop a realistic plan of material production and procurement to meet the master production schedule. However, as we can see at Subway, it is possible to ensure that exactly the right amounts are manufactured at exactly the right time and this approach is often called **lean production**.

In this chapter we shall look at implementing lean systems and their approach to respond to variations in demand. We can define a lean system as a highly efficient process that produces products and services in the desired quantities, exactly when they are needed. Lean systems are an extension of the **just in time (JIT)** approach, closely associated with Toyota, and so we start off by examining the Toyota Production System (TPS) before looking at the more widely applicable lean model. These methods are increasingly being used by firms for service delivery and also in the public sector for healthcare.

Inventory Control Classification

We have already seen the benefits of introducing control in the form of dependent demand systems such as MRP, but greater reductions in inventory can be obtained using lean systems.

Figure 10.1 Matching supply and demand: stock time charts for different systems

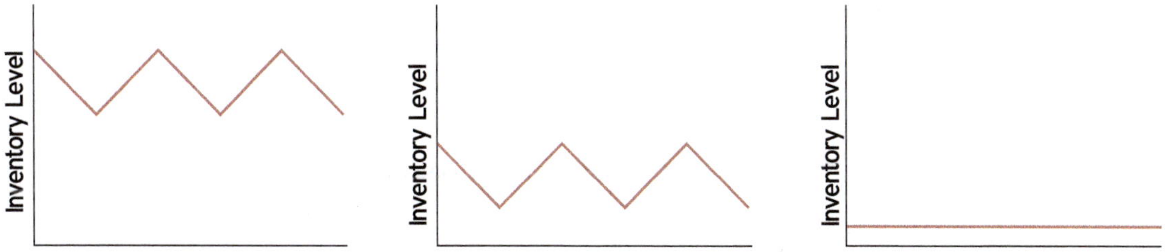

(a) **Traditional System**
Excess Stocks 'Just In Case'

(b) **ERP/MRP System**
Supply Matches Demand, Using Batches of EOQ

(c) **Lean System**
Match Supply and Demand, by Reducing Batch Size

Figure 10.1 shows the stock time charts for different systems. With traditional *independent demand* systems there is extra stock in the system to ensure there is always enough, and because managers may not accurately know the exact amount of material required (see Figure 10.1a).

With ERP systems, the MRP calculation sets production and delivery to achieve the predicted demand and so there is no excess stock left once the demand has been satisfied. However, as these systems normally utilize batching rules such as EOQ, parts are ordered as fixed quantities; hence we get the common sawtoothed pattern. The ERP approach helps to eliminate the problem of ordering excessive stock, so it can be beneficial to organizations, but it can still result in stockholdings while parts wait to be used on the production line as the batches of materials are consumed (see Figure 10.1b).

With lean systems, the EOQ rules are challenged to try and make parts in a **batch size of one** to further reduce the stockholding level. Reducing the batch size as far as possible gives a very low and constant inventory level. The inventory in a lean system is fixed and is made up of in-process material directly driven by demand from the customer. This is a very efficient system, with very low or near-zero inventories being held (see Figure 10.1c).

> **Batch of one:** a key element of the lean approach, which seeks to produce individual products, as this is normally what the customer orders.

Push and Pull Systems

Classifying the differences between inventory control systems in a more general manner, we can identify two distinct approaches known as *push* and *pull*.

Figure 10.2 shows how systems such as ERP and MRP are often 'push' in their approach, as the activities in the firm are planned centrally, with instructions and materials sent to individual workstations to push the product through the production stages.

The lean approach operates in a different way, with customer orders initiating production activities. This is a 'pull' approach as an operation responds to demand by pulling material through the operation towards the customer end of the supply chain as shown in Figure 10.2.

The contrast in the **push versus pull inventory control** approaches is useful in helping us appreciate the basic nature of lean systems. In essence, the push system makes a plan and then tries to coordinate the production of all the sub-assemblies and parts towards achieving the plan. We saw this clearly in the MRP system in Chapter 9 where the task is one of coordination of quantities and timings to deliver the MPS. Pull systems have no such detailed plans, but respond to an order when it arrives from a customer, or is generated by the manager of the system. In practice, this means that the last production station is first to respond by making the finished product and this prompts further workstations back up the chain to produce the parts that have been consumed.

> **Push–pull inventory control:** in push systems there is a central planning system that generates and programmes orders for the production line. With pull, orders come from customers, and the line reacts to the demand.

We can also see this pull approach in service environments. For example, when a new bank account is opened, the account services department request the production of the credit and debit cards from blank stock.

Chapter 9, p289

Figure 10.2 Differences between push–pull inventory control system

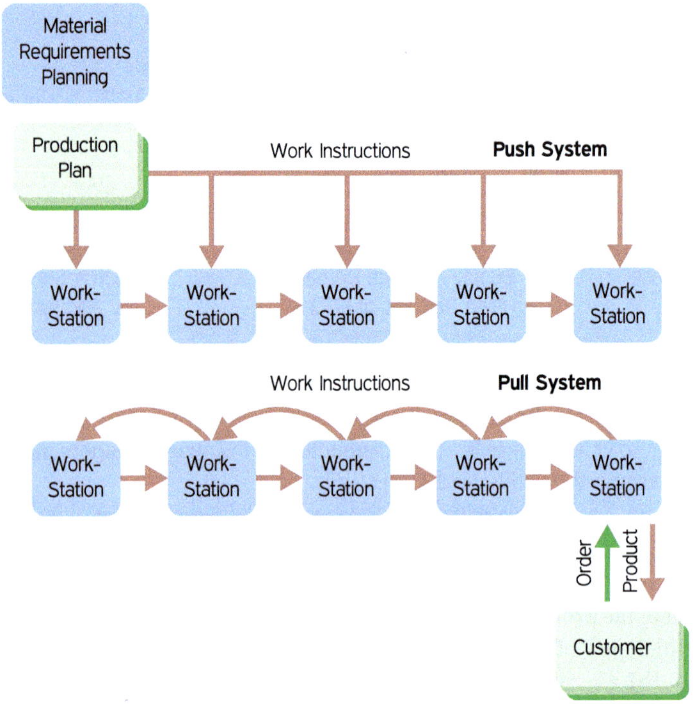

In summary, with pull the order initiates the flow of materials. However, making it work is complex and there are many elements needed in a lean implementation; we need to explore these in some detail to fully appreciate the way it operates.

It is worth noting that the process of producing the product is the same whether a push or pull system is used. Push or pull refers purely to how production is initiated.

Stop and Think

Think of the different types of food outlet you use: fast food, help-yourself buffet restaurant, supermarket, college shop. Which approach – push or pull – do they use?

Toyota Production System (TPS): the model for lean systems as developed at Toyota by Ohno and using JIT.

Just in time (JIT): the pull-based material control system used at Toyota, and the basis of developing the lean model.

Muda, muri, mura (waste): focus on waste at the heart of lean systems.

Lean Production

Lean production is based on a series of practices synonymous with Toyota called the **Toyota Production System** (TPS) and built on principles of **just in time** (JIT). Toyota developed TPS after studying Ford in the 1940s and it has been generalized and extended to other industries to become known as *lean production*. At the heart of the approach is a focus on eliminating waste and so it can also be seen as a focus on continuous operational improvement. Waste in this context does not just mean throwing away the not used, but that any time inventory is in storage (i.e. not being worked on) represents waste in terms of time as is the need for storage space. Other **wastes** include resources such as employees not working, machines standing idle or the mismatch between forecast and actual demand for the product.

History of Lean Systems

GLOBALIZATION

The father of the Toyota Production System is often seen as Taiichi Ohno who started developing the system when he was faced with difficulties because of poor supply conditions. He could not plan ahead as he was not sure which parts would be delivered by the suppliers. This caused cash flow problems as the factory had more and more unfinished vehicles while they waited for the late parts needed to finish them. The incomplete vehicles could not be sold and so the company was running out of money to pay its bills.

Holding excess inventory hides fluctuations in supply and so, in order to identify which parts were missing, Ohno developed a system linking production stages closely together to operate just in time. The tool is called **kanban**. Ohno's aim was not to develop a super-efficient revolutionary production system, but to highlight material shortages quickly. From this base, the whole TPS system evolved. Even today, Toyota still claims it is developing and learning about the system. By his own account, Ohno (1988) thinks it took 35 years to fully realize the potential of his approach.

Kanban: Japanese word for the card that is the essential vehicle for operation of the JIT system of production control.

The transfer of ideas about JIT, TPS and lean production gained popularity through a book by Womack *et al.* (1990), called *The Machine that Changed the World*. Much of the TPS and the JIT approach had already been described in books by Monden (1983), Cusumano (1985), Shingo (1985) and Ohno (1988), but *The Machine that Changed the World* spread the ideas to a wider audience.

It is best to think of the TPS, lean systems and just in time as parts of the same approach, implemented as production systems, business improvement philosophy or material control systems, and at the heart is the customer-driven pull approach.

Confusingly, lean often has other names, including:

- Zero inventory
- Batch of one
- Continuous flow manufacturing
- Increased value manufacturing

Some of these titles are slightly misleading, as will become clear as we get deeper into this chapter.

Just in Time

The TPS is concerned with making items only as and when they are required and in the quantities that are needed to satisfy immediate requirements – in other words 'just in time' (JIT). The principle must be applied at every stage of production from raw material delivery through to the finished product. There are many techniques used in the JIT system, but at the heart of it is the kanban system.

The Kanban System

Kanban is a technique developed by Toyota to help implement JIT. Kanban is a Japanese word meaning 'signpost' or 'signal' and is used widely throughout production and service delivery systems around the world.

In its simplest form, a kanban is a way of indicating to a workstation whether it is required to produce something. If there is no signal, then there is enough stock in the system and no more is needed. The signal can be an empty box (showing that the previous delivery of parts has been used) or an empty space marked on the floor (showing that more can be delivered). If the box or space is empty, then more parts are needed; if it is full, then there is no need for more parts.

So a kanban instruction causes parts to be produced and when the box is full or the outlined space is occupied, they stop. When the box becomes empty again it is time to make more. At McDonald's, the kanban is run by the metal flag in the row of burgers waiting to be served. When it reaches the front it is passed back to the kitchen to ask for more. Figure 10.3 shows the kanban process in operation.

In Figure 10.3 parts are used by operation A and more is pulled from operation B. If operation B has a box to put parts in it works. No box means that operation B has no instruction and so makes nothing. As B uses parts to satisfy the demand from A, it empties a box which becomes the kanban instruction for C. Designing the system involves making sure that there is enough inventory in the system to keep working until the previous worker has replaced an empty box with a full one. There are only two boxes for each operation thus limiting the inventory in the system.

The original kanban system at Toyota makes use of cards rather than boxes: the *production kanban* (or *P kanban*) and the *conveyance kanban* (or *C kanban*). Parts are kept in standard containers, to which one of the two types of kanban card are attached. The production kanban specifies the part number of the item, the quantity to be made and the tools required, whereas the conveyance kanban states the source of parts and the work centre to which

Figure 10.3 The kanban system

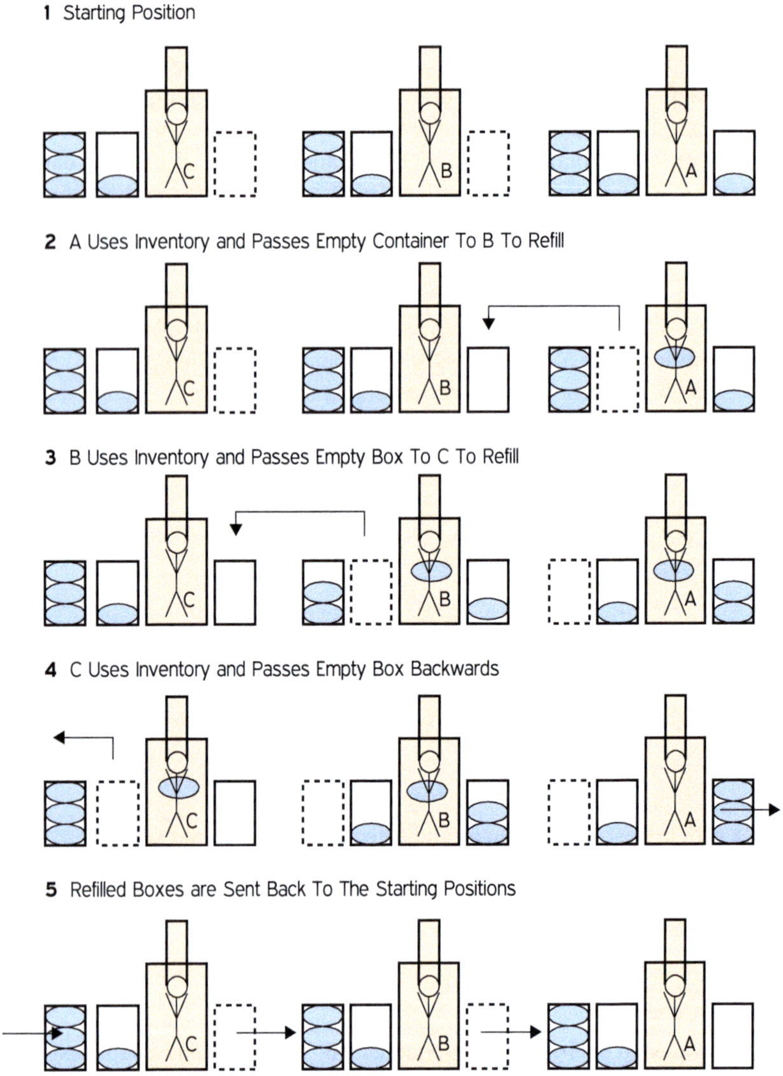

they should be delivered. The use of two cards means that the different jobs can be divided between workers: production staff and material handlers.

Every workstation needs to have a kanban link with its neighbours. The final assembly line, because it is the ultimate downstream activity, initiates and effectively controls all upstream activities right back to the suppliers and subcontractors in a chain reaction. You can now clearly see why this system is the 'pull' approach.

With kanban, there will always be a set amount of inventory in the system. This amount cannot be exceeded as there are only so many kanbans and it only produces items which have been used to make the customer's final product. In Subway they only pull the sandwich fillings from the cold store as and when they are required. So if everyone orders tuna, only this filling is pulled from storage.

Kanban is more than just an inventory control system; it is a means by which continual pressure is exerted over the whole of the production system to achieve improved productivity.

Calculation of Kanban Quantity

The amount of stock held in the kanban loop between workstations needs to be sufficient to cover the time taken for the replacement parts to be both manufactured and then delivered to the workstation. This needs to be worked out for all the production workstations and for each part.

The number of kanban containers placed between the workstations is given by the formula

$$N = \frac{D(T_w + T_p)(1 + c)}{a}$$

where:

N = the number of containers for the part
D = the planned usage rate for the part (parts per day).
T_w = the average waiting time for replenishment of parts. This is the time that the conveyance part of the kanban takes – moving the empty container to the supplying workstation and also moving the full container back to the demanding workstation (use a fraction of a day).
T_p = the average time to produce a container of parts. This is the production kanban time needed to make a container's worth of parts (use a fraction of a day).
a = the capacity of the container (number of parts). This should not be more than 10% of daily demand for the part; more than this and the kanban can start to operate as a buffer between the workstations rather than signalling demand.
c = a safety stock variable (expressed in the formula as a decimal fraction). Note how this value adds a safety margin to the calculation. It is set by the management and determined by company policy. It should not be set at more than 0.10, that is, a 10% margin; more than this and the kanban can start to operate as a buffer between the workstations rather than signalling demand.

WORKED EXAMPLE 10.1

Putting Kanban into Practice

A workstation undertaking the final assembly of a component has a planned daily usage rate of 240 parts per day and receives unfinished parts from the preceding station in containers that hold 5% of the day's demand. It takes 1 hour for the preceding station to fill a bin and 20 minutes for the filled bin to be delivered to the covering station.

Problem: *How many such bins are needed for the kanban loop to work efficiently in this production cell, given a single 8-hour shift per day and a risk factor of 8%?*

Approach: Kanban works by ensuring there is just sufficient stock between two stages in the production line so that, when the kanban request is issued, the replacement parts are delivered before the workstation runs out. It uses the formula

$$N = \frac{D(T_w + T_p)(1 + c)}{a}$$

Solution: In this example, the values to be used are:

$$D = 240 \text{ parts per day}$$
$$T_w = 20/(60 \times 8) = 0.04167$$
$$T_p = 1/8 = 0.125$$
$$c = 0.08$$
$$a = 5\% \text{ of } 240 = 12$$

And the calculation is therefore:

$$N = \frac{240 \times (0.04167 + 0.125) \times (1 + 0.08)}{12}$$
$$= \frac{240 \times 0.1667 \times 1.08}{12}$$
$$= 3.6$$

This means that the firm needs to have four containers of parts to make up the kanban stock. Having three containers would mean that there could be a delay, as parts might still be on the way when they were needed. This might not be a bad thing, as it would force the firm to look at the time taken to produce and deliver the parts and so force them to improve the process.

The key point is ...

that having more kanban stock than needed is a waste, but less may result in parts being short and thus delay production.

Stop and Think

Think of three possible problems that adopting the JIT system might generate.

SHORT CASE 10.1

Primark uses JIT

Source: ©dmitro2009/Shutterstock

In retail clothing operations there is a high risk that changing fashions can leave stores with high inventories of merchandise that is difficult to sell. Traditionally, the problem has been dealt with by markdowns and clearance sales. In an effort to improve operating efficiency, companies such as the UK's Primark adopt a more flexible 'quick response' (QR) approach.

The basic concept of QR in retailing is similar to that of JIT in manufacturing: to provide the right products, in the right quantities, in the quickest time, with minimum holding of inventory, at the lowest cost. Primark delays purchasing decisions until the season's fashions become clear. This requires suppliers to employ QR manufacturing, and Primark has weekly deliveries in order to compress lead times and provide maximum flexibility in adjusting the product mix. Sales information is shared across the suppliers and retailer by electronic data transfer. In this way it can respond quickly to what is happening in its stores by changing schedules to make more or less of the particular products, styles, colours and sizes current demand dictates.

Operating a QR system imposes pressure on the manufacturers supplying Primark as it means they have to accommodate highly volatile production schedules, much smaller production quantities and more frequent deliveries. Not surprisingly, not all manufacturers are up to the task, but those who have made the adjustment find that retailers such as Primark are prepared to pay premium prices for the QR service. This has given Primark a competitive edge over other cut-price suppliers who cannot match the QR requirement or get the latest fashions into the shops quickly enough.

Questions

1. How does QR help Primark achieve its corporate aims?
2. What problems will Primark face in trying to use QR as it expands its operations into Europe?

Sources: www.primark.co.uk/aboutus/FAQ, accessed 4 November 2019.

The Lean Focus on Reducing Waste

Along with value adding, the lean movement focuses on reducing waste at all levels. Ohno (1988) described three types of waste: *muda* ('non-value-adding work'), *muri* ('overburden') and *mura* ('unevenness'). This framework is central to many lean implementations:

- *Muda:* non-value adding tasks. This has been the focus of attention for most lean advocates, who state that the role of management is to examine and reduce muda. This is where the practice of removing waste is most evident.
- *Muri:* planning waste due to the poor design or implementation of the system. It represents things such as having to move heavy weights or having to work harder than usual. The highly stressed lean system becomes more prone to variation, which generates waste.
- *Mura:* imbalance as a result of poor implementation of the design. Toyota tries to smooth production activities and eliminate fluctuation at the scheduling or operations level, such as quality and volume, and also imbalance within work tasks.

Ohno added more detail by identifying seven muda wastes:

- *Transportation:* waste when moving products in the manufacturing process. This does not add value to the product and, apart from final delivery, is unimportant to the customer.
- *Inventory:* any type of inventory (components, work-in-progress or finished goods) represents products not being processed and leads to other problems such as obsolescence and the hiding of quality issues.
- *Motion:* waste generated when people or equipment move or walk. This does not add value to the product.
- *Waiting:* such as inventory. Holding inventory does not add value.
- *Overproduction:* producing an item before it is needed is a waste which generates waiting and inventory.
- *Overprocessing:* waste is generated if the equipment used is too complex or expensive for the task performed. Toyota uses the simplest machine for the job which often means older but well-maintained equipment.
- *Defects:* inspecting and fixing defects does not add value.

Recently there have been attempts to extend Ohno's list to include other wastes. Womack added the underutilization or misdeployment of employees – in particular, the waste that results when employees are asked to carry out manual tasks, but their employers do not make use of their ability to think about the task and how to improve the job itself. Conversely, using expensive highly trained staff to do menial tasks is a waste: for instance, it would be wasteful to use a highly trained lawyer to work on a simple car insurance claim.

It was once thought that effective muda reduction led to improvements in muri and mura, and therefore many managers concentrated purely on the seven muda wastes. However, managers are now realizing that better planning and implementation can be more effective steps to take than just concentrating on eliminating waste.

Stop and Think

It is important to stress that the lean system focuses the firm on thinking about the demands of the customer. Do you think that customers will define waste in the same way as the company? Think of a firm you use regularly. To you as a customer, what constitutes waste? Now put yourself in the position of the manager and think about what constitutes waste for the manager and for the firm. Are these the same? If not, why aren't they?

Characteristics of Lean Systems

There are many parts required to make a lean system work and all are equally necessary. Evidence for this can be seen in the work of Ferdows and De Meyer (1990) and the **sand cone principle**. The sand cone idea states that many advanced practices work only if they are based on sound foundations laid by other practices. The analogy is that a sand cone (or sand castle) will only stand up if it is standing on a solid foundation. Lean production follows the sand cone principle closely, as many elements are needed before a lean/JIT system will work properly. If any one element is missing, then the system may not function to the best of its ability. The foundation for lean/JIT is quality to ensure tasks happen as they are intended each and every time. This is the same as Ferdows and De Meyer who specifically

Sand cone principle: records the importance of certain practices building on others in a predetermined order.

Figure 10.4 Elements of the lean production system

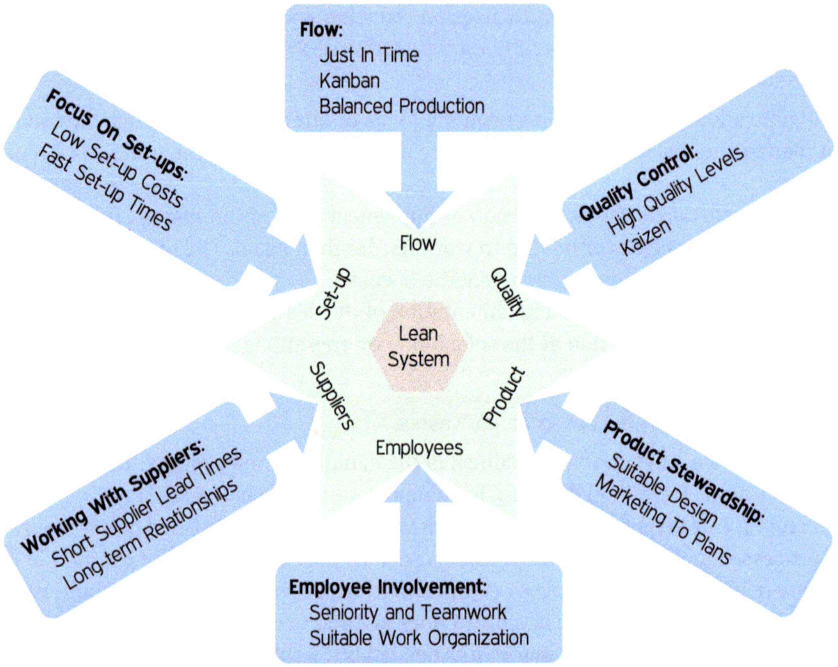

argue that quality is the first layer of the sand cone. Quality gives dependability, which allows speed, and these two together can enable flexibility – and only with all these in place can firms then achieve efficiency.

The elements of a lean system are summarized in Figure 10.4. Note that all the elements are needed for the whole system to work together, including not only production practices within the company, but also supplier involvement and most importantly quality as in the sand cone model.

Focus on Set-Ups

Economic order quantity (EOQ): fixed order (or production) amount that minimizes the total costs over a whole year.

SMED (single minute exchange of dies): approach to reduce machine changeovers to achieve batch size of one.

As mentioned previously, lean systems are different from other forms of inventory control in that they do not assume that there are optimum **economic order quantities**. Lean systems aim to produce all items in a batch size of one. This means that, in designing lean systems, managers need to examine the set-up activity for each operation in order to reduce the time associated with it. Remember: it is the cost of the set-up that makes it economical to produce in larger batches. There are several tools available to help with set-up reduction, but the most famous is **single minute exchange of dies (SMED)**. (Note: A 'die' is the part of a machine tool that is used to cut the shape of the end product.) SMED follows Shingo's work at Toyota, where pressing machines were adapted to reduce changeover time from hours to seconds (Shingo, 1985).

Chapter 7, p213

The concept has wide implications for both production and service delivery. Where firms have introduced these techniques effectively, batch sizes can be reduced towards a size of one: that is, the operator can press a button and the machine changes automatically to produce another type of part. We saw this in Chapter 7, where we talked about the difference between takt time and cycle time. The SMED approach seeks to make these the same, so reducing waste.

In a car factory for example, expensive, specially designed press machines can make any type of car body demanded by a kanban with a short production cycle time. An alternative approach also seen at Toyota is to use several old or very simple machines instead. It may be cheaper to have three simple machines set up for the three different parts produced and switch from one to another as demanded by the kanban rather than buy an expensive flexible machine. But whatever the approach, fast set-up is essential for the JIT system.

Suppliers

Much time is also lost in the delivery of items from suppliers and so lean systems demand that the suppliers cooperate and are located close to the manufacturer. The suppliers need to become an extension of the production line, delivering exactly what is required at very short notice and with perfect quality. If you were to stand outside a factory with a well-designed lean system, you would see many small vans making frequent deliveries, instead of infrequent deliveries being made by just a few large trucks. An inability to make suppliers deliver small batches rapidly is one of the main reasons for the poor success rate of JIT implementation in US and European companies.

Flow and Synchronization

In addition to the delivery of parts via kanban, a JIT system demands that advanced operating practices are used on the production line. One key focus of the system is smooth flow. This is in terms both of volume (a constant rate) and of product mix (an even and predictable plan). In order for the line to operate consistently, managers often intervene and smooth out variations in the product mix that arise from real customer demand. For example, a large order of high work content cars, such as those with air conditioning, is split up and interspaced with lower specification vehicles to spread the workload on the production line evenly. Manufacturing could not complete all the extra work of producing a long run of high work content products and keep to the average time taken per vehicle. In practice the real sequence of customer orders is manipulated to give a fixed repeating schedule for the production line. This process has the Japanese name *heijunka*.

Other tools developed by Toyota to help ensure smoothness include **jidoka** or *autonomation*. This is the in-process application of technology to identify and correct mistakes. The production line self-corrects and poor-quality parts are eliminated. With lean systems, poor quality quickly impacts on the next workstation disrupting the constant flow.

Jidoka: implementing self-checking to ensure a consistent flow of production.

Heijunka

Heijunka is a technique used to generate smooth, mixed production schedules. Using the heijunka technique, an assembly line or service delivers output with a predetermined order volume and variety irrespective of the real pattern or sequence of customer order arrival. The smoothed pattern is repeated over and over again. This gives the benefits of batch manufacture with economies of repetition and adds predictability which helps coordination of supply. However, designing a schedule that is able to produce a repeating pattern from random customer orders is complicated. This process is simplified if the number of products and combinations of options offered are also limited.

Heijunka: a method for developing a repeating schedule that produces the correct mix of products. It is important to spread the launch of products into the production line evenly to smooth the amount of work required.

Despite the complexities in establishing the schedule, its implementation can be simplified by using a *heijunka box* (as shown in Figure 10.5). A heijunka box is effectively a box full of different slots. Each slot represents a different product or service variant (e.g. the 'types' at the side of the box), and the sequence (or time) at which they will need to be produced (shown across the top of the box). The orders are placed in the next empty slot for the type of product demanded and so shuffled into the predetermined smooth sequence.

Figure 10.5 A heijunka box to help sequence product mix in a lean JIT system

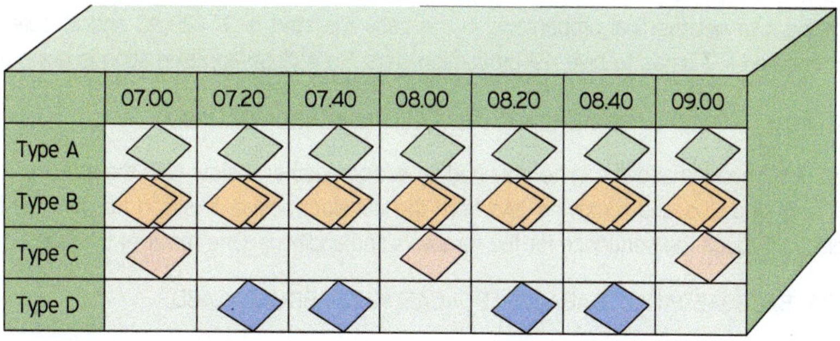

WORKED EXAMPLE 10.2

Heijunka: Smoothing Production Orders for Improved Flow

A production line runs a double 12-hour shift, which means it is working for 24 hours per day, 5 days a week and has a 4-week month.

The orders come at irregular intervals, but on average arrive in a month as shown:

Product A = 5,760

Product B = 4,800

Product C = 3,200

Product D = 2,880

Problem:

(a) What is the total monthly production volume and respective production mix?

(b) What is the production sequence schedule for products A, B, C and D?

Approach: Developing a production schedule from a list of known constraints is similar to working out the cycle time in line balancing. Managers work out how often to make a unit of each product, so that at the end of the schedule time they have made the right total number. With heijunka, the aim is to develop a repeating sequence that is able to produce the right quantities of products, but which mixes the orders up to smooth the demand on production and limit work in progress.

Solution: From above, the total production for the month will be 16,640: this can be met by levelling the production volume to 4,160 per week (832 per day or 416 per shift). This smooths the factory volume and sets a constant speed for the assembly line, the cycle time for line balancing.

The next step considers the mix of production for each model. In order to make that number of each over the month, they will need to make them at the following rates (20 days × 24 hours × 60 minutes divided by the demand for each product):

Product A = 20 × 24 × 60/5,760 = 1 every 5 minutes
Product B = 20 × 24 × 60/4,800 = 1 every 6 minutes
Product C = 20 × 24 × 60/3,200 = 1 every 9 minutes
Product D = 20 × 24 × 60/2,880 = 1 every 10 minutes

The lowest common factor for these rates is going to be 90 minutes and so the manager can develop a schedule which repeats every 90 minutes to produce exactly the right mix of parts. This list can be rewritten (90/how often one is produced) as producing:

Product A = 18 every 90 minutes (90/5 = 18)
Product B = 15 every 90 minutes
Product C = 10 every 90 minutes
Product D = 9 every 90 minutes

The final schedule can be set by looking at the ratios between the products and remembering that it will produce 416 per shift or 52 per 90 minutes. The sequence is developed by starting with an approximate sequence and then adjusting it to get the final proportions. In this case the start is 3A, 2B, 1C and 1D spread out as ABACABD and then repeated it 7 times to give 49 production slots. So a close approximation is going to be:

ABACABD ABACABD ABACABD ABACABD ABACABD ABACABD ABACABD

The full list of 52 needed above can be obtained by adding another 3 slots with the exact proportions achieved by adding 3Cs, 1B and 2Ds and removing 3As from the 49 slots above. This can be done by hand-picking equally spaced places through the sequence for the removals and additions. One result of the finished sequence might be:

ABACABDACBACBDABDACABCDABACBDABDACABDABCBABDCABACABD

However, the exact result depends on how the close approximation was generated and where in the sequence products were added and removed. This sequence will be the basis for the positioning of holes in the heijunka box and is repeated every 90 minutes.

Note: The above example shows the levelling of the variations in work and the generation of quite a complex sequence. Over the month the sequence will satisfy the volume and mix of orders, but at the same time it has generated an even and repeating production schedule. This is clearly more desirable than building a single large batch of A, followed by a single large batch of B, C and D, and changing the numbers of batches in each day.

Quality Control for Lean Systems

Within lean systems there is an emphasis on doing things quickly with very limited stocks of materials. There is no slack in the system and the impact of faulty components or delays in work is quickly felt further down the production process. Lean production therefore needs to have a clear focus on doing things right first time and so needs a very effective quality system. This system is often called **total quality management (TQM)**; it is so important that some people often refer to lean production as *JIT/TQM* to stress the importance.

TQM is covered in more detail in Chapter 13, however, to show its importance to lean production we will outline some basic quality ideas. The focus is that production processes are made as robust as possible to ensure smooth flow. One approach to this is called **kaizen**, which can be translated as 'continuous improvement'. In practice, when quality problems occur a new routine is developed to ensure that the problem cannot reoccur. Kaizen has already been mentioned in Chapter 5 in the context of value stream mapping.

Total quality management (TQM): quality system that is needed for effective lean production, and based on kaizen (continuous improvement).

Kaizen: continuous improvement approach to quality control.

Lean Quality Tools

Chapter 13, p429

Chapter 5, p139

Hansei, or 'reflection', is one key approach to quality which tries to ensure that managers and employees identify the root causes of any quality problem. This includes detailed forensic-style investigation, called *gemba*, to gather data from all sources so we do not just opt for the first solution we find which may not be the optimum. Another quality term important for lean production is *genchi genbutsu*, which means 'go and see for yourself'. This stresses how employees must not rely on reports from others to identify solutions, but should go and look themselves. It is not uncommon in non-lean organizations for oversimplified reports and conference calls to be used to try to solve problems, but these often miss something important as the manager making the decision hasn't been to see the problem first hand. Genchi genbutsu makes the investigation more robust and an incomplete solution less likely, thus promoting kaizen.

Another tool is the *5 Whys*. Instead of just identifying the first cause of a problem, employees ask the question 'Why?' as many times as is needed to get to the root cause. For example, if we find that the wheels fall off the cars we make, asking five whys might generate the following:

1. Why – because of loose nuts
2. Why were the nuts loose? – because of a badly calibrated torque wrench, which caused the nuts to be insufficiently tightened
3. Why wasn't the tool calibrated? – because the tool for calibrating the torque wrench was worn
4. Why was the calibrating machine worn? – because it hadn't been maintained properly
5. Why was it not maintained? – because there was no procedure for carrying out maintenance on the calibration machines.

The real cause of the problem is established (i.e. maintenance procedures) and instead of just retightening the nuts at the end of the line, a new calibration procedure would ensure that this type of error could not happen again.

When a solution is implemented, lean organizations follow the principles of *poka yoke*, which is 'fail-safeing' or 'mistake-proofing'. Here the emphasis is on designing a process that can only happen in one way – the correct way – and so mistakes cannot be made. A good example of this is fitting steering wheels on the production line. Toyota includes a keyed slot as well as a hexagonal nut and bolt. The keyed slot will only fit in one position and so it is impossible for the operator to fit the steering wheel in any other position than straight. Without the keyed slot, the wheel could be aligned with any of the six sides of the hexagonal nut. The same approach can be employed in services, when online forms automatically check to see whether data we have entered is correct. For example, if the form requires a telephone number to be entered in a particular box, it will check to see whether a valid set of digits has been entered and automatically reject letters. Getting the data right in the first place is much cheaper than having to correct it later when the fault is discovered at a critical moment.

Total productive maintenance (TPM): the application of TQM ideas to ensuring that machines operate effectively, and are always available.

Lean organizations take great care in looking after machines on the production line and often employ an approach called **total productive maintenance (TPM)**. TPM ensures that the important measure of overall equipment effectiveness (the time spent producing) is maximized by making employees responsible for maintenance and developing kaizen approaches to improving the reliability of machines. The employees own the maintenance of the machine and are much closer to the problems and solutions than relying on a visit from the maintenance team. TPM is much more than preventive maintenance and akin to TQM.

Another lean quality tool worth noting is *andon*. So that workers know what is happening in the production area, a series of lights are used that warn of quality issues elsewhere on the line and draw the attention of the nearby employees. This is not about finger pointing at mistakes, but ensuring all possible attention and help is given to quickly and permanently solve a problem.

Stop and Think

JIT converts say that 'a defect is a treasure'. What do they mean by this, and how does it relate to JIT?

Employee Involvement

Effective lean production, with its reliance on TQM, demands support from dedicated workers and places a high emphasis on training. The system is precise in nature with no excess capacity, meaning there is no place for people to learn on the job – such a notion is contrary to the ideas behind leanness. In the same way as we saw SMED externalizing set-up, so training takes place *off* the production line. Using someone in production who has not mastered their tasks is too big a risk. Employees in a lean organization receive far more training than in normal companies. This training enables employees to make their own decisions in developing kaizen and implementing quality solutions. The training includes many advanced quality tools to allow quality problems and variation to be analysed. Working in a JIT lean system can be a high-pressure and stressful environment as it offers little down time and this often requires a high level of physical fitness and mental alertness. Workers on production lines in lean plants are usually relatively young and are sometimes required to physically warm up before starting work.

Senpai–Kohai Authority System

Lean firms have an elaborate mentoring process to manage the relationships between employees and their superiors. The mentoring system at Toyota is called *senpai–kohai*. Senpai are the mentors and kohai the trainees. These relationships last beyond initial training and continue when people have moved on to other roles in the organization. This gives a well-developed system of learning where senior people remain connected to the organization and the kohai actively seek out their advice. The senpai–kohai approach reduces the all-too-common mistakes when a new generation re-tries approaches which failed previously. The same respect for seniority features in the gemba and genchi genbutsu approaches to investigating quality problems. These practices are the way lean firms build effective teams where each member is valued for his or her contribution.

Product Stewardship

Lean firms employ *value stream mapping* (see Chapter 5) as a key planning tool to analyse the value-added network required in bringing a product to the consumer. Lean organizations also make use of *simultaneous engineering* and work closely with suppliers, meaning a wide range of skills and resources can be employed in designing the product. As there are many different groups

Chapter 5, p139

involved, design decisions future proof production and service delivery processes. This is a closed-loop approach and it removes the need to redesign parts later when problems emerge in the manufacturing phase.

Lean organizations have a focus on product standardization and modularity (see Chapter 4), which not only make the product simpler by reducing complexity, but also ease the adoption of JIT and SMED. *The Machine that Changed the World* (Womack *et al.*, 1990) stated that Japanese firms could design a new car in half the time of their US competitors and using only half the resources.

Chapter 4, p105

SHORT CASE 10.2

Apple's iPhone

Source: ©NYC Russ/Shutterstock

The iPhone has been a remarkable success since its introduction in 2007, reaching 2.2 billion sales before Apple stopped reporting sales figures in November 2018. In 2005 Apple introduced the option for customers to order a customized iPhone with an engraved cover design. The product is produced by one of its subcontractor factories in China (run by Foxconn) and shipped to the USA in 90 hours.

Achieving this employs many of the steps from the TPS – in particular the focus on looking at value-adding steps and set-up reduction/SMED. Apple uses SCM practices such as long-term sole supply contracts with component makers in China and employs a specialist logistics operator (FedEx).

The iPhone is particularly suitable for lean production, as it is high value, produced from standardized parts and the customization can be carefully controlled. Given the fast-changing nature of the mobile phone market, running with little or no stocks also makes sense to Apple, as it reduces the risk of having outdated stocks and smooths out the introduction of new models.

This example illustrates that lean production is not just the application of one approach, but rather the adoption of an entire integrated toolbox of many techniques.

Questions

1. What advantages does Apple gain by operating its lean system?
2. How critical is the relationship with FedEx for the success of the customized iPod process?

Sources: www.apple.com

CRITICAL PERSPECTIVE

Lean or Mean?

Some implementations of the lean approach were not successful. One of the primary reasons is that managers failed to appreciate the needs of their business in being competitive. Focusing their attention on waste reduction is a good strategy. One term which is good to think about here is 'anorexic lean' where all flexibility or capacity used in emergencies is stripped out of the process. This limits future options.

However, many top-performing firms choose to be inefficient in certain instances to enable them to better serve their customers and differentiate themselves from competitors. Zara is a good example of a pull system which deliberately introduces inefficiency to enable responsiveness. For example, Zara's clothes are all pre-labelled and hanging as they leave the factory. This adds delivery cost in terms of extra weight and space, but means that the clothes can be taken straight from the lorry onto the shop floor for immediate sale.

Chapter 8, p249

We looked at the idea of decoupling points and push-pull boundary in Chapter 8.

Contemporary Thinking: Extending Lean to Other Industries

Previously we have considered lean as a production system but the focus on waste reduction generated interest far beyond the car industry. An updated book, *Lean Thinking* (Womack and Jones, 1996), repackages and extends the ideas originally documented by Ohno and Shingo. This section examines some of the broader ideas or philosophies that have become known as the lean system.

The Five Principles of Lean Thinking

BUSINESS INTEGRATION

Lean thinking focuses on improvement through five principles:

- *Concentrate on value for customers:* lean systems focus on reducing waste and satisfying the needs of customers.
- *Appreciate the value stream:* a lean organization should understand which activities add value for the customer and which are wastes to be eliminated.
- *Concentrate on improved flow;* flow should be smooth and constant to ensure efficient operations.
- *Adopt pull:* meet customer demand by reacting to them; pull systems do not produce unnecessary outputs.
- *Perfect quality:* lean systems target right first time and use kaizen.

By implementing the five principles, managers gain a greater understanding of how to run the system more efficiently.

The 5S Lean Implementation Framework

Another framework which is used within lean management is *5S*. This is a programme for reorganizing the workspace and workflow to improve efficiency and eliminate waste. 5S is an effective way to apply lean ideas to both production and service activities. They are Japanese terms that can also be translated into English words starting with S:

1. *Sort* (*seiri*): remove unnecessary items from the workplace.
2. *Set* in order (*seiton*): efficient and effective storage methods, including painted floors and marked-off work areas, so that workers do not waste time looking for things.
3. *Shine* (*seiso*): make the workplace clean, so that things remain in place and employees take pride in the area and in their work.
4. *Standardize* (*seiketsu*): encourage all employees in sharing and developing standardized best practices.
5. *Sustain* (*shitsuke*): the last step – continue to follow the other Ss.

CRITICAL PERSPECTIVE

Other Thinkers' Lean Ideas

Chapter 13, p429

The extension of lean production to a wider lean system is heavily dependent on Japanese ideas based on the Toyota-focused writings of Ohno (1988) and Shingo (1985) and has much in common with the quality gurus such as Deming, covered in Chapter 13.

Lean production ideas also came from Schonberger (1986), who studied and reported the sources of Japanese industrial power in the 1980s. At the University of Nebraska he based his ideas on observation of the Kawasaki motorcycle plant nearby. Schonberger's main thesis involved identifying nine lessons or practices that lay at the heart of the lean system. He described not only the operation of JIT, but also the rest of the system, along with TQM, the supply relationships and the role of employees. Shonberger showed the highly integrated nature of lean production, a message that was not appreciated at first, as many firms focused purely on kanban and found the results of their efforts disappointing (Pilkington, 1998).

The key point is ...

that some people claim that the lean approach is applicable to all firms and focus purely on its kaizen improvement and waste reduction approaches. But there are many additional elements that are necessary for it to work effectively as a production system and these are often overlooked by some firms seeking a fast transformation. As a result, their new systems do not deliver everything as expected. Look again at Figure 10.4 and the elements of the lean production system.

Stop and Think

How might JIT apply to a service like a hospital or department store?

Lean Services

Lean systems, and their presentation in terms of waste reduction strategies, make the approach appealing to non-manufacturing firms. There has been a rise in service firms and not-for-profit organizations implementing lean projects. Good examples of non-manufacturing firms adopting lean approaches include fast-food outlets such as Pizza Hut and McDonald's, logistics firms such as FedEx and DHL, e-businesses such as Amazon and Yahoo Shopping, and the emergency services. For these firms speed is an order winner and so generates an advantage over competitors.

When discussing the differences between manufacturing and service operations in Chapter 1 we described the intangible nature of services and the way that services do not exist before consumption by the consumer, require the consumer to be present and cannot be made in advance. All these features show that services are ideal for making use of lean systems which demand attention is paid to the customer and not to produce something until it is needed.

Chapter 1, p23

The main elements of lean systems can be applied to service environments using the lean thinking framework we saw earlier: customer value, the value stream, improve flow, use pull, and perfect quality. Many firms choose the 5S framework, with its focus on basic housekeeping, as it is immediately applicable and offers a clear set of steps. Getting things tidied and set out in the 5S framework is a quick return for services which previously may not have focused on efficiency. Following the lean method, and 5S in particular, generates sizeable improvements with little effort, and the spread of success stories has added impetus to the lean movement. According to Spear and Bowen (1999), the four rules of lean thinking are equally applicable to services and production. They are:

1. All work shall be highly specified as to content, sequence, timing and outcome. This eliminates any ambiguities in a process.
2. Every customer–supplier connection must be direct and there must be an unambiguous yes-or-no way to send requests and receive responses. This eliminates poor hand-offs between people and departments.
3. The pathway for every product and service must be simple and direct. This eliminates 'work-arounds' and extra work to compensate for poorly designed processes.
4. Any improvement must be made in accordance with the *scientific method*, under the guidance of a teacher, at *the lowest possible level* in the organization. This means that decisions must be based on evidence and fact, rather than on 'gut feelings', and that those operating the process need to be actively involved in its improvement.

All the rules require that activities, connections and processes have built-in controls to signal problems automatically. It is the continual response to problems that makes this seemingly rigid system so flexible and adaptable to changing circumstances in service and production.

SHORT CASE 10.3

Lean Adoption in the NHS

Source: ©BlurryMe/Shutterstock

The UK's National Health Service (NHS) has been working on lean ideas for several years and is a good example of how lean systems can be employed in service environments.

The NHS has an Institute for Improvement and Innovation, tasked with 'helping all NHS organizations achieve the same levels of quality and efficiency as top-performing organizations'. One way has been through the adoption of service transformation teams, which employ the 5S framework to implement ideas on wards and in clinics.

At the Hereford Hospitals NHS Trust a major problem was the time spent waiting for pathology results. A project was set up to understand and redesign the flow of work in the department, using lean principles.

The five-day project involved 50 staff and centred on mapping the existing journey of samples through pathology. This was then examined using gemba and genchi genbutsu (go and see the actual source) to remove obvious sources of waste, duplication and delays. This practice of walking through the entire process enlisted the support and encouragement of the staff. Such regular **gemba walks** have become the norm.

Gemba walk: The practice of regularly walking through a process to identify wasteful activities.

Previously, test samples had been collected together in a batch and so it was hard to identify the arrival order needed to provide consistent response times. Collecting samples from arrival was reduced from 13 minutes on average to just 1 minute by removing batching. Heijunka ideas of smooth flow meant that tests were then carried out immediately on arrival. Much time was found to be wasted looking for equipment: therefore simple visual tools such as putting taped outlines on the floor were employed to ensure that equipment had a clear location and that it was replaced after use.

Overall, a 40% reduction in process time resulted: from 62 minutes on average (but ranging up to 2 hours) to a consistently lower 38 minutes. Working more effectively and removing duplicated activities, such as having to re-mark samples as they moved around the department, generated savings of £365,000 per year. A by-product is that the department finishes its work 15 minutes earlier each day and can use this time to develop further quality improvements.

Questions

1. Which parts of the five principles of lean thinking have the improvement team employed?
2. Why do you think the pathology department were not able to introduce these changes themselves in the past?

Source: www.institute.nhs.uk/quality_and_value/lean_thinking/leean_case_studies.html

CRITICAL PERSPECTIVE

The Best System?

The attractions of lean systems make them tempting to all managers, but some care is needed as there are elements that cannot be implemented in every case. This section tries to assess when the full lean system is suitable. Many elements of lean can be applied to different situations and so it is not uncommon for firms to state that they have adopted lean principles without following JIT. In particular, the general housekeeping of 5S and much of the TQM approach are readily transferable, whereas adopting JIT can be harder.

Full Lean Is Not Always a Good Choice

Although we have seen that lean thinking has many benefits and can be applied to widely different situations, there are instances when JIT in particular, if it could be implemented at all, would be a poor choice. These issues may be related to difficulty in implementing elements such as: worker empowerment; supplier cooperation; the prohibitive expense of breaking the EOQ rules; reducing set-ups; or a lack of stable demand for the product. In these cases full lean production is not suitable for the firm and would not be a good choice. But these firms can still benefit from lean thinking and waste reduction. A good example is the Hoover washing machine plant in Merthyr Tydfil. It employs kanban and lean quality tools within the factory but is driven by a make-to-stock system. The result is that the factory itself is efficient and work moves smoothly and quickly, but the company does not have to invest in all the elements of the lean system or force suppliers to adopt the systems as well.

With push systems, changes in demand can be accommodated, as the plan can be changed to produce more items or it is possible to alter the product mix for the next production run. For example, many car makers have a 13-week MRP plan and so this is the longest a customer must wait for a vehicle. However, lean producers do not have this flexibility as the system is running at maximum capacity and new orders are added to the end of the production list. This queue can extend indefinitely if there is too much demand for one product.

Similarly, in service firms the concepts of pre-producing inventory and batching do not exist. These firms focus on the lean philosophy and general housekeeping as well as the customer.

The Volume and Variety Model

If we consider the Hayes and Wheelright (1979) model of **volume and variety**, (see Figure 5.4), the choice between implementing production in batches or with JIT becomes easier to identify. This is illustrated in Figure 10.6, which shows that the high volume and relatively low product varieties of Toyota and Burger King are suited to JIT.

With lower volumes, it is hard to justify the expense of setting up a dedicated, lean/JIT system and so small firms such as the local bakery find it too expensive. Similarly, if an organization is already operating a lean system, increasing product variety necessitates large numbers of extra kanban loops and increases stock adding cost. In these cases, batching and the push approach are more suitable as can be seen in firms such as Bentley or many in the aerospace industry, where the complex nature of the product excludes the adoption of JIT.

Volume and variety model: Hayes and Wheelright (1979) developed a model stating that volume carried out by an operation and variety or choice offered to customers is linked and results in the types of operation such as project, batch and mass production.

In practice, most companies employ a system that suits their own situation and it is likely to be a combination of MRP, kanban and push. The Synchro MRP system employed by Yamaha is one such example with JIT/kanban on the shopfloor to move materials and products around but an MRP system is used for the planning and push-style ordering of parts.

Figure 10.6 Hybrid JIT–MRP systems

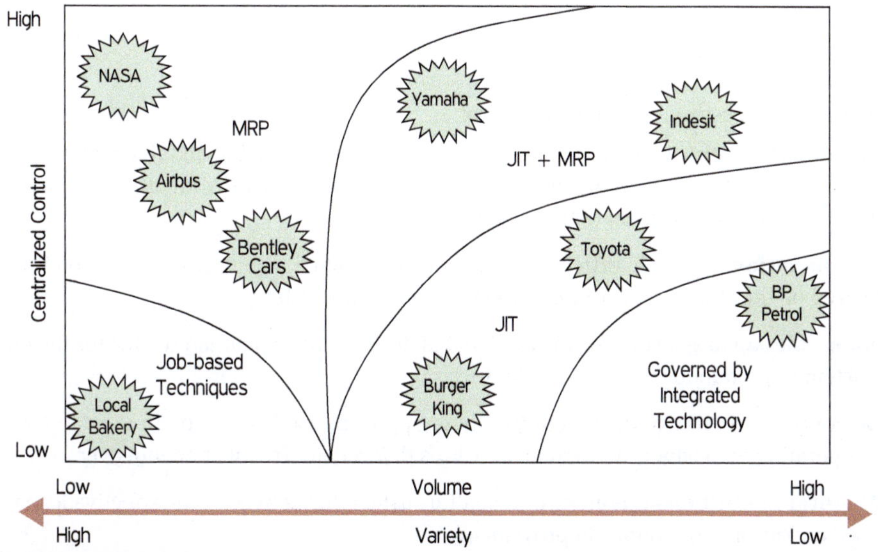

The key point is ...

that the lean system has many elements that need to be in place for it to function properly. If any of these cannot be introduced, then perhaps the firm should consider whether another approach is more suitable.

Summary

This chapter has looked at lean production by exploring the lean production system and its just-in-time system of production control.

The lean system coordinates activities in a different way from the push systems normally used with the ERP/MRP approach in the last chapter. One of the main aspects has to do with the initiation of the system and hence the distinction between 'pull' (JIT) and 'push'.

Lean production can be a very efficient system, but it is not suitable for all products, services or markets, and we have focused on selecting an appropriate system. Lean/JIT is very expensive to design, not least in the set-up time reduction activities and getting the suppliers of materials to make frequent small deliveries. These features are normally only present in large manufacturing organizations and many firms which have tried to adopt lean systems without understanding these ground rules found the results didn't deliver what they expected.

In this chapter we have looked at the very efficient systems adopted under the banner of lean production. Specifically we have:

- Dealt with how to classify pull systems
- Explored how kanban works
- Described the factors that are needed to support lean production
- Developed lean production to cover the notion of lean thinking and extended it to services
- Identified some weaknesses of lean production
- Employed the volume and variety model to identify the operating conditions suitable for each type of production control system.

Key Theories

The key theories discussed in this chapter were:

- **Push and pull inventory control** – in push systems, the production activities follow a programme from a central system. With pull, the line reacts to demand requests from other production cells, which all ultimately respond directly to the customer.
- **Lean production** – a highly efficient management approach with repeated focus on waste reduction and based on the ideas of the Toyota Production system and JIT.
- **Kanban** – the Japanese word for the card that is the essential signalling device for the operation of the JIT system of production and service delivery
- **Smooth production scheduling (heijunka)** – approach used to ensure an even and repetitive process when operating with small, short-run batch sizes that require frequent changeover
- **TQM (total quality management)** – a quality system that is needed for effective lean production and is based on kaizen (continuous improvement)
- **Lean thinking** – extending lean production to broader ideas or philosophies through a focus on waste reduction
- **Sand cone principle** – records the importance of certain practices building on others in predetermined order. This is important to ensure that lean systems work as intended
- **Volume, variety and control** – the best practice for controlling production and delivery processes.

Suggested Answers to Stop and Think Questions

1. **Push and pull:** The choice of push or pull depends on a range of factors, such as customer demand patterns and processing time. Fast food uses a pull approach, as the demand is constant and the preparation times are short. A traditional restaurant will employ a combination of both push and pull, as some preparation is completed in advance, and the food finished to the specific orders of the customer. That is why they often run out of popular dishes when they are busy (as experienced particularly in a 'help yourself'-style buffet restaurant). The supermarket and college shop will use a push approach, as the customers cannot wait for the products to be delivered if the shop runs out. There may well be some pull elements, as in the reorder level system we saw in Chapter 9, where a certain level of stock triggers (or pulls) a replenishment of the stocks.
2. **JIT implications:** Adopting the JIT system can produce many problems for managers. If we consider the kanban system first, there is a need for the manager to be certain about the level and consistency of demand for the product. As this is a pull system, it needs orders to generate reactions and so a constant demand is necessary. Other problems appear if the firm has a weak control of quality, as it needs to be able to use every part being produced. Running out of parts because some are unusable scrap will create problems. In practice, there are many different elements that need to be in place for the system to work properly and these are covered in the next section.
3. **Waste:** As systems become leaner, the excess resources are squeezed out of the system and so managers need to focus more closely on exactly meeting the needs of their customers. So whereas a manager may see excess staff as a waste, the customer looks at this as an extra cost they need to pay. Another example is the way that managers will see processing delays in production as costing staff time, whereas the customer sees this as an unmet delivery.
4. **Quality in lean systems:** When people talk of 'a defect as a treasure' they mean it forces them to improve the system. Something going wrong shows a situation that shouldn't be allowed to repeat, and so the system can be redesigned to prevent the problem recurring. The correction makes the system less likely to generate faulty products and thus becomes more robust, which is the aim of continuous improvement.
5. **Lean services:** JIT has been employed in many service environments. Becoming leaner, and therefore using fewer resources and delivering services exactly in the right amounts and quantities, can benefit everyone in the health care industry, as it improves quality of care and reduces costs. Similarly, in the department store, starting the lean journey leads to lower operating costs and so a more efficient process for customers. It can also improve product availability, as the accuracy of the stocks held increases, and deliveries can be satisfied more quickly.

connect

Review Questions

1. Describe the supporting factors needed for a kanban system to function effectively.
2. What conditions are needed for a JIT system to work, and do these prohibit the adoption of lean production in your country?
3. Discuss the merits and limitations of push versus pull approaches to managing inventory.
4. Describe the volume–variety model of Hayes and Wheelwright. With examples, explain whether you think the model is valuable to practising managers in selecting between MRP and lean production.

5. Use the volume and variety model to choose a production system for the following products and processes. Be sure to explain why you make your choice.
   (a) Car manufacturing
   (b) Washing machine production
   (c) Optician's workshop
   (d) Producing canned soup
   (e) A bakery
   (f) Sandwich bar
6. What is the 5S framework and how would it be applied to a university cafe?

Discussion Questions

1. Visit a nearby fast-food restaurant (McDonald's would be a good choice). Take time to watch what happens behind the counter, following the production of both the fries and the burgers. What controls the work, and how is an order for more food from the kitchen initiated?
2. Use the Internet to find out about the operations of Zara. Draw up a list of features of the TPS and see if you can work out how much of the system Zara uses.
3. Go to the Subway case at the start of the chapter. Look at the list of important elements of the Subway lean system and try and see how many are similar to those of the TPS. Compare the preparation process at Subway with another fast-food chain you know. Which do you think is the most lean, and why? As Doctor's Associates is a purely franchised operation, what risks does this present for maintaining its brand?
4. 'To be competitive today, companies must adopt just in time.' Discuss the validity of this statement by considering several different industry sectors.
5. Discuss, with examples, whether you think JIT can be used in a service environment.
6. Briefly describe the key components of MRP and JIT systems. Why must they be fully understood before selecting an appropriate production control system for a small manufacturing company?

Problems

1. The kanban system uses bins containing a fixed, small amount of WIP. The number of such bins of each part used in the production system depends on the usage, replenishment time and size of the container.
   (a) Produce the formula for the number of bins needed for one kanban loop between two cells.
   (b) A workstation covering seats for cars just-in-time has a planned daily usage rate of 320 seats per day and receives uncovered seats from another station in containers that hold 4% of the day's demand. It takes 1 hour for the preceding station to fill a bin and 30 minutes for the filled bin to be delivered to the covering station. How many such bins are needed for the kanban loop to work efficiently in this production cell, given a single 8-hour shift per day and a risk factor of 7%?
   (c) What changes to the system would be needed if the company were to start producing a racing-style seat in addition to the existing design?
2. A workstation binding books just-in-time has a planned daily usage rate of 600 books per day and receives leafbound books from another station in containers that hold 5% of the day's demand. It takes 1 hour for the preceding station to fill a bin and 30 minutes for the filled bin to be delivered to the covering station.
   (a) How many such bins are needed for the kanban loop to work efficiently in this production cell, given a single 8-hour shift per day and a risk factor of 8%?
   (b) What changes to the system would be needed if the company were to start producing a ring-bound version in addition to the existing design?

3. A workstation assembling the cases for pocket calculators just-in-time has a planned daily usage rate of 1,320 calculators per day and receives the insides of the calculators from another station in containers that hold 1% of the day's demand. It takes 1 hour for the preceding station to fill a bin and 15 minutes for the filled bin to be delivered to the casing station. How many such bins are needed for the kanban loop to work efficiently in this production cell, given a single 8-hour shift per day and a risk factor of 8%?

4. A workstation making water fountains just-in-time has a planned daily usage rate of 100 fountains per day and receives uncovered seats from another station in containers that hold 5% of the day's demand. It takes 2 hours for the preceding station to fill a bin and 1 hour for the filled bin to be delivered to the covering station. How many such bins are needed for the kanban loop to work efficiently in this production cell, given a 10-hour day?

5. A production line runs an 8-hour shift for 5 days per week. The orders come at irregular intervals, but on average arrive as shown in a month:

   Product A = 400

   Product B = 600

   Product C = 600

   Use heijunka to develop a smoothed production schedule for the products.

6. A production line runs a 12-hour shift for 5 days per week. The orders come at irregular intervals, but on average arrive as shown in a month:

   Product A = 200

   Product B = 400

   Product C = 300

   Use heijunka to develop a smoothed production schedule for the products.

7. A production line runs an 8-hour shift for 5 days per week. The orders come at irregular intervals, but on average arrive as shown in a month:

   Product A = 150

   Product B = 200

   Product C = 150

   Use heijunka to develop a smoothed production schedule for the products.

Further Reading

Bartezzaghi, E. (1999) 'The evolution of production models: is a new paradigm emerging?', *International Journal of Operations and Production Management,* **19**(2), 229–250.

Chapman, C.D. (2005) 'Clean house with lean 5S', *Quality Progress,* **38**(6), 27–32.

Hines, P., Holweg, M. and Rich, N. (2004) 'Learning to evolve: a review of contemporary lean thinking', *International Journal of Operations and Production Management,* **24**(10), 994–1011.

Holweg, M. (2007) The genealogy of lean production. *Journal of Operations Management,* **25**(2), 420–437.

Liker, J.K. (2004) *The Toyota Way: 14 Management Principles from the World's Greatest Manufacturer,* McGraw-Hill, London.

Liker, J. and Hoseus, M. (2008) *Toyota Culture: The Heart and Soul of the Toyota Way,* McGraw-Hill.

Swank, C.K. (2003) 'The lean service machine', *Harvard Business Review,* **81**(10), 123–129, 138.

Wu, Y.C. (2003) 'Lean manufacturing: a perspective of lean suppliers', *International Journal of Operations and Production Management,* **23**(11–12), 1349–1376.

References

Cusumano, M.A. (1985) *The Japanese Automobile Industry: Technology and Management at Nissan and Toyota.* Harvard University Press, Cambridge, MA.

Ferdows, K. and De Meyer, A. (1990) 'Lasting improvements in manufacturing performance: in search of a new theory', *Journal of Operations Management,* **9**(2), 168–184.

Hayes, R. and Wheelright, S.C. (1979) 'The dynamics of process-product life cycle', *Harvard Business Review,* **57**(2), 15–22.

Monden, Y. (1983) *Toyota Production System: Practical Approach to Production Management*, Industrial Engineering and Management Press, Norcross, GA.

Ohno, T. (1988) *Toyota Production System: Beyond Large-Scale Production*, Productivity Press, Cambridge, MA.

Pilkington, A. (1998) 'Manufacturing strategy regained: evidence for the demise of best practice', *California Management Review*, **41**(1), 31–42.

Schonberger, R. (1986) *World Class Manufacturing: The Lessons of Simplicity Applied*, Free Press, New York.

Shingo, S. (1985) *A Revolution in Manufacturing: The SMED System*, Productivity Press, Stamford, CT.

Spear, S. and Bowen, H.K. (1999) 'Decoding the DNA of the Toyota Production System', *Harvard Business Review*, Sep–Oct.

Womack, J.P. and Jones, D.T. (1996) *Lean Thinking: Banish Waste and Create Wealth in Your Corporation*, Simon & Schuster, New York.

Womack, J.P., Jones, D.T. and Roos, D. (1990) *The Machine that Changed the World*, Rawson Associates, New York.

11 Project Management

Learning Outcomes

After reading this chapter, you should be able to:

- Define the scope of activities involved in modern project management
- Use the basic tools available to plan and deliver projects on time, within budget and to specification
- Appreciate the move towards project-based organizations, and the use of project management frameworks such as PRINCE2 and PMBOK
- Describe the role of leadership in helping organizations adapt and change, to understand and meet the business challenges they face
- Describe various approaches to organizational design and consider the tensions between functional capabilities and project capabilities
- Outline the role and competencies of a project manager

Crossrail: A new railway under London

Source: ©Martin Hoscik/Shutterstock

The Crossrail project, to be known as the Elizabeth Line, was the largest civil engineering project in Europe, and the largest single addition to the London transport network for over 50 years. After many years of planning and false starts, work began in 2009 and was originally due to open in December 2018. After initial good progress the project was hit by many minor issues and it needed three more years before the first limited service could start running.

The project was a series of underground tunnels (21 km in total) and stations which extend the mainline services from the west of England and Heathrow Airport through the centre of the city, allowing direct access to key areas without the need to change train services.

The project was largely publicly funded. The two main contributors were Transport for London, which was to pay £7.7 billion, and the Department for Transport paying £5.6 billion. There were also smaller partners who have a stake in the project, including airport operator BAA, providing £230 million, and the Corporation of London, providing £200 million. In addition, Crossrail created a Tunnelling Academy to tackle the shortage of people with the necessary skills to work on the project, by providing training on the key skills required to work in and around a tunnel excavation and build environment.

Given the size of Crossrail, its organization was every bit as complex as the project itself. Three companies – Bechtel, Halcrow and Systra – were project delivery partners, and had contracts to complete major parts of the project.

These companies were overseen by Crossrail and had to work together where their parts of the projects overlap. They also had their own project management teams who worked out how their individual parts of the project were to be delivered, and employed a multitude of other contractors as needed.

The total cost of the project is expected to reach £18.25 billion when everything is finally wrapped up, more than £2 billion more than the original budget. Some of this budget overrun is £500 million per year lost revenue, while the rest is unforeseen extra work. The tunnels were completed on time and budget but delays and costs were added as key central stations were being fitted and the complexity of the building work, such as the 60m long escalators, became evident. A major problem – far more complex and expensive than envisaged – was the integration of the signalling systems with those of the pre-existing routes. This could not be hurried as it is critical for safety certification.

So there were many layers of project management, spanning several companies, which all needed to be coordinated to complete the project. This hints at the complexity of the management of the project, but says nothing of the engineering difficulties faced in designing and building not just one of the longest railway tunnels in the world, but one that passes through the complex network of existing tunnels and utilities in one of the busiest and most densely populated cities in the world.

Sources: https://www.newcivilengineer.com/latest/crossrail-details-revised-delivery-schedule-23-01-2020/; http://www.crossrail.co.uk/news/articles/crossrail-project-update

Introduction

With increasing pressure on organizations to complete work more rapidly and cost-effectively, the modern manager is expected to have a variety of skills that his or her predecessors may not have thought necessary. One fundamental change is the way in which initiatives and new developments are introduced through project management. It used to be enough to allow individual departments to introduce changes in an ad hoc way, but the advent of company-wide, process-dependent initiatives means that more rigorous methods of managing change are needed. The initiatives that a manager may now have to deal with require accurate control and coordination, and so demand formal project management techniques. These were originally developed for projects in manufacturing, construction and civil engineering.

However, many projects that make full use of formal techniques still fail, and often with very serious consequences. Projects can fail in different ways. Some fail when they are first launched, such as the Samsung Galaxy Note 7 which was prone to battery fires; some suffer long delays, such as the Berlin Brandenburg airport; and others, such as Crossrail, need ever-increasing sums of money to meet their deadlines. Why is this? There is no simple answer; projects fail for many different reasons. But regardless of the complexity or size of a project, three features are fundamental to success: **cost, performance and time**. There are many tools available for managing these three, and we shall see a few of these in this chapter.

Cost, performance and time: projects are normally subjected to these three performance criteria.

Care is needed as the employment of sophisticated project management tools and techniques alone is not enough to guarantee success. Project success can be measured using cost, performance and time, but project management is concerned with managing people within changing environmental and organizational contexts. These all have a profound and often unpredictable bearing on the project itself. Successful project managers are also project leaders, and have well-developed strategic and interpersonal skills. These are needed in addition to the technical skills associated with scheduling, resource allocation and decision-making in optimizing the three variables of cost, performance and time.

This chapter will focus on both tools and techniques, and will consider the challenges facing practising managers in order to help them understand the difficulties and complexities of managing projects by looking through multiple lenses and considering overlapping subjects. In particular, the chapter will first consider the strategic aspect of projects, such as project stakeholders, and the ways in which we can structure projects within the organization. It will then focus on the tools, by looking at the sequence of steps typically found in project management – the tools needed to develop plans, monitor project progress, manage the individuals in the project team, and ensure completion.

Alternative Views of Project Management

BUSINESS INTEGRATION

At one level, project management processes and techniques can be used to coordinate resources to achieve predictable results. However, it is important to understand that project management is not totally a science; there is no straightforward formula for success. Since projects involve people, there are always uncertainties that cannot be absolutely controlled, and so project management is partly an art that requires flexibility and creativity.

Projects are owned by a multiplicity of stakeholders, whose needs and aspirations must be accommodated. As can be seen in the Airbus NEO case (Short Case 11.1), organizational 'politics', the external environment, marketing pressures and the needs and objectives of a large number of individuals must be considered. Hence there must be regular interaction, especially when a project team is being set up, with 'commissioning executives', other stakeholders and interested parties. The purpose of this interaction is to define the boundaries of the project, and to keep its core objectives in focus. The significance of the motivation and commitment of individual team members should be recognized. Teamwork is vital because projects involve not only internal specialists but also external suppliers, subcontractors and end users.

Figure 11.1 shows how we can view project management from two alternative perspectives. The first is *inside* the project, looking outwards, where detail will dominate the life of the project manager and he or she is likely to be thinking mainly of the three project goals of time, performance and cost. Here the project manager is concerned with detail in planning and controlling the project.

The project manager may be responsible for achievement of the goals of the project, but normally his or her direct authority is often limited as he or she is responsible for just one project. Resources and support have to be negotiated with a wide network of more senior people inside and outside the organization. Often the project manager's authority is low at the outset, and must be built up and maintained if the project is to progress well and achieve its goals.

Our second perspective on project management is from *outside* the project looking in: here the stakeholders' views become more evident, and communications and relationships dominate. These views are from suppliers, commissioning managers, and other interested parties such as the general public. They tend to want to see the big picture, and how the project's progress will impact on them.

Think about how different your views on and involvement with the Crossrail project would be if you were the project manager, a building contractor, the Mayor of London, or a commuter: the views on when a project can be considered a success or failure also change with the perspective taken. The project manager will focus on the three performance criteria of cost, performance and time, whereas the commuters want as little disruption as possible and the work to be completed on time. The mayor is hoping it delivers the improvements promised and within budget, whereas individual contractors want to get their work done quickly, with as few complications as possible, while making a profit.

Stakeholders: the people who have a say in or are influenced by a project.

There is one aspect which is common to all the **stakeholders**, though, and which can be used to give a definition: project management relates to the management of a *temporary organization.*

Figure 11.1 The two perspectives of project management

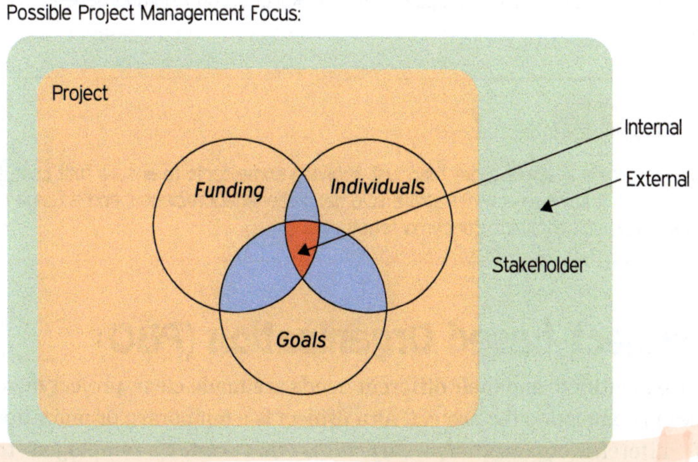

This has significant implications in understanding the task and tools of managing projects and the nature of organizations, as there are many different approaches to structuring the organization to deliver the project. One major and consistent development in the shift to more project management over the past few decades has been a move towards more dynamic and temporary organization structures. Gone are the days where people used to have a job for life; they are now more likely to find their jobs changing regularly, and this can be directly attributable to organizations managing change through project management. The possible alternative structures, and the advantages and disadvantages of these project organization types, are covered in the next section.

SHORT CASE 11.1

Airbus NEO Stakeholders

Source: ©Markus Mainka/Shutterstock

The A320/A321 NEO is the latest incarnation of the hugely successful Airbus narrow bodied airline. NEO stands for new engine option and is the firm's rival to the Boeing 737 MAX which itself has been beset with delays due to software issues which were found following two crashes of the new planes.

Soon after launch, the Franco-German Airbus stopped delivering A320neo jets powered by Pratt & Whitney geared-turbofan engines and halted pre-delivery test flights due to a series of problems with the engines. This came after a two-year delay following problems with the fuel efficient engines, and production issues at a factory in Germany. The firm's largest shareholders are the German and French states with 11% each and there is constant tension about where new factories are built.

At the same time, the chief procurement officer of the $50 billion supply chain, Klaus Richter, stepped down. Speculation about why he resigned surrounds several issues including the delay to the NEO and also the dynamics of the top managers:

> *Richter, once seen by some as a potential candidate for CEO, joins a long list of unconnected departures and his exit appears linked to matters of corporate structure and style rather than purely industrial issues, people close to the company said. (Hepher, 2019).*

Questions

1. Identify the stakeholders in the Airbus NEO project.
2. How much control do you think the chief procurement officer has over a major project like the NEO?
3. What advice would you give to Richter's successor about managing the stakeholders of the firm?

Source: https://www.reuters.com/article/us-airbus-delays/airbus-reshuffles-supply-chain-as-former-autos-executive-leaves-group-idUSKBN1XH1WX;https://www.bangkokpost.com/thailand/general/1410430/new-setback-for-airbus-a320neo

The key point is ...

that project management is about more than just applying some tools to ensure that cost, time and performance are met. It involves a wider strategic/organizational appreciation, and a range of skills that bring all the many players' and stakeholders' concerns together.

Towards the Project-based Organization (PBO)

Once the stakeholders are identified, and their different needs are made clear, project managers can start to think about the strategic issues in completing the project. As a project is a temporary organization, the managers need to consider a range of different organizational structures that can be employed to deliver the project.

Figure 11.2 Functional organization structure

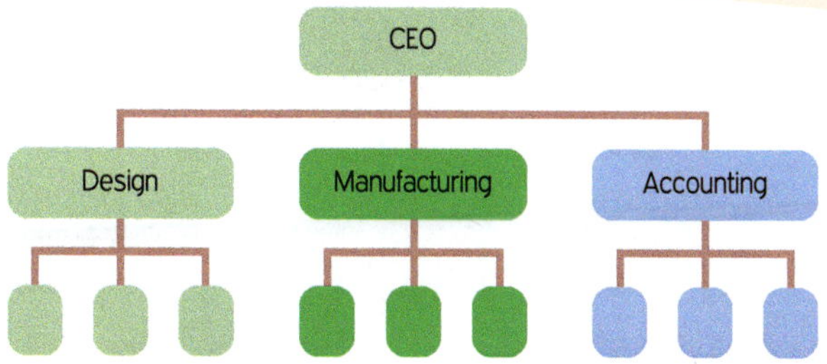

Some organization structures are better suited to projects than others. This section explores these different structures and identifies their benefits, with particular reference to accomplishing projects.

Designing a Project-based Organization

An organization can be defined as *the arrangement of people in a business so that they can act as one body.* The conventional approach to company management is the *line and staff* or functional approach, which separates skill sets such as product design, production, sales, marketing and accounting. This is the traditional hierarchical structure of organization as shown in Figure 11.2. It is possibly the oldest structure, and its persistence is due partly to its simplicity and partly, for many years, to the apparent absence of a better alternative. We now see that the conventional pyramidal hierarchy is considered unnecessarily authoritative. Several studies have highlighted weaknesses in the line and staff approach. There is a slow flow of information; the approach is impersonal, because of its inherent bureaucracy; it is slow to change, because of the inflexible and complex nature of the structure; an ever-increasing use and application of technology is required to assist organizational communication; and younger people are less keen on rigid line and staff authority.

Many organizations – Scandinavian Airlines (SAS), for example – have moved to a more customer-oriented organization. They believe that organizations should be focused on the workers who are in contact with the customer, and that these are supported at the sharp end by management. Another trend is to try to 'flatten' the layers between the decision-makers and the front-line employees who ultimately are the ones who deliver the service or add value. This increases the speed of communication between the customers and the managers.

With projects, the hierarchical and functional boundaries in the organization also act as constraints on communication, and so hinder the performance of the project. Instead of carrying out the project using whatever skills are needed at the time, projects operating within a functional organization require negotiation with the functional managers for access to skills and resources. For example, if a manufacturing-based project needs access to the sales computer system, the project manager has to enlist support from his superior to clear the way to talk to his opposite number in sales. Carrying out work for the manufacturing department is not what sales staff are there to do, and so there is understandable resistance and a delay in completing the work until it has been agreed by both departments.

As a result, it is usually possible to operate a project within a functional structure only if it is established as a separate part of the organization, temporarily staffed by the required experts drawn from the functions. This is shown in Figure 11.3. These project teams are normally championed by one function to provide the support and line management needed as there is no other place for the organization to locate the project in its hierarchy. These types of project are often weak in their impact as the members still focus on their functional responsibilities and are easily distracted by the needs and activities back in their home department. Staff are not always working towards the project goals.

There are alternatives to the functional organization that are more suited to managing projects. Figure 11.4 shows the **matrix organization**, which has staff reporting to two managers. The (vertical) responsibility is to the functional role, and the other (horizontal) responsibility is to a specific project. This structure can be stressful for staff, because working for more than one boss can result in divided loyalties and ambiguous lines of authority. However, it can help cross-functional teams secure ownership of the project.

> **Matrix organization:** combined organization structure that overlays functional and project-based styles.

Practitioners consider the matrix structure to be a two-dimensional system, where each project represents a potential *profit centre* and each functional department represents a *cost centre.* This interpretation can create conflict, because functional departments may feel they no longer have an input to corporate profits.

Figure 11.3 Typical cross-functional project team or task force

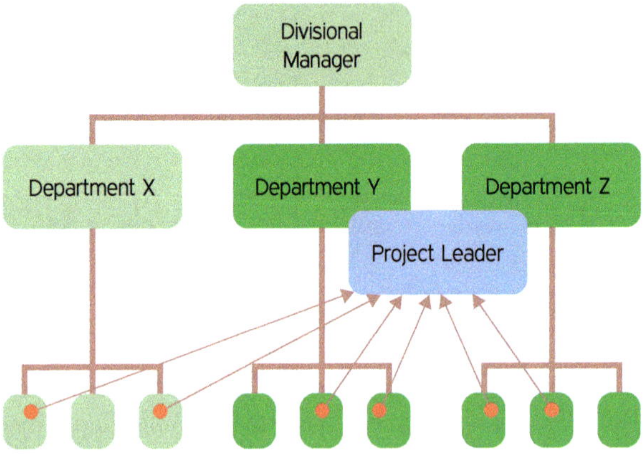

Figure 11.4 The matrix organizational structure

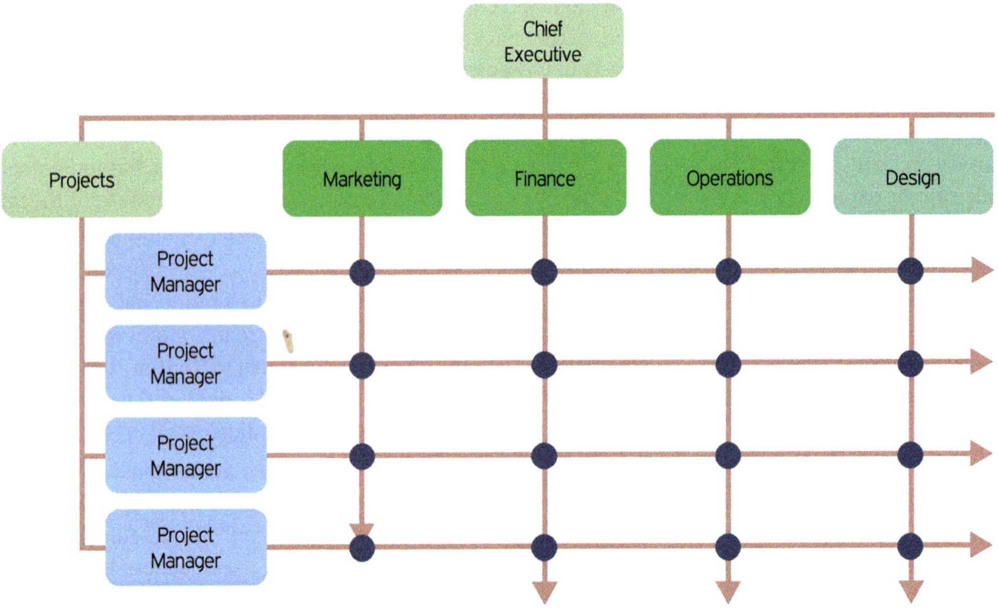

Generally there are three types of matrix structure:

- A *weak matrix arrangement,* where the project manager acts as a coordinator of the work and chairs meetings with the representatives of other departments involved in the project. Resources are allocated by consensus and the project manager is reduced to administering the project rather than leading it.
- A *middling matrix,* where there is an attempt to balance the power of the project manager with that of the line manager. The administration of the organization is such that the line manager applies resources to the activities that need to be carried out by the project: that is, the project provides a source of income for the functional department.
- A *strong matrix,* where functional departments have the role of providing resources through seconding people on a full-time basis to the project team. This arrangement operates only when the project is highly important to the organization. There are drawbacks as it may isolate an individual from their normal promotion or career development path. However, here the aims and needs of the project are paramount and so it is likely to be successful.

Some organizations take the matrix even further and lose the direct functional hierarchy, leaving central roles such as personnel, accounting and training as ancillary tasks. This can be seen in Figure 11.5.

Figure 11.5 A strong matrix structure with hierarchy only for support staff

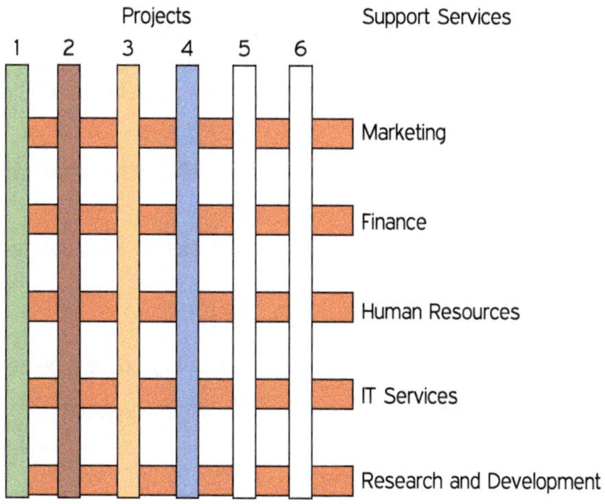

Figure 11.6 Wholly project-based organization

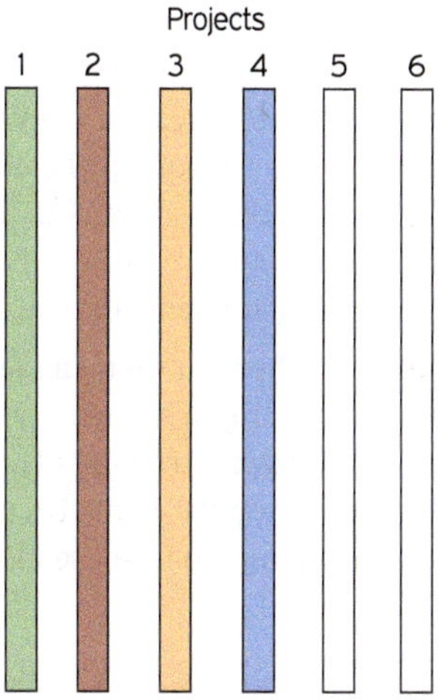

Recently, some firms have taken this approach still further into what is known as the **project-based organization** structure. As its name suggests, this organization is structured purely around projects; each is self-contained, with all its own staff and support skills (see Figure 11.6). The move towards virtual organizations and the emergence of new technologies allows this structure to operate and the only permanent staff are the senior executives and the project managers. The other staff are on fixed contracts and so are hired and used as needed. This allows the project to be the focus of the organization and offers greater flexibility to the firm as it can take on projects in a wide range of areas, just by recruiting staff with the necessary skills, and not having to worry about how to use its employees.

Project-based organization: represents a shift from functional organization structure, via the matrix organization, to one where the project is the focus of attention.

The problems with this approach are that there is greater duplication of roles across projects owing to a lack of central coordination. Also there are problems with learning as there is no guarantee that the staff from one project will be used in any others; and that acquiring the right skills may be difficult or expensive in times of shortages. Take, for example, the simultaneous Crossrail project (discussed in the opening case study) and the London Olympics. Both were looking for staff with similar skills for short-term temporary contracts in what were already shortage trades in London. This can only mean that the costs are higher for the organization than they could be if their staff were permanently employed. However, neither organization will exist after the completion of each project, and so does not need to appoint these staff permanently.

The key point is ...

that the format of an organization is important for carrying out the project, and there are certain structures that make managing projects easier than others. However, it is important to remember that projects, by definition, are only temporary. Therefore the project-based organization is not ideal for those firms where projects are used purely for occasional activities.

Stop and Think

You are setting up a new company that delivers training courses over the Internet. Which organization type would you use for the following activities in the firm?

(a) The head office, including the sales, IT and accounting departments.

(b) The commissioning department, which arranges for different experts to produce a package of materials.

(c) After five years of growth, a project to relocate to a new building with more space.

Managing the Project Life Cycle

So far we have seen the complexity of effectively managing projects and the strategic considerations of different stakeholders, as well as the way projects fit into existing organization structures. Now we shall start to look at some of the approaches that can help us deliver the project on time, in budget, and to specification. We have already defined a project as a temporary structure that is focused on delivering one objective. This can become more complicated if we think about how some firms have to co-manage the delivery of several projects with varying objectives at once, or as in the Human Genome Project in Short Case 11.2, when the tools to complete the project do not yet exist. A good starting point, though, for the techniques of project management is that every project goes through the same phases: definition, planning and resourcing, implementation, and wind-up or handover to the customer.

There are many frameworks that help us structure the way we manage projects. The best way to describe a project management framework is to think of a cookbook. If you are unsure of how to manage a project, simply refer to the recipe in the cookbook. There are two well-known structures (cookbooks) for managing projects. The first, *PRINCE2* (Projects in Controlled Environments), is popular in the UK and Europe, whilst the second, *PMBOK* (Project Management Body of Knowledge), is supported by the US-based Project Management Institute.

PRINCE Methodology

PRINCE2 is a project management methodology developed by the UK's Office of Government Commerce (OGC), which is an independent office of HM Treasury. OGC manages PRINCE2 and has adopted an 'open' strategy that makes it publicly available so that it can be used without the need for a proprietary licence or royalty payments of any kind. It has been revised several times, and should more accurately be referred to as PRINCE2 6th Edition, reflecting the current version.

Numerous major organizations currently use PRINCE2. They include The AA, Aviva, Network Rail, BT, Camel, GlaxoSmithKline, Hitachi, HM Land Registry, the Home Office, Hong Kong Telecom, TFL, the Danish Government, NatWest, the NHS, Philip Morris, the RAF, Reading Borough Council, Royal Mail, Tesco, TSB, and Unilever. Many of these organizations use only some elements of the methodology rather than the full package. The use of a cookbook doesn't guarantee a perfect meal; nor does it include all the information that might be needed. PRINCE2 is a framework within which to operate, and represents a set of guidelines and knowledge of best practice, in a similar vein to the ISO 9000 quality management system, which is covered in Chapter 13.

Chapter 13, p429

PRINCE2 is not intended to include all the subjects relevant to project management. Project management techniques and tools such as network planning are adequately covered elsewhere and are considered to be tried and tested techniques. PRINCE2 focuses on the management of the project and the resources involved in carrying out all the activities of that project. Thus PRINCE2 is a process-oriented approach to project management and it separates the management of a project into various key processes. Each is clearly defined and contains the essence of a system: inputs, outputs, objectives and feedback control. Figure 11.7 shows the key processes of the PRINCE2 methodology. Note the way that the processes themselves are linked in a certain rigid way.

Figure 11.7 The PRINCE2 process

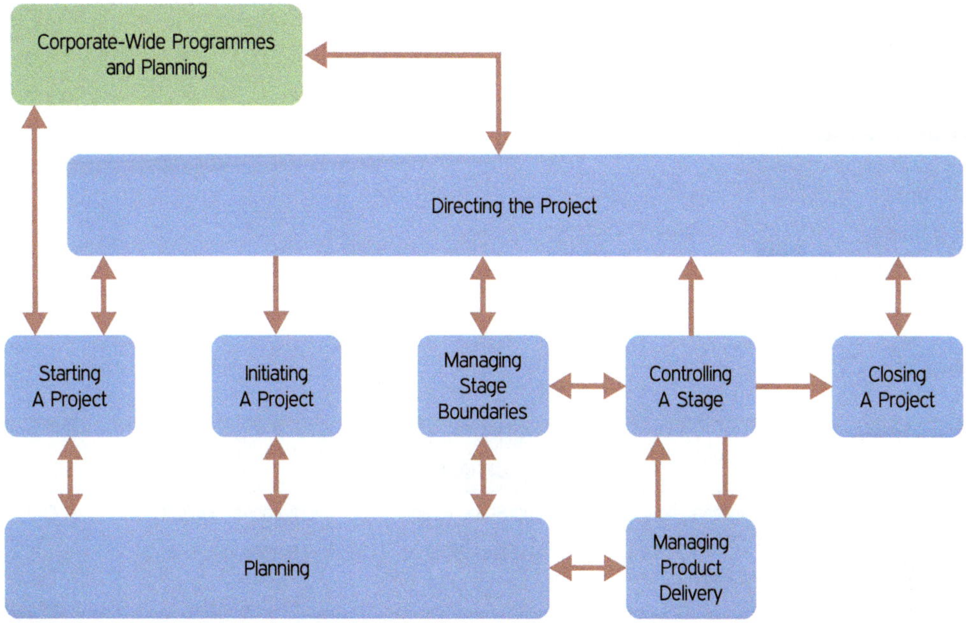

In more detail, PRINCE2 defines 45 separate activities, and groups these under the eight processes as shown in the diagram. Each process has a clear list of outputs, which represent key timing or decision points for a project. These are summarized in Figure 11.8, showing the different management levels that are responsible for each. The *directing* process is the responsibility of the *project board,* which is charged with an overview and integration with the rest of the business. The middle layer is concerned with *delivering* the project and is the responsibility of the team members, and the last line of the diagram shows the role of the project manager.

PRINCE2 Elements

PRINCE2 defines a programme as:

> *A portfolio of projects selected, planned and managed in a coordinated way which together achieve a set of defined business objectives. Programme management methods and techniques may also be applied to a set of otherwise unrelated projects bounded by a business cycle.*

PRINCE2 is designed for an environment where there are products, supported by a business case, commissioned by a customer and produced by a supplier, that are intended to produce benefits and are operated by a user. These terms are important, because they show the concerns and motivation of PRINCE2, along with its focus.

- *Business case:* a formal document that contains the information necessary to justify the project. It describes the costs and benefits of the project, and answers the question 'Why should this project be undertaken?' It should also contain the criteria for reviewing the progress of the project, and criteria for measuring satisfactory progress or terminating the project.
- *User:* this defines those who will ultimately operate the final product and should be identified separately from the customer.
- *Customer:* the person(s) who commissioned the project, and who should ultimately receive its benefits.
- *Product, deliverable* and *outcome:* these words are used interchangeably to describe project end points. They describe what has been or what should be achieved. Results of projects may vary enormously, from tangible items such as buildings to intangibles such as a culture change.
- *Project issues:* things that may adversely affect the successful outcome of the project – also known as problems.
- *Supplier:* a person or group providing specialist skills and resources to the project in order to create the project outcomes required by the customer and users.
- *Subcontractor:* a person or group who provides products and/or services to the supplier.

Figure 11.8 PRINCE2 process contents and level of responsibility

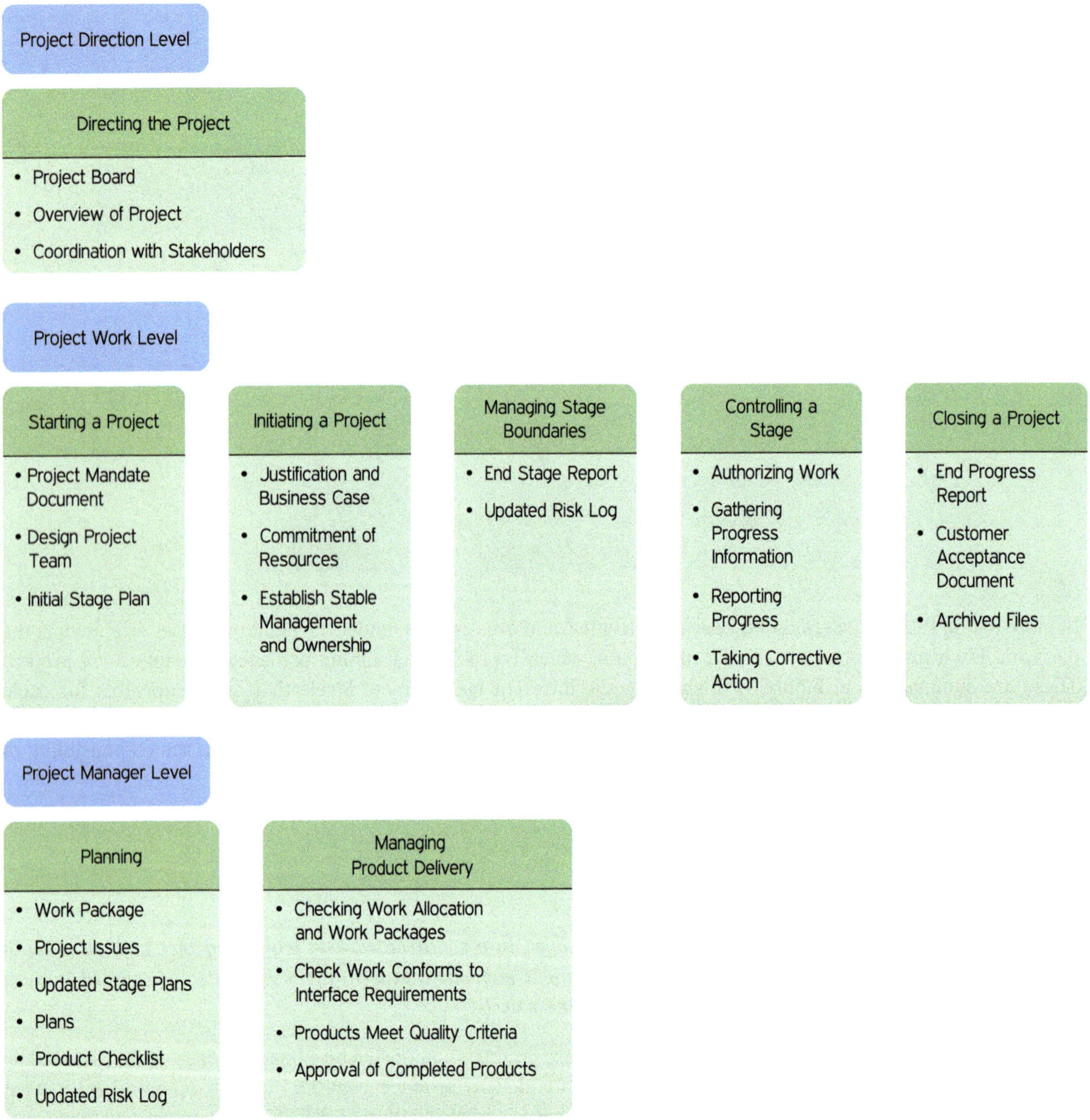

So PRINCE2 is about managing all projects in a programme or organization in a controlled manner. The recipe book has clear statements about how a project is initialized and recorded in the *project initiation document* (PID). This defines what the project will deliver, and a mechanism for managing the changes if the client wants additional work carried out.

The running of the project is also clearly defined, with *a project board* that manages the project for its whole duration. It consists of several members, each representing a major project interest. This is useful, as it generates cross-ownership of the project between the interested parties.

Under PRINCE2, projects are monitored by a *project assurance team* for the duration of the project. This covers both technical and administrative responsibilities. This ensures the continuity and integrity of the project are maintained, and involves a focus on the user.

Project managers are appointed for day-to-day management of the project, and PRINCE2 gives guidance on deciding how their duties should be allocated. A project manager may be appointed for the duration of the project, to plan the project and define responsibilities for each stage manager. Thereafter, the job involves ensuring that the project progresses to time and budget, managing the interface with other projects, reporting to the project board, and initiating any corrective action as necessary.

A *stage manager* may be appointed for each stage, and is given the task of ensuring that stage products are produced on schedule to acceptable quality standards and within budget. The stage manager is supported by the *stage team(s)* responsible for producing the products of the stage. At the discretion of the project board the same person may manage more than one stage, or the roles of project manager and stage manager may be undertaken by the same person. *Teams* are created during each stage to implement the project. The team organization, responsibility definitions and the allocation of those responsibilities to individuals will depend upon the size and nature of the project, and on the skill mixes available.

PRINCE2 helps ensure that a project is fully defined and scoped, by using *product breakdown structures* (PBS) to identify all necessary products, whether they are to be produced within the project, already exist, or are to be produced by another project. The structure has as its *origin* the product that the project has been commissioned to produce. This reflects the PRINCE2 distinction between management and technical activities, and the need for the quality control process to be independently auditable.

The project manager, the project board and the senior users have to put effort in 'up front' to make more of the project visible right from the start. But the effort put in at the beginning is repaid by a reduction in work later, both for the board and for the project team overall. It helps the project planners and auditors to identify, earlier rather than later, whether specific individuals or special tools need to be involved in the review or testing process.

Once the major products and the necessary activities to produce them have been defined, the project can be divided into stages. Each stage will end at a *key control point,* where a formal decision must be taken whether to proceed to the next stage, or to abandon (or suspend) the project. These key points will usually coincide with the completion of a major product, or product set, which then becomes the baseline for moving forward. Such a key point might be: when detailed user requirements have been established, and these need to be confirmed formally, with a commitment to meet them; or where tenders have been received, and acceptance of one of them will introduce a new set of circumstances and new commitments.

PRINCE2 requires a structured set of technical and resource plans to achieve effective technical and managerial control of a project, including:

- technical plans
- resource plans
- exception plans.

A *stage technical plan* is prepared for each stage of the project, and shows all products and technical activities within that stage. The stage technical plan is produced at the same time as, and to complement, the stage resource plan. Detailed technical plans will probably be necessary in all but the smallest projects. Typically, they are used for detailed planning and control of major activities (e.g. system test).

Individual *work plans* are produced as necessary from the stage and detailed technical plans to allocate detailed activities to specific people within a stage team. Actual progress is reported against these plans for later compilation of control reports.

Resource plans are used to identify the type, amount and period of use of the various resources required during the life of the project. *The project resource plan* is mandatory for all projects. It is a top-level plan produced during the initiation stage to quantify the resources needed for succeeding stages of the project. The *stage resource plan* contains details of all the required resources for a stage. It may be produced at two levels of detail: the first in summary form for approval by the project board; the second in more detail for the stage manager, and against which actuals are recorded. The initiation stage plan is prepared as early in the project as possible. Plans for each subsequent stage are prepared before the stage commences, in time for submission to the end stage assessment meeting of the previous stage.

The detailed resource plans are created as necessary to plan the required resources for a particular activity (e.g. system test).

The *exception plan* is required only when a significant deviation from the plans, in terms of cost or elapsed time, has exceeded or will exceed tolerances previously defined by the project board (e.g. if a significant request for change has to be implemented). It shows the action proposed to meet the deviation, and the consequences of the deviation and of the corrective action.

PRINCE2 provides a *control structure* to be applied during each stage. The control components cover all aspects of project activity, and allow the project board to assess project status before committing to further expenditure and/ or a revised timescale. Controls are applied via meetings of project management and project staff as required, each meeting producing a set of predefined documents. There are five types of control meetings following comprehensive reporting and change control procedures.

PRINCE2 includes guidance on getting the project firmly under control at the outset, and recognizes that this cannot usually be done in the context of a single meeting. What needs to be in place before any development starts – the project initiation document (PID) – is described in detail, as well as how to assemble the information required. The *mid* and *end stage assessments* (MSA and ESA) are mandatory management controls that occur at the midpoint and end of each stage. They consist of formal presentations by the project manager to the project board of the current project status, and requests for approval of the resource and technical plans for the next stage. Approval by the project board is needed before the project can proceed to the next stage.

The final stage of the PRINCE2 method is *project closure*. This addresses what needs to be handed on from the project to those who will be using, running and maintaining the system in the future; the project manager receives a project valuation report that reviews the conduct of the project and considers what lessons can be learnt; arranges for a post-implementation review to be held at the appropriate time and formally closes the project; and hands the resulting system over to the service manager and the users.

Managing all products as a single configuration is referred to generally as *configuration management*. This approach allows all participants to see the entire project as a configuration, where there is structure to the management of all information relating to the project. Configurations could be loaded onto databases and accessed by both internal and external staff. This presents the possibility of knowledge capture and ultimately knowledge management.

GLOBALIZATION

PRINCE2 Alternative: PMI PMBOK

PRINCE2 is not alone in offering a structured framework for managing projects. An equally popular approach giving advice on the successful completion of projects comes from the Project Management Institute (PMI). PMI offers its *Project Management Body of Knowledge* (PMBOK), which lists the roles and skills of project managers in much the same way as PRINCE2 lists the steps for effective project management. The PMI cites its mission as advancing the profession of project management, and was recognized by the US ANSI as an Accredited Standard Developer in 1988.

In PMBOK, PMI has a framework for professional development that describes the clusters of knowledge, skills, abilities, and other personal characteristics relevant to most, if not all, types of project. These skills can be acquired and improved through training and development programmes for project managers. PMI promotes project management as an individual skill, which must be based on a sound body of knowledge, and is directed towards the development of professional standards of both ability and conduct. PMI qualifications are available to employers as an indication of the fitness of an individual to manage projects.

The *PMBOK Guide's* fourth edition was released in 2008, and was a significant update as the body of knowledge had grown substantially. Like PRINCE, the PMBOK document seeks to spread and standardize project management practices, and since mid-2007 nearly a half-million *PMBOK Guides* have been purchased from the PMI website, or distributed to PMI members. The Institute of Electrical and Electronics Engineers has adopted the *PMBOK Guide* as IEEE Standard 1490 to further promote its adoption.

CRITICAL PERSPECTIVE

Project Management Frameworks

The description of PRINCE2 gives some idea of the meaning of a project management framework or recipe book. It shows the extent of the detailed descriptions and approaches contained within PRINCE2 and similar frameworks such as PMBOK.

Some organizations adopt the PRINCE2 approach in full, whereas others apply only parts which they integrate with internal procedures. This is due largely to the complete nature of PRINCE2, as it can be seen as a sledgehammer to crack a nut; smaller, simpler projects do not need the complete formal framework for successful completion.

Experienced project managers know the importance of the key steps that PRINCE2 and PMBOK represent, and so they intuitively manage their projects well. Without this experience, projects can and often do go astray.

Another criticism often levelled at systems such as PRINCE2 is that they do not address the nature of management structures, nor what software to use for project planning. They cover only the broad approach to the management of a project, and the stages and processes necessary to bring a project to completion. Such aspects of the organizational design and which specific tools are needed to meet the key elements in the framework must be addressed separately and decisions made by the project board. This detail of guidance is beyond PRINCE2, but is often needed in organizations inexperienced in project management.

Similarly, the frameworks ensure only that a firm covers the necessary steps; they do not offer the most elegant solution for a particular project.

The key point is ...

that complex projects require a formal process to ensure that all aspects are covered, but often a project is too small to warrant the full application of PRINCE2 or PMBOK.

SHORT CASE 11.2

The Human Genome Project

CSR

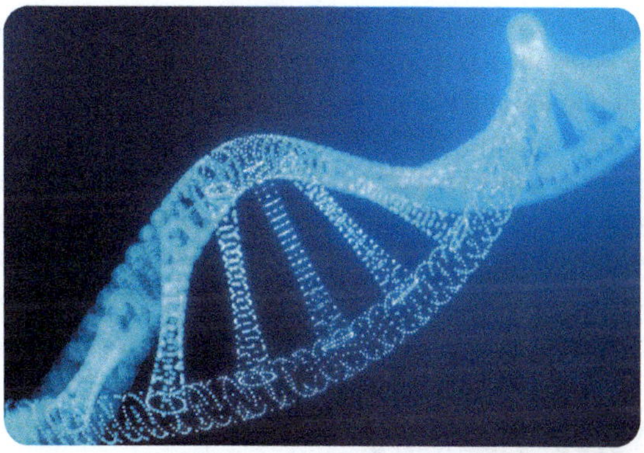

Source: ©Rost9/Shutterstock

One of the most remarkable scientific undertakings in recent years has been the human genome project (HGP). 'The ultimate goal of this initiative is to understand the human genome' and 'knowledge of the human as necessary to the continuing progress of medicine and other health sciences as knowledge of human anatomy has been for the present state of medicine'. The aim is to establish a map of the human genes, and then enable the identification of common variations that could be linked to the increased likelihood of specific diseases such as cancer or diabetes.

The $3 billion project, formally started in 1990, was a 13-year US National Institute of Health and UK Wellcome Trust funded initiative involving many international collaborators in universities and research centres from the United States, the United Kingdom, Japan, France, Germany, and China, as well as private firms. Initially the project was to last 15 years, but this was shortened as new technologies accelerated progress.

The specific goals were to:

- Determine the sequence of the 3 billion chemical base pairs in human DNA (consisting of protein combinations made up of four types, labelled A, T, C and G)
- Identify and appreciate the role of the 20,000–25,000 genes in human DNA (genes are the active significant part of the complete DNA sequence)
- Store and make available this information in accessible databases
- Develop tools to analyse the databases
- Involve private firms in developing the sequence and exploiting its potential
- Address the major ethical, legal and social issues arising from the project

Benefits of the project emerged even before the work was complete, as new tests were established for common genetic diseases such as breast cancer, liver disease and cystic fibrosis.

Organizing the work has been a major undertaking in project management, not only in determining who carries out what work, but also in how it is funded and how it might be exploited commercially.

Questions

1. How do you think the project goals set out above were developed into a more complete plan?
2. What problems do you think the project planners had in establishing their plan at the start, when they knew that the technologies they would employ needed to be developed as part of the project itself?

Source: US Department of Energy Genome Program, http://genomics.energy.gov.

The key point is ...

several things make a project difficult to manage. It could be the size of the project increasing the complexity as the number of organizations or individuals increase, meaning there is more to manage. For example, a student essay versus a team assignment, or the number of stakeholders in the Airbus NEO (Short Case 11.1). Or it could be the number of times the project or a similar one has been completed before, such as comparing a new railway line to a space expedition. Uncertainty of technology or relying on unknown solutions also add to the complexity, as can be seen in the Human Genome Project (Short Case 11.2). PRINCE2 is invaluable in the more complex projects as it forces a systematic approach where all aspects of the project delivery are stressed.

Project Management Tools

Project management frameworks such as PRINCE2 ensure that all the steps in the project life cycle are completed in a controlled and organized way. This is valuable in the management of a project, as it clearly identifies the relevant players and key milestones for the project. However, PRINCE2 does not go into the detail of planning the work for the project – just the major processes of the project itself. To enable the detailed planning and management of the project, there is a set of specific project management tools that can be employed. All of these involve generating plans and ensuring they are followed, or at least make the managers aware of when the plan is not being followed so that appropriate action can be taken. Sometimes, as can be seen in the Bolshoi Ballet Renovation (Short Case 11.3), good plans themselves are not sufficient for successful project management.

This section will look at these detailed project planning and monitoring techniques.

Project Planning

At the heart of project management is planning or – more accurately – coordinating activities in terms of timing and understanding the associated costs.

Planning should be considered only as a tool, as the project still has to be controlled and managed using appropriate measures and monitoring systems to ensure that the timings established in the plan occur.

Developing project plans is essentially a process of continuously opening up boxes to reveal more and more detail about the project – a bit like peeling back the layers of an onion. The PRINCE2 methodology gives us the outer layer, but we need to keep delving ever deeper until we have sufficient detail to map all the steps needed to complete the project. This is rarely simple; as there are often different ways to tackle an activity, each option may change the other activities needed to complete the project. For example, in building a bridge it is possible to choose to pour concrete sections on site as needed, but these take time to set. If the sections are made off site, they can be used as soon as they are delivered. The project manager needs to consider a wide range of things in deciding which route to adopt.

Developing a project plan is often made more complex when projects span several different organizations and involve many individuals and parties. The planning process can become unstructured, as plans often need to be updated as the work progresses.

Work breakdown structure (WBS): statement of all the work that has to be completed in a project.

The **work breakdown structure (WBS)** is a statement of all the work that has to be completed in a project. The project manager works closely with the other members of the project team to identify all work tasks. Major work elements are broken down into smaller components, and another level of detail is added: see Figure 11.9, which is for the Smart

Figure 11.9 Work breakdown structure (WBS)

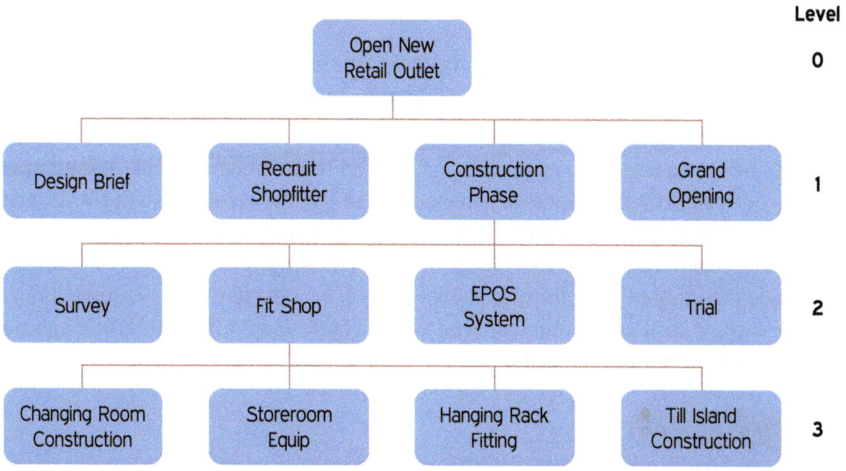

Togs company's opening of a new shop. Perhaps the most important contributor to delay in projects is the omission of work that is essential to the successful completion of the project. The WBS is essential for the project, as it is the document that lists the packages (or chunks) of work which need to be done for the project to be completed.

Each work package will consist of activities. An *activity* is the smallest unit of work effort, consuming both time and resources, that a project manager can schedule and control. Each package of work in the WBS must have an *owner* who is responsible for doing the work. Each task, in turn, must also have an owner. Ownership avoids confusion in the execution of activities, and assigns responsibility for timely completion. If an activity is without an owner, it is unlikely to get done. This also helps the PM track the project as it crosses between different organizations or functional groups that may be the source of conflict. The WBS can be redrawn as a *responsibility matrix* (Table 11.1) to show who is responsible for each activity, and when it changes hands.

Table 11.1 Responsibility matrix for Smart Togs shop opening (extract of fit shop phase)

Phase/tasks (partial)	Responsible staff				
	Mike	Jane	Harry	Melvin	Wendy
3. Construction phase					
3.1 Survey					
3.2 Fit shop					
3.2.1 Changing room construction	R			I	
3.2.2 Storeroom equip			R	C	A
3.2.3 Hanging rack fitting			I		R
3.2.4 Till island construction		R		C	A
3.3 EPOS system					
3.4 Trial					

R = responsible; C = consult; A = assist; I = inform.

The project manager can focus on these interfaces, once they are identified; they are often sources of problems, as communication may not be perfect across the organization units. PRINCE2 highlights these through its stage boundary process.

The responsibility matrix lists each activity, and the staff who are involved. They are assigned a letter to show their role on the activity, as shown in Table 11.1. Every task must have just one R or responsible person, whereas there can be any number of Cs (consults), As (assists) or Is (informs).

Once defined, the WBS becomes the basis of the project, and so it must be accurate; any errors or omissions will have serious knock-on effects. Project budgets are then set, based on the elements in the WBS, and so the impact of errors relates not only to timing, but also to cost. If the project costs are unreliable, then the impact on the contracting organization or the sponsor can be catastrophic, and far reaching. For example, Wembley Stadium was the subject of long delays as the main contractor and subcontractor for the steel work argued about who was responsible. Both suffered greatly, and it is still unclear who was at fault, even after the affair had degenerated into a series of claims and counterclaims in the courts.

Developing Budget Plans

Budgets are very important for project management. Because of the temporary nature of projects, there is no source of funds other than those assigned to the project and the activities in the WBS, and so the process of budgeting is more than just estimating the possible total cost of the project. Some firms have highly developed methods for estimating budgets, depending on their experience and the nature of what needs estimating. Architects, for example, can take the area of a building and multiply by a figure to give a very good approximation of the costs for normal construction. Similarly, software producers' estimates of budget are based on the number of lines of code required, and are calculated using standardized values.

As a project continues, a common method for monitoring progress is to compare the money spent on each activity against the budget allocated for that activity. Failure to assign the right funds to an activity at the beginning of the project means that later it may overspend. Then it either has to be completed in a different (cheaper) way, or needs to be funded from the budget of another activity. If the entire project has been under-budgeted at the outset, then this will lead to a cost overrun.

There are two ways for developing budgets: top-down and bottom-up.

Top-down Budgeting

One approach to setting budgets is to ask the senior managers to predict the cost. They draw on their experience, and formulate an overall guide figure for the project as a whole. This can then be given to others to divide the total amounts into ever-finer detail, and allocate them to work packages and activities. This is called breaking down the cost, and results in a *cost breakdown structure*. This is similar to developing the work breakdown structure mentioned earlier, and the two activities often happen at the same time.

A problem with this approach is that often it amounts to little more than senior management guesswork, and even if the overall budget is approximately correct, errors may creep in as the budget is broken down and allocated to work packages and activities.

Bottom-up Budgeting

With bottom-up budgeting, the individual elements of the work breakdown structure are costed separately. The overall project budget can then be calculated. These budgets can be very accurate, as each element represents a well-defined piece of work. Another benefit is that there are many people involved in developing these budgets, ensuring activities are not neglected. Also, there are benefits from including stakeholders early on, as their support and investment of time help the smooth running of the project itself.

However, developing a complete list of the tasks involved in the project can be difficult, and there is often pressure from senior management to cut budgets after they have been set. This can cause problems later in delivering all the stages of the project.

Top-down is more common than bottom-up, as senior managers see the importance of controlling the budgeting process and the organization as a whole. Also, it is such an important task that responsibility is rarely delegated to juniors.

Figure 11.10 Gantt chart

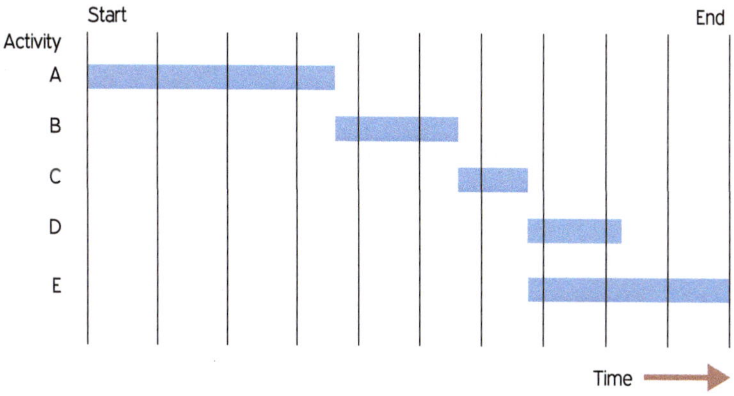

Scheduling Projects

Project Visualization Tools

Sometimes known as bar charts, **Gantt charts** are the simplest representation of project timing. Time is shown across the bottom of the chart, and the vertical axis lists the activities of the WBS. The activity start and durations are shown as coloured bars running across the chart, as shown in Figure 11.10. Gantt charts are easy to follow, but have one major drawback, in that they do not show relationships between activities, giving purely a picture of the timing.

Gantt chart: horizontal bar diagram showing activities and their duration.

Network Approaches

Gantt charts can be annotated to include information on the order of relationships between the project tasks. There are different ways of showing this information, but, regardless of the method used, the plan should show the interaction or dependence of events, and allow distinctions to be made between activities (things that need to be done), events (things that happen) and milestones (project-tracking or control points).

A *network diagram* representing a project is shown in Figure 11.11. The activities are represented by the nodes, and are given letters to identify them, but the order in which they need to be completed is shown by the lines. For example, activity A can start at once, and proceed without waiting for any other activity. Activities B and C, though, cannot start until activity A is finished, and similarly activity D needs both B and C to have completed before it can be started. The project will be finished only when all the activities are complete, with H being the last. This representation of the activity order is logical, as some jobs cannot be started before others are finished. If the project is to build a new house, the walls cannot be built until the foundations are laid, and similarly work on the roof cannot start until the walls are built.

There are two different sorts of notation used in network approaches: *activity on node*, as in Figure 11.11, and *activity on arrow*, as shown in Figure 11.12. This chapter will use both types of diagram, but the method of calculation is the same; it is just the notation that differs. It is very important that you know which one you are using, and do not mix them up.

Figure 11.11 Network activity diagram: activity on node representation

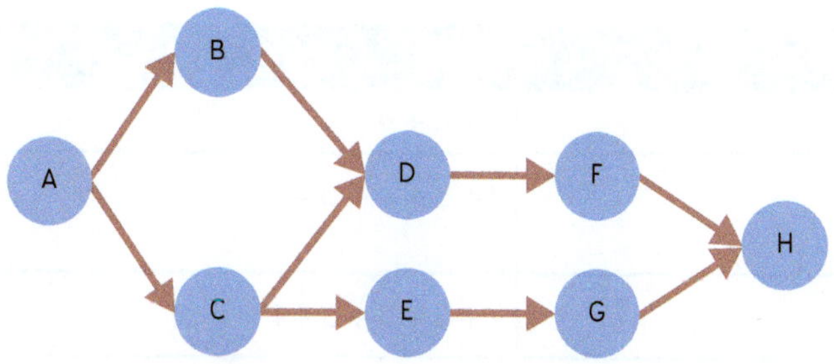

Figure 11.12 Network activity diagram: activity on arrow representation showing dummy activity

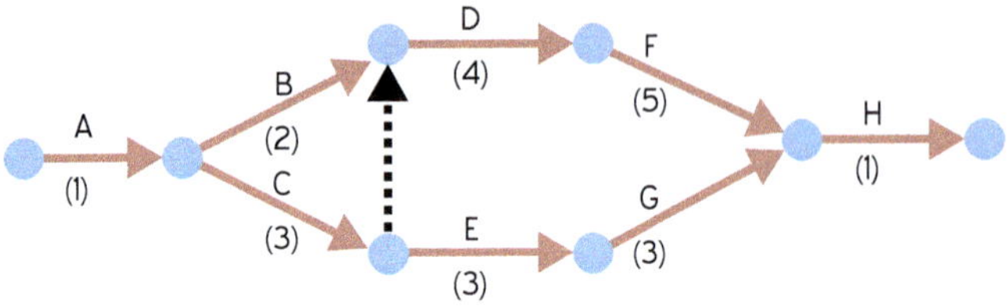

Figure 11.13 The critical path for a project network

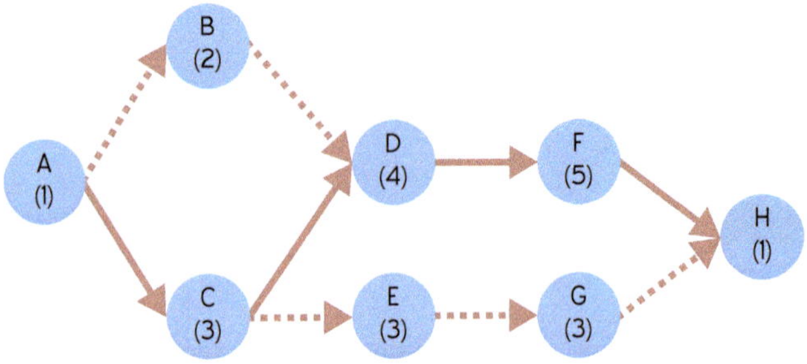

For some networks, dummy activities need to be used when there are two different paths in the network which are separate but dependent on one another. For instance, in Figure 11.12, activity D cannot start until both B and C are finished. To show this dependence, a dummy link needs to be shown, using a dotted line.

The Critical Path Method

The *critical path method (CPM)* is a project management tool that makes use of the network diagram. The first valuable role of the CPM technique is to identify the longest train of activities through the project network. As we saw above, some activities cannot start until others are finished, and if we add these together end to end, they show us the time needed to complete these tasks. The longest path through the network is known as the **critical path**, as it will determine the total time taken for the project to be completed. Activities that lie on the critical path need careful monitoring, as any delay will extend the end date for the whole project.

> **Critical path:** the chain of activities that determines the total duration of a project from start to finish.

> **Float:** the spare time an activity has before it will become on the critical path, and so allowing rescheduling without impact.

> **Slack:** the spare time an activity has before it will become on the critical path.

Figure 11.13 shows a network, with the times for each activity. If the times are added together through the network (see Table 11.2), it is easy to see that the longest path is A C D F H, and it needs 14 days to complete these activities. The possible paths and their times are shown in the following table.

Note the way the critical path is highlighted in the diagram. Activities not on the critical path have what is called **float** (or **slack**) time, which can be used without affecting the total length of the project. We need to be careful because if a non-critical path activity is delayed too much, it will then form a new critical path and so impact the entire project duration.

Table 11.2 The duration of the paths through the project network

Path	Times	Duration of path
A B D F H	1 + 2 + 4 + 5 + 1	13
A C D F H (critical path)	1 + 3 + 4 + 5 + 1	14
A C E G H	1 + 3 + 3 + 3 + 1	11

Figure 11.14 A node layout showing useful data on a network diagram

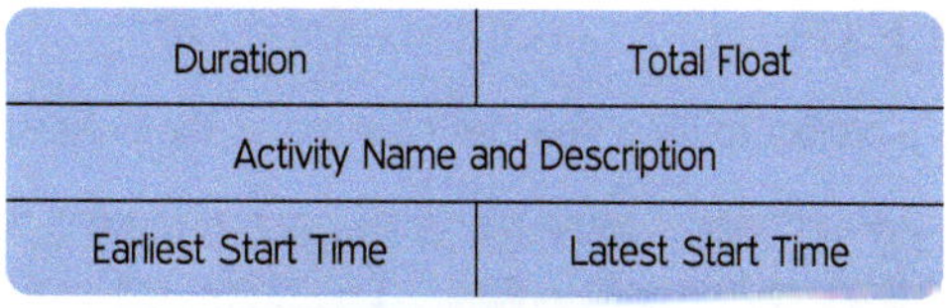

Figure 11.15 Network diagram showing critical path and activity float

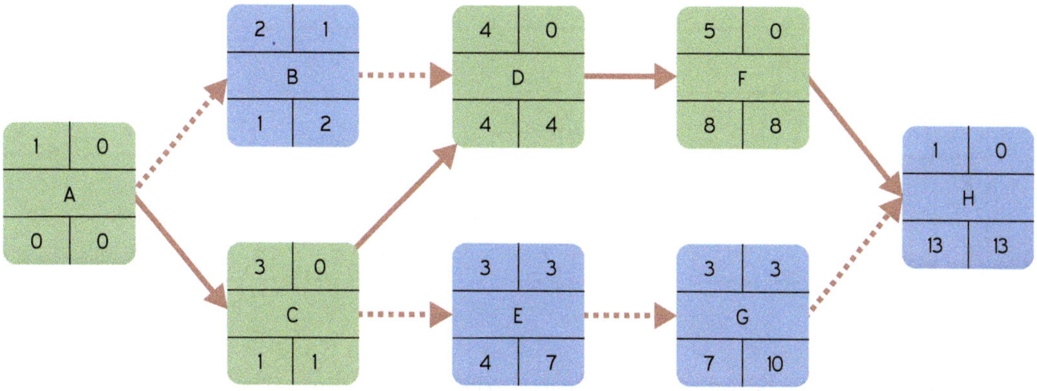

The critical path can be identified by inspection, but there is a rule that takes away any chance of our missing a path in the network. We start by working out the *earliest start times* (EST) for the activities through the network: work forwards from the first activity, adding the times for each of the activities and recording them. This gives the earliest possible start times for the activities. This calculation is then repeated backwards, starting with the completion time for the last activity, based on the longest path through the network. This gives the *latest start time* (LST) for each activity – the latest time it can start without affecting the total project duration. The critical path is the route through the network which has matching LST and EST times, and this is of course the longest path. Activities on the critical path have no slack or spare time, and must start when the previous activity is finished, otherwise the project will overrun.

Figure 11.14 shows the way we can now redraw the nodes of the network diagram to show all the information we would like to see at a glance, including the name of the activity, its duration, EST, LST and float. Using the convention in Figure 11.14, the network example from Figure 11.13 can now be redrawn, and is shown in Figure 11.15. It becomes clear which activities lie on the critical path and also how much slack or float time is available for each activity.

The forward and backward calculation approach effectively determines the float of activities – the amount of slack time between having to start the activity and getting the project finished on time, and the earliest possible time the activity could be started. This is useful for balancing the demand on resources without disturbing the total project time. For example, we might have two activities needing bricklayers scheduled for the same week. However, if one of the activities had a week of slack, then we could delay its start and use the same team for one run of two weeks instead of having to recruit two sets of bricklayers. This would be cheaper and less complex for us.

CPM: Crashing Times and Costs

Another important use of CPM is in exploring *trade-offs* between project time and cost. It is common for the duration of an activity to be reduced by extra investment (perhaps in more people, or in more or better machines), and CPM allows the project manager to balance this extra cost and total project time. A term used in this approach is *crashing* an activity. A crashed activity cannot be reduced further, no matter how much extra money is spent. For example, there is nothing we can do to cut the time for baking biscuits in the factory once we have invested in a new production line and ovens; biscuits need time to bake. Similarly, you cannot put more female resources together to help gestate a human baby quicker than 9 months.

A common example is when cost penalties arise as projects exceed certain dates and the manager has to determine whether it is worth spending money on crashing the project or taking the penalty.

WORKED EXAMPLE 11.1

University Gas Pipe

The table below describes a project to lay a new gas pipe across the university campus:

Activity	Precedes	Normal time (days)	Crash cost per day	Crash time (days)
A	B, C	10	50	6
B	D	6	30	3
C	E	2	–	2
D	F	4	40	3
E	D	6	80	4
F	–	8	100	5

Problem:

(a) *Construct the activity-on-node network diagram.*

(b) *Determine the ESTs, the LSTs, slack, the project duration and the critical path activities.*

(c) *Use the crash cost information to redesign the project so that the work will be completed two days earlier, in time for the start of term.*

Approach:

(a) Draw the network diagram so that the precedence of the activities can be established.

(b) Record the duration, calculate the forward and backward path lengths, and hence the EST, LST and floats. The critical path is where there is zero float.

(c) Concentrating on the critical path, try and reduce individual activity times using the cheapest option, taking care that the critical path is not extended to another route through the network.

Solution:

(a) Draw the diagram (Figure 11.16) by starting with the first activity and working forwards so that the logic shown in the table is transferred to the diagram. So, from above, activity A is first, and must be completed before B and C can start. D has to follow B and E, and E follows just C. F follows D alone.

(b) The duration of each activity is written in the node as shown (A lasts 10 days, etc.). Use these times to work out the EST for each activity/node. So the earliest B and C can start is when A is finished, that is,

Figure 11.16 Network diagram before crashing, showing the critical path

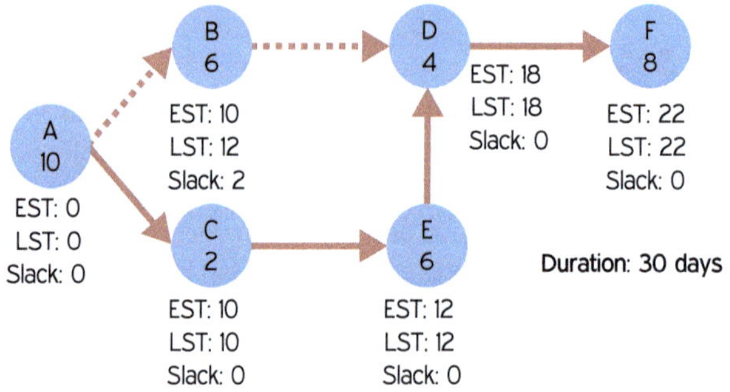

Figure 11.17 First step: showing network reduced by 1 day from D

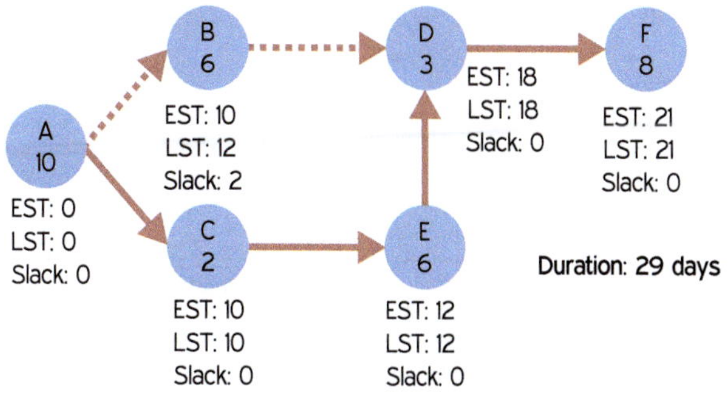

Figure 11.18 Solution showing the crashed network

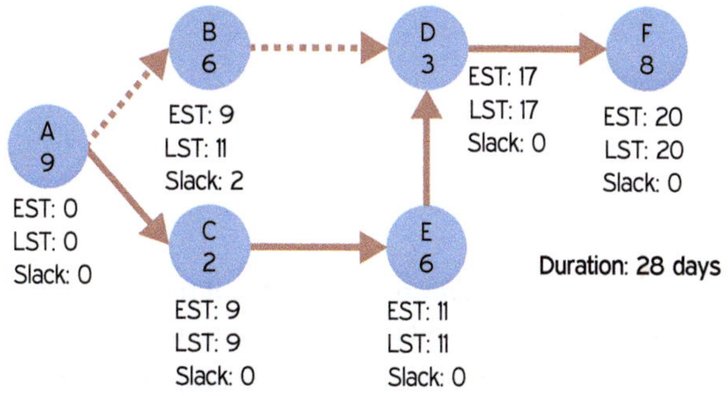

after 10 days. D can start after B, which would be 16 days (10 for A and 6 for B), but actually D cannot start until E is finished, which cannot be until 18 days (10 for A, 2 for C and 6 for D). F starts 4 days after D (D starts after 18 and takes 4 days itself). The total duration of the project is 30 days, as we need to add the 8 days for F to its start time of 22. This completes the forward pass.

To work out the LST, start at the end of the project with F and work backwards. As the project will take 30 days in total, the latest that F can start without the end time changing is 22 (30 less the 8 days for F). The LST for D is 18 (4 days before F needs to start). E must start at latest 6 days before D starts, which is 12 (18 for D, less 6 for E), and similarly for C and A: their LSTs are the same as their ESTs – they are on the critical path, as we can see. B, on the other hand, has an LST of 12, as it has to be finished for D to start, and D has to start at latest on day 18. Hence B can start on day 12 and still be finished without delaying D. Where the EST and LST are the same, this is the critical path, shown in Figure 11.16 in bold.

(c) The project duration needs to be reduced by 2 days. The cheapest and so the first choice to reduce the critical path is D, which is reduced by 1 day at a cost of £40. We should check and see whether the critical path has changed, in this case whether B has lost its float. Figure 11.17 is the new network diagram. B still has its 2 days' slack, so there is no change in the critical path. Now we can look for the next day to take out of the project.

D cannot be reduced any further, and so we need to look for the next cheapest on the critical path, which is A, which can be reduced by 1 day at a cost of £50. The new network is shown in Figure 11.18.

Final result: the project has been reduced by 2 days, at a total cost of £90.

The key point is ...

that we can nearly always change the duration of an activity by spending money. However, the project manager has to know whether this is a good use of his or her limited funds.

Figure 11.19 GANTT chart showing slack times and resource utilization

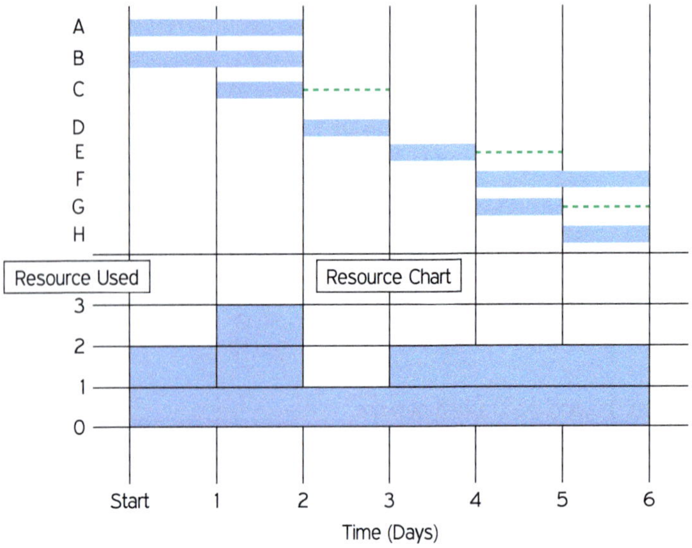

Resource Allocation

As well as defining the timing of activities and the overall length of the project, another important activity in scheduling is planning which resources are needed, and how much of each one.

If we think again about the London 2012 Olympics and Crossrail projects, in both cases it was realized early on that they would be unable to recruit the number of specialist trades that they needed. As a result, both project teams set up apprentice schemes to ensure they had sufficient trained resources to complete the project plan. An alternative approach to acquiring or training the necessary skilled resources is to examine the project plan and see whether changes to it might help with resource constraints.

Figure 11.19 shows how Gantt charts can be extended to show the loading of resources, or in this case the number of employees needed for the project. The section at the foot of the bar chart uses the same time axis to show the resource demand throughout the project.

The load diagram shows the usage of the resources as the project develops, and some constraints can be easily identified. In Figure 11.19 it is clear that we need three workers on the second day, but the rest of the project could be completed with one or two per day.

Resource Levelling

The above example is based on resource allocation against the earliest start times for the activities, but given the slack in the project it may be possible to schedule the activities to smooth the resource demand. The reason why we expressly calculated the float or slack time before was not only so that we could establish the critical path, but also to help identify when activities could be rescheduled to help with the loading of resources. Looking again at Figure 11.19, the dotted lines show which activities can be rescheduled within their float or slack time. Moving these activities would have no effect on the critical path or total length of the project.

Resource levelling: the practice of using float to improve the resources needed in a project.

Figure 11.20 shows that by considering the timing of one activity we can level the resource needed. By delaying the start time of activity C, the project can now be completed with a level resource usage of just two employees. **Resource levelling** has the advantage of keeping staffing levels constant, and so reducing the number of resources that need to be moved on and off the project.

Stop and Think

How might the ideas covered in this chapter on project scheduling help you complete a group project for your course?

Figure 11.20 Balancing resources by moving activities within slack

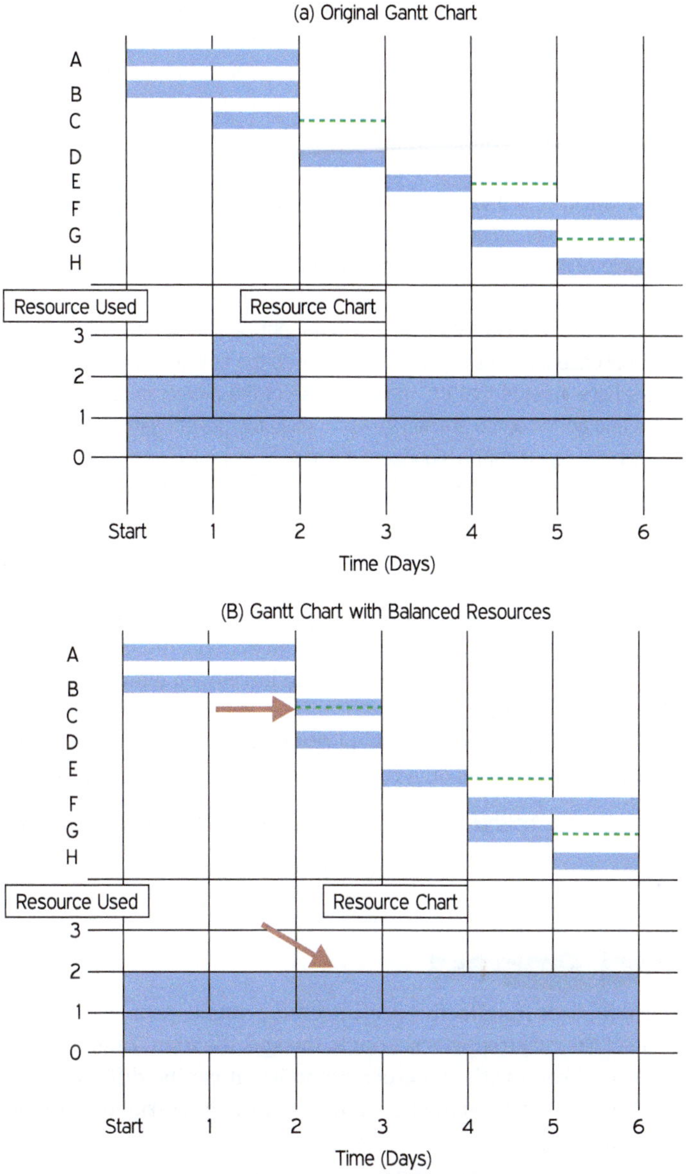

SHORT CASE 11.3

Bolshoi Ballet Renovation

Source: ©Mistervlad/Shutterstock

The world famous Bolshoi Ballet Company was founded in 1776 as the Imperial Bolshoi Theatre of Moscow. Its home is now in Theatre Square, Moscow, and the current building was designed by architect Andrei Mikhailov and built in 1824 to replace the Petrovka Theatre, which was destroyed by fire in 1805.

The Bolshoi Theatre was closed for a planned four-year restoration in 2005, but the project was beset with numerous problems. The theatre has been renovated several times in its history, but this project was the largest, and was initially budgeted at a cost of 15 billion roubles ($610 million). However, once engineers started work, they identified significant weaknesses with the existing foundation, which meant that 75% of it needed to be replaced. Additionally they discovered a river flowing through the foundation, which needed to be diverted. Much of the extra work on the foundation was the result of the unexpectedly poor condition of previous restoration work.

The renovation was intended to restore the theatre to its original acoustics, which were substantially changed during Soviet era renovations, and to do this the theatre's interior has been totally removed. This includes the 19th-century wooden fixtures, silver stage curtain and red velvet banquettes, which have all been removed for repair. The two-headed eagle of the original Russian coat of arms has been reinstalled in place of the Soviet hammer and sickle that was there before.

The project was further complicated by the involvement of the Russian authorities who funded the work, with their sense of national pride and artistic perfection adding to the stringent quality standards the project had to meet. These stakeholders have insisted that the main purpose of the project is to create an international treasure with excellent acoustics and performance ambience. As a result, the project saw important changes to the specification as it developed. Each change meant a significant rethink of the project, which in some cases led to the reworking of completed stages. It eventually reopened in 2011 and estimates of the total cost of the project are as high as $1.1 billion.

Questions

1. What were the sources of changes to the project plan? Think about both those from the uncertain nature of the work itself and also those from artistic and governance interventions.
2. Which of the changes you have identified could have been managed, and which were beyond the realm of the project manager?
3. How might the project manager have kept track of how the project was developing, and what would you like to see reported on a regular basis if you were in charge?

Sources: http://rt.com/news/bolshoi-theatre-restoration-delay/; www.bolshoi.ru/en/theatre/reconstruction/

Managing Project Progress

Given that there are three objectives for effective project management – to meet time deadlines, to stick to the costs set in the budget, and to meet the requirements set out in the specification – and given that the project may consist of a number of work packages, each with numerous activities, it can be difficult to report progress against this complex situation without giving long, detailed explanations. Imagine trying to report the delays in the Boshoi Ballet Renovation (Short Case 11.3).

For example, consider a project with a budget of £4 million, lasting 24 months, and with four goals set in the project specification. If the project is about halfway in month 12, the firm has spent £3 million, and one objective has been reached: is the project on time, within budget, and to specification? It is not possible to say with this information. To be able to give a clear explanation, the project manager must concentrate on the stakeholder group being addressed. Each group may have a different view of how the project's progress should be expressed. An internal audience may focus on cost, an external stakeholder may focus more on time, and the customer on all three objectives. In order to avoid ambiguity and information overload, there is a method that attempts to clarify the situation objectively: it is referred to as **earned value reporting (EVR)**.

Earned value reporting (EVR): a means of monitoring projects, based on key measures of completion against estimated cost or schedule.

Variance and Earned Value

Earned value is a tool to report how much work has been accomplished on a project, and can be used as a simple way to monitor progress. The term *variance* is used to describe deviation from the planned schedule or budget. Both the schedule and budget need to be considered simultaneously because:

- *Cost variance* refers only to the budget, and does not measure the differences or variances between scheduled work to be completed and actual work completed

Figure 11.21 Cost–schedule comparison

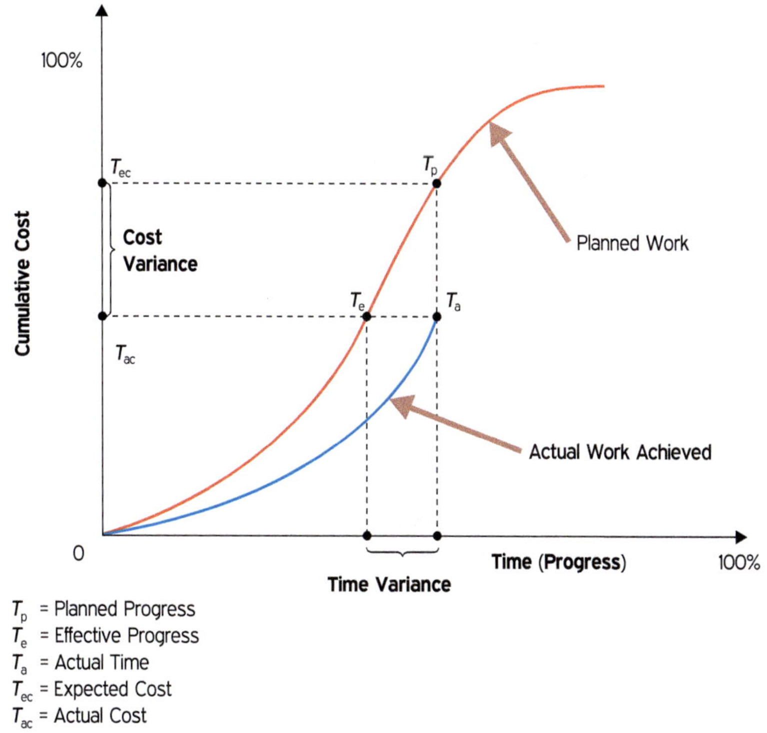

Figure 11.22 Cost–schedule speculation

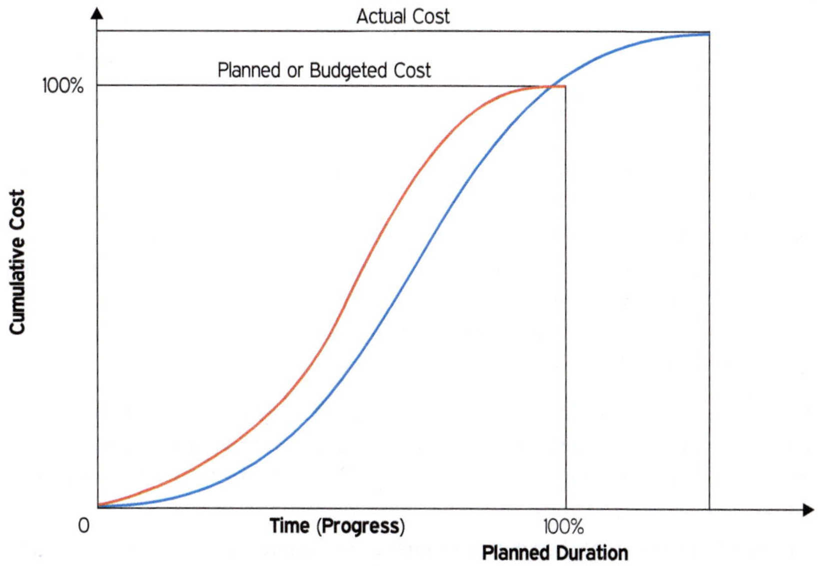

- *Schedule variances* provide a comparison between planned work completed and actual work completed, but do not report on cost.

These are shown in Figure 11.21, which compares the cost of the project with the time the project has been under way. The figure reviews progress at time T_a, and shows the project is currently behind schedule, as progress is less than planned. However, the expected cost to date (T_{ec}) was forecast in the project plan, and is less than the total actual cost (T_{ac}), as shown in the diagram. If we take the curve and extend it to the end, as in Figure 11.22, the project may be looking at late delivery, and in this case it looks like it may not be able to stick to the budget either. This is only speculation, but it shows how the EVR tool provides early warning of problems.

Figure 11.23 Earned value chart

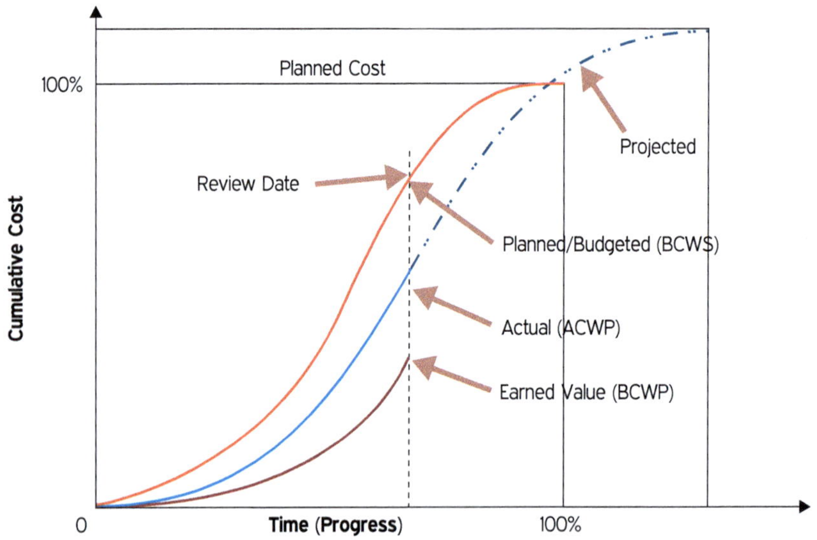

BCWS – Planned or Budgeted Cost of Work Scheduled
ACWP – Actual Cost of Work *Performed*
BCWP – Budgeted Cost of Work ***Actually Performed*** (or Earned Value)

A difficulty in comparing actual and budgeted expenditure is that, for a given period, the comparison fails to take into account the amount of work achieved in relation to the cost incurred. To help with this problem, the earned value of the work done (often expressed as the *value completed*) is found by multiplying the estimated percentage completion of work for each task/activity in progress by the planned cost of those tasks/activities. This can then be used to make an estimate of overall completion of the project, by adding all these calculations for all tasks completed plus those in progress.

In practice, there are some important questions to ask about a project, that help in understanding the relationships between cost and work:

- Actual costs are less than the budget. Is the project doing well, or is it behind schedule?
- The project's actual costs are higher than budgeted, and the project is only halfway complete. What is the project likely to cost at completion?
- The project manager continually tells us not to worry about the cost overruns. The rest of the work will cost less than budgeted. Is this probable?

EVR charts can be used to derive certain measures that allow us to quickly identify project status and so answer these questions. Earned value is accurately measured as *budgeted cost of work performed* (BCWP), and is normally compared with the *actual cost of the work performed* (ACWP) and *budgeted cost of work scheduled* (BCWS), as shown in Figure 11.23.

Typically, variances are defined so that they will give a negative number when the project is behind, or over budget. It is also possible to project the actual costs forward, with the assumption that if the performance continues, this is how the overall project might turn out. We can see that we are able to calculate the cost variance, as it is the difference between the amount budgeted for the work and that performed to date: budgeted cost of work performed or earned value (BCWP) minus the actual work performed (ACWP):

$$\text{Cost variance (CV)} = \text{BCWP} - \text{ACWP}$$

Similarly, we would also be interested in the variance in schedule, calculated as the difference between the budgeted cost of work performed or earned value (BCWP) and the budgeted cost of work scheduled (BCWS):

$$\text{Schedule variance} = \text{BCWP} - \text{BCWS}$$

Figure 11.24 Possible arrangements of ACWP, BCWP and the planned (BCWS)

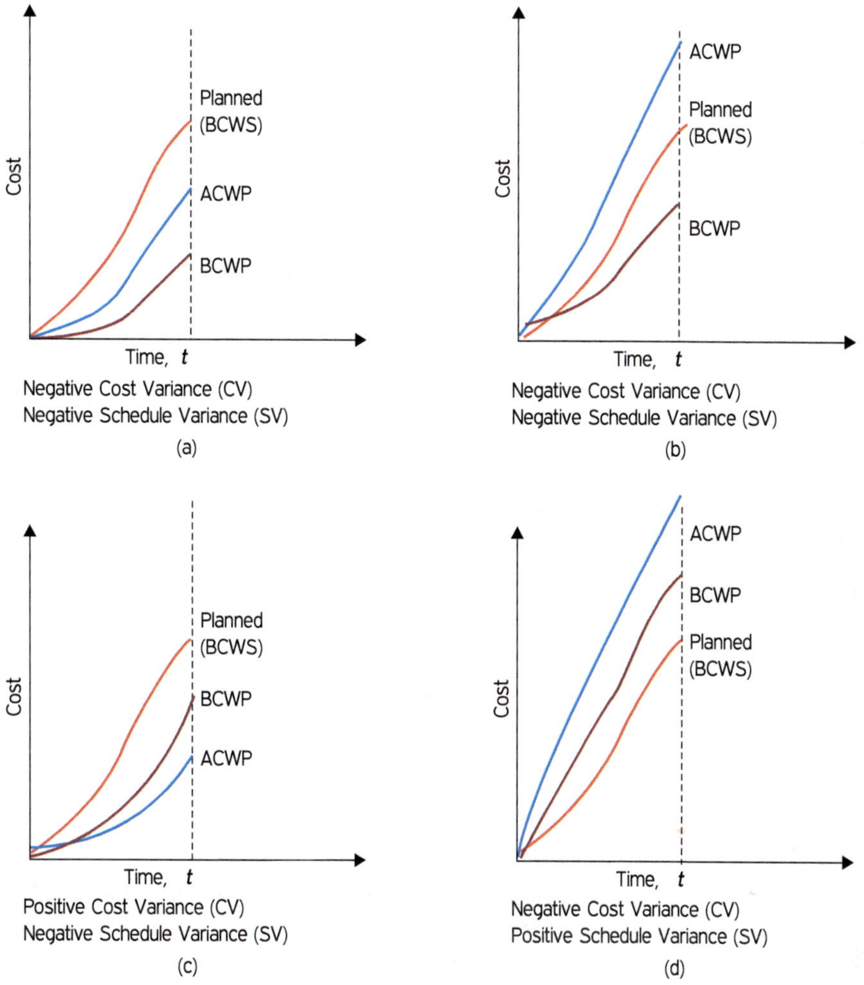

The different situations relating to the variances are shown in Figure 11.24. Note the way that the different measures give an indication not only of the source of the problem but also of its severity.

Tracking Project Ratios

Combining the values of variance into index values tells us even more quickly how the project is progressing. In general, indices of 1.0 show the project to be on schedule, whereas values below 1.0 are unfavourable. Again, as above, we are interested in both the cost and the schedule and so have one index for each, and also an overall measure for the project. These are:

$$\text{Cost performance index (CPI)} = \frac{\text{BCWP}}{\text{ACWP}}$$

$$\text{Schedule performance index (SPI)} = \frac{\text{BCWP}}{\text{BCWS}}$$

$$\text{Cost–schedule index} = \text{CPI} \times \text{SPI}$$

With these indices there is no need for a long, detailed explanation of progress, and the trend in value taken over time can be tracked. If the values are within accepted limits, then there is no need for managerial action.

WORKED EXAMPLE 11.2

EVR: Project Management Tracking Indices

Given a project with:

ACWP = £1,500
BCWS = £1,000
BCWP = £800 (earned value)

Problem: *Calculate the CSI index, and determine whether it is managerially satisfactory.*

Approach/solution:

$$\text{CSI} = \frac{£800}{£1{,}500} \times \frac{£800}{£1{,}000}$$
$$= 0.427$$

So CSI < 1, indicating a problem. We can see that we have spent nearly twice as much as planned for the work performed so far (CPI), and also that we are running behind schedule (SPI).

The key point is ...

that while we may have the most elaborate project plans and budgets, we need to be able to track progress, and tie this directly into what we expected to have achieved. Failure to do so means that the project is effectively out of control.

Managing People

This chapter started by talking about how many companies are re-engineering their functionally oriented organizations in order to focus on key business processes, and enable project-based working. Companies such as General Electric have stressed the need to promote flexible organization: 'The challenge, for us, is to strip and break down walls that cramp people, inhibit creativity and waste time' (GE's Annual Report, 2010). Companies such as DuPont, IBM, Hewlett-Packard, Renault and GM have launched major efforts to create high-performance teams using techniques such as kaizen and Six Sigma (explored in more depth in Chapter 13).

Chapter 13, p429

Within project-based organizations the pressure to perform is even greater, as each project is temporary and so needs to quickly set up, define its own structure and style, and then begin to perform. This section will look briefly at the ideas surrounding building and managing effective teams, as these are highly important to project managers trying to accomplish their three performance criteria of cost, time and specification.

Project Teams

Teams are groups of individuals who cooperate to carry out a joint task. They may be assigned to specific work roles, or operate a more flexible system where roles are shared. A *project team* is a group organized to work together to accomplish a set of objectives that cannot be achieved effectively by individuals. Organizational barriers, such as infrastructure, policies and procedures, all have an impact on how the team performs.

Forming Teams

There are some basic principles in team formation, and these are referred to as the *team paradigm:*

- Teams are task oriented rather than functionally focused
- Teams hold a single organization view, which promotes unity rather than conflict
- Teams have participative leadership rather than remote supervision
- In teams, power, conflict and emotion are seen as anti-productive forces.

So lines of command and control are replaced by links based on influence and common interest.

Three attributes are usually considered when building membership of a project team:

- Technological, business or commercial skill (professional orientation)
- Time and cost consciousness (goal orientation)
- Ability to work with different types of people (team orientation).

In choosing members of a team, technical skill is usually the first consideration, with the second attribute time and cost consciousness. It is often the case with operations managers and engineers that business or organizational skills are a poor relation to their armoury of technical skills. Indeed, 'soft' or people-related skills are often viewed with less enthusiasm than the 'harder' technical skills, but we have already seen the nature of projects, and the focus on a single goal demands that these are all equally important.

Team Roles

As a team is made up of a number of individuals, they typically include many patterns of behaviour, and a key aspect of success is ensuring the members interact effectively. This can be described as creating a *team spirit,* and is a source of synergy. Successful teams refer to themselves and colleagues in complimentary terms, as together they can achieve more than the sum of their individual contributions. There are four interlocking principles that guide team designers:

- There is a balance between functional roles and team roles
- Members of teams are able to adjust themselves to the relative strengths within the team, both in expertise and in specific team roles
- Personal qualities make team members suited to some team roles and weak in others
- A team can deploy its technical resources to best advantage only when it has a full range of team roles to ensure efficient teamwork.

There are a number of frameworks used to identify the roles. One of the most useful is that of Belbin (1981), which defined the characteristics of team members. These frameworks argue that most of the roles need to be present for a team to be effective. For example, a team made up solely of manager types, who are strong on coordinating, managing resources and monitoring the project, will not make progress without the creative and diligent types that design and carry out the work.

Belbin's team roles:

- *Plant:* creative, imaginative, unorthodox . . .
- *Resource investigator:* enthusiastic, communicative, extrovert . . .
- *Coordinator:* mature, confident . . .
- *Shaper:* challenging, dynamic, thrives on pressure . . .
- *Monitor evaluator:* sober, strategic and discerning . . .
- *Teamworker:* cooperative, mild, perceptive . . .
- *Implementer:* disciplined, reliable . . .
- *Completer:* painstaking, conscientious, anxious . . .
- *Specialist:* single-minded, self-starting . . .

Leading Teams

Leadership is crucial in projects for inspiration, motivation and direction. At its purest it generates an emotional connection between the leader and the team as can be seen in the SQ318 case (Short Case 11.4). There are various interpretations of leadership, which are summarized in Figure 11.25.

The difference between a manager and a leader is that leadership implies inspiration and directing from the front, whereas management is concerned with control. There are many examples of leadership, with the best political leaders able to mobilize support around their ideas and visions. They rarely instruct their colleagues, but inspire support based on the ideas they communicate.

Leaders have been shown to adopt a combination of the following roles when needed:

- *Directing:* autocratic style, appropriate to use with people who lack competence but are committed to their work.

Figure 11.25 Suggested graduations in leadership

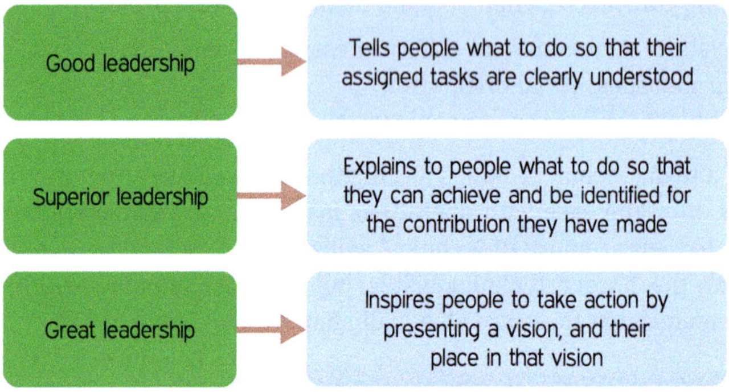

- *Coaching:* appropriate to use with people who have competence but lack commitment. A project manager should encourage decision-making, although the style would be directional. Explanations for decisions would be given, and suggestions would be solicited.
- *Supporting:* appropriate to use with people who have competence but lack motivation. A project manager need not always give direction, as an expert in a discipline will always know better, but support is important to boost confidence.
- *Delegating:* appropriate for people who have both competence and commitment.

Positive leadership is the single greatest factor contributing to a project's success or failure; therefore leadership is one of the most important competencies of a project manager. There are some fundamental leadership qualities among effective project managers.

- *Style:* use of a combination of directive and supportive relationships as appropriate. This is especially useful because project teams consist of individuals of widely varying expertise.
- *Analytical:* in order to achieve technical project goals, the project manager needs to be analytical, to understand the technical subtleties.
- *Collaborative:* to surmount the boundaries between the organizational units in order to accomplish something in the interest of the larger organization. Avoiding negative criticism; always preferring constructive criticism.
- *Organizational know-how:* project managers need to be sensitive to the needs of the senior managers, recognize cultural barriers, build networks, and develop an organizational insight.
- *Negotiative:* project managers should be accomplished negotiators. They are required to negotiate with the functional department managers for resources – both people and material. They must also negotiate when overcoming obstacles, driving towards project goals, and dealing with poor performance.
- *Affable:* in general, if you are to work with people, then you must be able to get on with them. Getting on means being a good listener, understanding differing points of view, and above all being culturally sensitive. Cultural sensitivity addresses issues of differences and ensuring thoughtfulness and inclusiveness.

Stop and Think

Think of a person you regard as a great leader. Do they exhibit all or just some of the roles seen above? Do they need to be exemplary in all to complete their job?

SHORT CASE 11.4

Mr Chai's SQ318 Team and Singapore Airlines

When Mr Jones got on flight SQ318 from Singapore's Changi Airport to London Heathrow after a successful business trip, he was thinking about how he might best run the new luxury hotel project he had just signed. As the trip unfolded, he was given much inspiration.

At first glance, the work of a super-jumbo cabin crew may not seem a good example of a project, which can be defined as a temporary organization with one purpose. However, as the crew members are all brought together for just one trip, and each trip may have a different number of passengers and route, it could be called a project.

What struck Mr Jones most about his flight was the way the In-flight Supervisor, Mr Chai, set a tone of professionalism and focus on service that permeated his crew of 24 and made the trip exceptional. Right from the start, it was clear that this crew was working well as a team, with each knowing their own tasks, but also freely helping each other, and being relaxed and confident in providing for the needs of the customers. Mr Chai came on the intercom as the plane taxied, and as well as the usual safety messages, he introduced the key team members in each cabin, welcomed his guests and in particular the newlyweds in 33E and F, and thanked the passengers for choosing Singapore Airlines.

Mr Chai's leadership style was to lead by example, as he seemed to be all over the plane, serving the food, collecting rubbish and crockery, and chatting with nearly every one of the 450 passengers on the packed flight. Mr Chai's demeanour spread through his colleagues, who all followed his lead – from the very attentive and personal service for the passenger in seat 51C, who didn't get the choice of meal he wanted, but was showered with extra bread rolls and desserts to take his mind off it, to the help given to the families with babies, making the trip as comfortable as possible for them, and also for their neighbouring passengers.

As the plane landed in London, Mr Chai was again on the intercom, passing on the wishes of his crew to the passengers, leaving no one out from those returning home, going on holiday, returning to study after the break, undertaking business, and of course the honeymooners. He received a round of applause from both the passengers and his crew as he finally signed off.

Mr Jones was impressed, and then remembered that Singapore Airlines has received numerous awards for its standard of service, and claims to be 'The World's Most Awarded Airline'. He now understood how they had achieved this, with a focus on service that was epitomized by Mr Chai and delivered by his team.

Questions

1. Think about Belbin's list of team roles, and list which of them relate to the different jobs of the cabin crew.
2. Which of the list of fundamental leadership styles did Mr Chai use on the flight?

Source: www.singaporeair.com/mediacentre/pacontent/news/NE_5307.jsp

Ending Projects

We have already seen in the PRINCE2 methodology that the end of a project is equally as critical as the other stages. Ending a project is about ensuring that all the objectives have been met, that the resources and contractual obligations have been completed, that personnel have found new projects to work on, and that the organization has recorded the important aspects learnt in carrying out the project. A key part of this is the *project audit,* which is a formal inquiry into the project to validate the original business feasibility studies, to reassure top management of the completion and effective running of the project, and to confirm the organization's readiness to move on to the next project or phase. An organization needs to store the lessons learned from one project to apply to another, and prevent making similar mistakes again.

Projects by their nature are temporary, and so each one will have its own measure of success. The primary measure is to what extent it has achieved its objectives. Again, PRINCE2 makes this exercise of reviewing success an explicit part of the project process. A major reason why projects fail is called *scope creep;* this happens when stakeholders keep changing the specification of the project as it progresses, as demonstrated earlier in the Bolshoi Ballet example in Short Case 11.3. There are many public sector projects where changes in political leadership mean that the aims or content of the project often change. Such revisions to the project goals make managing the work itself virtually impossible, and often work packages become distorted and do not fit together, and so the project eventually becomes unmanageable. An example of this was the UK's attempt at electronic patient records in the National Health Service, where the original aim of digitizing records was constantly revised as the original needs of the family doctor were changed to accommodate hospitals and the changing layers in management systems of the health service. Another example is the delays to the certification phase in the building for the World Cup (Short Case 11.5).

The key point is ...

that as organizations move towards project-based work, they need to introduce ways to capture and learn experiences for future work, as the individuals may not stay within the firm.

SHORT CASE 11.5

QATAR 2022 World Cup Stadium Delay

Source: ©EQRoy/Shutterstock

Progress for the QATAR World Cup initially progressed well. Two new stadiums were completed on time in 2019, the brand new 40,000-capacity Al-Janoub stadium and the 45,350 seat Education City stadium. Five other new stadiums were also nearing completion and the previous national stadium, Khalifa International, had been refurbished.

However, plans for inauguration matches in the new venue for the final, the Education City stadium, were delayed. It was due to hold the World Club Cup finals in December 2019 but the certification process was not completed in time and so the matches were played at Khalifa International.

'Construction at Education City stadium is complete and the venue is now operational', FIFA said in a 2019 statement. However, the necessary certification process took longer than expected and therefore the stadium was unable to host the required full capacity test events prior to the semi-final and final of the FIFA Club World Cup. 'The priority is to ensure an enjoyable experience for all fans so it was decided to open the stadium at a later date.'

Questions

1. Why do you think the final stages of building the stadium, gaining certification, have been given as the reason for the delay?
2. Would adopting a methodology like PRINCE2 have made the organizers more aware of the problems than not using a structured approach?

Source: https://www.thenews.com.pk/latest/580038-certification-problems-delay-launch-of-qatars-new-2022-world-cup-stadium

Summary

This chapter has examined project management, an area of growing importance in operations management. It started with a definition that projects are temporary organizations, tasked with carrying out just one purpose. It is important for people involved in projects to appreciate that there is more than one way to look at the project. Often people focus on purely the internal view of achieving the cost, time and performance targets of the project, but neglect the importance of thinking like an outside stakeholder. Looking at the project from the point of the outside stakeholders allows the project management team to meet its commitments to those whom the project ultimately serves.

Projects make unusual demands on the organization, as there are alternative ways in which the firm can be organized to deliver the project. Many organizations are looking to adopt flatter structures, which focus the power to make decisions on front-line staff, and moving towards the project-based organization is one way to achieve this.

Successful project managers need a high level of both technical and leadership skills, including familiarity with scheduling and resource allocation techniques. But while tools such as PRINCE2 ensure that all the key steps in projects are completed in a controlled manner, project management involves much more than step-by-step problem-solving. There is a high degree of complexity and uncertainty involved in all but the simplest of projects, and understanding teams and developing leadership skills are vital for handling complexity and overcoming uncertainty.

Key Theories

The key theories discussed in this chapter were:

- **Project-based organization** – a shift from functional organization structure, via the matrix organization, to one where the project is the focus of attention.
- **Project management framework** – a structured approach, such as PRINCE2 or PMBOK, to ensure that all steps are covered and stakeholders considered in completing a project.
- **Critical path management** – an approach to managing projects that focuses on the activities that determine the total length of the project.
- **Belbin's team roles** – a list of team member characteristics, the inclusion of which ensures a balance between doers and planners.

Key Equations

$$\text{Float for an activity} = \text{Latest start time} - \text{Earliest start time}$$

$$\text{Cost variance (CV)} = \text{BCWP} - \text{ACWP}$$

$$\text{Schedule variance} = \text{BCWP} - \text{BCWS}$$

$$\text{Cost performance index (CPI)} = \frac{\text{BCWP}}{\text{ACWP}}$$

$$\text{Schedule performance index (SPI)} = \frac{\text{BCWP}}{\text{BCWS}}$$

$$\text{Cost–schedule index} = \text{CPI} \times \text{SPI}$$

where BCWS = planned or budgeted cost of work scheduled; ACWP = actual cost of work *performed;* and BCWP = budgeted cost of work *actually performed* (or earned value).

Suggested Answers to Stop and Think Questions

1. **Different organization forms for different situations:** (a) The head office, including the sales, IT and accounting departments, are very functionally focused, and so this kind of structure is probably more suited. (b) The commissioning department, which arranges different experts to produce a package of materials, is effectively managing a number of projects simultaneously, and so a matrix structure would work well. (c) Relocating to a new building is a pure project activity, with its temporary structure and single purpose.
2. **Applying project scheduling to an assignment:** Being able to develop and produce a plan for the project, including a schedule to complete by the deadline, is useful in monitoring progress. Regular meetings will show when something is running late and some more resource might be needed to get back on track.

3. **Identifying leadership style:** Leaders come from many different walks of life, and some can be successful with only a few of the roles. Charismatic and autocratic style can be sufficient for political leaders, whereas business leaders normally need to exhibit technical skills to be able to control their organization, and maintain the support and respect of others.

connect

Review Questions

1. What is the definition of a project?
2. Name the organization styles as they move from the functional to pure project-based form.
3. What can increase the complexity of a project?
4. List the eight processes of the PRINCE2 framework, and give an example for each one.
5. What is the critical path for a project?
6. Why is the critical path important?
7. Why does EVR have both schedule and cost variance elements?
8. List Belbin's team roles, and identify which one(s) you most regularly carry out in class work.
9. Why do you think the ending of projects is often overlooked?

Discussion Questions

1. Why do you think there are more projects today than ever before?
2. Why would an 'outside looking in' approach provide a useful perspective on project management?
3. Discuss three projects you are aware of that have not been delivered on time, or within budget, or have not met the planned outcome or specification. Why did they fail?
4. Why are matrix structures difficult to manage?
5. Are PRINCE2 and PMBOK the same or different? Discuss.
6. How do project managers develop a project schedule?
7. Using EVR to monitor and report project progress is dependent on the accuracy of the information fed into the measures. Is this an accurate critique?
8. Of all of the competencies and preferred behaviours of a project manager, which do you think are the most difficult to develop or achieve?
9. Evaluate the problems not closing a project properly can generate for the organization.

Problems

1. Table 11.3 shows a list of activities needed to develop a new vaccine along with their immediate predecessors and their durations.

Table 11.3 Activity precedence and durations

Activity	Immediate predecessors	Duration (days)
A	–	2
B	–	3
C	A	4
D	A	5
E	C	6
F	D	3
G	D and B	4
H	E	7
I	F	2
J	F and G	3

(a) Using the information in Table 11.3, construct a Gantt chart.

(b) Use the information in Table 11.3 to:

(i) Draw a critical path network for these using the 'activity on arrow' notation.

(ii) Calculate the earliest start times.

(iii) Calculate the latest start times.

(iv) Calculate slack time.

(v) Define the critical path.

(vi) Given the resource available in Table 11.4, state how the resource requirement could be smoothed by 'floating' some of the activities.

Table 11.4 Resource available

Activity	Number of people
A	2
B	3
C	3
D	4
E	5
F	4
G	5
H	6
I	4
J	4

(c) Table 11.5 shows the times by which the activities in Table 11.3 can be crashed (e.g. A cannot be reduced at all, whereas B can be reduced by 1 day maximum), and the cost of doing so. Is it possible that the project can be finished in 17 days, and if so, how much more would that cost?

Table 11.5 Details of crash times possible and cost

Activity	Days to crash	Cost per day (£)
A	0	–
B	1	60
C	2	80
D	0	–
E	1	40
F	0	–
G	1	90
H	2	90
I	0	–
J	1	20

2. The tasks for developing a new game are shown in Table 11.6, with their immediate predecessors and their durations:

Table 11.6 Activity precedence and durations

Activity	Immediate predecessors	Duration (days)
A	–	3
B	A	2
C	A	4
D	A	5
E	B and C	2
F	C	3
G	D	6
H	E F and G	4
I	H	5

(a) Using the information in Table 11.6, construct a Gantt chart.

(b) Using the data in Table 11.6:

(i) Draw a critical path network for these, using the 'activity on node' notation.

(ii) Calculate the earliest start times.

(iii) Calculate the latest start times.

(iv) Calculate slack time.

(v) Define the critical path.

(vi) Given the resource available in Table 11.7, state how the resource requirement could be smoothed by 'floating' some of the activities.

Table 11.7 Resource available

Activity	Number of people
A	4
B	2
C	2
D	3
E	5
F	1
G	2
H	4
I	1

(c) Table 11.8 shows the times by which the activities in Table 11.6 can be crashed (e.g. A can be reduced by 1 day maximum, and B not at all), and the cost of doing so. Is it possible that the project can be finished in 20 days, and how much more would that cost?

Table 11.8 Resource available

Activity	Days to crash	Cost per day (£)
A	1	20
B	0	–
C	2	50
D	1	70
E	0	–
F	0	–
G	2	40
H	1	30
I	0	–

3. A project to design a new website is represented in Table 11.9 which lists the required activities, their immediate predecessors and their durations.

Table 11.9 Activity precedence and durations

Activity	Immediate predecessors	Duration (days)
A	–	2
B	–	3
C	A	1
D	B	4
E	C and D	1
F	D	3
G	E	2
H	F	4
I	G and H	3

(a) Using the information in Table 11.9, construct a Gantt chart.

(b) Using the data in Table 11.9:

(i) Draw a critical path network for these, using the 'activity on node' notation.

(ii) Calculate the earliest start times.

(iii) Calculate the latest start times.

(iv) Calculate slack time.

(v) Define the critical path.

(vi) Calculate the float time. Given the resource available in Table 11.10, state how the resource requirement could be smoothed by 'floating' some of the activities.

Table 11.10 Resource available

Activity	Number of people
A	10
B	20
C	10
D	30
E	40
F	50
G	10
H	30
I	10

(c) Table 11.11 shows the times by which the activities in Table 11.9 can be crashed (e.g. A can be reduced by 1 day maximum, and C not at all), and the cost of doing so. Is it possible that the project can be finished in 15 days, and how much more would that cost?

Table 11.11 Resource available

Activity	Days to crash	Cost per day (£)
A	1	90
B	1	80
C	0	–
D	1	70
E	0	–
F	1	90
G	1	90
H	1	80
I	0	–

4. A firm is developing a new vaccine. Based on the project information in Table 11.3 (question 1 above), after 7 days the project should have activities A, B, C and D completed, and 1/6 (16.7%) of activity E completed. Using the budgeted costs, actual costs and percentage completion for each activity given in Table 11.12:

Table 11.12 Earned value information

Activity	Days' duration	Budget (€)	Actual costs (€)	% complete
A	2	600	680	100
B	3	300	270	100
C	4	800	On budget	80
D	5	400	On budget	25
E	6	400		0

(a) State the BCWS, ACWP and BCWP.

(b) Calculate the schedule variance. Comment on your findings.

(c) Calculate the cost variance. Comment on your findings.

(d) Calculate the CPI. Comment on your findings.

(e) Calculate SPI. Comment on your findings.

(f) Calculate CSI. Comment on your findings.

5. The project manager for the new game project which is detailed in Table 11.6 (question 2 above) wishes to know how well things are going. After 7 days the project should have activities A, B, and C completed, and 4/5 (80%) of activity D completed. Using the budgeted costs, actual costs and percentage completion for each activity given in Table 11.13:

Table 11.13 Earned value information

Activity	Days' duration	Budget (€)	Actual costs (€)	% complete
A	3	500	300	100
B	2	700	790	100
C	4	300	On budget	80
D	5	400	On budget	80

(a) State the BCWS, ACWP and BCWP.

(b) Calculate the schedule variance. Comment on your findings.

(c) Calculate the cost variance. Comment on your findings.

(d) Calculate the CPI. Comment on your findings.

(e) Calculate SPI. Comment on your findings.

(f) Calculate CSI. Comment on your findings.

6. The tasks needed to design a website are shown in Table 11.9 (question 3 above). After 5 days the project should have activities A, B, and C completed, and 2/4 (50%) of activity D completed. Using the budgeted costs, actual costs and percentage completion for each activity given in Table 11.14:

Table 11.14 Earned value information

Activity	Days' duration	Budget (€)	Actual costs (€)	% complete
A	2	9,000	12,000	100
B	3	10,000	21,000	60
C	1	8,000	On budget	100
D	4	20,000	On budget	0

(a) State the BCWS, ACWP and BCWP.

(b) Calculate the schedule variance. Comment on your findings.

(c) Calculate the cost variance. Comment on your findings.

(d) Calculate the CPI. Comment on your findings.

(e) Calculate SPI. Comment on your findings.

(f) Calculate CSI. Comment on your findings.

Further Reading

Davies, A. and Hobday, M. (2005) *The Business of Projects*, Cambridge University Press, Cambridge.

Maylor, H. (2017) *Project Management*, Pearson, Harlow.

Meredith, J. R., Shafer, S. M., & Mantel, S. J. (2019) *Project Management: A Managerial Approach*, John Wiley & Sons, Hoboken, NJ.

Morris, P. W. G., Pinto, J. K., & Söderlund, J. (2018) *The Oxford Handbook of Project Management*, Oxford University Press, Oxford.

Pinto, J. K. (2016) *Project Management: Achieving Competitive Advantage*, Pearson, Boston.

PMI (2017) *A Guide to the Project Management Body of Knowledge (PMBOK Guide)*, Project Management Institute, Newtown Square, PA.

References

Belbin, M. (1981) *Management Teams*, Heinemann, London.

Hepher, T. (2019) Airbus reshuffles supply chain as former autos executive leaves group, *Reuters*. https://www.reuters.com/article/us-airbus-delays/airbus-reshuffles-supply-chain-as-former-autos-executive-leaves-group-idUSKBN1XH1WX (accessed 1 June 2020).

PART 4 Improving

Contents

JOBS

WANTED

Strategic Operations Development Director

We are a global company undergoing tremendous growth. As Strategic Operations Development Director, you will have a vital role in executing policy and strategic development in our organization. You will be responsible for improvement projects – such as the adoption and implementation of new technology and world-class practices.

This position has responsibility for developing and implementing innovative operations strategy, including: (1) developing and maintaining systems to measure key performances against established standards; (2) liaising and cooperating with management, external providers and standards bodies (e.g. ISO, government bodies); (3) establishing necessary communication strategy for the improvement and awareness of quality and innovation across all departments; (4) workforce planning, recruiting, coaching and mentoring operations staff; and (5) being responsible for the constant improvement of organizational performance.

The right candidate will have a relevant master's degree with a minimum of five years of experience in an engineering, manufacturing, service, or performance and quality improvement management role. They are likely to have professional qualifications and a chartered status. They should have a successful track record in process improvement, have effective people skills, and be able to implement change within large teams and inspire others.

How can an Operations Manager improve performance?

We speak to Trevor Stocker, Operations Manager, at Nottingham Express Transit (NET) to find out.

What does NET do?
NET runs a world-class tram network for Greater Nottingham, a large city in the East Midlands of the UK. NET's mission is to get people from A to B as quickly, smoothly and safely as possible – hassle free! Trams are environmentally friendly and low floored, making them accessible for all!

What are you responsible for?
I am responsible for making sure that trams run to schedule, are safe, and well maintained. I ensure staff are trained and available and we meet all performance objectives set by our various stakeholders. I also make sure all our operational processes and IT systems are fit for purpose.

What are the key measures of success?
As part of our operating franchise, we schedule almost a thousand trams services per day, only stopping for Christmas day. NET carries approximately 18 million customers per year and we have a business target to complete 96% of all scheduled trips on time. Therefore attentive management of the network infrastructure, trams, employees (those working on trams and back at the depot), IT systems, scheduling and safety systems are required. We also link with regulatory bodies and community partners. NET is a performance led organization, and data from reporting processes drives constant service improvements.

What are the consequences of poor performance?
If NET does not meet its performance targets as defined in our operating franchise, we will be financially penalized by Nottingham City Council – the owners of the tramway. Poor performance can lead to negative customer feedback affecting our overall patronage and satisfaction levels. Ultimately, if we fail to deliver on our contractual obligations, we can be stripped of the franchise to operate and maintain the tramway. It is therefore imperative that we identify problems quickly and develop clear corrective action plans.

What are NET's future improvement plans?
We aim to continuously improve the quality of our service by analysing our performance data, investing and using our IT systems to capture real-time data and ensuring our staff are highly trained. The management team evaluates business performance in weekly 'visual management' meetings. For instance, we work with the local highways team to ensure better traffic management around the tramway and we are currently implementing 'smart' road signalling solutions.

Why do you like being an operations manager?
My role is very challenging and wide-ranging. For the 15 years I have worked for NET, I feel like I have always been able to make a valuable contribution to the company and to the community served by the tramway. My job requires the ability to work effectively with people, to be able to analyse data, adopt the latest technology and of course, let us not forget the basics, drive a tram!

12 Performance and People Management

Learning Outcomes

After reading this chapter, you should be able to:

- Examine the role of performance management in ensuring effective business performance
- Devise and use performance measures to inform the performance management system
- Analyse and evaluate different performance management methodologies
- Demonstrate how important human resources are to operations performance
- Analyse and implement workforce management plans
- Recruit and motivate a workforce

W.L. Gore & Associates: Gore-Tex Manufacturer

Source: ©Phonix_a Pk.sarote/Shutterstock

Achieving operational excellence is the goal of all organizations, yet very few will ever achieve it. One company which might legitimately claim to perform excellently is W.L. Gore and Associates.

Origins

The company was founded in 1958 in Newark by Wilbert (Bill) Lee Gore and his wife Genevieve. Bill had previously spent 16 years with the DuPont Company specializing in fluoropolymer research. While working in his basement, he developed a process for insulating a series of parallel electrical wires using polytetrafluoroethylene (PTFE) and this led to the company's first patent. The resulting product was named Multi-Tet cable and, demonstrating that in business timing is everything, it found application in the relatively new, but fast growing, industries of computers, communications, and process control equipment.

The company operated from the basement of the Gores' home until 1960, when an order from the Denver Water Company for seven and a half miles of Multi-Tet cable made it necessary to expand manufacturing capacity. A new facility was therefore built in Delaware and by 1970, Gore and its subsidiary companies had manufacturing plants for wire and cable in Arizona, Scotland, Germany and Japan.

While the company was busy finding considerable success manufacturing cable insulation, the product for which W.L. Gore is best known was already in the pipeline. In 1963 Bill and Genevieve's son Bob, a chemical engineer, joined the company. By 1969, he was researching a process for stretching extruded PTFE to make pipe-thread tape. During a series of unsuccessful experiments in which he was attempting to stretch rods of PTFE by slowly applying force to heated PTFE, he applied a sudden, accelerating yank that unexpectedly caused the PTFE material to stretch to around 8 times its original length. This counterintuitive and somewhat surprising result led to a process for transforming solid PTFE into a microporous structure.

The company initially referred to this new material as 'fibrillated PTFE'. Thankfully, a year later, it was given the much more user-friendly name of 'Gore-Tex expanded PTFE' and the product for which the company is best known was born.

Today, expanded PTFE (ePTFE) is the basis for the vast majority of the company's products and W.L. Gore is one of the 200 largest privately held companies in the United States employing almost 10,500 people across the world. In 2019 it posted sales of $3.7 billion.

Organization

While W.L. Gore has become a household name due to a combination of its technical skill and its brand, it is also well known for its operational performance and this is largely due to the way it structures its organization and manages its people. From 1984 to 2017, W. L. Gore earned a position on *Fortune* magazine's annual list of the US '100 Best Companies to Work For'.

Crucial to gaining these awards was Gore's unique structure, which evolved from the company's success with small teams during its early years. This approach was based on Bill Gore's experience with 'task force teams' while he was employed at DuPont. Such groups were usually multidisciplinary and typically operated for short periods of time outside of the company's formal management hierarchy.

Bill Gore first presented the concept of a 'lattice' organization to Gore 'associates' in 1967. He later refined his ideas and presented what he termed 'culture principles' in a paper entitled 'The Lattice Organization – A Philosophy of Enterprise' in 1976.

Unlike a traditional hierarchy Bill Gore proposed a flat, lattice-like organizational structure where everyone shares the same title of 'associate'. There are neither chains of command nor predetermined channels of communication. Leaders replace bosses and associates choose to follow leaders rather than have bosses assigned to them.

Bill Gore articulated four culture principles:

- Associates have the freedom to encourage, help and allow other associates to grow
- Associates should demonstrate fairness to each other and everyone
- Associates are provided with the ability to make one's own commitments and are expected to keep them
- A waterline situation involves consultation with other associates before undertaking actions that could impact the reputation or profitability of the company.

In the lattice organization, associates are encouraged to communicate directly with each other and are accountable to fellow members of their teams. Teams typically organize around opportunities, new product concepts or businesses. As teams evolve, leaders frequently emerge as they gain followership. This unusual organizational structure and culture has been shown to be a significant contributor to company performance, associate satisfaction and retention.

Performance

Despite this unusual degree of freedom Gore doesn't tolerate associates who do not contribute. Indeed, within Gore, the pressure to contribute can be exhausting. People are assumed to be multifaceted, with a wide range of abilities, and no-one is expected to devote all of their time to a single task. Each year, every associate receives a comprehensive peer review. This is shared with a compensation committee comprising individuals from the employee's work area. Each associate is then ranked against every other associate in the business unit. This ranking determines compensation. Seniority has no place in Gore's compensation system, a business leader might be paid less than a scientist. The formula is fixed: the greater the contribution the greater the reward.

While this system clearly differentiates between those who add value and those who don't, the company also strives for inclusivity. Every associate is a shareholder. After their first year at Gore, new associates are awarded 12% of their salary in the form of stock. For many associates Gore stock is their single biggest financial asset. Most associates therefore feel they have a big stake in the company.

Sustainability

As well as performing well as a business, in recent years Gore has committed to performing well as a corporate citizen. As a chemical company Gore's processes have the potential to be damaging to our planet. Over the last 10 years Gore has undertaken a number of initiatives to help save the environment. In 2011 it re-engineered its durable water repellency treatment to be more environmentally friendly; in 2013, it completed the elimination of Perfluorooctanoic Acid (PFOA) from raw materials used in the manufacture of consumer and professional apparel; and in 2015 it launched a social responsibility programme partnering with customers to improve conditions for the workers that make finished products from its fabrics. Currently it is Gore's goal to completely eliminate perfluorocarbons (PFCs) of environmental concern from the life-cycle of all of its consumer laminates by 2023.

Sources: www.gore.com; www.fortune.com; Hamel, G., (2007) *Building an Innovation Democracy*, Path Institute.

Introduction

Performance management can be practised in a number of different ways. The W.L. Gore & Associates case illustrates how one company manages its performance. It is a good example of how high performance can be created using a holistic approach that begins with the corporate strategy and involves the entire organization. All aspects of the organization – for example, the structure, the operating model and the reward system – are included.

Performance management: systematic measuring, monitoring and decision-making geared towards fulfilling organizational objectives.

Perhaps the majority of companies are not as innovative and dynamic when managing performance as W.L. Gore & Associates. But what is clear from this case is that there must be a strong link between performance management and business strategy and it is important to note that how an organization approaches the development and implementation of each impacts on both.

The purpose of this chapter is to introduce the concept of performance management as a conduit for the proactive achievement of organizational objectives. The first step in managing performance successfully is to define what is to be achieved. For this, managers must set over-arching strategic objectives for the organization and ensure these objectives are flowed down to all levels so that they make sense to people wherever they are in the organization and whatever their role is. If the workforce understand clearly what is expected of them, they will be more likely to do it successfully, therefore people and the performance of operations are inseparable. This chapter links directly with the material that was introduced in Chapters 1 and 2 that explained how corporate strategy and operations strategy are created and aligned. It explains how the performance of the operation is measured and managed as managers attempt to implement these strategies.

Chapter 1, p23
Chapter 2, p55

This chapter begins by explaining the mindset that must be adopted when managing performance. It goes on to explain what is required to build and implement a performance management system before describing some of the more well-known performance management models. Then the chapter introduces and explores techniques that ensure people are managed effectively and sympathetically within a high performance operational environment.

What Is Performance Management?

The Performance Management Mindset

Organizational performance can be compared to sporting performance. In sports, the difference between success and failure is usually very clear: there is a competition to be won and the most capable athlete or team will prevail. The outcome of the competition will be measured objectively – for example, the football team that scores the most goals will win the match, the runner who covers the distance most quickly will win the race. Indeed, even in more intangible pursuits such as figure skating or boxing, tangible **performance measures** are used where points are awarded for various aspects of the performance.

Performance measures: factors that the customer will use to judge the performance of a product or service.

In many ways, measuring business performance is similar to measuring sporting performance. Simple, 'outcomes-based' measures are present: the company that sells the most units of product or gains the greatest market share may be considered the most successful. Though it must be stressed that in business and in organizations in the public and not-for-profit sectors, things may be a bit more complex and more subtle measures may be required to allow a useful analysis to be made.

In sports, while outcomes-based measures that indicate who wins and who loses are the most visible manifestation of performance, they provide only part of the picture. An athlete's capability must also be measured. As the athlete trains s/he must have some ongoing indication of how they are likely to perform in future contests. Often capability might be assessed using process-based measures. Process-based measures are generally more numerous than outcomes-based measures and data may be gathered more frequently, sometimes on a daily basis, as the athlete carries out their activities during the process of training. This form of measurement can be complicated as capability is rarely measured in only one way, there are a number of elements to consider, such as strength, speed and endurance. Each element may itself have numerous parameters, each with a different performance measure. In addition, athletes who compete in different sports may use similar measures but aim to meet a different target. For example, the strength required of a particular muscle-group for athletes who compete in weightlifting will be different from that required of the same muscle-group for athletes that compete in long-distance running.

Chapter 2, p55

Like athletes, organizations must measure their capability on an ongoing basis as only by doing this will they be able to assess how fit they are to compete in their markets. In Chapter 2, we introduced the five generic performance objectives of *cost, quality, dependability, speed* and *flexibility*. As operations managers, we must define measures that tell us something useful about our company's performance against these objectives. These measures must be appropriate to the industry context and operational activity in question. For example, we would not measure the dependability of the services provided in a hospital in exactly the same way that we might measure the dependability of the services provided in a hotel.

Performance management systems must be appropriate to their context and they must provide relevant and usable information. Remember, the reason we gather performance data is so we can use it to inform our decision-making about which of our operational capabilities needs to be improved. The basis of all operational improvement programmes is the understanding we gain from analysing the performance data we have collected. This data tells us how we are performing against standards set by ourselves or by industry regulators or by competitors in the market.

As well as ensuring our performance management system gathers appropriate data we must also ensure it gathers data that can tell us something about the future so plans can be made with greater certainty. As operations managers we search for predictability, we want to know how our operation will perform in future yet, rather frustratingly, we can only access data that tells us how it performed in the past. A good performance management system will help us to bridge the gap between past and future performance.

While gathering performance data appropriate to our operational context and ensuring some level of predictability are important, it is also essential to consider the 'manageability' of the performance management system itself. Sometimes the effort expended in the collection of large amounts of performance data can begin to affect the efficient running of the operation. For instance, having a **human resource management** (HRM) system that requires personnel to devote a significant amount of time to gathering, sorting, classifying and analysing data on employees' performance may be counter-productive. Performance management activities must not get in the way of the core operational activity. A performance management system must complement and enhance operational activity without obstructing it.

Human resource management (HRM): the organizational function that deals with issues related to its workforce. HRM may also be seen as a particular perspective on people management and people related issues.

So, in summary, the purpose of a performance management system is to create a flow of useful data that informs management about every facet of the business and it must do this without itself detracting from operational performance by adding unnecessary cost or complexity.

Performance Management's Contribution to Competitive Advantage

Chapter 2, p55

One of the major challenges faced by organizations is to establish coherence between long-term strategic objectives and ongoing operational activity. In practice, what tends to happen is that senior management is clear about corporate objectives, but the rest of the workforce is less well informed. This situation must be avoided and, in Chapter 2, we discussed how operations strategy is generated, and explained how it forms the link between corporate strategy and operational activity. Part of the activity involved in implementing an operations strategy is in ensuring that performance measures are coherent and aligned from the top to the bottom of the organization.

Although a rather hackneyed cliché, it is true to say that 'what gets measured gets done'. Therefore, using performance measures to guide operational activity will ensure that the work being done in all parts of the organization is in line with the overall corporate strategy.

Without a clear 'line of sight' between the strategic objectives set at the top of the company and the operational activity that is happening on the shop-floor, offices and work-centres, individual parts of the organization may begin to wander and eventually may even take their own course. The result is that an organization may lack inter-departmental coherence or, in other words, all parts of the company may not be pulling together to achieve strategic objectives. Different sections may, in effect, be working to their own agendas.

This fragmentation is not always easy to see, it may appear that individual departments are doing well as they are meeting those targets they have set themselves. However, the overall company will be achieving sub-optimally, in other words, from a performance point of view it will be less than the sum of its parts. For example, a single process within a manufacturing system may be producing a large number of parts but if the rate of production in this process is higher than the rest of the system can keep up with, an excess of inventory held in the form of work-in-progress may result. A large amount of work-in-progress is generally considered an indicator of poor performance.

An effective performance management system provides the 'line-of-sight' that prevents parts of the organization from taking their own path.

Stop and Think

What aspects of your organizational structure might make it difficult to ensure performance objectives are aligned throughout your business?

In the Hayes and Wheelwright model introduced in Chapter 2 (see Figure 2.3), one of the main considerations in moving from Stage 1 to Stage 4 is achieving this 'line of sight', across separate parts of the organization. Using this model, one can see that performance management is not just about measuring and gathering data, the model performs a much more useful role in two fundamental ways. First, it is a mechanism to help align objectives vertically within the organization and second, it provides a coordinating role by pulling departments together horizontally across the business. This vertical and horizontal integration, and the coherence it brings to operational activity, is a significant contributor to a company's ability to gain competitive advantage.

Chapter 2, p55

SHORT CASE 12.1

Performance Management Crisis

On 18 March 2009, the *Daily Telegraph* ran the front page headline 'Targets blamed for 1,200 deaths at hospital', and a BBC-televised news programme opened with the same story. There has probably not been a more damning headline implicating performance targets in organizational failure.

Patients admitted for emergency treatment at an NHS Trust in the UK were subjected to 'shocking and appalling' care that included untrained receptionists carrying out medical checks and heart monitors being switched off, a newspaper report stated.

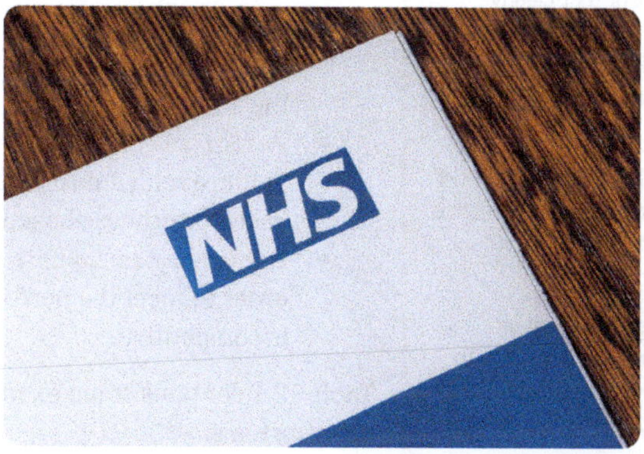

Source: ©chrisdorney/Shutterstock

The Healthcare Commission, the NHS standards watchdog, contended that evidence suggested that as many as 400 deaths at the Mid-Staffordshire NHS Foundation Trust could have been prevented. The commission's investigation, based on more than 300 interviews and an examination of more than 1,000 documents, uncovered inadequately trained staff who were too few in number, junior doctors left in charge at night, operations were repeatedly cancelled and patients were left without food, drink or medication. The Commission heard that some patients were left in soiled bedding for several hours at a time, and were not given their regular medication. Receptionists with no medical training were also expected to assess patients coming into A&E.

Describing the episodes as a 'gross and terrible breach of trust of the patients the NHS seeks to serve', Sir Bruce Keogh, medical director of the NHS, said the report showed there had been a 'complete failure of leadership' at the Trust. He added that: 'I'm proud of the NHS but actually I'm really saddened by this report.'

A consequence of this performance was that the trust's chief executive, Martin Yeates, and its chairman, Toni Brisby, resigned.

One of the reasons proved for this situation was that in order to achieve coveted Foundation status, the Trust management had become obsessed with meeting government targets rather than looking after the sick in its care. David Kidney, the MP for Stafford, suggested that the hospital was too enthusiastic in cost-cutting.

The Commission stated: 'An analysis of the trust's board meetings from April found discussions were dominated by finance.'

This case is set in a time of normal demand. In times of crisis, such as during the global COVID-19 pandemic, performance metrics need to rapidly change so more suitable measures (such as number of tests carried out and medical equipment availability) are captured in favour of the regular administrative measures (such as adherence to budget).

Questions

1. Who are the key stakeholders in a hospital?
2. What performance measures should the Trust have been focusing on?

Sources: *The Times*, 17 March 2009; *Daily Telegraph*, 22 March 2009.

Building a Performance Management System

Components of Performance Management

Now that we have explained the crucial role of performance management in the success of an organization, we must consider what is involved in creating a Performance Management System (PMS) that will provide all the information required, allowing managers to make informed and timely decisions that can steer an organization in the right strategic direction.

Performance objective: a statement that clearly explains what is to be achieved by an operation or part of an operation.

Performance measures: factors that the customer will use to judge the performance of a product or service.

Performance target: this states the level of operational performance to be achieved in order to meet the performance objective.

There are three fundamental components of a PMS. These are performance objectives, performance measures and performance targets.

- **Performance objectives** are statements that clearly explain what is to be achieved by an operation or part of an operation. These will be linked directly to the strategic objectives of the company.
- **Performance measures** are numerical representations of aspects of an operation that are relevant to meeting a performance objective. These may be outcomes-based or process-based.
- **Performance targets** state the level of operational performance to be achieved in order to meet the performance objective. These must be set to ensure the company is competitive.

Table 12.1 contains some examples of how this thinking might be incorporated into operations systems.

Table 12.1 Examples of objectives, measures and targets

Sector	Objective	Measure	Target
Manufacturing	To ensure no unplanned machine stoppages	Number of breakdowns	Zero breakdowns
Manufacturing	To achieve the scheduled production output	Number of products completed	E.g. 100 units
Transport	To provide a reliable service	Lateness measured in minutes after scheduled time of arrival	E.g. < 3 minutes
Transport	To maintain clean vehicles	Number of customer complaints	Zero complaints

CRITICAL PERSPECTIVE

Scoring a Bullseye on the Wrong Target

Setting the correct performance target is crucial. Without knowing what the correct level of performance should be, it is impossible to judge whether actual performance achieved is good, bad or indifferent. For instance, in a call centre, if the performance target is 90% of calls answered within 15 seconds, and the result at month-end showed that 91% of calls had been answered in 15 seconds, this performance might be considered as good.

However, this performance would seem less of a triumph if it was subsequently revealed that the competition consistently achieved 95%; or last month's average had been 98%; or customers expected every call to be answered within 10 seconds.

Conversely, it may also have been revealed that only 50% of calls answered resulted in a satisfactory outcome for the caller during the first call. On further consideration, it may have been better to have a lower response rate with a higher customer resolution outcome during the first call. These different targets could result in different operator behaviour, fewer calls taken but greater caller satisfaction.

The key point is ...

that performance targets must be carefully considered from a number of points of view to ensure that they meet the expectations of all stakeholders.

Principles that Guide Performance Management

We have explained that each part of an operation must be managed against a set of objectives that are linked to the strategic objectives of an organization. Performance against these objectives must be assessed and to do this we must agree the measures to use and the targets to aim for. While there is a lot to consider when deciding on measures and targets, there are four general principles that should be considered when developing a PMS to ensure it is fit for purpose and easy to use.

Simplicity

Measures must be clear and easy to understand. This normally means capturing the data we require using as few measures as possible. Remember that the more measures we have, the more time and effort is required to gather the data and to interpret it. Complexity causes delay between data collection and subsequent action.

Tangibility

While many aspects of an operation may seem intangible and difficult to measure, such as culture or employee motivation, the data we gather must be usable, so where possible we must ensure that data collected can be objectively quantified. Analysis of quantitative data is generally much easier than qualitative data. However, here there is the obvious caveat commonly attributed to Albert Einstein that 'Not everything that can be counted counts, and not everything that counts can be counted.' Therefore, though data on certain aspects of performance may, by its nature, be subjective, it does not mean that an organization should avoid collecting it. More effort must be put into making this data usable.

Suitability

Chapter 2, p55

While utilizing measures that are suitable might seem an obvious thing to do, there is a complication here that is often missed. As an organization becomes more mature, it will need to alter its measures. Again referring to Hayes and Wheelwright's model introduced in Chapter 2, the measures deployed in Stage 1 may focus on capturing quality performance, but when the operation has reached a higher stage of maturity, and quality is achieved much more reliably, less effort may be required in this area. A more sophisticated measuring system may be deployed to gather the numerous detailed measures and combine them into fewer aggregate measures. This will allow management effort to be focused on gathering detailed measures in another aspect of the operations performance. For example, once the quality of output is achieved reliably, performance management effort may be more usefully applied to improving efficiency, a parameter more associated with Stage 2 of the Hayes and Wheelwright model.

Consistency

Like many aspects of operations management consistency is important. Here, there are two aspects to be considered. First, consistency across the organization: are all departments gathering data on a particular measure in the same way? If they are not, the integrity of comparisons made with this data will be compromised. Second, consistency across time: is the data being gathered in the same way this year as it was last? If not, it will be impossible to analyse trends. One must also consider a consistent method of aggregating data from an operational level to tactical and strategic levels to avoid loss of context as not all operational units are the same. However, there is a caveat here, as time moves on and organizations mature, measures may have to change as some measures become obsolete. In this case, the principle of suitability (previously explained) should take precedence over the principle of consistency.

CRITICAL PERSPECTIVE

What Is Key about KPIs?

When building a PMS, each measure that is included should indicate something useful about an aspect of operational performance. If it does not, then it should not be included in the PMS as the effort expended in gathering data on this measure will be wasted.

Key Performance Indicator (KPI): a particular measure that has been deemed of crucial importance in managing the performance of the operation.

Rather confusingly, the term **Key Performance Indicator (KPI)** has entered the lexicon of operations management and is often used to denote a measure that is particularly important to management decision-making. Some might argue that as all the measures built into the PMS have been selected because of their importance then attributing the additional label of KPI seems superfluous. However, others might argue that not all measures are equal. Some measures, due to contingencies within the business at certain times, may assume greater importance.

In addition, and somewhat ironically, as time has passed the term KPI has become overused to the point where it has become almost meaningless, with many managers applying it as a matter of convenience to all measures within their PMS.

The key point is ...

that organizations must not get caught up in terminological debates which will do nothing but detract from the effectiveness of their PMS. If an organization is going to allocate a greater level of importance to some measures and allocate the term KPI to them then it must be made clear what the measures are and why they are 'key'.

Devising Useful Performance Measures

Composite Measures

Our five generic performance objectives of quality, cost, speed, flexibility and dependability can be thought of as composites. To meet the customers' expectations each may comprise a number of components. For instance, when measuring the speed of an operation we may need to aggregate order processing time, manufacturing time and delivery time. Each of these is a component of the overall speed; added together, they indicate what the customer will experience. So while the composite measure may be all that the customer is interested in, as operations managers we may need to look at things in more detail.

Fundamental Measures

While many important operational performance measures are composites made up of a number of different elements, we tend to find that as we delve more deeply into the operation and begin to measure at increasing levels of granularity within processes and even at the level of individual tasks, the measures become much simpler and more fundamental. For example, 'number of calls answered in a day' in a call centre is a fundamental measure and it is difficult to see how this can be usefully broken down much further.

Ratiometric Measures

Some composite measures are made up of the ratio of one measure against another measure. One that is common in operations management, and the one that operations managers talk about most is productivity. Productivity is a simple, yet for some reason often misunderstood, term.

Productivity: the ratio of output produced by an operation to the input resources used to produce it

Productivity expresses the relationship between the outputs (in the form of goods and services) and the inputs (resources used to create the outputs). The most commonly understood formula for productivity is the following:

$$\text{Multi-factor productivity} = \frac{\text{Output from the operation}}{\text{All inputs to the operation}}$$

This is a very simple form of productivity calculation. It includes all outputs and all inputs and as such is often called multi-factor productivity as it includes all factors used as inputs to the conversion process. Multi-factor productivity has no standard dimensional unit such as kilometre, amp or gram although is sometimes expressed as a percentage.

A more specific expression of productivity is called single-factor productivity; in this formula the denominator is replaced with a single form of input – this, for example, might be *labour*.

$$\text{Single-factor productivity} = \frac{\text{Output from the operation}}{\text{Single input to the operation}}$$

Worked Example 12.1 calculates single factor productivity using labour hours.

WORKED EXAMPLE 12.1

Calculating Productivity

A table manufacturer currently makes 100 tables a week for their main customer, a national furniture retailer. The customer wishes to increase the order to 135 tables a week. Currently there are four carpenters working a 40-hour week (in total 160 person hours per week).

Problem: *Assuming that inputs, that is, labour hours are fixed, what productivity increase is required to achieve the required manufacturing schedule?*

Approach:

(a) Calculate current productivity level.

(b) Calculate the productivity level required to meet the new schedule.

(c) Calculate the difference between the current and the required.

Solution:

$$\text{Productivity} = \frac{\text{Output(s) from the operation}}{\text{Input(s) to the operation}}$$

(a) Using the single-factor of labour hours and the single-factor productivity formula:

Current productivity = 100 tables /160 person-hours

Current productivity = 0.625 tables per hour

To put this another way, it takes 1 hour and 36 minutes of labour to make 1 table.

(b) Use the formula in order to calculate the required productivity:

Required productivity = 135 tables/160 person hours

Required productivity = 0.84 tables per hour

To put this another way, to meet the new schedule the manufacturing time for each table must be reduced to 1 hour and 11 minutes.

(c) Productivity must increase from 0.63 tables per hour to 0.84 tables per hour or to put this another way each carpenter must reduce the time it takes to manufacture a table by 25 minutes. This would represent a productivity increase of around 26%.

In this example we have assumed a single fixed productivity factor (i.e. labour hours), therefore to reach the new level of productivity each carpenter would have to either work more quickly or find some way of making the process more efficient to facilitate a reduction in manufacturing time.

In Worked Example 12.1, productivity can be expressed using the combined dimensions of the numerator and the denominator, for example output per labour hours. Alternatively, if the production was completely automated we might need to use a different single factor denominator, such as 'robot hours used' or 'energy used'. To be useful as a performance measure, productivity within an operation – and how it is quantified and interpreted – must be made specific to the nature of that operation.

Productivity data is often used for making comparisons. For example, productivity last year against productivity this year, or productivity of one manufacturing site against another, or one company against that of a competitor.

Productivity is also used by governments as an economic measure. The UK Office for National Statistics (ONS) provides a formula (and a web-based calculator) that businesses can use to calculate their productivity. The ONS formula is:

$$\text{ONS productivity} = \frac{\text{Turnover} - \text{Intermediate consumption}}{\text{Number of workers}}$$

Intermediate consumption: the value of the goods and services consumed as inputs by a process of production, excluding fixed assets. In other words, resources that become part of the end product or service delivered to the customer.

This ONS formula (ONS, 2018) is slightly more complex as it introduces another term 'Intermediate consumption'. **Intermediate consumption** is defined as the value of the goods and services consumed as inputs by a process of production excluding fixed assets; in other words, the value of transformed resources. However, this formula simply represents another form of single-factor productivity, in this case worker productivity.

The ONS also helpfully provide a set of comparison figures to allow each business to judge its performance against industry standards. This is a useful tool to allow companies to benchmark their performance against industry norms.

Although there may be a number of metrics that can be used to measure productivity there are three fundamental ways to improve productivity using the ONS formula if other factors remain equal:

- Decrease the level of transformed inputs to the end product or service
- Increase the level of transformed output of the end product or service
- Reduce the level of fixed assets employed – those transforming resources that do not become part of the end product or service (e.g. people employed).

Simply speaking, if an operation improves its productivity it produces more output using the same amount of resources.

Although productivity is probably the most significant ratiometric productivity measure, other ratios also apply. There are too many different ratios to create an exhaustive list, but some examples of useful ratios are given below.

$$\text{Sales performance} = \frac{\text{Actual units sold per period}}{\text{Planned units sold per period}}$$

$$\text{Process quality} = \frac{\text{Error rate}}{\text{Number of products manufactured}}$$

$$\text{Service quality} = \frac{\text{Number of complaints}}{\text{Number of transactions}}$$

Testing the Usefulness of Performance Measures

Hopefully by this point it will be clear that measuring performance is always context sensitive. As explained in the last few pages, the most important part of setting up a performance management system is in selecting the correct measures. There is no one-size-fits-all solution. While some measures may be useful to a number of organizations, some organizations may need to develop measures that are only useful to them. Whatever business you are in, the trick is in selecting the correct measures for you. To help with this, there are nine tests that you can apply to your selected measures to help you decide whether or not to use them. Think of these tests as a form of due diligence on the efficacy of your chosen measures.

- The *truth test:* Is the measure definitely measuring what it's meant to measure?
- The *focus test:* Is the measure only measuring what it's meant to measure?
- The *consistency test:* Is the measure dealt with in the same way whenever the data is gathered or whoever gathers the data?
- The *access test:* Can the data be readily communicated and easily understood?
- The *clarity test:* Is any ambiguity possible in interpretation of the data?
- The *'so what' test:* Can, and will, the data be acted upon?
- The *timeliness test:* Can the data be analysed soon enough for action to be taken?
- The *cost test:* Is it worth the cost (effort) of collecting and analysing the data?
- The *gaming test:* Will the measure encourage any undesirable behaviours?

Implementing a PMS

As we have discussed all the necessary elements needed for a PMS, we will now discuss how to put these together to create a PMS.

- *Step 1:* Gather the strategic objectives defined by both the corporate and operations strategies.
- *Step 2:* Communicate these objectives throughout the organization.
- *Step 3:* Define performance measures that are relevant to each of these objectives.
- *Step 4:* Set performance targets that are relevant to each performance measure.
- *Step 5:* Implement a process that enables timely and accurate data to be gathered on the chosen measures.
- *Step 6:* Implement a review system that enables consideration of the resulting performance data.

There are several questions that need to be answered around the practicalities of implementing a PMS particularly in relation to Steps 5 and 6. Some of these are:

- How will the data be collected?
- Who or what will collate and sort the data?
- Who or what will analyse the information?
- How will the information be distributed?

Again, as with many aspects of performance measurement, there is no single answer; however, there are two broad approaches. First, if your organization is relatively small and your PMS quite simple, it may be best to allocate these 'data gathering and number crunching' tasks to those closest to the data-gathering points, particularly if the data is to be acted upon locally. Second, if your organization is large and your PMS more comprehensive, it may be best to set up a department whose function is purely to manage the PMS.

Regardless of how you choose to do this, though, there will need to be a formal review process to allow data to be communicated and acted upon.

Figure 12.1 illustrates a simple process. The key point to note here is that the emphasis of this process is in taking the gathered data and identifying the areas of variance. In other words, where the actual performance measured does not meet the planned performance, as defined by the targets set, corrective action must be taken. Performance data must be used to inform the business improvement activity that is taking place within the organization.

Figure 12.1 Performance review process

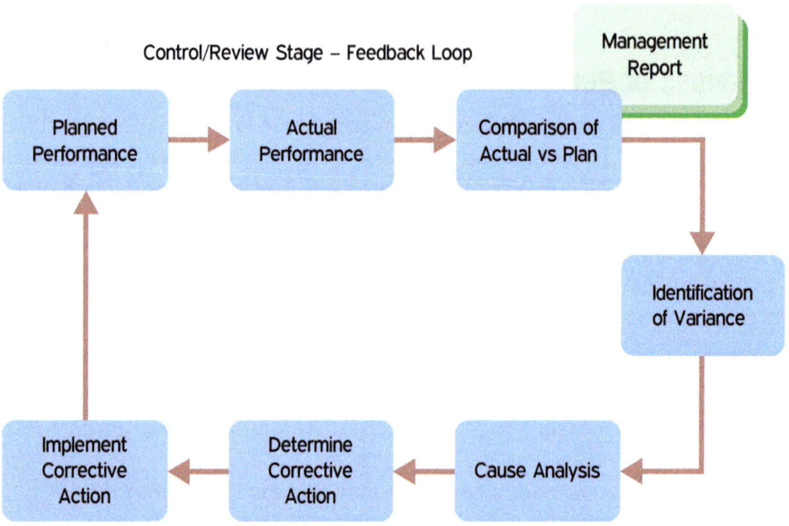

Stop and Think

What are the main performance measures that the customers (i.e. the passengers) of an airline might be interested in?

Thus, performance measurement is a means to an end, not an end in itself. The real benefits of managing operational performance in this way come from ensuring that appropriate improvements in business performance take place and are based on empirical data. Management reports are used to summarize overall performance of each section or department within an organization, against predetermined targets.

CRITICAL PERSPECTIVE

Performance Management and Trade-Offs

We introduced the concept of trade-offs in Chapter 2. Performance measures can help us to identify and manage these. For example, let's consider two performance measures commonly used in a call centre, 'customer satisfaction' and 'number of calls taken per hour'.

Chapter 2, p55

Generally speaking, customers are satisfied if they have their query dealt with fully at the first time of asking so that they do not have to ring back about the same subject. A second call could be considered a form of unnecessary rework. Call centres tend to use this as an *outcome* measure. However, they also measure number of calls per hour each call-handler takes, a *process* measure.

Call-handlers may decide to prioritize the target set for the *process* measure over the target set for the *outcome* measure. By doing so they may well cut short a call or pass the customer on to someone else, or simply give the customer the briefest (but not the best) answer. These actions will generally result in rework and an unhappy customer.

Customer satisfaction versus number of calls per hour is therefore a trade-off which might be better managed if decisions are supported by performance data analysis. For example, taking longer to complete a call while fully answering the customer's query may, over the long term, result in less time spent answering calls and greater productivity.

The key point is ...

decisions on trade-offs must, where possible, be made using tangible information and considered in relation to both long-term and short-term outcomes.

SHORT CASE 12.2

The Consequences of Misreporting Performance

Source: ©VladKK/Shutterstock

Severn Trent Water, part of Severn Trent Plc, is the world's fourth largest privately owned water company. Its vision is to deliver the highest possible service performance for customers, while also offering the lowest prices. To support this vision, in its 2020–2025 strategic plan, it has set itself a number of ambitious performance targets including: reducing sewer flooding by 8%; ensuring 95% of low pressure water issues are fixed first time; reducing water leakage by 15%; reducing pollution by 17%; and improving 2,100 km of river.

Yet, in October 2007, the company was charged by the Serious Fraud Office (SFO) in relation to data it provided to Ofwat (the water services regulation authority in England and Wales). The SFO brought three charges against Severn Trent Water of providing false information concerning leakage data in the company's June returns of 2000, 2001 and 2002. The charges stem from an investigation Ofwat carried out after a Severn Trent employee made allegations in 2004 concerning false reporting at the company.

Separately, Ofwat brought two fraud charges over another issue: misstated customer relations data. Severn Trent Water's customer relations department deliberately misreported some of its customer service data to hide its true performance in 2005 and in earlier years. This issue, not subject to any criminal procedures, was a problem that Severn Trent itself uncovered in 2006, and to which it drew the regulator's attention. The company identified that it had provided false information to Ofwat regarding customer service data, such as information on how quickly the company dealt with supplier interruptions and customer queries or complaints.

In a monopoly where the majority of customers have no choice of supplier, the only protection that they have is from the regulator. The availability of reliable, accurate and complete performance information is critical for Ofwat to be able to protect consumers. By deliberately misrepresenting its performance, Severn Trent Water prevented Ofwat from identifying failures in the company's customer service and taking action to improve that service.

This deception, combined with poor internal processes and controls within the company, meant that customers of Severn Trent Water received a service that was of a lower standard than that reported, and in many cases was below the statutory minimum. The outcome was that Severn Trent was fined 2.9% of its 2006/2007 turnover (£34.7 million) for deliberately misreporting some key customer service information, and 0.1% of its 2005/2006 turnover (£1.1 million) for providing sub-standard services to customers in 2005–2006.

Note: The regulator sets restrictions on how much water companies can charge customers, based on how effectively they treat their customers. By overstating its customer service performance, the company was allowed to charge higher prices than if it had provided correct figures.

Questions

1. Why did the company misrepresent data to Ofwat?
2. What would you say was the key performance driver for this company in the early 2000s and how has this changed more recently?

Source: John O'Doherty, *Financial Times*, 22 November 2007, http://cachef.ft.com/cms/s/0/ad46048a-98ca-11dc-bb45-0000779fd2ac.html; *Times Online*, 8 April 2008, http://business.timesonline.co.uk/tol/business/industry_sectors/utilities/article3703915.ece; Severn Trent Code of Practice 2018, www.stwater.co.uk/server.php?show=ConWebDoc.3403

Performance Management Models

Introduction, p.1

Performance management is not new. Taylor (1911), who we met in the Introductory Chapter, with his system of scientific management used it in a rudimentary form. Since this early work, the imperative to manage performance proactively using a data-driven method has increased, with companies in all industry sectors coming to understand its usefulness.

A criticism of this early work, though, is that it tended to concentrate rather narrowly on the process-based aspects of the business. In addition, the growing need to comply with accounting regulations and particularly to report financial performance resulted in a focus on financial measures.

The idea of using a comprehensive set of measures to gather performance data about more than just process and financial performance was first proposed by Drucker (1955). More recently, this idea has come of age and various models have been developed to guide operations managers and help them ensure that their PMS gathers a comprehensive set of measures which inform decision-making on all aspects of the business.

This section introduces three models, each of which attempts to overcome the limitations that measuring only financial and process performance brings. The models discussed are:

- The Performance Pyramid
- The Balanced Scorecard
- The Performance Prism

It is worth pointing out that these models have been developed individually but some evolution in sophistication can be seen as we move from the earliest model, the Performance Pyramid, through the Balanced Scorecard to the latest, the Performance Prism. It could be argued that each is so different in conceptualization from the others that any attempt at finding any points of commonality or difference through which to define any form of lineage is rather pointless. However, it is useful to compare and contrast their approaches as each has something to offer.

As previously highlighted, customization to context is all important and the choice of which model to use will depend very much on where it is intended to be used.

The Performance Pyramid

The performance pyramid shown in Figure 12.2, developed by Lynch and Cross (1991), is structured as a hierarchy of performance measures. The pyramid structure is a useful diagrammatic representation as it illustrates movement from a small number of broad measures which capture strategic performance at the top of the pyramid to a larger number of more specific measures which capture the detail of operational performance as we move down the pyramid.

Figure 12.2 The Performance Pyramid

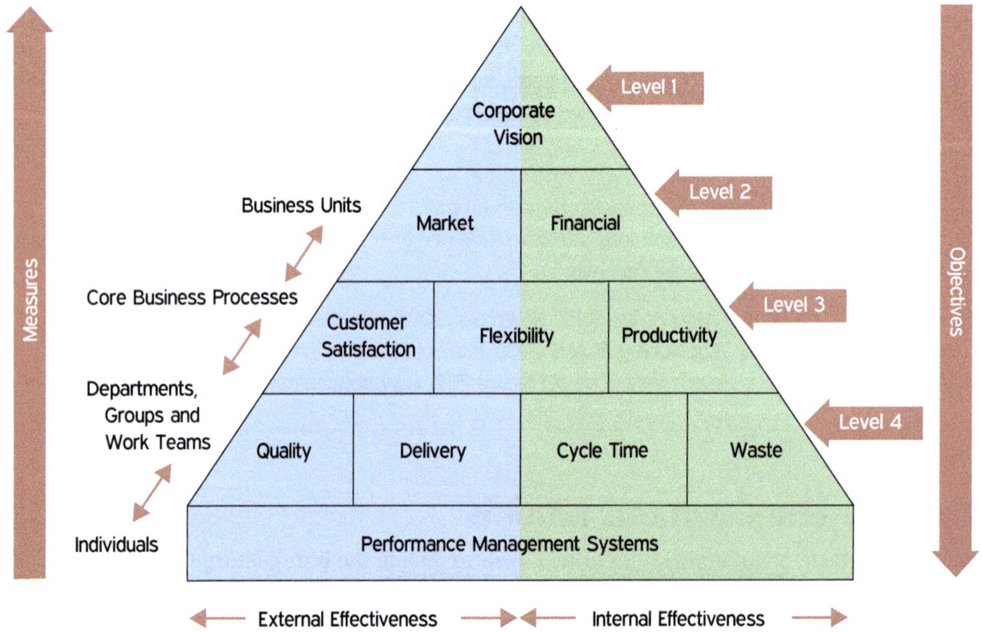

Source: Adapted from Lynch and Cross (1991).

The Performance Pyramid can be most easily explained by considering each of its four levels.

Level 1 contains the corporate vision which states where the organization wants to be and what it wants to achieve.

Level 2 focuses on measuring the organization's performance in terms of market-related measures and financial measures. How an organization performs financially and within markets will clearly indicate how likely it is to achieve its corporate vision. Here we may want to deploy measures that tell us about the proportion of available market we have captured or the profit we are making on each sale.

Level 3 focuses on measuring customer satisfaction, operational flexibility and productivity. These are the aspects that will influence market and financial performance.

Level 4, in turn, then focuses on measuring lower level, process performance such as quality, delivery time, cycle time and waste.

The left-hand side of the pyramid contains measures which have an external focus and which are predominantly non-financial. Those on the right-hand side are focused on the internal efficiency of the organization and are predominantly financial.

While the performance pyramid does encourage a more holistic view of performance and does hint at the integrated nature of performance management it does tend to concentrate on two groups of stakeholders, that is, shareholders and customers. It is necessary to ensure that measures are included which relate to other stakeholders as well.

The Balanced Scorecard

Perhaps the most ubiquitous of performance management models is Kaplan and Norton's Balanced Scorecard (Kaplan and Norton, 1996, 2008). While the Performance Pyramid is rather two dimensional, the Balanced Scorecard very much encourages the inclusion of measures that tell us about all aspects of the business. It can be thought of as both a process and a tool. As a thinking process it helps us identify what activities are important to the success of our business and as a communications tool, it provides performance information for all aspects of the organization.

As illustrated in Figure 12.3, Kaplan and Norton suggest that to cover an entire business, measures must be found that provide useful data on four perspectives of the business. These perspectives, Kaplan and Norton would argue, provide a useful categorization system that encapsulates all business activity. Considering all four perspectives helps to avoid a narrow concentration on only financial or process-based measures (the criticism of

Figure 12.3 The Balanced Scorecard

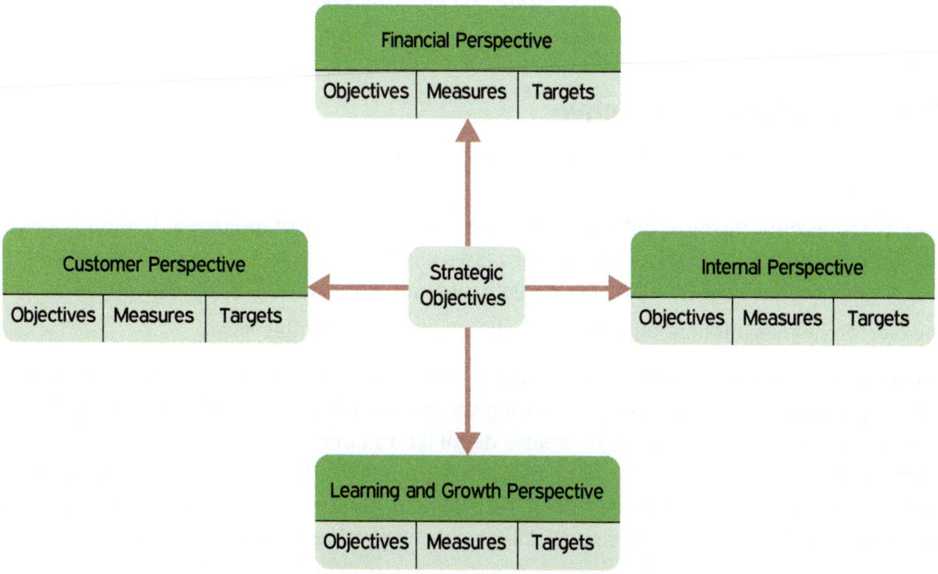

Source: Adapted from Kaplan and Norton (1996).

early performance measurement) or on only shareholders and customers (the criticism levelled at the Performance Pyramid).

In addition, each of the measures within each perspective must be linked directly to the strategy of the business. In other words, each must tell us something about how likely we are to achieve what we have set out to. Adding the term 'balanced' to the name does tend to cause some confusion, this term suggests a balanced view of business performance should be sought but does not suggest that the same number of measures must be used in each perspective. Each of these perspectives is explained below.

The Financial Perspective

The information collected here will help us answer the question: how do we look to shareholders?

This perspective is a relatively simple one to understand. It recognizes that while (possibly) in the past financial measures may have received too much attention at the expense of other measures, they are still an important part of the information that is needed. These measures will be easily recognizable from our financial reports and might include revenue, profit and cash flow. Indeed any measures required by our accounting systems may be included here.

The Customer Perspective

The information collected here will help us answer the question: how do our customers see us?

This perspective has become more visible in the last few years, as customer focus has increased across all industries. These measures may include aspects of performance that are important to individual customers that relate directly to features of products (such as reliability) and services (such as delivery time) or may include more general measures, such as market share, that tell us something about our performance in the market.

This can be a difficult perspective to collect numerical data on, as the elements that make up customer satisfaction can sometimes be rather intangible. Often, customer satisfaction surveys are carried out which utilize scaling and ranking systems to create some degree of quantification.

The Internal Perspective

The information collected here will help us answer the question: what must our operation excel at?

This perspective is sometimes rather erroneously called the operational perspective. This can be confusing as this label suggests that it only refers to the operational core of the business, such as the production line or the call centre, but this perspective actually refers to all the process-based activity in the organization. Again, like the financial perspective, most organizations will have had considerable experience with these measures as they may have been using them for a long time. Here, measures characterize the performance of all aspects of our internal delivery systems and processes. So rework, time lost through machine breakdown, all forms of product/service output measure, levels of work in progress, customer queuing time, are all examples of measures that can be included here.

Innovation and Growth Perspective

The information collected here will help us answer the question: how can we continue to build our organizational capabilities?

This perspective is perhaps the most difficult to make sense of. One way of looking at it, though this may be viewed by some as an oversimplification, is as a set of measures used to characterize the performance of the more intangible assets of your organization that do not fit easily into any of the other three perspectives.

Kaplan and Norton help us out here by suggesting three types of intangible asset.

- **Human capital** refers to the skill, talent and know-how that the organization has at its disposal and this may be quantified by, for example, measuring the levels and types of qualification help by employees. We will focus on human resources in greater detail later in this chapter.
- **Information capital** refers to the data and information that is held by the organization and this may include intellectual property measured by, for example, number of patents held, or information gained from expert analysis of particular market segments or of other areas of interest.

- **Organizational capital,** or put more simply culture, is the most difficult to quantify of the three types of 'capital', but again, this can be done using survey and interview methods which use scaling and ranking techniques to measure, for example, employee motivation and commitment.

The Performance Prism

The Performance Prism, illustrated in Figure 12.4 adopts a different approach. Neely *et al.* (2002) argue that deriving measures from strategy is wrong. They suggest that the reason an organization has a strategy is to help it deliver value to stakeholders, therefore the foundation of any PMS has to be an understanding of these stakeholders. Only when this understanding is gained is it possible to explore the issue of what strategies should be put in place to ensure the wants and needs of the stakeholders are satisfied.

The Performance Prism consists of five interrelated facets:

- The **Stakeholder satisfaction facet** asks the question: who are the stakeholders and what do they want and need? This facet forces us to think more broadly beyond only shareholders and customers. Here, stakeholders might include suppliers, regulators, government, in fact any individual or entity that has some stake in the organization.
- The **Stakeholder contribution facet** asks the question: what can our stakeholders contribute to us? This facet has been included as a separate component as it illustrates that a relationship is reciprocal. Organizations deliver value to their stakeholders and they expect something in return. For example, customers have many expectations in relation to such things as quality and cost but in return they may be expected to supply loyalty.
- The **Strategies facet** asks the question: what are the strategies we need to ensure the wants and needs of our stakeholders and of our organization are satisfied? For each of our strategic objectives it should be possible to implement measures that allow us to determine if we are on target to achieve them within the timescales set.
- The **Processes facet** asks the question: what are the processes we have to put in place in order to allow our strategies to be delivered? For each of our processes, it should be possible to identify specific measures that allow us to assess their performance.
- The **Capabilities facet** asks the question: what are the capabilities we require to operate our processes? This facet is perhaps the least widely understood. Capabilities are the combination of people, practices, technology and infrastructure that together enable execution of the processes. As soon as this question has been answered, then it becomes possible to identify measures that allow the organization to assess whether it possesses the required capabilities.

Figure 12.4 The five facets of the Performance Prism

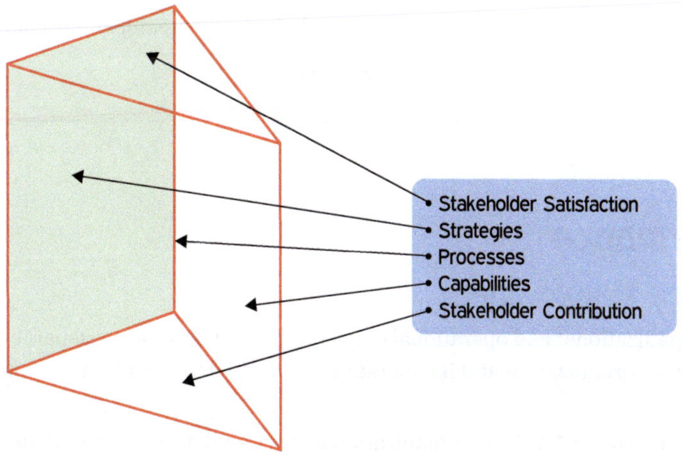

Source: Neely *et al.* (2002).

SHORT CASE 12.3

Performing Well for Intangible Results

BUSINESS INTEGRATION

Four Seasons Health Care is one of the UK's largest independent health care providers caring for more than 10,000 people across the UK.

Four Seasons' origins date back to the late 1980s. Since then, the company has achieved growth through acquisitions and the construction of new care facilities.

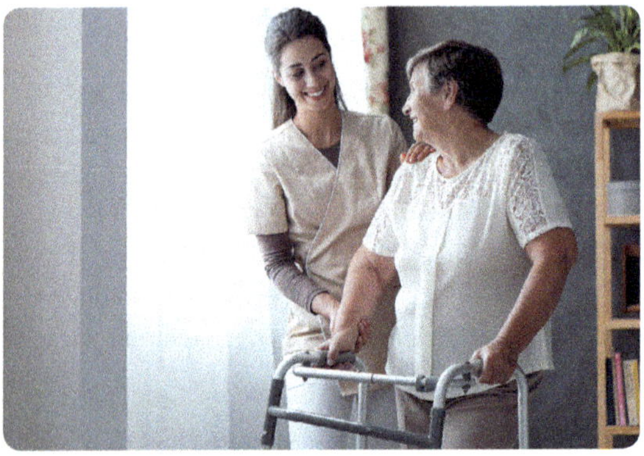

Source: ©Photographee.eu/Shutterstock

The care home sector in the UK is fragmented: 80% is made up of small companies in domestic-type home environments; the remaining 20% of the sector is made up of four relatively large organizations. The sector is heavily regulated and quality control is key because a single mistake can affect a resident's general comfort and well-being. Staff represent 60% of the operating cost base with most staff earning minimum wage. It is a low-tech, high-touch business. The remainder of the cost base comprises around 20% on food and 15% on utilities, with the balance on consumables, medical supplies and so on. Fixed overheads are high, and margins are tight, in the region of 2%.

If good performance management stems from understanding your strategic objectives, then this industry is given a clear message by the way revenue is generated. About 80% of the revenue comes from the public purse, which for most of the period 2010–2020 has been seeking to cut expenditure. Therefore the focus has been to grow profit through finding efficiencies. Recognizing where you need to improve is the first step in performance improvement. This is made possible by having a good performance management system and accepting the difficult messages that come from it.

The care-home service is about stakeholder management. The business is about providing homes to people: fundamentally, care homes rent out rooms. Residents are a critical stakeholder – they are not necessarily the customer, though. Sometimes the customer is a relative of the resident, and their perception of the service required is different from the perception of the person receiving it. As a regulated industry, the sector must conform to a myriad of quality standards and requirements, and any care home can be subjected to random checks with little notice given. Staff and management work in small homes, even those that are part of a larger organization. At the operational level, the strategic objective of the business can be realized only through recognizing that in practical terms there are a number of business systems that converge to make one operation. Hospitality and catering, housekeeping and cleaning, medical and pharmaceutical are just a few that may work across more than one care home (i.e. operating unit) within a business.

Question

1. How can a performance management system help this company achieve its strategic objectives?

Sources: www.fshc.co.uk/company-information/about-four-seasons

People Performance

Human Resource Management

The management of organizational and operational employee performance are inseparably linked as the productivity and performance of an organization and its operation is hugely dependent on its employees' skills, knowledge and motivation.

Human resource management (HRM) is the organizational function that deals with issues related to its workforce. HRM may also be seen as a particular perspective on people management – one that emphasizes a strategic and integrated approach. The management of people as a human resource is not, however, restricted to just the HRM function but is also the responsibility of operations managers, strategic managers and employees themselves.

Table 12.2 shows some common HR activities. For explanatory purposes, these are arranged into four broad categories: operational, strategic, administrative and employee focused. It should, however, be considered that this categorization system is by no means definitive – it could be argued that some activities fit into more than one of these categories. Indeed, the interpretation and implementation of these activities varies greatly between different organizations depending on their size, sector, country of location and culture. For instance, some small-to-medium sized organizations might not have a dedicated HR function, some organizations might not have a strategic-level input, and some may have a controlling rather than developing perspective on their employees.

The list of activities in Table 12.2 is not exhaustive and is given here to show the context that operations managers work in, the HR activities they engage with directly and indirectly and those employee-related activities which operations tend to hand off to other specialist functions. In the remainder of this chapter we will consider why the activities in Table 12.2 are undertaken and how they are implemented. While it is not the intention of this chapter to cover the in-depth activities of the HRM function itself, the relative importance of HR activities for operation management will be explained.

At this point, it is useful to provide a definition of HRM. Storey (2007) defines HRM as 'a distinctive approach to employment management which seeks to achieve competitive advantage through the strategic deployment of a highly-committed and capable workforce using an array of cultural, structural and personnel techniques'. The definition of HRM is somewhat contested, but this version is commonly cited and generally accepted based on the following assumptions that HRM:

- is a people-centric perspective or philosophy
- has a strategic role to play in helping organizations achieve sustained competitive performance
- requires ongoing investment, through effective policies and practices, to ensure that productivity and other measures of performance are met.

HRM presents a unitaristic view of the employment relationship. In other words, the achievement of organizational goals and objectives is the sole purpose of employers and employees, and it is commitment to these goals that is sought from all stakeholders in an organization. This is in contrast to the pluralistic view of 'employment relations', which recognizes the importance of different and often competing goals of different external stakeholders – for example, trade unions, shareholders and governments.

The Evolution of Human Resource Management

As with many management terms, HRM has evolved through the decades. Fifty or sixty years ago one would be hard pushed to have found the term HRM being used. Most managers and academics believe that the term began around the 1950s in the USA. A summary article by Kaufman (2014) highlights the complex and multi-faceted development of the field. This development can be simplified into three key stages.

Table 12.2 HR activities

Operations-based HR activities	Strategic-led HR activities	Administrative HRM functional activities	People-centric HR activities
• Business partnering • Advice to line managers • Recruitment • Selection • Learning and development • Training • Management development • Reward and benefits management • Performance management • Disciplinary and grievance proceedings • Dismissals • Redundancy • Organization (job) design	• Executive board membership • Strategic decision making • Workforce planning • Succession planning • Talent management and development • Policy development	• Employment law advice • HR-related administration • Upkeep of personal records • Pay and managing the payroll system • Pensions • Health and safety • Equal opportunities and diversity monitoring	• Employee engagement and motivation • Career management • Counselling • Occupational psychology • Occupational health • Change management

The Social Reform Movements and Emergence of Industrial Relations and Personnel Management (ca 1890s–1930s)

During this period, working conditions were appalling. Social reformers such as the Cadbury's chocolate company in the UK worked to improve working conditions. Great strides were made in regulating and legislating on reducing working hours, use of child labour, and improving health and safety at work. These issues resulted in a growing labour management problem for operations as mass production and large-scale employment became common practice – which manifested itself in greater conflict (and thus poorer relations) between employees and management – and saw a growing interest in the effective management of the labour force through what now is known as 'classical management theory'.

Classical management theory, in particular the notions of bureaucracy (Weber, 2009 [1946]), the division of labour (Henri Fayol, 1841–1925) and Frederick Taylor's principles of scientific management (Taylor, 1911), is recognized as one of the most influential theoretical and, ultimately, practical people management developments of this period. For instance, scientific management argues that greater workplace productivity is achieved through more rationalized and efficient modes of production. In short, Taylor and disciples of Taylorism place their faith in a scientific, statistically based analysis of the workplace and, with this, constantly strive for ever-greater efficiency in the production process. Efficiency, it was concluded, may be attained through increasing the mechanization of the workplace, the simplification and routinization of work and the extrinsic output-focused, reward-based motivation of employees.

New work practices driven by these principles of scientific management were required to engage more fundamentally than ever before with issues of effective job design, workforce planning, training, reward and performance measurement – and are all core activities associated with the burgeoning field of 'personnel management', as it was known at the time.

Taylor's scientific management principles are often criticized for not putting employees-as-people at the forefront of management practice. Taylor simply concluded that motivation, and thus the efficient performance of employees, could be gained through the design of clear, simple and repetitive tasks, and the use of reward systems based on being paid for piecework. Taylor neglected many of the more people-centric features of managing employees. Despite these criticisms, many of these scientific principles are still evident today in less developed countries, and in casual and low paid jobs.

The Human Relations Movement and Expansion of Organizational Behavior as an Academic Discipline (ca 1930s–1970s)

Towards the middle of the 20th century, and with its genesis in the Hawthorn studies of the 1930s, there was an increase in academic research in the overlapping fields of industrial and organizational psychology and industrial anthropology and sociology that began to influence performance management theory and personal management practice.

A key theme in this research became known as the human relations movement. This took a behavioural, psychological and emotional perspective on the employment relationship rejecting, at least on the surface, the 'rationale economic [wo]man' assumptions of Taylorism and scientific management. This research in the human relations field was focused on exploring the potential relationships between organizational efficiency, organizational performance and employees' positive emotions, attitudes and behaviours at, and towards, work.

Today this work is commonly attributed to the field of organizational behaviour that includes topics such as leadership, organizational culture, team or group working effectiveness, interpersonal relations at work, job satisfaction and engagement, job design, and so on. Organizational behaviour is concerned with the improvement of working lives and the potentially positive effects on individual, team and organizational effectiveness. It is within this period that contemporary notions of HRM – and indeed the term HRM – began to emerge.

From Personnel Management to Strategic HRM (ca 1970s–the present)

Within academic literature and practice, a dichotomy is often presented between notions of personnel management and HRM, with the more strategic and business-focused HRM often presented as evolving from the more operational, administrative and employee-focused personnel management (Storey, 1989). Notions of strategic HRM, as opposed to more operational and functional personnel management grew in the 1960s and 70s. Strategic HRM emphasized the importance of a close alignment between a firm's business and the HR strategy and the

Table 12.3 Key differences between personnel management and HRM

Personnel management		HRM
Control of employee	→	Participation of employee
Operational and administrative	→	Strategic
Reactive	→	Proactive
Fragmented and ad-hoc policies and practices	→	Integrated and coordinated policies and practices
Focus on performance measurement	→	Focus is on added value

development of a highly committed workforce. This was considered to be in contrast to 'personnel management practices', that were viewed as a rather ad-hoc collection of more bureaucratic, controlling and reactive people management policies. Table 12.3 summarizes these differences.

At the same time, and closely paralleling debates around the transitions from personnel management to HRM, was the identification of 'hard' and 'soft' variants of HRM,

Hard HRM emphasizes the efficient utilization of the workforce and views employees as a 'resource' that needs to be effectively deployed to achieve organizational goals, much like any other transforming resource (e.g. production machinery, warehouse space, digital analysis capacity, data storage). Hard HRM therefore tends to focus on those HR activities and tools related to the close control and coordination of employees – for example, HR planning, clear goal- and target-setting and, most important of all, continuous performance measurement and assessment. Hard HRM is regarded as being closely aligned to the more mechanical and deterministic principles of personnel management.

Soft HRM, on the other hand, is said to place a greater emphasis on those people management practices and activities that are aimed at gaining the effective, or in other words, emotional, commitment of employees. Employees are thus viewed in the more humanistic way, extolled by advocates of the human relations, strategic HRM and 'high-commitment work practices' approaches. Tight control of employees is thus potentially less important because highly committed employees are more self-regulating (Truss, 1997). Table 12.4 summarizes the main differences between hard and soft HRM ideologies.

Hard HRM: HR practices and policies that enable the close control and co-ordination of employees and views employees as an organizational resource to be effectively utilized

Soft HRM: HR practices and policies aimed to elicit the affective (emotional) commitment of employees to the organization and its goals.

Today it is considered that effective HRM practices and policies are those that engage with both hard and soft HRM – and thus the principles of personnel management and strategic HRM – and that these approaches are not mutually exclusive. After all, hard HRM, which is associated with tighter control practices such as performance measurement and management, may provide greater work-related clarity and focus for both employers and employees. At the same time, a greater involvement in decision making and flexibility – soft HRM – may present more enriching and rewarding work for employees and the associated attitudinal and behavioural benefits for employers.

Sustainable HRM (2000s–the present)

Currently there may also be a fourth stage of HRM emerging. The recent focus placed on business ethics and social and environmental sustainability is encouraging organizations to focus on delivering HRM goals within a wider economic, social and environmental setting (Freitas *et al.*, 2011).

Table 12.4 Contrast between hard and soft HRM

Hard HRM		Soft HRM
Employees are a resource to be utilized	→	Employees are a source of competitive advantage
Deployment	→	Development
Control	→	Commitment
Direction	→	Involvement
Rigidity	→	Flexibility
Performance management	→	Performance enabling

High-profile ethical and environmental issues (e.g. zero hours contracts, pension scandals, carbon reduction and work-life balance initiatives) have driven this trend, and many organizations have reacted by focusing on these via a strategic approach to HRM. Thus strategic HRM now seeks a balance between 'economic prosperity, social equity and environmental integrity' (Freitas *et al.*, 2011, p. 32).

Stop and Think

What sort of person do you think is best suited to working in operations primarily focused on hard HRM practices and what type of person is best suited to working in operations primarily run using soft HRM practices? Why are these so?

Workforce planning (WP): an integral part of strategic and operational planning in organizations; a core process of HRM to ensure that an organization has the right number of people at the right time, in the right place with the right skills, which are aligned to the strategic and operational strategy.

Workforce intelligence planning: matching organizational needs with the right number of employees with the right knowledge, skills and behaviours in the right place at the right time. Sometimes referred to as WIP.

Strategic workforce planning: having workforce planning to include the right number of people at the right time, in the right place with the right skills and behaviours, which are aligned to the strategic and operational strategy and financial budget planning.

Workforce Planning

Workforce planning (WP) is an integral part of strategic and operational planning in organizations. It is regarded as a core process of HRM to ensure that an organization has the 'right' number of people at the 'right' time, in the 'right' place with the 'right' skills, which are aligned to the strategic and operational strategy. The addition of behavioural considerations to the workforce plan, the creation of measures of performance and finally the conversion of these into implementable actions is known as **workforce intelligence planning**. **Strategic workforce planning** includes both types of workforce planning as well as highlighting the importance of planning to a financial budget, whether maintaining, flexing, up-sizing or down-sizing an organization.

This section will outline and critique workforce planning in respect to operations management performance. Workforce planning is crucial because an organization's people are inextricably linked to operational delivery performance.

Historically, workforce planning has been referred to as manpower planning, but manpower planning tends to be associated with a more centralized, number-crunching exercise with attempts to computationally forecast future requirements. Manpower planning has been criticized for being too mechanistic and softer workforce intelligence planning methods are currently preferred.

The Process of Workforce Planning

As discussed in the section above, the key to WP is defining what 'right' means in the context of 'the right employees with the right skills at the right place at the right time' – also who defines 'right' and how do they define 'right'? In effect, WP is a process in which an organization attempts to estimate the demand for labour and evaluate the size, nature and sources of supply which will be required to meet the demand. Regardless of how 'right' is defined, WP aims to help organizations meet the challenges associated with operating in an environment that is subject to dramatic changes.

Larger departments of an organization, such as operations, will have a significant role in defining what 'right' means as demand for labour volume, skills levels and knowledge capabilities will perhaps be better understood by the operations of a company rather than the core HR Department.

Workforce plan: how many people of what type at what skill levels are needed at any particular time in an organization depending on internal and external factors.

When all the 'rights' have been defined in a workforce planning process, involving operational functions and HR, a **workforce plan** will be produced. In general a workforce plan will be designed to be short term (one year), medium term (three years) or long term (five years plus).

It is worthwhile being cautious about optimizing such workforce plans 'too firmly' in organizations where planning can be regarded as continuously changing – due to both internal and contextual specific external factors – and the flexibility to re-plan 'on-the-fly' is often required. Thus, in order to maximize operational workforce performance, an organization must have a workforce that is engaged with its strategy and able to react quickly to changing workforce requirements.

Workforce planning for operations should:

- Obtain and retain the quality and quantity of people needed to achieve strategic objectives
- Make the best use of human resources
- Anticipate the problems of potential surpluses or deficits of people through gap and demand analysis
- Develop a well-trained, flexible and agile workforce that can adapt to an uncertain and changing environment
- Reduce dependence on external recruitment when key skills are in short supply.

Factors that need to be considered during the process of workforce planning include:

- Business plans and scenario planning
- Product and service demand forecasting
- Organizational structure and redesign
- Succession management for key positions
- Talent management and career planning
- Recruitment and retention planning
- Creation of an agile and flexible workforce through multi-skilling and building continuous learning, training and development
- Skills acquisition
- Senior leadership and line manager development
- Employee engagement techniques.

Whichever HR factors are included, it is important to note that WP, WIP and SWP are seen as dynamic HR tools. A precursor to WP, WIP and SWP is the agreement of the organization's senior management team, engagement and buy-in from managers and HR that are 'joined up' and integrated. Once the plan has been prepared, then communications with and engagement of the organization's leaders and line managers will be critical success factors. From the above discussion, you can see that the process of workforce planning is complex, uncertain and ongoing, and is something that operations managers need to strongly grasp.

WORKED EXAMPLE 12.2

Workforce Allocation: Getting Academics to Teach Classes

A workload allocation process might happen as follows for a university teaching department – where teaching is being allocated to academic members of staff for a forthcoming academic year.

Every year from January to March the head of an academic department (in this case the Operations Management Department) needs to allocate teaching for the forthcoming academic year starting the following September. Different sources of information are gleaned: person specifics come from the HR Department (see blue section) and details on classes to be taught come from the Programme Administration Office (with input from other academic departments – see white section). It then falls to the head of the academic department, using their specialized local knowledge, to allocate teaching to specific staff members based on individuals' knowledge, skills, attributes and other characteristics.

Problem: *Use the information in Figure 12.5 to complete the workload allocation for the Operations Management Department (using the empty white sections). The management jobs have already been allocated (see yellow section).*

Approach

Apply the following work standards:

- more than one member of staff must be allocated to each class (module) – to minimize risks due to sickness, resignation and travel/weather issues
- maximum of four teaching modules per year for teaching-only staff and a maximum of two modules per year for staff who do research and teaching – to prevent over-loading
- allow for part-time or full-time employment (e.g. Tina Sun is only 50% employed)
- allow for other management responsibilities.

This is a process of trial and error: it can be done manually, or by using a simple spreadsheet.

Figure 12.5 Workforce allocation tool – the 'problem'

Work Allocation for Operations Dept. at the 'Global Business School'

Teaching load norms: teaching and research staff up to 2.0, and teaching only upto 4 modules per year

Module Code	Module name	Students expected	Module Credit	Teaching Period/ Term/ Session	Claire Comet	Peter Saturn	Leo Starr	John Moon	Tina Sun	TOTAL
				full time equivalent (FTE)	1.00	1.00	1.00	1.00	0.50	4.50
				position	Teaching Fellow	Professor	Lecturer	Snr. Lecturer	Professor	
				name	Claire Comet	Peter Saturn	Leo Starr	John Moon	Tina Sun	TOTAL
Management load	HoD (2.0)							2.00		2.00
	Programme Director (1.0)						1.00			1.00
	Deputy Head (1.0)				1.00					1.00
	Group Leader (0.5)								0.50	0.50
	Ethics Committee (0.1)							0.10		0.10
	Convenor / Outreach Champion (0.5)				0.50					0.50
Under graduate 1st year										
B111	Applications Development	45	15	TP2						0.00
B115	Principles of Operations Management (A and B occurances - runs twice)	646	15	TP2						0.00
Under graduate 2nd year										
B220	Business Operations Excellence	74	15	TP2						0.00
B229	Optimisation and Decision Analytics	18	15	TP1						0.00
Under graduate final year										
B331	Operations Strategy	111	20	TP1/2						0.00
B332	Managing Information Technology in a Global Context	98	10	TP2						0.00
Post Graduate										
BP130	MSc Business Analytics Dissertation	?	50	TP1/2/3						0.00
BP863	Business Analytics in Practice	?	15	TP2						0.00
Online: part-time distance-learning										
BO864	Software amd Systems Analytics (MSc)	30	15	March-Sept						0.00
BO863	Business Analytics in Practice (MBA)	30	15	TP2						0.00
Foundation course										
BF008	Business Model Generation	56	15	TP2						0.00
BF006	E-Business	56	15	TP2						0.00
	Actual teaching load				1.50	0.00	1.00	2.10	0.50	
	Normal teaching load				4.00	2.00	2.00	2.00	1.00	
	Difference (minus is underloaded, positive is overloaded, +/- 0.5 is okay)				-2.50	-2.00	-1.00	0.10	-0.50	
	Number of modules				0	0	0	0	0	

Solution

Figure 12.6 shows an acceptable workable solution by applying the above work standards (e.g. for 'Operations Strategy' there are two teachers with a 50:50 split allocation between John Moon and Tina Sun) and process of trial and error. Percentage of employment has been considered and other management activities.

Figure 12.6 Workforce allocation tool – the 'solution'

Work Allocation for Operations Dept. at the 'Global Business School'

Teaching load norms: teaching and research staff up to 2.0, and teaching only upto 4 modules per year

Module Code	Module name	Students expected	Module Credit	Teaching Period/ Term/ Session	Claire Comet	Peter Saturn	Leo Starr	John Moon	Tina Sun	TOTAL
				full time equivalent (FTE)	1.00	1.00	1.00	1.00	0.50	4.50
				position	Teaching Fellow	Professor	Lecturer	Snr. Lecturer	Professor	
				name	Claire Comet	Peter Saturn	Leo Starr	John Moon	Tina Sun	TOTAL
Management load	HoD (2.0)							2.00		2.00
	Programme Director (1.0)						1.00			1.00
	Deputy Head (1.0)				1.00					1.00
	Group Leader (0.5)								0.50	0.50
	Ethics Committee (0.1)							0.10		0.10
	Convenor / Outreach Champion (0.5)				0.50					0.50
Under graduate 1st year										
B111	Applications Development	45	15	TP2			0.20	0.80		1.00
B115	Principles of Operations Management (A and B occurances - runs twice)	646	15	TP2	0.40	1.00			0.60	2.00
Under graduate 2nd year										
B220	Business Operations Excellence	74	15	TP2				0.60	0.40	1.00
B229	Optimisation and Decision Analytics	18	15	TP1	0.80		0.20			1.00
Under graduate final year										
B331	Operations Strategy	111	20	TP1/2				0.50	0.50	1.00
B332	Managing Information Technology in a Global Context	98	10	TP2	0.10		0.90			1.00
Post Graduate										
BP130	MSc Business Analytics Dissertation	?	50	TP1/2/3			0.20	0.80		1.00
BP863	Business Analytics in Practice	?	15	TP2	0.50		0.50			1.00
Online: part-time distance-learning										
BO864	Software amd Systems Analytics (MSc)	30	15	March-Sept					0.50	0.50
BO863	Business Analytics in Practice (MBA)	30	15	TP2	0.25		0.75			1.00
Foundation course										
BF008	Business Model Generation	56	15	TP2	0.90				0.10	1.00
BF006	E-Business	56	15	TP2			1.00			1.00
	Actual teaching load				4.45	1.00	4.75	4.80	2.60	
	Normal teaching load				4.00	2.00	2.00	2.00	1.00	
	Difference (minus is underloaded, positive is overloaded, +/- 0.5 is okay)				0.45	-1.00	2.75	2.80	1.60	
	Number of modules				6	1	7	4	5	

The proposed work plan shown in Figure 12.6, however, is not perfect and could be further improved. For instance, while Claire Comet has a suitable workload, Peter Saturn is under-loaded and Leo Star, John Moon and Tina Sun are all slightly overloaded. The Head of Department should perhaps try to make this fairer by reallocating some of Tina's load to Peter and recruiting another teaching-only member of staff to remove load from Leo and John.

Overall, the department is currently understaffed. Recruitment and selection of new employees does, however, take time and is prone to much uncertainty, especially for specialized experienced staff, and this is why this planning exercise had to be done well before the start of the new academic year.

Worked Example 12.2 could have contained hundreds of different classes (rows) and staff (columns). Complexity in work force planning arises when detailed factors need to be included (e.g. difference in class sizes, class credit value, timetabling clashes, part-time working and other staff duties). Ever-changing issues will cause ongoing iteration and refinement of work plans.

A similar work planning process to that shown in Worked Example 12.2 can be applied to other organizations. For instance, a technical sales department in an electronics company may change 'classes' for 'products' or 'sales regions' and allocate these to different 'sales people' rather than teachers. The work-allocation process remains fundamentally similar.

Why Are WP, WIP and SWP Important?

A **workforce plan**, as seen in Worked Example 12.2 will provide workforce visibility in to the future; it will determine recruitment and retention, training and development, and influence reward and recognition for the workforce. It can also be used as a day-to-day management tool to control work reallocation, productivity and performance management.

To be fully successful, a workforce plan will also need to provide insights into succession planning for senior teams and to organization design and it will also contribute to setting the desired culture. This is far more difficult to achieve via a mechanized workforce allocation tool but can, in part, be set up by putting suitable people in the correct management roles. The yellow section in Worked Example 12.2 shows who will do certain management roles – John Moon is Head of Department and sits on the Ethics Committee and will be responsible for setting a suitable strategy and upholding standards so becomes very influential in its culture – in this way the softer side of HR planning can be addressed.

Further soft workforce planning factors, beyond the scope of a simple tool, must be addressed, such as:

- At a strategic level, the workforce plan will show what an organization needs to do in respect of its human assets to achieve competitive advantage. It will show which aspects of talent management require most attention, whether there are sufficient skills in key areas and where there is a need for HR interventions.
- At an operational level, the workforce plan will provide intelligence on recruitment over the period of the plan or changes in business. It will provide visibility on redeployment or redundancy as the business strategy evolves and emphasis is placed on different things (such as closing down departments, introducing new products and services or developing new locations of work). It will provide insights on training needs in both the short and the long term.

Other more general issues need to be considered – such as the ethnicity, diversity and age of the workforce – and these issues need to be built into future plans. Changing demographic realities, employment laws, technological advances, and ever-evolving globalization dictate that it is time to get focused and serious about creating diverse and inclusive workforce plans that drive performance and spark innovation.

Furthermore, a resilient workforce plan will increase workforce agility meaning that a workforce has 'the ability to stay open to new directions and be continually proactive, helping to assess the limits or risks of existing approaches and ensuring that leaders and followers have an agile and change-ready, mind-set to enable them, and ultimately the organisation, to keep moving, changing, adapting' (CIPD, 2011, p. 6).

CRITICAL PERSPECTIVE

Workforce, Productivity and Economic Measures?

Measures of productivity are generally based on a formula that considers 'value of transformed outputs' minus the 'value of transformed inputs' per 'unit(s) of transforming resource' that *are not* part of the end product or service (e.g. people, production machines, facilities, etc.). The accuracy of a productivity calculation depends on exactly how each of these factors are defined. All too often, over-simplified single factor productivity calculations are used. In particular, using number of people in the workforce as a single denominator, as in the ONS formula.

The problem with using only the number of people in the workforce as a denominator is that the fewer people that a company employs, the more productive an organization looks, at least in the short term. However, people are often replaced by technology which may not cost in terms of salary but costs in terms of capital expenditure, interest on loans, depreciation, maintenance, errors, training, installation and obsolescence. Therefore, having fewer employees in the long term does not necessarily give more productivity – as a multi-factor denominator would demonstrate. In the long term, reducing the number of employees can reduce production capacity and therefore output and hence productivity.

The key point is ...

that a significant problem occurs because different measures of productivity are often used by economists/governments (who favour the ONS single-factor employee denomination) and operations managers/company directors (who favour more organizational specific multi-factor definitions). Perhaps a more standard, usable and accurate formula for productivity is needed?

SHORT CASE 12.4

Workforce Intelligence Planning at Higgs & Sons Solicitors

Higgs & Sons is a successful legal firm that employs in excess of 200 people. The HR Department has engaged the workforce in a 'My Future' HR initiative, and to maintain a cutting edge in HR in support of the firm's business strategy the firm's Managing Partner and HR Director agreed to introduce workforce intelligence planning (WIP) into Higgs & Sons. The first phase of WIP has been designed to:

Source: © Alexander Supertramp/Shutterstock

- establish WIP in the HR Department and align it to the firm's business plan
- engage senior leadership in the design
- engage all employees, both legal and support staff, in the design of a 'One Team' initiative
- include a focus on the wider enterprise; to ascertain how changes in wider stakeholders' needs (e.g. courts, insurance companies, Ministry of Justice) are changing and could affect WIP in Higgs & Sons
- understand the future client context by engaging with the wider enterprise
- conduct a formative and subsequent evaluation to ensure dynamism
- design a workforce-planning model which includes internal and external factors.

In order to engage the workforce and partners in the workforce intelligence plan's design and implementation, interviews and focus groups were initially undertaken with business owners and staff members to identify their needs and identify innovative approaches from their experience. The findings highlighted many different employee and senior management ideas. The findings have informed a 'One Team' plan, which has been developed and put into practice along with an annual survey, to measure the impact of the plan. For example, the evaluation survey will identify the success of 'boundary spanning' employees, who work across different departments, and understand how this improves the client base and agility of the workforce.

The intention of this HR initiative was to extend WIP to include the behaviours of external stakeholders and clients who are not part of Higgs & Sons, but whose changing requirements may affect the overall number, type of skills, and behaviours of the Higgs & Sons workforce. Understanding these exogenous forces should help strategic WIP implementation. For instance, it is possible that some clients may move towards wanting fixed-priced legal work which may require a behavioural change in Higgs & Sons' culture towards a 'Managed Professional Business' (MPB) type operation in some services rather than following a more traditional 'Professional Partnership' (P2) type operation (Pinnington and Morris, 2003). Inevitably, this will have a dramatic impact upon WP, WIP and SWP.

Questions

1. What are the implications of the co-development of the workforce plan?
2. How will HR ensure that the WIP is sustainable?
3. Why and how can external factors be effectively included in the WIP?

Source: Higgs & Sons, 2017.

Stop and Think

Workforce planning has in the past been seen as a mechanical and computational exercise focusing on headcount, especially in more knowledge-based industries, but the practice is becoming softer. Increasing emphasis is now being placed on skills, fit and culture. Likewise appraisals, reward and remuneration must be aligned. What practice do you think should prevail: 'hard' or 'soft'?

Recruitment and Selection

Based on job analysis and activity within the workforce planning process an organization may decide to reallocate workers from one job to another, reduce the number of workers or recruit new workers. While it is easy to understand the need for systematic and strategic recruitment and selection, developing an understanding of how to implement it at an organizational level is more difficult. This is particularly true in the context of strategic HRM because the vast majority of the recruitment and selection literature adopts a micro-HRM perspective, focusing on narrow issues and specific techniques. This can lead to poor practice and a failure to apply a rigorous approach to attracting and selecting competent people. In this section we will review key issues for operations managers who need to be involved in recruitment activities to make sure a suitable workforce is provided for operations. The process of recruitment should be evidence-based, systematic and strategic as shown in Figure 12.7.

In systematic approaches to selection, a sequential process is followed that applies research (e.g. job market conditions) and problem-solving logic (e.g. recruitment tests) to recruitment and selection (see Figure 12.7). The process begins with job analysis, in which various HR and operations management techniques are applied to determine the work to be done and the various knowledge, skills, abilities and other characteristics/competencies that are required to deliver the work.

Job analysis: a systematic process designed to determine what a job role involves and what makes for an effective worker in that role. It produces either a job description (work orientated job analysis) or a person specification (worker orientated analysis).

Based on the **job analysis**, recruitment activities are carried out to advertise and communicate job vacancies, and attract applicants by describing the tasks and person requirements alongside benefits and other information. Job analyses also guide decisions about selection criteria (i.e. upon what information will a selection decision be made?), and ultimately the assessment techniques used to make the selection. Information about the reliability and validity of assessments also guides decision-making about which techniques to use.

While robust selection helps to ensure that people are recruited with as suitable competencies as can be reasonably expected, the processes of performance management, and training and learning help people to ultimately integrate into the organization and become more purposeful.

Figure 12.7 The recruitment and selection process

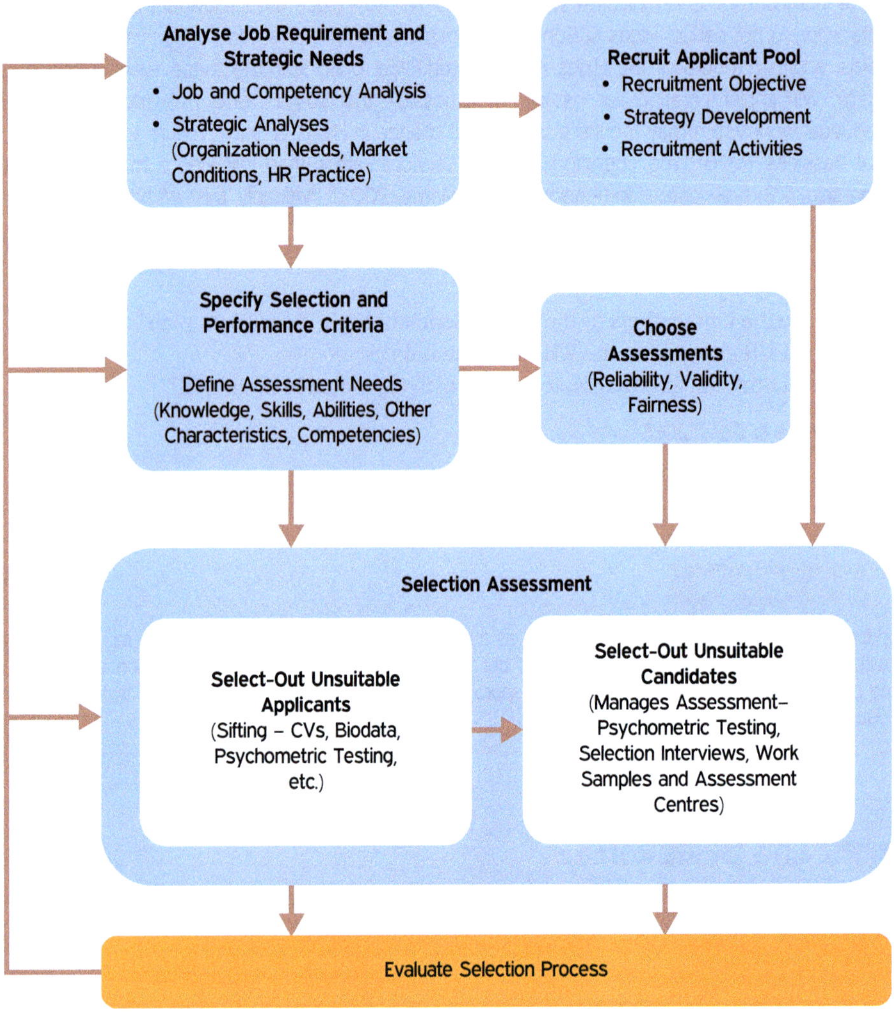

Source: Adapted from Woods and West (2014).

Recruitment: Attracting People to Jobs

For systematic recruitment the following factors need to be considered:

- *Recruitment objectives:* identifying the specific recruitment need, the kinds of individuals to be recruited, the time-frame for processes, and the required levels of performance and retention needed from the process
- *Recruitment activities:* application of specific methods of recruitment to attract the applicant pool, typically involving decisions about who will do the recruitment, whether it will be outsourced, the nature of the information to be conveyed and the use of various media
- *Strategic development:* working out a strategy for the recruitment activity, in which key questions about who and where to recruit, how to reach targeted people and what to communicate during the recruitment are all considered.

Schneider's Attraction-Selection-Attrition (ASA) model (Schneider, 1987) describes how people are attracted to organizations principally on the basis of their judgement about whether they fit with the job and organization. Initial decisions may be based on perceptions of job fit, but, according to the ASA model, during the recruitment and selection phase, applicant and organization both enter into a kind of fact-finding exercise, designed to determine the degree of fit between them. When the person-to-organization fit is high, the applicant is more likely to be selected.

Once within the organization, employees who are a poorer fit are more likely to leave (attrition). The result of this is that, over time, an organization will gradually become populated with people who fit well with the organization. There are many benefits to this, such as employees tending to show high levels of job satisfaction and organizational commitment. Schneider's ASA model recognizes the importance of subjective 'fit' perceptions in HRM decision making, with specific implications for how jobs are marketed during recruitment.

Selection: Fitting People Competences to Job Descriptions

Before we can assess whether or not a candidate is suitable for the job we are recruiting for, we first need to establish what we require. In the first instance, we would probably have a fairly clear idea of the kind of things that make an operations manager effective in their job (for instance, they need to be analytical, output focused, good at managing teams and competent at using technology). But what if we are recruiting to a role that we know little about? Then we would need to follow a process called job analysis. Job analysis is the foundation of all selection processes. It is the systematic process by which HR professionals seek to better understand what a job role involves and what makes for an effective worker in that role.

There are two broad approaches to conducting job analysis. These approaches differ in their focus, the methods you might use to conduct them and their resultant outputs:

- *Work-orientated job analysis* seeks to break the job down into its elements, the smallest units of work that it consists of, such as pressing a button on a machine, opening an application on a computer, or selecting an appropriate tool. These elements are grouped into job tasks, all of which may themselves be grouped together to produce a 'job description'.
- *Worker-orientated job analysis* focuses on defining the knowledge, skills, abilities and other attributes/characteristics (KSAOs) that make a worker effective in a particular role. KSAOs cover a very diverse range of characteristics of the job holder's knowledge, skills learnt for a particular job task, more generalized innate cognitive and physical abilities, motivation, attitudes, values, and personality traits. Once defined, these attributes are drawn together to form a detailed 'person specification'.

In contemporary HRM practice, a very widely used approach to job analysis is competency modelling or profiling. Competencies can be defined as observable workplace behaviours that can form the basis of differentiated measurements of performance. The job analyst, either using their own expertise or through consultation with subject matter experts, identifies the competencies that best reflect the required behaviour in a particular role. The identified behaviours then inform the behaviours that will need to be demonstrated during the selection process by the successful applicant for the role. For example, for the role of a customer service office manager, the job analyst might reason that the competencies that the job-holder required might be as follows: organizing their own time and that of others, managing resources and budgets and communicating effectively. A competency framework would inform the job analyst of the level of each competency required, and would detail the kinds of behaviour that would be demonstrated by someone performing at this level in a similar role. The successful applicant for the role would then be required to demonstrate behaviour at this level at selection, perhaps assessed through their performance on a trial period.

From a practical point of view, standardized competency models (e.g. typing skills, language skills, numerical reasoning, and logic tests) help practitioners to understand the broad competency domain, but specific companies typically have their own emphasis and contextual information to add, making competency models organization- and job-specific.

By nature, competencies are flexible, allowing them to be applied across jobs at different levels of seniority, and to remain relevant as job requirements change over time. For these reasons, the recent trend is for senior managers to favour the competency approach over other forms of job analysis (Campion *et al.*, 2011). The task of the HRM practitioner, together with the operations manager, is to devise competency models, develop descriptions of relevant behavioural content, and then identify specific competencies required for specific jobs and positions in the organization.

Stop and Think

Organizational human resource requirements are always changing based on internal factors such as strategy, technological advances and external factors such as legislation, market conditions and seasonality. How can more certainty be brought into recruitment and selection of the workforce?

Employee Performance Management

Purpose and Process

In order to meet strategic objectives, organizations need to capitalize on a number of critical resources, including financial, technical and human resources. Some managers may argue that the human resources of an organization are often its chief source of sustainable competitive advantage, especially in the global arena. However, in order to ensure that employees are able to perform their tasks at optimal levels, organizations need to manage their performance in a systematic fashion, using appropriate human resource strategies.

In HR terms **performance management** is the process through which organizations can ensure that individual employees are working towards organizational goals by monitoring and guiding their performance. **HR performance management systems** (PMSs) are the primary vehicle through which organizations: (1) allocate work through **job assignment** (2) set goals through a **goal setting** process (3) establish **performance standards** (4) provide **feedback** (5) conduct **performance appraisal**, and (6) distribute and allocate outcomes (rewards and punishments).

Furthermore, PMSs help organizations successfully implement their business strategy. In other words, organizations need to design and implement sophisticated PMSs in order to be able to get optimal performance from all employees. To do this, they need to ensure that all stages of PMSs are put in place, implemented and reviewed on a regular basis.

While the concepts of performance management and performance appraisal are often used interchangeably, essentially the performance appraisal is just one piece of the overall human resource performance management system. We discuss each of these components in detail below, while also examining the importance of two intervening variables that may have a significant impact on the performance management process, namely employee motivation and supervisor-subordinate relationships. The final PMS aspect we must consider is human performance in a global context, which we will do at the end of this chapter.

Performance management (of human resources): the process through which organizations can ensure that individual employees are working towards organizational goals by monitoring and guiding their performance.

(HR) performance management system (PMS): the process by which organizations ensure that employees are working towards achieving a company's strategic objectives, This includes job assignment, goal setting, coaching, feedback, rewards/punishment and performance appraisal.

Job assignment: matching individuals' competences with job requirements, so as to achieve the best fit.

Goal setting (HR): assigning work tasks to individuals so that they are clear on what is expected of them. To be effective, the goals should be specific, measurable, attainable, realistic and time-bound.

Performance standards (HR): specific performance expectations and levels against which employees performance will be judged – thus, it should be clear to the employees what level(s) of performance would be deemed unacceptable, acceptable and surpassing expectations.

Feedback (HR): the process by which individuals are informed of the degree to which they are meeting desired or expected levels of performance.

Performance appraisal (HR): evaluating an individual's past performance for a specific period, usually one year.

Work Assignment

As discussed in the previous section, work assignment is about recruiting and selecting new people to join the organization. Inevitably there is rarely a perfect fit between a person and a job specification and individuals will need training and/or guidance to bridge the skills and abilities gaps. Even in cases where an organization has hired an individual who is a perfect fit for the job, the organization needs to be aware that both individuals and the content of jobs evolve. In other words, someone who was a perfect fit at the time of hiring may not be such a good fit a few months later since the job's demands may have changed. Clearly, the bigger the gap between the individual's skills and abilities and the job requirement, the greater the need for performance management. Goal setting, feedback, coaching and other developmental activities are all components or outcomes of the performance management process, which seeks to bridge the gap between achieved and desired performance. This iterative ongoing process is designed to help employees perform the work content of their jobs more productively and purposefully.

Goal Setting

In order for individual employees to know what is expected of them, it is crucial that they are set clear and unambiguous goals. It is well documented that individuals who have been provided goals are able to work more efficiently and are also more effective at their assignments than those who are not given goals and must figure these out from their own understanding of the job. Having goals that are clearly defined helps employees understand what is expected of them, and assists them in planning and prioritizing their work accordingly. However, in order for goal setting to be effective and for the individual to use the goals in accomplishing his or her work, these goals should be: (i) specific; (ii) measurable; (iii) attainable; (iv) relevant/realistic; and (v) time-bound. Thus, for example, a goal that states 'reduce shipping costs by 3% over the next six months' is likely to be more helpful to an individual than simply a goal that states 'reduce costs'.

Performance Standards

Once clear goals have been set, it is essential that clear performance standards are established so that the employee is aware of how his or her performance will be judged and rated. Each employee can then be measured, during the performance review against the established standards. For instance, let us say that a rating of 'five' on the dimension of 'quality of customer service' (on a five-point scale, with five being the highest possible level of performance and one being the lowest possible level) can only be attained by individuals who have served at least 50 customers within a given time period (e.g. one work-shift) and got, on average, ratings of 4.5 or above. Such customer feedback is now often sought immediately in service industries by emoji button style feedback machines. By this measure those individuals who have on average less than 4.5 will get a rating of '4'.

One of the biggest advantages of providing clear standards is that it reduces unnecessary and unpleasant surprises and makes it easier for employees to keep track of how they are performing by regularly assessing their achievements against the established standards. In addition, this practice can motivate employees to be more proactive and seek out feedback, so they know more about how they could improve their performance to enable them to earn the desired rating level.

Providing Feedback

Feedback is the mechanism through which an individual can be informed of how he or she is doing on the job. As one might expect, this process is rather complicated and stressful, it is often avoided by both supervisors and subordinates, especially where the supervisor is required to share feedback that is negative. However, it is crucial that supervisors provide regular feedback to employees, since timely and directed feedback to employees can help employees correct performance deficiencies and prevent future errors. Further, it is very important that managers provide feedback on a consistent basis and deliver it with a view to helping the subordinate improve his or her performance, and do not use it as an opportunity to 'punish' the subordinate and/or make him or her look foolish. Feedback delivered in a spirit of fairness is likely to be accepted by the subordinate. Whereas if the subordinate feels that the feedback is insincere, or designed as an excuse to punish, then s/he is likely to reject it, thus defeating the purpose of giving the feedback.

Clearly, organizations need to create a culture where feedback is easily accepted by those concerned and is seen as a critical part of the performance management process. In cases where managers deliver insufficient feedback, human resource departments may need to institute policies that mandate feedback, perhaps by requiring documentation of their feedback meetings and follow-up with subordinates.

Performance Appraisal

Performance appraisal refers to the formal evaluation of employees, conducted to determine the degree to which they are meeting specified objectives. The primary purpose of performance appraisals tends to be administrative – determining merit/ salary raises, promotions and so on. There is, however, another purpose for which organizations use performance appraisals: to determine the developmental needs of individual employees. A developmental approach to appraisals is particularly important as it holds out the prospect of improving future performance rather than simply measuring past performance.

In either case, for the performance appraisal process to proceed smoothly and to serve the desired purpose, it is essential that the organization design and implement comprehensive, fair and transparent systems and processes that are explicitly shared with both supervisors and subordinates. All employees, both appraisers and appraisees, should be familiar with the appraisal purpose and process, the appraisal documentation, the relevant dimensions of evaluation and the standards that will be used to rate performance. By doing this all parties know what to expect and when to expect it. Communicating the purpose and process of appraisal is an important aspect of performance management for an operations manager, and comprehensive support from the HR function is needed to define contemporary key practices of the process.

SHORT CASE 12.5

Why GE Is Stopping its Numerical People Performance Appraisal

Source: © Sundry Photography/Shutterstock

In 2015, GE abandoned its annual performance review, joining Microsoft, Accenture and Adobe and other leading companies that are looking for alternatives to the traditional performance management system. Famous for its use of a quantitative, forced ranking system, the hard-driven style of performance at GE and elsewhere has been criticized by academics, practitioners, managers and employees. The recent financial downturns at GE has led to some question about the future efficacy of traditional HR PMSs and a recent article in *Fast Company* predicted that 'half of Fortune 1000 companies will drop numerical performance ranking for people as a basis for annual performance reviews'.

Instead, performance management at GE is becoming more continuous, more developmental, less formal and less quantitative. With regard to the frequency of appraisal, 'the world isn't really on an annual cycle any more for any thing', said GE's Head of Human Resources, Susan Peters. The annual appraisal, according to Peters, 'had become more a ritual than moving the company upwards and forwards'. Instead, in part due to generational preferences, the company is adopting an instantaneous feedback model, which Peter says is 'more frequent, faster, and mobile-enabled'. The programme, called 'PD@GE' or 'performance development at GE', assigns each employee short-term goals. Rather than annual reviews or quantitative rankings, managers are expected to frequently monitor progress towards the completion of priorities following a philosophy of continuous improvement rather than ranking. An 'app' serves as a central note-taking repository for managers and employees, who can also request to receive, or give, feedback at any point. The language has also changed: goals are 'priorities', performance conversations are 'touch-points' and feedback is done through 'insights'. Coaching has replaced ranking as the operative verb in the process.

And the annual performance review? It is still in place at GE, although now it is a summary conversation held in December, in which managers and employees can look back with the benefit of data gathered throughout the year and set goals for the future without the fear and stress of having a once-a-year appraisal that determines a person's career prospects or future pay. GE still rewards performance through pay, a process referred to as differentiation. As Peters puts it: 'One thing we do know is that we will maintain our culture of meritocracy and differentiation. . . . We're trying to figure this out and keep some of the fundamentals of the culture and also move to a place where it's more contemporary.'

Questions

1. What do you think of organizations doing away with numerical ratings? Will it help boost morale and productivity, or cause ambiguity and confusion?
2. If you were managing a team, how would you compare team-member performance without using numbers?

Source: 'Why the annual performance review is going extinct', *Fast Company*, 21 October 2015; and 'Why GE had to kill its annual performance reviews after more than three decades', *Quartz*, 13 August 2015.

Distributing/Allocating Outcomes

Individuals generally work for an organization in exchange for appropriate compensation and rewards. Thus, an individual who performs better than a colleague should have a reasonable expectation that s/he will get rewarded at a higher level than the said colleague. Indeed, the performance appraisal process plays a critical role in this determination. However, it is important that the organization has fair and transparent procedures so that employees have a clear understanding of what kinds of reward are likely to be associated with the relevant level of performance. Rewards may be financial (e.g. more salary, shares, bonus, etc.) or non-financial (e.g. more recognition, autonomy, holiday, better office, etc.). It is also important that the organization adhere to the stated policies and procedures.

Employee Motivation

According to Pritchard and Ashwood (2008) motivation is the 'process used to allocate energy to maximize the satisfaction of needs'. Indeed, almost all scholars agree that motivation is guided by individual needs. So, when someone is hungry, they need food to satisfy that hunger and are thus motivated to find food. On the other hand, if someone believes they need a bigger house they will find ways to earn more money to buy one. Of course, one might argue that often what motivates people is their wants (e.g. luxury items) and not their needs (basic necessities like food, shelter and clothing). Nonetheless, people are driven to achieve whatever they believe they need, and not everyone is motivated by the same things.

Thus operations managers who understand what motivates their subordinates will be better able to manage their performance by addressing those needs. Of course, not all employees' needs can be easily fulfilled by organizations. Take, for example, two employees – the first needs a half day off to carry out family care issues, while the second wants (or may argue needs) promotions every year. In both cases, performance will begin to suffer if the needs are not met. However, while the organization may be able to fulfil the first employee's need without too much trouble, the second employee's need may be impossible to meet.

Pritchard and DiazGranados (2008) present a useful model that summarizes the potential connection between performance management and employee motivation (or need satisfaction) – see Figure 12.8. Essentially, their model mirrors Vroom's classical (1964) expectancy theory, where motivation is viewed as a 'future-orientated concept' and individual behaviour is driven by the expected receipt of desirable rewards.

Performance → Results

It is critical that individuals perceive a strong match between their abilities and the results expected of them. Perhaps an example would help illustrate this best. Several years ago, an author of this book was asked to teach an undergraduate course on database design, and he was required to start almost immediately as the previous instructor had suddenly died. Since he had recently completed a doctorate in a different subject and not studied database design since being an undergraduate nearly 10 years before, he perceived this link to be very weak, and thus had no motivation to take on this assignment. In other words, he believed that no matter how hard he worked, he would not be able to achieve the desired results in the time-frame specified. Conversely, if individuals perceive that they have the necessary abilities to perform a work task, and believe their performance will lead to the desired results, they will be motivated to take on and try to do well in new tasks.

Results → Appraisal

Once individuals have achieved the desired results, it is essential that a formal, structured evaluation is conducted at the appropriate time, and that detailed descriptive feedback is provided to the individuals. In other words, it is critical that once the results have been achieved the supervisor explains to the subordinate, supported by facts and figures, why his or her performance exceeds expectations on some dimensions, meets expectations on others, and is perhaps below expectations on yet others. Such feedback will allow the subordinate to improve his or her abilities and request relevant guidance and or training, where necessary. The critical issue here is that subordinates must believe that their achievements and related results will be fairly and accurately appraised.

Appraisal → Outcomes

Once the appraisal is done, another important link (appraisal to outcomes) must be recognized by subordinates as real and valid. In other words, if the subordinate has been rated as exceeding expectations and yet receives an average reward (e.g. merit case and/or bonus), the subordinate is likely to see this link as broken. Thus it is absolutely critical that an organization follows fair and transparent procedures when deciding raises and bonuses, and these

Figure 12.8 Performance management and employee motivation

Source: Adapted from Pritchard and DiazGrandos (2008).

should mirror the appraisal ratings. Far too often supervisors are tempted to over-reward subordinates they like by awarding them higher than deserved rates; or conversely, under-reward subordinates they don't like with lower than deserved rates. If information on this type of anomaly becomes common knowledge, employees' trust in the performance management system is likely to diminish and they will see this link as broken, with the attendant negative impact on motivation.

Outcomes → Needs Satisfaction

The final link, outcomes to needs, is perhaps the most important of the four in this model. No matter what outcomes the organization offers, if those outcomes do not meet the employees' needs then the employee will not be motivated. Of course, as previously noted, not all individuals have the same needs. This poses a dilemma for an organization which is: how do you come up with a reward system that can satisfy each individual employee's needs? Furthermore, too often an employee's needs are beyond an organization's capacity to meet, in which case an employee may have outgrown or become mismatched to an organization's work requirements and may have to move to another more appropriate organization. While this might indeed be true in some cases, the fact remains that effective performance management requires that organizations try to meet as many of their employees' needs as is practicably possible.

Overall the above model presents one of the clearest representations of motivation at work. Organizations and operations managers that truly care about performance management would do well to understand the individual components and work on ensuring that the links are seen as real and valid and are put into practice.

The key point is

that to be motivated, a workforce needs to be culturally, emotionally and practically engaged with an organization's best interests. If this is not happening at all levels and within all areas, a workforce is not positively contributing. A focus on people and their individual positivity can drive the collective benefit for the whole organization.

Summary

In this chapter we have introduced the concept of performance management systems (PMSs) as a mechanism to help organizations achieve their strategic objectives. PMSs help managers think about the practicalities of what to measure and when to take measurements so they can control and change organizations.

Real-time access to data on business goals, key performance indicators and business processes is one of the critical elements for a successful performance management system. Since organizational performance cannot be measured independently of people performance an integrated systems approach, with suitable supporting IT, is required for both people performance and organizational performance – as seen in each level of the performance pyramid.

Multiple deployments of PMSs, such as experienced by multinational enterprises (MNEs) and increasingly longer global supply chains make establishing PMSs more challenging. Too often, global organizations treat PMSs for their international operations as a mere extension of their domestic systems without taking into account cultural, societal and environmental differences. Given that culture and context of work can vary significantly from country to country, or indeed location to location within a single country, PMSs should be tailored to each unique business environment.

Longer global supply chains make performance issues more inter-dependent and context sensitive and PMS problems can be exacerbated if they are not carefully adapted across a supply chain. So, for example, supplier and customer PMSs developed by a UK company for a UK supply chain cannot necessarily be transferred, without adaptation, to measure supplier or customer performances in Eastern Europe or India.

Overall, PMSs are about establishing a baseline performance for any given metric, and once established, improvements can then begin. The improvement of performance measures is the subject of *quality management* and is dealt with in a separate chapter in this book.

Key Theories

The key theories discussed in this chapter were:

- **Organizational alignment** – through performance measurement
- **Scientific management and operations performance objectives** – Taylorism and the foundations of people management
- **Components of a performance management system (PMS)**
- **Performance management frameworks:**
  - The Performance Pyramid
  - The Balanced Scorecard
  - The Performance Prism
- **Human resource management** for operations management managers
- **Workforce planning** – approaches, cases and tools
- **Recruitment and selection approaches** – of people to operations management jobs
- **Performance management and motivation** of people in operations management

Key Equations

$$\text{Multi-factor productivity} = \frac{\text{Output from the operation}}{\text{All inputs to the operation}}$$

$$\text{Single-factor productivity} = \frac{\text{Output from the operation}}{\text{Single input to the operation}}$$

$$\text{ONS productivity} = \frac{(\text{Turnover} - \text{Intermediate consumption})}{\text{Number of workers}}$$

Suggested Answers to Stop and Think Questions

1. **Alignment of performance measures:** Ensuring alignment throughout an entire business can be tricky. There are many different types of organizational structure. In a hierarchy with many levels, scope of responsibility of each department may be clear but the number of levels may make a clear flow-down from top to bottom very difficult as objectives become increasingly vague as they are translated for use at each layer. On the other hand, a shallow structure may make flow-down easier but broader responsibilities may make measurement in each department more difficult. More sophisticated structures such as matrix or product-oriented structures add another level of difficulty as objectives may not always flow vertically down the structure from the strategic apex but may also flow horizontally across the structure from customer-facing project teams or product groups.
2. **Airline performance measures:** While there are a number of possibilities here, generally speaking there are two measures that customers are interested in. First, the number of delayed or cancelled flights: this is generally known as dispatch reliability. This measure is useful in any transport business. And second, the safety record, which may be composed of a number of measures such as fatalities, crashes or on-board accidents. A safe and reliable airline is possibly what most customers would want and they may be prepared to pay a premium for this. Although a safe and reliable system is generally an efficient (and therefore low cost) system so there should be no premium paid to gain access to this system.

3. **Hard HRM practices verses soft HRM practices, why so?** Hard HRM practices will be best suited to workers who have not bought into high level company goals (such as temporary staff), or who do a simple mechanical repetitive job, or those who find lack of supervision difficult to deal with; hard HRM may also be applied to more junior members of staff or those with little or no work experience. People better suited to soft HRM tend to be highly educated and experienced people, those who have bought into high level company vision, those who can work effectively alone, self motivated consciousness workers. Applying the wrong practices will result in lack of productivity of both types.
4. **What practice do you think should prevail: 'hard' or 'soft'?** This depends on the industry and the volume of people being managed. Industries with many 'hard' metrics need to rely on the clarity, precision and immediacy that hard metrics can bring (e.g. mass production or mass services provision). Industries that are more professional, knowledge intensive with longer-term visions should rely more on 'soft' measures. In reality, all industries tend to have both types, with people becoming more driven by softer measures as they become more senior.
5. **How can more certainty be brought into recruitment and selection of the workforce?** This requires HR and operations managers to be aware of new products and services being developed and new strategies being adopted. Management need to have professional HR people aware of new employment legislation, marketing need to be aware of changing consumer demands, plus a general awareness of new and disruptive technology needs to be considered. Getting this wrong can lead to an incorrectly skilled workforce.

connect

Review Questions

1. What are the five key factors for performance measurement?
2. What are the productivity formulas?
3. What are good tests for checking the usefulness of performance measures?
4. Name and describe three classic performance management models.
5. List HR activities that positively contribute to performance.
6. What is the difference between 'hard' and 'soft' HRM?
7. What is workforce planning?
8. When recruiting, what are the two broad approaches to job analysis?
9. What are the four main transitions in people performance management?

Discussion Questions

1. Discuss why performance management must be a top-down process.
2. What are the cultural challenges that organizations might face when attempting to introduce a performance management system?
3. What are the advantages and disadvantages of different performance management models with respect to actual company performance?
4. How can employees in an organization be encouraged to be more productive?

5. Why is recruitment and selection so important for operations?
6. People performance management is an ongoing process; what difficulties will managers incur during this process?

Problems

1. The Washclean company makes 1,200 washing machines per week and employs 50 people who cost a total of £60,000 a week to employ. Washclean uses £200 of materials per machine. Other costs (e.g. overheads) are estimated at £100 per machine. Washclean sells machines for £500 each. For one week of production:

   (a) using the multi-factor productivity formula, calculate productivity for all factors based on cost

   (b) using single-factor productivity formula, calculate productivity for number of machines per person

   (c) using the ONS productivity formula calculate productivity.

2. The Hapidaze insurance company sold 1,000 insurance policies in a month to 1,000 different customers (one each). It planned to sell 1,500 policies in that month. It had 150 complaints from customers about errors in their policies. (a) What is Hapidaze's sales performance? (b) What is Hapidaze's service quality?

3. The Strongsafe building company needs to allocate 'units of work' to craftsmen to building jobs for the next month. Buildsafe has five full-time employees and five jobs. The rules Buildsafe applies to work allocation are as follows:

   - Each job needs at least two people to work on it – for safety reasons
   - Craftsmen can only work on their qualified occupation – for trade union reasons
   - Each person can have between two and five jobs at any one time – to control travel
   - Each person is allocated whole (1.0) or half (0.5) units of work, and each person can have between 3.0 and 5.0 units of work across all their jobs.

   Employees are skilled as below:

   - John – contract manager and general builder
   - Brian – bricklayer
   - Anita – plumber
   - Mo – carpenter
   - Sarah – electrician

   For this month no one job can have more than 10 units of work allocated to it otherwise the job will not make a profit as workers get paid by completed units of work.

   Using the workload allocation matrix below and a process of trial and error allocate workers to jobs so that all work allocation rules are obeyed.

Work Allocation for Buildsafe - Month X

		full-time equivalent	1.00	1.00	1.00	1.00	1.00	5.00
		position	Contracts/General	Bricklayer	Plumber	Carpenter	Electrician	
		name	John	Brian	Anita	Mo	Sarah	TOTAL
Job	**Skills needed**		units of work					
ONE	contracts/general, bricklaying, plumbing, carpenter, electrician							
TWO	contracts/general, bricklaying, carpenter, electrician							
THREE	contracts/general, bricklaying, plumbing, carpenter							
FOUR	contracts/general, bricklaying							
FIVE	contracts/general, bricklaying, plumbing, carpenter, electrician							
	Actual work load							
	Number of jobs							

Further Reading

Armstrong, M. (2017) *Armstrong on Reinventing Performance Management: Building a Culture of Continuous Improvement*, London, Kogan Paul.

Crawshaw, J. R., Budhwar, P., and Davis, A. (2017) *Human Resource Management: Strategic and International Perspectives*, 2nd edn, Sage, London.

Kaplan, R. S. and Norton, P. N. (2004) *Strategy Maps: Converting Intangible Assets into Tangible Outcomes*, Harvard Business School, Boston, MA.

Kaplan, R. S. and Norton, P. N. (2008) *The Execution Premium: Linking Strategy to Operations for Competitive Advantage*, Harvard Business School, Boston, MA.

Lucianetti, L., Battista, V., & Koufteros, X. (2019) Comprehensive performance measurement systems design and organizational effectiveness. *International Journal of Operations & Production Management*, **39**(2), 326–356.

Neely, A. (2007) *Business Performance Measurement: Unifying Theory and Integrating Practice*, Cambridge University Press, Cambridge.

Neely, A., Adams, C. and Kennerly, M. (2002) *The Performance Prism: The Scorecard for Measuring and Managing Business Success*, FT Prentice Hall, London.

Neely, A., Yaghi, B. and Youell, N. (2008a) *Enterprise Performance Management: The Global State of the Art*, Cranfield University, School of Management.

ONS (2018) 'How productive is your business?' https://www.ons.gov.uk/employmentandlabourmarket/peopleinwork/labourproductivity/articles/howproductiveisyourbusiness/2018-07-06#business-calculator-compare-your-business-to-others-in-great-britain

Pinnington, A, and Morris, T. (2003) 'Archetype change in professional organizations: Survey evidence from large law firms', *British Journal of Management*, **14**(1), 85–99.

Pritchard, R. D. and Ashwood, E. (2008) *Managing Motivation*, Taylor and Francis, New York.

References

Campion, M. A., Palmer, D. K. and Campion, J. E. (2011) 'A review of structure in the selection interview', *Personnel Psychology*, **50**(3), 655–702.

CIPD (2011) *HR Outsourcing Fact-sheet*, Chartered Institute of Personnel and Development, London.

Drucker, P. F. (1955) *The Practice of Management*, Heinemann, London.

Freitas, W. R. de S., Jabbour, C. J. C. and Santos, F. C. A. (2011) 'Continuing the evolution towards sustainable HRM and sustainable organisations', *Business Strategy Series*, **12**(5), 226–234.

Kaplan, R. S. and Norton, D. P. (1996) *The Balanced Scorecard: Translating Strategy into Action*, Harvard Business School Press, Boston, MA.

Kaplan, R. S. and Norton, D. P. (2008) 'Mastering the management system', *Harvard Business Review*, **86**(1), 62–77.

Kaufman, B. E. (2014) 'The historical development of American HRM broadly viewed', *Human Resource Management Review*, **24**(3), 196–218.

Lynch, R. and Cross, K. (1991) *Measure Up! Yardstick for Continuous Improvement*. Blackwell, Oxford.

Pritchard, R. D. and DiazGrandos, D. (2008) 'Motivation and performance management', in A. Varma, P. S. Budhwar and A. S. DeNisi (eds.), *Performance Management Systems: A Global Perspective* (Global HRM Series), Routledge, London, pp. 40–54.

Schneider, B. (1987) 'The people make the place', *Personnel Psychology*, **40**(3), 437–453.

Skinner, W. (1974) 'The Focused Factory', *Harvard Business Review*, **52**(3), 113–121.

Storey, J. (1989) 'Introduction: From personnel management to human resource management', in J. Storey (ed.), *New Perspectives on Human Resource Management*, Blackwell Business, London, pp. 1–18.

Storey, J. (2007) 'Human resource management today: An assessment', in J. Storey (ed.). *Human Resource Management: A Critical Text*, 3rd edn, Routledge, London, pp. 3–19.

Taylor, F.W. (1911) *The Principles of Scientific Management*, Harper, New York.

Truss, C., Gratton, L., Hope-Hailey, V., McGovern, P. and Stiles, P. (1997) 'Soft and hard models of human resource management: A reappraisal', *Journal of Management Studies* **34**(1), 53–73.

Vroom, V. (1964) *Work and Motivation*, Wiley, New York.

Weber, W. (2009 [1946]) 'Characteristics of bureaucracy', in *From Max Weber: Essays in Sociology*, Routledge, London, pp. 196–198.

Woods, S. A and West, M. A. (2014) *The Psychology of Work and Organizations*, 2nd edn, Andover, Cengage Learning EMEA.

13 Quality Management

Learning Outcomes

After reading this chapter, you should be able to:

- Define what quality is, and explain why it is important to organizations
- Describe different philosophies of leading quality experts
- Explain the history of quality management
- Give examples of quality dimensions in services and products
- Apply the tools of quality to organizational situations
- Describe the costs involved in providing a quality service or product

Coca-Cola's Dasani

Source: ©Keith Homan/Shutterstock

Dasani is the Coca-Cola Company's bottled water, which first launched in the US in 1999 to compete with Pepsi's Aquafina brand. It was described as bottled, purified water that was 'enhanced with minerals for a pure, fresh taste'. It had appealing packaging, with attractive recyclable light-blue tinted bottles. Dasani's promotional campaign carried the punch line 'Treat yourself well. Everyday', as the company wanted to emphasize the emotional and physical satisfaction provided by a healthy lifestyle. Dasani quickly captured a huge market share in bottled water, second only to Aquafina.

Coca-Cola spent £7 million launching Dasani in the UK on 10 February 2004, with the rather unlikely punch line 'The more you live life, the more you need Dasani.' It was a huge investment.

Within five weeks of its launch, Coca-Cola voluntarily recalled its entire stock of Dasani bottled water – about 500,000 bottles. The recall was made after a potentially harmful chemical, bromate, was found to exceed local legal standards. The UK's food quality regulator, the Food Standards Agency (FSA), claimed that long-term exposure to high levels of bromate could increase the risk of cancer. The limit for bromate in bottled and tap water differs across countries. In the UK the limit is 10 parts per million (ppm), whereas the limit in Europe is 25 ppm. Dasani was tested to be between 10 and 22 ppm, too high for the UK.

A reporter discovered that the source of Dasani was actually tap water, not natural spring water. The water came from Thames Water, and was processed at Coca-Cola's factory in south-east London. The story quickly made it to the leading newspapers, which accused Coca-Cola of selling processed, bottled water to the public for 95 pence (for a half-litre bottle), so making a profit of 3,166 times!

The FSA stated that Dasani did not comply with British labelling guidelines on the use of the term 'pure', as it should be used only with reference to 'single ingredient foods or to highlight the quality of ingredients'. Since Dasani added calcium (according to UK regulations), magnesium and sodium bicarbonate to the water to improve its taste, it could not be labelled or advertised as 'pure'. The FSA further accused the company of misleading consumers through erroneous advertisements: if bottled water was not labelled as mineral water or spring water, it was considered simply bottled drinking water.

When the story broke, Coca-Cola's marketing department explained that the tap water they used went through four stages of production before it was bottled. The purification process (adopted from NASA) removed any impurities, such as bacteria, viruses, salts, minerals, sugars, proteins, and toxin particles. This process would make the water tasteless: so, in order to enhance the taste of the purified water, minerals were added.

To support Coca-Cola's claim, it was stated that Dasani water had passed 99.92% of quality tests conducted by the Drinking Water Inspectorate of England and Wales. Coca-Cola worked closely with all regulatory bodies to solve the controversy, and was fully confident that Dasani complied with all guidelines and regulations in the UK. Canadean, an independent beverage research company, stated that at least two out of every five bottles of water sold around the world were like Dasani's 'purified' water, albeit with different purification processes. Canadean emphasized that the purity treatments were exactly the same as the treatments that normal tap water undergoes to satisfy public health requirements.

Coca-Cola had to halt the launch of Dasani in France and Germany but despite the recall, the company remained adamant about the high quality of its bottled water: 'In the packaged water business, people pay for a product because they know it is safe, high quality, available, and convenient. When the Coca-Cola Company sells drinking water in its various forms, it is not charging for the water per se, but rather for the value we add to the water to make it a branded beverage.'

Source: K.Y. Aparna (2005) 'Coca-Cola's Dasani in the UK', ECCH case study, ref no. 505-040-1, 2005.

Introduction

We can see from the Dasani case that even large corporations such as Coca-Cola can make quality management mistakes. In the eyes of customers, any mistake made by a firm can cause dissatisfaction. From a company's perspective, customer dissatisfaction is a quality problem. No organization can be 100% sure that it can provide the quality that the customers expect. Many firms also realize that quality has become a central issue for value creation and competitiveness. However, quality standards are challenging to manage.

There are several interpretations of what 'quality' means. In this chapter we shall show that there are different approaches that an organization can adopt in order to raise quality levels and prevent defects and failures occurring in its processes, products and services.

We will explore how quality management paradigms have been changing in order to comply with competitive challenges shaped by innovation, technology and services. We will address the dilemmas that many firms face when choosing the most suitable quality management approach. We will also show how quality performance can be measured, monitored and controlled.

Quality management can contribute to improved profitability by helping companies to design products and services that conform to specifications that define exactly what the customer wants. Quality products, processes and services also create greater value for customers, thus obtaining increased market share and revenue growth for the company. All this can lead to improved profitability, as shown in Figure 13.1.

Defining Quality

'Quality' is a highly subjective term. If you went around and asked a number of people to articulate what quality is, you would probably get many different answers. You would probably hear comments such as 'things that don't break', 'right the first time', 'customer value', 'conformance to standards', 'customer satisfaction' or 'no defects', for example. There are also short-, mid- and long-term quality expectations of products. For instance, it is acceptable that clothes might fade within a year if worn and washed a lot, but you would expect your washing machine to last

Figure 13.1 Quality's contribution to profitability

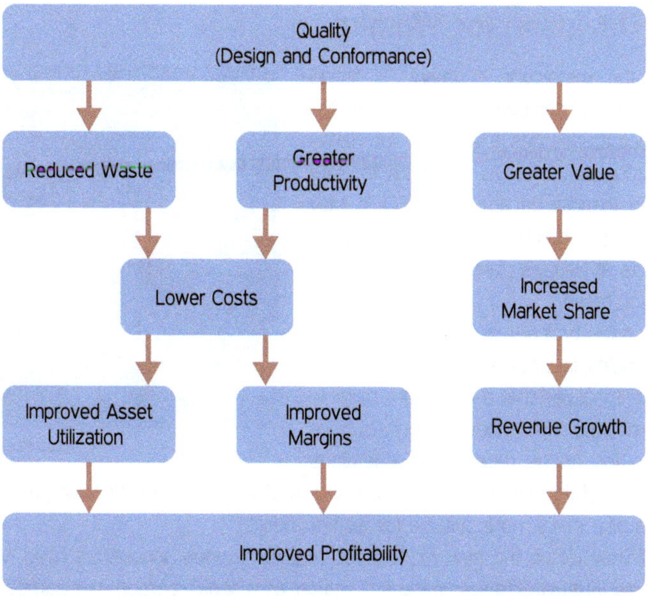

Source: Adapted from George and Weimerskirch (1998).

at least 5 years. The perceived quality of a product might also depend on what the product is made from; after all, a silk shirt feels nicer than polyester, and organic vegetables supposedly taste better than non-organic ones.

Our perception of service quality is even more subjective. It is likely that we have all been sick, or have required help from a doctor or hospital, at some point in our lives. In that situation, we would obviously prefer not to wait too long for consultations or treatment. Our perception of the experience is also affected by the behaviour of the doctors and nurses – whether they seem caring and are able to give us enough attention.

Quality is one of the most critical issues in satisfying the customer. Given the variations in expectations of quality, an organization has to make decisions about what level of quality it will aim to provide for its customers.

An initial challenge when attempting to improve quality levels is to define what is meant by quality. Garvin (1987) identifies five different approaches:

- The *transcendent approach* views quality as synonymous with innate excellence. This is the traditional dictionary definition. Examples might be a Rolex watch, or a British Airways first class flight.
- The *manufacturing-based approach* assumes that quality is all about making or providing error-free products or services, and is also known as the *production perspective*. Examples might include the Japanese car industry.
- The *user-based approach* assumes quality is all about providing products or services that are *fit for their purpose*, and is also known as the *customer perspective*. For instance, a watch needs to keep time, and a plane needs to fly from one destination to another.
- The *product-based approach* views quality as a precise and measurable set of characteristics, and is also known as the *engineering perspective*. For example, watches need to keep time, but may have many other features designed in.
- The *value-based approach* defines quality in terms of value to the customer, and is also known as the *economic perspective*. Some may consider a cheap product or 'no-frills' service to be better than an expensive one if it delivers value for money. For instance, Ryanair could be better than British Airways, or a Swatch watch better than a Rolex.

The key point is ...

that quality is always defined by the customer, and a product should be fit for purpose and should conform to specification.

SHORT CASE 13.1

Harley-Davidson for Women

Source: ©Ken Wolter/Shutterstock

Harley-Davidson, the motorcycle company, is facing some challenges to stay competitive and grow. Registration of new motorcycles has fallen 36% for Harley since 2007. Its production level has also sunk to 2001 levels. Since Keith Wandell became the CEO in May 2009, he has made several changes, including reworking labour contracts at Harley's plants, and streamlining the Harley-Davidson brand.

Harley bikes have typically appealed to middle-aged, rich, white males. In a riders' event in Orlando in May 2009, Wandell realized that a bike more suitable to women is something that Harley customers have long been asking for. As he recalls, 'Ten questions were asked and nine of them were from women, and all of them were really asking the same thing: When are you going to design a bike that's more suitable for women riders?'

Harley is definitely taking the new market potential for women seriously. It hired Marisa Miller, a model who appeared in *Sports Illustrated*'s swimming suit edition, as a spokesperson. The company also doubled its spending on marketing activities, including the introduction of the Super Low.

However, while much work is being done on marketing, the key issue here is actually operational. Most of the bikes are designed for male bikers, and as men and women have considerably different physiologies – women tend to be shorter, weigh less and have wider hips than men – the customer requirement is therefore different. This means that a bike designed to a specification based on a woman's physiology will be different from one designed to a specification based on a man's physiology. Selling a bike designed for a man to a woman therefore leads to a quality problem. Essentially, the bike and the customer do not fit together properly!

Questions

1. Can Harley-Davidson benchmark its current practices to enhance the appeal of new bikes for women?
2. What challenges should Harley-Davidson consider in order to ensure that the same quality standards (in both the bikes and the service levels) are maintained?

Source: *Bloomberg Businessweek*, 4–10 October 2010.

Dimensions of Quality

Over the years, various concepts and tools have been developed to help companies improve their operations. When a firm designs a product or service, certain performance characteristics and features need to be handled carefully in order to make sure that they can fulfil customers' expectations.

Product Quality

Quality has many dimensions, including performance, features, reliability, durability, conformance, serviceability, aesthetics and perceived quality (Garvin, 1987). Table 13.1 lists eight dimensions, and provides examples of these dimensions in a car.

Service Quality

Many aspects of quality are subjective, and depend on the customer's expectations, but it is easier to meet the expectations for products than for services. Customers can see and touch most products before buying them, and

Table 13.1 Dimensions of product quality

Dimension	Meaning	Example in a car
Performance	A product's primary operating characteristics	Acceleration; braking distance; steering; handling
Features	The 'bells and whistles' and secondary characteristics	Power options; CD player or iPod adaptor; antilock breaking system; leather seats
Reliability	The probability of a product operating over a specific period of time under stated conditions of use	A car's ability to start on cold days; frequency of failures
Durability	The amount of use one gets from a product before it physically deteriorates, or until replacement is preferable	Corrosion resistance; the long wear of upholstery fabric.
Conformance	The degree to which a product's design and operating characteristics meet established standards	All electronics components in a car have to work within −40°C and +85°C.
Serviceability	The speed, courtesy and competence of repair work	Access to spare parts; the number of miles between major maintenance services; the cost of servicing
Aesthetics	How a product looks, feels, sounds, tastes or smells	A car's colour; instrument panel design; control placement; the 'feel of the road'
Perceived quality	Past performance and reputation	A customer might be influenced by their personal experience and that of acquaintances, as well as written reviews by other users

Source: Adapted from Crosby *et al.* (2003).

manufacturers can inspect the quality of the products before releasing them for purchase. Many aspects of a product's quality can be subjective, though. For example, how long you expect your mobile phone to work may depend on how quickly you plan to switch to a newer model, but manufacturers can influence customers' expectations by the length of guarantee they offer.

Services differ from products in four ways:

- *Intangibility:* most services cannot be counted, measured, inventoried, tested or verified in advance of sale to ensure their quality, as in having a consultation with a doctor, for example. Services cannot be protected through patents, and prices are difficult to set.
- *Heterogeneity:* the performance of services differs between producers, and what the firm intends to deliver might be entirely different from what the customer receives.
- *Inseparability:* the production and consumption of services occur simultaneously.
- *Perishability:* services cannot be stored or inventoried. For example, an empty seat in a bus or airplane is a sale lost forever.

Because of these differences there are additional dimensions that we might use to judge the quality of products and services (Parasuraman *et al.*, 1985, p. 47):

- *Reliability:* involves consistency of performance, and dependability. It means the firm performs the service right first time. It also means that the firm honours its promises.
- *Responsiveness:* concerns employees' willingness or readiness to provide service.
- *Competence:* means possession of the required skills and knowledge to perform the service.
- *Access:* involves approachability and ease of contact.
- *Courtesy:* involves politeness, respect, consideration, and friendliness of contact personnel.

- *Communication:* means keeping customers informed in language they can understand, and listening to them. It may mean that the company has to adjust its language for different consumers – for example, increasing the level of sophistication with experienced users but speaking simply and plainly with a novice.
- *Credibility:* involves trustworthiness, believability, honesty. It means having the customer's best interest at heart.
- *Security:* is the freedom from danger, risk, or doubt.
- *Understanding/knowing the customer:* involves making the effort to understand the customer's needs.

Service quality deals with the company's ability to meet customers' expectations. See Short Case 13.2 for more coverage of this topic. However, as service quality can be hard to measure, a useful method is to look at the difference between what we expect and what we actually receive. So if the service we receive is less than we were expecting, we shall be disappointed. Similarly, if the company exceeds our expectations we are likely to be pleased. Word of mouth, personal needs and past experience shape our expectations of the quality of services (ES). We tend to be satisfied when perceptions exceed the expectations of a service (ES < PS), but unhappy when the expectations are not met (ES > PS).

The *service quality model* (Figure 13.2) illustrates various possible sources in the process of service delivery that may result in gaps between customers' expectations and the quality of the services delivered:

1. *Consumer expectation/management perception gap:* the managers of a service firm do not always know what features to provide to consumers in advance, and what levels of performance on those features are needed in order to deliver a high-level service.

Figure 13.2 The service quality model

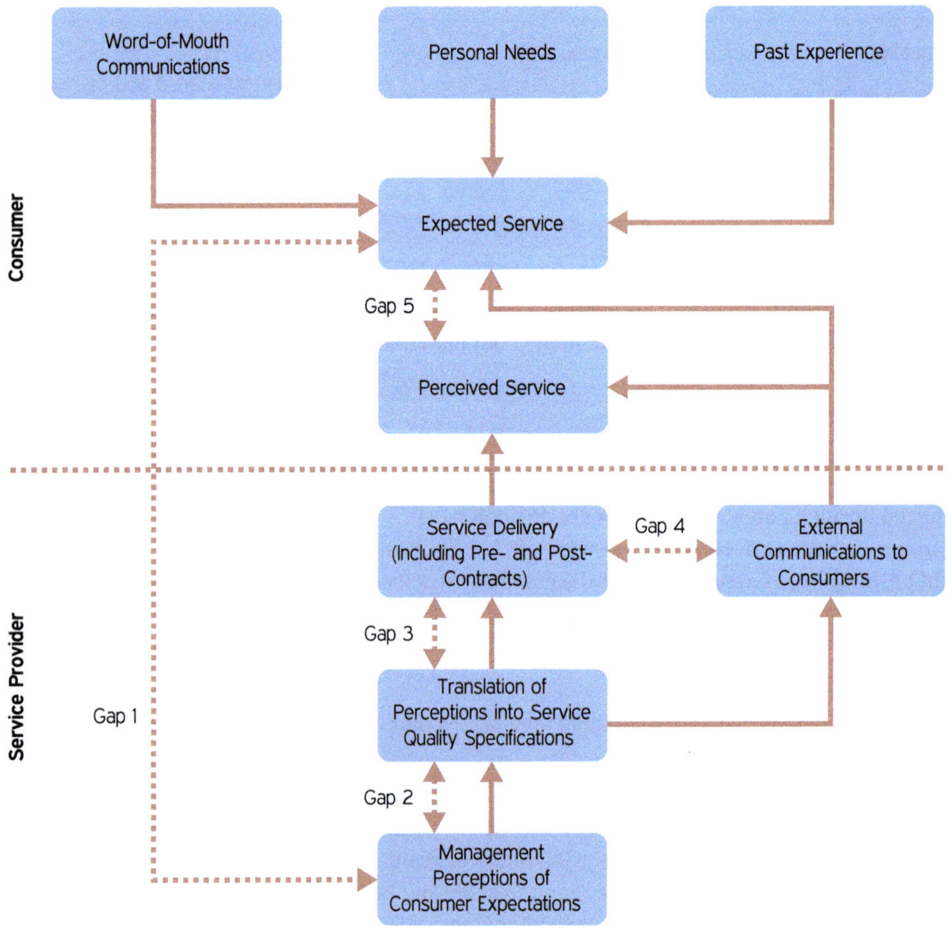

Source: Adapted from Parasuraman et al. (1985).

2. *Management perception/service quality specification gap:* it is often difficult for managers to match or exceed consumer expectations, often because there is an absence of management commitment to service quality.
3. *Service quality specifications/service delivery gap:* there is no guarantee that high-quality service performance can be attained, even when guidelines exist and the personnel treat the consumers correctly. Service firms' employees often exert a strong influence on the quality of the service delivered. Because employees are human beings, their performance cannot always be standardized.
4. *Service delivery/external communications gap:* the media, advertising and other communications channels can affect consumer expectations. When a firm promises more than it can deliver, it raises initial expectations. However, when it cannot fulfil the expectations, the perceptions of quality will be significantly lower.
5. *Expected service/perceived service gap:* the key to ensuring good quality of service is meeting and exceeding what consumers expect from the service. This gap is arguably the most important, as it is the resulting effect of all the others, and is judged by the customer.

SHORT CASE 13.2

7-Eleven, Japan

Source: ©Chalermphon Srisang/Shutterstock

There are 7-Eleven convenience stores in many different countries around the world, but the experiences we expect as consumers vary from country to country. For instance, in Asian stores one can get kimchi-flavoured rice balls, one of the store's most popular items. Kimchi is a traditional Korean fermented dish – typically made with napa cabbage, chilli and garlic– but rice balls would probably not be very popular items in Europe or North America.

The Japanese 7-Eleven stores focus on providing good-quality service to customers. As early as the 1980s, 7-Eleven introduced computers that displayed graphic data and interactive registers in order to transmit information between the headquarters and the stores to ensure that high-selling items would not go out of stock. For instance, popular items such as cooked rice could be delivered to the stores as frequently as three times a day.

By the mid-1990s it was possible for customers to pay for mail order purchases at the stores. Stores also started to offer all kinds of innovative services, including sales of ski-lift vouchers, international phone cards, colour photocopying, games software, and more.

In 2007, 7-Eleven introduced a web shopping service, which combined Internet shopping with existing store services and infrastructure. The corporation's goal is to create products and services that provide new value for customers and franchises, and by doing this service quality is also enhanced. With innovations in information technology, 7-Eleven is able to fulfil customers' expectations and create a better shopping experience for the customers at its stores.

In 2019, its stores have solar panels and LEDs. Moreover, with its Omni 7 online service shopping, customers can order all kinds of goods by mobile, and have the items delivered or picked up.

Questions

1. How difficult would it be for 7-Eleven stores worldwide to be as good at ensuring quality as 7-Eleven in Japan?
2. Which factors enable 7-Eleven Japan to grow and continuously satisfy its customers?

Source: www.sej.co.jp

Philosophical Approaches to Quality

The notion of quality management started in the 1950s in Japan. During that time, Japan employed consultants from the US and Europe to assist in the process of its industrial reconstruction after the Second World War. The best known of these consultants were W. Edwards Deming and Joseph Juran. Later, Western organizations also embraced quality, using approaches advocated by Philip Crosby and Armand V. Feigenbaum. The philosophies of these four Americans, often referred to as the *quality gurus,* have considerably influenced the development of quality management in organizations across the world.

Deming's Philosophy

Deming's approach to quality is considered as the cornerstone of modern quality management. He saw quality as a way to satisfy customers – not merely to meet their expectations, but to exceed them. He stressed the need for organizations to stay ahead of customers. The means to improve quality rests with the organization's ability to control and manage systems and processes properly. Deming emphasized that it is management's responsibility to take care of changing processes. The management should establish clear standards that are considered acceptable, and also provide tools to carry out that work.

Deming's philosophy is mostly associated with the Shewhart cycle, or the *PDCA* (plan, do, check, act) cycle of continuous improvement, shown in Figure 13.3:

Plan (P): the cycle starts with the planning stage, when the necessary objectives and processes are established in order to deliver the results according to the expected output.
Do (D): once the plan has been agreed, the next stage is the implementation of the processes, when the plan is tried out in the operation.
Check (C): the next stage of the cycle is when the processes are measured and the results are compared against the expected performance improvement.
Act (A): this is the last stage of the cycle. During this stage, the differences between the trials and expected performance are analysed to determine their cause. Once the cause is determined, the cycle starts again until the desired performance improvement is achieved.

In addition, Deming advocated the use of *statistical process control* (SPC) to ensure that processes were robust and in control.

Deming (1986) expressed his philosophy towards quality through his famous 14 management principles:

Principle 1: Create constancy of purpose to improve products and services – take a longer-term view, and innovate.
Principle 2: Adopt the new philosophy – accept the management style that promotes constant improvement.
Principle 3: Cease dependence on mass inspection – concentrate on improving processes.
Principle 4: End the practice of awarding business on price tag alone; build up relationships with fewer suppliers to understand jointly specifications of and uses for materials and other inputs.

Figure 13.3 The PDCA cycle

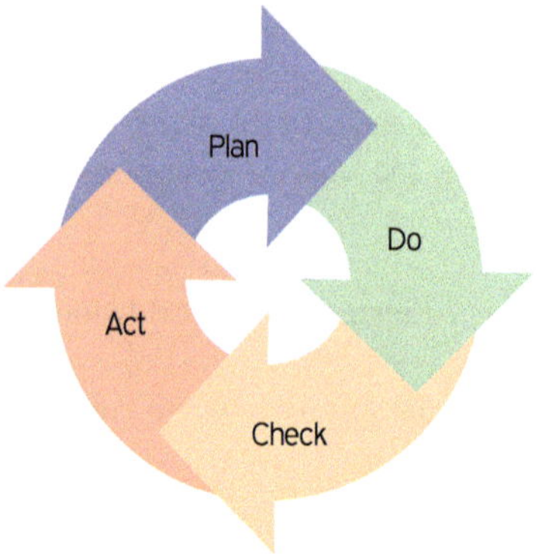

Principle 5: Constantly and forever improve the system – search continually for problems in all processes. It is management's job to work on the system.
Principle 6: Institute modern methods of training on the job – for all, to make the best use of every employee.
Principle 7: Institute leadership – institute modern methods of supervision for managers to focus on quality, not numbers.
Principle 8: Drive out fear – so that people work more effectively.
Principle 9: Break down barriers between departments – teamworking to tackle problems.
Principle 10: Eliminate slogans and exhortation – make reasonable requests of the workforce.
Principle 11: Eliminate work standards and numerical quotas – focus on quality, and provide support.
Principle 12: Remove barriers that rob workers of pride in their work – for example, defective materials, poor tools, lack of management support.
Principle 13: Institute a vigorous programme of education and training – for continual updating and improvement.
Principle 14: Create a top management structure to push every day on the above 13 points. Top management commitment is where it begins and ends.

We can see that these principles all fit together, and lead managers and employees to change the way they deliver quality to the customer.

Juran's Philosophy

For Juran, quality begins with who will use the company's products or services, and how and why these customers will use them. All improvement activities should be customer focused. Juran defined quality as 'fitness for purpose or use', which has five major quality dimensions: quality of design, quality of conformance, availability, safety, and field of use:

1. **Quality of design** is concerned with how well the design concept and its specifications match the intended use of the product or service.
2. **Quality of conformance** deals with how well the actual product or service delivery matches the design intended.
3. **Availability** also includes how the company manages reliability and maintainability.
4. **Safety** is concerned with whether there is any risk to the customer when they use the product or receive the service.
5. With **field of use**, the company seeks to understand how well the product conforms to specifications after it reaches the customers.

Juran introduced the idea of a quality trilogy: *planning, control* and *improvement*. Like Deming, he emphasized the importance of management involvement and the need for a supportive infrastructure. Juran, however, argued that quality is not free, and that companies must reduce the cost of quality. His philosophy of quality is summarized in the following 10 points (Juran, 1988):

Point 1: Build awareness of the need and opportunities for improvement.
Point 2: Set goals for improvement.
Point 3: Organize to reach the goals, such as establish a quality council, identify problems, select projects, appoint team, and designate facilities.
Point 4: Provide training throughout the organization.
Point 5: Carry out projects to solve problems.
Point 6: Report progress.
Point 7: Give recognition.
Point 8: Communicate results.
Point 9: Keep the score.
Point 10: Maintain momentum by making annual improvement part of the regular system and processes of the company.

For Juran it is all about developing a planned approach to managing quality in the organization.

Quality of design: concerned with how well the design concept and its specifications match the intended use of the product or service.

Quality of conformance: deals with how well the actual product or service delivery matches the design intended.

Availability: the actual amount of time that a resource can be used for its intended purpose

Safety: concerned with whether there is any risk to the customer when they use the product or receive the service.

Field of use: the company seeks to understand how well the product conforms to specifications after it reaches the customers.

Crosby's Philosophy

Crosby (1979) advocated the philosophy that 'quality is free'. He defined quality as *conformance to requirements.* He argued that organizations should seek to produce zero defects – that is, to make the product right the first time. Higher-quality products reduce costs and raise profits. It is much more expensive to correct errors or to pay for scrap, rework or failures in the field.

Crosby's programme has 14 steps that focus on how to change the organization, and offers action plans for implementation (Ghobadian and Speller, 1994, p. 60).

Step 1: Management commitment – make clear where management stands regarding quality.
Step 2: Quality improvement team – set up a team to run the quality improvement programme.
Step 3: Quality measurement – provide a display of current and potential non-conformance problems in a manner that permits objective evaluation and corrective action.
Step 4: Cost of quality evaluation – define the ingredients of the cost of quality, and explain its use as a management tool.
Step 5: Quality awareness – provide a method of raising the personal concern felt by all personnel towards product/service conformance and the reputation of the company.
Step 6: Corrective action – provide a systematic method of resolving quality problems that have been identified through the previous steps.
Step 7: Zero-defect planning – examine, identify and implement the actions necessary prior to the launch of a zero-defect programme.
Step 8: Employee education – identify and introduce the training that employees need in order to carry out their part in the quality improvement process.
Step 9: Zero-defects day – create an event that will let all employees know, through personal experience, that there has been a change.
Step 10: Goal setting – turn pledge and commitment into actions, by encouraging individuals to establish improvement goals for themselves and their groups.
Step 11: Error cause removal – give the individual employee a method of communicating to management the situations that make it difficult for the employee to meet the pledge to improve.
Step 12: Recognition – appreciate those who actively participate.
Step 13: Quality councils – bring together the professional quality people for planned communication on a regular basis.
Step 14: Do it over again – emphasize that the quality improvement process never ends.

For Crosby, quality is all about *right first time.*

Feigenbaum's Philosophy

Armand V. Feigenbaum saw quality as the 'total composite product and service characteristics of marketing, engineering, manufacture and maintenance through which the product and service in use will meet the expectations of the customers' (Feigenbaum, 1986). To him, quality is a way of managing an organization, and it is everyone's responsibility. He believed that effective management of quality represented the best return on investment for the firm.

One of Feigenbaum's major contributions is on the cost of quality. He identified three categories of quality costs:

1. *Failure costs:* these are costs caused by defective materials and products that do not meet company quality specifications.
2. *Appraisal costs:* these are costs related to maintaining company quality levels by means of formal evaluations of product quality, such as inspection, testing and quality audits.
3. *Prevention costs:* these are costs related to keeping defects from occurring in the first place, such as quality control engineering, employee quality training, and quality maintenance of patterns and tools.

He also identified 10 benchmarks for quality success:

1. Quality is a company-wide process.
2. Quality is what the customer says it is.

3. Quality and cost are a sum, not a difference.
4. Quality requires both individual and team zealotry.
5. Quality is a way of managing.
6. Quality and innovation are mutually dependent.
7. Quality is an ethic.
8. Quality requires continuous improvement.
9. Quality is the most cost-effective, least capital-intensive route to productivity.
10. Quality is implemented with a total system connected with customers and suppliers.

Feigenbaum was the first to coin the term *total quality,* suggesting that quality is the responsibility of all in the organization and so needs a high degree of coordinated effort.

The Evolution of Quality Management

Managing quality can be extremely challenging, depending on the situation and the tasks being controlled. The practice of quality management has evolved over recent decades. Modern operations management is considered to have evolved since the 1920s. The evolution has progressed, beginning with inspection, before moving on to quality control, and then quality assurance, before reaching total quality management, and Six Sigma (see Figure 13.4).

Each subsequent evolution has subsumed those that have come before it. The characteristics of these evolutionary steps are summarized in Table 13.2, and are explored further in this section.

Figure 13.4 The evolution of quality management

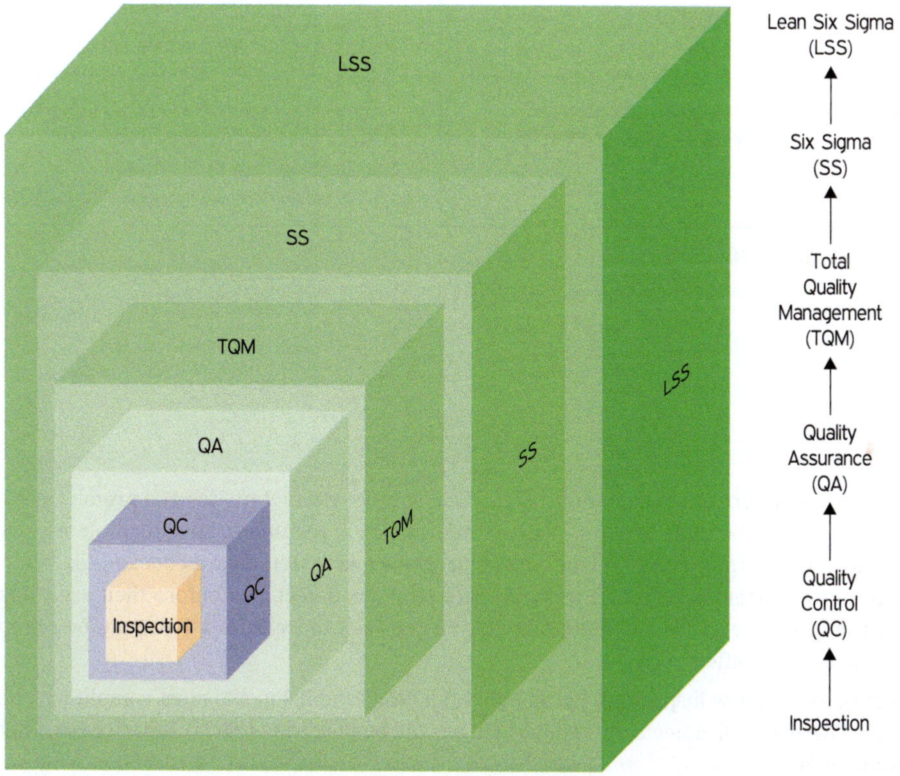

Table 13.2 Main tasks of quality management levels

Level of quality management	Characteristic actions of this level
Inspection – retrospective checking for quality after tasks have been completed. This is mainly done just by quality inspectors	• Salvage • Sorting, grading, re-blending • Corrective actions • Identify sources of non-conformance • Limited to a small number of police-like inspectors
Quality control (QC) – a system to detect quality problems as they occur, normally limited to operations	• Develop quality manual • Process performance data • Self-inspection • Product testing • Basic quality planning • Use of basic statistics • Paperwork controls
Quality assurance (QA) – a system that is proactive with some emphasis on improvement, normally limited to operations and directly related areas	• Quality systems development • Advanced quality planning • Use of quality costs • Failure mode and effect analysis (FMEA) • Statistical process control (SPC) • Use of quality as a unique selling point for marketing
Total quality management (TQM) – a proactive approach involving everyone in an organization.	• Policy deployment • Involve suppliers and customers • Involve all operations • Process management • Performance measurement • Teamwork • Employee involvement throughout the organization
Six Sigma – a proactive approach involving everyone in an organization, which has low failure rates	• Linkage to personal performance reviews and career progression • Emphasis on the reduction of errors • Application of Six Sigma tools to reduce process variation
Lean Six Sigma – a proactive approach combining Six Sigma and Lean, aiming at low failure rates and waste reduction	• Become faster and more responsive to customers • Strive for Six Sigma capability level • Operate at low costs of poor quality • Achieve greater flexibility throughout the business

Source: Adapted from Dale *et al.* (2007, p. 24).

Inspection

Inspection is the simplest process of a quality system. One or more characteristics of a product, service or activity are examined to assess and identify sources of non-conformance in relation to specification or performance standards. For example, in a manufacturing plant, incoming goods and materials are checked (sometimes visually or sometimes with more sophisticated tools) to make sure they are defect-free before they are transported to the assembly line. The incoming goods and materials that do not meet the specifications may be returned, salvaged, scrapped, reworked, or modified.

Service industries, too, can use inspection. For instance, all food establishments must comply with health and sanitation standards. These establishments are regularly inspected by governmental bodies to check whether they have violated the standards.

SHORT CASE 13.3

Beer Tasting Is a Serious Business

Source: ©Rido/Shutterstock

Three times a week, at 11 o'clock in the morning, a quality assurance tasting panel, comprising nine or ten specially trained tasters, sit in Carlsberg's Research Centre (CRC) in Copenhagen, Denmark, to ensure that a Carlsberg beer tastes like a Carlsberg, regardless of where it is brewed. Every company that brews Carlsberg beers under licence has to send samples once a month to the tasting panel. They have to submit samples of every type of beer, especially if the beers are packaged in different bottles or cans, or brewed to different strengths.

The panel measure the beers against an international beer 'flavour wheel', which itemizes and numbers 140 different base flavours and aromas, ranging from fruits and flowers to nuts and grains. If the the tasters recognize any other flavours, CRC can identify the faults and report back to the brewer.

The tasters are chosen from within the company. New tasters are required to attend seven training sessions, where they are taught to recognize different flavours, beers and aromas. They also have to score at least 60% in all their taste tests, and participate in panels on a trial basis for their first 3–6 months. Interestingly, the flavour receptors that are most sensitive to beer are at the back of the tongue, which means that the tasters have to swallow the beer being tested!

Questions

1. How difficult is it for Carlsberg to monitor and control the taste of its beers?
2. Should there be other standards and/or procedures to ensure quality at Carlsberg?

Source: www.carlsberggroup.com

Quality Control

GLOBALIZATION

With *quality control* (QC), a more sophisticated approach is used to manage quality. At this level quality standards are set, and quality manuals with detailed product and performance specifications are developed. Basic statistics are also used in quality control measures in order to achieve greater process control and lower incidences of non-conformance. Self-inspection against internationally recognized standards (such as those of the International Organization for Standardization) is also used.

We often take standards for granted in our daily lives. However, if standards were absent, we would soon notice. For example, it would be frustrating if your favourite chocolate drink tasted different every time you bought it. We also rely on standards to ensure that we aren't harmed by things we are not capable of noticing, such as contamination in our drinking water, or electromagnetic radiation from high-voltage power cables. Standards make sure that the characteristics of products and services, such as quality, environmental friendliness, safety, reliability, efficiency and interchangeability, meet desired specifications.

The **International Organization for Standardization (ISO)** is the world's largest standards organization, and has 162 members worldwide. Since 1947 it has published more than 17,500 standards. Perhaps the best-known ISO standards are the ISO 9000 series. ISO 9000 certifies that a company meets certain industry standards. Its objective is to give customers assurance that the quality of the products and services provided by a supplier meets their requirements. It also ensures that organizations have a quality policy, with standardized procedures to ensure that defects are monitored, there are corrective and preventive action systems, and all systems are reviewed by the management.

International Organization for Standardization (ISO): the world's largest standards-developing organization.

The ISO 9000 series consists of the following main standards:

- *ISO 9000: Quality Management Systems – Fundamentals and Vocabulary:* describes the fundamentals of quality management systems.
- *ISO 9001: Quality Management Systems – Requirements:* provides the requirements that an organization needs in order to achieve customer satisfaction through consistent products and services that meet customers' expectations.
- *ISO 9004: Quality Management Systems – Guidelines for Performance Improvements:* provides guidance on how an organization can plan for continual improvement.

CRITICAL PERSPECTIVE

Advantages and Disadvantages of ISO Standards

In order to attain ISO accreditation, an organization has to prove that every step of a process is documented and subsequently adhered to. The process of recording and documenting can be tedious and extremely frustrating for companies that do not have a standard way of doing things. ISO accreditation can be obtained only through an approved certifying body by paying a fee. Although the fee is relatively small, the cost of obtaining accreditation can be relatively expensive, because a lot of time and effort can go into developing a comprehensive quality system.

However, many organizations are willing to invest in getting ISO certification. Although it is not a legal requirement, it is becoming a requirement of doing business in the European Union. One of the biggest advantages is that the third party audit ensures that the quality management of the organization is on a par with the rest of the industry. As ISO certification is the most common type of certification, implementation of new systems becomes easier. The process of certification forces the organization to analyse its internal processes objectively, resulting in more efficient and cost-effective processes.

The key point is ...

that although quality accreditation is important, it can be onerous and expensive to gain.

Quality Assurance

BUSINESS INTEGRATION

Quality assurance (QA) embraces activities that provide confidence that the organization will fulfil the requirements of quality. Whereas inspection and quality control focus on the detection of mistakes, QA aims to prevent them from occurring.

Finding and solving a problem is not enough to ensure quality excellence; the root causes of the problem need to be eliminated too. The focus at this stage shifts from detection to the prevention of non-conformance. This requires the support of top management, to encourage all departments and functions to work together. Here we see the biggest impact of the quality gurus, who were all concerned not just that existing systems should be made to work the way they were designed to, but that managers should be constantly working on a systematic approach for improvement. QA therefore represents an advance over QC, as it includes all parts of the firm, not just the operations, in delivering the service or producing the product.

QA is often seen as little more than a step in the journey towards total quality management.

Total Quality Management

Total quality management (TQM) embraces all aspects of inspection, quality control and quality assurance. TQM is an approach that involves the whole organization, with the focus on producing high-quality goods and services. It is a quality management approach based on the participation of all its members, aimed at the long-term success of an organization through customer satisfaction. Because of this, teamwork and employee involvement become a crucial part of the TQM process, although customers and suppliers are also involved. Successful TQM implementation brings benefits to all members of the organization and society.

There are eight TQM principles (Dale *et al.*, 2007, p. 30):

1. *Customer focus:* organizations depend on their customer needs, meet customer requirements, and strive to exceed customer expectations.
2. *Leadership:* leaders establish unity of purpose and the direction of the organization. They should create and maintain the internal environment in which people can become fully involved in achieving the organization's objectives.
3. *Involvement of people:* people at all levels are the essence of an organization, and their full involvement enables their abilities to be used for the organization's benefit.
4. *Process approach:* a desired result is achieved more efficiently when activities and related resources are managed as a process.
5. *Systems approach to management:* identifying, understanding and managing interrelated processes as a system contributes to the organization's effectiveness and efficiency in achieving its objectives.
6. *Continual improvement* (kaizen): continual improvement of the organization's overall performance should be a permanent objective of the organization.
7. *Factual approach to decision-making:* effective decisions are based on the analysis of data and information.
8. *Mutually beneficial supplier relationships:* an organization and its suppliers are interdependent, and a mutually beneficial relationship enhances the ability of both to create value.

Properly implemented TQM systems have improved the performance of many firms, resulting in fewer defects, lower inventory levels, reduced lead times, higher flexibility, and increased employee satisfaction. However, the implementation of TQM can be very challenging. In a study of American companies, Salegna and Fazel (2000) identified the following obstacles:

- A lack of a company-wide definition of quality
- A lack of a formalized strategic plan for change
- A lack of a customer focus, poor inter-organizational communication
- A lack of real employee empowerment
- A lack of employee trust in senior management
- A view of quality programmes as a quick fix
- A drive for short-term financial results, politics and turf issues
- A lack of strong motivation
- A lack of time to devote to quality initiatives
- And a lack of leadership.

CRITICAL PERSPECTIVE

Why TQM Doesn't Always Work

GLOBALIZATION

Is TQM a fad or just a buzzword? Japanese companies seem to have been more successful in implementing TQM than Western companies. So what are the underlying reasons for the successful implementation of TQM? TQM was based primarily on Japanese experiences in the automotive and electronic industries. Today, the aim of TQM is to increase external and internal customer satisfaction with fewer resources (Hellsten and Klefsjö, 2000), regardless of the type and nationality of the companies.

TQM transformation is a long-term process, often requiring a fundamental shift in management practice and organization culture, which needs a huge investment in money and time. Senior management in many firms feel that quality improvement efforts have not boosted their capacity to compete, have not resulted in implementation of a significant number of practices associated with TQM, and have not focused TQM improvements on providing better products and services (Beer, 2003).

Top management adopts TQM programmes typically with the goal of improving performance. However, TQM will fail if they are not committed or if they lack understanding of the programme. Hence it is essential that the senior team has the capacity to:

1. Develop commitment to the new TQM direction and behave and make decisions that are consistent with it
2. Develop the cross-functional mechanisms, leadership skills, and team culture needed for TQM implementation
3. Create a climate of open dialogues about progress in the TQM transformation that will enable learning and further change. (Beer, 2003, p. 623)

The key point is ...

that TQM needs top management support even though it is primarily delivered by all employees.

Stop and Think

Should all companies (regardless of their size or reputation) adopt TQM?

Six Sigma

Six Sigma is an evolution of TQM that was pioneered by Motorola in the 1980s. A senior engineer there introduced the concept in response to increasing complaints from the field salesforce about warranty claims. The Six Sigma methodology made Motorola one of the first companies to win the Malcolm Baldrige National Quality Award in 1988, a prestigious award that is given to US corporations that have demonstrated outstanding quality in their products and processes. Since then, many companies have tailored the Six Sigma method to their own programmes, including General Electric (GE), Texas Instruments, Kodak, Xerox and Ford. GE, for example, launched its Six Sigma programme in 1995, and over a four-year period was able to achieve a 20% margin improvement and a 12% reduction in headcount per year (Basu, 2004).

In essence, Six Sigma is a quality concept with the goal of value creation through quality improvement. Many objectives in Six Sigma are similar to those in TQM, such as customer satisfaction, continuous improvement, team-based activities, education and training, and problem-solving methodologies. One distinct characteristic of Six Sigma, though, is that it places statistical analysis centrally in quality management. The Greek letter σ is the symbol for standard deviation, and Six Sigma is represented as 6σ. The aim of Six Sigma is to reduce defects to less than 3.4 per million opportunities/outputs **(DPMO)**.

DPMO: defects per million opportunities.

The DMAIC Cycle

Six Sigma is a continuous improvement, or kaizen methodology, based on the DMAIC cycle (Figure 13.5), which is an extension of Deming's PDCA wheel.

Figure 13.5 The DMAIC cycle

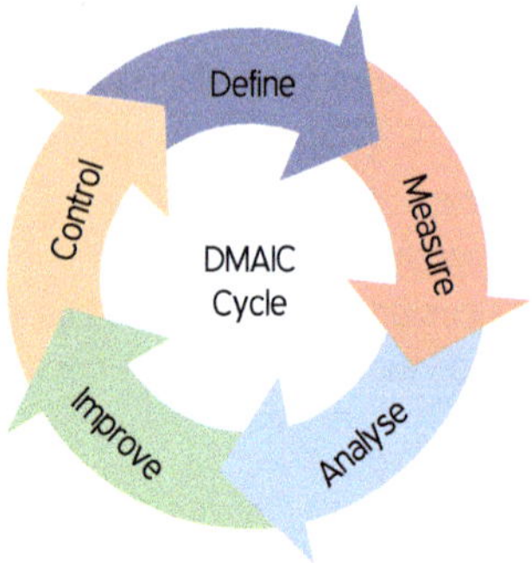

The DMAIC cycle can be broken down as follows:

Define (D): The cycle starts with the problems, project goals and processes being defined. Here the organization identifies the customers and their priorities, as well as its business objectives. Often the target for performance is determined at this stage.

Measure (M): This stage determines how to measure the process and its performance. Relevant data are collected. It is important to measure performance in order to know whether anything is improved by our actions.

Analyse (A): Once the measurements are set, they can be analysed. It is here that cause-and-effect relationships and the most likely causes of defects are revealed. It becomes crucial to identify the key variables that create process variation, and in turn result in product and service delivery variation, which can cause dissatisfaction in customers.

Improve (I): Once the causes of defects are identified, work can begin to improve the processes to remove these causes. At this stage the maximum acceptance ranges of the key variables, and how to measure the deviations of the variables, are set.

Control (C): This is the final stage of the cycle. The improved process needs to be continuously controlled and monitored, to make the improvements sustainable. Then the process starts all over again, to achieve further improvements or redesign the process as customer requirements change.

As with previous approaches to quality management, for Six Sigma to succeed it is crucial that there is support from all levels of the organization. The management needs to provide strong leadership, define performance metrics, select projects that have a high probability of yielding good business results, and provide appropriate training for all employees. Depending on the level of expertise attained, practitioners or employees are known as green belts, black belts or master black belts:

- *Green belts:* these are professionals with at least three years of experience using the Six Sigma methodology and tools, who wish to lead a process improvement or quality improvement team.
- *Black belts:* these are experts in Six Sigma philosophies and principles. They also have basic knowledge of lean enterprise concepts, so they are able to identify non-value-added processes and activities. They have team leadership skills, and act as coaches for the green belts.
- *Master black belts:* these are the ultimate experts in the methodologies, tools, and applications in strategic implementation of Six Sigma within an organization. They have extensive training in statistics and the use of quality tools. They are also qualified to train the black belts and the green belts. These are usually full-time quality professionals.

Training and certification for Six Sigma belts can be obtained from external bodies.

Lean Six Sigma

Lean Six Sigma is the most comprehensive level of quality management. It includes key concepts from lean management and Six Sigma tools.

BUSINESS INTEGRATION

Traditional quality management systems have worked well for many firms. However, with increasing outsourcing activities and globalization, the role of quality management has to be redefined. Many firms are combining Six Sigma with lean production methodologies, resulting in Lean Six Sigma, in order to improve process capability and eliminate waste. The integrated approaches should enable firms to become faster and more responsive to customers, to operate with lower costs of poor quality, and to achieve greater flexibility throughout the business (Antony *et al.*, 2003). Table 13.3 compares the tools used by the two methodologies.

It is worth noting that there is some overlap between these methodologies, and ideally they should be used together for the best results. Practitioners and academics are still trying to agree on the best way of doing this.

Stop and Think

What do you think TQM is lacking, and why do you think it has been usurped by Lean Six Sigma?

Table 13.3 Tools used by Six Sigma and lean production

Six Sigma tools	Lean production tools
• Belt system (green belt, black belt, and master black belt) • DMAIC cycle • Statistical process control • Process capability analysis • Quality function deployment • Failure mode and effect analysis • Root cause analysis • Process mapping • Change management tools	• Workplace management • Pull system (kanban) • Total productive maintenance • 5S practice • Value stream mapping • Just-in-time • Production flow balancing • Waste identification and elimination • Kaizen • Change management tools

Source: Adapted from Antony *et al.* (2003).

European Foundation of Quality Management (EFQM) Excellence Model

There are several alternative frameworks to Lean Six Sigma that aim to help firms implement quality improvement in a structured way. The *EFQM model* was formed by 14 leading West European companies in 1988 to recognize quality achievements, especially for public sector organizations and SMEs (small and medium enterprises). In 2004 a study by Basu revealed that EFQM had 19 partner organizations in Europe, and over 20,000 member companies, which include 60% of the top 25 companies in Europe.

The EFQM model (see Figure 13.6) is a non-prescriptive framework based on nine criteria. Five of these criteria are *enablers* (leadership, people, policy and strategy, partnership and resources, and processes) and four are *results* (people, customer, society, and key performance). Whereas the enablers cover what an organization *does*, the results cover what an organization *achieves*. Innovation and learning help to improve enablers that, in turn, lead to improved results. The EFQM model is used for self-inspection, allowing firms to rate their performance, and the EFQM criteria are very similar to those used in competitions to rate firms' quality systems. In North America, for example, the prestigious Baldridge Award is given to one firm per year to recognize their efforts, and Japan has an equivalent, called the Deming Prize.

Table 13.4 shows an example of how EFQM is applied by a care provider. The weighting for each of the results and enablers may vary for each application.

Figure 13.6 The EFQM excellence model

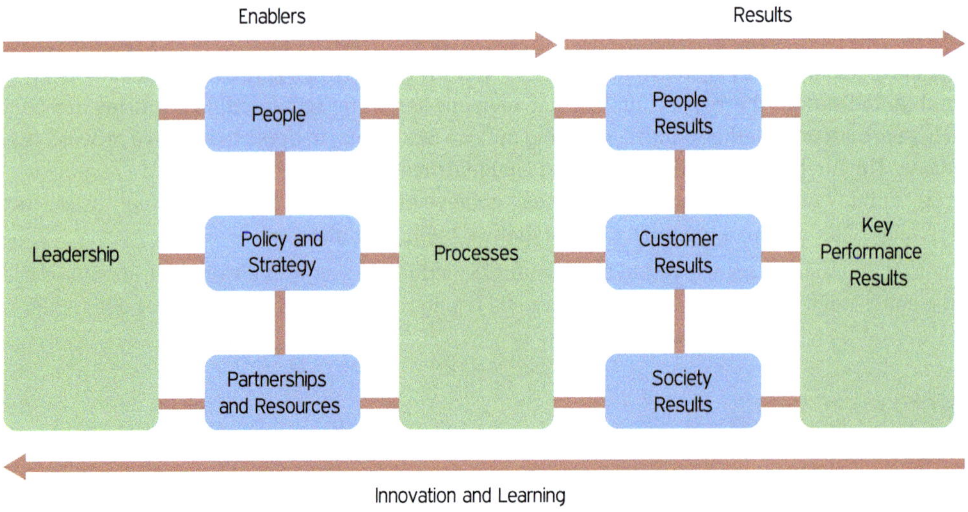

Table 13.4 Application of EFQM by a care provider

Criteria		Example
Results	Key performance	Key outcomes: • Outcomes for adults, carers, children and families • Performance against national and local targets
	Customer	Impact on people who use our services: • Experience of individuals, children and their parents and carers who use our services
	People	Impact on employees: • Motivation and satisfaction • Employees' ownership of vision, policy and strategy
	Society	Impact on the community: • Community perception, understanding and involvement • Impact on other stakeholders • Community capacity
Enablers	Processes	Delivery of key processes: • Access to services • Day-to-day planning and resource allocation • Assessment, care management and statutory supervision • Risk management and accountability • Personalized approaches • Inclusion, equality and fairness in service delivery • Joint and integrated delivery of services
	Policy and strategy	Policy and service development, planning and performance management: • Development of policy and procedures • Operational and service planning • Strategic planning including partnership planning • Involvement of users, carers and other stakeholders • Range and quality of services • Quality assurance and continuous improvement
	People	Management and support of employees: • Recruitment and retention • Employee deployment and teamwork • Development of employees
	Partnership and resources	Resources and capacity building: • Financial management • Resource management • Social work information systems • Partnership arrangements • Commissioning arrangements
	Leadership	Leadership and direction: • Vision values and aims • Leadership of people • Leadership of change and improvement Capacity for improvement: • Global judgement based on evidence of all key areas, in particular, outcomes, impacts and leadership direction

Source: Adapted from www.efqm.org (2003).

Quality Tools

Quality philosophies, approaches and frameworks are high-level ways of thinking about quality issues. At a more practical level, quality managers need tools and techniques to collect, analyse and fix operational problems. There are many tools; this section highlights some of the most popular and effective ones.

SIPOC (supplier–input–process–output–customer) diagram: maps the processes a company (or a person) goes through in order to satisfy a customer's requirements in the context of the supply chain.

Flow chart: provides a visual representation of all major steps in a process.

The Seven Basic Tools of Quality

SIPOC Diagram

SIPOC (supplier–input–process–output–customer) diagrams are used to map operational processes. Figure 13.7 shows a simple SIPOC diagram for making coffee. The diagram allows us to record and then analyse the different roles, parties and processes involved in the operation.

Flow Chart

A **flow chart** is a series of connected supplier–input–process–output diagrams. It provides a visual representation of the different steps in a process. Flow charts can provide a common language or decision plan for a process. Figure 13.8 shows a flow chart for getting out of bed.

Figure 13.7 SIPOC diagram

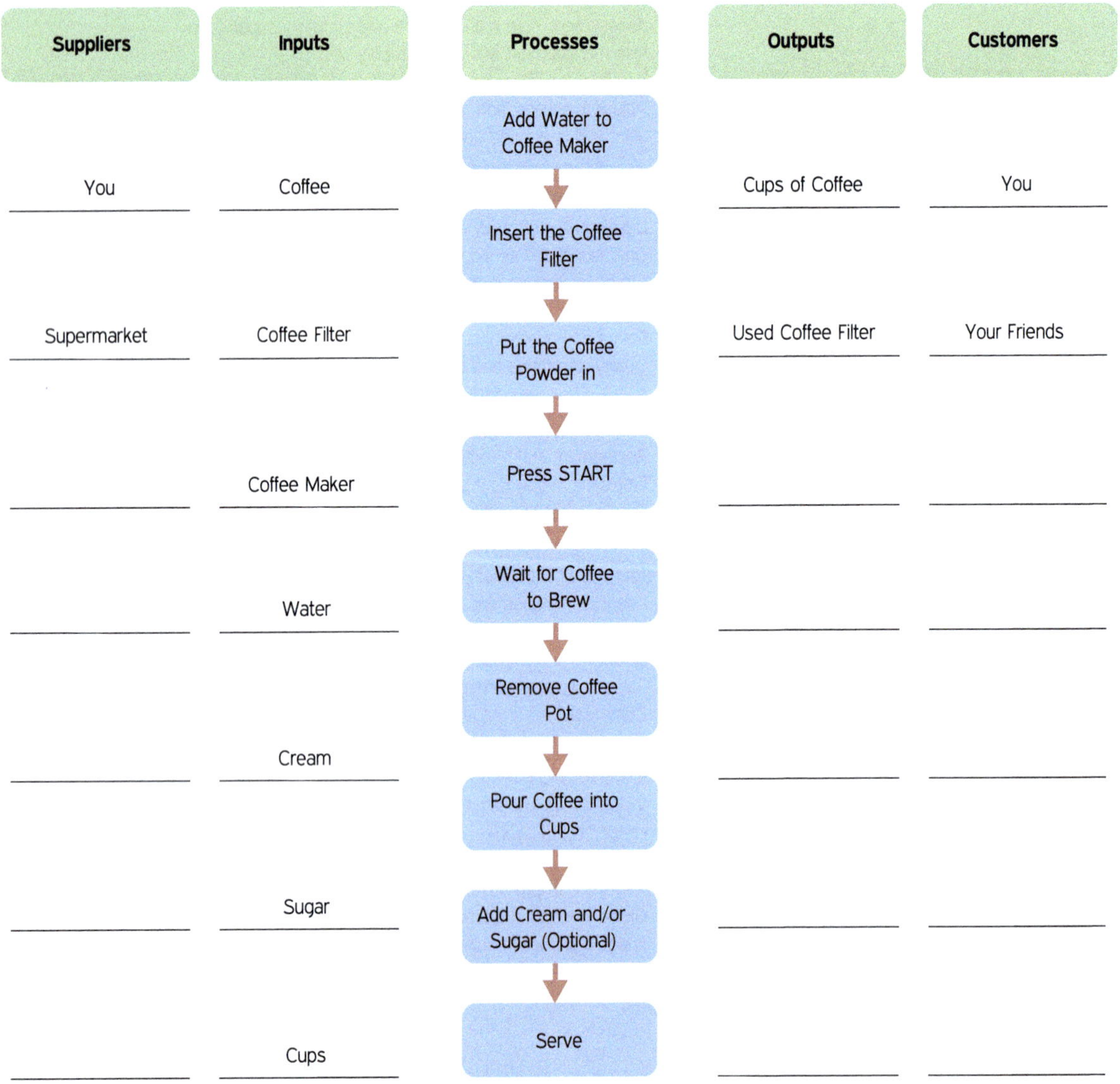

Figure 13.8 A flow chart of getting out of bed

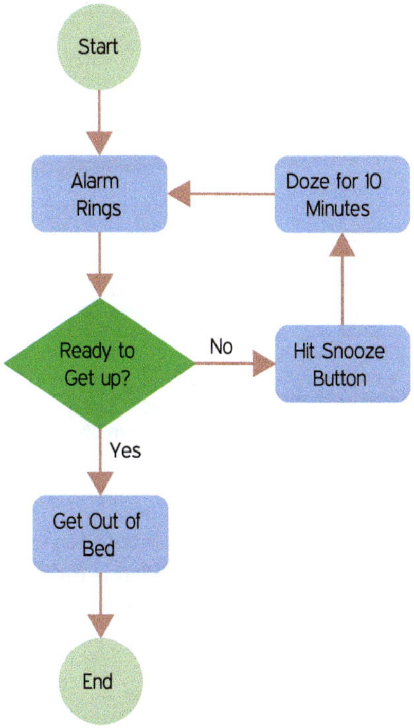

Histogram and Measles Chart

Histograms are used to record the type and frequency of data occurring. They can be used in connection with data capturing tools such as 'measles charts'. Figure 13.9 shows a spanner being produced, which is then inspected for faults. If a fault is found it is then marked with a 'measle' to show exactly where the error has occurred. The frequency of each type of fault occurring is then recorded on the histogram.

This simple tool helps us to identify patterns. If all the defects are focused in one area a root cause may then be revealed.

Pareto Analysis

A **Pareto diagram** arranges categories from highest to lowest frequency of occurrence. A Pareto analysis of quality problems would start by listing the problems identified, then recording the number of times each occurred (the *frequency*), and then ordering them, with the most frequent problem listed first so that addressing this problem could be prioritized. For instance, there are many reasons why luggage gets lost by airlines: flight delays, meaning that passengers miss connecting flights; luggage tags accidentally getting torn off; or simple loss through human error).

Pareto diagram: arranges categories from highest to lowest frequency of occurrence.

Figure 13.10 is a Pareto diagram for luggage lost by an airline.

Figure 13.9 A histogram and a measles chart

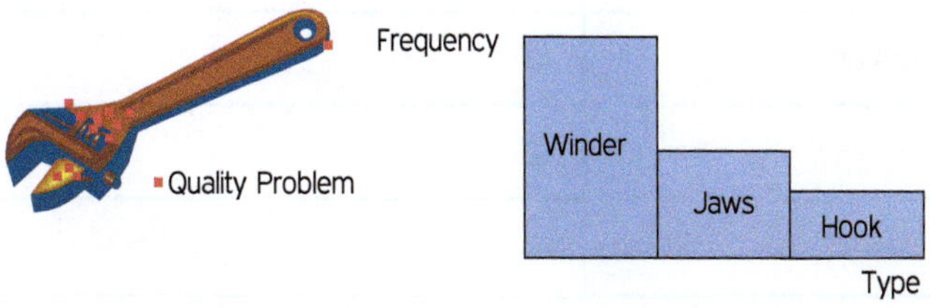

Figure 13.10 Pareto diagram showing reported reasons for lost luggage

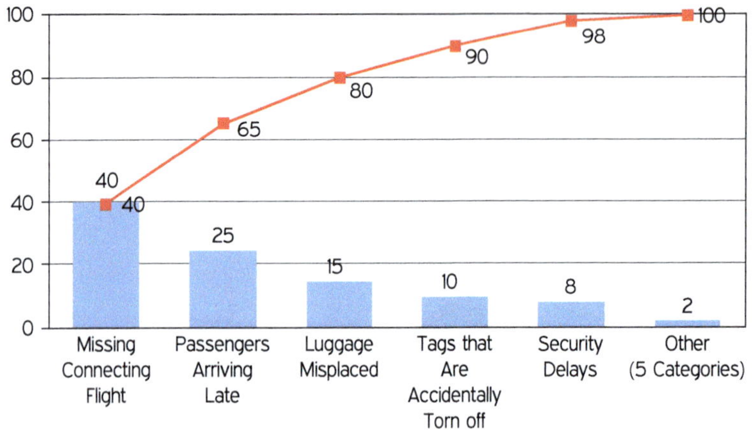

Table 13.5 displays the percentage of incidents that can be attributed to each cause, and the cumulative percentage. In this example, although there are perhaps many different reasons for luggage getting lost, as described above, an airline could prevent 65% of instances of luggage loss if it addressed the two most common reasons – those caused by passengers arriving late or missing connecting flights.

Scatter Diagram

Scatter diagram: shows the degree and direction of the relationship between two variables.

Scatter diagrams show the correlation between two variables – for example, the correlation between customer satisfaction in a five-star restaurant and variables such as waiting time and presentation of food (ratings scored by traveller reviews such as Trip Advisor), as shown in Figure 13.11. Here it can be seen that there is a high degree of correlation between presentation of food and satisfaction (Figure 13.11b), but much less correlation between customer satisfaction and waiting time (Figure 13.11a). These relationships may be very different in a different context. For instance, in a fast-food restaurant the relationships may be reversed, as customers prefer speed over presentation.

Cause-and-Effect Diagram

Cause-and-effect diagram: structural approach to finding of possible cause(s) of a problem.

The **cause-and-effect diagram** (also known as an *Ishikawa* or *fishbone diagram*) is a structured approach to finding the possible cause(s) of a problem. Figure 13.12 shows the causes for lack of responsiveness to customers. Consider an IT company that supplies

Table 13.5 Pareto analysis of reasons for lost luggage

Problem	Percentage of incidences	Cumulative percentage
Missing connecting flight	40	40
Passengers arriving late	25	65
Luggage being misplaced	15	80
Tags that are accidentally torn off	10	90
Security delays	8	98
Other (5 categories)	2	100

Figure 13.11 Scatter diagram correlating customer satisfaction with waiting time (a) and presentation (b)

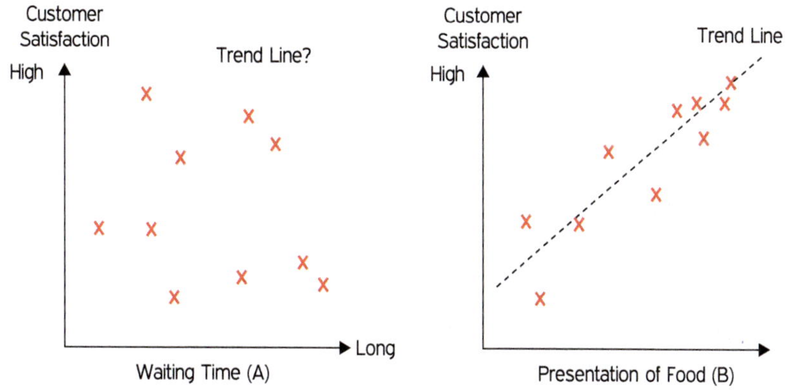

printers and related services (such as maintenance) to a university. Recently, the marketing department received lots of complaints from customers for its 'lack of responsiveness to customers'. The top management asked the marketing and sales managers to look into possible reasons for the customer complaint (the effect). A cause-and-effect diagram was drawn consisting of a 'backbone' and 'fish bones' – for example, manpower, machines, methods and materials – to identify possible causes. Each of the fish bones may have more bones. For instance, manpower was identified as one cause that needed further investigation. One of the reasons might be related to having too few trained staff.

Figure 13.12 Cause-and-effect diagram

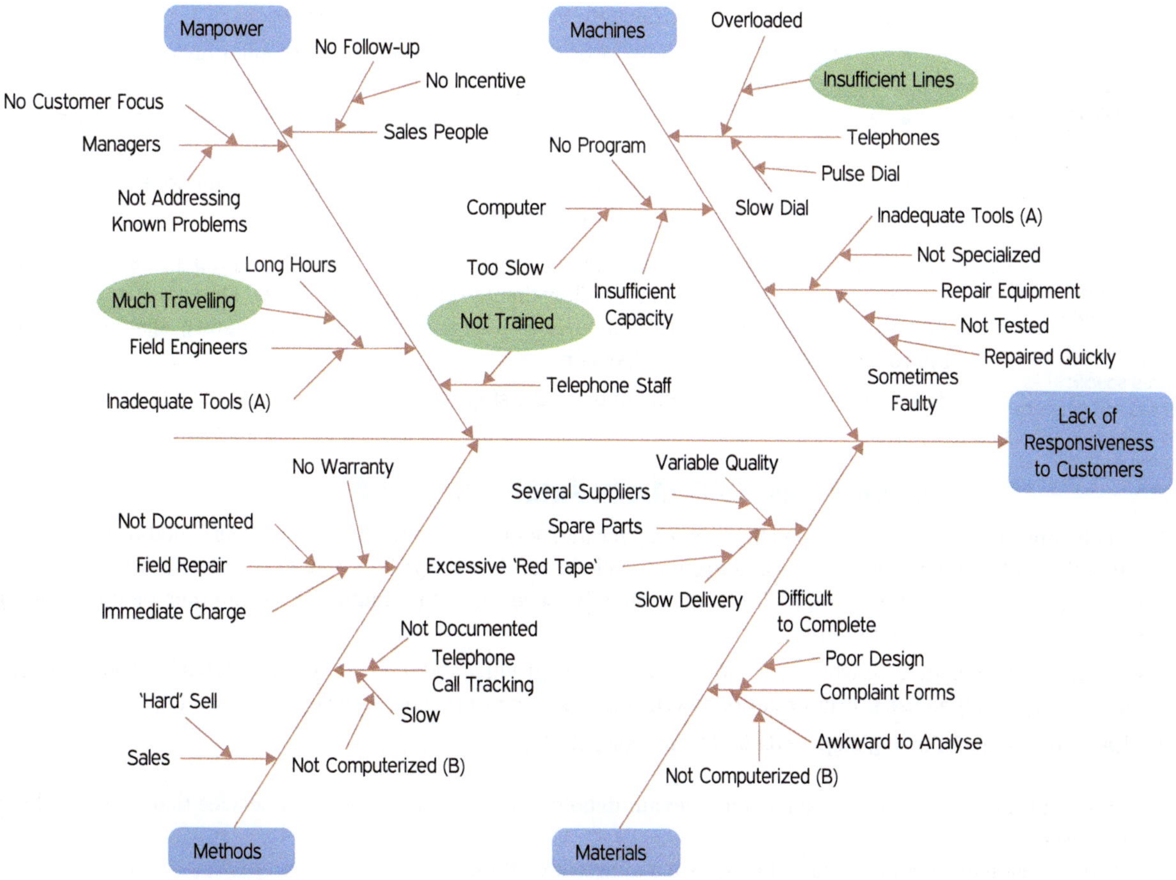

Source: www.syque.com.

Figure 13.13 A run chart of straw lengths produced on two different machines

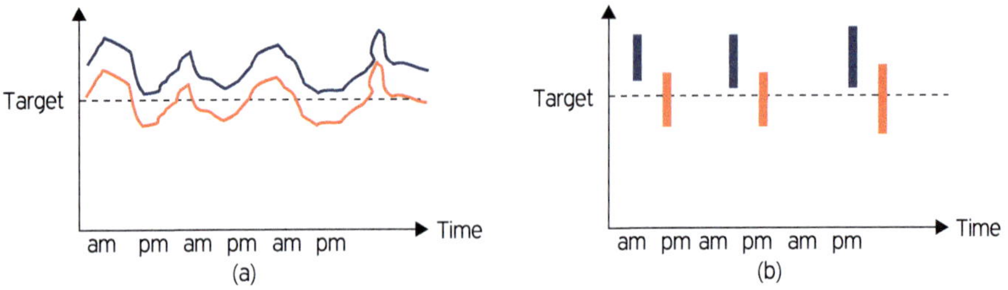

Run and Multi-Vari Charts

Run chart: shows the trends in data over time.

A **run chart** shows trends in data over time and can be used to identify evolving changes to the system, or differences that repeat or occur at certain times. Figure 13.13a shows readings from two machines making drinking straws over a three-day period. The blue line shows that this machine is operating in a similar pattern to the machine producing the output displayed by the orange line, but that it is producing, on average, longer straws, which are in general further away from the target length. In Figure 13.13b a *multi-vari* diagram is shown displaying the same information in a different way: it shows the difference between the longest and shortest output (the range) for each machine, for each day.

Benchmarking

Benchmarking originated from the Rank Xerox Corporation in the 1980s as an improvement method to compare performances. It is a popular technique that has been widely adopted. Today, benchmarking is used by companies to compare best practices. Its goal is to provide knowledge in different specific areas about which company is the 'best in class', and how its performance compares with that of other organizations (Basu, 2004).

Internal benchmarking: provides a comparison among similar operations or processes within a company's organization.

Competitive benchmarking: compares the company's performance against that of the competitors.

Functional benchmarking: compares specific processes and functions across different industries to find the 'best in class'.

Benchmarking can be classified into three categories (Dale, 1999):

- **Internal benchmarking**: provides a comparison among similar operations or processes within a company's organization.
- **Competitive benchmarking**: compares the company's performance with that of the competitors.
- **Functional benchmarking**: compares specific processes and functions across different industries to find the 'best in class'.

For example, the Rover Group employed internal benchmarking to compare its three manufacturing sites' reject rates, and so allow them to share practice ideas. The same firm also used functional benchmarking to compare its machine spare parts inventory system with the approach used by Marks and Spencer.

The process of benchmarking involves the steps shown in Figure 13.14.

Failure Mode and Effect Analysis (FMEA)

The technique of FMEA was developed by the aerospace and defence industries in the 1960s as a method of identifying possible failures that might occur in a product while in service (the *failure mode*), predicting what effect the failure might have should it occur, and then analysing the severity of that failure. Work can then be done during the design phase to stop that failure from occurring.

Essentially, the team identify what could go wrong with the product and then rate these failures by likelihood and severity. They can then use this information to prioritize solving or preventing the event happening.

FMEA involves the following steps (adapted from Basu, 2004, p. 149):

Step 1: Form a team and flow-chart the relevant details of the product, process or service that is selected for analysis.
Step 2: Assign each component of the system a unique identifier.
Step 3: List all the functions that each component of the system performs.

Figure 13.14 Benchmarking processes

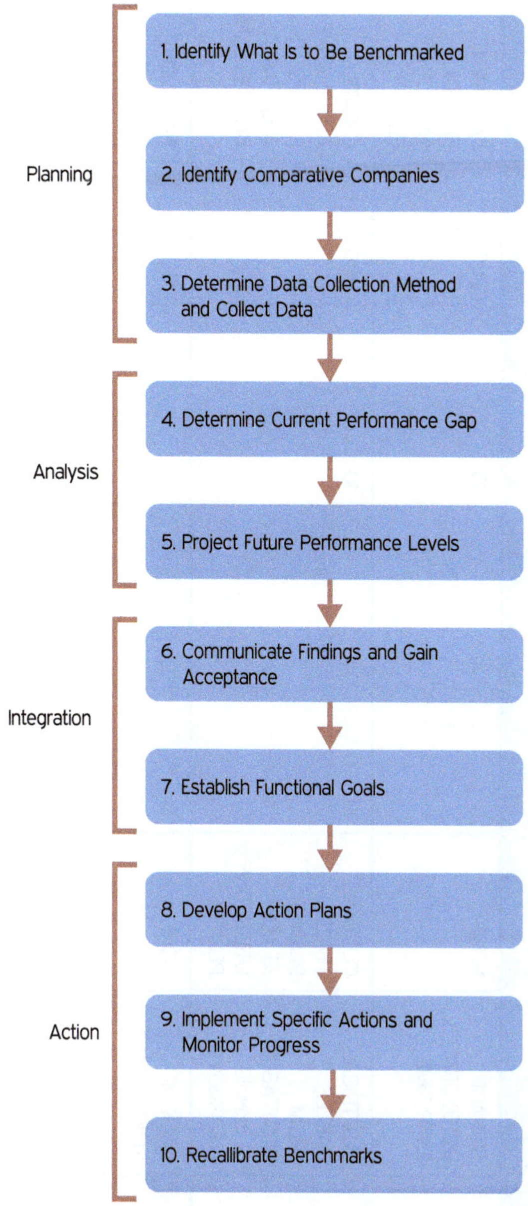

Source: Adapted from Chen and Paetsch (1998).

Step 4: Identify potential failure modes for each function listed in step 3.
Step 5: Describe the effects of each failure mode, especially the effects perceived by the user.
Step 6: Examine and summarize the causes of each failure mode.
Step 7: Identify and assess current controls to detect a potential failure mode.
Step 8: Determine the severity (S) of the potential hazard of the failure to personnel or system, on a scale.
Step 9: Estimate the relative likelihood of occurrence (O) of each failure.
Step 10: Estimate the ease with which the failure might be detected (D).
Step 11: Determine the risk priority number (RPN) for each failure, which is attained by multiplying the numbers obtained in steps 8, 9 and 10 (RPN = S × O × D). The potential failure modes in descending order of RPN should be the focus of the improvement action to minimize the risk of failure.
Step 12: Monitor the recommendations and corrective actions that have been put in place to eliminate or reduce failures, for continuous improvement.

Figure 13.15 provides an illustration of FMEA used on assessing the hotel services of a ski resort. The RPN values indicate that poor quality ingredients from the restaurant should take priority in managing the risks of failure; we

Figure 13.15a A FMEA of hotel services of a ski resort

SYSTEM COMPONENT	POTENTIAL FAILURE MODE (What could go wrong)	POTENTIAL FAILURE EFFECT (What happens to the customer if the failure occurs)	POTENTIAL CAUSES(S)	CURRENT CONTROLS (What systems are in place to prevent failure)	SEVERITY (How significant is the failure's effect to the customer)	OCCURRENCE (How likely is this failure to occur)	DETECTABILITY (How likely is it that the existing system will detect/ prevent failure - i.e. probability of non-detection)	RISK PRIORITY NUMBER (RPN)	ACTIONS TO BE TAKEN
RECEPTION	UNCLEAR SIGNAGE	CUSTOMER CONFUSION - LEADS TO COMPLAINT	SIGNAGE DETERIORATES OVER TIME	NONE	5	4	10	200	IMPLEMENT PERIODIC INSPECTION PLAN
	TRIPPING HAZARDS	CUSTOMER TRIP - LEADS TO INJURY	ELECTRICAL CABLES FROM PORTTABLE CLEANING EQUIPMENT	CLEANING TIMES PLANNED AT LOW UTILISATION PERIODS	10	4	10	400	CREATE ALTERNATIVE ROUTES TO AVOID AREAS BEING CLEANED
RESTAURANT	REFRIGERATOR FAILS	FOOD SPOILS – LEADS TO WASTE AND INCREASED COST	LACK OF MAINTENANCE	NONE	8	2	10	160	IMPLEMENT PERIODIC INSPECTION PLAN PROVIDE ANOTHER REFRIGERATOR
	POOR QUALITY INGREDIENTS	CUSTOMER BECOMES ILL	POOR CONTROL OF SUPPLY	NONE	10	5	10	500	IMPLEMENT SUPPLIED QUALITY PROGRAM

Figure 13.15b Scaling grid for FMEA

Rating	Severity (S)	Occurrence (O)	Detectability (D)
	How significant is this failure's effect to the customer?	How likely is the cause of this failure to occur?	How likely will the existing system detect the cause if it occurs? ***Note: p is the estimated probability of failure not being detected.***
1	Customer won't notice the effect or will consider it insignificant.	Not likely	Nearly certain to detect before reaching the customer ($p >> 0$)
2	Customer will notice the effect.	Documented low failure rate	Extremely low probability of reaching the customer ($p < 0.01$)
3	Customer will become irritated at reduced performance.	Undocumented low failure rate	Low probability of reaching the customer without detection ($0.01 < p < 0.05$)
4	Customer dissatisfaction will take place because of reduced performance.	Failures occur film time to time	Likely to be detected before reaching the customer ($0.05 < p < 0.20$)
5	Customer's productivity is reduced.	Documented moderate failure rate	It might be detected before reaching the customer ($0.20 < p < 0.50$)
6	Customer will complain. Customers are likely to request repair or return the product. Internal costs (scrap, rework, etc.) will increase.	Undocumented moderate failure rate	Unlikely to be detected before reaching the customer ($0.50 < p < 0.70$)
7	Customer loyalty will be reduced. Internal operations will adversely be affected.	Documented high failure rate	Highly unlikely to detect before reaching the customer ($0.70 < p < 0.90$)
8	Customer goodwill will be completely lost. Internal operations will be disrupted.	Undocumented high failure rate	Poor chance of detection ($0.90 < p < 0.95$)
9	Customer or employee safety is compromised. Regulatory compliance becomes questionable.	Failures common	Extremely poor chance of detection ($0.95 < p < 0.99$)
10	Catastrophic. Customer and/or employee are endangered without warning. Violation of law or regulation might occur.	Failures nearly always occur	Nearly certain that failure won't be detected

don't want customers to become ill due to poor control of supply. On the other hand, with the lowest RPN value, the failure is not as severe if the refrigerator fails. Figure 13.15b provides a scaling grid to measure S, O and D. Sometimes O is measured in terms of frequency and D in percentage (%). It is important to stay consistent with the measures throughout the columns.

Quality Function Deployment

Quality function deployment (QFD) is sometimes referred to as the House of Quality (because the diagram looks like a house). It helps to build in quality, as defined by the customer at the beginning of the design process. This tool is applicable whether a service or a product is being designed.

QFD is typically used at the beginning of a design process to help capture customer requirements for a new product or service. QFD captures the *voice of the customer* (VOC) by producing a detailed list of what the customer wants. These WHATs are then prioritized in terms of relative importance, possibly benchmarked against competitors, and then the design team has to decide HOW they could deliver what the customer has asked for. The final – and perhaps the most important – step is then to see how well the solutions (the HOWs) correlate with WHAT the customer has asked for.

It comprises the following elements, as shown in Figure 13.16:

- *The WHATs:* creates a list of customer requirements. Their importance is scored and prioritized on a scale.
- *The HOWs:* compiles a list of design requirements necessary to achieve the customer requirements listed as WHATs.
- *Relationship matrix:* shows the relationship between the WHATs and the HOWs.
- *Correlation matrix:* is the roof of the house. It captures the interrelationship between the design requirements. This is important when design features are being bundled together (e.g. a new mobile phone can be used to make calls, access the Internet and take pictures).
- *Analysis of competitors:* determines how the customers perceive competitors' abilities to meet the requirements.
- *Technical attributes and evaluation:* ranks the technical importance of each design requirement (usually shown as an absolute score, and a relative ranking).

Let's consider the QFD function of the Apple iPhone (Figure 13.17) and ask ourselves what it is that consumers want from an iPhone. Some of the requirements – the WHATs – are size, technology, features, storage capacity, battery life and price. Consumers also value these requirements differently. Price, for instance, means more (priority 10) than being environmentally friendly (priority 5). From the technical design's perspective, Apple needs to evaluate the design requirements for iPhones (the HOWs), such as technical requirements for case, screen, memory, software, camera and battery.

Once the HOWs and WHATs are gathered, Apple needs to find out the relationship between them. The Relationship Matrix shows, for instance, that the size of the iPhone has a strong relationship with the camera, but a weaker relationship with the case, screen, and battery.

Figure 13.16 Quality function deployment

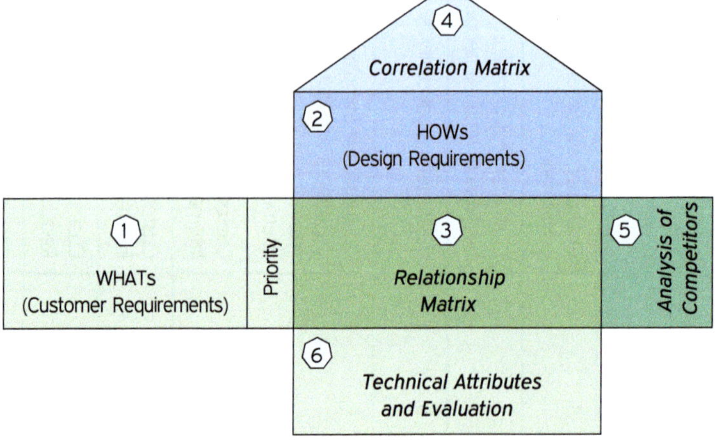

The roof shows that there is a *strong positive* correlation between case and screen (i.e. a design improvement in the case will contribute strongly to the improvement of the screen, and vice versa), whereas the correlation between battery and camera is only *positive* (i.e. a design improvement in the battery will contribute to the improvement of the camera, and vice versa, but not significantly). There is no correlation between screen and camera (i.e. a design improvement in the screen will not contribute to improvement of the camera, and vice versa).

The right-hand side of the matrix indicates how the competitors perform in satisfying the WHATs. The iPhone is superior to its competitors in terms of technology, design and features, but it is considerably more expensive than other phones in the market. This high-tech product also has a superior case, screen, memory and software elements (ranked the best in technical evaluation). The QFD provides a comparative analysis of the iPhone in relation to the competitors' products.

QFD matrices can be linked together to show how customer attributes flow through and influence other parts of the operation, such as the production process. The HOWs of one matrix become the WHATs of the next matrix (Figure 13.18). For a manufacturing plant, the engineering characteristics of House 1 become the customer attributes of House 2 in order to understand their influence on parts deployment. The design requirements need to be assessed in relation to the parts characteristics. The houses can be interlinked with as many houses as the company sees fit.

Figure 13.17 Example of iPhone

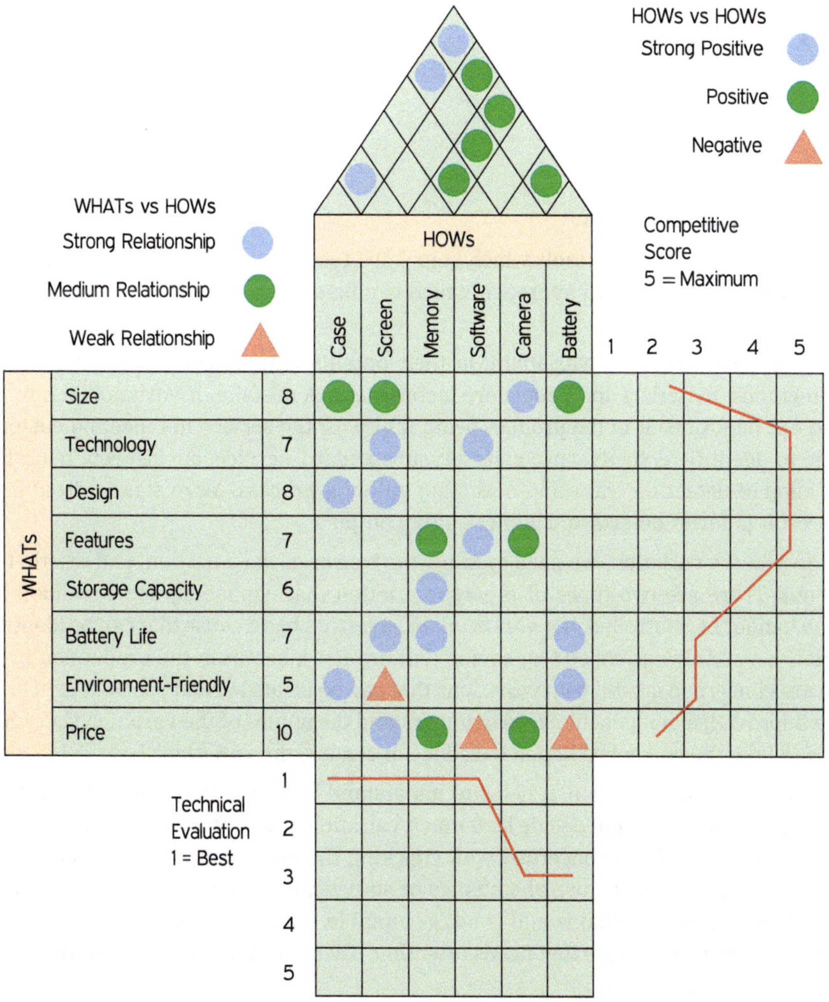

Source: http://blogs.warwick.ac.uk/ssanchez

Figure 13.18 Linked houses of quality

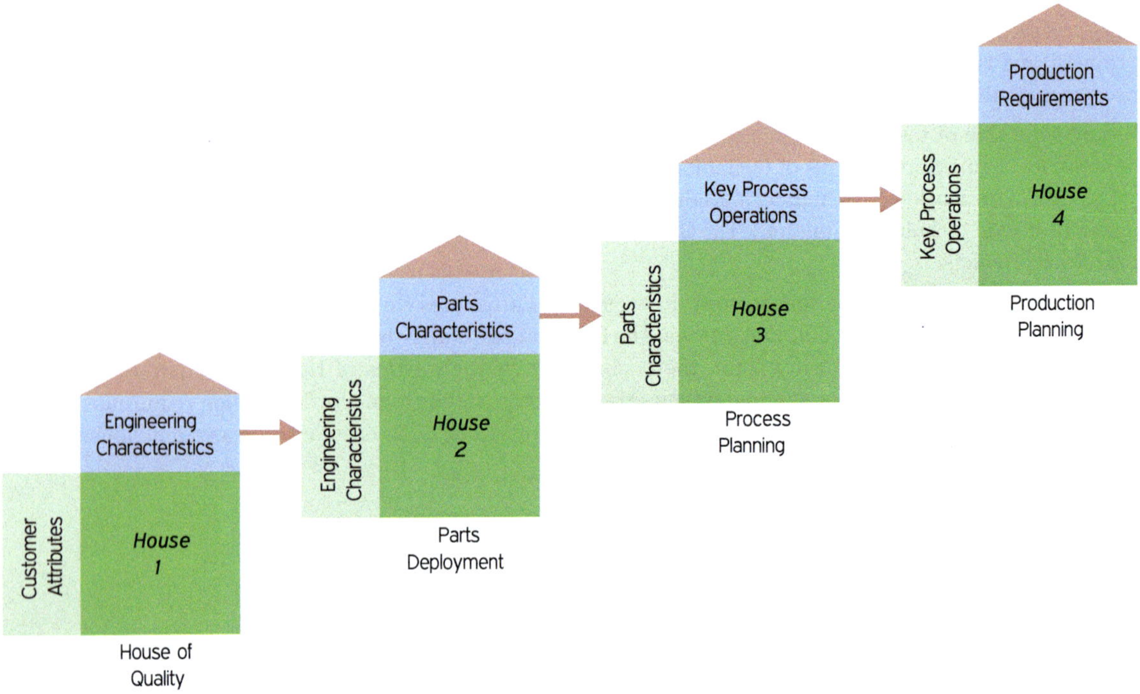

Source: Adapted from Hauser and Clausing (1988).

Statistical Process Control

So far, we have seen some of the many tools which help firms focus and improve the quality of their products and services. In this section we focus on an approach which can be used to control the quality of the process, called *statistical process control* (SPC).

All processes exhibit some degree of variability in their outputs (e.g. a product or a service). This is because machines, tools, methods, materials and people are inconsistent. A mistake or variation in how any one part of a process is carried out might result in the product being faulty, or the service not meeting customer expectations. Rather than wait to identify defective products or substandard service by inspection or through customer complaints, SPC aims to detect the variation occurring within a process. More standardized processes with less variation should result in fewer defects and higher-quality outputs.

In order to manage process variation, we need to know the source of the variation, and whether the variation can be controlled or not. There are two types of process variation that commonly occur: random and non-random. *Random variation* cannot be controlled, but *non-random variation* has a cause that can be identified and assigned. Non-random variations are always caused by events that are not inherent in the production process. For quality management, we are concerned mostly with variations that can be identified and controlled. In order for the quality of a process to be improved, management needs to understand the nature of the variation (i.e. whether it is random or non-random), and take the corrective action to reduce or remove the variation.

Before we can start controlling variation, it helps to understand how variation occurs. Statistical models help us predict likely patterns of variation, and decide how much variation is acceptable, and what change is likely to be a symptom of a faulty process. SPC is concerned with checking the quality characteristics of a product or service while it is being produced, through the use of statistics or statistical methods. It identifies the natural variation of the process, and sets the limits for what is and is not acceptable. Any variation beyond the acceptable level indicates a non-random or assignable cause that needs attention. There are four main uses of SPC (Basu, 2004):

- To achieve initial process stability
- To provide guidance on how the process may be improved by the reduction of variation

Figure 13.19 Normal distribution curves

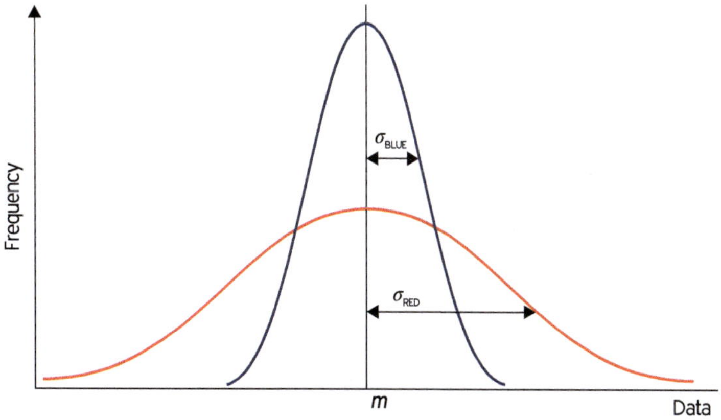

- To assess the performance of a process and increase process capability
- To provide information to assist with management decision-making.

Normal Distributions

SPC models are based on measurements that vary according to a statistical distribution. The exact statistical distribution depends on whether we are measuring *attributes* or *variables*.

Let us initially deal with measuring variables, which follow a *normal* (or bell-shaped) distribution. In a normal distribution, measurements are distributed continuously, but tend to cluster around a set point, with more extreme measurements being less likely to occur. This produces a bell-shaped curve called the *normal curve*, such as those shown in Figure 13.19.

Two key characteristics describe the **population** in a normal curve: the *mean* (μ) and the *standard deviation* (σ). The mean (μ), pronounced 'mu', is the average of the population measurements. The population is defined as every member of a *set* – for instance, all students currently registered at your university, or all the invoices sent to customers in a particular month, or all eggs produced by a farm in a week. The standard deviation (σ), pronounced 'sigma', is a measure of the variation of the population measurements. A small sigma, as exhibited in the blue curve, means that most of the data are centred on the mean, and hence have less variation than the red curve, which has a larger value of sigma.

Population: in a statistical distribution, the entire set of things that make up what is being measured. Samples are taken from a population.

If a population has mean m and standard deviation σ, and is described by a normal curve, then the following empirical rules apply, as illustrated in Figure 13.20:

- *Rule 1:* 68.26% of the population measurements are within one standard deviation (1σ) from the mean in either direction. Therefore 31.74% of the data is more than one standard deviation from the mean. That is, 15.87% of the data will fall below –1 standard deviation, and 15.87% will be above +1 standard deviation.
- *Rule 2:* 95.44% of the population measurements are within two standard deviations from the mean in either direction. Therefore 4.56% of the data is more than two standard deviations from the mean. That is, 2.28% of the data will fall below –2 standard deviations, and 2.28% will be above +2 standard deviations.
- *Rule 3:* 99.73% of the population measurements are within three standard deviations from the mean in either direction. Therefore 0.27% of the data is more than three standard deviations from the mean. That is, 0.135% of the data will fall below –3 standard deviations, and 0.135% will be above +3 standard deviations.

These proportions are fixed, and are described in statistical tables: so once we know the mean and standard deviation of a measurement, we know what proportion of the population is likely to fall within any particular range of measurements. Suppose that the distribution of heights of men between the ages of 18 and 26 is approximately normal, with a mean of 170 centimetres (μ = 170 cm) and standard deviation of 8.5 centimetres. Using the empirical rule, we would have the following statistics, as shown in Figure 13.21:

- 68.26% of men are between 161.5 and 178.5 cm tall
- 95.44% of men are between 153 and 187 cm tall
- 99.73% of men are between 144.5 and 195.5 cm tall

Figure 13.20 Empirical rule for a normally distributed population

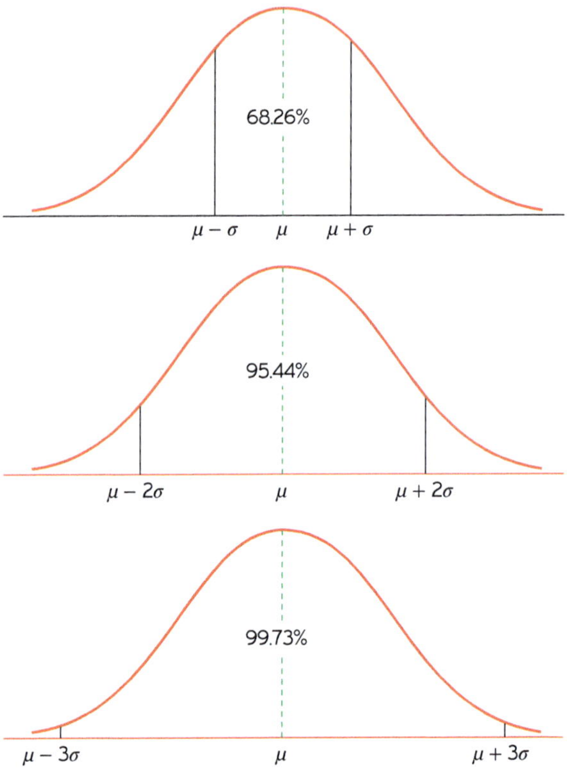

We often interpret the three sigma interval ($\pm 3\sigma$) to be the interval that contains almost all the measurements in the population, and this has traditionally been considered an acceptable quality level. In practice, this means that if the specification limits of a product are set equal to $\pm 3\sigma$, we could expect 0.27% defective parts, or 2,700 defective parts per million (ppm), to be produced. *Six Sigma* is so called because it aims to reduce the variability of a process so that outputs that lie within $\pm 6\sigma$ of the mean fall within the specification limits. This means

Figure 13.21 Example of empirical rule

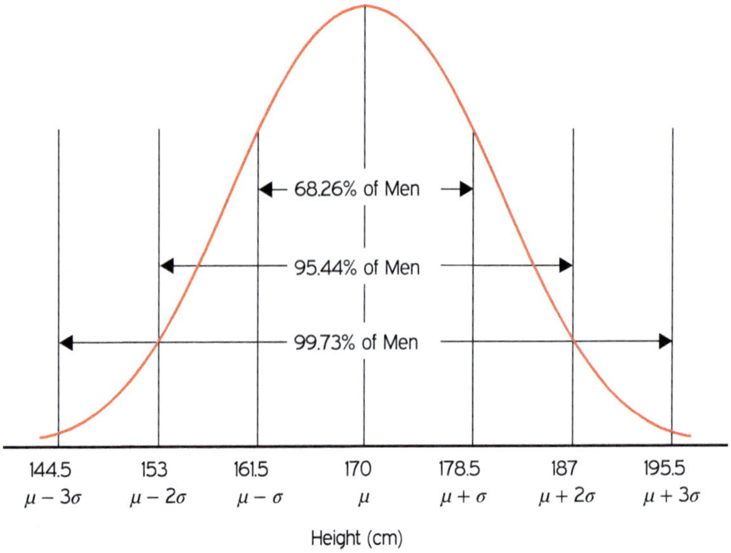

Figure 13.22 Comparison of curves within and outside specification limits

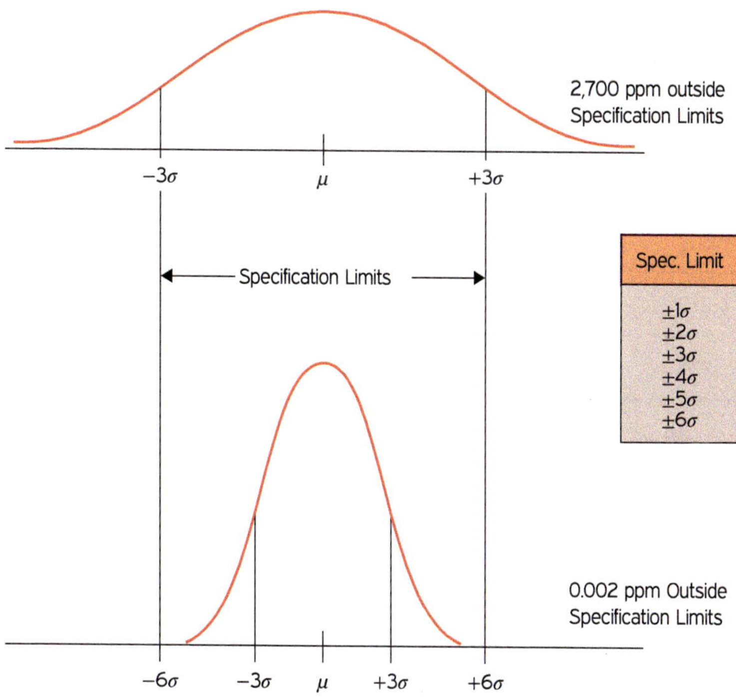

Spec. Limit	Percentage	Defective ppm
$\pm1\sigma$	68.26	317,400
$\pm2\sigma$	95.44	45,600
$\pm3\sigma$	99.73	2,700
$\pm4\sigma$	99.9937	63
$\pm5\sigma$	99.999943	0.57
$\pm6\sigma$	99.9999998	0.002

that only 3.4 parts per million will be beyond the specification limits, which for most operational purposes is as close to zero as is required.

In Six Sigma the terms *defects per million opportunities* (DPMO) is used, which means the number of defects a process would produce if there were a million opportunities to do so. This is slightly different from defects per number of parts produced, as each part may have more than one way in which it can be defective.

For any company these tighter tolerances mean that there are fewer faulty products being made, and this in turn means lower costs of rework and scrap. For example, if the designers of a product state that all the good, non-defective parts need to be within specification range, and the process producing the parts needs to operate within 6σ limits, then we have a process that should produce only 3.4 parts per million that we cannot use. This is a very low scrap rate. It is shown in Figure 13.22, where the process described by the bottom curve is less likely to produce faulty parts. The top curve, however, shows a higher likelihood of producing unusable parts – those that fall outside the specifications – and so we should continuously need to inspect the parts. The lower curve needs less monitoring, as there is less variation or change in the process. This situation is the ultimate aim of the Six Sigma approach: the reduction of variation in a process's output.

CRITICAL PERSPECTIVE

Is Six Sigma 3.4 Defects per Million Opportunities?

The table in Figure 13.22 lists the 6σ defect rate as 0.002 DPMO, but the Six Sigma philosophy indicates that a 6σ process will produce 3.4 DPMO. This is because the architects of Six Sigma built a 1.5σ shift into their statistical calculations to capture the variations in 'the voice of customer', believing that over time the process would drift, so eroding its integrity from 0.002 DPMO to the more realistic 3.4 DPMO. This shift of course alters the process integrity for all σ values, as shown in Table 13.6.

Table 13.6 DPMO, defect and yield percentages with a 1.5σ shift incorporated

+ and –	DPMO	Defect percentage	Yield percentage
1σ	691,462	69%	30.9%
2σ	308,538	31%	69.1%
3σ	66,807	6.7%	93.3%
4σ	6,210	0.62%	99.38%
5σ	233	0.023%	99.977%
6σ	**3.4**	**0.00034%**	**99.99966%**
7σ	0.019	0.0000019%	99.9999981%

The key point is ...

that regardless of the absolute values used, a 6σ process is the ultimate goal for a process designer.

Using SPC

If we apply the information above, we can ensure our process is producing only good parts by ensuring that the output curve of the process fits within the tolerances set by the engineers designing the product, as shown in Figure 13.23.

In practice, ensuring the output is always within tolerance needs two steps. The first step is to ensure that the output is stable and producing within tolerance as shown in Figure 13.23. When we first turn on a hot tap, for example, the water temperature may vary before becoming stable; this is because there may be cold water in the pipe between the hot water tank and the tap. So we need to run the process to ensure it is stable before testing if it is producing within tolerance. The second step uses SPC charts to monitor the process and see whether there is any evidence that the mean or standard deviation is changing as a result of assignable causes. If there is no indication that the process is varying, then we can continue operating it and use the parts it produces with confidence. As the parts were within specification when we started, there is no evidence that the process has changed and so the parts will still be within specification. We repeat this second check frequently to be sure we catch any change in the process as soon as it occurs.

Figure 13.23 A process output curve fitting well between the specifications set by the designer

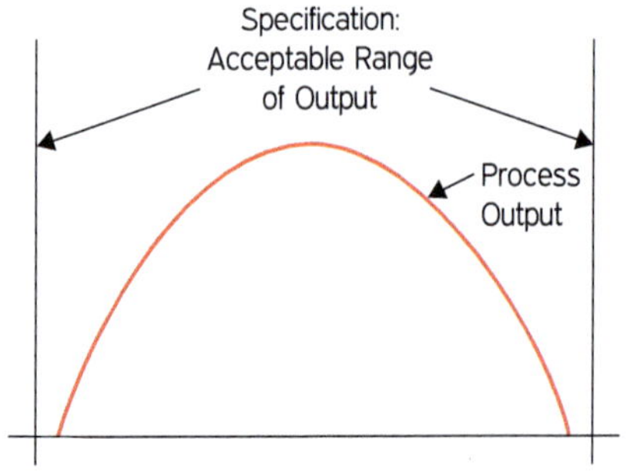

Measuring Process Capability

Process capability measures how much yield (output) a process can produce within pre-specified tolerance limits. Traditionally, a process is capable if all its outputs as measured using 3σ limits fall within the specified tolerance limits. However, using 6σ thinking, we know that this may not be good enough for today's quality requirements and so some firms choose the tighter measure by insisting production measured at the 6σ level is within specification. Whether a process is capable or not can be determined by visual inspection (from a chart), or by calculation.

Customers normally state their requirements in terms of a target value with some specified *tolerances* (also called *specifications*), to give a range of what would be acceptable. For example, the output voltage specification of many semiconductors is set at 5 volts $\pm 5\%$, which means that as long as the voltage measurements are between 4.75 and 5.25 volts, the semiconductors meet the specifications, and hence are acceptable.

To measure the process capability we use an index number called Cp calculated as shown in the Process Capability Ratio below. This compares the width of the tolerance range to the width of the process output. Note that the 6σ process output shown as the denominator in the equation below is the plus or minus 3σ level: 3σ either side of the mean equals a total of 6σ – not to be confused with the 6σ process we have been discussing, which would be $+6\sigma$ or -6σ either side of the mean, totalling 12σ.

$$\text{Process capability ratio, } C_p = \frac{\text{Upper specification level (USL)} - \text{Lower specification level (LSL)}}{6\sigma}$$

Referring to Figure 13.24, a ratio of less than 1 ($C_p < 1$) indicates that outputs will be outside the predefined specification or tolerance limits (as the width of the process output is wider than the range specified by the designers). A ratio greater than 1 ($C_p > 1$) indicates that the outputs are within the specification, as shown. However, we would not want the ratio to be too close to 1.0, as this implies a tight fit, and would leave little margin for error. Typically, the process aim is set at 1.33, to allow some leeway. A ratio of 2 would signify that 6σ levels (as defined by the quality philosophy) have been reached.

The C_p ratio takes into account only the variance or width of the process output; it does not measure the location of the values. To measure location and variance we need to use a more sophisticated measure, known as the C_{pk} ratio. This takes into account whether the process output is central to the specification or, if it isn't, how far from central is it. We can see in Figure 13.25 that it is possible to have a good C_p value but still produce many defective parts if the process output is too far from the centre of the acceptable values as set in the specification.

The C_{pk} ratio is calculated as follows. Note that the 'min' and the square brackets indicate we are interested in the minimum value of either possible calculation:

$$C_{pk} = \min\left[\frac{\overline{X} - \text{LSL}}{3\sigma}, \frac{\text{USL} - \overline{X}}{3\sigma}\right]$$

where $\overline{X}$ is the average of the process output (its centrality); LSL and USL are the lower and upper specification limits (set by the designers); and 3σ is the process output range over three standard deviations. If:

$C_{pk} = C_p$ the process mean is centred between the specification limits

$C_{pk} > 1.0$ the process is capable

$C_{pk} < 1.0$ the process is not capable

Figure 13.24 C_p values and how they compare process output and specification limits

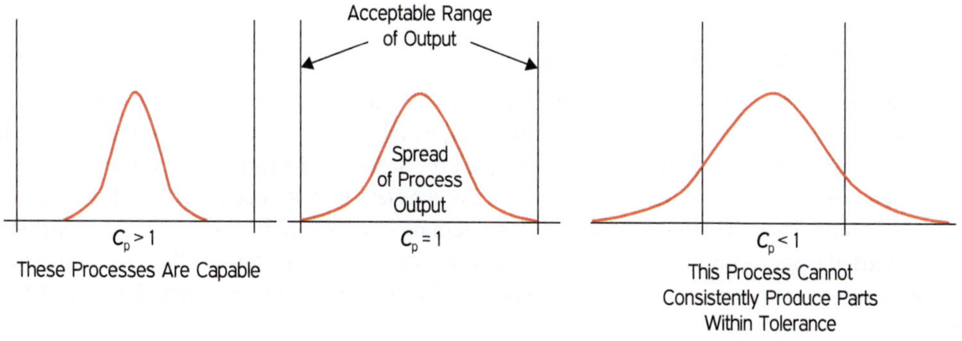

Figure 13.25 Representation of possible C_{pk} results

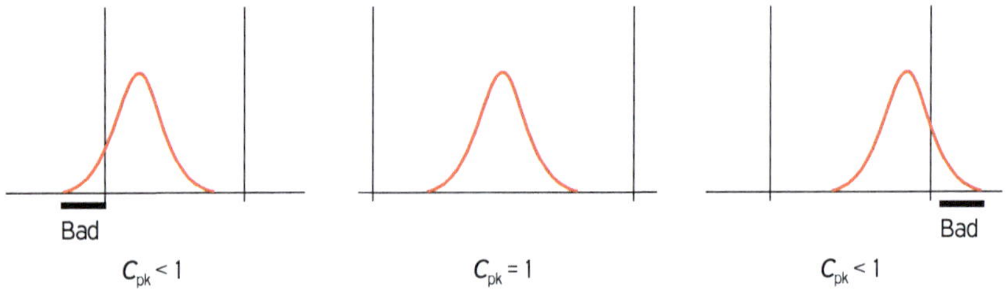

For example, assume a manufacturing process that produces the above-mentioned semiconductors has a mean of 4.9 volts and a standard deviation of 0.1 volts:

$$C_{pk} = \min\left[\frac{4.9 - 4.75}{3 \times 0.1}, \frac{5.25 - 4.9}{3 \times 0.1}\right]$$
$$= \min(0.5, 1.17)$$

Hence the lowest value of C_{pk} is 0.5, which means that the process is not capable of always producing semiconductors that are within the specification – the situation that is represented in the left-hand diagram of Figure 13.25.

So C_p and C_{pk} are indices that tell us whether the process is producing all its output (or, rather actually 99.73% or more, as we have adopted the 6σ limit) within specification. This means the process is producing only good parts.

SPC Charts

Control chart: used to plot sample means, average means and ranges over time; indicates the lower and upper control limits.

An SPC chart is a **control chart** that graphically presents samples of output taken from the total output (the population) being produced by the process. Its job is to test the output and see whether this has varied from when the process was capable (i.e. passing both the C_p and C_{pk} tests). If the SPC chart reveals a variation in the output of the process, then we no longer have the same output, and so could be producing faulty parts. Our reaction is to stop using the process and find out what has changed. As there are different types of measurement we can apply to samples, there are therefore different types of chart. The process of establishing which control chart to use is determined by the following steps:

- *Step 1:* Consider whether you are collecting variable data or attribute data. *Variables* refer to data that are measured on a continuous scale, such as weight, height, volume, or time. *Attributes* refer to situations, such as yes/no, on/off, or right/wrong.
- *Step 2:* Choose the type of chart to be used. A variables chart is used to control individual, measurable characteristics. Attribute charts are used to control the number of defective units or defects in a unit. You also need to consider whether the sampled population or sample space is constant, or varies. Figure 13.26 shows a decision tree for choosing which chart to use to measure a process.
- *Step 3:* Once the type of chart to be used is established, one can take samples and calculate means of samples, and upper and lower control limits using the appropriate formula. The principles for every chart are the same; however, the formulae vary due to different distributions being used (attributes follow a binomial distribution whilst variances follow a normal distribution).

SPC Charts for Variables: $\overline{X}$ and Range

If the process can be measured using a continuous variable such as length, height or time, the chart employed is the $\overline{X}$ and range chart. An example is shown in Figure 13.27, which identifies the top part as showing the mean ($\overline{X}$, or average) and how it varies over time, and the lower part the same for the range (spread or standard deviation). Both charts have a central line to help us record the data and assess how it is changing, and they also have upper and lower control limits. These are there to warn us if something unexpected happens. If either chart suggests that the process has varied from its previous (capable) state, then we need to take action. If there is no evidence of any change to the process, then we can continue to operate the process, confident that the output is still within specification.

Figure 13.26 Which control chart to use?

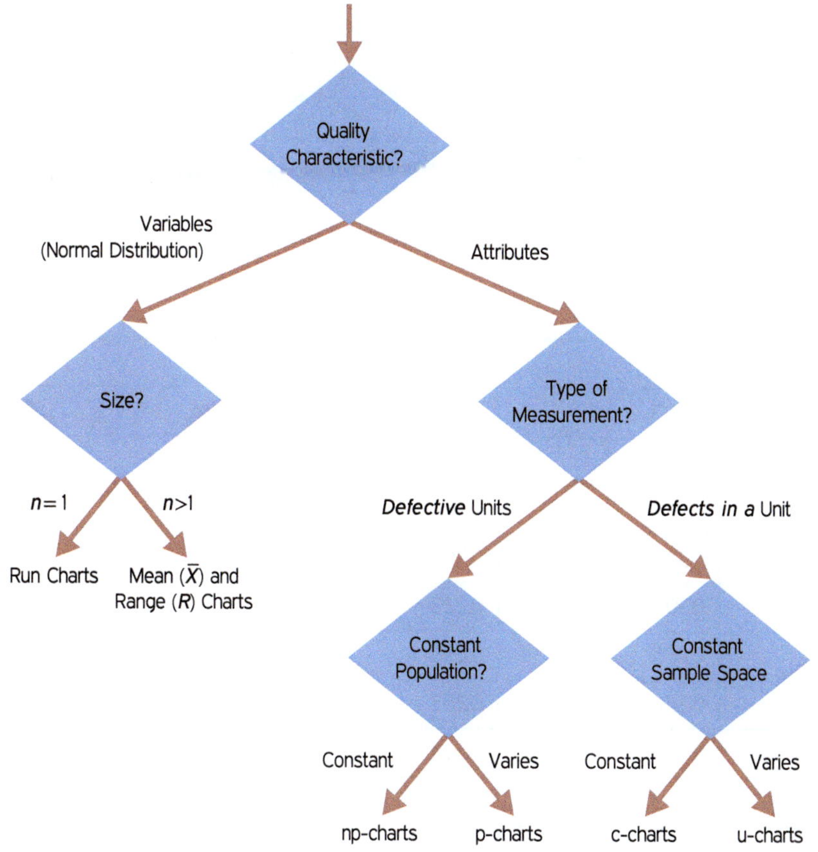

Source: Adapted from Bicheno (2002, p. 38)

Figure 13.27 The main parts of the $\bar{X}$ and range chart

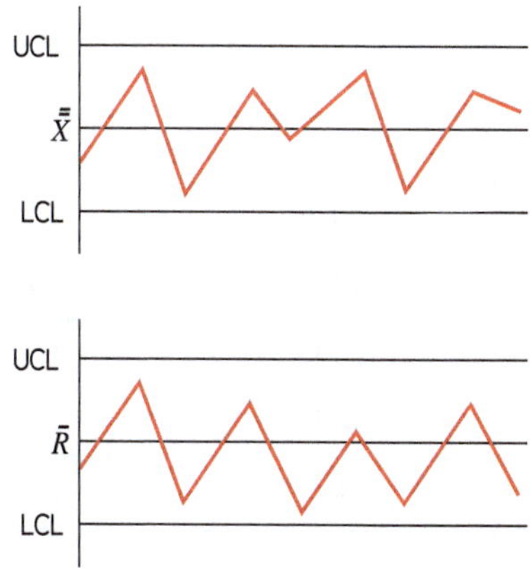

The $\bar{X}$ (or X-bar) chart monitors the average (mean) of the samples being measured, and the range (or R) chart the variance (standard deviation) in the samples. The $\bar{X}$ and R charts are used together in a sampling plan to monitor repetitive processes and see whether the output curve has changed.

An $\bar{X}$ chart plots the means of the samples taken from the outputs of a process. Each sample mean will be an approximation to the population mean (μ). The larger the sample is, the more closely it will represent the population (e.g. a sample of 10 football diameters from a total population output of 1,000 will give a less accurate approximation of the population mean than if 100 were sampled). This potential error is corrected using pre-calculated values from a table such as Table 13.7.

Table 13.7 Factors for determining control limits for $\overline{X}$ and R

No. of observations in subgroups, N	Factor for $\overline{X}$ chart	Factors for R chart		
		Lower control limit	Upper control limit	Divisor estimate of standard deviation
	A_2	D_3	D_4	d_2
2	1.880	0	3.267	1.128
3	1.023	0	2.574	1.693
4	0.729	0	2.282	2.059
5	0.577	0	2.114	2.326
6	0.483	0	2.004	2.534
7	0.419	0.076	1.924	2.704
8	0.373	0.136	1.864	2.847
9	0.337	0.184	1.816	2.970
10	0.308	0.223	1.777	3.078
11	0.285	0.256	1.744	3.173
12	0.266	0.283	1.717	3.258
13	0.249	0.307	1.693	3.336
14	0.235	0.328	1.672	3.407
15	0.223	0.347	1.653	3.472
16	0.212	0.363	1.637	3.532
17	0.203	0.378	1.622	3.588
18	0.194	0.391	1.608	3.640
19	0.187	0.403	1.597	3.689
20	0.180	0.415	1.585	3.735
21	0.173	0.425	1.575	3.778
22	0.167	0.434	1.566	3.819
23	0.162	0.443	1.557	3.858
24	0.157	0.451	1.548	3.895
25	0.153	0.459	1.541	3.931

The centre line of an $\overline{X}$ chart is the average of the sample means, $\overline{\overline{X}}$ (this is known as the *grand mean* or as X-bar-bar), or a target value for the process.

$$\text{Mean of the sample, } \overline{X} = \frac{\sum_{i=1}^{n} X_i}{n}$$

$$= \frac{X_1 + X_2 + \ldots + X_n}{n}$$

where i is the item number, and n is the total number of items in the sample.

$$\text{Average of the means of the samples, } \overline{\overline{X}} = \frac{\sum_{j=1}^{m} \overline{X}_j}{m} = \frac{\overline{X}_1 + \overline{X}_2 + \ldots + \overline{X}_m}{m}$$

where j is the sample number, and m is the total number of samples.

$$\text{Average range, } \overline{R} = \frac{\sum_{j=1}^{m} R_j}{m} = \frac{R_1 + R_2 + \ldots + R_m}{m}$$

where R is the difference between the maximum and minimum values of each sample.

The upper and lower control limits for $\overline{X}$ charts are:

Upper control limit for $\overline{X}$, $\text{UCL}_{\overline{X}} = \overline{\overline{X}} + A_2\overline{R}$
Lower control limit for $\overline{X}$, $\text{LCL}_{\overline{X}} = \overline{\overline{X}} - A_2\overline{R}$

The upper and lower control limits for range charts are:

Upper control limit for R, $\text{UCL}_R = D_4\overline{R}$
Lower control limit for R, $\text{UCL}_R = D_3\overline{R}$

The process standard deviation can be estimated (again as we only have a small sample and not the whole population, using Table 13.7) as:

$$\text{Standard deviation, } \sigma = \frac{\overline{R}}{d_2}$$

The values for A_2, D_3 and D_4 vary with the number of observations in subgroups, as listed in Table 13.7. Essentially, as the values change and the more observations we have, the more true the value, and so we can see smaller variations before needing to take action.

WORKED EXAMPLE 13.1

Grommets: Calculating Sample Carton

A materials inspector wants to know whether a special component called a grommet meets the length specification required for manufacturing. The specification limits for the grommet are between 24 and 36 mm. He collects 25 samples with 4 observations in each, as shown in Figure 13.28.

Problem: *Are the samples in control? Should the inspector be concerned?*

Approach: Figure 13.28 provides an example of how $\overline{X}$ and R charts are used. The chart shows the data collected from the measurements of the process. There are 25 samples (m = 25) with 4 observations each (n = 4). The mean of each sample, $\overline{X}$, and range R are calculated for each sample. The centre line, upper limits and lower limits for each of the charts are calculated as follows:

$$\overline{\overline{X}} = \frac{\sum_{j=1}^{m} \overline{X}_j}{m} = \frac{\overline{X}_1 + \overline{X}_2 + \ldots + \overline{X}_m}{m}$$

$$= \frac{731.25}{25} = 29.250$$

$$\overline{R} = \frac{\sum_{j=1}^{m} R_j}{m} = \frac{R_1 + R_2 + \ldots + R_m}{m}$$

$$= \frac{217}{25} = 8.680$$

Figure 13.28 An example of completed $\overline{X}$ and R charts

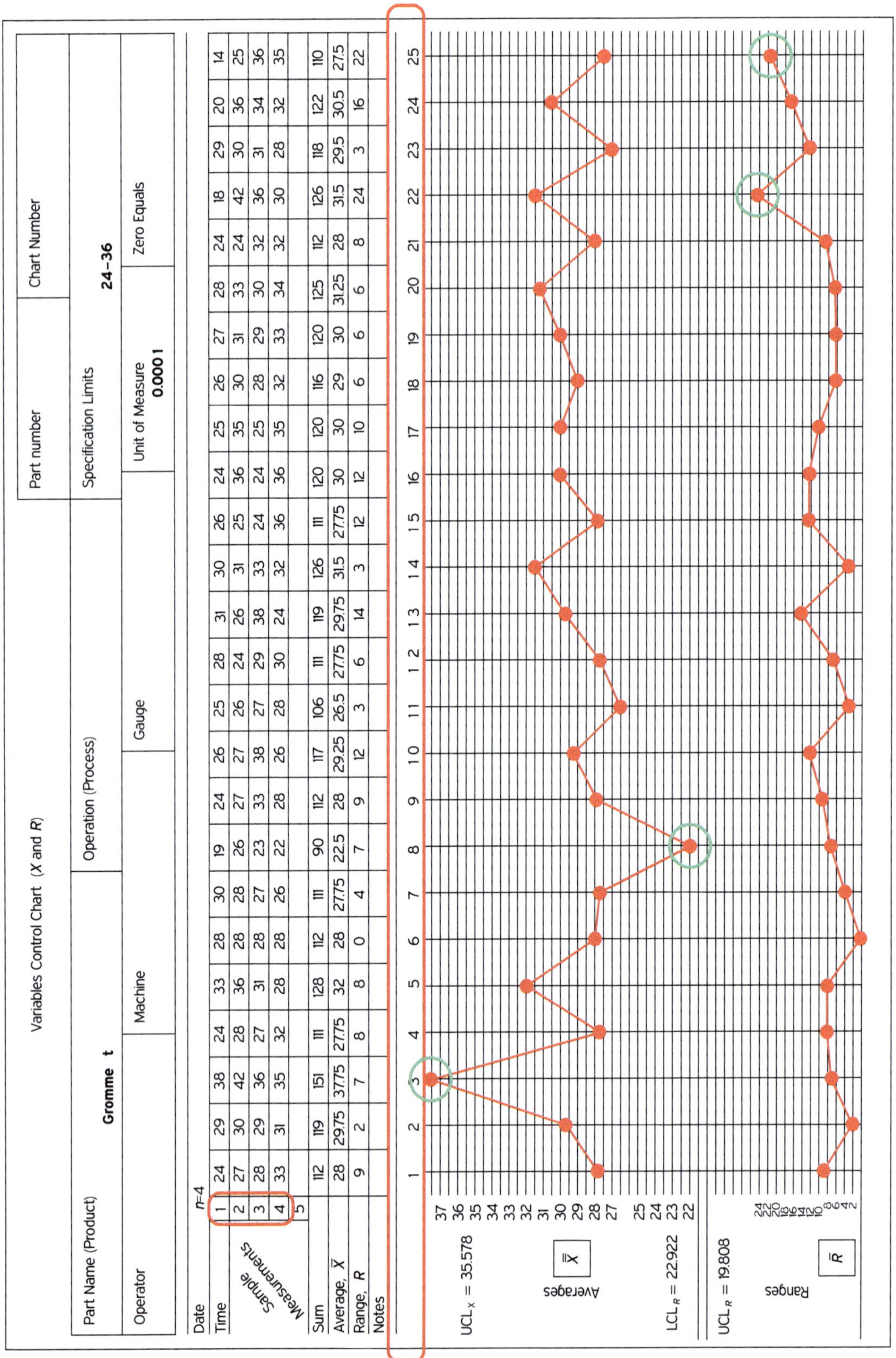

	1	2	3	4	5	6	7	8	9	10	11	12	13	14	15	16	17	18	19	20	21	22	23	24	25
Date																									
Time																									
Sample Measurements 1	24	29	38	24	33	28	30	19	24	26	25	28	31	30	26	24	25	26	27	28	24	18	29	20	14
2	27	30	42	28	36	28	28	26	27	27	26	24	26	31	25	36	35	30	31	33	24	42	30	36	25
3	28	29	36	27	31	28	27	23	33	38	27	29	38	33	24	24	25	28	29	30	32	36	31	34	36
4	33	31	35	32	28	28	26	22	28	26	28	30	24	32	36	36	35	32	33	34	32	30	28	32	35
5																									
Sum	112	119	151	111	128	112	111	90	112	117	106	111	119	126	111	120	120	116	120	125	112	126	118	122	110
Average, $\overline{X}$	28	29.75	37.75	27.75	32	28	27.75	22.5	28	29.25	26.5	27.75	29.75	31.5	27.75	30	30	29	30	31.25	28	31.5	29.5	30.5	27.5
Range, R	9	2	7	8	8	0	4	7	9	12	3	6	14	3	12	12	10	6	6	6	8	24	3	16	22
Notes																									

Source: Foster (2010, p. 369).

Using Table 13.7, and knowing that $n = 4$, we have $A_2 = 0.73$, $D_3 = 0$ and $D_4 = 2.28$. So:

$$\begin{aligned} UCL_{\bar{X}} &= \bar{\bar{X}} + A_2\bar{R} \\ &= 29.25 + (0.729 \times 8.68) \\ &= 35.578 \end{aligned}$$

$$\begin{aligned} LCL_{\bar{X}} &= \bar{\bar{X}} - A_2\bar{R} \\ &= 29.25 - (0.729 \times 8.68) \\ &= 22.922 \end{aligned}$$

$$\begin{aligned} UCL_R &= D_4\bar{R} \\ &= 2.282 \times 8.68 \\ &= 19.808 \end{aligned}$$

$$\begin{aligned} LCL_R &= D_3\bar{R} \\ &= 0 \end{aligned}$$

Solution: The chart shows that there are four samples that require further investigation, as they are outside the control limits: samples 3, 8, 22 and 25. This could be due to machine, material or human error, or some other factor. Note that each point plotted on the $\bar{X}$ chart is the average of a mean, and each point plotted on the range chart is the range of a sample.

Any point outside the control limits would not normally occur, and so would indicate that the process had changed in some way. If we had already tested C_p and C_{pk}, any variation would tell us that we were now possibly producing parts out of specification.

SPC Charts for Attributes

When we are recording attribute data such as counts or proportions, rather than variables such as height or length, we need to use different charts.

The *p*-chart is used to illustrate the *proportion of defectives* (or percentage non-conforming) in each subgroup – for example, the proportion of dissatisfied customers in a survey of train commuters. It is the most universal chart, based on the proportion of non-conforming items within a chosen set of items. Other possible applications of *p*-charts include late deliveries, incomplete orders, accounting errors, typing errors, or misspellings.

An *np*-chart plots the *number of defectives* (or the number of non-conforming items) in each subgroup (using the same sample size each time). The use of an *np*-chart is essentially the same as the use of a *p*-chart, except that *np*-charts use integer numbers (e.g. 0, 1, 2) rather than proportions (e.g. 0.5, 1.1, 2.5).

A *c*-chart is used to monitor the *number of non-conformities* (or defects) in a discrete unit, *not* the number of items found to be conforming. It requires a constant sample space, which means that the space for finding defects must be the same for each unit. Typical situations when a *c*-chart is used include flaws in a specific length of fabric, flaws in an auto finish (for a particular model), defects in a paint finish (if all cars are of the same size), the number of flaws in a standard A4 paper, or number of incorrect responses on a standardized test.

When the sample space varies (such as in inspection for flaws in different models of car within a model family), a *u-chart* is used. In this case the *average number of non-conformities* is charted. For instance, you might decide to inspect the end-of-line scratches in the paint on all cars of differing sizes in a production line – for example, a saloon, an estate or a coupé. Consider in this example that the car is the unit. As all cars (units) are of different sizes (i.e. different surface area of paint to check), checking *defects per unit* is a far more useful measure than just the *number of defects*.

As for $\bar{X}$ and R charts, for all these charts the upper control limit (UCL) and lower control limit (LCL) are usually established at ±3 standard deviations from the centre line (unless Six Sigma tolerances are being used, in which

Table 13.8 Control limit formulas for attribute data

Chart type	Data type	Centre line	Upper control limit	Lower control limit
p	Percentage non-conforming, where p is proportion defective, $\bar{p}$ is average proportion defective	$\bar{p}$	$UCL = \bar{p} + 3\sqrt{\frac{\bar{p}(1-\bar{p})}{n}}$	$LCL = \bar{p} - 3\sqrt{\frac{\bar{p}(1-\bar{p})}{n}}$
np	Number of non-conforming items, where p is proportion defective, $\bar{p}$ is average proportion defective	$n\bar{p}$	$UCL = n\bar{p} + 3\sqrt{n\bar{p}(1-\bar{p})}$	$LCL = n\bar{p} - 3\sqrt{n\bar{p}(1-\bar{p})}$
c	Number of non-conformities, where c is number of defects	$\bar{c}$	$UCL = \bar{c} + 3\sqrt{\bar{c}}$	$LCL = \bar{c} - 3\sqrt{\bar{c}}$
u	Number of non-conformities per item, where u is process average number of non-conformities or defects per unit, n is average sample size	$\bar{U}$	$UCl = \bar{U} + 3\sqrt{\frac{\bar{U}}{n}}$	$UCl = \bar{U} - 3\sqrt{\frac{\bar{U}}{n}}$

tolerance limits will be set at ±6 standard deviations from the centre line). The formulae for the attribute data are listed in Table 13.8.

Interpretation of Charts

In addition to identifying data points outside the control limits, we need to look out for unusual patterns on SPC charts, such as data points that exhibit non-random variation in the process. These indicate that the process may be going out of control and becoming incapable – a capable process passed C_p and C_{pk} and is only able to produce parts within specification. Figure 13.29 illustrates various scenarios of non-random variation that can occur, and which can be identified using an SPC chart. Even when there is too little variation, we should investigate why the data points are so close to the mean value.

Cost of Quality

Managing quality is not cheap. It has been estimated that in 2001 it cost General Electric (GE) somewhere between \$11 billion and \$16 billion to implement its quality management strategy (www.isixsigma.com). As quality management evolves from being reactive (i.e. fixing problems after detection) to proactive (i.e. preventing failures from occurring in the first place), the nature of what constitutes quality costs is changing as well. Quality costs can be classified into three categories: *prevention costs*, *appraisal costs* and *failure costs* (internal and external), as detailed in Table 13.9.

The traditional view of the costs of quality was that there was an optimum level of investment in quality prevention and appraisal, after which there were diminishing returns to failure reduction, as shown in Figure 13.30. The contemporary view of the cost of quality demonstrates that investment in cost of quality prevention and appraisal will always result in some improvement – that is, some reduction in internal or external failure.

Traditionally, the costs of quality were perceived by many manufacturing companies as costs related to running the quality assurance department and costs relating to scrap. Similarly, it was estimated that companies in the 1980s typically spent between 5% and 25% of their annual sales turnover on quality-related costs, and 95% of this was spent on appraisal and failures (Dale and Plunkett, 1990).

Figure 13.29 Scenario of non-random variation in processes

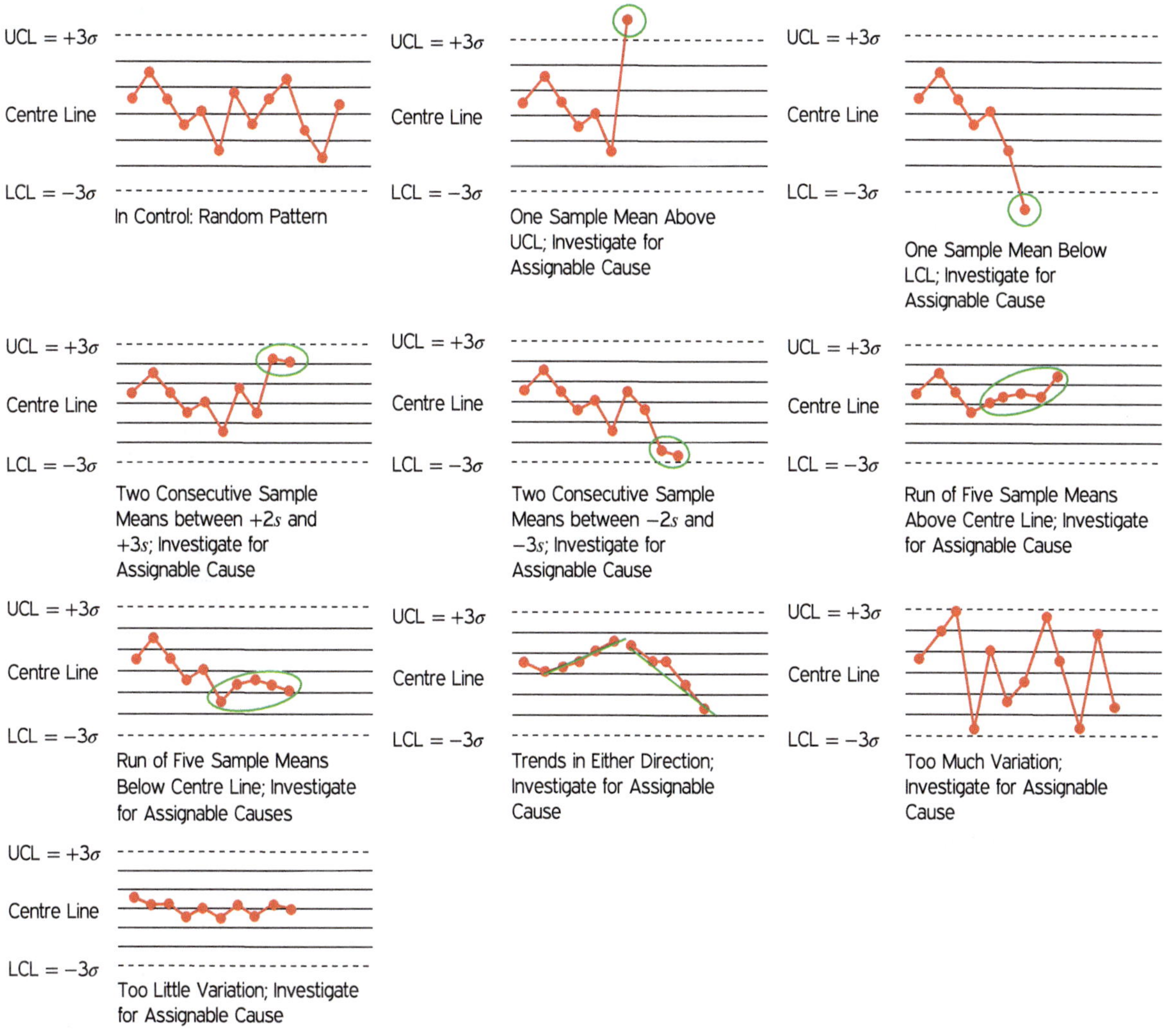

Source: Adapted from Hansen (1963, p. 65).

Contemporary Thinking: Quality Control and Corporate Social Responsibility

Recently, firms have started to consider the quality costs related to environmental factors, and how they impact on sustainable operations management practice. Various organizations are developing standards for corporate social responsibility (CSR). ISO 26000 is an ISO initiative for CSR standardization. It is intended for both the public and private sectors in developed and developing countries. Its purpose is to:

- Develop an international consensus on what social responsibility means, and the CSR issues that organizations need to address
- Provide guidance on translating principles into effective actions
- Refine best practices that have already evolved, and disseminate the information worldwide for the good of the international community.

In addition to ISO 26000, two other prominent standards are AA 1000 and SA 8000. The *AA 1000 standard* has been developed by the Institute of Social and Ethical Accountability, with the purpose of improving the accountability

Table 13.9 Definitions of quality costs

Category	Description	Examples
Internal failure costs	Costs related to deficiencies discovered before delivery that are associated with the failure to meet explicit requirements or implicit needs of customers	Scrap, rework, lost of missing information, failure analysis, 100% sorting inspection, re-inspection, re-testing, redesign of hardware and software, and downgrading
External failure costs	Costs related to deficiencies that are found after the customer receives the product. The costs also include lost opportunities for sales revenue	Warranty charges, complaint adjustments, returned material, allowances, penalties due to poor quality, rework on support operations, revenue losses in support operations, and customer defections
Appraisal costs	Costs incurred to determine the degree of conformance to quality requirements	Incoming inspection and test, in-process inspection and test, document review, examination of accounts, product quality audits, maintaining accuracy of test equipment, inspection and test materials and services, and evaluation of stock
Prevention costs	Costs incurred to keep failure and appraisal costs to a minimum	Quality planning, new products review, process planning, process control, quality audits, supplier quality evaluation, and training

Source: Adapted from Gryna *et al.* (2007).

Figure 13.30 Cost of quality prevention and appraisal

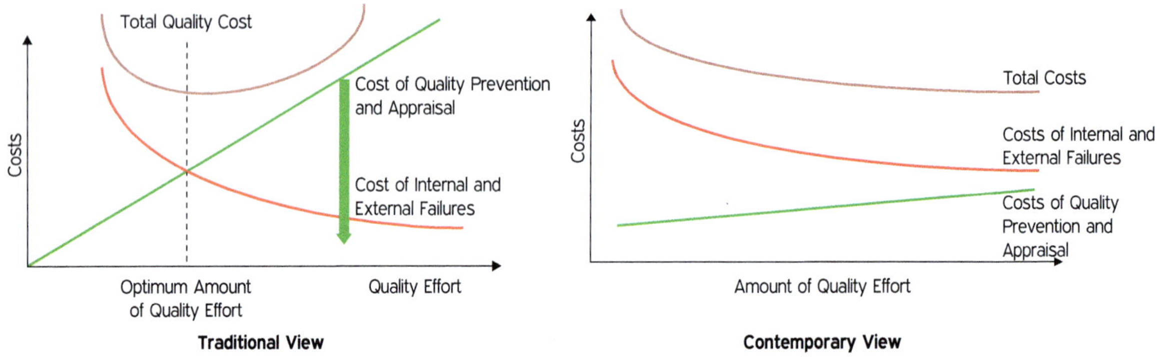

Figure 13.31 The changing profile of quality costs

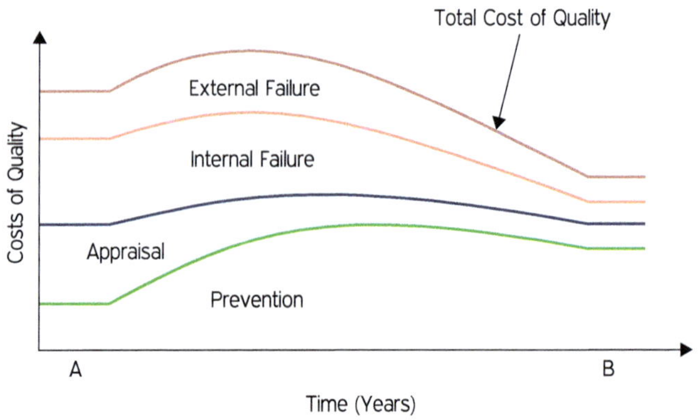

and overall performance of organizations through increased quality in social and ethical accounting, auditing and reporting, through management of the system, individual behaviours and the impact on stakeholders.

SA 8000, developed by Social Accountability International, is a social accountability standard for child labour, forced labour, health and safety, freedom of association and the right to collective bargaining, discrimination, working conditions, and workers' rights. It specifies requirements for social accountability so that a company can develop, maintain and enforce policies and procedures in order to manage those issues that it can control and influence.

Stop and Think

Is compliance with ISO standards a sufficient criterion to guarantee that a company can produce products and services of a desired quality? Does it guarantee that the company is ethical?

Summary

In this chapter we have explained how difficult it is to define quality, and have highlighted the importance of quality performance for organizations. Quality is embedded in all aspects of our lives, ranging from the physical products we use to the services we consume.

The philosophies of quality management have been outlined, and its fundamental principles indicated. The evolution of quality management over recent decades was explained. It is important to understand this, as it mirrors the 'quality journey' that many organizations undertake as they strive to practise better-quality management and raise their standards.

As well as philosophies there are also many operational tools that managers can use to assess and improve quality, such as FMEA, QFD and SPC. The tools are typically structured into a methodological approach such as TQM or Six Sigma.

Views about quality management have changed in recent decades, and this can be demonstrated by the different way in which the costs of quality are assessed. The contemporary view is that it is always good to continuously invest in quality.

An emerging issue is the impacts of digitalization and corporate social responsibility on corporate strategy, which add complexity to quality management.

Key Theories

The key theories discussed in this chapter are:

- **European Foundation of Quality Management (EFQM)** – a framework for quality management based on nine criteria: five are enablers (leadership, people, policy and strategy, partnership and resources, and processes) and four are results (people, customer, society, and key performance).
- **Failure mode and effect analysis (FMEA)** – an advanced method to conduct reliability analysis. It provides detailed insights into the system's interrelationships and potential sources of failures.
- **Lean Six Sigma** – the integrated approach of combining Six Sigma with lean production methodologies to improve process capability and eliminate waste.
- **Quality Function Deployment (QFD)** – sometimes referred to as the House of Quality; a tool to capture customer needs in product designs.
- **Six Sigma** – a method for standardizing the way defects are counted. It applies statistical methods to achieve no more than 3.4 defects per million opportunities in any process, product or service.
- **Total Quality Management (TQM)** – a quality management approach centred on the participation of all its members, aiming at the long-term success of an organization through customer satisfaction.

Key Equations

Measuring process capability:

$$\text{Process capability ratio, } C_p = \frac{\text{Upper specification level (USL)} - \text{Lower specification level (LSL)}}{6\sigma}$$

$$C_{pk} = \min\left[\frac{\overline{X} - \text{LSL}}{3\sigma}, \frac{\text{USL} - \overline{X}}{3\sigma}\right]$$

$\overline{X}$: the average of the process output (its centrality)

LSL: lower specification limit

USL: upper specification limit

σ: standard deviation

$\overline{X}$ and range charts:

$$\text{Mean of the sample, } \overline{X} = \frac{\sum_{i=1}^{n} X_1}{n} = \frac{X_1 + X_2 + \ldots + X_n}{n}$$

i: the item number

n: the total number of items in the sample

$$\text{Average of the means of the samples, } \overline{\overline{X}} = \frac{\sum_{j=1}^{m} \overline{X}_j}{m} = \frac{\overline{X}_1 + \overline{X}_2 + \ldots + \overline{X}_m}{m}$$

j: the sample number

m: the total number of samples.

$$\text{Average range, } \overline{R} = \frac{\sum_{j=1}^{m} R_j}{m} = \frac{R_1 + R_2 + \ldots + R_m}{m}$$

R: the difference between the maximum and minimum values of each sample

Upper control limit for $\overline{X}$, $\text{UCL}_{\overline{X}} = \overline{\overline{X}} + A_2\overline{R}$

Lower control limit for $\overline{X}$, $\text{LCL}_{\overline{X}} = \overline{\overline{X}} - A_2\overline{R}$

Upper control limit for R, $\text{UCL}_R = D_4\overline{R}$

Lower control limit for R, $\text{CLR}_R = D_3\overline{R}$

Standard deviation, $\sigma = \dfrac{R}{d_2}$

A_2, D_3 and D_4 : factors for $\overline{X}$ chart and R chart.

Answers to Stop and Think Questions

1. **TQM:** TQM is a management approach centred on quality that is based on the participation of the organization's people, aiming at long-term success. If an organization seeks to follow the eight quality management principles (customer focus, leadership, involvement of people, process approach, system approach to management, continous improvement, factual approach to decision-making, and mutually beneficial supplier relationships), then it should adopt TQM. In fact, we can say that virtually all organizations (small and large) apply these principles. However, more recent developments in quality management, such as Lean Six Sigma, claim to be more effective.

2. **Lean Six Sigma:** For firms trying to use TQM as an approach to quality, it is often criticized for a lack of structure. As TQM is a collection of the ideas of the quality gurus, it is not owned or defined by any individual or organization, and so there is no blueprint to follow. Along with TQM, Lean Six Sigma shares the benefits of a focus on continuous improvement and the many tools available for zero defects and right first time, but includes a more prescriptive framework from the many consultants offering advice. This means that firms may find it easier to implement Lean Six Sigma.
3. **ISO standards:** ISO certification has become the minimum requirement for many organizations to be accepted in an industry. It provides a certain level of reputation for organizations. However, no quality manuals or procedures are comprehensive enough to guarantee that an organization can provide defect-free products and customer satisfaction 100%, all the time. The organization needs to match its quality objectives with the appropriate quality management tools. Although ISO certification is seen as a minimum standard by many, the downside is that it can also stifle any future changes, because of the extensive documentation and procedural constraints it introduces.

connect

Review Questions

1. Would you consider poor service as a failure? How would you go about getting rid of the failures and improve the service? (a) Discuss poor service as a failure, and (b) identify the gaps in the Service Quality Model.
2. Name five products that, in your opinion, have a high degree of quality. Are these products produced by large corporations? How do the corporations ensure the high degree of quality?
3. Should companies consider ISO 9000 as the first step to approaching quality management? If so, why?
4. You are helping your best friend to plan his/her wedding. How are you going to make sure that nothing goes wrong? Which decision tools can you use to ensure a successful wedding?
5. Describe your decision criteria for buying your most recent mobile phone. Would you replace your phone soon? (a) Discuss how the next generation of phones can be best developed, and (b) identify the elements in the Quality Function Deployment framework.
6. You have recently been hired as the Quality Director for a leading pharmaceutical company to combat a Coronavirus epidemic and have learned that Six Sigma and Lean can be useful tools to do this. Why is this? Can you combine Six Sigma and Lean together?
7. You have been asked by your parents and friends to tell them about Quality Gurus and their philosophies on quality. Describe the quality philosophies the gurus are associated with.

Discussion Questions

1. Discuss Six Sigma and lean production methodologies. Can you apply Lean Six Sigma to services?
2. Describe your holiday experiences from various countries and cities. What kinds of transportation mode did you use (e.g. taxis, buses, rental car)? Did the taxi ride experience, for instance, differ from those in your home country? Discuss the different aspects of an experience such as a taxi ride (e.g. the interior technologies installed, smell, cleanliness, comfort, safety) and compare them with the quality standards you might expect in your country.

Problems

1. Suppose that $\bar{p} = 0.3$ and $n = 200$. Calculate the upper control limit (UCL) and lower control limit (LCL) of the corresponding p-chart.
2. Suppose that $\bar{c} = 26$. Calculate the upper control limit (UCL) and lower control limit (LCL) of the corresponding c-chart.

3. An organization wants to study the fraction of incorrect sales invoices that are sent to its customers. A random sample of 100 sales invoices for 40 weeks is collected. It reveals that the total number of incorrect sales invoices from all samples is 97.
   (a) Calculate the fraction of incorrect sales invoices.
   (b) Calculate the centre line (CL) for the p-chart.
   (c) Calculate the upper control limit (UCL).
   (d) Calculate the lower control limit (LCL).
4. The manager of a printing shop wishes to monitor the number of non-conformities (missing characters, miscolouring, smearing, etc.) produced by a high-speed printing machine. The manager inspects 3 pages of the text output from the printing machine every day for 40 days. The recorded nonconformities are listed in Table 13.10.

Table 13.10

Inspection unit	Number of non-conformities	Inspection unit	Number of non-conformities
1	0	21	3
2	2	22	2
3	2	23	1
4	0	24	0
5	0	25	0
6	3	26	0
7	5	27	2
8	1	28	3
9	1	29	4
10	0	30	3
11	3	31	1
12	0	32	0
13	0	33	0
14	1	34	0
15	1	35	2
16	2	36	0
17	2	37	1
18	2	38	1
19	0	39	3
20	1	40	0

   (a) Construct a c-chart for the printing machine's non-conformities.
   (b) Discuss whether the manager should be concerned about the situation.
5. You have been asked to test whether the manufacturing process of a mass production of chocolate cookies is capable or not. According to the specification, each cookie is to weigh 75 grams with 5% tolerance. After collecting samples of the cookies over a month, you found that the manufacturing process of producing the

cookies has a mean of 74 grams and a standard deviation of 2 grams. Calculate the process capability ratio C_{pk} to find out whether the manufacturing process is capable or not.

6. You noticed that some skiing resorts are offering medical services, particularly tailoring to those with skiing injuries. As the General Manager of a newly built hotel with a medical centre, you want to assess the potential failures that can occur if a medical centre is offered as an additional service. You know that it will be catastrophic to the customers if staff are not available at the medical centre because customers will be not treated on time. Currently, there are no controls in place to prevent the failure. This failure has a documented high failure rate, and it is nearly certain that the failure won't be detected.

   (a) Using the FMEA template shown in Figure 13.15a and the scaling grid in Figure 13.15b, create a FMEA for the ski hotel's service system with a medical centre.

   (b) Explain the result of your assessment and propose action(s) to be taken.

Further Reading

George, M.L., Rowlands, D., Price, M. and Maxey, J. (2005) *Lean Six Sigma Pocket Tool Book,* 1st edn, McGraw-Hill, New York.

Hayler, R. and Nichols, M.D. (2007) *Six Sigma for Financial Services: How Leading Companies Are Driving Results Using Lean, Six Sigma and Process Management,* McGraw-Hill, New York.

Juran, J.M. and Godfrey, A.B. (1999) *Juran's Quality Handbook,* 5th edn, McGraw-Hill, New York.

Martin, J.W. (2007) *Lean Six Sigma for Supply Chain Management: The 10-Step Solution Process,* McGraw-Hill, New York.

Ohno, T. (2013) *Taiichi Ohnos Workplace Management,* 1st edn, McGraw-Hill.

Rampersad, H.K. and El-Homsi, A (2007) *TPS-Lean Six Sigma: Linking Human Capital to Lean Six Sigma,* IAP, Charlotte, NC.

References

Antony, J., Escamilla, J.L. and Caine, P. (2003) 'Lean Sigma', *Manufacturing Engineer,* April, 40–42.

Basu, R. (2004) *Implementing Quality: A Practical Guide to Tools and Techniques,* Thomson, London.

Beer, M. (2003) 'Why total quality management programs do not persist: The role of top management quality and implications for leading a TQM transformation', *Decision Sciences,* **34**(4), 623–642.

Bicheno, J. (2002) *The Quality 75; Towards Six Sigma Performance in Service and Manufacturing,* PICSIE Books.

Chen, I.J. and Paetsch, K. (1998) 'Benchmarking: A quest for continuous improvement', in *Handbook of Total Quality Management,* C.N. Madu (ed.), Kluwer Academic, London, pp. 409–424.

Crosby, P.B. (1979) *Quality Is Free,* McGraw-Hill, New York.

Crosby. L.B., DeVito, R. and Pearson, J.M. (2003) 'Manage your customers' perception of quality', *Review of Business,* Winter, 18–24.

Dale, B.G. (1999) *Managing Quality,* Blackwell, Oxford.

Dale, B.G. and Plunkett, J.J. (1990) *The Case for Costing Quality,* Department of Trade and Industry, London.

Dale, B.G., van der Wiele, T. and van Iwaarden, J. (2007) *Managing Quality.* 5th edn, Blackwell Publishing, Oxford.

Deming, W.E. (1986) *Out of Crisis,* MIT Press, Cambridge, MA.

Feigenbaum, A.V. (1986) *Total Quality Control,* 3rd edn, McGraw-Hill, New York.

Foster, S.T. (2010) *Managing Quality: Integrating the Supply Chain,* 4th edn, Prentice Hall, Boston, MA.

Garvin, D.A. (1987) 'Competing on the eight dimensions of quality', *Harvard Business Review,* November–December, 101–109.

George, S. and Weimerskirch, A. (1998) *Total Quality Management,* John Wiley & Sons, New York.

Ghobadian, A. and Speller, S. (1994) 'Gurus of quality: A framework for comparison', *Total Quality Management,* **5**(3), 53–69.

Gryna, F.M., Chua, R.C.H. and DeFeo, J.A. (2007) *Juran's Quality Planning and Analysis,* 5th edn, McGraw-Hill, New York.

Hansen, B.L. (1963) *Quality Control: Theory and Application,* Pearson Education, Upper Saddle River, NJ.

Hauser, J.R. and Clausing, D. (1988) 'The House of Quality', *Harvard Business Review,* May–June, 63–73.

Hellsten, U. and Klefsjö, B. (2000) 'TQM as a management system consisting of values, techniques and tools', *TQM Magazine,* **12**(4), 238–244.

Juran, J.M. (1988) *Quality Control Handbook,* 4th edn, McGraw-Hill, New York.

Parasuraman, A., Zeithaml, V.A. and Berry, L.L. (1985) 'A conceptual model of service quality and its implications for future research', *Journal of Marketing,* **49**(Fall), 41–50.

Salegna, G. and Fazel, F. (2000) 'Obstacles to implementing TQM', *Quality Progress,* **33**(7), 53–57.

www.efqm.org

www.isixsigma.com

14 Future Directions in Operations Management

Learning Outcomes

After reading this chapter, you should be able to:

- Summarize current themes and topics in operations management
- Discuss emerging challenges faced by operations managers
- Discuss future directions for operations management
- Evaluate the future personal characteristics required by operations managers.

Beth's Chocolate Ambitions

BUSINESS INTEGRATION

Source: ©ju_see/Shutterstock

Beth is a recent university graduate with a degree in business and technology management, which included a placement year with a large international company producing a variety of confectionery products. She took the operations management themed electives in her degree, including operations management, supply chain management, operations research, data analytics, and IT for businesses, and passed with distinction. She is now working as an assistant operations manager with a small but ambitious company that makes boutique-style chocolate products, which it sells online and through magazines to customers all around the world. As the food and drink industry is the largest part of the UK manufacturing sector (14.6% when Beth graduated), she saw a 'tasty' future ahead of her.

During her placement year in the confectionery company she spent short periods in the strategic planning, purchasing, sales and marketing, and production departments, which gave her a great overview of how important operations management is to everything that a company does. For instance, on one occasion while she was working in sales, an unexpectedly large order for Sticky Lollies was received from a large and important chain of high street stores, and she was tasked with making sure that the order was fulfilled correctly to the customer's wishes. However, because the order had not been anticipated by strategic planning, there was a shortage of ingredients. This meant she had to talk to the purchasing department to get suppliers to amend their delivery volumes at short notice. It also meant that she had to talk to the production manager and warn him that he should take on some more short-term staff from a temping agency. After resolving these urgent issues, she also let strategic planning know that the situation could happen again the following year, as the order had seemed to coincide with the store's new Back to School promotions.

She had initially found it ironic that even though she was in the Sales Department at the time, she had been very involved in many production and operations management decisions. Her experience stood her in good stead for her job interview after graduation, where she described how she had been so crucial in bringing in and delivering such a big order.

Now working as assistant operations manager for the small chocolate company, she had a strong grasp of the similarly complex and challenging issues that they faced. She knew that she was in a key role, and that she had to be a quick thinker, a good communicator, a good planner, a team player and a leader. She found opportunities to demonstrate these skills soon after starting, which got her noticed by the operations director, who had given her a new project to set up the production line for a new chocolate cake product.

She was very excited about this, because it would be an interesting challenge – and would obviously mean testing and eating a lot of chocolate cake to ensure that quality levels were just right! Also, she knew that the current chief executive officer had started out in just the same way, and had been promoted after making several new product launches operational successes. After many other successes, such as his adoption of online technologies, his development of new overseas markets, becoming a chartered manager and completing a part-time MBA, he had eventually got the top job. Over coffee one day Beth found out that he put most of his success down to understanding the operations of the company, its capabilities, and how to deliver what the customer had asked for. Beth could see that, in addition to these factors, further advances in Internet-based technologies and data analytics were needed by the company's operations. If Beth took all this on board, and could implement these future changes, then perhaps one day she too might get the top job!

Introduction

The opening case demonstrates how demanding the role of an operations manager is, the wide variety of skills needed, and how rewarding it can be when good products and services get delivered to happy customers. The role of operations managers is rapidly changing as more demands are placed on them by macro trends in the social, environmental, political, economic, legal and technological areas. As a result, we believe that the role of the operations manager will become increasingly strategic over the forthcoming decades. In addition to being aware of external macro trends, operations managers also require an appreciation of all the other organizational functions if they are going to be able to make effective operations decisions.

In the past, the operations manager's job was perhaps seen as the least glamorous of the managerial functions in industry, with poor working conditions, limited career prospects, and low pay. Operations managers were not well qualified, and the operations role failed to attract ambitious people. The current position is changing as operations managers are now becoming more highly qualified and highly paid, and find their jobs challenging and interesting.

This chapter looks ahead to the future of operations management and outlines the likely changes to this role and the new skills it will require. Operations management jobs will require higher levels of conceptual, interpersonal and analytical skills (Gunasekaran and Ngai, 2012). These requirements have significant implications for management education. Graduating students from schools of business management or engineering disciplines will need knowledge in core areas of business, along with mathematics, computer and communication skills. Business schools are likely to respond by increasing the number of field trips, internships and industry-based projects to form part of their business programmes. Students will need to develop a greater understanding of strategy and technology. Along with subjects in the core operations management area, newer subjects such as business analytics, innovation, humanitarian and crisis management, CSR, and the management of workforce (e.g. ethics, law, diversity, etc.) may become important parts of the core curriculum. In tandem, companies may also encourage apprenticeship schemes for school leavers and graduates (CABS, 2019).

In this chapter we pick up on the three themes threaded throughout the book, and explore them in more detail. These themes are important; they touch upon many different topics and, therefore, cannot be limited to single chapters. They epitomize what is currently happening in operations management, and point towards what might happen in the future. These themes will make operations more demanding, and require more educated and skilful operations managers.

- *Globalization* – which addresses the fact that companies increasingly have to adopt common standards and practices throughout the world, but take cultural differences, commercial and technical histories into account.

- *Business integration* – which includes the use of information technology, data-sharing, structure, strategy issues, function-to-function process integration within an organization, and supply/demand/partner integration between different organizations.
- *Corporate social responsibility (CSR)* – which considers environmental, ethical and social issues.

This chapter will briefly explore each of these themes, point to how they are relevant to previous chapters, discuss their current impact on operations management and, where possible, discuss the implications for the future. In doing so we shall show how important it is for operations managers to continually learn and develop themselves, and to contribute towards developing the practice and the theories of operations management.

This chapter also contains a short section specifically on operations managers and their careers. This is because many new graduates start off in an operations management role, even though they may not actually be called 'operations managers'. The intention of this section is to help you become more successful in your career more quickly. It will help you realize what personal skills are valued by potential employers, and to become more aware of wider trends in operations management, so that you can prepare for the future directions operations management may take.

Globalization

Globalization is increasing global connectivity, integration and interdependence in the economic, social, technological, cultural, political and ecological spheres. The globalization of industry should allow for better worldwide production networks to provide broad access to goods and services for consumers, and the globalization of financial institutions should allow for better access to funds and credit for consumers, companies and government agencies. Similarly, the globalization of transportation and communication systems should allow for a better flow of goods, people and information among nations.

GLOBALIZATION

Throughout this book the theme of **globalization** and global issues has been prominent. Part One discussed how strategy and innovation is becoming increasingly global. Part Two discussed how operations design should achieve an appropriate portfolio of competencies in suitable geographic locations; how operations are influenced by supply and demand forces; and how operations managers are becoming accountable for more than just delivering products and services. Part Three highlighted why capacity and work are assigned to particular locations, the risks of distributing suppliers across the globe, efficiency and effectiveness, and the issues associated with globally sized projects. Part Four looked at how performance measurement systems, people performance, and quality improvement, can affect business units, regions and nations.

Globalization: increasing global connectivity, integration and interdependence in the economic, social, technological, cultural, political and ecological spheres.

The negative side of globalization and interconnected operations systems is that any disruption propagates through nations at a very rapid rate. For instance, any unscheduled blockage of ships at one of the world's major ports, such as Hong Kong, Amsterdam, Singapore or Dubai, can affect the availability and prices of many essential goods around the world. Similarly, any changes in currency exchange rates (e.g. the euro against the dollar) can affect both the demand for and the supply of goods and services across the world. The credit crunch in 2008 was probably the most high-profile example of globalization gone wrong, where poor-quality, 'toxic' financial products were circulating in the global financial supply chain, damaging all economies that they touched, regardless of location. More recently the effects of changing political borders (e.g. the United Kingdom leaving the European Union – 'Brexit') and global pandemics (e.g. Ebola and Covid-19) have had dramatic effects on nations and global operations.

The positive effects of globalization mean that we can benefit from efficient production and distribution systems; we get the benefits of using goods manufactured at locations around the world that have been delivered to us in a cost-effective manner. Also, advances in information and communications technology and data analytics are now allowing companies to deliver a wide range of services, from financial transactions to customer service to medical diagnostics, to customers all around the world. While there are costs and risks associated with managing and operating a globalized organization, globalization is also attractive to organizations for a variety of other reasons:

- *Access to cheaper labour and operating costs:* US and European companies are now setting up in China, Malaysia, India and South Africa
- *Access to knowledge and skills:* some firms locate in Germany, the UK and Japan to gain access to knowledge in these countries despite higher labour costs
- *Access to natural resources:* certain companies locate facilities in African nations to draw upon their natural resources

- *Access to new markets:* by locating facilities in new countries, firms can market their products and services to a new set of customers. For example, Dyson, Jaguar Land Rover and Black & Decker moved their production to China, partly to access the Chinese market
- *To establish facilities at strategically international locations* so that logistic and distribution costs can be reduced. Intel has a distribution centre in Amsterdam that serves the whole of Europe
- *To take advantage of tax and financial incentives* provided by local governments. For example, Honda and Aston Martin moved into South Wales and Nissan to the north-east of England.

In addition, globalization is sometimes driven by other political and industry-specific reasons (Stiglitz, 2017). For example, by locating a production facility in a country, providing employment and participating in community activities, a firm can be perceived as local rather than foreign – as in the move by US companies Ford or Amazon to the UK, for example.

Approaches and Stages of Globalization

According to Ghemawat (2007), when firms globalize, they can consider three different approaches: adaptation, aggregation or arbitrage. Each of these approaches has a slightly different purpose, and is suitable for different strategic and operational scenarios. A firm uses:

Adaptation (in a globalization context): boosting revenue and market share by maximizing local presence in a country.

- **Adaptation** to boost revenue and market share by maximizing its local presence in the country. In doing this, the firm will try to adapt its products and services to be more in tune with the new host nation. It will, however, retain its overall, global strategy, corporate identity, core competencies and values. For example, Tesco adapted the look and feel of its stores as it sought to globalize its operations: in Thailand they were called 'Tesco Lotus', and in the USA they were called 'Fresh and Easy'. In the USA, Fresh and Easy was subsequently sold at a loss to a US company due to poor performance in the global recession around 2008. In Thailand, a successful sale to a Thai grocery chain is likely due to a revised Tesco strategy focusing more on home markets as cheap value-based supermarkets (e.g. Lidl and Aldi) have eroded Tesco's strong UK market position.

Aggregation (in a globalization context): achieving economies of scale by creating regional or global operations.

- **Aggregation** to achieve economies of scale by creating regional or global operations. In doing this, the firm tries to boost the size of its output. There is little attempt to adapt to local cultures and values, and companies can sometimes be criticized for being too powerful and too insensitive to local needs, or have been accused of exploiting natural resources and local workforces. For example, McDonald's has in the past been accused of destroying Brazilian rainforests to raise beef cattle for its burgers sold elsewhere in the world.
- **Arbitrage** to exploit the differences among national or regional markets. This is achieved by locating separate parts of supply chains in different places. For instance, two different sources of coal (Australian and South American) may be used to ensure that prices remain competitive. Labour arbitrage is used by companies such as Jaguar Land Rover to make sure labour cost can be controlled (e.g. labour costs in Slovakia and China are far cheaper than in the United Kingdom).

Arbitrage (in a globalization context): the exploitation of differences among national or regional markets, often by locating separate parts of supply chains in different places.

Further differences between the features of these approaches are shown in Table 14.1.

In reality, firms tend to use a mixture of these three approaches. However, the aggregation approach has to be used sensitively, as nations are becoming increasingly aware of the negative effects that large globalizing organizations can have. In contrast, the adaptation approach is currently seen as more politically correct.

Another view of globalization is provided by Farrell's (2004) five-stage model. Farrell takes a different view, based upon the *level* of globalization that a company wants to achieve, as it must be remembered that not all companies will want to 'conquer the world', and will settle for a less global presence. Farrell's model suggests five stages, which are not necessarily sequential, but achieve various levels of globalization: these are shown in Figure 14.1. Stage 1, the lowest level of globalization, achieves entry into a new market. Stage 2 involves relocating part of a company's operations to a new country. Stage 3 involves the development of an extended supply network spanning several countries. Stage 4 is reached when companies become reliant on their core processes operating across the globe. Stage 5, the most advanced level of globalization, allows new products and services to be designed by drawing on

Table 14.1 Features of different approaches to globalization

	Adaptation	Aggregation	Arbitrage
Competitive advantage Why should we globalize at all?	To achieve local relevance through national focus while exploiting some economies of scale	To achieve economies of scale and scope through international standardization	To achieve economies through international specialization
Configuration Where should we locate operations overseas?	Mainly in countries that are similar to the home base, to limit the effects of culture, administrative, geographic and economic distance		In a more diverse set of countries, to exploit some elements of distance
Coordination How should we connect international operations?	By country, with emphasis on achieving local presence within borders	By business, region, or customer, with emphasis on horizontal relationships for cross-border economies of scale	By function, with emphasis on vertical relationships, even across organizational boundaries
Controls What types of extreme should we watch for?	Excessive variety or complexity	Excessive standardization, with emphasis on scale	Narrowing or fragmentation of activities spreads
Change blockers Whom should we watch out for internally?	Entrenched countries	All-powerful unit, regional, or account heads	Heads of key functions
Corporate diplomacy How should we approach corporate diplomacy?	Address issues of concern, but proceed with discretion, given the emphasis on cultivating local presence	Avoid appearance of homogenization or hegemonism (particularly Americanization by the USA)	Address the exploitation or displacement of suppliers, channels or intermediaries that are potentially most prone to political disruption
Corporate strategy What strategic levers do we have?	Scope selection Variation Decentralization Partitioning Modularization Flexibility Partnership Recombination Innovation	Regions and other country groupings Product or business Function Platform Competence Client industry	Cultural (country-of-origin effects) Administrative (taxes, regulations, security) Geographic (distance, climate differences) Economic (differences in prices, resources, knowledge)

Source: Adapted from Ghemawat (2007).

the whole global network of resources and skills, and which can be delivered to new markets in a timely and efficient manner.

As with Ghemawat's model, Farrell's model is only indicative of what organizations may do. The stages can occur in different sequences, and the model could be deployed differently for any nation that an organization chooses to include in its globalization strategy.

Functions Commonly Globalized

As a result of globalization, many activities can now be performed at locations far from an organization's home country.

Manufacturing

Manufacturing products and their components at locations far from the home country is perhaps the most common function of a global firm. This can be done to remain competitive: for instance, firms often locate their factories close to a source of cheap labour, such as Taiwan or Poland, or a source of inexpensive raw material. Large-scale contract manufacturers such as Foxconn provide high technology, high volume outputs at low unit prices for innovative design companies such as Apple and Sony.

Figure 14.1 Farrell's globalization stages

The five stages of global restructuring				
Industries and companies tend to globalize in phases; at each stage, there are different opportunities for creating value. In the first three stages, value comes from the basic improvements to typical business practices. In the last two stages, it comes from true process innovations and market expansion. The stages are not necessarily sequential.				
1. Enter new markets	2. Move production abroad	3. Disaggregate the value chain	4. Re-engineer the value chain	5. Create new markets
Companies use production models similar to the ones they deploy at home to enter new countries and expand their customer bases	Companies relocate their production processes to take advantage of cost differentials; they export finished goods globally	Companies' individual product components are manufactured in different locations or regions; countries may specialize in component manufacturing, assembly, or both	Companies redesign their production processes, taking into account, to maximize efficiencies and cost savings	Given lower costs due to globalization, companies can offer new products at lower prices, and can penetrate new market segments or geographies, or both
Less global ⟷ Highly global				

Source: Farrell (2004).

SHORT CASE 14.1

Intelligent Manufacturing at Foxconn

BUSINESS INTEGRATION

GLOBALIZATION

As the rise of new technologies such as AI, Big Data, IoT and Cloud Computing disrupt traditional manufacturing models, the term 'intelligent manufacturing' has gained prominence in recent years. Intelligent manufacturing refers to the process, system and models of advanced manufacturing that possess intelligent characteristics such as self-sensing, self-adaptive and self-decision-making features. Intelligent manufacturing consists of: an intelligent factory platform that directs the scale and scope of manufacturing with intelligent production lines at its core, and an end-to-end data flow, which is supported by interconnected networks.

Source: © rafapress/Shutterstock

Enterprises can fully leverage these cutting-edge technologies to maximize reliable, predictive and intelligent competencies that bring real value to the business and ensure resilience to potential risks. Building upon the concept of the industrial Internet centred on 'cloud computing, mobile terminal, Internet of things (IoT), big data, artificial intelligence (AI), network, and robots', Foxconn harnesses the benefits of AI to extract meaningful analytical insights from production lines and merge them with various flows, including human flow, process flow, information flow, technical flow and money flow, optimizing efficiency for our clients across the globe, improving quality and reducing cost of manufacturing.

Among all advanced technologies deployed across operations, the five 'lights-out' factories at Foxconn exemplify the potential of an emerging manufacturing model which is fully integrated with intelligent capabilities. With a fully automated manufacturing process that engages over 60,000 robots and 5,000 types of testing equipment, Foxconn operate in a centralized big data repository that stores all kinds of data extracted from manufacturing processes, leveraging an industrial AI system that maximizes the benefits of industrial Internet applications such as HRM (PMSs), flexible factory set-ups and reliable logistics systems. The model has effectively reduced the cost of labour, enabled smooth and barrier-free communication between staff, end-to-end equipment and the AI centres, and optimized sensor-equipped robotic operations in factories. Such a model has been named by the World Economic Forum as the 'factory of the future'.

Questions

1. How has globalization been facilitated at Foxconn?
2. What is meant by the term 'lights out' and what are the implications for global operations?

Source: https://www.foxconn.com/

Procurement

In a non-globalized environment, a firm buys materials and components from suppliers located close to production facilities. However, the ease of transportation and the reduction in other associated purchasing costs in a global economy make it possible for companies to purchase their supplies from vendors located far from their home countries.

Maintenance and Monitoring

Advances in information technology mean that it is becoming possible to monitor and maintain manufacturing and products remotely. For instance, the Rolls-Royce engines of an aircraft can be monitored while in-flight from service centres (e.g. Singapore), which liaise with destination airports anywhere in the world to ensure, if necessary, that spare parts are readily available when the aircraft lands.

Logistics and Distribution Services

As companies, products and services are becoming spread around the world, logistics and distribution services have become more important. For instance, TNT, the Dutch logistics company, was once a part of the Dutch national postal services, but now is a global business in its own right, moving and managing other organizations' products around the world.

Customer Service

Customer service and support provided by telephones or via the Internet (e.g. chatbots, talk apps, instant messaging, track and trace apps, and emails) has seen an explosion in globalization during the last decade; it is now common to talk to someone in India or South Africa if you ring a help desk in Europe.

Technical Expertise

With the advance in information technology and the spread of education worldwide, it is now possible to locate facilities for complex and knowledge-based business processes internationally. For example, using the Internet, health-care facilities can make patients' records available to medical experts who might be located far from the home country. Similarly, many complex financial and legal functions can also be performed remotely.

Research and Development

Many companies are increasingly locating their own facilities, or outsourcing production activities, in foreign countries to facilitate product development and innovation. As mentioned in Chapter 4, product development in goods and service industries is a long-term and complex process. However, effective product development is essential for a firm's long-term success. Globalization has allowed many firms to locate product development activities abroad. For example, Microsoft, IBM, Oracle and many other Western companies have located their facilities in several different countries to take advantage of the local talent pools for their product development efforts.

Chapter 4, p105

Globalization is a strong theme in operations management, and this is likely to continue for the foreseeable future. Smart operations managers will ensure global forces are used to their advantage.

CRITICAL PERSPECTIVE

Is Globalization a Good Thing?

Globalization poses a dilemma for most organizations. On the positive side, they must globalize to be able to gain benefits from standardization (lower costs, speedier delivery, and enhanced reliability), foster and integrate new knowledge to raise industry standards (without eroding competitive advantage), reach new markets, and achieve strategic change (by adopting new practices and discontinuing old ones). However, on the negative side, those who seek to globalize must:

- Strike the right balance between local specialization achieved by integrating knowledge into local activities and maintaining a global product or service (e.g. McDonald's now tries to adapt its products, depending on the country or region it is in, while maintaining standardized processes).
- Maintain ethical issues about work allocated to lower-wage economies. Typically dirty, dangerous or highly repetitive work is given to developing nations (e.g. recycling hazardous materials); is this right? People with a social conscience want to make sure that people in developing nations are not exploited. (e.g. in 2006, the clothing giant GAP was found to be using child labour in one of its 'unapproved' subcontractors).
- Work with local trade unions, who often oppose the 'exportation of jobs' from their countries.
- Minimize the negative social impact of products (e.g. Nestlé caused problems when it introduced powdered baby milk into African nations), and assess whether the trade is 'fair'.
- Fit products and services correctly to different cultures and religions (e.g. financial products in Islamic cultures must be Shariah compliant, and beef products cannot be made or consumed in Hindu nations).
- Ensure the safety of workers and nearby residents in developing nations, which is not always done (e.g. the Union-Carbide chemical disaster at the Bhopal plant in India, which killed and seriously injured thousands).
- Minimize language and interpretation misunderstanding (e.g. the move of UK call centres to India has not been totally successful because accents cannot be understood by international customers).
- Familiarize themselves with cyber security and data protection laws. For instance, new General Data Protection Regulation (GDPR) laws in the European Union prevent sharing of a person's personal data with another party, or for using it for a purpose for which it was not given.
- Steer clear of bribery and corruption (e.g. payments to local officials in host nations who claim to 'ease' deals).

The key point is ...

that many of these global issues are complex, as they have problematic ethical and social dimensions.

Stop and Think

Why do some organizations choose to globalize and others choose not to? In the opening case, how do you think globalization will affect Beth's company and her career?

Business Integration

BUSINESS INTEGRATION

Business integration is an operations management theme that covers systems (including IT systems), staff, style (cultural, personal), skills, strategy and higher level super-ordinate goals such as philanthropic aspirations, or wider industrial or national contributions. This is applicable to all levels of operations, from an individual's fit within a department, to departments fitting together in an organization, to organizations fitting together in wider supplier relationships. Put simply, it is about getting the various parts, people, processes and systems to work together better.

The theme of business integration is prominent throughout this book, and is important at all levels in and beyond single organizations. It must be practised in temporary teams, functional departments, entire companies and company-to-company relationships if systems and processes are going to work effectively and efficiently.

For instance, in Part One of this book we highlighted how customer requirements should drive the strategy and systems of the organization, and that a holistic view needs to be taken that neither sub-optimizes an organization nor neglects to incorporate the right competencies within its extended suppliers and partners. In Part Two of the book we discussed how information systems (e.g. enterprise resource planning – ERP) must join together seamlessly; and how products and processes need to be designed with ease of delivery in mind. In Part Three of the book we demonstrated why business integration is essential to plan capacity, integrate suppliers, practise lean thinking and just-in-time operations, and deliver projects successfully. Part Four of the book shows why and how performance, people quality and improvement initiates are affected by the degree of business integration.

McKinsey's 7S Framework Applied to Business Integration

Many different facets of business integration can be put forward; we are going to use an adapted version of the McKinsey 7S framework (Waterman *et al.*, 1980) to show why business integration is so important at all levels. Figure 14.2 shows the 7S framework, which considers strategy, structure, systems (including IT systems)/processes, staff, style, skills, and superordinate goals as important strategic factors. All these factors affect individuals, departments, companies and inter-company structures to some extent.

Table 14.2 shows how each of the 7S factors relates to operations management and success factors for maximizing business integration. If an organization fails to apply the correct level of business integration, at best it can result in organizational inefficiency and ineffectiveness. At worst an organization can make dangerous and fatal mistakes. For instance, train operating companies could cause trains to crash. Lack of business integration in hospitals has seen patients mistreated, viruses spreading out of control and patients even accidentally killed as incorrect treatments are applied. Lack of integration in government has seen illegal activities such as immigration go undetected. Similarly, lack of systemic business integration in chemical and scientific organizations has resulted in large-scale explosions such as the Chernobyl nuclear power plant disaster in Russia, or oil spillages such as BP's Deepwater Horizon oil rig in the Gulf of Mexico.

The Role of Information Technology in Business Integration

Over recent years developments in information technology (IT) have dominated discussion about business integration, and are likely to continue to do so in the foreseeable future, so it is worth looking at IT and its role in business

Figure 14.2 The 7S model applied to business integration

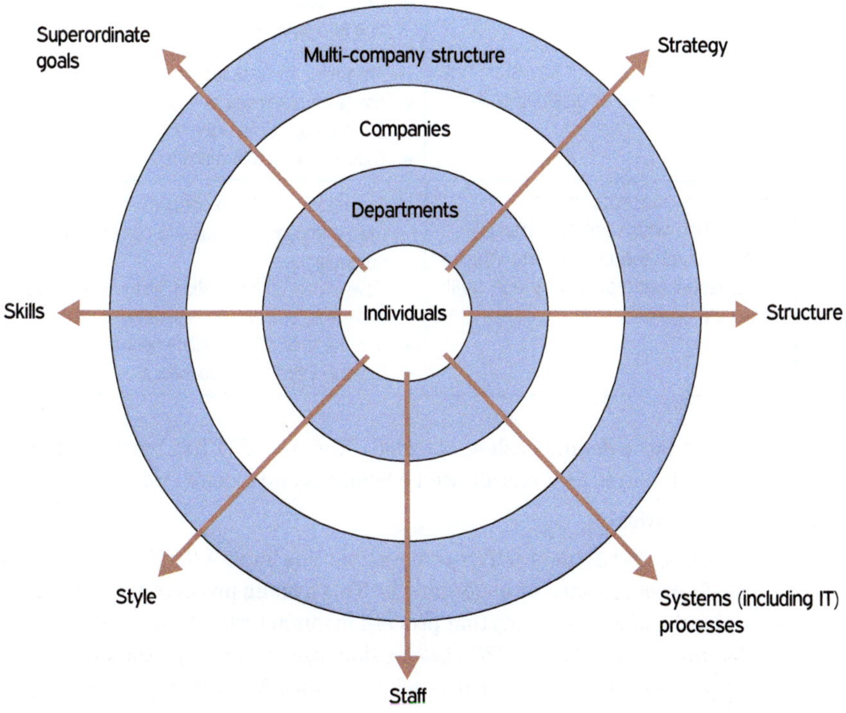

Source: Adapted from Waterman *et al.* (1980).

Table 14.2 Application of the 7S framework in an operations management context, with key success factors for business integration

Element of 7S model	Relevance in an operations management context	Key success factors for business integration
Strategy	The contribution of operations management in influencing and supporting organizations' strategy	• Make all departments' roles clear in delivering or supporting customer-facing process • Define what the company is going to do, and what it is going to outsource • Budget provided for integrative activities with other functions (e.g. marketing and purchasing)
Structure	The modification of organizational structure to support operations	• Be predominantly process dominated, not functionally dominated • Be as flat as possible • Multi-site companies are clear on their individual roles and interdependencies
Systems (including IT systems)/ process	The development of specific processes and information systems to support operations management	• Lean and agile processes • Driven by customer-pull signals using the value stream concept • Information systems (e.g. ERP – Chapter 9) use single-point real-time data, which is available to all those that need it, including those outside the organization when necessary • Well-designed supply and demand chains Chapter 9, p289 • Just-in-time thinking is used • Performance measurement systems encourage integrative behaviour • Unifying reporting
Staff	The characteristic of staff in terms of their background, age and sex and characteristics such as engineering background or service background, use of contractors/consultants	• Well informed through good communication channels up and down between all levels of management • Willingness to work with suppliers, customers and partners to make whole supply chain better • Recruit good staff; train and retain them • Role of operations manager becomes enlarged
Style	Includes how key managers behave in achieving the organization's goals and the cultural style of the organization as a whole	• Culture should include teamworking • Need joint reward systems for productivity • High levels of trust and professionalism • Clear leadership • Shared values and beliefs
Skills	Distinctive capabilities of key staff, but can be interpreted as specific skill-sets of teams	• Are teams multi-skilled and cross-functional? • Are team players at all levels? • Strong project management practices • Endorse the quality management ethos
Superordinate goal	The guiding concepts of the organization which are also part of shared values and culture. The internal and external perception of these goals may vary	• Organization looks to partner with external organizations to form multi-company structures to complement its own core competencies • Have joined-up information systems (e.g. inventory management, and sales, ordering processes) • Use the enterprise management concept • Develop integrative capabilities

integration in more detail (Cash *et al.*, 2008). The use of IT has particularly increased since the advent of the Internet, as it has allowed e-business and e-commerce to develop.

> **E-business:** electronically mediated information exchanges, both within an organization and with external stakeholders, supporting the entire range of business processes.

E-business allows:

- *Business-to-business (B2B) integration:* this implies that both sides are businesses, non-profit organizations or governments. This usually involves the linking up of core operational ERP systems that process manufacturing or service delivery transactions
- *Business-to-employee (B2E) integration:* used by an organization to communicate with its employees for activities such as scheduling work, communication, and provide shared workspace for common work files. Such systems are sometimes known as a *staff intranet.*

E-commerce allows:

- *Business-to-consumer (B2C) integration:* facilitating transactions in which buyers are individual consumers
- *Consumer-to-consumer (C2C) integration:* a scenario in which consumers sell directly to other consumers (e.g. eBay) via a neutral third-party organization
- *Consumer-to-business (C2B) integration:* where individuals make business propositions to businesses (e.g. Priceline's 'name your own price' facility).

E-commerce: electronically mediated information exchanges between an organization and its external stakeholders, concerned predominantly with buying and selling.

E-business and e-commerce helps achieve higher levels of integration by developing:

- *Channels to sell a product or service through:* such as Amazon.com, which sells exclusively through the Internet
- *Supplementary channels:* where 'click and mortar' retailers have extended their catchment areas through the Internet (e.g. Amazon in other domains other than a buyer's country of residence)
- *Technical support:* customers can solve problems regarding the products or services they have purchased (e.g. MS Windows help and automatic system updates)
- *Advanced manufacturing services:* for instance, manufacturers such as MAN Trucks can provide advanced services for fleet operators to monitor factors such as fuel, tyre and brake usage to reduce operating costs
- *Enhancements to existing services:* customizing product or services, or tracking orders (e.g. automatic 'Internet-of-Things' print cartridge renewal service for HP home printers)
- *A means to convey further information:* such as product/service details, customer accounts or supplier ratings (e.g. online newspaper subscriptions).

Higher levels of integration are achievable by using employees' and consumers' mobile electronic devices (e.g. tablets and smart phones) through what is known as **mobile commerce** (or M-commerce) through 'apps' so that people can be reached when they are away from their desktop or laptop computer. Further to this, location-based services such as Google Maps are a particular growth area as high-speed 5G network coverage improves.

Mobile/M-commerce: electronically mediated information exchanges using mobile electronic devices.

The capabilities of the Internet have transformed many traditional operations into online or virtual operations where it has been feasible and desirable to do so. For instance, an organization that has a dynamic and interactive website is able to market, integrate, operate, trade, engineer and exchange data more effectively with its suppliers, customers and partners. A successful example is the Driver and Vehicle Licensing Agency (DVLA) in the UK. It has a system that allows you to buy car tax online, and the system is clever enough to check whether you have a valid road-worthiness certificate and motor insurance policy by automatically linking up with other organizations' systems before issuing the tax. This saves the government lots of time and money, and reduces fraud.

To decide which aspects of an operation are best suited to become an online e-operation, the **information intensity** of the operation needs to be considered in respect to the agents or people operating it, the way the process is delivered, and the type of product or service being delivered.

Information intensity: the degree to which an organization's products/services, processes, people/agents and transactions in general are reliant on digital assets – the more reliant an organization is on digital assets the higher their information intensity.

Figure 14.3, the information intensity cube, shows three main types of business integration in respect to their information technology.

- *Traditional commerce,* with low information intensity, which involves a real person dealing with a physical product using a physical process that involves machines, cash payments and interfaces face-to-face with a customer. This is what we might see in a fast-food, street vendor (e.g. hamburgers). In a situation like this the use of customer-facing IT is limited, although we now see some street vendors taking contactless payment from smart phones, as these are easier to deal with than cash. The back-end supply systems are likely to use electronic ordering systems, and for larger fast food outlets these are likely to be highly automated. The customer delivery process is now, even for small food vendors, able to be partially digitalized through companies such as Deliveroo and Just Eat.
- *Total e-business* with a high information intensity, such as a digitized product like a music MP3 or MP4 video file, delivered automatically through an online subscription service provider using a standard high-speed streaming process (e.g. Netflix, BBC iPlayer, Amazon Prime). This is a perfect solution for online revenue generation (e.g. e-business), because it has taken what once was a physical product (a CD or record) and made it into a digital computer file, which can then be sold online without any physical transaction. Taking

Figure 14.3 Information intensity cube

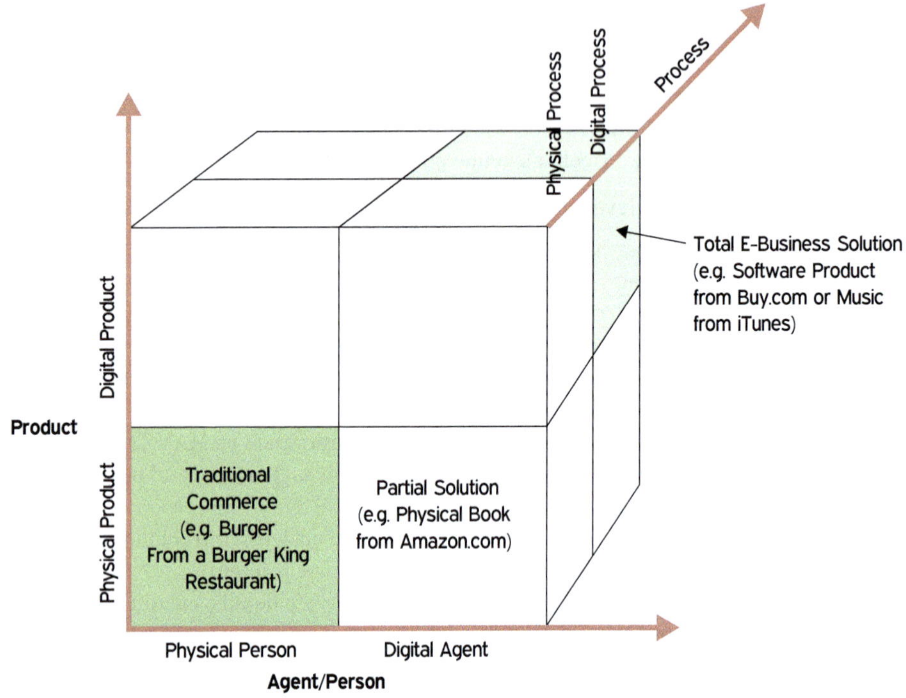

Source: Adapted from Negroponte (1995).

this to a more advanced level can allow companies to integrate their automated processes and sell complementary products and services together – for instance, the purchase of travel tickets, hotels and car hire from different companies through a single online travel company such as Expedia.

- *The partial solution*, with medium information intensity, where physical products are delivered to the customer but ordering and payment are carried out online. This partial solution, pioneered by companies such as Amazon, is fast being adopted by all retailers of easily movable goods. Companies who can't adopt such as business model (e.g. hairdressers, charity/thrift shops, coffee shops) are those that now dominate our high streets as others increasingly go online.

Although it needs to be stressed that information technology is not the only thing that has contributed to business integration, it has been the most significant development in recent years, and it is generally thought that this will continue to be the case in the future. Therefore operations managers need to be aware of the information intensity of their operation, products and services if they wish to apply IT appropriately.

More recently financial aspects of processes transactions are being radically changed as blockchain (sometimes also known as digital distributed ledger technologies – DLT) accompanied with crypto-currencies (such as Bitcoin, Ethereum or Libra) are beginning to change financial supply chain transactions.

Stop and Think

In the opening case, how would Beth's placement year job have been easier if the confectionery company had had more integrated processes and IT systems?

SHORT CASE 14.2

BUSINESS INTEGRATION

Walmart and other Food Giants Team up on IBM's Blockchain

Walmart and a group of food giants are teaming up with IBM to explore how to apply blockchain technology, also known as distributed ledger technology, to their food supply chains.

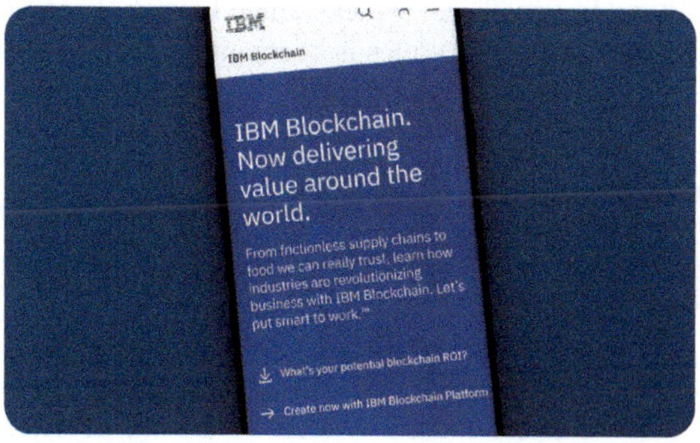

Source: © Grey82/Shutterstock

The coalition includes retailers and food companies such as Unilever, Nestlé, Kroger and Dole. They will be aiming to use blockchain, a technology that facilitates crypto-currencies, such as Bitcoin, to maintain secure digital records and improve the trace-ability of their foodstuffs, like chicken, chocolate and bananas. Walmart has already run two blockchain experiments in partnership with IBM. The first involved tracking Chinese pork. The second involved tracing Mexican mangoes. For the trials, Walmart used Hyperledger Fabric, a blockchain originally built by IBM, which was housed by the Linux Foundation's Hyperledger group. This is the preferred blockchain of IBM, who have been encouraging clients to try the tech across industries as varied as private equity, banking, government and health care. The vice president of food safety at Walmart was so pleased by the pork and mango trials that he rallied peers to join the cause. 'We were so encouraged that we really quickly started reaching out to other suppliers and retailers as well.'

Kroger's VP of corporate food technology and regulatory compliance, said that Walmart's experience with the software gave the tech 'legitimacy'. 'The food industry is ripe for a solution like that', he said. Indeed, the food giants like the idea of simplifying their supply chains with automatic tracking of important information, such as temperature and quality of goods, shipment and delivery dates, and safety certifications of facilities. IBM, meanwhile, is keen on selling subscriptions to blockchain-related services that integrate with its cloud business.

'We're asking companies to join to help evolve the solution and guide and steer its direction', said HP's vice president of blockchain at IBM. 'We'll do PoCs [proofs-of-concept] later down the line.'

Businesses are already putting blockchain technology to the test in a variety of industries, including cargo shipping, poultry and diamonds. The new food group is set to bring the technology one step closer to production.

Questions

1. What benefits does blockchain (distributed ledger) technology bring to supply chains such as those in the food industry?
2. What challenges and opportunities do crypto-currencies, such as Bitcoin, bring to organizations?

Source: Adapted from Robert Hackett (2017), https://fortune.com/2017/08/22/walmart-blockchain-ibm-food-nestle-unilever-tyson-dole/.

Corporate Social Responsibility

Corporate social responsibility (CSR) in operations management means having an operations strategy that will meet the requirements of current needs without compromising the ability of future generations to meet their own needs. This means considering environmental, ethical and social issues on a par with financial and more traditional operational performance measures. Companies have traditionally focused their aims on creating profit for their shareholders, and other performance measures relating to CSR issues have typically been much less important. However, the shareholders and stakeholders of companies have currently become much more interested in the factors that impact on wider social and environmental issues.

CSR

The shareholders are those individuals or companies that legally own one or more shares in a company. Stakeholders are those individuals or organizations who are influenced, either directly or indirectly, by the actions of the company. This expanded view of organizational accountabilities means that the scope of a firm's strategy must not only include economic viability but should also consider the natural environment and social impact on its stakeholders.

Throughout this book CSR has been a prominent theme. For instance, in Part One we highlighted increasing customer concerns about ethical practices and the exploitation of vulnerable nations and people. In Part Two we highlighted how ethical and environmental issues have become more important in product design and service delivery. In Part Three we explained how CSR can add to industry and planetary sustainability. Part Four of the book describes how ethics is becoming an increasingly important part of performance measurement and quality management systems.

SHORT CASE 14.3

CSR

Fast Fashion Growth Must Slow Down

Scientists have warned that the fashion industry must make urgent and fundamental changes to their business models in order to prevent devastating environmental impacts.

The fashion industry is the world's largest industrial polluter after the aviation sector, and is estimated to be responsible for 10% of all global pollution. The environmental impact of the fashion industry – particularly the so-called 'fast-fashion' market, which is based on a rapid cycle of cheap, mass-manufactured, disposable garments often made from artificial fibres – has been brought to mainstream attention in recent years. However, fast fashion continues to grow and accelerate, largely driven by the popularity of budget online retailers.

Source: © Ernest Rose/Shutterstock

Environmental impacts through excessive water use (1.5 trillion litres), chemical pollution, high carbon emissions, textile waste (more than 92 million tones), and overuse of plastics that fill our oceans are just a few of its harmful effects.

Even more seriously, the fast fashion industry frequently relies on child, prison, bonded and forced labour.

A systemic transition towards slower fashion requires a slowdown in manufacturing volumes, the introduction of more ethical and sustainable practices throughout the supply chain and a shift in consumer behaviour to reduce the amount of new clothing being purchased.

Question

1. How can a systemic permanent transition towards 'slower' more ethical and sustainable fashion be achieved?

Source: 'Fast fashion growth must slow, scientist warn', *Engineering and Technology Magazine*, 15(4), May 2020, p. 11, eandtmagazine.com

The Triple Bottom Line

Triple bottom line: considers the social and natural environmental impact of a company's strategy as well as the more conventional economic impact.

To capture an expanding view of stakeholders and their expectations concerning CSR, the phrase the **triple bottom line** has been coined (Elkington, 1994): see Figure 14.4.

The triple bottom line evaluates the firm's performance against social, economic and environmental criteria. The following expands on the meaning of each dimension of the triple bottom line framework.

Social

This pertains to fair and beneficial business practices towards labour, the community and the region in which a firm conducts its business. A triple bottom line company seeks to benefit its employees, the community and other social entities that are affected by the firm's existence. A company should not use child labour, should pay fair salaries to its workers, should maintain a safe working environment with tolerable working hours, and should not otherwise exploit its community or labour force. A business can also give back by contributing to the community through health care, education and other special programmes. But consumers must also play their part, ensuring that items and

Figure 14.4 The triple bottom line

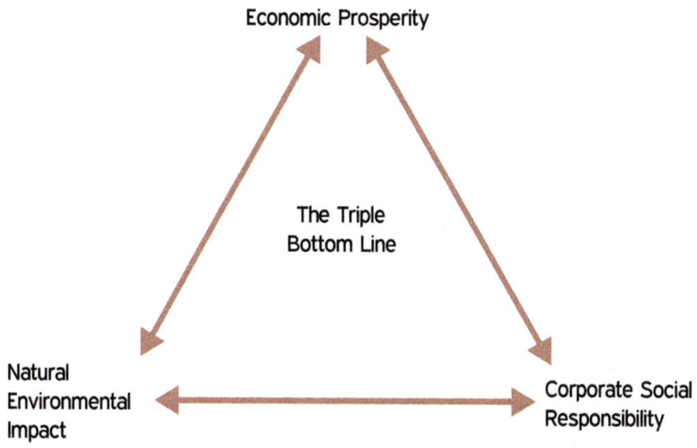

Source: Elkington (1994).

services that they purchase are used, maintained and reused suitably, and are recycled once they are no longer usable. The aim for consumers should be to apply the '4Rs' in the following order: **r**educe consumption, **r**euse items as much as possible,**re**-manufacture items where possible and only **r**ecycle if the former options are not available.

Land Rover (based in the UK), which make off-road sport utility vehicles (SUVs), is often criticized for making fuel-inefficient vehicles, but over 60% of the Land Rovers ever made are still on the road. Therefore Land Rover claim that they are excellent at conserving the raw materials from which they are made, in contrast to an average vehicle that might last only 10 years. In 2020 Land Rover replaced its classic 'Defender' model due to changing environmental legislation, after more than 60 years in production, for a radically different, more environmentally friendly model.

Economic

The firm is obligated to compensate shareholders who provide capital through stock purchases and other financial investments via a competitive return on their investment. Company strategies should promote growth and increase long-term value for this group in the form of profit. Within a sustainability framework, this dimension goes beyond just profit for the firm, and should also provide lasting economic benefit to society, such as through local and national tax payments to government. This is so important that in many countries economic CSR is carefully defined in law and regulated (e.g. the Sarbanes-Oxley Act in the USA, which came into being after the collapse of Enron). So, is a company really practising CSR if it just adheres to the basic requirements? Some people certainly think so, but they also think that extra voluntary steps should also be taken, such as protecting pension schemes for employees and making prompt payment to smaller suppliers.

Natural Environment

This refers to the firm's impact on the natural environment. The company should protect the environment as much as possible. Managers should move to reduce a company's ecological footprint by carefully managing its consumption of natural resources, and by reducing waste, as well as ensuring that the waste is not harmful before disposing of it in a safe and legal way. Many businesses now conduct 'cradle-to-grave' assessments of products to determine what the true environmental costs are – from the processing of the raw materials, to manufacture, to distribution, and to eventual disposal by the final customer. For instance, all wood- and paper-based products in the UK must now conform to Forest Stewardship Council (FSC) regulations to show they have come from sustainable sources.

Another emerging standard in recent years has been ISO 14000, from the International Organization for Standardization. This is a three-section environmental management system that covers initial planning, implementation, and objective assessment. Although it has had some impact, it has largely been limited to Europe. ISO 14000 states a number of specific requirements, including:

- A commitment by top-level management to environmental management
- The development and communication of an environmental policy
- The establishment of relevant legal and regulatory requirements
- The setting of environmental objectives and targets

- The establishment and updating of a specific environmental programme, or programmes, geared to achieving the objectives and targets
- The implementation of supporting systems such as training, operational control and emergency planning
- Regular monitoring and measurement of all operational activities
- A full audit procedure to review the working and suitability of the system.

The application of initiatives such as ISO 14000 should help with issues such as:

- reducing use of *non-recyclable plastics* – plastic waste going into seas must be minimized and reusable materials (i.e. glass) may be more ecologically friendly
- reducing use of *unnecessary packaging* – too much packaging uses valuable resources and costs more to transport (e.g. Apple are very sparing with their packaging)
- reducing reliance on *fossil fuels* and moving to sustainable fuel sources combined with better insulation on factory and office buildings – thus decelerating global warming
- encouraging the concept of the *circular economy* where products no longer have an 'end-of-life' state but instead have a point where they feed into another supply chain. For instance, old tyres can be shredded to make rubber matting for children's playgrounds instead of going into landfill. Alternatively, products get returned to their original manufacturer to be refurbished (e.g. printer cartridges, or internal combustion engine blocks)
- emphasizing the concept of *industry symbiosis* – where one industry's by-product becomes another industry's valued core input. For instance, decaffeinated coffee manufacturers do not need the caffeine but have a valuable by-product that can be sold to energy drink manufacturers (e.g. Redbull)
- creating *greater visibility* in supply chains for *accountability* reasons (e.g. undeclared horse meat found in human food is unacceptable, and potential virus sources of COVID-19 need to be tested and traced back to source).

CRITICAL PERSPECTIVE

Is CSR Really Any Good for Business?

Conventional operations strategy focuses on just the economic part of the triple bottom line. But because many of the processes that fall under the domain of operations and supply chain management have social and environmental impacts, it is important that these are also considered. Therefore the whole topic of CSR is rising swiftly up the corporate agenda. In 2008 the Economist Intelligence Unit found that the majority of managers surveyed believe CSR is of either 'high' or 'very high' importance, which contrasts with 2004, when the majority of managers surveyed thought it was of 'moderate', 'low' or 'very low' importance. The likelihood is that it will grow to be even more important in the future. It is estimated that around 35% of the world's largest corporations publish reports on their environmental policies and performance (Kolk, 2000). This may be partly motivated by an altruistic desire to save the planet. However, what is also now clear to companies is that 'green reporting' also makes sound business sense.

Although most strategists believe that improving society and preserving the environment are good things, some still disagree, citing the potential loss of profit or efficiency. Others argue that companies operating in rich countries can afford to contribute to society and the environment, whereas a company in a poor or developing nation must focus purely on survival. In the developing world the economic benefit realized by the use of abundant local resources may be viewed as worth their destruction. For example, cutting down trees in the Amazon rainforest to sell for timber and clear space to graze cattle may seem reasonable to the Brazilian government, but currently unreasonable to Europeans, who in the past have cut down their own forests to power their industries.

Some people believe that CSR is nothing more than just ***greenwash*** (a term used to describe practising CSR for cynical or disingenuous reasons, because it is currently fashionably to do it rather than because one actually believes in its genuine purpose), and that CSR is being used as a marketing strategy to increase brand value and sell more products and services – which results in greater consumption of scarce resources and ironically may make the situation worse; such issues are the subject of ongoing research (Walker ***et al.***, 2014).

The key point is ...

that the jury still seems to be out on whether CSR is good business sense, or whether it is one step too far in 'political correctness'.

Stop and Think

Is corporate social responsibility just a cynical marketing ploy to make us think organizations care about us and the planet, or is there some real substance to it? In the opening case, how does CSR affect Beth's job?

SHORT CASE 14.4

Sustainable Forestry: Is There such a Thing as Good Wood?

CSR

GLOBALIZATION

Source: ©Kletr/Shutterstock

Royal Houthandel G. Wijma & Zonen BV is a Dutch timber company established in 1897. The company has a long tradition in managing the supply chain from timber harvested in the forest, via timber processing and trade to the final user. Approximately 70% (by volume) of the wood traded by Wijma comes from its own production facilities (sawmills). The other 30% is purchased from third parties, particularly from West Africa, where Wijma has been active for many years. As a result of redevelopment after the Second World War, there was a large demand for hardwood in Europe. Azobé timber was introduced by the Dutch government as a good, cheap alternative to European oak. In 1968 the supply of this timber from West Africa was secured for them by establishing a purchasing office in Cameroon. Today, hard wood is still much in demand in European construction for items such as bridge, lock, pier and dock construction.

However, since the 1990s, Wijma has been involved in a conflict between the timber industry and various environmental organizations calling for a boycott on the use of tropical timber. Later Wijma changed its position, and the emphasis was placed on promoting certified sustainable forest management based on the principles of the FSC (Forest Stewardship Council). For various reasons the implementation of sustainable forestry takes place very slowly. Many countries in the Southern hemisphere lack the experience, knowledge and financial resources found in Western countries that make this type of activity possible. In addition, developing countries find it difficult to understand the reasons why this action is necessary, mainly because of the diversity of opinions held by the various stakeholders, such as scientists, politicians and pressure groups in various countries.

In 2001 Wijma gained an area of long-term concessions in Cameroon (currently a total of 190,000 hectares for the next 30 years), with areas designated as 'production forests' by the government. A management plan was required to state how the forest manager will operate it in a sustainable way, taking into consideration the socio-cultural, economic and ecological aspects of the forest.

By 2005 Wijma had completed the pioneering work of full FSC certification in Africa. Mark Diepstraten, the CEO, explained the lesson learned by Wijma from the above experiences as follows: 'We should not turn down social discussions, but participate in them. We must communicate our chosen path clearly and transparently. You must, as a company, communicate what you do, why you do it and how you are going to achieve it . . . The new director in Cameroon is more open, because he understands how important it is to make a link between the market requirements in Europe and timber extraction in Cameroon'.

Further, full FSC 'forest management' and 'chain of custody' certifications were granted in 2012. By 2020, Wijma managed over 315,000 hectares of FSC-certified forest across five sites in West Africa and was the first company with a group certificate in Africa.

Questions

1. Why should companies in developed countries care about where their raw materials come from and how they are produced?
2. Are governments right to intervene in business and operations practice?
3. Could companies in developing countries take a different approach, rather than exporting raw materials as demonstrated in this case?

Sources: Adapted from J. Cramer (2006) 'Timber extraction by Koninklijke Houthandel Wijma in Cameroon', in *Corporate Social Responsibility and Globalisation: An Action Plan for Business*, Greenleaf Publishing, pp. 81–84; and wijma.co.uk (2020).

Operational Learning for Operations Managers

During the past two decades significant changes have occurred in the job of the operations manager, mainly in response to the introduction of new process technologies, data analysis capabilities and management philosophies. Trends indicate that the operations manager will have a much greater role to play in setting the strategic direction of the company, and in defining competitive priorities. The ability to gather and interpret information from the external environment and quickly react to it will become more critical. Competitive and consumer pressure will force operations managers to concentrate on improving CSR and sustainability.

As globalization continues to increase, there will be greater choice over where to buy, produce and sell goods and services. Globalization has blurred the economic distinctions between countries and companies, creating an increasingly 'borderless' or 'flat' world in which economic decisions are made without reference to company or country boundaries (Friedman, 2005). The ability to manage people and resources within and across national boundaries will become an important part of the operations manager's role. Organizations will increasingly focus on core competencies, and outsource most of the non-core activities. In addition, organizations will focus more on the management of their supplier relations to improve profitability. To achieve a balance between costs and consumer satisfaction, operations managers will have to think more about the integration of organizations. Operations managers will also have to recognize that business processes, not functions, create value for the customer, and that such processes typically transcend functional units and organizational boundaries.

In the future, sustainability issues will become more important, and operations managers will be required to design and implement ecologically sound manufacturing and service delivery practices. Operations managers will play an increasing role in deciding the types of product to manufacture and the materials that should be used, and will increasingly help to design processes that can reduce waste and harmful emissions.

As more firms embrace the goal of lean and agile manufacturing, technology will play an increasingly prominent role in the future. Continuous developments are happening in flexible automation, computer-integrated manufacturing and computer-aided design tools. The use of artificial intelligence, conference systems, virtual reality, digital twins, data and process analytics, 3D printers, digital learning environments, drones, and use of co-bots further build on these existing technologies. While Internet technologies greatly improve relationships and communications between organizations, customers, suppliers and partners if suitably applied through the Internet of Things (IoT).

All this implies that, in the future, operations managers will have to be more highly trained, and should have the ability to understand and use complex manufacturing and service technologies and systems (CABS, 2019). It may be more important to become a member of a professional institution that can help disseminate the latest changes in the field and to engage in ongoing professional development. In terms of job content, operations managers will have more opportunities to exercise personal initiative, improve efficiency, be innovative and be among the first to adopt exciting new technologies.

As cross-functional linkages between manufacturing, marketing, engineering and human resources increase, operations managers will be required to possess an increasing breadth of management knowledge. With the increasing focus on lean and agile thinking, the span of control of operations managers will inevitably increase. In addition, the rapid move towards the use of the Internet has resulted in the growth of **knowledge workers**, who are highly educated and skilled. Thus the traditional function of *supervision and control* is likely to change to that of a *specialist* providing assistance to employees and teams. This implies that organizations will have to spend a considerable amount of time and money to enhance the managerial skills and experiences of operations managers. Currently, it is generally thought that most operations managers need more training in leadership, business and management in order to be more successful in their future careers. However, on the positive side, these changes will inevitably provide new and more exciting career paths for operational managers.

Knowledge workers: employees whose skills are based more on what they know than on what they can physically do.

In summary, the rapid increase of technology and the advent of the knowledge worker will require highly qualified individuals to manage the operations of organizations effectively. As companies increasingly focus on their manufacturing and service delivery operations to gain competitive advantage, the operations manager of the future will play a key strategic role in enhancing organizational performance.

SHORT CASE 14.5

The Apprentice: Could You Be Hired by Lord Sugar?

Lord Alan Sugar was originally famous for building up the Amstrad group, and lately – and perhaps more widely known – for fronting the hit TV show ***The Apprentice*** in the UK. He is a charismatic leader, who has always known the value of good operations management. He left school at an early age to set up his own business, selling things such as boiled beetroot, car aerials and related electronics products. His entrepreneurial drive has led to the development of innovative home computing and entertainment products, and more lately an extensive property portfolio. His value proposition to the consumer has always been 'innovative products at reasonable prices'. To deliver these, he focused on low costs of manufacture by using innovative manufacturing processes, ensuring that components were bought at competitive prices, and adopting a no-nonsense management style. As someone who has risen from humble beginnings to head a diverse portfolio of businesses worth in excess of £800 million he has always known the value of good operations management, and ***The Apprentice***, believe it or not, is very much aimed at, among other things, developing excellent operations management skills!

Source: London Entertainment/Alamy Stock Photo

Questions

1. What personal skills does a good operations leader, such as Lord Sugar, require?
2. What operational principles has Lord Sugar adopted?
3. Do you think you could become a successful operations director or manager? Why, and how might you do this?

Stop and Think

There can be a lot of pressure on operations managers to 'get everything right first time'. What do you think they should do to prepare themselves for such challenges?

Summary

This final chapter concentrates on the main cross-chapter themes of the book. These are all themes that are too significant to be left to just one or two chapters, as they epitomize the current state of operations management and point towards its future. Table 14.3 picks out the main points from each chapter.

Table 14.3 Summary of the key themes in this book

Chapter topic area	Business integration	CSR	Globalization
Strategy and customer orientation	Customers' requirements drive overall organizational strategy	Increasing customer CSR concerns are addressed	Used to positively affect all stakeholders

continued

Table 14.3 *(continued)*

Chapter topic area	Business integration	CSR	Globalization
Operations strategy	Holistic systems perspective is taken of the business	Does not exploit vulnerable workers, natural resources or developing nations	Correct balance of centralization versus decentralization and duplication versus robustness
Innovation and competitive advantage	Incorporate a network of research and development competencies	Seeks the use of new materials, methods and technology to improve CSR	Seeks to reduce unnecessary waste and preserve future planet
Product and service design	Correct level of duplication and robustness is built into the product service delivery system	These are designed with ethical and environmental and waste reduction issues in mind	Organization has units at points of natural resource, human resource, knowledge bases and end markets, and draws upon them appropriately
Process design	Processes are customer facing, lean and data driven	Delivers financial gain, preserves natural resources and work-life balance	Demonstrates responsible management, accountability, digitization and empathy with all stakeholders
Supply network and enterprise design	ICT is used to connect operations together	Does not exploit vulnerable workers or developing nations, looks to reduce global carbon footprint	Appropriate portfolio of competencies is built, and these are in the right geographical locations as per PESTEL factors
Capacity planning and management	Work allocated to suitable business unit, depending on volume and competencies – inbuilt flexibility	Flexible while not exploiting vulnerable workers, natural resources or developing nations	Work allocated to suitable business unit, depending on volume and competencies and proximity to end market
Supply chain management	Supply chains highly integrated, and tend towards multi-organization enterprises	Global whilst not exploiting vulnerable workers, natural resources or developing nations	Draws upon production and service delivery networks to be lean and agile and minimizes logistics risks
Lean operations and JIT	Customer-driven processes, with continuous flow and levelled loading	Improves business and sector sustainability and reduces waste	Lean thinking extends to partners, suppliers and customers.
Inventory planning and management	Minimum inventory, made to order whenever possible	Accurate accounting, storage, transportation and use of recycled materials	No overproduction
Project management	Establish core competencies and commonality between projects	Meet all project stakeholders' criteria – not just traditional time, cost and quality	Drawn on global resources as necessary
Performance and people measurement	Accurate, real-time data available to all	Ethical, human and environmental impact is measured	Net effects for nations, companies and business units is known
Quality and performance improvement	Organization has a 'total quality management' philosophy and people have a 'right first time' attitude	Meet all organizational stakeholders' criteria – not just traditional time, cost and quality	Globalization should enhance overall sector standards while maintaining competitive advantage

Now that you have studied this book, we hope that you are a great deal more prepared in terms of your knowledge, skills and personal aspirations to go forth and become an excellent operations manager. Why not go forth and change the world through excellent operations management?

Suggested Answers to Stop and Think Questions

1. **Globalization:** It is appropriate for some companies to globalize if their products and services are generic and widely marketable, have high set-up costs, and will benefit from a large scale of economy. Globalization can be part of market development for successful mature products and services (e.g. Coca-Cola, Fedex, Tesco). However, some products and services are not well suited to globalization, particularly those that serve niche markets, and are difficult or expensive to transport (e.g. real ale, health service facilities).

   The chocolate products in the opening case could be part of a globalization strategy. From an operational point of view it would mean that the chocolates had to conform to international standards for content and production. It may be the case that new production facilities are set up abroad, or that the products are made under licence by another company if production and transportation costs are prohibitive.

2. **Information technology:** Good IT integration should facilitate better communication within and between organizational departments, as well as between different organizations that work closely together (e.g. retailers, importers/exporters and manufacturers). If the chocolate company had had an IT system that linked up prospective and actual sales orders, accessible in real time by the purchasing, production and strategic planning departments, the shortfall in ingredients and staff might have been avoided, and the customer might have been served better. In addition, an advanced system (using big data analysis and artificial intelligence) might have been able to detect trends like this occurring throughout the annual demand pattern, and forewarn the strategic planners.

   For Beth, such an IT system (sometimes known as a sales ordering process system, as part of a larger enterprise resource planning – ERP – system) could have made her job a lot less stressful; it might have meant that instead of spending time correcting things that had gone wrong or not thought of, she could have concentrated on developing exciting new products and processes.

3. **Corporate social responsibility:** Looking after our natural environment and resources is unquestionably an important thing to do. Similarly, it is also important to respect cultural, political and social differences. Both of these, along with making sustainable profit, are necessary for organizations. However, CSR can sometimes be used for marketing purposes without actually having any real impact; you should consider how companies' and governments' CSR claims would actually make a difference. For instance, is putting more tax on petrol or air flights really going to stop people travelling? Will people stop buying cheap products if they know workforces are being exploited?

   Beth, working in the chocolate factory, would need to consider the following factors. Are ingredients obtained from sustainable forests? Are suppliers treating their workforces ethically? Are developing countries getting a fair share of the profits? And are machines using power economically? Wider issues involve customers' health and marketing messages (e.g. is chocolate really good for you, or should it contain health warnings?).

4. **Right first time:** To have a successful career, operations managers must always be aware of all the latest developments in management thinking, tools, techniques and technology. This usually requires a combination of continuing professional development and the implementation of competitive practices.

   However, even the best operations managers get it wrong at times. The important point is not to hide or ignore problems, but to resolve them as a team within the organization, to learn from them, and not to make them again. In this way organizations and practice will continually improve, and organizations will become more competitive and sustainable.

Review Questions

connect

1. Describe the key success factors for business integration.
2. Explain why some businesses are more appropriate to be supported by information technology than others, and why some will never be pure online businesses.
3. Discuss the benefits of globalization in respect to: (a) individual organizations; (b) nations; (c) Planet Earth.
4. Can globalization and corporate social responsibility be simultaneously deployed ?
5. Is corporate social responsibility adding to unnecessary organizational costs and complexity?
6. How can we ensure that the workforce of the future is adequately prepared for the future challenges of operations managers?
7. What are the triple bottom line factors?

Discussion Questions

1. The Internet-of-Things is everywhere in the modern world and it affects our everyday personal lives and work place activities. Discuss devices that have become an indispensable part of the Internet-of-Things.
2. Look at the mission statements of HSBC (bank), EE (mobile phone operator), the John Lewis Partnership (retailer) and Starbucks (coffee houses). State the similarities and differences and why they might be considered cynical.
3. Characterize the personal consumer behaviour of your peer group. How do you think you can influence the corporate social responsibilities of large organizations?
4. Look at job recruitment sites such as www.monster.com, and see the skill sets that are required by operations managers. Do you think you have them?

Further Reading

Benedettini, O., Clegg, B., Kafouros, M. and Neely, A. (2010) *The Ten Myths of Manufacturing,* AIM executive briefing paper (www.aimresearch.org).

Binder, M. and Clegg, B. T. (2010) *Sustainable Supplier Management in the Automotive Industry: Leading the 3rd Revolution through Collaboration,* Nova Science Publishers, New York.

Branson, R. (2017) *Finding my Virginity,* Amazon Media.

Burcher, P. G., Lee, G. L. and Sohal, A. S. (2004) 'The changing roles of production and operations managers in Britain from the 1970s to the 1990s', *International Journal of Operations and Production Management,* **24**(4), 409–423.

Cramer, J. (2006) *Corporate Social Responsibility and Globalisation: An Action Plan for Business,* Greenleaf Publishing, Sheffield.

D'Netto, B. and Sohal, A.S. (1999) 'Changes in the production manager's job: past, present and future trends', *International Journal of Operations and Production Management,* **19**(2), 157–181.

Geary, J. (2017) *How to Be a Chief Operating Officer: 16 Disciplines for Success.* Kindle Direct Publishing.

Vance, A. (2015) *Elon Musk: How the Billionaire CEO of SpaceX and Tesla is Shaping our Future.* Virgin Digital.

The *Sunday Times, The Independent* and other quality newspapers: job advertisements for operations managers and directors.

References

CABS (2019) *The Changing Shape of Business Education,* Chartered Association of Business Schools, London. charteredabs.org (accessed June 2020).

Cash, J. I., Earl, M. J. and Morison, R. (2008) 'Teaming up to crack innovation and enterprise integration', *Harvard Business Review,* November, 1–11.

Economist Intelligent Unit (2008) *Why CSR?* Economist Intelligent Unit, London.

Elkington, J. (1994) 'Toward the sustainable corporation: Win-win-win business strategies for sustainable development', *California Management Review,* **36**(2), 90–100.

Farrell, D. (2004) 'Beyond offshoring: Assess your company's global potential', *Harvard Business Review,* **82**(12), 82–90.

Friedman, T. (2005) *The World Is Flat: A Brief History of the 21st Century,* Farrar, Straus and Giroux, New York.

Ghemawat, P. (2007) 'Managing differences: The central challenge of global strategy', *Harvard Business Review,* **85**(3), 58–68.

Gunasekaran, A. and Ngai, E. W. T. (2012) 'The future of operations management: An outlook and analysis', *International Journal of Production Economics,* **135**(2), 687–701.

Kolk, A. (2000) *The Economics of Environmental Management,* FT Prentice Hall, Harlow.

Negroponte, N. (1995) *Being Digital,* Vintage Books, New York.

Stiglitz, J. E. (2017) 'The overselling of globalization', *Business Economics,* **52,** 129–137.

Walker, H., Suering, S., Sarkis, S. and Klassen, R. (2014) 'Sustainable operations management: Recent trends and future directions', *International Journal of Operations Management,* **34**(5). https://doi.org/10.1108/IJOPM-12-2013-0557

Waterman, R. H., Peters, T. J. and Philips, J. R. (1980) 'Structure is not organization', *Business Horizons,* **23**(3), 14–26.

Glossary

A

ABC – system for ranking inventory into parts to control closely and parts that don't merit undue effort in monitoring.

Actual capacity – the expected output of an operation, considering both planned stoppages and unplanned stoppages.

Adaptation (in a globalization context) – boosting revenue and market share by maximizing local presence in a country.

Aggregate planning – a top-level look at demand for the operation as a whole; does not differentiate between different products and services.

Aggregation (in a globalization context) – achieving economies of scale by creating regional or global operations.

Agile supply – use of market knowledge and the virtual corporation to exploit profitable opportunities in a volatile marketplace.

Arbitrage (in a globalization context) – the exploitation of differences among national or regional markets, often by locating separate parts of supply chains in different places.

Availability – the actual amount of time that a resource can be used for its intended purpose

B

Back-office activities – activities that are hidden from the customers.

Batch of one – a key element of the lean approach, which seeks to produce individual products, as this is normally what the customer orders.

Bill of materials (BOM) file (or product structure or product tree file) – lists the description of the product (such as the material, components and quantity) and the sequence in which the product is to be assembled.

Business process – sequence of tasks to get things done.

C

Capacity – the maximum goods or services that an operation can produce.

Capacity requirements planning (CRP) – MRP module that examines workloading on workstations to identify shortfalls.

Cause-and-effect diagram – structural approach to finding of possible cause(s) of a problem.

Centre of gravity method – approach that uses the physical analogy of a 'balancing point' to determine the geographical location of an operation relative to others that it has a direct relationship with.

Chase demand – capacity strategy in which the operation expands and contracts its capacity to follow demand changes.

Circular Economy – When firms look at the resources they use and seek to keep re-using them rather needing more fresh materials.

Closed-loop MRP – use of the MRP calculation to examine whether the plans it produces are achievable, given limits in capacity or supply times and other constraints.

Collaborative enterprise governance – method of controlling parts of many different organizations simultaneously, in order to deliver products and services with agility and efficiency.

Competitive advantage – what sets a firm apart from its rivals, making it the supplier of choice for customers within a particular market.

Competitive benchmarking – compares the company's performance against that of the competitors.

Constraint – a restriction on the running of an operation.

Control chart – used to plot sample means, average means and ranges over time; indicates the lower and upper control limits.

Core competencies – competencies that contribute directly to business goals.

Corporate responsibility – the awareness, acceptance, and management of the wider implications of management decisions.

Cost, performance and time – projects are normally subjected to these three performance criteria.

Critical path – the chain of activities that determines the total duration of a project from start to finish.

Customer contact – refers to the physical presence of the customer in the system, or the percentage of the time that the customer is in the system relative to the total service time.

Customer relationship management (CRM) – ERP tools where all relevant information about a customer can be presented in one place, thus offering a transparent way of supporting customers.

Customer value elements – factors that, when combined, define the value proposition.

Customer value proposition – statement of precisely what the customer values and will therefore buy in the form of a product.

Customization point – the point where a process output becomes linked to a specific customer order.

Cycle time – the actual time a process or task in a process takes to produce a unit of output.

Cyclical review – inventory review system that determines the amount to be ordered at set intervals.

D

Degree of variation – the variation in the provision of a service, where customization for and interaction with customers are common sources of variation

Demand – the quantity of goods and services demanded by consumers.

Demand management – capacity strategy in which the operation attempts to manipulate demand to smooth the peaks and troughs; used in conjunction with the marketing department.

Dependent demand – demand for a part that is normally directly related to that for some others, and ultimately to the aggregate production plan.

Dependent demand – reasonably predictable demand, linked or associated with another factor, which may have a clearer future pattern.

Design capacity – the expected output of an operation when there are no stoppages.

Development – activity that involves systematic but non-routine technical work directed towards producing new or improved materials, products or services.

Distinctive competencies – competencies so unique that they create competitive advantage.

DPMO – defects per million opportunities.

Dynamic capability – a firm's ability to upgrade and reconstruct its capabilities in response to the changing environment, therefore attaining and sustaining its competitive advantage.

E

E-business – electronically mediated information exchanges, both within an organization and with external stakeholders, supporting the entire range of business processes.

E-commerce – electronically mediated information exchanges between an organization and its external stakeholders, concerned predominantly with buying and selling.

e-Service – the delivery of service using online media, which can be delivered in a virtual environment with little or no human interaction.

Earned value reporting (EVR) – a means of monitoring projects, based on key measures of completion against estimated cost or schedule.

Economic batch quantity (EBQ) – another name for EPQ.

Economic order quantity (EOQ) – fixed order (or production) amount that minimizes the total costs over a whole year.

Economic production quantity (EPQ) – extension of the EOQ that includes the effect of producing parts.

Effective capacity – the expected output of an operation considering planned stoppages for maintenance, shift changeovers etc.

Efficiency – actual output shown as a percentage of the operation's effective capacity; demonstrates how well the operation is working to expectations.

Endogenous theories – theories about an organization that focus on the organization and its links to the business environment.

Engageability – the ability to attract partners and the means to deliver value.

Enterprise integrator/orchestrator – organization that takes the lead role in transforming a loose supply network into a tightly integrated enterprise.

Enterprise resources planning (ERP) – ERP systems are corporate-wide information systems that present data as if from a central single entity source.

Exogenous theories – theories about an organization that focus on its internal workings, resources and skills.

Extended enterprise – semi-permanent group of organizations working towards joint strategic objectives.

F

FANG – Collective term for e-businesses: Facebook, Amazon, Netflix, Google

Feedback (HR) – the process by which individuals are informed of the degree to which they are meeting desired or expected levels of performance.

Field of use – the company seeks to understand how well the product conforms to specifications after it reaches the customers.

Finished goods inventory – completed products awaiting shipment or built for stock.

Finite capacity scheduling – advanced MRP II system including routines to try and solve any capacity problems.

Float – the spare time an activity has before it will become on the critical path, and so allowing rescheduling without impact.

Flow chart – provides a visual representation of all major steps in a process.

Flow diagram – a drawing used to analyse the flow of people and materials.

Forecast – predicting the future, normally based on historical data with some interpretation.

Front-office activities – activities where there is direct customer contact, whether face to face, or by email, telephone, or letter.

Functional benchmarking – compares specific processes and functions across different industries to find the 'best in class'.

G

Gantt chart – horizontal bar diagram showing activities and their duration.

Gemba walk – The practice of regularly walking through a process to identify wasteful activities.

Globalization – increasing global connectivity, integration and interdependence in the economic, social, technological, cultural, political and ecological spheres.

Globalization – the increasing integration of internationally dispersed economic activity, and the extension of an organization's operational activity to cover the whole world.

Goal setting (HR) – the process of assigning work tasks to individuals so that they are clear on what is expected of them. To be effective, the goals should be specific, measurable, attainable, realistic and time-bound.

H

Hard HRM – HR practices and policies that enable the close control and co-ordination of employees and views employees as an organizational resource to be effectively utilized

Heijunka – a method for developing a repeating schedule that produces the correct mix of products. It is important to spread the launch of products into the production line evenly to smooth the amount of work required.

Holistic thinking/holism – considering a system to be more than a sum of its parts.

Human resource management (HRM) – the organizational function that deals with issues related to its workforce. HRM may also be seen as a particular perspective on people management and people related issues.

I

Incremental innovation – change that moves things on in small steps.

Independent demand – a less predictable demand pattern as it is not easily linked to other factors.

Independent demand – demand that is treated as unrelated to anything else.

Information intensity – the degree to which an organization's products/services, processes, people/agents and transactions in general are reliant on digital assets – the more reliant an organization is on digital assets the higher their information intensity.

Innovation outcome – the output that is new or different.

Interface specifications – define the protocol for the fundamental interactions across all components constituting a technological system.

Intermediate consumption – the value of the goods and services consumed as inputs by a process of production, excluding fixed assets. In other words, resources that become part of the end product or service delivered to the customer.

Internal benchmarking – provides a comparison among similar operations or processes within a company's organization.

International Organization for Standardization (ISO) – the world's largest standards-developing organization.

Inventory – the materials and finished products that are present in the firm, and also in its supply chain. In general, inventory represents a waste, and should be avoided if possible.

Inventory records file – information about the part, including sources, and the stock levels. A key part of the MRP calculation.

Inventory turn – the time taken for a firm's entire inventory to be used and replaced.

J

Jidoka – implementing self-checking to ensure a consistent flow of production.

Job analysis – a systematic process designed to determine what a job role involves and what makes for an effective worker in that role. It produces either a job description (work orientated job analysis) or a person specification (worker orientated analysis).

Job assignment – the process of matching individuals' competences with job requirements, so as to achieve the best fit.

Just in time (JIT) – the pull-based material control system used at Toyota, and the basis of developing the lean model.

K

Kaizen – continuous improvement approach to quality control.

Kanban – Japanese word for the card that is the essential vehicle for operation of the JIT system of production control.

Key Performance Indicator (KPI) – a particular measure that has been deemed of crucial importance in managing the performance of the operation.

Knowledge push – innovation driven by advances in technology that create new products.

Knowledge workers – employees whose skills are based more on what they know than on what they can physically do.

L

Layout – the physical configuration of departments, work centres, and equipment in an operation.

Lead time – the time it takes to design, make, and deliver a product or service.

Leagile supply – combination of a lean supply chain and an agile supply chain.

Lean production – highly efficient management approach with repeated focus on waste reduction, and based on the ideas of the Toyota Production System and JIT.

Lean supply – seeks to develop a value stream to eliminate all waste.

Lean thinking – extending lean production to broader ideas or philosophies. Based on five-step framework: concentrate on value for customers, appreciate the value stream, concentrate on improved flow, adopt pull, perfect quality.

Level production – capacity strategy in which the operation produces to a consistent level; unsold product is stored, and sold when demand peaks.

Little's Law – Total process throughput time = No. of work-in-progress items x Item cycle time

Logistics – the process of planning and implementing the movement and storage of goods in the supply chain.

Long-term capacity plan – a relatively high level plan covering strategic decision 1–3 years ahead.

M

Make to order (MTO) – where planning, procurement and production wait until there is an order from a customer before starting.

Make to stock (MTS) – where production happens before an order has been received.

Manufacturing resource planning (MRP II) – extension of MRP that not only identifies the amounts and times for delivery for components but also includes capacity checks, and extends the calculations to cover the scheduling of production.

Market-based view – the strategic approach that prioritizes what the market wants in its decision-making.

Master production schedule (MPS) – a formal list of the products to be sent to customers, plus detailed specifications and delivery dates; the start of the MRP calculation.

Material requirements planning (MRP) – a way of calculating the demand and timing for component deliveries in order to make the products listed in the master production schedule.

Matrix organization – combined organization structure that overlays functional and project-based styles.

Medium-term capacity plan – a capacity plan covering tactical decisions 3–12 months ahead.

Mobile/M-commerce – electronically mediated information exchanges using mobile electronic devices.

Muda, muri, mura (waste) – focus on waste at the heart of lean systems.

Multi-organization enterprise – a group of different companies, or group of parts of different companies, working together to deliver a product or service in a highly integrated way.

N

Need pull – customer identification of gaps in the market that provide an opportunity to innovate and create a product.

O

Obsolescence – the state of becoming obsolete, or out of date.

Operations strategy – the set of major decisions about core competencies, capabilities and processes, technologies, resources and key tactical activities necessary in the function or chain of functions that create and deliver product and service combinations.

Order-qualifying criteria – the required standards that, if not achieved, will disqualify a product or service from consideration by the customer.

Order-winning criteria – the key reasons to buy a product or service.

original equipment manufacturer – refers to a company that develops or manufacturers a component or product that is sold by another company

Outsourcing – process of giving part of your operations to another organization.

Overall equipment effectiveness (OEE) – actual capacity when applied to individual machines; tells the operation how well the equipment is being used.

Overall professional effectiveness (OPE) – actual capacity when applied to individual workers; tells the operation how well the employee is performing.

P

Pacemaker task – the task that dictates the speed of the overall process.

Pareto diagram – arranges categories from highest to lowest frequency of occurrence.

Performance appraisal (HR) – the process of evaluating am individual's past performance for a specific period, usually one year.

Performance management (of human resources) – the process through which organizations can ensure that individual employees are working towards organizational goals by monitoring and guiding their performance.

Performance management – systematic measuring, monitoring and decision-making geared towards fulfilling organizational objectives.

(HR) performance management system (PMS) – the process by which organizations ensure that employees are working towards achieving a company's strategic objectives, This includes job assignment, goal setting, coaching, feedback, rewards/punishment and performance appraisal.

Performance measures – factors that the customer will use to judge the performance of a product or service.

Performance objective – a statement that clearly explain what is to be achieved by an operation or part of an operation.

Performance standards (HR) – specific performance expectations and levels against which employees performance will be judged – thus, it should be clear to the employees what level(s) of performance would be deemed unacceptable, acceptable and surpassing expectations.

Performance target – this states the level of operational performance to be achieved in order to meet the performance objective.

Population – in a statistical distribution, the entire set of things that make up what is being measured. Samples are taken from a population.

Postponement – delaying the timing of crucial processes in which end products assume their specific functionalities, features and identities

Process quality – the integrity of the operational system that creates the output.

Process servers – the points of sale or stations at the front of the queue where the customer is served.

Product life cycle – generalized model of the buying behaviour of customers over time; used to predict demand for a product or service.

Product platform – set of interconnected subsystems that form a common structure, from which a stream of derivative products can be developed and produced.

Product quality – the quality of the output of the operation, whether it is a tangible product or an intangible service.

Productivity – the ratio of output produced by an operation to the input resources used to produce it

Productization of services – the process of convergence of services to include product content.

Project-based organization – represents a shift from functional organization structure, via the matrix organization, to one where the project is the focus of attention.

Push–pull inventory control – in push systems there is a central planning system that generates and programmes orders for the production line. With pull, orders come from customers, and the line reacts to the demand.

Q

Quality of conformance – deals with how well the actual product or service delivery matches the design intended.

Quality of design – concerned with how well the design concept and its specifications match the intended use of the product or service.

R

Radical innovation – extreme, game-changing progress.

Raw materials – materials purchased but not processed.

Relative throughput time – the interval of time between availability for use and completion of the service encounter

Reorder level (ROL) – the trigger level used in the reorder point inventory system (Q type), which generates the ordering of a fixed amount (normally the EOQ) with an irregular interval.

Reorder point – level of inventory that indicates the time to order a batch of the EOQ in a reorder level system.

Research – scholarly or scientific investigation or inquiry; generally categorized as either basic or applied.

Resource levelling – the practice of using float to improve the resources needed in a project.

Resource-based view – the strategic approach that prioritizes the capability of the firm in its decision-making.

Reverse logistics – addresses key issues related to how companies can become more environmentally efficient through recycling, reusing and reducing the amount of materials used.

Rough-cut capacity planning – CRP applied at the aggregate level to try and ensure the plan is close to achievable with existing capacity limits.

Run chart – shows the trends in data over time.

S

Safety – concerned with whether there is any risk to the customer when they use the product or receive the service.

Safety stock – extra inventory used to cover uncertainty or delivery times so that the system can keep operating.

Sand cone principle – records the importance of certain practices building on others in a predetermined order.

Scatter diagram – shows the degree and direction of the relationship between two variables.

Service – any activity or benefit that one party can offer to another that is essentially intangible, and does not result in the ownership of anything.

Servitization – the addition of services to complement the sale of a manufactured product

Servitization of products – the process of convergence of products with service content.

Short-term capacity plan – an active and often reactive plan covering all the detail needed to carry out the operation.

SIPOC (supplier–input–process–output–customer) diagram – maps the processes a company (or a person) goes through in order to satisfy a customer's requirements in the context of the supply chain.

Slack – the spare time an activity has before it will become on the critical path.

SMED (single minute exchange of dies) – approach to reduce machine changeovers to achieve batch size of one.

Soft HRM – HR practices and policies aimed to elicit the affective (emotional) commitment of employees to the organization and its goals.

Stakeholders – the people who have a say in or are influenced by a project.

Stock time chart – chart showing how the inventory of a part or component changes over time.

Stock-out – When an organisation runs out of material this is often called a stock-out and can be expensive as the operations have to wait until more inventory is delivered.

Strategic alignment – the alignment of all decisions made at different levels of the organization with the overall strategic goals.

Strategic workforce planning – having workforce planning to include the right number of people at the right time, in the right place with the right skills and behaviours, which are aligned to the strategic and operational strategy and financial budget planning.

Supplier network – loose group of organizations that collectively deliver parts and services to an end customer.

Supply base rationalization – reduction of suppliers in order to become more efficient.

Supply chain management (SCM) – the management of activities, organization and processes involving all the stakeholders, from the end customers (i.e. downstream) to the supplier that produces the raw material (i.e. upstream).

Sustainable competitive advantage – competitive advantage that is based on a valuable, rare, imperfectly imitable and non-substitutable resource that is specific to the company, and cannot be transferred.

System – a complex whole, the functioning of which depends on its parts and the interactions between those parts.

T

Takt time – the time allowed by the customer for each unit of output to be produced.

Third-party logistics (TPL) – a TPL provider can be treated as an external supplier that performs some or all parts of a company's functions, especially logistics services.

Threshold competencies – competencies that allow the firm to exist and operate, but provide no competitive advantage.

Total productive maintenance (TPM) – the application of TQM ideas to ensuring that machines operate effectively, and are always available.

Total quality management (TQM) – quality system that is needed for effective lean production, and based on kaizen (continuous improvement).

Toyota Production System (TPS) – the model for lean systems as developed at Toyota by Ohno and using JIT.

Trade-offs – factors that cannot exist concurrently in their best state; the optimization of one necessitates a compromise in another.

Transaction costs – the price associated with buying or selling goods or services.

Transformed resources – materials to be converted into products for sale, and information.

Transforming resources – facilities such as buildings, equipment and tools and process technology; all the staff involved in the conversion process; and the capital that is needed to buy materials, and pay for the facilities and staff.

Triple bottom line – considers the social and natural environmental impact of a company's strategy as well as the more conventional economic impact.

U

Utilization – actual output shown as a percentage of the operation's design capacity; demonstrates how well the operation is working to expectations.

V

Value matrix – a framework of generic operations strategies called value propositions that informs the set-up of the operation.

Value Stream – sequence of activities designed to create value and eliminate waste

Vertically integrated enterprise – almost permanent and extremely well-integrated group of organizations; very similar to a single legal entity.

Virtual enterprise – temporary group of organizations exploiting a short-term, high-risk opportunity.

Volume and variety model – Hayes and Wheelright (1979) developed a model stating that volume carried out by an operation and variety or choice offered to customers is linked and results in the types of operation such as project, batch and mass production.

W

Weighted score technique – used for comparing the attractiveness of alternative operational locations that allocates a weighted score to each relevant factor in the decision.

Work breakdown structure (WBS) – statement of all the work that has to be completed in a project.

Work in progress – Work in progress (WIP) is inventory which is in the manufacturing process and so no longer raw material but not yet a finished product.

Workforce intelligence planning – matching organizational needs with the right number of employees with the right knowledge, skills and behaviours in the right place at the right time. Sometimes referred to as WIP.

Workforce plan – defines how many people of what type at what skill levels are needed at any particular time in an organization depending on internal and external factors.

Workforce planning (WP) – an integral part of strategic and operational planning in organizations; a core process of HRM to ensure that an organization has the right number of people at the right time, in the right place with the right skills, which are aligned to the strategic and operational strategy.

Y

Yield management – a group of methods that assist an operation with fixed capacity to maximize its revenue and utilize the capacity it has to best advantage.

Index

D

E

G

H

I

J

Q

R

X

Y

Z